McCALL'S BIG Book of CHRISTMAS KNIT & CROCHET

McCALL'S
BIG Book
of CHRISTMAS
KNIT & CROCHET

**The Editors of
McCall's Needlework & Crafts Magazine**

CHILTON BOOK COMPANY
RADNOR, PENNSYLVANIA

Copyright © 1982 by ABC Needlework and Crafts Magazines, Inc.
All International Rights Reserved
Published in Radnor, Pennsylvania 19089, by Chilton Book Company

Manufactured in the United States of America

Library of Congress Cataloging in Publication Data

Main entry under title:
McCall's big book of Christmas knit and
    crochet.
    (The Chilton needlework series)
    Includes index.
    1. Knitting. 2. Crocheting. 3. Christmas
decorations. I. McCall's needlework & crafts.
II. Title: Big book of Christmas knit and
crochet. III. Series.
TT820.M483 1982   746.43'041   82-70537
ISBN 0-8019-7252-3   AACR2

2 3 4 5 6 7 8 9 0   1 0 9 8 7 6 5 4 3

CONTENTS

475 Projects (With Complete Instructions for All)

General Directions and Finishing Instructions

CHRISTMAS PALS
Tiny dolls make the scene for a shelf, mantelpiece, or a holiday table centerpiece. Stitch crocheted Christmas Carolers, see page 17.

Carolers by Catherine Rhoades   Photography by Arthur Klonsky

Angels from around the world stand on a mantel
or hang from your Christmas tree. Eight inches
high, they wear knitted dresses over Styrofoam

GREETINGS

bodies; felt wings and trims; gold cord halos and belts. Make several and place before arches on your mantel. See International Angels, page 19.

FAMILY PORTRAIT

North Pole family
poses for the
camera! In rows of
easy single crochet,
bodies are flat
pieces sewn together,
stuffed. Reindeer
is 16″ tall. North
Pole Family, page 19.

FAMILY FRIENDS

Happy snowman in warm scarf, hat and mittens
frolics with one of Santa's reindeer, in
harness, ready for his trip South. Both toys
are easy to make in single crochet. Directions
for Snowman, page 20, and Santa's Reindeer, page 21.

HOLIDAY NEEDLEWORK

'Tis the season for stitching the wonderful
little touches that make Christmas so merry.

Knit three socks:
Joy and Tree motifs
are embroidered
(pages 21 and 22),
Heart-and-Tree
motif is knit-in
(page 22). Crochet
large and small
Granny Square
Stockings, pages 22
and 23.

Crochet a tree skirt. Eight-pointed star radiates with chevron stripes; at each point add a thick tassel (see page 23).

Crochet Santa in every size and shape. Left to right, Triangular Santa, page 23; Tiny 11″ Santa, page 24; Santa with tuna-can tummy and disc limbs, page 24.

Santas and knitted stockings by Jane Slovachek
Photography by Arthur Klonsky

GETTING IN ON THE ACT

Finger puppets (below) are fun by the handful! Single crochet the entire cast: left to right, Panda, Teddy, Pig, Mouse, Reindeer, Puppy, Snowman, Elephant, Santa and Frog—all fabric-trimmed (see page 25). Set the scene for more fun with Yarn Loop Dolls (inset). Loop the yarn into bodies (6"–7½") made of nylon stockings stuffed with fiberfil (see page 26).

Finger puppets by Rose M. Blomer.
Photography by Arthur Klonsky.

CHILD'S CHRISTMAS AFGHAN

The twelve days of Christmas, from the partridge in a pear tree to twelve drummers drumming. Child's coverlet is crocheted in afghan-stitch squares, merrily embroidered in cross-stitch with pretty birds and festive folk. Child's Christmas Afghan, 42" × 56", page 27.

CHRISTMAS CAROLERS
Shown on page 7

SIZE: 6" to 7" high.

MATERIALS: Knitting worsted weight yarn, 1 oz. each of eggshell and dark red for woman, 1 oz. each of gray, black, tan and white for man, 1 oz. each of yellow, wine, and variegated lilacs for girl. Sport yarn, 1 oz. pink for heads and hands; small amounts of dark red, yellow, brown. Crochet hooks sizes C and E. Foam rubber balls, two 2¼" diameter, one 1¾" diameter. Lightweight cardboard. Glue. Toothpicks.

GAUGE: 5 sc = 1"; 6 rows = 1" (size E hook).

Note: Use E hook with worsted weight yarn, C hook with sport yarn.

WOMAN: BODY: With eggshell, ch 50. Sl st in first ch to form ring. Working in rnds of sc, work 4 rnds even.

Next Rnd: Dec 2 sc evenly spaced around. Repeat last rnd until piece is about 4¼" from start and there are about 10 sc in rnd. End off.

SLEEVES (make 2): With eggshell, ch 16. Sl st in first ch to form ring. Working in rnds of sc, work 5 rnds even. * Dec 2 sc in next rnd, work 1 rnd even, repeat from * twice more. End off.

With dark red, work edging around bottom of each sleeve: Sc in sc, * ch 2, sc in next sc, repeat from * around.

SIDE PANEL OF DRESS (make 2): With eggshell, beg at front edge, ch 9.

Row 1: Sc in 2nd ch from hook and in each ch—8 sc. Ch 1, turn each row.

Row 2: Sc in each sc.

Row 3: 2 sc in first sc, sc in each sc across.

Row 4: Repeat row 2.

Rows 5–10: Repeat rows 3 and 4—12 sc.

Rows 11 and 12: Work even on 12 sc.

Row 13: Sk first sc, sc across.

Row 14: Sc in each of 10 sc.

Row 15: Sk first sc, sc across. End off.

With dark red, work edging around 3 sides of panel; do not work on straight (top) edge: Sc in sc, * ch 3, sc in next st, repeat from * around.

CAPE: With dark red, ch 16.

Row 1: Dc in 3rd ch from hook and in each ch across. Ch 2, turn.

Row 2: Sk first dc, 2 dc in each dc to last dc, dc in last dc. Ch 2, turn.

Row 3: Repeat row 2. End off.

HEAD: With pink yarn and C hook, ch 3; sl st in first ch to form ring.

Rnd 1: 6 sc in ring.

Rnd 2: 2 sc in each sc around.

Rnd 3: (Sc in next sc, 2 sc in next sc) 6 times.

Rnd 4: (2 sc in next sc, sc in 2 sc) 6 times.

Rnds 5–7: * Sc in 5 sc, 2 sc in next sc, repeat from * 10 times—35 sc in rnd. Work 10 rnds even. Then dec as follows: (Sk 1 st, sc in next 5 sts) 15 times. While working decreases, insert ball.

(Sk 1 st, sc in next 3 sts) 4 times. (Sk 1 st, sc in next 2 sts) 4 times. End off.

BONNET: Back: With eggshell, ch 2.

Rnd 1: 6 sc in 2nd ch from hook.

Rnd 2: 2 sc in each sc around.

Rnd 3: (Sc in next sc, 2 sc in next sc) 6 times.

Rnd 4: (Sc in 2 sc, 2 sc in next sc) 6 times.

Rnd 5: Sc in each sc around. Ch 1, turn.

Rnd 6: Sc in next sc, (2 sc in next sc, sc in next sc) 11 times. End off.

Front: With eggshell, ch 35.

Row 1: Sc in 2nd ch from hook and in each ch—34 sc. Ch 1, turn.

Row 2: Sc in each sc across. Ch 2, turn.

Row 3: Dc in each sc across. Ch 1, turn.

Row 4: Sc in next dc, hdc in next dc, dc in each dc across to last 2 sts, inc 2 dc at center of row, hdc and sc in last 2 sts. Ch 1, turn.

Row 5: Sl st across 3 sts, hdc in next st, 2 dc in next st, dc across, inc 3 dc in row, end 2 dc in 5th st from end, hdc in next st, sl st in next st. End off. Sew front to back, picking up back lps only.

With dark red, make a ch long enough to fit inside edge of bonnet. Sew inside front edge of bonnet. Attach 6" strands of yarn to each side of bonnet for ties.

HANDS (make 2): With pink yarn and C hook, ch 6. Work in rows of 5 sc for 5 rows.

Row 6: Work 2 sc tog, sc in next sc, work 2 sc tog.

Row 7: Sc in 3 sc.

Row 8: 2 sc in each sc—6 sc. Work even on 6 sc for 8 rows. End off.

BOOK (make 4 pieces): With wine and C hook, ch 7. Work even on 6 sc for 7 rows. End off. Cut 2 squares of cardboard slightly smaller than crocheted pieces. Sew 2 pieces tog over each cardboard. Sew 2 book pieces tog. Cut a few paper "pages" to fit in book. Stitch to center fold of book.

FINISHING: Using larger size pattern for cone, cut piece from cardboard. Shape cone, overlapping 2 edges about 2" at base. Staple or sew tog. Insert cone in body. Fold under first rnd of crocheted piece and glue or sew in place. Sew top of sleeves flat. Sew a sleeve to each side of body. Insert hands; sew in place. Sew skirt panels to each side of body.

Insert a wooden toothpick halfway through base of head, the other half through top of cone. Tack head to body.

Cut long strands of yellow yarn for hair. Sew some to top of head at left side, bring across right side and sew in place, forming some loops over "ears" for curls. Repeat in opposite direction.

Embroider eyes and mouth. Tie bonnet to head. Sew cape closed at neck over doll. Sew book to hands.

MAN: BODY: Work as for Woman, working first 13 rnds in tan, remainder in white.

SLEEVES: Work as for Woman, mak-

ing sleeves gray. Work 1 rnd of black hdc around lower edge.

COAT: With gray, ch 51.

Row 1: Sc in 2nd ch from hook and in each ch across. Ch 1, turn each row.

Rows 2–4: Work even in sc.

Rows 5–21: Work in sc, dec 2 sc evenly spaced each row. End off. Work 1 row of black hdc around lower edge. With gray, work 1 row sc along each front edge.

CAPE: With gray, ch 35. Repeat rows 1–4 of Coat.

Rows 5–11: Work in sc, dec 2 sc evenly spaced each row. End off. Finish as for Coat.

COLLAR: With black, ch 16. Hdc in 3rd ch from hook and in each ch across. Ch 2, turn. Sk first hdc, 2 hdc in each st across to last st, hdc in last st. End off.

HEAD: Work as for Woman's Head.

HAT: Top: With gray, ch 2.

Rnd 1: 6 sc in 2nd ch from hook.

Rnd 2: 2 sc in each sc around.

Rnd 3: (Sc in next sc, 2 sc in next sc) 6 times.

Rnd 4: (Sc in 2 sc, 2 sc in next sc) 6 times.

Rnd 5: (Sc in 3 sc, 2 sc in next sc) 6 times.

Rnd 6: (Sc in 4 sc, 2 sc in next sc) 6 times. End off.

Sides: With gray, ch 36. Sl st in first ch to form ring. Work even on 36 sc for 8 rnds.

Rnds 9–11: Inc 6 sc evenly around each rnd. Sl st in next st. End off.

Hatband: With black, ch 36. End off. Sew sides of hat to top. Sew band around hat at rnd 8.

HANDS: Work as for Woman's Hands.

BOOK: Work as for Woman's Book.

FINISHING: Using larger size pattern for cone, cut piece from cardboard. Shape cone, overlapping 2 edges about 2" at base. Staple or sew tog. Insert cone in body. Fold under first rnd of crocheted piece and glue or sew in place.

Embroider black buttons on white "shirt" and long straight stitches down center front of tan section. Tack coat around neck edge of body. Sew top of sleeves flat. Sew a sleeve to each side of body. Insert hands; sew in place.

Insert a wooden toothpick halfway through base of head, the other half through top of cone. Tack head to body. Sew cape and collar in place.

Cut strands of brown yarn for hair; sew to head. Stuff hat. Sew to head over hair. Embroider eyes and mouth. Sew book to hands.

GIRL: BODY: With yellow, ch 40. Sl st in first ch to form ring. Working in rnds, work 3 rnds even.

Next Rnd: Dec 2 sc evenly spaced around. Repeat last rnd until piece is about 3" from start and there are about 8 sc in rnd. End off.

COAT: With wine, ch 42, sl st in first

ch to form ring. Working in rnds, work 2 rnds even. Dec 3 sc evenly spaced each rnd for 10 rnds—12 sc. Ch 1, turn. For collar, work 2 sc in each of 11 sc. Ch 2, turn. Sc in first sc, * ch 2, sc in next sc, repeat from * across. End off.

SLEEVES: With wine, work as for Woman's Sleeves, end off after row 9.

HANDS: Work as for Woman's Hands.

MUFF: With variegated lilacs, ch 7. Work in rows of 6 sc for 12 rows. Sew first and last rows tog. Fringe this seam. Make a ch 7″ long; run ch through muff; join ends of ch.

SCARF: With variegated lilacs, ch 4. Work in rows of 3 sc until scarf is 10″ long. Fringe ends.

HEAD: With pink yarn and C hook, ch 3; sl st in first ch to form ring.

Rnd 1: 6 sc in ring.

Rnd 2: 2 sc in each sc around.

Rnd 3: (Sc in next sc, 2 sc in next sc) 6 times.

Rnd 4: (2 sc in next sc, sc in 2 sc) 6 times.

Rnds 5–10: Work even on 24 sc. Then dec as follows: * Sk 1 st, sc in next 5 sts, repeat from * 10 times. While decreasing, insert ball. Dec as necessary to cover ball. End off.

HAT: With variegated lilacs, ch 2.

Rnd 1: 6 sc in 2nd ch from hook.

Rnd 2: 2 sc in each sc around.

Rnd 3: (Sc in next sc, 2 sc in next sc) 6 times.

Rnd 4: (2 sc in next sc, sc in 2 sc) 6 times.

Rnd 5: (Sc in 3 sc, 2 sc in next sc) 6 times.

Rnd 6: (Sc in 4 sc, 2 sc in next sc) 6 times.

Rnds 7 and 8: Sc in each sc around— 36 sc. End off. Make a small pompon; attach to top of hat.

FINISHING: Using smaller size pattern for cone, cut piece from cardboard.

Shape cone, overlapping 2 edges about 1¼″ at base. Staple or sew edges tog. Insert cone in body. Fold under first rnd of crocheted piece and glue or sew in place.

Place coat over body. Sew top of sleeves flat; sew a sleeve to each side of body. Insert hands; place muff ch around neck; place hands in muff; sew hands in place.

Insert a wooden toothpick halfway through base of head, the other half through top of cone. Tack head to body.

Cut strands of yellow yarn for hair; sew to top of head at center; bring strands to side; tack in place. Embroider eyes and mouth. Sew hat to head each side. Tie scarf around neck.

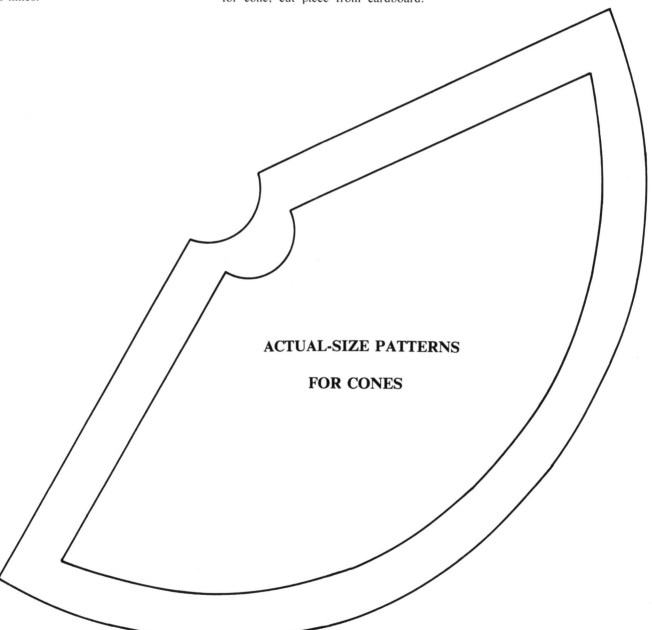

ACTUAL-SIZE PATTERNS

FOR CONES

INTERNATIONAL ANGELS
Shown on pages 8 and 9

SIZE: About 8½" high.

MATERIALS: Knitting worsted, ¾ oz. robe color, ¼ oz. hair color. Set of double-pointed needles No. 5. 6" styrofoam cone. 2" styrofoam ball. Gold cord. Felt for wings, robe trimmings, face, arms and features. Chenille sticks, 2 for each angel. Fabric cement or all-purpose glue.

GENERAL DIRECTIONS: Knitted Robe: Cast on 45 sts; divide evenly on 3 needles. Join, k 2 rnds.

Next Rnd: K 2 tog at beg of each needle—42 sts. K 2 rnds even. Repeat last 3 rnds until 6 sts remain. K 2 rnds. Bind off.

Sleeve (make 2): Cast on 18 sts; divide evenly on 3 needles. Join, k 8 rnds.

Next Rnd: K 2 tog at beg of each needle—15 sts. K 8 rnds even. Repeat dec rnd—12 sts. K 6 rnds even. Bind off.

Pull robe over cone, stretching to fit. Run yarn around bottom, pull to fit. Run yarn back and forth across bottom to hold robe tight; fasten. Glue felt circle over bottom.

Enlarge patterns for wings, arms and face by copying patterns on paper ruled in 1" squares.

Arms: Run chenille stick through cone ½" from top. Slip sleeves on; sew to robe. Cut off stick to protrude ½" below sleeves. Cut 4 arms from felt; glue over stick.

Head: Cut face from felt. Put a line of glue down center; glue to ball. Put glue all over back of face and gently shape to ball, easing out wrinkles. Run 3" piece of chenille stick through head; bend over ½" at top. If angel has collar, cut felt circle same size as cone bottom, cutting out with pinking shears. Put small hole in center of collar; put over top of cone. Glue spot in front and back of collar to hold down. Stick head into top of cone with protruding end of chenille stick.

Hair: Cut strips of yarn 6" or 7" long. Arrange strands crosswise, side by side, on 4½" strip of masking tape. Stitch down center for center hair part (or to one side for side part.) Strip off tape, fold hair piece in half, glue together along stitching. For bangs, glue short strands across front of head before adding hair. Glue hair to head, folded edge at front.

Features: Cut eyes, pupils, and mouth from felt in desired colors. Glue to face. Freckles on red-headed angel are made with felt-tipped marker.

Wings: Cut 2 wings from felt. Cut 2 pieces of felt about 1" square. For each wing, put glue on one side of a square, glue to inner edge of wing with a 1½" piece of chenille stick between it and

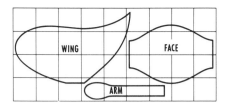

wing, chenille stick protruding about ¾". When dry, push stick into body to hold wing.

Halo: Cut piece of gold cord 6½" long; join ends by wrapping with transparent tape or thread. Push pin through joining into head.

Trimming: Cut strips of felt with pinking shears and glue in place around bottom of robe, down front and around sleeves, as desired. Make belt or necklace of gold cord or soutache braid. Add felt cross, if desired.

NORTH POLE FAMILY
Shown on page 10

SIZES: About 16" high, plus Santa's hat, reindeer's antlers.

MATERIALS: Knitting worsted weight yarn, 3 ozs. red (R), 1 oz. each of white (W), pink (P), and black (B) for Santa; 3 ozs. red (R), 2 ozs. white (W), 1 oz. pink (P) and ¼ oz. black (B) for Mrs. Santa; 3 ozs. brown, ¼ oz. each of black (B) and red (R) for reindeer. Crochet hook size E. Stuffing. Scraps of felt: red, black, pink, blue, for Santa and Mrs. Santa. Brown felt, 9" x 12", for reindeer. Craft glue. Three black shank buttons, 6 silver jingle bells, two 12" chenille sticks, for reindeer.

GAUGE: 5 sc = 1".

Note: Toys are worked in sc throughout.

SANTA: Beg at tip of hat, with R, ch 3.

Row 1: Sc in 2nd ch from hook and in next ch. Ch 1, turn each row.

Rows 2-7: Work even.

Row 8: Inc 1 sc—3 sc.

Rows 9-11: Work even.

Rows 12-23: Repeat rows 8-11, 3 times.

Row 24: Inc 1 sc—7 sc.

Row 25: Work even.

Rows 26-31: Repeat rows 24 and 25, 3 times.

Row 32: Inc 1 sc each side—12 sc.

Row 33: Work even.

Row 34: Repeat row 32—14 sc.

Rows 35 and 36: Work even.

Row 37: Repeat row 32—16 sc.

Rows 38-41: Work even.

Face: Change to P, work 12 rows even. Dec 1 st each side of next 2 rows—12 sc. Work 2 rows even.

Suit: Change to R.

Rows 1 and 2: Work even.

Row 3: Sc across 12 sc, ch 21 for arm.

Row 4: Sc in 2nd ch from hook and in each ch, sc in 12 sc, ch 21.

Row 5: Sc in 2nd ch from hook and in each ch, sc in 32 sc—52 sc.

Rows 6-12: Work even.

Row 13: Sc in 36 sc. Ch 1, turn.

Row 14: Sc in 20 sc. Ch 1, turn.

Rows 15-18: Work even.

Row 19: Inc 1 sc each side—22 sc.

Rows 20-23: Work even.

Rows 24-38: Repeat rows 19-23, 3 times.

Row 39: Sc in 12 sc for leg. Ch 1, turn.

Row 40: Sc in 10 sc, work 2 sc tog.

Row 41: Work even—11 sc.

Row 42: Sc to last 2 sc, work 2 sc tog.

Row 43: Work even—10 sc.

Rows 44-46: Repeat rows 42, 43, 42.

Rows 47-52: Work even—8 sc.

Boot: Change to B, work 9 rows even.

Next Row: Sc across, ch 8.

Next Row: Sc in 2nd ch from hook and in each ch, sc in 8 sc. Work 6 rows even. End off. Work 2nd leg to correspond on last 12 sc of row 38, reversing shaping.

Mittens: Join B and work 9 sc across end of arm. Work 3 more rows even.

Next Row: Dec 1 sc each side. Work 3 rows even.

Next Row: Dec 1 sc each side. End off. Make another Santa the same. Sew pieces tog, stuffing firmly as you sew.

Buttons (make 3): With W, ch 2. Work 6 sc in 2nd ch from hook. Work 2 sc in each sc around—12 sc. Work 1 rnd even. Stuff buttons lightly before sewing on. For hat pompon, make 2 buttons; sew tog over tip of hat.

Trims: With W, make ch long enough to fit around piece to be trimmed. Work 2 rows of sc. For button suit trim, work 3 rows. Sew trims in place. Sew hat trim on after working hair.

Collar: With W, ch 27. Work 3 rows of sc. Sew to neck with points free in front.

Belt: With B, make ch long enough to fit around waist. Work 1 row sc. Sew belt to suit.

Features: From felt, cut blue eyes, black pupils, pink round nose, red crescent mouth. Glue on.

Hair: Work long straight sts on back of head from cap to pink neck. For beard, wind yarn several times around finger, sew loops in groups to face. For moustache, wind yarn several times around 3 fingers; sew to face at center of loops. Eyebrows are short W strands, glued on.

MRS. SANTA: Front: Beg at top of head, with P, ch 11.

Row 1: Sc in 2nd ch from hook and in each ch—10 sc. Ch 1, turn each row.

Rows 2-5: Inc 1 sc each side.

Rows 6-17: Work even—18 sc.

Rows 18-21: Dec 1 sc each side.

Rows 22 and 23. Work even—10 sc.

Dress: Row 1: Change to R, work across, inc 2 sc evenly spaced; ch 21 for arm.

Row 2: Sc in 2nd ch from hook and in each ch, sc in 12 sc, ch 21 for arm.

Row 3: Sc in 2nd ch from hook and in each ch, sc in 32 sc.

Rows 4-7: Work even—52 sc.

Row 8: Sc in 20 sc, inc 1 sc in each of next 2 sc, sc in 8 sc, inc 1 sc in each of next 2 sc, sc in 20 sc—56 sc.

Row 9: Sc in 21 sc, inc 1 sc in each of

ANTLER PATTERN

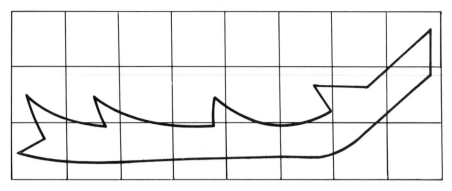

next 2 sc, sc in 10 sc, inc 1 sc in each of next 2 sc, sc in 21 sc.

Row 10: Work even—60 sc.

Row 11: Sc 45 sc. Ch 1, turn.

Row 12: Sc 30 sc. Ch 1, turn.

Rows 13 and 14: Work even.

Row 15: Sc in 6 sc, work 2 sc tog twice, sc in 10 sc, work 2 sc tog twice, sc in 6 sc.

Row 16: Sc in 5 sc, dec 2 sc as before, sc in 8 sc, dec 2 sc, sc in 5 sc.

Rows 17-19: Work even—22 sc.

Row 20: Dec 4 sc evenly across.

Rows 21-23: Work even—18 sc.

Rows 24-35: Inc 1 sc each side of next row, work 2 rows even, 4 times.

Row 36: Inc 1 st each side—28 sc.

Rows 37-41: Work even.

Row 42: Repeat row 36.

Rows 43-58: Work even—30 sc. End off.

Back: Work as for front, through row 7 of dress.

Rows 8-10: Work even.

Row 11: Sc in 37 sc. Ch 1, turn.

Row 12: Sc in 22 sc. Ch 1, turn.

Rows 13-19: Work even. Work as for front from row 20.

Boots: Join B in 7th sc from side edge on lower edge of front, sc in same sc and in 6 more sc. Work even for 4 rows.

Row 6: Sc in 7 sc, ch 7.

Row 7: Sc in 2nd ch from hook and in each ch, sc in 7 sc. Work 5 rows even. End off. Work other boot to correspond. Work same on back.

Hands: With P, work 7 sc on end of arm. Work 4 more rows even. Dec 1 sc each side of next row. Work 2 rows even. Dec 1 st each side of next row. End off.

Sew front and back tog, stuffing firmly as you sew.

Apron: With W, ch 21. Work 24 rows even on 20 sc. End off. Join W and sc in 5th sc from end, sc in next 11 sc. Work 12 rows even on 12 sc. End off. For top strap, ch 40 and work 1 row sc. Sew ends to top of apron. For waist strings, ch 25 and work 1 row sc. Make another string same. Sew an end of each to sides of apron. Tack tog at center back, leaving ends hang. For bow at back, ch 6. Work 2 rows of 5 sc. Dec 1 sc each side of next row. Work 2 rows even. Dec 1 sc on next row. Work 1

row even. Inc 1 sc on next row. Work 2 rows even. Inc 1 sc each side of next row. Work 2 rows even. End off. Sew to center back over strings.

Work W trims and collars as for Santa. Make features as for Santa. Add rosy cheeks with felt marker.

Hair: Work long straight sts from top of head to neckline. For top, cut 15 W strands 1 yard long. Knot tog at center. Divide into 3 groups of 10 strands and braid. Coil braid around (about 3 coils); sew securely to top of head.

REINDEER: With brown, beg at top of head, ch 11.

Row 1: Sc in 2nd ch from hook and in each ch. Ch 1, turn each row.

Rows 2-5: Inc 1 sc each side each row.

Rows 6-19: Work even—18 sc.

Rows 20 and 21: Dec 1 sc each side.

Rows 22 and 23: Work even—14 sc.

Row 24: Sc across, ch 21.

Row 25: Sc in 2nd ch from hook and in each ch, sc across, ch 21.

Row 26: Sc in 2nd ch from hook and in each ch, sc in 34 sc—54 sc.

Rows 27-31: Work even.

Row 32: Sc in 38 sc. Ch 1, turn.

Row 33: Sc in 22 sc. Ch 1, turn.

Rows 34-39: Work even.

Row 40: Dec 1 sc each side.

Rows 41-60: Work even—20 sc.

Row 61: Sc in 9 sc for leg. Ch 1, turn.

Row 62: Work even.

Row 63: Sc in 7 sc, work 2 sts tog.

Rows 64-66: Work even—8 sc.

Row 67: Sc in 6 sc, work 2 sts tog.

Rows 68-70: Work even—7 sc.

Row 71: Sc in 3 sc, work 2 sts tog twice.

Rows 72-85: Work even—5 sc. End off. Work other leg to correspond.

Hoof: With B, work 6 sc up outer edge of leg. Work 3 rows even.

Next Row: Sc in 3 sc. Turn.

Next Row: Sk 1 sc, sc in 2 sc. Ch 1, turn.

Next Row: Sc in first sc. End off. Work other point to correspond. Work hooves the same at end of arms, leaving a small part of lower arm free.

Make another Reindeer the same.

Nose: Ch 21. Sc in 2nd ch from hook and in each ch. Work 2 rows even.

Next Row: Dec 4 sc evenly across. Work 4 rows even—16 sc.

Next Row: Work 2 sts tog across—8 sc. End off. Sew up and stuff. Sew to one reindeer piece.

Ears (make 2): Ch 4. Sc in 2nd ch from hook and in each ch. Work 1 row even. Inc 1 sc on each of next 2 rows. Work 2 rows even—5 sc. Dec 1 sc on each of next 3 rows—2 sc. Work 2 sts tog. End off. Sew to head after reindeer is stuffed.

Antlers: Enlarge pattern for antler on paper ruled in 1″ squares. Draw around pattern twice on folded felt. Pin felt tog, stitch around lines leaving bottom open. Cut antlers close to stitching. Bend ends on chenille sticks, push end of each into an antler. Twist ends that come out tog. Sew reindeer pieces tog, stuffing firmly as you sew, leaving top open. Insert ends of antlers in open head of stuffed reindeer, sew up head seam with antlers in place, sewing through felt ends.

Cut felt ovals for eyes; sew button eyes to felt. Glue eyes to face. Sew button on tip of nose. Glue on red felt crescent mouth.

Harness: With R, ch 91. Work 1 row of sc. End off. Put harness around neck and waist; crossing in front; sew ends tog under front cross and tack harness to body. Sew on jingle bells.

SNOWMAN
Shown on page 11

SIZE: 15″ high.

MATERIALS: Knitting worsted weight yarn, 1 4-oz. skein white; 1 oz. each of black, red, green, orange. Crochet hook size G. Stuffing. Yarn needle.

GAUGE: 7 sc = 2″.

SNOWMAN (make 2 pieces): With white, ch 15. **Row 1:** Sc in 2nd ch from hook and in each ch across—14 sc. Work in sc throughout, ch 1, turn each row.

Rows 2 and 3: Inc 1 sc each side—18 sc.

Rows 4 and 5: Work even.

Rows 6-9: Repeat rows 2-5—22 sc.

Rows 10 and 11: Repeat row 2— 26 sc.

Rows 12-26: Work even.

Rows 27 and 28: Dec 1 sc each side.

Rows 29 and 30: Work even—22 sc.

Rows 31-38: Repeat rows 27-30 twice —14 sc.

Row 39: Dec 1 sc each side.

Rows 40-42: Inc 1 sc each side.

Rows 43-51: Work even—18 sc.

Rows 52 and 53: Dec 1 sc each side.

Rows 54-67: Change to black. Work even on 14 sc for 14 rows. End off.

HAT BRIM: With black, ch 28. Sl st in first ch to form ring. Sc in first ch, * 2 sc in next ch, sc in next ch, repeat from * around. Sew brim to beg of hat when toy is stuffed.

ARM: Join white at bottom of 3rd rib (6 rows) down from first inc for head.

Ch 10; sc in 2nd ch from hook and each ch to end, sl st in next row down on side of body. Turn, sk sl st, sc in each of 9 sc. Ch 1, turn. Sc in 9 sc, sl st in next row down on side. Turn, sk sl st, sc in each of 9 sc. Ch 1, turn. Sc in 7 sc, work last 2 sc tog, sl st as before. Work 2 rows of 8 sc. End off.

Mitten: With red, work 7 sc on end of arm. Work 6 rows even. Dec 1 st each side for 2 rows. Work 1 row even. End off. Join red on upper edge of mitten 3 rows from bottom, work 3 sc on edge toward mitten tip. Work 1 row even. Dec 1 sc on next row; work 2 sc tog on last row. End off.

Sew bodies tog, right sides out, stuffing as you go.

SCARF: With green, ch 9. Work even in sc on 8 sts for 20 rows. Dec 1 st each side of next row. Work 45 rows even on 6 sts. Inc 1 st each side of next row. Work 20 rows even on 8 sts. End off.

EYES: With black, ch 2; 4 sc in 2nd ch from hook. Sew to face, forming a half circle.

BUTTONS: With black, ch 2; 6 sc in 2nd ch from hook. Sew 3 to front, forming circles.

NOSE: With orange, ch 6. **Row 1:** Sc in 2nd ch from hook and in each remaining ch.

Rows 2 and 3: Dec 1 sc each row.

Row 4: Work even.

Row 5: Dec 1 sc.

Row 6: Work even.

Row 7: Work 2 sc tog. End off. Sew up side seam. Sew nose to face.

Embroider red smiling mouth in outline stitch.

REINDEER
Shown on page 11

SIZE: 9″ long.

MATERIALS: Knitting worsted weight yarn, 2 ozs. light brown; 1 oz. each of dark brown and red; few yards of black. Crochet hook size G. Polyester stuffing. Two black shank type buttons. Seven 12″ chenille sticks. Yarn needle.

GAUGE: 4 sc = 1″.

REINDEER: BODY (make 2): With light brown, ch 16. **Row 1:** Sc in 2nd ch from hook and in each remaining ch. Work in sc throughout; ch 1, turn each row.

Rows 2-7: Work even—15 sc.

Row 8: Work 2 sc tog, sc across.

Row 9: Sc in 12 sc, work 2 sc tog.

Rows 10-14: Work even—13 sc.

Row 15: Dec 1 sc each side.

Rows 16-18: Work even—11 sc.

Row 19: Inc 1 sc at end of row.

Row 20: Inc 1 sc each side.

Rows 21 and 22: Work even on 14 sc. At end of row 22, ch 13.

Row 23: Sc in 2nd ch and in each ch across, sc in each sc—26 sc.

Row 24: Inc 1 sc in last sc.

Rows 25-32: Work even—27 sc.

Rows 33 and 34: Dec 1 sc each side—23 sc.

Row 35: Sc in 8 sc. Ch 1, turn.

Rows 36-39: Work even.

Rows 40-42: Dec 1 sc each side. End off.

Sew bodies tog, right sides out, stuffing as you go.

EAR: With light brown, ch 6. **Row 1:** Sc in 2nd ch from hook and each ch across.

Row 2: Sc in 3 sc, sl st in 2 sc, ch 2, sl st to tip of ear. Sew an ear to each side of head 1″ below top of head, 5 rows from back of head.

TAIL: With light brown, ch 8. **Row 1:** Sc in 2nd ch from hook and in each ch across.

Row 2: Sc in 7 sc, sc, ch 2, sc in end of tail, sc in 7 ch on opposite side of starting ch. End off. Sew on tail.

BACK LEG: With light brown, ch 2. **Rnd 1:** 6 sc in 2nd ch from hook.

Rnd 2: 2 sc in each sc around.

Rnds 3 and 4: * Sc in next sc, 2 sc in next sc, repeat from * around—27 sc.

Rnd 5: Sc in each sc around. Ch 14.

Row 1: Sc in 2nd ch from hook and next 12 ch, sl st in edge of circle. Ch 1, turn.

Rows 2-5: Sc in each of 13 sc. Ch 1, turn each row. End off. Fold chenille stick in half, bend sharp ends under a bit. Place on leg, extending into circle. Sew side seam of leg and across bottom, stuffing lightly. Sew circle to side of toy at back, stuffing as you go. Sew over end of leg with black yarn in straight sts for hoof.

FRONT LEG: With light brown, ch 17. **Row 1:** Sc in 2nd ch from hook and in each ch across. Ch 1, turn each row.

Rows 2-5: Work even in sc. End off. Fold chenille stick as for back leg, sew and stuff, but sew up only 13 sc; sew top of leg flat to body. Stitch hoof.

ANTLERS: With dark brown, ch 8. **Row 1:** Sc in 2nd ch from hook and in each ch across.

Row 2: Sl st in 4 sc, ch 30.

Row 3: Sc in 2nd ch from hook and in next 3 ch; ch 4; sc in 2nd ch from hook and in next 2 ch; sc in each ch of long ch. End off. * Count 8 sts from end of long ch, join yarn in 8th ch, ch 4; sc in 2nd ch from hook and next 2 ch, sl st in next st of long ch. End off. Repeat from * once more, counting from other end of long ch. Make 3 more antlers the same. Sew 2 antlers tog with chenille stick between. Cut pieces for inside prongs and twist to main stick. Sew antlers to head above ears.

FINISHING: Sew buttons to head for eyes. Embroider red nostrils and mouth with straight sts.

Harness: With red, ch 31. Work 2 rows of 30 sc. Sew ends tog around body. Make another piece the same. Sew ends to each side of first strip.

EMBROIDERED JOY STOCKING
Shown on page 12

MATERIALS: Knitting worsted weight yarn, 3 ozs. red (MC), 1 oz. white (CC). Knitting needles, 1 set double-pointed, size 6. Crochet hook size G.

GAUGE: 5 sts = 1″; 13 rows = 2″.

CUFF: With CC, cast on 46 sts. Divide sts on 3 needles, having 15 sts on first needle, 16 sts on 2nd needle, 15 sts on 3rd needle. With care not to twist sts, join and k 1 rnd. Work in garter st (p 1 rnd, k 1 rnd) for 23 rnds more. Cut CC, join MC.

LEG: Work in stockinette st (k each rnd) for 84 rnds, about 13¼″ from last cuff rnd. Cut MC.

Divide for Heel: Sl last 4 sts of first needle to 2nd needle, sl last 11 sts of 3rd needle to first needle—22 sts for heel. Divide remaining sts on 2 needles for instep.

HEEL: Beg on right side and working back and forth on heel sts only, join CC and work in garter st (k each row) for 21 rows, end with right side row. Cut CC.

Turn Heel: Row 1: Wrong side facing, join MC, p 13, p 2 tog, p 1. Turn.

Row 2: Sl 1, k 5, k 2 tog, k 1. Turn.

Row 3: Sl 1, p 6, p 2 tog, p 1. Turn.

Row 4: Sl 1, k 7, k 2 tog, k 1. Turn.

Row 5: Sl 1, p 8, p 2 tog, p 1. Turn.

Row 6: Sl 1, k 9, k 2 tog, k 1. Turn.

Row 7: Sl 1, p 10, p 2 tog, p 1. Turn.

Row 8: K 12, k 2 tog, k 1—14 sts.

Gusset: With MC, pick up and k 11 sts along left side edge of heel and sl to needle with heel sts; k all instep sts to one needle, dec 1 st each side; with free needle, pick up and k 11 sts along right side edge of heel, k first 7 sts of heel to same needle—58 sts; 18 sts on first needle, 22 sts on 2nd needle, 18 sts on 3rd needle.

Rnd 1: On first needle, k to within last 2 sts, k 2 tog; on 2nd needle, k across; on 3rd needle, sl 1, k 1, psso, k to end.

Rnd 2: K around. Repeat last 2 rnds 5 times more—46 sts. Work even for 25 rnds. Cut MC, join CC.

Toe: Rnd 1: On first needle, k to within last 2 sts, k 2 tog; on 2nd needle, sl 1, k 1, psso, k to within last 2 sts, k 2 tog; on 3rd needle, sl 1, k 1, psso, k to end.

Rnd 2: P around. Repeat last 2 rnds 6 times more—20 sts. With 3rd needle, k sts of first needle—10 sts each needle. Weave toe tog with Kitchener st.

FINISHING: Hanging Loop: With hook and CC, make ch 4″ long. Fold and sew ends to inside back corner of cuff.

EMBROIDERY: Work "Joy" in duplicate st on front of stocking, beg top of J on 20th row below cuff. With scrap of green yarn, work a 4-petal lazy daisy st flower in center of O. Make white French knot center. See Contents for Stitch Details.

HEARTS AND TREES STOCKING
Shown on page 12

MATERIALS: Knitting worsted weight yarn: Color A (white), 3 ozs.; Color B (Red), 1 oz.; Color C (Green), 1 oz. Knitting needles, size 8. Set of double-pointed needles, size 8. Crochet hook, size G. Yarn bobbins.
GAUGE: 9 sts = 2″; 6 rows = 1″.
Note: When knitting in patterns, use a separate 2-yd. strand for each motif or use bobbins, 6 each of Colors A and B. When changing colors, always bring color to be used from under color last used to prevent a hole. Carry Color A loosely across wrong side.
CUFF: With B, cast on 42 sts. K 4 rows. Cut B, join A. Work in stockinette st (k 1 row, p 1 row) for 8 rows. Cut A, join C. K 4 rows. Cut C, join A.
Leg: Work in stockinette st for 2 rows.
Pattern: Row 1: K 1 A, * k 2 B, k 1 A, k 2 B, k 2 A; repeat from * across, end last repeat k 1 A.
Row 2: P 1 A, * p 5 B, p 2 A; repeat from * across, end p 1 A. Following chart, work rows 3–30. Repeat rows 1–30 once more, then rows 1–24 once. Change to dp needles dividing sts as follows: From right side, k first 10 sts to one needle for heel, sl next 11 sts to 2nd needle for one half of instep, sl next 11 sts to 3rd needle for 2nd half of instep, sl last 10 sts to 4th needle, then to back end of first needle—20 sts on first needle for heel.
HEEL: Working back and forth on heel sts only, p 1 row, k 1 row for 16 rows, end with k row.
TURN HEEL: Row 1: P 12, p 2 tog, p 1. Turn.
Row 2: Sl 1, k 5, k 2 tog, k 1. Turn.
Row 3: Sl 1, p 6, p 2 tog, p 1. Turn.
Row 4: Sl 1, k 7, k 2 tog, k 1. Turn.
Row 5: Sl 1, p 8, p 2 tog, p 1. Turn.
Row 6: Sl 1, k 9, k 2 tog, k 1. Turn.
Row 7: Sl 1, p 10, p 2 tog. Turn.
Row 8: K 11, k 2 tog.
GUSSET: Along left side edge of heel, pick up 9 sts and sl to heel needle; k all instep sts to one needle, working pat as follows: k 3 A, * k 2 C, k 5 A; repeat from * twice more, end last repeat k 3 A; with free needle pick up 9 sts along right side edge of heel, with same needle k first 6 sts from heel needle—15 sts on first needle, 22 sts on 2nd needle, 15 sts on 3rd needle.
Rnd 1: On first needle, k to within last 2 sts, k 2 tog; on 2nd needle, k across in pat following chart row 26; on 3rd needle, sl 1, k 1, psso, k to end.

Rnd 2: K around, working pat across 2nd needle following chart row 27. Repeat last 2 rnds 4 times more, working pat across sts of 2nd needle following chart rows 28–30, then chart rows 1–5—42 sts. Work 1 rnd more omitting dec on first and 3rd needles, complete pat and dec 1 st at each end of 2nd needle—40 sts. With A only, work 25 rnds even.
TOE: Rnd 1: On first needle, k to within last 2 sts, k 2 tog; on 2nd needle, sl 1, k 1, psso, k to within last 2 sts, k 2 tog; on 3rd needle, sl 1, k 1, psso, k to end.
Rnd 2: K around. Repeat last 2 rnds 4 times more—20 sts. With 3rd needle, k sts of first needle. Break yarn leaving a 12″ end. Weave toe tog with Kitchener st.
FINISHING: Sew back seam. Weave in all ends neatly. With G hook and A, make a ch 4″ long. Fasten off. Fold in half forming lp and sew to inside back corner of cuff.

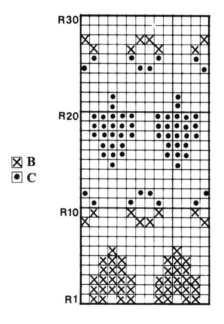

R30

R20

R10

R1

⊠ B
⊡ C

EMBROIDERED TREES STOCKING
Shown on page 12

MATERIALS: Knitting worsted weight yarn, 3 ozs. white. For embroidery, 3 yds. of red and 2 yds. of green. Knitting needles, 1 set double-pointed, size 6. Crochet hook size G.
GAUGE: 5 sts = 1″; 13 rows = 2″.
CUFF: Cast on 52 sts. Divide sts on 3 needles having 17 sts on first needle, 18 sts on 2nd needle and 17 sts on 3rd needle. With care not to twist sts, join and k 1 rnd. Work in garter st (p 1 rnd, k 1 rnd) for 21 rnds more.
LEG: Work in stockinette st (k each rnd) for 10 rnds.
Rnd 33: K 2 tog, k 24, k 2 tog, k to end—50 sts. K 17 rnds even.
Rnd 51: K 2 tog, k 23, k 2 tog, k to end—48 sts. K 37 rnds even.

Divide for Heel: K first 12 sts of first needle for heel, sl remaining 3 sts to 2nd needle, sl last 12 sts of 3rd needle to first needle with 12 heel sts—24 sts for heel; divide remaining sts on 2 needles for instep.
HEEL: Work back and forth on heel sts only in garter st (k each row) for 24 rows, end with right side row.
TURN HEEL: Row 1 (wrong side): P 14, p 2 tog, p 1. Turn.
Row 2: Sl 1, k 5, k 2 tog, k 1. Turn.
Row 3: Sl 1, p 6, p 2 tog, p 1. Turn.
Row 4: Sl 1, k 7, k 2 tog, k 1. Turn.
Row 5: Sl 1, p 8, p 2 tog, p 1. Turn.
Row 6: Sl 1, k 9, k 2 tog, k 1. Turn.
Row 7: Sl 1, p 10, p 2 tog, p 1. Turn.
Row 8: Sl 1, k 11, k 2 tog, k 1. Turn.
Row 9: Sl 1, p 12, p 2 tog. Turn.
Row 10: K 13, k 2 tog—14 sts.
GUSSET: Pick up and k 12 sts along left side edge of heel and sl to needle with heel sts; k all instep sts to one needle; with free needle, pick up and k 12 sts along right side edge of heel, k first 7 sts from heel needle to same needle— 19 sts on first needle, 24 sts on 2nd needle, 19 sts on 3rd needle.
Rnd 1: On first needle, k to within last 2 sts, k 2 tog; on 2nd needle, k across; on 3rd needle, sl 1, k 1, psso, k to end.
Rnd 2: K around. Repeat last 2 rnds 6 times more—48 sts. Work even for 26 rnds more.
TOE: Rnd 1: On first needle, k to within last 2 sts, k 2 tog; on 2nd needle, sl 1, k 1, psso, k to within last 2 sts, k 2 tog; on 3rd needle, sl 1, k 1, psso, k to end. Work 1 rnd even. Repeat last 2 rnds 6 times more—20 sts. With 3rd needle, k across sts of first needle—10 sts on each needle. Weave toe tog with Kitchener st.
FINISHING: With red, embroider along top and bottom edge of cuff in outline st. Embroider around garter st heel in outline st. With green, embroider tree trunks in outline st and branches in straight st. With red, work pots at base of trees in straight st, using 2 long horizontal sts at top and 1 short horizontal st at bottom. See Contents for Stitch Details.
HANGING LOOP: With hook, make ch 4″ long. Fold and sew ends to inside back corner of cuff.

LARGE GRANNY SQUARE STOCKING
Shown on page 12

SIZE: 15″ long.
MATERIALS: Knitting worsted, 4-oz. skeins, 1 skein each of red, green, and white. Susan Bates or Marcia Lynn crochet hook size G-6. Yarn needle.
GAUGE: 1 square = 5″.
GRANNY SQUARE (make 8): With red, ch 6; join with a sl st to form ring.
Note: Always ch 3 for first dc of rnd.

Row 1: * 3 dc in ring, ch 1; repeat from * 3 times, join with a sl st. Sl st across to next ch-1 sp.

Row 2: 3 dc, ch 1, 3 dc (corner) in same sp, * 3 dc, ch 1, 2 dc in next sp; repeat from * 2 times, join with a sl st. End off.

Rows 3–5: Repeat row 2 with white, green and red, having one more 3-dc group between corners in each row.

HALF SQUARE (make 3): With red, ch 4; join with a sl st to form ring.

Row 1: Ch 4, * 3 dc in ring, ch 1, repeat from * once more, 1 dc in ring; ch 4, turn.

Row 2: 3 dc in first sp, 3 dc, ch 1, 3 dc in next sp (corner), 3 dc in next sp, ch 1, 1 dc in same sp. End off.

Row 3: Join white in first sp of last row, ch 4, 3 dc in sp, 3 dc in next sp, 3 dc, ch 1, 3 dc in next sp, 3 dc in next sp, 3 dc in next sp, ch 1, 1 dc in same sp. End off.

Rows 4 and 5: Repeat row 3 with green and red, having one more 3-dc group each side of corner in each row.

FINISHING: With red, sl st squares tog by inserting hook from front under two top threads of each st of last row of squares, following diagram for square placement. Leave top edge open. Dash lines indicate fold lines of squares. With yarn needle, draw red through open edge of toe half square, pulling yarn tight to close.

With red, work 6 rows sc around top edge, working a ch-20 lp at back on last row for hanger.

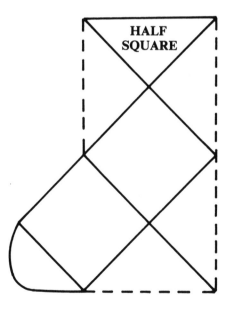

HALF SQUARE

SMALL GRANNY SQUARE STOCKING
Shown on page 12

SIZE: 9″ long.
MATERIALS: Knitting worsted, 4-oz. skeins, 1 skein each of white, red, and green. Susan Bates or Marcia Lynn crochet hook size G-6.

GAUGE: 1 square = 3¾″.
GRANNY SQUARE (make 6): With red, ch 6; join with a sl st to form ring.
Note: Always ch 3 for first dc of rnd.
Row 1: * 3 dc in ring, ch 1; repeat from * 3 times, join with a sl st in top of first dc. Sl st across to next ch-1 sp.
Row 2: 3 dc in ch 1, 3 dc in same sp, * 3 dc, ch 1, 3 dc in next sp (corner), repeat from * 2 times. End off.
Rows 3 and 4: Repeat row 2 with white and green, having 1 more 3-dc group between corners on each row. End off.
FINISHING: With green, sl st squares tog as pictured by inserting hook under two top threads of last row of squares, leaving top and front edges of top two squares open for lacing.

With red, work 5 rows sc on top edge for border, working a ch-20 lp at back on last row for hanger. Work 1 row sc down front of border and down front of square, up side of other square and up border. End off.

With white, make a ch to measure 26″. Lace through last row of red sc. Tie a knot in each end of lacing.

CHRISTMAS TREE SKIRT
Shown on pages 12 and 13

SIZE: 46″ diameter.
MATERIALS: Knitting worsted weight yarn, 4-oz. skeins, 3 skeins each of white (W) and green (G), 4 skeins red (R). Susan Bates or Marcia Lynn crochet hook size J-10. Susan Bates Adjustable "Trim-Tool" for tassels.
GAUGE: 4 sc = 1″; 4 rows = 1″.
Note: Work all rows from right side.
SKIRT: With R, ch 51.
Row 1: Sc in 2nd ch from hook, sc in next 2 sts, * dec 1 st (to dec, pull up a lp in each of next 2 sts, yo and through 3 lps on hook), sc in next 2 sts, (sc, ch 2, sc) in next st for point, sc in next 2 sts, repeat from *, end sc in last 3 sts. End off. There are 8 points, including both ends.
Row 2: With W, 2 sc in first st, sc in next 2 sts, * sk 1 st, sc in next 3 sts, (sc, ch 2, sc) in ch-2 sp, sc in next 3 sts, repeat from *, end last repeat sk 1 st, sc in last 3 sts, working 2 sc in last st. End off.
Row 3: With G, 2 sc in first st, sc in each sc across, working (sc, ch 2, sc) in each ch-2 sp and 2 sc in last st. End off.
Row 4: With R, inc in first st, sc in next 3 sts, * dec 1 st, sc in next 4 sts, (sc, ch 2, sc) in ch-2 sp, sc in next 4 sts, repeat from * across, end last repeat dec 1 st, sc in last 4 sts, working 2 sc in last st.
Note: Decs fall in center 2 sts between 2 points.
Row 5: With W, inc in first st, sc in each st across, skipping each dec st of last row and working (sc, ch 2, sc) in each ch-2 sp, end inc in last st. End off.

Row 6: With G, inc in first st, sc in each st across, work (sc, ch 2, sc) in each ch-2 sp, end inc in last st. End off.
Rows 7–9: Keeping to color sequence of R, W, G, and working in hdc rather than sc, repeat rows 4–6. **Note:** As sts are added between points, there will be more sts worked between decs on row 4. Always work decs in center 2 sts between points.
Rows 10–12: Keeping to color sequence and working in dc rather than sc, repeat rows 4–6.

Continue to repeat rows 4–6 in color sequence, working 2 rows of each color in dc, then (3 rows of each color in dc) twice, then 3 rows each of R and W in dc, then 1 row each of G and R in dc.
FINISHING: Work 1 row dc with R along sides and opening. With "Trim-Tool," make eight 4″ tassels; attach a tassel to each point.

TRIANGULAR SANTA
Shown on page 13

SIZE: 10″ high.
MATERIALS: Worsted weight yarn, 1 oz. red, ½ oz. white, ½ oz. pink. Crochet hook size G. Stuffing. Blue and black embroidery floss. Yarn needle.
GAUGE: 5 sc = 1″.
SANTA: Beg at top of hat, with red, ch 3.
Row 1: Sc in 2nd ch from hook and in next ch. Ch 1, turn each row.
Row 2: Inc 1 sc in row.
Row 3: Work even.
Rows 4–17: Repeat rows 2 and 3—10 sc.
Rows 18–23: Change to pink, repeat rows 2 and 3—13 sc.
Rows 24 and 25: Work even.
Row 26: Change to red, work even.
Rows 27–36: Repeat rows 2 and 3—18 sc. End off. Make another piece the same. Sew tog at sides, leave bottom open.
Bottom: With red, ch 7.
Rnd 1: Sc in 2nd ch from hook and in each of next 4 ch, 3 sc in last ch. Working on opposite side of starting ch, sc in 4 ch, 2 sc in last ch. Work around in sc, inc 2 sc each end each rnd until piece fits into opening. Stuff body; sew in bottom.
Arms (make 2): With red, ch 7. Work 5 rows of 6 sc. Change to white. Dec 1 sc in next row, work 4 rows even. Dec 2 sc in next row. Run yarn through last sts. Sew up side seam. Stuff arm; sew on.
Legs (make 2): With red, ch 9. Work 10 rows of 8 sc. Sew up back seam and across top. Stuff.
Feet (make 2): With white, ch 8. Work same as leg for 5 rows. Sew toe and sole seam. Stuff; sew to bottom of leg. Sew leg to front of body.
Pompon: With white, ch 2.

Rnd 1: 5 sc in 2nd ch from hook.

Rnd 2: 2 sc in each sc around. Work even on 10 sc for 2 rnds. Gather edge, stuff and pull tight to form ball. Sew to top of hat.

Hatband: With white, ch 26. Work 1 row of 25 sc. Sew to bottom of hat.

Suit Trim: With white, ch 36. Work 1 row of 35 sc. Sew to bottom of body.

Nose: With pink, ch 2, 4 sc in 2nd ch from hook. Sew into a ball; sew to face.

Hair: With white, embroider straight vertical sts from hatband to top of suit around sides and back of face. Embroider beard with lazy daisy sts worked closely tog. Mustache is straight sts from nose to sides of beard.

Features: Embroider black satin st pupils, blue straight st eyes, white straight st eyebrows, red straight st mouth. See Contents for Stitch Details.

TINY SANTA
Shown on page 13

SIZE: 11" high.

MATERIALS: Knitting worsted, small amounts of red, white, black, pink. Crochet hook size D. Stuffing. Craft glue. Felt scraps, red and black. Yarn needle. White sewing thread.

GAUGE: 9 sc = 2"; 5 rows = 1".

SANTA: BODY: With red, ch 21.

Row 1: Sc in 2nd ch from hook and in each remaining ch—20 sc. Ch 1, turn each row.

Rows 2–11: Work even in sc. End off. Sew side edges tog (center front). Sew top edges tog, stuff and sew bottom edges tog.

LEG (make 2): Beg at top, with red, ch 7.

Row 1: Sc in 2nd ch from hook and in each remaining ch—6 sc. Ch 1, turn each row.

Rows 2–10: Work even in sc. Change to black. Work 5 rows even. End off. Roll leg over stuffing. Sew side edges tog. Sew top edge flat. Sew to bottom of body so legs swing freely.

FOOT (make 2): Beg at back edge, with black, ch 7. Work even on 6 sc for 5 rows. End off. Sew up and stuff foot, rounding toe end. Sew foot to leg.

ARM (make 2): With red, ch 6. Work even on 5 sc for 12 rows. Change to black. Work even for 5 rows. End off. Sew up over stuffing, rounding both ends. Sew to sides of body at shoulder so arms swing freely.

HEAD (make 2 pieces): Beg at neck, with pink, ch 4.

Row 1: Sc in 2nd ch from hook and in next 2 ch. Ch 1, turn.

Row 2: Sc in each sc—3 sc. Ch 4, turn.

Row 3: Sc in 2nd ch from hook and in next 2 ch, sc in each of 3 sc. Ch 4, turn.

Row 4: Sc in 2nd ch from hook and in next 2 ch, sc in each of 6 sc. Ch 1, turn.

Rows 5–10: Work even on 9 sc. Change to red.

Rows 11 and 12: Work even.

Row 13: Dec 1 sc each end—7 sc.

Row 14: Work even.

Row 15: Repeat row 13.

Rows 16 and 17: Work even.

Row 18: Repeat row 13—3 sc.

Rows 19–25: Work even.

Row 26: Dec 1 sc.

Rows 27–29: Work even. Work 2 sc tog. End off. Sew pieces tog, stuffing as you go. Sew neck to top of body.

TRIMMING: With 2 strands of white held tog, make a ch long enough to go down front of body, around lower edge and up front to neck. Sew, right side down, to body. Trim around boots, cuffs and cap in same way.

FINISHING: Cut black eyes, red mouth from felt. Glue on. Thread white yarn in needle, make hair and beard with straight stitches; beard can be stitched into top of trimming on suit. For mustache, cut 2½" piece of white yarn. Glue center over mouth, curl up ends; glue in place. For pompon, with 2 strands of white, ch 15. Sew into a ball; sew to top of hat.

DISK SANTA
Shown on page 13

SIZE: 16" high.

MATERIALS: Knitting worsted weight yarn, 2 ozs. red, ½ oz. each white, pink and black. Crochet hooks sizes E and J. Tunafish can. Cardboard. Stuffing. Yarn needle. Masking tape.

GAUGE: 5 sc = 1".

SANTA: BODY: Draw around open top of can on cardboard. Cut out circle. Tape to open top, cover entire can with tape. With red and E hook, ch 2. **Rnd 1:** 7 sc in 2nd ch from hook.

Rnd 2: 2 sc in each sc around.

Rnd 3: * Sc in next sc, 2 sc in next sc, repeat from * around.

Rnd 4: 2 sc in each sc around.

Rnds 5 and 6: Work even—42 sc.

Rnd 7: (Sc in next 6 sc, 2 sc in next sc) 6 times—48 sc. End off. Piece should come almost to edge of can all around. Make another piece the same.

With red and E hook, ch 10. Sc in 2nd ch from hook and in each ch across. Ch 1, turn each row. Work even on 9 sc for 47 rows or until strip, when stretched, covers sides. Sew ends tog on can. Sew circles to strip, catching back lp of each sc on edge of circles.

ARMS AND LEGS: With J hook, work disks same as for body through rnd 2. Make 11 red disks for each arm and leg, 2 white disks for each arm and leg and 4 black disks for each leg.

Make 1 white disk for Santa's hat and 2 for buttons.

SHOE (make 2): With black and E hook, ch 12. Sc in 2nd ch from hook and in each ch across. Ch 1, turn each row. Work 10 more rows of 11 sc. Fold in half, sew first and last rows tog for top of shoe. Close toe and heel ends, stuffing lightly with yarn scraps.

MITTEN (make 4 pieces): With black and E hook, ch 6. Sc in 2nd ch from hook and in each ch (thumb). Ch 1, turn each row.

Row 2: Sc in 2 sc, ch 6.

Row 3: Sc in 2nd ch from hook and in 4 ch, sc in 2 sc.

Rows 4–7: Work even on 7 sc. At end of row 7, ch 2. Working along bottom of mitten, work 5 sc across. Ch 1, turn. Work 2 rows even. End off. Sew 2 tog for each hand, stuffing lightly.

To Join Legs and Arms: Sew center of 18" piece of red yarn to center side of body where each arm and leg should be. String disks on double yarn. Push up disks. Sew back top corner of foot to yarn of leg and last black disk. Sew top of mitten to yarn of arm and last white disk.

HEAD: With pink and E hook, ch 2. Work 6 sc in 2nd ch from hook.

Rnd 2: 2 sc in each sc around. Work 1 rnd even.

Rnd 4: (Sc in next sc, 2 sc in next sc) 6 times. Work 1 rnd even—18 sc.

Rnd 6: (Sc in 2 sc, 2 sc in next sc) 6 times. Work 1 rnd even—24 sc.

Rnd 8: (Sc in next sc, 2 sc in next sc) 12 times. Work 3 rnds even—36 sc.

Rnd 12: (Sc in 8 sc, 2 sc in next sc) 4 times. Work 4 rnds even—40 sc.

Rnd 17: * Sc in each of 2 sc, pull up a lp in each of next 2 sts, yo and through 3 lps on hook (1 dec), repeat from * around. Work 2 rnds even—30 sc.

Rnd 20: Work 2 sc tog around. Work 2 rnds even—15 sc. End off. Stuff head; sew to body.

HAT: With white and J hook, ch 25. Sl st in first ch to form ring.

Rnd 1: Sc in each ch around.

Rnds 2–4: Sc in each sc.

Rnd 5: (Sc in 3 sc, work 2 sc tog) 5 times. Work 4 rnds even—20 sc.

Rnd 10: (Sc in 2 sc, work 2 sc tog) 5 times. Work 2 rnds even—15 sc.

Rnd 13: (Sc in next sc, work 2 sc tog) 5 times. Work 5 rnds even—10 sc.

Rnd 19: (Sc in 3 sc, work 2 sc tog) twice. Work 3 rnds even—8 sc.

Rnd 23: (Sc in 2 sc, work 2 sc tog) twice. Work 3 rnds even—6 sc. Work 2 sc tog around. End off.

Sew white disk to top of hat; sew hat to head.

FINISHING: Sew buttons to body. Embroider white hair in 1" long vertical sts around sides and back of head. Embroider black eyes outlined with blue, white straight eyebrows. Embroider red horizontal st for nose, triangular mouth. Take long sts from side to nose and back to side for mustache; form loops at side. Stitch loops around chin for beard.

FINGER PUPPETS
Shown on pages 14 and 15

SIZE: 4″ high.
MATERIALS: Knitting worsted in small amounts (colors given with individual puppets). Crochet hook size G. Iron-on tape.
GAUGE: 4 sc = 1″.
PUPPETS: BODY: Ch 2.
Rnd 1: 6 sc in 2nd ch from hook.
Rnd 2: 2 sc in each sc around.
Rnds 3–5: Work even on 12 sc.
Rnd 6: Work 2 sc tog around—6 sc.
Rnd 7: 2 sc in each sc around.
Rnd 8: Sc in 3 sc, ch 4 for arm; sc in 2nd ch from hook and next 2 ch, sc in next 5 sc, ch 4 for 2nd arm; sc in 2nd ch from hook and next 2 ch, sc in next 4 sc.
Rnd 9: Sc in 3 sc, sc in 3 ch, sc in 3 sc of arm, sc in 5 sc, 6 sc around 2nd arm, sc in 4 sc.
Rnd 10: Work even on 24 sc.
Rnd 11: Sc in 3 sc, sk 6 sc of arm, sc in 6 sc, sk 6 sc of arm, sc in 3 sc.
Rnds 12–16: Work even on 12 sc. End off.
BEAR: Work body with brown.
Ears (make 2): With brown, ch 3.
Rnd 1: 5 hdc in 3rd ch from hook. End off. Sew ears to head.
FINISHING: Use black iron-tape for round eyes, triangular nose. Embroider red mouth.
MOUSE: Work body with gray. Work only 14 rnds, then ch 14; attach ch to puppet's arm.
Ears (make 2): With gray, ch 2.
Row 1: 5 sc in 2nd ch from hook. Ch 2, turn.
Row 2: 2 hdc in first sc, hdc in 3 sc, 2 hdc in last sc. End off. Sew to head.
FINISHING: Line ears with pink iron-on tape. Use dark pink iron-on tape for round eyes, triangular nose. Make black whiskers of sewing or embroidery thread.
PIG: Work body with pink. Work only 14 rounds.
Snout: With pink, ch 2; 5 sc in 2nd ch from hook.
Rnd 2: Sc in back lp of each sc around. End off; sew to face.
Ears (make 2): With pink, ch 3, sl st in 2nd ch from hook, 2 dc in next ch. End off; sew to head.
FINISHING: Use black iron-on tape for round eyes. Embroider mouth with red yarn.
ELEPHANT: Work body with gray, working rnd 11 same as rnd 10 to make bigger arms, then working rnds 11–14 of body. End off.
Ears (make 2): With gray, ch 2.
Row 1: 2 sc, 2 hdc, 1 dc in 2nd ch from hook. Ch 2, turn.
Row 2: 3 dc in dc, 3 hdc in next st, 2 sc in next st, sl st in each sc. End off; sew to head.

Trunk: With gray, ch 2.
Rnd 1: 3 sc in 2nd ch from hook.
Rnds 2 and 3: Work in sc, inc 1 sc each rnd—5 sc.
Rnds 4 and 5: Work even.
Rnd 6: Inc 1 sc in rnd. End off. Stuff; sew to face, curving trunk up.
FINISHING: Use black iron-on tape for round pupils, white for oval eyes. Embroider mouth with red yarn.
LION: Work body with gold.
Ears (make 2): With gold, ch 2. Work 4 sc in 2nd ch from hook. Sew to head.
Mane: With gold, ch 22. Sl st in first ch to form ring. Join brown. With gold and brown tog, loop st in each ch around. End off. Sew mane around head.
FINISHING: Use brown iron-on tape for round eyes, triangular nose. Make black whiskers with thread.
FROG: Work body with green through rnd 2.
Rnd 3: (Sc in next sc, 2 sc in next sc) 6 times.
Rnds 4 and 5: Work even on 18 sc.
Rnd 6: Dec 6 sc in rnd.
Rnd 7: Dec 5 sc in rnd—7 sc.
Rnd 8: Work even.
Rnd 9: Inc 2 sc in rnd—9 sc.
Rnd 10: Sc in 4 sc, ch 7; sl st in 2nd ch from hook and in next 5 ch, sc in next 5 sc, ch 7; sl st in 2nd ch from hook and in next 5 ch.
Rnd 11: Sc in 4 sc, sl st in 6 sts on arm, 3 dc in end of arm, 6 sl sts on other side of arm, sc in 5 sc. Work 2nd arm same as first arm.
Rnd 12: Sc in 4 sc, inc 1 sc; sk arm; sc in 5 sc, inc 1 sc; sk arm.
Rnds 13–17: Sc in each sc around. End off.
Eyes (make 2): With green, ch 2.
Rnd 1: 4 sc in 2nd ch from hook.
Rnd 2: Inc 1 sc in rnd—5 sc.
Rnd 3: Work even. End off. Sew to head.
FINISHING: Use white and black iron-on tapes for round eyes and pupils. Embroider mouth with pink yarn.
DOG: Work body with variegated yarn for 15 rnds.
Ears (make 2): With variegated yarn, ch 3.
Row 1: Sc in 2nd ch from hook and in next ch. Ch 1, turn. Work even for 2 rnds.
Row 4: Inc 1 sc in row. End off. Sew to head.
FINISHING: Use brown iron-on tape for round eyes and triangular nose, red tape for tongue. Tie narrow red ribbon around neck.
PANDA: Work body with white through rnd 6, with black through rnd 10, with white through rnd 13.
Rnds 14–16: With black, work as for rnds 8–10. End off. Sew legs tog for 3 sts each side.
Ears (make 2): With black, work as for bear.

FINISHING: Use black iron-on tape for round eyes, triangular nose; use red for semicircular mouth.
REINDEER: Work body with brown for 15 rnds.
Ears (make 2): With brown, ch 2.
Row 1: Sc in 2nd ch from hook. Ch 1, turn each row.
Rows 2 and 3: Inc 1 sc each row.
Row 4: Dec 1 sc.
Row 5: Work 2 sc tog. Sew to sides of head.
Antlers (make 2): With beige yarn, ch 6; sl st in 2nd ch from hook and in next ch; ch 3; sl st in 2nd ch from hook and in next ch, sl st in last 3 ch. End off; sew to head.
FINISHING: Use small red pompon for nose. Use black iron-on tape for round eyes.
SNOWMAN: With white, work body through rnd 7.
Rnd 8: (Sc in next sc, 2 sc in next sc) 6 times.
Rnd 9: Sc in 4 sc, ch 3; sc in 2nd ch from hook and in next ch, sc in 9 sc, ch 3; sc in 2nd ch from hook and in next ch, sc in 5 sc.
Rnd 10: Sc in 4 sc, 4 sc on arm, sc in 9 sc, 4 sc on arm, sc in 5 sc. Work even for 1 rnd.
Rnd 12: Sc in 4 sc, sk 4 sts of arm, sc in 9 sc, sk 4 sts of arm, sc in 5 sc. Work 1 rnd even.
Rnd 14: Working over a doubled #30 rubber band (2″ long), sc in each sc around. End off.
Hat: With black, ch 2.
Rnd 1: 5 sc in 2nd ch from hook.
Rnd 2: 2 sc in each sc around.
Rnd 3: Sc in back lp of each sc.
Rnds 4 and 5: Sc in each sc around.
Rnd 6: Sc in front lp of each sc.
Rnd 7: 2 sc in each sc around. End off. Stuff hat with scraps of black yarn; sew to head.
FINISHING: Use black iron-on tape for round eyes, nose and buttons.
SANTA: With peach yarn, work body through rnd 6.
Rnd 7: With red, work rnd 7 of body.
Rnd 8: Inc 1 sc in next st, sc in 2 sts, ch 3 for arm; sc in 2nd ch from hook and in next ch, (2 sc in next st, sc in next st) twice, 2 sc in next st, ch 3 for 2nd arm; sc in 2nd ch from hook and in next ch (2 sc in next st, sc in next st) twice.
Rnd 9: Sc in 4 sc, work 4 sc around arm, sc in 8 sc, work 4 sc around arm, sc in 6 sc. Work 1 rnd even.
Rnd 11: Sc in 4 sc, sk 4 sc of arm, sc in 8 sc, sk 4 sc of arm, sc in 6 sc.
Rnds 12 and 13: Work even. Cut red.
Rnd 14: With white, working over a double #30 rubber band (2″ long), sc in each sc around. End off.
Hand (make 2): With peach, ch 2. Work 5 sc in 2nd ch from hook, then work 1 rnd on 5 sc. End off; sew to end of arm.

Cuff (make 2): With white, ch 7. Sew to arm above hand.

Belt: With black, ch 25. Sew to body around waist.

Hat: With red, ch 2.

Rnd 1: 3 sc in 2nd ch from hook.

Rnds 2–5: Inc 1 sc each rnd—7 sc.

Rnds 6–9: Inc 2 sc each rnd—15 sc. Cut red.

Rnds 10 and 11: With white, work even. Sew to head.

Pompon: With white, ch 2. Work 4 sc in 2nd ch from hook; work 1 rnd on 4 sc. End off. Close opening. Sew to top of hat, fold top of hat over; sew to side.

Beard: With white, ch 15. Sl st in 2nd ch from hook and in next ch, sc in next 2 ch, hdc in next ch, dc in 4 ch, hdc in next ch, sc in next 2 ch, sl st in last 2 ch. End off. Sew beard to face.

FINISHING: Using black iron-on tape for eyes, red for nose, make round eyes and nose.

YARN LOOP DOLLS
Shown on pages 14 and 15

SIZE: About 6¾" to 7½" tall.

MATERIALS: Flesh-tone nylon stocking. Coats & Clark Red Heart 4 Ply Handknitting Yarn, one 3½-ounce skein each of the following colors: Lt. Gold #603, Cashmere #323, Pantile Brown #283, Jockey Red #902, Emerald #676; one 1-ounce skein each: White #1, Off-White #3. Coats & Clark Red Heart Persian Type Needlepoint and Crewel Yarn, one 12-yard pull skein Black #050. Felt: one 9" × 12" sheet each of rose and black; scraps of pink, lime, light brown, and dark brown. Scraps of lightweight cardboard. Silver metallic round braided trim ¹⁄₁₆" diameter, ¾ yard. Sewing thread. Fiberfill for stuffing. Pink crayon. Black felt-tip marking pen. White craft glue. For Bear: Green satin ribbon ⅜" wide, piece 12". For Clown: Pink satin ribbon: ⅞" wide, piece 11"; ½" wide, piece 13". For Santa: Scrap of gold foil, about 1" square.

DIRECTIONS: Cut out body pieces from single thickness of nylon stocking as follows: Body: 4" square; head: 3"-diameter circle (5" circle for Santa); nose: 1" circle (omit for Bear); arms: 2" square (2" × 2½" for Clown); legs: 2" × 2½" (2" × 3" for Lion and Clown.)

Body: Fold piece in half, bringing two opposite sides together to form a pouch; stuff pouch with fiberfill. Slip-stitch edges of stocking together, enclosing fiberfill. As you stitch, mold object to resemble a small potato with seam in back (see Figure 1).

Head: Hand or machine-baste around raw edges; pull basting, gathering nylon to form a pouch; stuff pouch with fiberfill. Pull thread tightly, enclosing fiberfill, and tie off for neck. For all except Santa, mold fiberfill with hands so head is round; for Santa, elongate head top for hat. To make nose for all except Bear, gather piece same as for head; compress cotton-ball sized piece of fiberfill and stuff into opening; tie off. Place nose on head about ¾" above tied-off neck. Stitch in place securely with invisible stitches.

Arms and Legs: Fold piece in half lengthwise with edges even; for Bear's arm, fold in half widthwise. Hand or machine-stitch across long raw edge and one short edge; turn to right side. Stuff with fiberfill. Turn raw edge to inside; slip-stitch end closed. For Lion's foot, bend bottom 1" of leg, following Figure

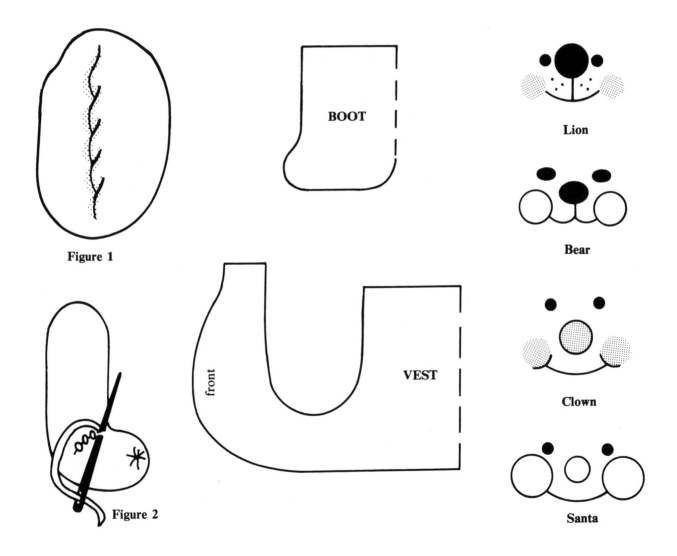

Figure 1

Figure 2

BOOT

VEST · front

Lion

Bear

Clown

Santa

2. Make a few stitches to secure the foot in position, as shown.

To Assemble: Pin tied-off neck edge on head to top end of body, centering body seam in back. Stitch head in place securely so tied-off neck is invisible. Stitch arms and legs to body.

Loopy Coat: Cover doll with ¼" loops, unless otherwise directed; follow photograph for colors and leave faces bare. Use doubled strand of 4-ply yarn in needle. To begin a strand, draw yarn through stocking and fiberfill, burying end inside stocking. Work about four backstitches per inch, leaving ¼" loop between each stitch; do not pull stitches taut. To end a strand, clip off excess yarn close to stocking. Change directions of stitches often so that loops have a natural random appearance; work loops densely so no stocking shows through. At joining of arms, legs, and head to body, work loops over joined edges, securing appendages firmly to the body.

Clothing: Trace and complete actual-size half patterns; cut out.

LION: Referring to face diagram, use one strand black persian yarn to work French knots for eyes and straight stitches for mouth. Use black felt-tip pen to mark whiskers and blacken nose. "Rouge" cheeks with pink crayon. Cover head with ½" loops; do not work loops on bottoms of feet. For tail, cut three 10" lengths from Lt. Gold yarn. Thread lengths through stocking at rump so all ends are even; braid. Cut an 8" × ¼" strip from rose felt; tie into bow around end of tail. Use pattern to cut vest from rose felt. Glue vest fronts to vest back at shoulders. Glue silver braid trim around edges of vest; place vest on lion and glue 2" lengths of silver braid across front of vest as shown. From dark brown felt, cut four ½"-diameter circles and two ¾" × 1⅛" ovals. Glue two circles to head for ears; glue two circles to bottoms of arms; glue ovals to bottoms of feet.

BEAR: Referring to face diagram, cut eyes and nose from black felt; cut cheeks from pink felt. Glue in place as shown. Work mouth in outline stitch, using one strand black persian yarn. For tail, use Cashmere yarn to make a 1"-diameter pompon; stitch in place at rump. From light brown felt, cut two ¾"-diameter circles for outer ears; from dark brown felt, cut two ½"-diameter circles for inner ears. Glue one inner ear, centered, to each outer ear. Glue ears to top of head. Tie green ribbon in bow around neck.

CLOWN: Referring to face diagram, use one strand black persian yarn to work French knots for eyes and outline stitch for mouth; work two small straight stitches at each end of mouth, as shown.

"Rouge" cheeks and nose with pink crayon. Do not cover soles of feet and ½" at bottom of arms (hands) with loops. Work Pantile Brown hair. For shoes, cut four 1⅛" × 1⅜" ovals from lime felt; glue pairs of ovals together with edges even. Glue shoes to bottoms of feet. Make bows from narrow pink ribbon tied with silver trim; glue to shoe fronts. For cuffs, cut remaining narrow pink ribbon in half widthwise. Baste along one long edge of each length; gather to fit around bottom of arm just below loops; slip-stitch in place. Overlap short ends; glue. Use wide pink ribbon to make collar as for cuffs; stitch in place around neck joining, overlapping ends at center back. Cut two 2½" lengths from silver trim. Tie in bows and stitch to body front, as shown.

SANTA: Referring to face diagram, use one strand black persian yarn to work French knots for eyes and outline stitch for mouth. Cut cheeks from pink felt; glue in place. Use White yarn to work a single row of loops for sleeve, pants, and hat cuffs, and bottom of jacket. (Cover remainder of body with red loops.) Shape and glue on bits of fiberfill for hair, mustache, beard, and eyebrows. Use pattern to cut two boots from black felt. Fold each boot in half with edges even; whipstitch together around sole and toe, leaving straight edges above toe open. Stuff toe with small amount of fiberfill. Slide boot onto leg so that toe faces forward and stocking is covered; whipstitch front edges of boot together; tack boot top to leg. For belt, cut a 7½" × ¼" strip from black felt. Place belt around body, overlapping ends at center front; glue. Glue gold foil to cardboard scrap; cut out a ½" × ⅝" buckle as shown; glue on belt.

CHILD'S CHRISTMAS AFGHAN
Shown on page 16

SIZE: 42" x 56".
MATERIALS: Red Heart 4 Ply Hand Knitting Yarn, 10 4-oz. skeins Emerald Green (EG), 1 skein each Paddy Green (PG) and White (W). Afghan hook size H. Crochet hook size H. For embroidery: Red Heart Persian Type Needlepoint & Crewel Yarn, 1 12-yd. skein each of Cocoa Brown 126, Fawn Beige 132, Yellow 042, Black 050, Red 010, Pink 860, Royal Blue 740. Red Heart 4 Ply Hand Knitting Yarn, 1 1-oz. skein each Yellow 230 and Skipper Blue 848. Tapestry needles.
GAUGE: 10 sts = 3"; 3 rows = 1".
AFGHAN: SQUARE (make 12): With

EG, ch 45. Work in afghan st as follows:

Row 1: Pull up a lp in 2nd ch from hook and in each ch across, keeping all lps on hook.
To Work Lps Off: Yo hook, pull through first lp, * yo hook, pull through next 2 lps, repeat from * across until 1 lp remains. Lp that remains on hook always counts as first st of next row.
Row 2: Keeping all lps on hook, pull up a lp under 2nd vertical bar and under each vertical bar across. Work lps off as before. Repeat row 2 until there are 42 rows. End off. Steam-press squares.
NOTE: See charts for embroidery.

EMBROIDERY: Count number of squares on width and length of each chart to be embroidered. With pins, mark off section on crocheted square where embroidery will go, arranging design for best effect. Following charts and color key, embroider squares in cross-stitch, using 2 strands of Persian type yarn or single strand of 4-ply yarn in needle. For white and paddy green embroidery, use yarn from 4-oz. skeins. On chart 8, for handle of milk pail, bring beige yarn up at one top edge of pail, pass yarn under pink hand and down at other top edge of pail. On chart 11, embroider yellow pipe in satin stitch; embroider straight lines of black notes in straight stitches, fill in solid sections with outline stitch worked from the center out. On chart 12, outline drum with single strand of black; make 2 large cross-stitches over front of drum. With red, make 2 long straight stitches for drumsticks, bringing yarn up above pink crosses for hands, under pink stitches and down at black outline for top front of drum, crossing ends of sticks. Work yellow number in top right corner of each square, 2 sts in from right edge and 2 rows down from top.

FINISHING: EDGING FOR SQUARE: Rnd 1: With PG, make lp on hook; 3 sc in corner, sc in next st, * long sc in st 3 rows or 3 sts below, sc in each of next 3 sts, repeat from * around, working 3 sc in each corner. Sl st in first sc. End off.
Rnd 2: With W, sc in each sc around, working 3 sc in each corner st. Sl st in first sc. End off.

JOINING SQUARES: Lay squares out in right order: 1, 2 and 3 for top row, 4, 5 and 6 for next row, etc. To join squares, working from left to right in back lps only of W sc, with PG, sc squares tog with reverse sc. When squares are joined horizontally and vertically, work 1 rnd of reverse sc in PG around entire outer edge, working in both lps of W sc.

 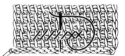

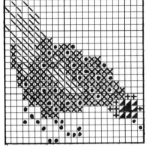

CROSS-STITCH ON AFGHAN STITCH

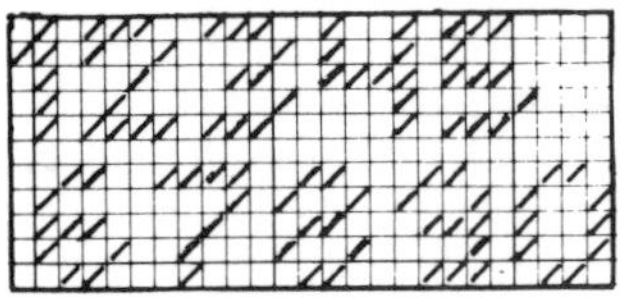

CHART 2

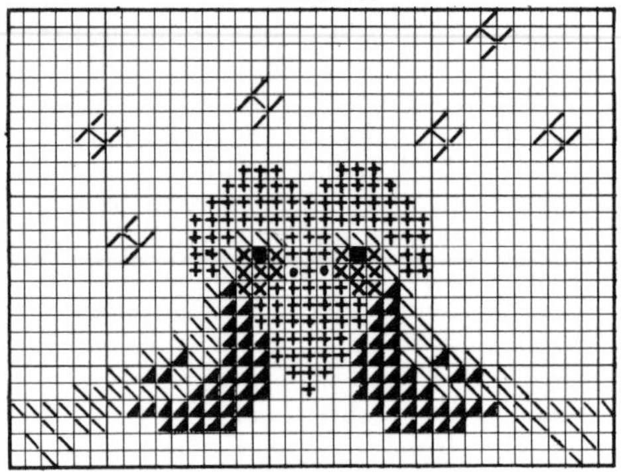

CHART 1

CHART 3

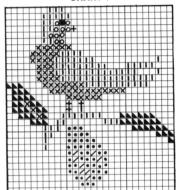

CHART 5

CHART 6

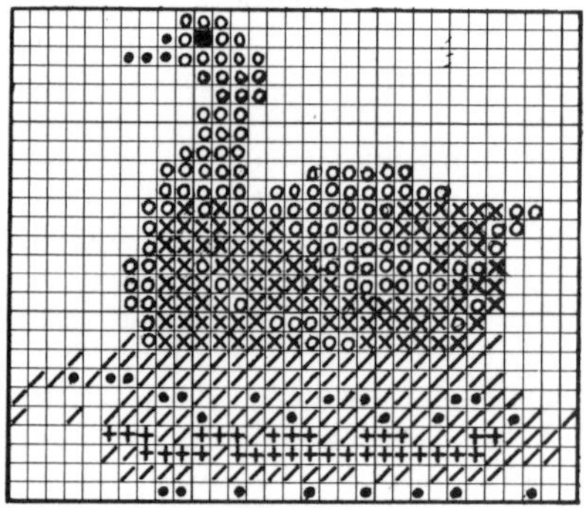

CHART 4

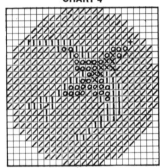

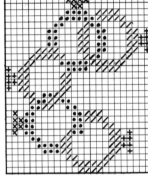

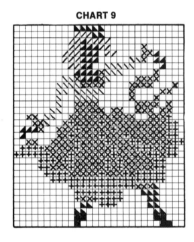

CHART 8

CHART 9

CHART 7

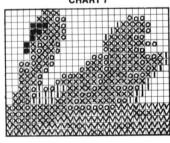

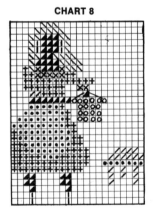

CHART 11

CHART 10

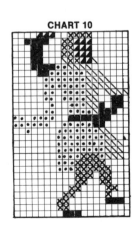

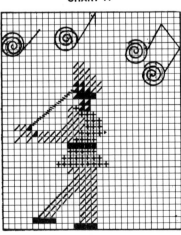

CHART 12

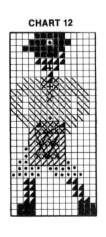

☒	WHITE
⬧	LT. YELLOW
⊡	DK. YELLOW
⥊	BROWN
▣	BLACK
◨	BEIGE
⊞	RED
◪	PINK
◩	ROYAL BLUE
☑	SKIPPER BLUE
◩	PADDY GREEN

28

SNOW CRYSTALS
Shown on page 33

SIZE: 3" to 3½".
MATERIALS: White mercerized knitting and crochet cotton. Steel crochet hook No. 8 (1.25 mm). Silver seed beads or small sequins (optional). Starch or sugar water. All-purpose glue.

1. CHRISTMAS DAISY: Ch 9, sl st in first ch to form ring. **Rnd 1:** Ch 5, dc in ring, (ch 2, dc in ring) 6 times, ch 2, sl st in 3rd ch of ch 5—8 sps.
Rnd 2: Ch 24, sc in same ch with sl st, * sc in next sp, ch 12, sl st in 4th ch from hook for picot, ch 8, sc in same sp with last sc, sc in next dc, ch 24, sc in same dc, repeat from * around, end sl st in first ch of ch 24 at beg of rnd. End off.

2. ROSE WINDOW: Ch 10, sl st in first ch to form ring. **Rnd 1:** Ch 6, dc in ring, (ch 3, dc in ring) 6 times, ch 3, sl st in 3rd ch of ch 6—8 sps.
Rnd 2: Sl st in next sp, ch 2, 2 hdc in same sp, (ch 2, 3 hdc in next sp) 7 times, ch 3, sl st in top of ch 2.
Rnd 3: Ch 1, turn; sc in first sp, ch 7, sc in same sp, (ch 8, sc in next sp, ch 7, sc in same sp) 7 times, ch 8, sl st in first sc.
Rnd 4: Sl st to 3rd ch of first lp; hdc in lp, (ch 3, sc in 3rd ch from hook for picot, hdc in same lp) twice, * ch 2, sc in next lp, ch 2, hdc, picot, hdc, picot, hdc in next lp, repeat from * around, end ch 2, sl st in first hdc.
Rnd 5: Ch 1, turn; sc in first sp, * ch 4, sc in next sp, ch 5, dc in hdc between 2 picots, ch-3 picot, ch 5, sc in next sp, repeat from * around, end ch 5, sl st in first sc. End off.

3. FROST CRYSTAL: Ch 12, sl st in first ch to form ring. **Rnd 1:** Ch 1, * sc in ring, (ch 5, sl st in 4th ch from hook for picot) 4 times, ch-4 picot, sl st in same ch with last picot, sl st in next ch, (ch-4 picot, sl st in same ch with next picot, sl st in next ch) 3 times, sc in ring, ch 24, repeat from * 5 times, end sl st in first sc. End off.

4. CHRISTMAS ROSE: Ch 8, sl st in first ch to form ring. **Rnd 1:** Ch 7, dc in ring, (ch 5, dc in ring) 4 times, ch 5, sl st in 2nd ch of ch 7—6 sps.
Rnd 2: Sl st in next lp, ch 4 (counts as 1 tr); holding back last lp of each tr on hook, make 3 tr in ch-5 lp, yo and through 4 lps on hook (4 tr cluster), * ch 9, 4 tr cluster in next lp, repeat from * 4 times, ch 9, sl st in top of first cluster.
Rnd 3: * Ch 7, sl st in 4th ch from hook for picot, ch 9, sl st in 4th ch from hook for picot, ch 3, sl st in top of cluster; in ch-9 lp work sc, hdc, 4 dc, hdc, sc, sl st in top of next cluster, repeat from * around, end sl st in sl st at beg of rnd. End off.

5. BUTTERFLY: Ch 8, sl st in first ch to form ring. **Rnd 1:** Ch 4, (dc in ring, ch 1) 7 times, sl st in 3rd ch of ch 4.
Rnd 2: Ch 1, sc in same place as sl st, ch 9, sc in 4th ch from hook for picot, ch 13, sc in sc of picot, ch 4, sc in 4th ch from hook for picot, sl st in ch with previous picot, ch 5, sc in same place as first sc, * (sc in next sp, sc in same sp) twice, sc in next dc, ch 9, sc in 4th ch from hook for picot, ch 13, sc in sc of picot, ch 4, sc in 4th ch from hook for picot, sl st in ch with previous picot, ch 5, sc in same dc of ring, repeat from * around, sl st in first sc. End off.

6. SERENADE: Ch 15, sl st in first ch to form ring. **Rnd 1:** Ch 1, 24 sc in ring. Sl st in first sc.
Rnd 2: Ch 1, sc in first sc, (ch 5, sk 2 sc, sc in next sc) 7 times, ch 5, sl st in first sc.
Rnd 3: Sl st in next 2 ch, sc in lp, (ch 5, sc in same lp, ch 5, sc in next lp) 8 times, end sl st in first sc.
Rnd 4: Ch 1, turn; sl st in lp; ch 3, 2 dc, ch 3, 3 dc in same lp, sc in next lp, * (3 dc, ch 3, 3 dc) in next lp, sc in next lp, repeat from * around, end sc in last lp, sl st in top of ch 3.
Rnd 5: Ch 1, turn; sc in sc, * ch 3, 3 dc, ch 3, 3 dc in next ch-3 lp, ch 3, sc in next sc, repeat from * around, sl st in first sc. End off.

7. GEORGIANA: Ch 7, sl st in first ch to form ring. **Rnd 1:** Ch 6, (dc in ring, ch 3) 7 times, sl st in 3rd ch of ch 6—8 sps.
Rnd 2: Sl st in next sp; ch 3, 2 dc in sp, (ch 3, 3 dc in next sp) 7 times, ch 3, sl st in top of first ch 3.
Rnd 3: Ch 7, sk 1 dc, dc in next dc, * ch 4, dc in next dc, ch 4, sk 1 dc, dc in next dc, repeat from * around, end ch 4, sl st in 3rd ch of ch 7.
Rnd 4: Sl st in first sp, ch 4, 2 tr in same sp, ch 4, sc in 4th ch from hook for picot, sl st in last tr, 2 tr in same sp, ch 3, sc in next sp, * ch 3, 3 tr, picot, 2 tr in next sp, ch 3, sc in next sp, repeat from * around, end ch 3, sl st in top of ch 4. End off.

FINISHING: Starch ornaments, pin into shape; let dry. Glue on beads or sequins.

SNOWBIRDS
Shown on page 34

SIZES: Directions are given for small bird (3½" long). Changes for large bird (4½" long) are in parentheses.
MATERIALS: J. & P. Coats Knit-Cro-Sheen, 1 ball. Steel crochet hook No. 6 (2). Absorbent cotton. Starch.
GAUGE: 7 sc = 1" (6 sc = 1").
BIRD: HEAD: With No. 6 hook (No. 2 hook), ch 4; sl st in first ch to form ring.
Rnd 1: 8 sc in ring.
Rnds 2–4 (5): * Sc in next sc, 2 sc in next sc, repeat from * around until there are 24 (30) sc. Work even until piece is 1¼" (1½") from start. * Sc in next sc, work next 2 sc tog, repeat from * around for 3 rnds, stuffing head before opening is too small. Pull last sts tog to close opening.
BODY: Work as for head through rnd 1.
Rnd 2: (Sc in next sc, 2 in next sc) 4 times.
Rnd 3: Sc in each sc around—12 sc.
Rnd 4: (Sc in next sc, 2 sc in next sc) 6 times.
Rnd 5: (Sc in next sc, 2 sc in next sc) 9 times—27 sc.
For large bird only, continue to inc in every other sc until there are 51 sc. Work even on 27 (51) sc until piece is 2¼" (4") from start.
Dec Rnd: (Sc in next sc, work next 2 sts tog) 6 (8) times, finish rnd. Work 1 rnd even. Repeat dec rnd. End off.

Stuff body; sew back opening with decs spaced evenly around bottom.
SMALL WING: With No. 6 hook, ch 15.
Row 1: Dc in 5th ch from hook, (ch 1, sk 1 ch, dc in next ch) 5 times. Ch 3, turn.
Row 2: Dc in next dc, ch 1, dc in next dc, 5 dc in next sp, drop lp off hook, insert hook in first dc of 5 dc, pull dropped lp through (popcorn made), dc in next dc, (ch 1, dc in next dc) twice. Do not work over last sp. Turn.
Row 3: Sl st to next dc, ch 3, dc in next dc, (ch 1, dc in next dc) 3 times. Work 1 rnd sc all around, keeping wing flat. Work 2nd wing the same but in working popcorn, insert hook from back to front in first dc, pull dropped lp through. (Popcorn forms on reverse side.)
LARGE WING: With No. 2 hook, ch 9 loosely.
Row 1: Dc in 5th ch from hook (V st), ch 1, sk 1 ch, 3 dc, ch 1, 3 dc in next ch (shell), ch 1, sk 1 ch, dc, ch 1, dc in last ch (V st). Ch 4, turn.
Rows 2 and 3: Dc, ch 1, dc in first ch-1 sp (V st), ch 1, shell of 3 dc, ch 1, 3 dc in ch-1 sp of shell, ch 1, V st of dc, ch 1, dc in last V st. Ch 4, turn.
Rows 4 and 5: 2 dc, ch 1, 2 dc in first ch-1 sp, ch 2, shell of 4 dc, ch 1, 4 dc in ch-1 sp of shell, ch 2, 2 dc, ch 1, 2 dc in last ch-1 sp. Ch 4, turn.
Row 6: 3 dc, ch 1, 3 dc in first ch-1 sp, ch 3, shell of 5 dc, ch 1, 5 dc in ch-1 sp of shell, ch 3, 3 dc, ch 1, 3 dc in last ch-1 sp. Ch 4, turn.
Row 7: Sc in first ch-1 sp, ch 5, sc in 2nd ch of ch 3, ch 5, sc in 3rd dc of shell, ch 5, sc in ch-1 sp of shell, ch 5, sc in 8th dc of shell, ch 5, sc in 2nd ch of ch 3, ch 5, sc in next ch-1 sp, ch 5, sl st in top of ch 4 turning ch. End off. Make 2nd wing the same.
BEAK: With No. 6 hook (No. 2 hook), ch 8. Sc in 2nd ch from hook and in each ch. End off.

CREST: With No. 6 hook (No. 2 hook), * ch 6, sc in 2nd ch from hook and in each ch, repeat from * twice. End off.

TAIL: Work as for crest.

FOOT (make 2): Work as for crest.

FINISHING: Starch beak, crest, tail, feet and wings. Fold beak in half. Sew to front of head. Sew crest to top of head. Sew tail to top back point. Sew feet to bottom of bird to extend out each side. Sew front point of wings to side of bird. Insert pins or sew on beads for eyes.

LACY SATIN BALLS
Shown on page 34

SIZE: 3″ diameter.

MATERIALS: J. & P. Coats Knit-Cro-Sheen, 1 ball white. Steel crochet hooks Nos. 6 and 7. Satin-covered plastic foam balls, 2½″ diameter. For flowers and leaves, six-strand embroidery floss (colors given with individual directions). Satin and metallic cords. White pearls. Blue beads. Starch. Straight pins.

GAUGE: 10 dc = 1″; 4 rnds = 1″.

BALL COVER (make 2 pieces): With white and No. 7 hook; ch 4.

Rnd 1: 9 dc in 4th ch from hook. Sl st in top of starting ch.

Rnd 2: Ch 3, dc in same place as sl st, (2 dc in next dc) 9 times. Join with sl st in top of ch 3.

Rnd 3: Ch 3, dc in same place as sl st, (2 dc in next dc) 19 times. Join.

Rnd 4: Ch 3, dc in same place as sl st, dc in next dc, (2 dc in next dc, dc in next dc) 19 times. Join.

Rnd 5: Ch 3, dc in next dc and in each dc around. Join.

Rnd 6: Ch 3, dc in same place as sl st, dc in next 2 dc, (2 dc in next dc, dc in next 2 dc) 19 times. Join.

Rnds 7 and 8: Repeat rnd 5—80 dc.

Rnd 9: Working in front lps, ch 1, * sc in next 2 sc, ch 3, sl st in top of last sc, repeat from * around. Join. Working in back lps of rnd 8, ch 1, sc in each st around. Join; end off. When making 2nd section, leave length of thread for sewing.

Note: Flowers and leaves are made with No. 6 hook.

PURPLE AND PINK BALL: Violet (make 7): With lavender or purple, ch 5. Sl st in first ch to form ring.

Rnd 1: (Ch 4, 2 tr in ring, ch 4, sl st in ring) 3 times, (ch 5, 2 dtr in ring, ch 5, sl st in ring) twice. End off.

Large Leaf (make 3): With dark green, ch 12. Tr in 4th ch from hook, tr in next 3 ch, dc in next 2 ch, hdc in next ch, sc in next ch, sc, ch 1, sc in last ch. Working along opposite side, sc in next ch, hdc in next ch, dc in next 2 ch, tr in next 4 ch, ch 3, sl st in last ch. End off.

Pink Flower (make 4): Ch 6; join to form ring.

Rnd 1: Ch 1, 12 sc in ring; join.

Rnd 2: Working in back lp, 2 sc in each sc; join.

Rnd 3: Working in back lp, * ch 2, sl st in next sc, repeat from * around. End off. Join thread in any front lp of rnd 1, repeat rnd 3.

Small Leaf (make 3):With light green, ch 9. Sl st in 2nd ch from hook, sc in next ch, hdc in next ch, dc in next 2 ch, hdc in next ch, sc in next ch, sl st in last ch, ch 3. Working along opposite side, sl st in first ch, sc in next ch, hdc in next ch, dc in next 2 ch, hdc in next ch, sc in next ch, sl st in next ch. End off.

BLUE AND WHITE BALL: Blue Flower (make 8): With light or dark blue, ch 4. Join to form ring.

Rnd 1: * Ch 7; holding back on hook last lp of each tr, 3 tr in 6th ch from hook, yo and through all lps on hook, sc in ring, repeat from * 4 times— 5 petals. End off.

White Flower (make 5): With white, ch 2.

Rnd 1: 8 sc in 2nd ch from hook; sl st in first sc.

Rnd 2: Sc in same place, * ch 2, 2 dc, sc, 2 dc in next sc, ch 2, sc in next sc, repeat from * around—4 petals.

Large Leaf (make 6): With emerald green, ch 10. Sc in 2nd ch from hook, dc in next 7 ch, sc, ch 1, sc in end ch. Working on opposite side of ch, dc in next 7 ch, sc in last ch.

Small Leaf (make 6): With lime green, ch 9. Dc in 4th ch from hook and in next 3 ch, sc in next ch, sc, ch 2, sc in end ch. Working on opposite side of ch, sc in next ch, dc in next 5 ch, sl st in base of ch 3.

CORAL BALL: Light Coral Flower (make 10): With light coral, ch 5. Dc in 4th ch from hook, ch 3, sl st in same st, sc in next ch (center of flower), (ch 4, dc in 4th ch from hook, ch 3, sl st in same st, sc in same center st) 4 times— 5 petals.

Dark Coral Flower (make 6): With dark coral, * ch 4; 2 tr in 4th ch from hook, ch 3, sl st in same ch, repeat from * 9 times—10 petals. End off; leave end for sewing. Thread needle; run thread through base of strip, pull tight to form cluster. Tack tog at base.

Leaf (make 6 each of lime and dark green): Same as small leaf of blue and white ball.

POINSETTIA BALL: Flower (make 5): With scarlet or dark red, ch 2.

Rnd 1: 8 sc in 2nd ch from hook. Join.

Rnd 2: * Ch 7, sc in 2nd ch from hook, hdc in next ch, dc in next 4 ch, sl st in next sc, repeat from * 7 times—8 petals.

Leaf (make 6): With dark green, ch 12. Sc in 2nd ch from hook, hdc in next ch, dc in next ch, tr in next 3 ch, dc in next ch, hdc in next ch, sc in next 2 ch, sc, ch 2, sc in last ch. Working back in each ch on opposite side, work 2 sc, hdc, dc, 3 tr, dc, hdc, sc.

GOLD BALL: Flower (make 10): With light, medium or dark gold, ch 5. Join to form ring.

Rnd 1: Ch 1, 12 sc in ring. Sl st in first sc.

Rnd 2: * Ch 3, 5 tr in next sc, drop lp from hook; insert hook in top of ch 3, pull dropped lp through, ch 3, sl st in next sc, repeat from * 5 times—6 petals.

Leaf (make 10): With medium or dark green ch 10. Sc in 2nd ch from hook, sc in next ch, hdc in next ch, dc in 4 ch, hdc in next ch, sc, ch 3, sc in last ch. Working back in each ch on opposite side, work hdc, 4 dc, hdc, 2 sc.

ROSE BALL: Irish Rose (make 4): With dark rose, ch 5. Join to form ring.

Rnd 1: Ch 1, 12 sc in ring. Sl st in first sc.

Rnd 2: Ch 1, sc in same place, * hdc, 3 dc, hdc in next sc, sc in next sc, repeat from * 5 times. Join.

Rnd 3: Ch 1, sc in same place, * ch 3, sc in back lp of sc between petals, repeat from * 5 times.

Rnd 4: In each lp make sc, hdc, 5 dc, hdc, sc. End off.

Pink and Rose Flowers (make 9): Work as for light coral flowers.

Leaves (make 8): With dark green, work as for small leaf of blue and white ball.

FINISHING: Wash ball covers, flowers and leaves. Starch using medium starch, 1 part starch, 3 parts water. Cover a plastic foam slab with wax paper. Stretch and mold each ball section over a plastic foam ball, remove carefully to retain shape and set on slab. Stretch and shape all flowers and leaves; pin to slab. Dry thoroughly. Sew ball halves tog over ball. Trim with hanging loop and bows of cord attached with pins. Push pins through pearls or beads, then through flowers centers. Arrange leaves and flowers as desired and pin to balls.

SNOWFLAKES
Shown on page 35

SIZE: 5½″–6″ in diameter.

MATERIALS: J. & P. Coats Knit-Cro-Sheen, 1 ball white. Steel crochet hook No. 6. Starch.

DIAMOND-EDGED SNOWFLAKE (1): Ch 6, sl st in first ch to form ring.

Rnd 1: Ch 5, dc in ring, (ch 3, dc in ring) 4 times, ch 3, sl st in 3rd ch of ch 5.

Rnd 2: (Ch 9, sc in next dc) 5 times, ch 9, sc in sl st at beg of rnd.

Rnd 3: Sl st to 5th ch of ch 9, (ch 9, sc in 5th ch of next ch 9, ch 5, sc in same st) 6 times.

Rnd 4: Sl st to 5th ch of ch 9, (ch 12, sc in 5th ch of next ch 9) 6 times.

Rnd 5: * (Ch 6, sc in 3rd ch from hook for picot) 3 times, ch 3, sc in sc made at beg of picot lp, ch 13, sc in next sc, repeat from * around, end ch 13, sl st in first sc. End off.

When starching snowflake, form diamond shapes from picot lps.

TREE-EDGED SNOWFLAKE (2): Ch 8, sl st in first ch to form ring.

Rnd 1: (Ch 2, dc, tr, dc, ch 2, sc in ring) 6 times.

Rnd 2: Sl st to tr, (ch 5, sc in next tr) 6 times.

Rnd 3: Ch 4, dc in same sc, (ch 5, dc, ch 1, dc in next sc) 5 times, ch 5, sl st in 3rd of ch 4.

Rnd 4: Sl st to ch-1 sp, ch 3, dc, ch 1, 2 dc in sp, (ch 5, 2 dc, ch 1, 2 dc in next ch-1 sp) 5 times, ch 5, sl st in top of ch 3.

Rnd 5: Sl st to next ch-1 sp, sc in sp, * ch 11, sc in 11th ch from hook, ch 9, sc in 9th ch from hook, ch 7, sc in 7th ch from hook, ch 4, sc in 4th ch from hook, sc in sc of ch-7 lp, ch 7, sc in same sc of ch-7 lp, sc in sc of ch-9 lp, ch 9, sc in same sc, sc in sc of ch-11 lp, ch 11, sc in same sc, sc in ch-1 sp, ch 9, sc in next ch-1 sp, repeat from * around, end ch 9, sl st in first sc. End off.

BELL-POINT SNOWFLAKE (3): Ch 9, sl st in first ch to form ring.

Rnd 1: (Ch 5, sc in ring) 6 times.

Rnd 2: Sl st to 3rd ch of first ch 5, (ch 7, sc in 3rd ch of next ch 5) 6 times.

Rnd 3: Sl st to 4th ch of first ch 7, ch 3, 4 dc in same st, (ch 5, 5 dc in 4th ch of next ch 7) 5 times, ch 5, sl st in top of ch 3.

Rnd 4: * Ch 8, sc in 3rd ch from hook for picot, ch 5, sc in last dc of 5-dc group, ch 8, sc in 3rd ch from hook for picot, ch 5, sc in first dc of next 5-dc group, repeat from * around, end sc in sl st at beg of rnd.

Rnd 5: * Ch 7, sc in next picot, ch 10, sc in same picot, ch 7, sc in next sc between picot lps, repeat from * around. Join; end off.

STAR SNOWFLAKE (4): Ch 5, sl st in first ch to form ring.

Rnd 1: Ch 4, tr in ring, (ch 5, 2 tr in ring) 5 times, ch 5, sl st in top of ch 4.

Rnd 2: Sl st to center of ch 5, sc in 3rd ch, (ch 7, sc in 3rd ch of next ch 5) 5 times, ch 7, sl st in first sc.

Rnd 3: Sl st to center of ch 7, sc in 4th ch, (ch 3, sc in same ch, ch 9, sc in 4th ch from hook for picot, ch 5, sc in 4th ch of next ch 7) 5 times, ch 9, sc in 4th ch for picot, ch 5, sl st in first sc.

Rnd 4: Sl st in back of ch-3 lp at beg of rnd, * ch 12, sc in 3rd ch from hook, ch 9, sl st in back of same ch-3 lp, ch 6, sc in 3rd ch from hook, (ch 8, sc in 3rd ch from hook) twice, ch 3, sc in back of next ch-3 lp, repeat from * around. Join; end off.

HEART-EDGED SNOWFLAKE (5): Ch 9, sl st in first ch to form ring.

Rnd 1: Sc in ring, (ch 7, sc in ring) 5 times, ch 7, sl st in first sc.

Rnd 2: Sl st to center of first lp, (ch 5, sc in next lp, ch 4, sc in same lp) 6 times.

Rnd 3: Sl st to 3rd ch of ch 5, (ch 3, 2 dc, ch 1, 2 dc in next ch-3 lp, ch 3, sc in 3rd ch of next ch-5 lp) 6 times.

Rnd 4: (Ch 7, sc in next ch-1 sp, ch 7, sc in next sc) 6 times.

Rnd 5: Sl st across ch 7, sc in sc, * (ch 10, sc in 4th ch from hook for picot) 3 times, ch 6, sc in same sc made before picot lp, (ch 9, sc in next sc) twice, repeat from * around, end sl st in first sc. End off.

When starching snowflake, turn center picot of each picot lp toward center, forming a heart-shaped design.

GOODY HOLDERS

Shown on pages 36 and 37

SIZE: 2½″ high.

MATERIALS: Small amounts of worsted weight yarn. Crochet hook size F (4 mm). Scraps of felt. Yarn needle. Two chenille sticks for reindeer. Cardboard tubes 1½″ diameter (toilet tissue rolls). White craft glue.

SANTA: Face: With pink, beg at bottom, ch 24. Sl st in first ch to form ring. Ch 1, sc in each ch around—24 sc. Working in each sc, work 7 rnds pink, 2 rnds white and 2 rnds red. Sl st in next st, end off. Cut tube to 2″. Put a line of glue at top, slide face up to cover tube.

Bottom: With pink, ch 2; 6 sc in 2nd ch from hook. **Next Rnd:** 2 sc in each sc around—12 sc. **Next 2 Rnds:** * Sc in next sc, 2 sc in next sc, repeat from * around—27 sc. End off. Sew to bottom of tube cover.

Finishing: With white, ch 24; sl st in first ch to form ring. Ch 1, sc in each ch around. Sl st in first sc. Sew around face over white rnds. For hair, cut 24 strands of white yarn 4″ long. Fold in half. Run a piece of yarn through the fold of all pieces. Sew folded edge around back of head under white trim. Make beard as for hair. Sew from side to side of face in a curve. Cut black semicircle eyes, red nose, red crescent mouth from felt; glue on. Highlight eyes with white dots. Glue 3 strands of white yarn under nose for mustache.

Cap: With red, ch 10; sc in 2nd ch from hook and in each remaining ch. Ch 1, turn each row. Work 1 row even on 9 sc. Dec 1 sc each side of next row. Work 1 row even. Repeat last 2 rows twice—3 sc. Work 2 rows even. Dec 1 sc on next row. Work 1 row even. Work 2 sc tog. End off. Sew cap to side of face at top. Sew a white pompon to tip.

Knot ends of red yarn strand to top sides of face for hanger.

ELF: Face: Work as for Santa, working last 2 rnds in green. Work bottom as for Santa.

Finishing: Finish as for Santa, making hair and beard red. Omit mustache. Make cap and hanger green.

CLOWN: Face: With white, beg at bottom, ch 24. Sl st in first ch to form ring. Ch 1, sc in each ch around—24 sc. Working in sc, work 9 rnds. Sl st in next st, end off. Cut tube to 2″. Put a line of glue at top, slide face up to cover tube.

Bottom and Collar: With white, work as for bottom of Santa. Do not end off. Work 2 dc in each sc around. With blue, work * sc in next sc, 2 sc in next sc, repeat from * around. End off. Sew bottom around tube cover.

Finishing: With green, ch 24; sl st in first ch to form ring. Ch 1, sc in each ch around. Sl st in first sc. Sew around top of face. For hair, cut 12 strands of red yarn 4″ long. Form 2 bunches of 6 strands, sew center of each bunch to side of face under green trim. From felt, cut blue diamond eyes, black pupils, red nose, red crescent mouth, yellow cheeks. Glue on. With blue, make cap as for Santa. Add green pompon, green hanger.

REINDEER: Face: With brown, work as for Santa, making 10 rnds of sc. When gluing face to tube, insert ends of 2 chenille sticks between tube and face 1″ apart at back. Bend sticks to form antlers.

Nose Bottom: With brown, work as for Santa. With brown, ch 16, sl st in first ch to form circle. Ch 1, sc in each ch around. **Next 2 Rnds:** Dec 3 sc in each rnd—12 sc. Work 2 sc tog around—6 sc. Stuff; sew on. With black, close opening at front of nose.

Ear: With brown, ch 6. Sc in 2nd ch from hook and next 4 ch. Ch 1, turn. Sc in 3 sc; end off. Sew an ear to each side of head.

Glue on black felt circles for eyes. Dot with white paint. Add brown yarn hanger.

SHEEP: Face: With white, ch 24. **Row 1:** Loop st in 2nd ch from hook and in each ch across. (To make loop st, hold ½″ wide strip of cardboard in back of work, wrap yarn around strip, work sc in st.) Ch 1, turn. **Row 2:** Sc in each st across. Ch 1, turn. **Row 3:** Loop st in each sc across. Ch 1, turn. Repeat rows 2 and 3 until there are 5 loop st rows. End off. Sew side seam to form tube. Cut cardboard tube to 2″. Put a line of glue at top, slide face up to cover tube.

With white, work bottom as for Santa.

Nose: With gray, ch 13; sl st in first ch to form ring. Ch 1, sc in each ch around. Work in sc, dec 3 sc in next rnd—10 sc. Work 2 sc tog around. End off. Sew up hole. Stuff nose; sew on. Glue a small oval of black felt to top of nose. Glue on 2 black felt circles for eyes. Dot each with white paint.

Ear: With gray, ch 5. Sc in 2nd ch from hook and in next 3 ch. Ch 1, turn. Sc in 2 sc; end off. Sew an ear to each side of head. Add white yarn hanger.

TREE ORNAMENTS

Shown on pages 36 and 37

SIZES: 3" to 6".

MATERIALS: Small amounts of worsted weight yarn. Crochet hook size F.

Stuffing: 12" chenille sticks. Red crayon. Yarn needle.

SANTA: Face: With pink, ch 2; 6 sc in 2nd ch from hook. **Rnd 2:** 2 sc in each sc. **Rnd 3:** (Sc in next sc, 2 sc in next sc) 6 times. **Rnd 4:** (Sc in 2 sc, 2 sc in next sc) 6 times—24 sc. Sl st in next sc. **Hat:** Change to red. Ch 1, sc in 9 sc. Ch 1, turn. **Rows 2-4:** Dec 1 sc each side. **Rows 5-9:** Work even on 3 sc. **Row 10:** Dec 1 sc. **Row 11:** Work 2 sc tog. **Row 12:** Sc in 1 sc. End off.

Beard: Join white in last red sc next to face; working around face, * sc in 2 sc, 2 sc in next sc, repeat from * around, sl st in first red sc of hat. Ch 1, turn. **Row 2:** Loop st in each sc, sl st in hat; end off. To make loop st, insert hook in st, wind yarn back over right index finger, catch yarn under finger with hook, pull through st, remove finger from loop, finish sc. From wrong side, work another row of loop st from 5th st on one side to 5th st on other side of face.

Back: With white, work as for face. Work back of hat as for front. With matching yarn, sew front and back tog with stuffing between, folding beard back between the 2 loop-st rows.

For nose, with pink, ch 2; work 4 sc in 2nd ch from hook. Sew into a ball; sew to face. Wind several loops of white yarn for mustache, sew center of windings under nose. Make a white ch for hat trim, sew around hat. Sew a white pompon to tip of hat. Embroider red mouth in outline st, blue eyes with black pupils in satin st.

ELF: Work as for Santa, making hat green, beard red. For nose, with pink, ch 2; work 3 sc in 2nd ch from hook. Work even on 3 sc for 2 rnds. Sew to face. Make eyes green. Add red eyebrows in straight st.

SNOWMAN: Head: With white, ch 2; 6 sc in 2nd ch from hook. **Rnd 2:** 2 sc in each sc. **Rnd 3:** (Sc in next sc, 2 sc in next sc) 6 times. **Rnd 4:** (Sc in 2 sc, 2 sc in next sc) 6 times. **Rnd 5:** (Sc in next sc, 2 sc in next sc) 12 times—36 sc. End off. Make another piece the same. Sew pieces tog, stuffing lightly.

For nose, cut a 1" piece of chenille stick. With orange, working over stick, work ch from one end to the other; turn, work back in ch st. Sew nose to center of face. For eyes, with black, ch 2; work 2 sc in 2nd ch from hook; sew into ball, sew to head. Embroider red mouth in outline st.

For scarf, with green, ch 4. Working in sc, work even on 3 sc for 7". Add fringe to end. Sew to bottom of head.

Hat: With black, ch 22. Join to make ring; work around on 22 sc for 6 rnds. * Sc in next sc, 2 sc in next sc, repeat from * around for 2 rnds. End off. Sew top of hat flat across. Sew hat to head.

STAR (make 2): With yellow, ch 2. Work 5 sc in 2nd ch from hook. **Rnd 2:** 2 sc in each sc. **Rnd 3:** (Sc in next sc, 2 sc in next sc) 5 times. **Rnd 4:** (Sc in 2 sc, 2 sc in next sc) 5 times—20 sc. **Form Point:** 2 sc in first sc, sc in each of next 2 sc, 2 sc in next sc. Ch 1, turn. Working in sc, dec 1 sc at center of each row until 2 sc remain. Work 2 sc tog. Sc in 1 sc. End off. Make other 4 points the same. Sew 2 pieces tog, stuffing as you go.

TREE: With green, ch 15. Work loop st in 2nd ch from hook and in each ch across. To make loop st, insert hook in st, wind yarn back over right index finger, catch yarn under finger with hook, pull through st, remove finger from loop, finish sc. Alternating 1 row of loop st and 1 row of sc, dec 1 sc each side of every sc row until 2 loop sts remain. Dec 1 sc on next row. Work 1 loop st. Work 1 sc. End off. Make another piece the same.

Trunk: With brown, ch 6. Sc in 2nd ch from hook and in each ch across. Ch 1, turn. Work even on 5 sc for 1 row. Dec 1 sc each side of next row. Work even on 3 sc for 3 rows. End off. Make another piece the same. Sew pieces tog with stuffing inside. Sew sides of tree tog, stuff. Place trunk at center of bottom edge; sew bottom edge.

Ornaments: With any color, ch 2; work 4 sc in 2nd ch from hook. Sew into a ball; sew to tree.

Star: With yellow, ch 2; work 5 sc in 2nd ch from hook. In each sc around work (sc, ch 4, sc). Sl st in first sc; end off. Sew to top of tree.

WREATH: With green, ch 33. Work 1 row of loop st (see Tree). End off. Beg in first loop st of first row, * work loop st in 2 sts, dec 1 loop st in next 2 sts (to dec, pull up a lp in next st, insert hook in next st, make loop st drawing yarn through 3 lps on hook), repeat from * across. End off. Make another piece the same. Sew pieces tog over a ring of chenille stick. With red, make a ch 9" long. Form a bow; sew on.

ANGEL: Face: With pink, ch 2; 6 sc in 2nd ch from hook. **Rnd 2:** 2 sc in each sc. **Rnd 3:** (Sc in next sc, 2 sc in next sc) 6 times. **Rnd 4:** (Sc in 2 sc, 2 sc in next sc) 6 times. **Rnd 5:** (Sc in next sc, 2 sc in next sc) 12 times—36 sc. Sl st in next st. End off. Make another piece the same for back of head. Sew pieces tog with stuffing between.

Hair: Wind yellow yarn in one layer only down around a pencil. Cut yarn, leaving an 8" end. Thread end in needle, run yarn through center of each strand of yarn all the way to last winding. Slip off pencil, pull up and sew curls to head. Make as many windings as needed to cover top, sides, and back of head.

Nose: With pink, ch 2; 3 sc in 2nd ch from hook. Sew into a ball, sew to face.

Embroider blue eyes in satin st. Glue on black felt pupils. Embroider mouth in red outline st.

Wing (make 2): With yellow, ch 14. **Row 1:** Sc in 2nd ch from hook and in each remaining ch. Ch 1, turn each row. **Rows 2 and 3:** Sc in 11 sc. **Rows 4 and 5:** Sc in 9 sc. **Rows 6 and 7:** Sc in 7 sc. **Rows 8 and 9:** Sc in 5 sc. End off. Press wings with warm steam iron. Sew to back of head.

For halo, work ch in yellow yarn over a piece of yellow chenille stick. Sew ends tog; sew to back of head.

JEWEL-TONE TRIMS

Shown on page 38

SIZE: 5½" long.

MATERIALS: D.M.C Perle Cotton #5, 53 yd. balls in assorted colors. Steel crochet hook size 00.

Note 1: Ornament is worked with double strand of cotton. Wind each ball into a double-strand ball.

Cluster St: (Yo hook, pull up a lp in same st) 4 times, yo hook and through all lps on hook, ch 1 (eye of cluster.)

ORNAMENT: Rnd 1: With double strand of thread (see Note 1), ch 16; sl st in back lp of 2nd ch from hook and in next 4 ch, continue working in back lps only, sc in each of next 4 ch, hdc in each of next 3 ch, dc in each of next 2 ch, 10 dc in last ch; working on opposite side of ch, dc in next 2 ch, hdc in next 3 ch, sc in next 4 ch, sl st in remaining 5 ch; sl st in first st. End off.

Rnd 2: Join another color in back lp of last st of rnd 1, work 2 sc in same st; working in back lps only, sc in each of next 9 sts, hdc in each of next 6 sts, 2 hdc in each of next 10 sts, hdc in next 5 sts, sc in each of next 8 sts, join with a sl st in first st. End off. Turn to wrong side.

Rnd 3: Join another color in 2nd st of rnd 2, 2 sc in this st, cluster st (see Cluster St) in next st, 2 sc in next st, sc in next st, * cluster st in next st, sc in each of next 2 sts, repeat from * around, end last repeat with sc in next st, sl st in first sc—17 clusters. End off. Turn to right side.

Rnd 4: Join another color with sc in st before first cluster, do not work in eyes of clusters, 2 sc in next st, sc in next 10 sts, hdc in next 4 sts, dc in next 2 sts, (2 dc in next st, dc in next 3 sts) 5 times, 2 dc in next st, dc in next 2 sts, hdc in next 4 sts, sc in next 8 sts, 2 sc in next st, sl st to first sc. End off.

Rnd 5: Join another color with sc in last st of last rnd, sc in next 2 sts, 2 sc in next st, sc in next 8 sts, hdc in next 8 sts. (2 hdc in next st, hdc in next 3 sts) 7 times,

Continued on page 41

Lacy, feathery snowflakes
decorate your tree
in beauty
with
sparkling
white.

SNOW
CRYSTALS

Crochet designs of cotton; starch, trim with beads.
See Snow Crystals, page 29.

A little lace adds
a delicate touch to
your Christmas tree.
Snowbirds are
crocheted, with
openwork wings
(page 29).

Crochet covers
for satin balls;
satin shows
through the lacy
pattern. Add
pretty sprays of
flowers (page 30).

ADD A
TOUCH
OF
LACE

Snowflakes can be
crocheted in a
variety of lovely
patterns. A strong
solution of starch
keeps them crisp
looking. For
patterns shown
here, see page 30.

COLORFUL TREE TRIMS

in crochet, with cardboard lining to hold
yummies, the holders will bring delighted
"oohs" and "ahs" from the children.
Directions on page 31.

Seven crocheted,
lightly padded
ornaments are cheery and unusual notes
for your tree. See Tree Ornaments, page 32.

JEWEL-TONE ORNAMENTS

Glowing pear drops are crocheted in the oval, enhanced
with puff stitches and picots. See Jewel-Tone Trims, page 32.

Knit a colorful stocking the Scandinavian way for the good kids who expect a visit from Santa.

Stocking for girls features snowflakes, boy and girl figures; for boys, trees, reindeer. See page 41.

Designed by
Tita Lillegraven-Mallory

FOR THAT SPECIAL NIGHT

Granny-like squares are quick to crochet and assemble
for stockings that will hold lots of surprises. Directions
for Christmas Red and Christmas Green Stockings,
page 42. Jolly Santa, yule tree, felt holly leaves, and the
name of your favorite little one pattern the merriest of
knitted Christmas stockings. See Santa and Tree
Stockings, page 42. Three tiny friends—Santa, elf, and
clown—are made in rounds of single crochet, for perfect
stocking stuffers (see directions for Wee Dolls, page 43).

JEWEL-TONE TRIMS
Continued from page 32.

hdc in next 6 sts, sc in next 6 sts, 2 sc in next st, sc in next 2 sts, sl st to first st. End off.

Rnd 6: Join another color in back lp of top st on small end, * ch 3, sl st in last sl st made (picot made), sk next st, sl st in back lp of next st, repeat from * around, sl st in same st as first sl st. Drop 1 strand of cotton; with single strand, make a ch 5½″-6″ long, sl st in first st. End off.

FINISHING: Weave in all yarn ends on wrong side. Block.

SCANDINAVIAN STOCKINGS
Shown on page 39

SIZE: 25″ long.

MATERIALS: Note: Materials are for boy's stocking marked "Sean". Any changes for girl's stocking marked "Megan" are in parentheses. Knitting worsted or 100% acrylic yarn, 4-ply weight, 1 4-oz. skein white (A) for each stocking; small amounts of burgundy (forest green)–(B), orange (dark pink)–(C), lime (peach)–(D), yellow (orange)–(E), pink (burgundy)–(F), dark orange (gold)–(G), forest green (bright red)–(H), aqua–(I), light blue (light green)–(J), dark blue (yellow)–(L), kelly green (pink)–(M), turquoise (N), light green (orchid)–(O), gold (purple)–(P), bright red (lavender)–(Q), brown (dark blue)–(R), coral (olive green)–(S), orchid (brown)–(T), (blue ombre)–(U). Set of dp needles No. 4 (3½ mm). Large-eyed tapestry needle.

GAUGE: 6 sts = 1″; 6 rnds = 1″.

Notes: Directions are given for boy's stocking. Changes for girl's stocking are in parentheses. Always change colors on wrong side, picking up new strand from under dropped strand. When more than 5 sts between colors, twist colors every 3rd st. Cut and join colors when necessary. Some designs (tree ornaments, names, reindeer, boys and girls) are embroidered in duplicate st when stockings are completed.

STOCKING: Beg at top with B, cast on loosely 72 sts; divide sts evenly on 3 needles. Put and keep a marker on needle between last and first sts of rnd. Join, being careful not to twist sts.

Rnds 1-6: Work in ribbing of k 2, p 2.

Rnds 7-9: * K 2 C, p 2 B, repeat from * around. Working in stockinette st (k each rnd), work remainder of stocking as follows:

Rnd 10: With C, knit.

Rnd 11: K 3 D, * k 1 E, k 7 D, repeat from * around, end last repeat k 4 D.

Rnd 12: K 2 D, * k 3 E, k 5 D, repeat from * around, end last repeat k 3 D.

Rnd 13: K 1 D, * k 5 E, k 3 D, repeat from * around, end last repeat k 2 D.

Rnd 14: * K 7 E, k 1 D, repeat from * around.

Rnds 15-20: K 1 rnd each of F and G; 2 rnds C, 1 rnd G, 1 rnd F.

Rnds 21-24: Repeat rnds 14, 13, 12, 11.

Rnd 25: With C, knit.

Rnds 26-28: * K 2 C, k 2 A, repeat from * around.

For Boy's Stocking Only: Rnd 29: With A, (k 24, k 2 tog) twice, k 20–70 sts.

Rnds 30 and 31: With A, knit.

Rnd 32: K 5 A, * k 1 H, k 9 A, repeat from * around, end last repeat k 4 A.

Rnd 33: K 4 A, * k 3 H, k 7 A, repeat from * around, end last repeat k 3 A.

Rnd 34: K 3 A, * k 5 H, k 5 A, repeat from * around, end last repeat k 2 A.

Rnds 35 and 36: Repeat rounds 33 and 34.

Rnd 37: K 2 A, * k 7 H, k 3 A, repeat from * around, end last repeat k 1 A.

Rnds 38 and 39: Repeat rnds 34 and 37.

Rnd 40: * K 1 A, k 9 H, repeat from * around.

Rnds 41 and 42: K 5 A, * k 1 R, k 9 A, repeat from * around, end last repeat k 4 A.

Rnd 43: With A, (k 2 tog, k 33) twice –68 sts.

For Girl's Stocking Only: Rnds 29-42: With A, knit.

Rnd 43: With A, (k 16, k 2 tog) 4 times –68 sts.

For Both Stockings: Rnd 44: * K 1 G (J), k 1 E (L), repeat from * around.

Rnd 45: * K 1 E (L), k 1 G (J), repeat from * around.

Rnds 46-52: With J (M), knit.

Rnd 53: Repeat rnd 45.

Rnd 54: Repeat rnd 44.

Rnd 55: With A, knit.

Rnd 56: With A, (k 15, k 2 tog) 4 times–64 sts.

Rnds 57-59: * K 2 M (N), k 2 A, repeat from * around.

Rnd 60: With M (N), knit.

Rnds 61-64: Repeat rnds 11-14, working with O (G) instead of D and N (C) instead of E.

Rnds 65-70: K 1 rnd each of P (I) and Q (R), 2 rnds S (Q), 1 rnd each of Q (R) and P (I).

Rnds 71-74: Repeat rnds 64, 63, 62, 61.

Rnd 75: Repeat rnd 60.

Rnd 76-78: Repeat rnds 57-59.

Rnd 79: With A, (k 14, k 2 tog) 4 times –60 sts.

Rnds 80-93: With A, knit.

Rnd 94: With A, (k 13, k 2 tog) 4 times –56 sts.

Rnds 95-97: * K 2 A, k 2 B, repeat from * around.

Rnd 98: With B, knit.

Rnds 99-102: Repeat rnds 11-14, working with E (J) instead of D and G (I) instead of E.

Rnds 103-108: K 1 rnd each of J (L) and L (E), 2 rnds T (D), 1 rnd each of L (E) and J (L).

Rnds 109-112: Repeat rnds 102, 101, 100, 99.

Rnd 113: Repeat rnd 98.

Rnds 114-116: Repeat rnds 95-97.

Rnd 117: With A, knit.

Rnd 118: With A, (k 12, k 2 tog) 4 times–52 sts. With A, k 11 rnds.

Shape Heel: K 14, sl last 28 sts worked to one needle for heel, hold remaining 24 sts on 2 needles for instep.

Row 1: Working from wrong side on heel sts, sl 1, p 16, p 2 tog, p 1, turn; sl 1, k 7, k 2 tog, k 1, turn; sl 1, p 8, p 2 tog, p 1, turn; sl 1, k 9, k 2 tog, k 1, turn; sl 1, p 10, p 2 tog, p 1, turn; sl 1, k 11, k 2 tog, k 1, turn. Continue in this way having 1 st more before dec on each row until there are 18 sts left, end p row. Turn; k across heel sts.

Foot: Working on all 42 sts, k around until foot measures 6″ from center back, dec 2 sts evenly spaced across

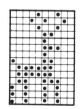

CHART 1

CHART 2

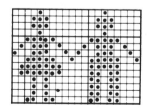

CHART 3

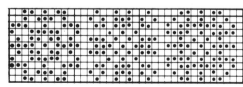

instep sts on last row, end center of sole—40 sts. Place 10 sts on first needle, 20 sts on 2nd needle, 10 sts on 3rd needle.

Shape Toe: First Dec Rnd: K to within 3 sts of end of first needle, k 2 tog, k 1; on 2nd needle, k 1, sl 1, k 1, psso, k to last 3 sts, k 2 tog, k 1; on 3rd needle, k 1, sl 1, psso, k to end—4 sts dec. K 1 rnd. Repeat these 2 rnds until 16 sts remain. K 4 sts of first needle to 3rd needle. Cut yarn, leaving 16″ length. Weave 8 sts of sole and 8 upper sts tog with Kitchener st.

Embroidery: For Boy's Stocking: Using duplicate st and any desired colors, embroider tree ornaments on Christmas tree as pictured. With L, following alphabet chart, embroider child's name once or twice across rnds 47-51. Alternating R and P, following chart 1, embroider reindeer around rnds 80-93.

For Girl's Stocking: Following chart 2, using duplicate st and U, embroider snowflakes around rnds 31-41. With F, following alphabet chart, embroider child's name across rnds 47-51. Following chart 3, using D for all faces, hands and girl's legs, T for shoes, any remaining colors for bodies, embroider boys and girls around rnds 80-93. Run in yarn ends on wrong side. Make 1 3″ chain lp; attach to upper back edge of stockings. Steam-press lightly.

CHRISTMAS RED STOCKING
Shown on page 40

SIZE: 20″ long.
MATERIALS: Knitting worsted weight yarn, 1 4-oz. skein red (R), 1 2-oz. skein white (W). Crochet hook size J.
GAUGE: Square = 4¾″.
STOCKING: SQUARE (make 10): With R, ch 4, sl st in first ch to form ring.
Rnd 1: Ch 2, 2 dc in ring; remove hook from lp, insert hook in top of ch 2, then in dropped lp, yo hook and through 2 lps on hook, ch 2, * 3 dc in ring, drop lp on hook, insert hook in first of 3 dc, then in dropped lp, yo and through 2 lps on hook, ch 2, repeat from * 6 times, sl st to top of ch 2—8 clusters. End off R.
Rnd 2: Join W in any ch-2 sp. Ch 2, 2 dc in sp, ch 1, * in next sp work 3 dc, ch 2, 3 dc; ch 1, 3 dc in next sp, ch 1, repeat from * twice; in last sp, work 3 dc, ch 2, 3 dc; ch 1, sl st to top of ch 2 at beg of rnd. End off W.
Rnd 3: Join R in any ch-2 corner sp; ch 2, 2 dc, ch 2, 3 dc in sp, * ch 1, 3 dc in next sp, ch 1, 3 dc in next sp, ch 1, 3 dc, ch 2, 3 dc in next corner sp, repeat from * twice, ch 1, 3 dc in next sp, ch 1, 3 dc in next sp, ch 1, sl st to top of ch 2. End off R.

Rnd 4: With W, sc in each dc around, working sc, ch 2, sc in each corner sp. Sl st in first sc. End off.
FINISHING: For each side of stocking, sew 5 squares tog, being sure to reverse position of toe square on 2nd side. Sew through back lps of sc only with white yarn. With R, work 1 row sc around one side of stocking, increasing at corners, decreasing at instep corner to keep work flat. Join. Ch 1, turn. Work another row of sc in same way. Work 2 extra rows across top. At front of foot, with R, work 20 sc across. Ch 1, turn. Work in rows of sc, dec 1 st each side each row until there are 8 sc. End off. Repeat sc edges and toe rows on 2nd side of stocking. Sew sides tog leaving open at top. For hanger, ch 30. Sc in 2nd ch from hook and in each ch across. Sew two ends tog to inside of back seam.

GREEN STOCKING
Shown on page 40

SIZE: 17″ long.
MATERIALS: Knitting worsted weight yarn, 2 ozs. green (G) and 2 ozs. white (W). Crochet hook size J.
GAUGE: Square = 4″.
STOCKING: SQUARE (make 10): With G, ch 4, sl st in first ch to form ring.
Rnd 1: Ch 3, 15 dc in ring, sl st to top of ch 3.
Rnd 2: Ch 4, * dc in next dc, ch 1, repeat from * around, end ch 1, sl st in 3rd ch of ch 4. End off.
Rnd 3: Join W in any ch-1 sp; ch 3, dc in same sp, (2 dc in next sp) twice, * 2 dc, ch 2, 2 dc in next sp, (2 dc in next sp) 3 times, repeat from * twice, 2 dc, ch 2, 2 dc in last sp, sl st to top of ch 3. End off W.
Rnd 4: With G, sc in each dc around, 3 sc in each corner sp. Join to first sc. End off G.
FINISHING: With G, sewing through back lps of sc only, sew 5 squares tog, for each side of stocking, being sure to reverse position of toe square on 2nd side. With W, from right side, work 1 row sc around one side of stocking, increasing at corners, decreasing at instep corner to keep work flat. Join. Ch 1, turn. Work 2 more rows of sc in same way. Join and turn each row. Work 2 more rows across top edge only. At front of foot, with W, work 16 sc across. Ch 1, turn. Work in rows of sc, dec 1 st each side each row until there are 6 sc. End off. Repeat sc edges and toe rows on 2nd side of stocking. Sew sides tog leaving open at top. For hanger, ch 22. Sc in 2nd ch from hook and in each ch across. Sew two ends tog to inside of back seam.

SANTA AND TREE STOCKINGS
Shown on page 40

SANTA: MATERIALS: Knitting worsted, 2 oz. green (G); 1 oz. each of white (W), red (R), gold (GO); small amounts of black (B), pink (P); 4 yards white angora (WA). Knitting needles No. 7. Black, gold, white and red sequins. Small glass beads. Sewing thread. Bead needle; tapestry needle. Two bells. Two stitch holders.
GAUGE: 5 sts = 1″; 6 rows = 1″.
Notes: Name is embroidered in duplicate st when stocking is completed. When working chart, k from right to left on right side rows; p from left to right on wrong side rows. Use a separate strand of yarn for each color change. Always change colors on wrong side, picking up new strand from under dropped strand. Cut and join colors as needed.
STOCKING: Cuff: Beg at upper edge with G, cast on 60 sts. Work in ribbing of k 1, p 1 for 6 rows. With W, work in stockinette st (k 1 row, p 1 row) for 10 rows. Work 2 G rows. Following chart, work to top of chart, dec 1 st each side on rows 43, 52, 61 and 73—52 sts. When chart is completed, work 6 G rows, end k row.
Divide for Heel: Left Heel Half: Row 1: With R, purl 13 sts.
Sl next 26 sts on a stitch holder (instep), sl last 13 sts on another stitch holder for right heel half. Work on left heel half sts only.
Row 2: Sl 1, k 12. Repeat last 2 rows 8 times.
Next Row: P 2, p 2 tog, p 1, turn; sl 1, k 3 turn; p 3, p 2 tog, p 1, turn; sl 1, k 4, turn; p 4, p 2 tog, p 1, turn; sl 1, k 5, turn; p 5, p 2 tog, p 1, turn; sl 1, k 6, turn; p 6, p 2 tog, p 1—8 sts. Cut R; sl sts on a safety pin.
Right Heel Half: Sl sts of right heel to needle, join R at beg of k row.
Row 1: Knit.
Row 2: Sl 1, p 12. Repeat last 2 rows 8 times.
Next Row: K 2, sl 1, k 1, psso, k 1, turn; sl 1, p 3, turn; k 3, sl 1, k 1, psso, k 1, turn; sl 1, p 4, turn; k 4, sl 1, k 1, psso, k 1, turn; sl 1, p 5, turn; k 5, sl 1, k 1, psso, k 1, turn; sl 1, p 6, turn; k 6, sl 1, k 1, psso, k 1—8 sts. With R, pick up and k 9 sts on side of right heel, k 26 sts on instep holder, pick up and k 9 sts on inner edge of left heel half, k 8 sts on safety pin—60 sts.
Shape Gussets and Instep: Row 1 and All Odd Rows: Purl.
Row 2: K 14, k 2 tog, k 28, sl 1, k 1, psso, k 14.
Row 4: K 13, k 2 tog, k 28, sl 1, k 1, psso, k 13.
Row 6: K 12, k 2 tog, k 28, sl 1, k 1, psso, k 12.

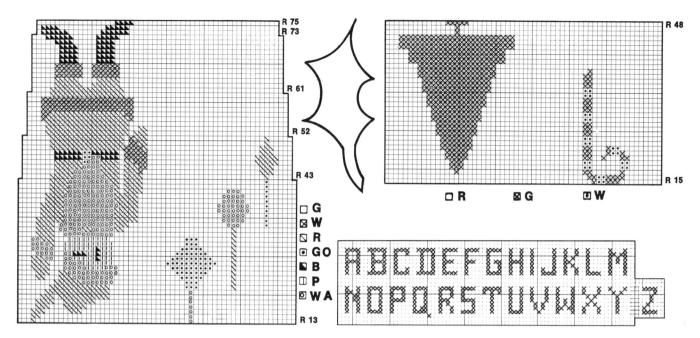

Row 8: K 11, k 2 tog, k 28, sl 1, k 1, psso, k 11.

Row 10: K 10, k 2 tog, k 28, sl 1, k 1, psso, k 10.

Row 12: K 9, k 2 tog, k 28, sl 1, k 1, psso, k 9—48 sts.

Row 13: Purl.

Foot: Working in stockinette st, work 4 W rows, dec 1 st each side of last row —46 sts. Work 10 GO rows, 4 W rows. Cut W; join G.

Shape Toe: Row 1: K 9, k 2 tog, k 1, put a marker on needle, k 1, sl 1, k 1, psso, k 16, k 2 tog, k 1, put a marker on needle, k 1, sl 1, k 1, psso, k 9—4 sts dec. P 1 row.

Row 3: (K to within 3 sts before marker, k 2 tog, k 1, sl marker, k 1, sl 1, k 1, psso) twice, k remaining sts—4 sts dec. Repeat last 2 rows 6 times—14 sts.

EMBROIDERY: With R, embroider name in duplicate st on W stripe at top of stocking.

FINISHING: Run in yarn ends on wrong side. Block. Sew back and sole seams; weave toe tog. Attach a small R pompon to nose of Santa; a medium W pompon to top of cap. Outline Christmas balls on back of stocking, Santa's eye and belt buckle with matching sequins. Make 3″ G chain; attach to top of stocking for hanging. Sew two bells to tip of toe.

TREE: MATERIALS: Knitting worsted, 2 oz. red (R); 1 oz. each of white (W) and green (G). Knitting needles No. 7. Two stitch holders. Assorted round and Christmas sequins. Small glass beads. Bead needle; tapestry needle. Green felt. Sewing thread. Two bells.

GAUGE: 5 sts = 1″; 6 rows = 1″.

Notes: Same as for Santa stocking.

STOCKING: Beg at upper edge, with R, cast on 60 sts. Work in ribbing of k 2, p 2 for 7 rows.

Pattern: With W, work in stockinette st (k 1 row, p 1 row) for 10 rows. Work 4 R rows. Following chart, work to top of chart. Work 9 rows, 10 W rows, 4 R rows; at the same time, dec 1 st each side every 4th row 4 times—52 sts.

Divide for Heel: Work same as for Santa stocking—13 sts remain on needle. With R, work left half of heel, right half of heel, gussets and instep same as for Santa stocking—48 sts.

Foot: Working in stockinette st, work 6 W rows, 8 R rows, 6 W rows.

Shape Toe: With R, work same as for Santa stocking.

EMBROIDERY: With G, embroider name in duplicate stitch on W stripe at top of stocking.

FINISHING: Run in yarn ends on wrong side. Block. Sew back and sole seams; weave toe tog. Cut three felt leaves using actual size pattern; sew to white stripe under tree. Make 3 R French knots on each side of leaves. Outline tree with sequins. Sew a bead to center of each sequin. Sew Christmas sequins to tree and around candy cane. Make 3″ R chain; attach to top of stocking for hanging. Sew two bells to toe.

WEE DOLLS
Shown on page 40

SIZE: About 8″ high.

MATERIALS: Knitting worsted, about 2 ozs. of main color for each: red for Santa, rainbow for Clown, green for Elf; small amounts of beige, black, white, yellow. White angora for Santa. Crochet hook size G. Stuffing. Four buttons to match toy for attaching arms and legs. For eyes, buttons, plastic eyes, felt scraps or embroidery floss. Button

and carpet thread. Three small jingle bells for Elf.

GAUGE: 5 sc = 1″.

SANTA: Head and Body: With beige, ch 2.

Rnd 1: 6 sc in 2nd ch from hook.

Rnd 2: 2 sc in each sc around.

Rnd 3: (Sc in next st, 2 sc in next st) 6 times—18 sc.

Rnd 4: (Sc in next 2 sts, 2 sc in next st) 6 times—24 sc.

Rnds 5-9: Work even.

Rnd 10: (Sc in next 2 sts, work 2 sc tog) 6 times—18 sc.

Rnd 11: (Sc in next st, work 2 sc tog) 6 times—12 sc.

Rnd 12: Work even. Cut beige; join red.

Rnd 13: Repeat rnd 3—18 sc.

Rnd 14: Repeat rnd 4—24 sc.

Rnds 15-23: Work even.

Rnd 24: Repeat rnd 10. Work 1 rnd even.

Rnd 26: Repeat rnd 11. Work 1 rnd even. End off.

Leg (make 2): With black, ch 6.

Rnd 1: Sc in 2nd ch from hook and in next 3 ch, 5 sc in last ch; working on opposite side of ch, sc in each of next 3 ch, 2 sc in last ch.

Rnds 2 and 3: Work even on 14 sc.

Rnd 4: Sc in 5 sc, (work next 2 sts tog) twice, sc in 5 sc.

Rnds 5 and 6: Work even on 12 sc. Cut black.

Rnd 7: With red, sc in 4 sc, 2 sc in next sc, sc in 2 sc, 2 sc in next sc, sc in 4 sc.

Rnds 8-14: Work even on 14 sc.

Rnd 15: (Work 2 sc tog, sc in 3 sc, work 2 sc tog) twice. End off.

Arm (make 2): With beige, ch 2.

Rnd 1: 6 sc in 2nd ch from hook.

Rnd 2: 2 sc in each sc. Work 2 rnds even. Cut beige. With red, work 9 rnds even. End off.

Hat: With red, ch 2.

Rnd 1: 6 sc in 2nd ch from hook. Work 1 rnd even.

Rnd 3: 2 sc in each sc. Work 3 rnds even.

Rnd 7: (Sc in next st, 2 sc in next st) 6 times. Work 3 rnds even on 18 sts.

Rnd 11: (Sc in each of 2 sc, 2 sc in next sc) 6 times. Work 3 rnds even on 24 sts. Cut red. With white, work 2 rnds even. Attach small white pompon to tip of hat.

FINISHING: Stuff head and body, arms and legs. Sew up bottom of body and tops of arms and legs. Attach legs to body with strong thread: * through body, right leg, button, right leg, left leg, button, left leg, repeat from * once. Fasten securely. Attach arms in same way. Sew on eyes. Embroider nose and mouth with red; satin stitch circle for nose, straight stitch for mouth. Knot angora strands around face, on back of neck, and between nose and mouth for hair, beard and moustache. Sew on hat.

CLOWN: Work head and body as for Santa, changing to rainbow at end of rnd 12. Work arms as for Santa, using rainbow instead of red.

Leg (make 2): With black, ch 7.

Rnd 1: Sc in 2nd ch from hook and in each of next 4 ch, 5 sc in last ch; working on opposite side of ch, sc in each of next 4 ch, 2 sc in last ch.

Rnds 2 and 3: Work even on 16 sc.

Rnd 4: Sc in 4 sc, (work next 2 sc tog) 4 times, sc in 4 sc—12 sc.

Rnds 5 and 6: Work even. Cut black.

Rnd 7: Join rainbow; sc in 4 sc, 2 sc in next sc, sc in 2 sc, 2 sc in next st, sc in 4 sc—14 sc.

Rnds 8-15: Work as for rnds 8-15 of Santa.

Collar: With white, ch 15. Dc in 3rd ch from hook, 2 dc in each remaining ch.

Nose: With red, ch 2. Work 6 sc in 2nd ch from hook. Draw up sts.

FINISHING: Stuff and attach arms and legs as for Santa. Sew on eyes and nose. Embroider red straight stitch mouth. Knot strands of yellow yarn over head for hair. Sew collar around neck.

ELF: Work head and body as for Santa using green instead of red.

Arm (make 2): With beige, ch 2.

Rnd 1: 5 sc in 2nd ch from hook.

Rnd 2: 2 sc in each sc. Work 2 rnds even on 10 sc. Cut beige. With green, work 10 more rnds. End off.

Leg (make 2): With red, ch 9.

Rnd 1: Sc in 2nd ch from hook and in each of next 7 ch; working on opposite side of ch, work sc in each ch—16 sc.

Rnd 2: Sc in 6 sc, (work 2 sc tog) twice, sc in 6 sc.

Rnd 3: Sc in 5 sc, (work 2 sc tog) twice, sc in 5 sc.

Rnd 4: Sc in 4 sc, (work 2 sc tog) twice,

sc in 4 sc. Cut red. With green, work 12 rnds even on 10 sc. End off.

Hat: With green, ch 2. Work as for Santa's hat through rnd 3. Work 2 rnds even.

Rnd 6: (Sc in next st, 2 sc in next sc) 6 times. Work 2 rnds even on 18 sc.

Rnd 9: (Sc in each of 2 sc, 2 sc in next sc) 6 times. Work 2 rnds even. Cut green. With red, work 2 rnds even. End off.

Ear (make 2): With beige, ch 5. Sl st in 2nd ch from hook, sc in each of next 2 ch, hdc in last ch. End off.

FINISHING: Stuff and attach arms and legs as for Santa. Sew on eyes. Make 2 black dots for nose, red straight stitch mouth. Make red collar as for Clown's collar; sew on. Sew ears to sides of head. Knot some yellow strands to top front of head for hair. Sew on hat. Sew bells to toes and hat.

POCKET PALS
Shown on page 66

SIZE: About 4".

MATERIALS: Knitting worsted weight yarn, 1 oz. pink for Santa, elf, girl, and clown; 1 oz. brown for bear, 1 oz. white for snowman. Smaller amounts of other colors. Crochet hook size J. Felt scraps. Fabric cement.

GAUGE: 7 sc = 2".

HEAD (make 2): Ch 2.

Rnd 1: 6 sc in 2nd ch from hook.

Rnd 2: 2 sc in each sc around.

Rnd 3: * Sc in next sc, 2 sc in each of next 2 sc, repeat from * around—20 sc.

Rnd 4: * Sc in 3 sc, 2 sc in next sc, repeat from * around—25 sc.

Rnd 5: * Sc in 4 sc, 2 sc in next sc, repeat from * around—30 sc.

Rnd 6: * Sc in next sc, 2 sc in next sc, repeat from * around—45 sc.

Rnd 7: Sc in each sc. End off. Sew 2 head pieces tog around edges, leaving 2½" open at top.

HANGER: Ch 45. Sew ch to opening at sides.

SANTA: Make head with pink, hanger with white.

Cap: With red, ch 16. Sc in 2nd ch from hook and in each ch. Ch 1, turn each row. Work in sc, dec 1 sc at end of each row until 5 sc remain. Work 5 rows even. * Dec 1 sc on next row. Work 3 rows even. Repeat from * once. Dec 1 sc on next row. Work 2 rows even. Work 2 sc tog. End off. Sew cap across front of head. For cuff, with white, ch 17. Work 2 rows of 16 sc. Sew to cap edge, turning ends to back. For pompon, with white, ch 7. Work 5 rows of 6 sc. Gather edges and stuff with white yarn; pull into a ball; sew to cap.

Nose: With pink, ch 2. Work 6 sc in 2nd ch from hook. Work 2 rnds of 6 sc. Stuff with pink yarn; sew to center of face.

Work hair with double strand of white, using straight sts. Glue white yarn on for looped mustache and forelock. Sew white loops on in 2 rows for beard. Cut blue eyes, black pupils, red crescent mouth from felt; glue on.

ELF: Make head with pink, hanger with white. With green, make cap same as for Santa.

Nose: With pink, ch 4. Sc in 2nd ch from hook, sc in each ch. Work 3 more rows of 3 sc. Gather starting end to a point and sew side seam, stuffing with pink yarn scraps. Sew nose to center of face.

Ears (make 2): With pink, ch 7. Sc in 2nd ch from hook and in each ch. Ch 1, turn. Sc in 4 sc. End off. Sew to sides of face with pointed end up.

With red, make hair and beard as for Santa with only 1 row of loops for beard. From felt, cut green eyes, black pupils. Glue on.

GIRL: Make head and hanger with pink.

Collar: With blue, ch 15. Work 3 rows of 14 sc. Sew to bottom of face with edges open at front.

Nose: With pink, ch 2. Work 6 sc in 2nd ch from hook. Work 1 rnd even. Stuff with pink yarn, pull into a ball, sew to face.

Hair: Cut 18 strands of gold yarn 24" long. Sew 9 strands tog at center to center top of front. Repeat with 9 strands on back. Glue hair down along sides. Sew to face with a stitch at bottom. Braid ends from front and back tog. Tie ends with yarn bows.

Features: Cut short pieces of gold yarn for eyebrows; glue on. From felt, cut blue eyes, navy pupils, red cheeks, red crescent mouth. Glue in place.

CLOWN: Make head and hanger with pink.

Ears (make 2): With pink, ch 5. Sc in 2nd ch from hook and in each ch. Ch 1, turn. Sc in 3 sc, 3 sc in last sc. Sew to side of face.

Nose: With red, work nose as for Santa's; work 1 more rnd.

Bow: With green, ch 6. Work 10 rows of 5 sc. For center piece, ch 6. Work 2 rows of 5 sc. Wrap around center of bow and sew tightly. Sew to bottom of face.

Hair: Form loops of orange yarn over fringe; sew on loops.

Features: From felt, cut green and red triangles for eyes, black pupils, red mouth, orange circles for cheeks. Glue in place.

BEAR: With tan, work first 3 rounds of face, finish head with brown. Work back and hanger with brown.

Ears (make 2): With brown, ch 5. Sc in 2nd ch from hook and in next 2 ch, 2 sc in last ch; working on opposite side of ch, sc in each ch. Ch 1, turn. Sc in each sc around. Sew to head.

Bow: With red, make bow as for Clown's.

Features: From felt, cut black eyes and nose, pink mouth. Glue on.

SNOWMAN: Make head and hanger with white. With orange, make nose as for elf.

Hat Brim: With black, ch 23. Work 2 rows of 22 sc. Sew across top of head; turn under ends and sew to make brim stiffer.

Hat Top: With black, ch 20. Work 9 rows of 19 sc. Fold piece in half; sew edges tog; sew to top of brim.

Scarf: With green, ch 31. Work 4 rows of 30 sc. Weave double strand of white through all rows; knot ends, leaving a fringe. Sew scarf around back and under chin.

Features: From felt, cut black eyes, red mouth. Glue on.

CORNUCOPIAS
Shown on page 67

SIZE: 4″ to 5″ long.
MATERIALS: Knitting and crochet cotton, such as J. & P. Coats Knit-Cro-Sheen, small amounts of any colors. Steel crochet hook size 5.
SQUARE: Ch 3; sl st in first ch to form ring.
Rnd 1: Ch 3 (counts as dc), 2 dc in ring, (ch 1, 3 dc in ring) 3 times, ch 1, sl st in top of ch 3.
Rnd 2: Sl st to next ch-1 sp, ch 3, 2 dc in sp, (ch 1, 3 dc, ch 1, 3 dc in next ch-1 sp) 3 times, ch 1, 3 dc in first sp, ch 1, sl st in top of ch 3.
Rnd 3: Ch 3, 2 dc in corner sp, (ch 1, 3 dc in next sp, ch 1, 3 dc, ch 1, 3 dc in next corner sp) 3 times, ch 1, 3 dc in next sp, ch 1, 3 dc in first sp, ch 1, sl st in top of ch 3.
Rnd 4: Work as for rnd 3, having 1 more group of 3 dc on each side.

Work 1 or more rnds in this way, changing colors as desired.
FINISHING: Join 2 sides of square to make cone shape. Sc around top edge of cone, then work picot edge: * ch 2, sl st in 2nd ch from hook; sc in next sc, repeat from * around, working ch 15 at top of cone for hanger. Starch cone.

CANDY CADDIES
Shown on page 68

MATERIALS: Knitting worsted weight yarn, 1-oz. balls of white, yellow, blue, pink, green, lime green, red, few yards black, orange. Set of dp needles No. 5. Masking tape. Fabric glue. Yarn needle. For each character caddy: Scraps of felt in colors shown. Tomato paste cans, 6 oz. size, with one lid. Styrofoam ball, 2″ diameter. Two 12″ chenille sticks. Two black chenille sticks for reindeer; cotton batting for Santa; 3 white, 5 blue, 6 green ball fringe pompons; 8″ piece of white ball fringe trim. For peppermint holder:

One tomato sauce can with one lid, 2½″ diameter, 3″ high.

CHARACTER CADDY: GENERAL DIRECTIONS: BODY: Cast on 24 sts; divide evenly on 3 needles. Join; k around for 26 rnds. Bind off in same tension as sts.

HEAD: Cast on 6 sts; divide on 3 needles. Join.
Rnd 1 and All Odd Rnds: Knit.
Rnd 2: (K 1, inc 1 st in next st) around.
Rnd 4: (K 2, inc 1 st in next st) around.
Rnd 6: (K 3, inc 1 st in next st) around.
Rnd 8: Repeat rnd 4—20 sts.
Rnd 10: Repeat rnd 6—25 sts.
Rnds 11-16: Knit.
Rnd 17: (K 3, k 2 tog) around. K 2 rnds even. Cut yarn, draw through sts, pull up and fasten securely.

Pull head over styrofoam ball. Draw up cast-on sts at bottom; fasten. Cut a 2½″ piece of chenille stick; insert 1″ into bottom of ball leaving 1½″ protruding.

Cover can with masking tape so printing does not show through. Slip cover over can with bound-off edge at top. Sew back and forth across bottom to keep cover on. From felt same color as body, cut and glue on circle to fit can bottom. After completing caddy, put masking tape over chenille stick protruding from head. Tape to inside of can.

Directions for arms, legs, wings, ears, etc. are given in individual directions. Work with 2 needles in stockinette st (k 1 row, p 1 row). After last row, cut yarn leaving 12″ end. Draw through remaining sts, pull up tightly and fasten. Sew seam with same yarn. Insert a piece of chenille stick. Sew cast-on edge in place.

Patterns are actual size. Complete half-patterns indicated by dash lines.
SANTA: Following General Directions, make red body, pink head.
Arms: Beg at upper edge with red, cast on 8 sts. Work back and forth in stockinette st for 12 rows; change to pink.
Dec Row: Dec 1 st each side of next row. P 1 row. Repeat dec row. Work 3 rows even. See General Directions for finishing.
Legs: Beg at top edge with red, cast on 9 sts. Work in stockinette st for 11 rows. Change to black. Work 1 row, then dec 1 st each side of next row. Work 9 rows even, then repeat dec row—7 sts. Work 1 row even. See General Directions for finishing. Form half of black section into feet.
Hat: With red cast on 24 sts; divide evenly on 3 dp needles. Join; k 4 rnds.
Rnd 5: Dec 1 st at beg of each needle. K 3 rnds even.
Rnd 9: Repeat rnd 5. K 2 rnds even.
Rnds 12-14: Repeat rnds 9-11.
Rnd 15: Repeat rnd 5. K 4 rnds even.

Rnds 20-29: Repeat rnds 15-19 twice—6 sts.
Rnd 30: (K 2 tog) 3 times. Cut yarn, draw through sts; fasten. Sew hat to head.
Felt Trims: Cut black strip ¼″ wide for belt, white strips for front, leg, arm and hat trim. Glue on. From black, cut two tiny circle eyes, red circle nose, red crescent mouth. Glue on. Glue on cotton batting moustache, hair, beard, as shown.
ELF: Following General Directions, make green and white body working 11 rnds green, 15 rnds white. Make pink head.
Arms: Beg with white, work as for Santa's arms.
Legs: With green, work as for Santa to last dec row—7 sts. Work 1 row, then dec 1 st each side. Work 3 rows even. See General Directions for finishing.
Hat: With green, work as for Santa. Attach a white ball fringe pompon to top.
Felt Trim: From red, cut front trim as shown. Glue on. Cut and glue on features as for Santa. Sew on loops of red yarn for beard and hair. Sew on hat.
RABBIT (made entirely in blue yarn): Following General Directions, make body and head.
Arms: Cast on 6 sts. Work in stockinette st for 8 rows. See General Directions for finishing.
Legs: Cast on 8 sts. Work in stockinette st for 11 rows. See General Directions for finishing.
Ears: Cast on 6 sts. Work in stockinette st for 6 rows.
Row 7: Inc 1 st at beg and end of row —8 sts. Work even for 11 rows.
Row 19: Dec 1 st at beg and end of row. Work 3 rows even.
Rows 23-26: Repeat rows 19-22. See General Directions for finishing.
Felt Trims: Cut long, narrow oval strip of pink. Glue over seam of ear. Sew cast-on edge of ear to head. Cut tiny black circle eyes, nose, 1″ wide white tie, small white teeth. Sew on two white pompons for nose. Glue on remaining features as shown. Sew a few loops of yarn between ears.
DUCK (made entirely in yellow yarn): Following General Directions, make body and head.
Wings (make 2): Cast on 8 sts. Work in stockinette st for 4 rows.
Row 5: Inc 1 st each side. Work 5 rows even.
Row 11: Dec 1 st each side. Work 3 rows even.
Row 15: Dec 1 st each side. P 1 row.
Row 17: K 2 tog across. See General Directions for finishing.
Tail: Cast on 12 sts. K 1 row, p 1 row.
Row 3: K, dec 1 st each side. P 1 row. Repeat last 2 rows until 2 sts remain.

See General Directions for finishing. Sew a few loops of yarn to tip of tail, top of head, and front.

Felt Trims: Using patterns, from orange, cut 2 feet and bills. If desired, glue paper to feet to stiffen. Cut tiny black circle eyes. Glue on features.

ROOSTER (made entirely in white yarn): Following General Directions, make body and head. Following Duck directions, make wings and tail.

Felt Trims: Using patterns, cut red comb and wattle, 2 yellow bills, feet; finish feet as for duck. Glue on. Cut tiny black eyes, cut narrow strips of brown, yellow, red for front, longer strips for tail. Sew on as shown.

CLOWN: Following General Directions, make lime green body, white head. Following Santa directions, make green arms with white hands, green hat.

Legs: With lime green, cast on 9 sts. Work in stockinette st for 16 rows. Change to white. Dec 1 st each side of next row, work 5 rows even. Repeat dec row. P 1 row. See General Directions for finishing.

Trims: Sew a few loops of orange yarn to head. Sew on hat. From felt, cut tiny blue circle cheeks, green triangle eyes, black circle pupils, orange triangle nose and mouth. Glue on as shown. Glue on white ball fringe trim and blue pompons as shown.

REINDEER: Following General Directions, make brown head and body. Following directions for Santa, make arms and legs in brown and black.

Ears: With brown, cast on 6 sts. Work 2 rows in stockinette st.

Row 3: K, inc 1 st each side. Work 3 rows even.

Row 7: Dec 1 st each side. P 1 row. Repeat last 2 rows once. See General Directions for finishing.

Nose: With brown, cast on 12 sts. K 1 row, p 1 row.

Row 3: K 2 tog at beg and end of row. P 1 row. Repeat last 2 rows twice. See General Directions for finishing, inserting yarn scraps instead of chenille stick.

Felt Trims: Cut black circle eyes, half oval nose, strips of red for belt and reins. Glue on. Glue green ball pompons on belt. Twist black chenille sticks into antler shapes. Insert one in each side of hand.

PEPPERMINT HOLDER: With red, cast on 30 sts; divide evenly on 3 needles. Join; k around for 23 rnds. Bind off in same tension as sts.

Slip cover over can with bound-off edge at top. Sew back and forth across bottom to hold cover in place. From red felt, cut and glue on circle to fit bottom of can. With pinking shears, cut green strips; glue on top and bottom edges of can. From pattern and felt, cut green leaves, red berries. Glue on.

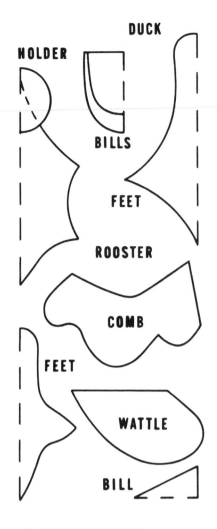

HOLDER · DUCK · BILLS · FEET · ROOSTER · COMB · FEET · WATTLE · BILL

POINSETTIA WREATH
Shown on page 69

SIZE: 14″ diameter.
MATERIALS: Susan Bates "Fashion-Tone" Mercerized Cotton (300-yard balls), 2 balls #0402 white, 1 ball each #047 carmine, #0227 emerald and #0289 canary yellow. Susan Bates or Marcia Lynn Jumbo Pom-Pon Maker. Susan Bates or Marcia Lynn Crochet hook size C-2 (2¾ mm). 12″ styrofoam wreath ring. Five yards ⅝″ green ribbon. Five green satin balls (25 mm). White glue. Liquid fabric starch. Yarn needle. Small piece of green felt.

WREATH: With white, make twelve 4½″ Pom-Pons, wrapping each half 400 times. Glue all around wreath ring.
SMALL POINSETTIA (make 2): **Petals** (make 5): With carmine, ch 14.
Row 1: Dc in 3rd ch from hook, (2 tr in next ch, tr in next ch) 3 times, 2 dc in next ch, dc in next ch, hdc in next ch, sc in next ch, sl st in last ch. Working on opposite side of ch, sc in same ch as sc, hdc in next ch, dc in next ch, 2 dc in next ch, (tr in next ch, 2 tr in next ch) 3 times, dc in next ch, sl st in ch at beg of row. End off; leave 6″ end.
Leaves (make 5): With emerald, work as for petal, but weave in end.

Center: With yellow, ch 5, sl st in first ch to form ring. * Ch 5, sl st in ring, repeat from * 4 times. End off; leave 6″ end.

FINISHING: Soak petals and leaves in a heavy starch solution, spread out and let dry. Cut a 1½″ felt circle, glue ends of leaves all around circle. With yarn needle, pull thread ends of petals through center of felt; tie ends tog on back to secure. Pull thread end of yellow center through center of felt; secure with knot. Make a two-loop bow with ribbon. Glue poinsettia to center of bow.

LARGE POINSETTIA (make 1): **Petals** (make 5): With carmine, ch 16. **Row 1:** Hdc in 2nd ch from hook and in each ch across. Ch 1; working on opposite side of ch, hdc in each ch across. Ch 3, turn.
Row 2: Dc in first hdc, (tr in next st, 2 tr in next st) 3 times, tr in next st, dc in next st, 2 dc in next st, dc in next st, hdc in next st, sc in each of next 2 sts, sl st in next st, sl st in ch-1 sp. Working on other side of row 1, sl st in first hdc, sc in each of next 2 sts, hdc in next st, dc in next st, 2 dc in next st, dc in next st, (tr in next st, 2 tr in next st) 3 times, tr in next st, dc in last st, sl st in base of foundation ch. End off; leave 6″ end.
Leaves (make 5): With emerald, work as for petals, but weave in end.
Center: With yellow, ch 7, sl st in first ch to form ring. * Ch 9, sl st in ring, repeat from * 6 times. End off; leave 6″ end.

FINISHING: Starch and assemble poinsettia as for small poinsettias. Make a three-loop bow with ribbon. Glue poinsettia to center of bow. Glue large poinsettia to center bottom of wreath, then glue small poinsettia to each side of center. Glue green balls around remainder of wreath.

CHRISTMAS TREE
Shown on page 69

SIZE: 19″ high.
MATERIALS: Susan Bates "Fashion-Tone" Mercerized Cotton, 4 300-yard balls emerald. Susan Bates or Marcia Lynn 5-in-1 Pom-Pon Maker. Styrofoam cone, 4″ diameter, 12″ high. Four yards ¼″ metallic gold ribbon. Wooden dowel, ½″ diameter, 8″ long. White plastic flower pot, 3″ diameter, 2¾″ high. Plaster of Paris. Gold glitter. White glue. White paint. Cardboard, 6″ x 4″. Toothpick.
TREE: Sharpen one end of dowel to point. Insert point into center bottom of styrofoam cone, leaving 5″ extended. Remove dowel from cone.

Mix plaster of Paris and fill pot. Allow to harden slightly, then insert straight end of dowel through center to bottom of pot. Allow to harden completely, keeping dowel straight up. Paint dowel with white paint. Spread glue around entire pot and on top of plaster. Sprinkle glitter over glue.

Cut 2 stars from cardboard using pattern. Glue together with toothpick between, one half of toothpick extended. Cover star with glitter as for pot. When dry, insert toothpick into top of cone.

Make about 64 Pom-Pons, using the inner and middle rings together. Glue Pom-Pons all over cone. Make ribbon bows and glue to tree. Insert dowel into hole at base of tree.

POMPON ORNAMENTS
Shown on page 70

SIZE: 5″ to 6″ high.
EQUIPMENT: Susan Bates or Marcia Lynn 5-in-1 Pom-Pon Maker. Susan Bates or Marcia Lynn crochet hook size G-6. White glue. Nylon thread. Scissors. Yarn needle.
SANTA: MATERIALS: Knitting worsted, red, white, black and off-white. Two 7 mm moveable eyes. Small piece polyester stuffing. Cardboard. Green paper. Narrow ribbon.
Body: Make a 1¾″ red Pom-Pon.
Head: Make a 1½″ off-white Pom-Pon. Glue head to body, leaving tying end of body at bottom.
Legs: With red, ch 21. Working in top lp of ch only, work 3 sc in 2nd ch from hook and in each ch across. End off. Twist to form coil. Attach center of legs to body with tying end. Make 2 black 1½″ Pom-Pons for boots. Trim to 1″; attach to leg ends.

Hat: With red, ch 2. **Row 1:** 2 sc in 2nd ch from hook. Ch 1, turn each row. **Row 2:** 2 sc in each sc. **Row 3:** 2 sc in first sc, sc in each sc across, 2 sc in last sc—6 sc. Repeat row 3 until there are 20 sc. Cut red. With white, work 2 rows even. End off. Sew shaped edges tog for back seam. Make a 1½″ white Pom-Pon. Trim to ¾″; attach to top of hat. Glue hat to head.
Arms: Make 2 red 1½″ Pom-Pons; glue to body.

Glue eyes to head below hat. Glue a piece of stuffing below eyes for beard. Cut 3 pieces of cardboard 1″ square, tape together in 3 layers, wrap and tie into a gift package, glue between arms. Attach nylon thread to hat for hanger.
ELF: MATERIALS: Knitting worsted, green and off-white. Two 7 mm moveable eyes. Scrap of green felt. Jingle bell. One red, one white chenille stem. ⅛″ red ribbon.
Body: Make a 1¾″ green Pom-Pon.
Head: Make a 1½″ off-white Pom-Pon. Cut 2 collars from green felt. Leaving tying end of body at bottom, glue collars to top of body, then glue head over collar.
Legs: With green, make as for Santa's legs and attach to body. Make 2 green 1½″ Pom-Pons. Trim to ¾″, attach to ends of legs. Tie 2 small ribbon bows around ankles.
Hat: With green, make as for Santa's hat; do not change color. Sew bell to tip; glue hat to head.

Glue eyes in place. Make 2 green 1½″ Poms-Pons. Trim to 1″ for arms. Twist chenille stems tog lightly, cut to 3″ length, bend to shape candy cane. Glue arms to body; glue candy cane between. Attach nylon thread to hat for hanger.

REINDEER: MATERIALS: Knitting worsted, light brown, red and white. Two 7 mm moveable eyes. Scrap of brown felt. Black 12″ chenille stick. Two green chenille stems. ¼″ red ribbon. Small red sequins.
Body: Make a 2″ brown Pom-Pon.
Head: Make a 1¾″ brown Pom-Pon.

Glue tog, leaving tying end of body at bottom.
Legs: With brown crochet 2 sets of legs same as for Santa; attach to body. Make 4 brown 1½″ Pom-Pons. Trim to 1″; attach to leg ends.

Make a red 1½″ Pom-Pon. Trim to ¾″; glue to head for nose. Glue eyes in place. Make a 1½″ white Pom-Pon. Trim to 1″; glue to back for tail. To make wreath, twist green stems tog lightly, then form a 2½″ circle. Twist ends to secure; cut away excess. Attach a small ribbon bow and sequins to wreath. Place wreath around neck.
Antlers: For each antler, fold 6″ black chenille stick in thirds, then twist one end tog. Trim and bend other ends to form 3-pronged antler. Glue to head. Cut ears from felt, using pattern; glue to head. Attach nylon thread to head for hanger.
TREE: MATERIALS: Knitting worsted in green. 24″ piece of narrow gold rickrack. Large gold star sequin.

Make a 1½″, 2″ and 2½″ Pom-Pon. Glue tog in sequence, then trim to tree shape. Wrap rickrack around tree, tacking ends and several spots with glue. Glue star to top. Attach nylon thread through hole in star for hanger.

PACKAGE TRIMS
Shown on page 71

SIZES: 2½″ to 4½″.
MATERIALS: Scraps of worsted weight yarn. Crochet hook size F. Felt scraps. Brown chenille sticks. Tiny gold bell. Red sequins. Craft glue. Yarn needle. Clear Con-tact plastic, ½ yard. Gold metallic thread.
WREATH: With green, ch 15. Sl st in first ch to form ring. **Rnd 1:** 2 sc in each ch around, sl in first sc. **Rnd 2:** * 2 sc in next sc, sl st in next sc, repeat from * around. Tie a bow with red yarn; sew on. Glue on red sequins.
SNOWMAN: Body: With white, ch 2. 6 sc in 2nd ch from hook. **Rnd 2:** 2 sc in each sc. **Rnd 3:** (Sc in next sc, 2 sc in next sc) 6 times. **Rnd 4:** Sc in each sc around. End off. For head, work through rnd 3. End off. Sew head to body.
Scarf: With red, ch 25. Sc in 2nd ch and in each ch across. Knot some fringe in each end. Sew around neck.

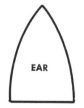

ORNAMENTS

EAR

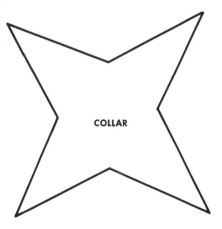

COLLAR

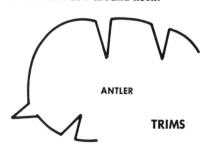

ANTLER

TRIMS

Hat: Brim: With black, ch 10. Sc in 2nd ch and in each ch across. End off. For crown, ch 5. Sc in 2nd ch and each ch across. Ch 1, turn. Work 2 more rows even. Sew to brim; sew hat to head.

Glue pieces of chenille stick to back for arms. Bend as desired. From felt, cut black buttons and eyes, red crescent mouth. Glue on.

ANGEL: With white, ch 10. Sc in 2nd ch and in each ch across. Ch 1, turn. Working in sc, dec 1 sc at center of each of next 4 rows—5 sc. Work 2 rows even. Dec 1 sc on next row. Work 1 row even. Dec 1 sc each row twice more. End off.

Face: With pink, ch 2; 6 sc in 2nd ch from hook. **Next Rnd:** 2 sc in each sc—12 sc. End off.

Hands (make 2): With pink, ch 2; 4 sc in 2nd ch from hook. End off.

Sleeve (make 2): With white, ch 4. Sc in 2nd ch and in each ch across. Ch 1, turn. Work 2 more rows even. **Next Row:** Dec 1 sc at center—2 sc. End off. Sew to robe. Sew hands to ends of sleeves. Sew face to robe.

Wings (make 2): With double strand of gold thread, ch 8. Sc in 2nd ch and in each of next 5 ch. Do not work in end ch. Ch 1, turn. Sk first sc, sc in each of next 5 sc. Ch 1, turn. Sc in 4 sc. Ch 1, turn. Sk first sc, sc in 3 sc. End off. Glue to back.

Glue on yellow yarn for hair. If halo is desired, glue on a notary seal. From felt, cut blue eyes, pink mouth. Glue on.

DEER: With brown, beg at bottom of body, ch 11. Sc in 2nd ch and in each ch across. Ch 1, turn. Work even on 10 sc for 4 more rows. At end of row 5, ch 3, turn. Sc in 2nd ch and in next ch (tail), sc in 10 sc. Ch 5 for head. Sc in 2nd ch and in next 3 ch, sc in 2 sc. Ch 1, turn. Work 2 rows even on 6 sc. Sc in first 4 sc. End off.

Legs (make 2): Ch 7; sc in 2nd ch and in each ch across. Sew to body.

Ear: Ch 3; sc in 2nd ch and last ch. Sew into ear shape with end of yarn; sew to head.

Antler: Bend 6″ chenille stick as shown in diagram. Push notches tog. Sew to top of head.

Make halter of red yarn. Sew on red sequins. Eye is black felt circle.

SHEEP: With white, beg at bottom of body, ch 11. Sc in 2nd ch and in each ch across. Ch 1, turn. Work even on 10 sc for 4 more rows. Ch 3, turn. Sc in 2nd ch and next ch (tail), sc in 10 sc. Ch 3 for head. Sc in 2nd ch and next ch, sc in 2 sc. Ch 1, turn. Work 2 rows even on 4 sc. Sc in 2 sc. End off.

Nose: Tie in gray at bottom of head, work 4 sc across front of head to top. Working in sc, dec 1 sc on each of next 2 rows. End off.

Legs (make 2): With gray, ch 6; sc in 2nd ch and in each ch across. Sew to body.

Ear: With white, ch 3; sc in 2nd ch and last ch. Sew into ear shape with end of yarn; sew to head.

Make a ch long enough to go around neck. Sew on a bell. Make eye of black felt; glue on.

STOCKING: With white, ch 10; sc in 2nd ch and in each ch across. Ch 1,

Continued on page 281

PERUVIAN TREE ORNAMENTS
Shown on page 72

MATERIALS: Small amounts fingering yarn, 3 ply (colors given in individual direction). Set of dp needles No. 2. Steel crochet hook No. 4. Cotton batting or scraps of yarn for stuffing. Tapestry needle.

GAUGE: 7 sts = 1″; 12 rows = 1″.

1: GOOSE: Beg at tail, working with 2 dp needles, with light brown, cast on 7 sts.

Row 1 (wrong side): K 1, (p 1, k 1) 3 times.

Row 2: P 1, (k 1, p 1) 3 times.

Rows 3-6: Repeat rows 1 and 2 twice.

Row 7: Repeat row 1, cast on 3 sts at end of row—10 sts.

Row 8 (right side): Working in ribbing as established, cast on 3 sts at end of row for lower edge of breast—13 sts.

Body and Head: Divide sts on 3 dp needles.

Rnd 1: From right side, working with 4th dp needle, join; k 1 rnd. Mark end of rnds.

Rnd 2: K 4, inc 1 st in next st, k 2, inc 1 st in next st, k 5—15 sts. K 1 rnd.

Rnd 4: K 2, inc 1 st in next st, k 1, inc 1 st in next st, k 4, inc 1 st in next st, k 1, inc 1 st in next st, k 3—19 sts. K 1 rnd.

Rnd 6: K 5, inc 1 st in next st, k 6, inc 1 st in next st, k 6—21 sts. K 1 rnd.

Rnd 8: K 2, inc 1 st in next st, k 2, inc 1 st in next st, k 8, inc 1 st in next st, k 2, inc 1 st in next st, k 3—25 sts. K 8 rnds.

Rnd 17: K 1, k 2 tog, k 19, k 2 tog, k 1—23 sts.

Rnd 18: K 1, k 2 tog, k 17, k 2 tog, k 1—21 sts.

Rnd 19: K 1, k 2 tog, k 5, k 2 tog, k 1, k 2 tog, k 5, k 2 tog, k 1—17 sts.

Rnd 20: (K 1, k 2 tog) 5 times, k 2 tog—11 sts. K 9 rnds.

Shape Beak: Rnd 30: K 2, sl 1, k 1, psso, k 4, k 2 tog, k 1—9 sts.

Rnd 31: K 1, sl 1, k 1, psso, k 3, k 2 tog, k 1—7 sts.

Rnd 32: Sl 1, k 1, psso, k 2 tog, k 1, k 2 tog—4 sts. K 1 rnd.

Rnd 34: (K 2 tog) twice.

Rnd 35: K 2 tog. End off.

FINISHING: Stuff head and body firmly. Sew cast-on sts at lower edge of body to tail. With blue, work two French knots above beak for eyes; five

beige and six brown French knots above eyes as pictured. Beg one row above tail, following chart 1, work French knots across back of bird. With brown, work three French knots on each side of lower edge of body for legs. Attach a strand of yarn to back for hanging.

2: CHICKEN: Beg at tail, working with 2 dp needles, with black, cast on 8 sts. Working in garter st (k each row), k 8 rows.

Row 9: K 1, (k 2 tog) 3 times, k 1—5 sts.

Row 10: K 1, (inc 1 st in next st) 3 times, k 1—8 sts. Cut black.

Rows 11 and 12: With white, k 1 row, p 1 row.

Row 13: Cast on 4 sts, k across tail sts, cast on 4 sts—16 sts.

Body and Head: Divide sts on 3 dp needles.

Rnd 1: From right side, working with 4th dp needle, join; k 3, inc 1 st in next st, k 8, inc 1 st in next st, k 3—18 sts.

Rnd 2: K 3, inc 1 st in next st, k 10, inc 1 st in next st, k 3—20 sts. K 1 rnd.

Rnd 4: K 3, inc 1 st in next st, k 12, inc 1 st in next st, k 3—22 sts. K 1 rnd.

Rnd 6: K 3, inc 1 st in next st, k 14, inc 1 st in next st, k 3—24 sts. K 1 rnd.

Rnd 8: K 3, inc 1 st in next st, k 16, inc 1 st in next st, k 3—26 sts. K 1 rnd.

Rnd 10: K 3, inc 1 st in next st, k 18, inc 1 st in next st, k 3—28 sts. K 1 rnd.

Rnd 12: K 3, inc 1 st in next st, k 20, inc 1 st in next st, k 3—30 sts. K 3 rnds.

Rnd 16: K 3, inc 1 st in next st, k 22, inc 1 st in next st, k 3—32 sts.

Shape Body and Head: Rnd 17: K 1, k 2 tog, k 26, k 2 tog, k 1—30 sts.

Rnd 18: K 1, k 2 tog, k 24, k 2 tog, k 1—28 sts.

Rnd 19: K 1, k 2 tog, k 22, k 2 tog, k 1—26 sts.

Rnd 20: K 1, k 2 tog, k 20, k 2 tog, k 1—24 sts.

Rnd 21: K 1, k 2 tog, k 18, k 2 tog, k 1—22 sts.

Rnd 22: K 1, k 2 tog, k 16, k 2 tog, k 1—20 sts.

Rnd 23: K 1, k 3 tog, k 12, k 3 tog, k 1—16 sts.

Rnd 24: K 1, k 3 tog, k 8, k 3 tog, k 1—12 sts. K 8 rnds.

Shape Top: Rnd 33: K 2 tog, k 8, k 2 tog—10 sts. K 1 rnd. Bind off.

WINGS (make 2): Working with 2 dp needles, with white, cast on 7 sts. Work in garter st for 8 rows. Dec 1 st at beg of next 5 rows—2 sts. K 2 tog. End off.

FEET (make 2): Beg at lower edge, with white, cast on 8 sts and divide on 3 dp needles. Join; k 4 rnds. Bind off.

BEAK: With 2 dp needles, with black cast on 5 sts. P 1 row.

Row 2: K 2 tog, k 1, k 2 tog—3 sts. P 1 row.

Row 4: Sl 1, k 2 tog, psso—1 st. End off.

FINISHING: Stuff head and body firmly. Sew cast-on edge of body to upper edge of tail; weave top of head tog. Fold cast-on edge of beak tog; weave to top of head. Work two blue French knots for eyes. Fold cast-on edge of legs tog; weave to body. Work black French knots around lower edge of each leg; work black French knots on each wing, white French knots on back of body as pictured. Sew cast-on edge of wings to body. From right side, with white, work one row sc around each wing. Attach a strand of yarn to back for hanging.

3: BLUE FISH: Beg at tail, with 2 dp needles, with light blue, cast on 11 sts. Work in garter st, dec 1 st each side every other row 3 times—5 sts. Cast on 5 sts at end of last row for lower edge of fish—10 sts on needle.

Body: Divide sts on 3 dp needles.

Rnd 1: From right side, working with 4th dp needle, join; k 5 rnds. Mark end of rnds.

Rnd 7: K 3, inc 1 st in next st, k to within last 3 sts, inc 1 st in next st, k 2—12 sts. K 3 rnds.

Rnd 11: Repeat rnd 7—14 sts. K 3 rnds.

Rnd 15: Repeat rnd 7—16 sts.

Rnd 16: Knit.

Rnds 17-26: Repeat rnds 15 and 16, 5 times—26 sts.

Shape Head: Rnd 27: K 11, k 2 tog, k 8, k 2 tog, k 3—24 sts.

Rnd 28: K 10, k 2 tog, k 3, k 2 tog, k 7—22 sts.

Rnd 29: K 9, k 2 tog, k 5, k 2 tog, k 4—20 sts.

Rnd 30: K 8, k 2 tog, k 7, k 2 tog, k 1—18 sts.

Rnd 31: K 7, k 2 tog, k 4, k 2 tog, k 3—16 sts.

Rnd 32: K 6, k 2 tog, k 5, k 2 tog, k 1—14 sts.

Rnd 33: K 5, k 2 tog, k 1, k 2 tog, k 4—12 sts.

Rnd 34: K 4, k 2 tog, k 3, k 2 tog—10 sts. Bind off.

Lower Fin: With 2 dp needles, with blue, cast on 7 sts. K 1 row. Bind off in k.

Side Fins (make 2): With 2 dp needles with blue, cast on 3 sts.

Row 1: K 1, inc 1 st in next st, k 1—4 sts.

Row 2: K 2, inc 1 st in next st, k 1—5 sts.

Row 3: K 2, inc 1 st in next st, k 2—6 sts. K 1 row. Bind off in k.

FINISHING: Stuff body and head firmly. Sew cast-on edge of body to tail. Weave front of head tog. Sew cast-on edge of lower fin in place. Leaving 4 sts at upper and lower edge of body free, beg on rnd 13, work French knots in each st every other rnd on each side of body, working 9 raspberry knots, 8 royal blue knots, 7 dark orange knots, 6 orange knots, 5 orange knots, 4 yellow knots, 3 black knots (see picture). Work green knots for eyes. Sew cast-on edge of side fins in place. Attach a strand of yarn to back for hanging.

4: OWL: Beg at tail, working with 2 dp needles, with brown, cast on 6 sts. K 8 rows.

Row 9: K 2, k 2 tog, k 2—5 sts. K 3 rows, cast on 5 sts at end of last row for lower edge of breast—10 sts.

Body and Head: Divide sts on 3 dp needles.

Rnd 1: From right side, working with 4th dp needle, join; k 1 rnd.

Rnd 2: Inc 1 st in first st, k 2, inc 1 st in next st, k 6—12 sts. K 1 rnd.

Rnd 4: Inc 1 st in first st, k 4, inc 1 st in next st, k 1, inc 1 st in next st, k 2, inc 1 st in next st, k 1—16 sts. K 1 rnd.

Rnd 6: Inc 1 st in first st, k 6, inc 1 st in next st, k 1, inc 1 st in next st, k 4, inc 1 st in next st, k 1—20 sts. K 1 rnd.

Rnd 8: Inc 1 st in first st, k 8, inc 1 st in next st, k 1, inc 1 st in next st, k 6, inc 1 st in next st, k 1—24 sts. K 1 rnd.

Rnd 10: Inc 1 st in first st, k 10, inc 1 st in next st, k 1, inc 1 st in next st, k 8, inc 1 st in next st, k 1—28 sts. K 1 rnd.

Rnd 12: K 15, inc 1 st in next st, k 10, inc 1 st in next st, k 1—30 sts.

Rnds 13-19: K 7 rnds.

Shape Head: Rnd 20: K 2 tog around—15 sts. K 9 rnds.

Shape Top: K 4, turn; k 4, turn; bind off 4 sts. K next 4 sts, turn; k 4, turn; bind off 4 sts. Bind off remaining 7 sts.

WINGS (make 2): With 2 dp needles, with brown, cast on 6 sts. Work in garter st for 6 rows. Dec 1 st at beg of next 5 rows—1 st remains. End off.

FINISHING: Stuff head and body firmly. Sew cast-on edge of body to tail; weave top of head tog, leaving the 4 garter sts free on each side of head for ears. Work yellow French knots for eyes, brown French knot for beak on front of head. Work four yellow, three hot pink, four raspberry French knots on back of head. Beg at row above tail, following chart 2, work French knots across back of owl. Weave cast-on edge of wings to back. Work 1 row sc around each wing.

FEET (make 2): With brown, ch 6; working under strand at back of each ch, sl st in each of first 3 ch, (ch 3, sl st in each of 3 ch just made) twice, sc in last 3 ch. Attach feet to owl. Attach a strand of yarn to back for hanging.

5: TROPICAL BIRD: Beg at tail, working with 2 dp needles, with raspberry, cast on 8 sts. Working in garter st, k 8 rows.

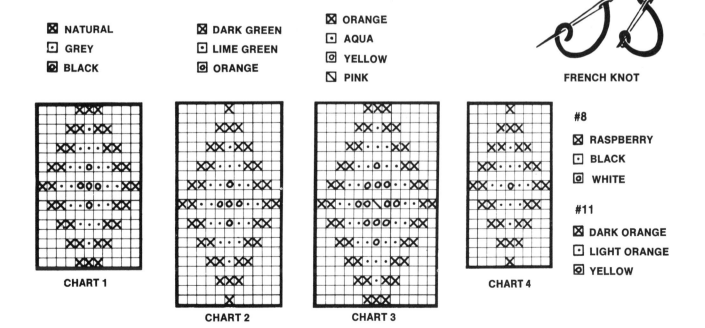

⊠ **NATURAL**
⊡ **GREY**
◪ **BLACK**

⊠ **DARK GREEN**
⊡ **LIME GREEN**
◙ **ORANGE**

⊠ **ORANGE**
⊡ **AQUA**
◙ **YELLOW**
◲ **PINK**

FRENCH KNOT

CHART 1

CHART 2

CHART 3

CHART 4

#8
⊠ **RASPBERRY**
⊡ **BLACK**
◙ **WHITE**

#11
⊠ **DARK ORANGE**
⊡ **LIGHT ORANGE**
◙ **YELLOW**

Dec 1 st each side of next row—6 sts. K 1 row, cast on 6 sts at end of last row for lower edge of breast—12 sts.

Body and Head: Divide sts on 3 dp needles.

Rnd 1: From right side, working with 4th dp needle, join; k 1 rnd. Mark end of rnds.

Rnd 2: K 6, inc 1 st in next st, k 4, inc 1 st in next st—14 sts. K 1 rnd.

Rnd 4: Inc 1 st in first st, k 4, inc 1 st in next 2 sts, k 6, inc 1 st in next st—18 sts. K 1 rnd.

Rnd 6: K 8, inc 1 st in next st, k 8, inc 1 st in next st—20 sts. K 1 rnd.

Rnd 8: Inc 1 st in first st, k 6, inc 1 st in each of next 2 sts, k 10, inc 1 st in next st—24 sts. K 1 rnd.

Rnd 10: K 10, inc 1 st in next st, k 12, inc 1 st in next st—26 sts. K 1 rnd.

Rnd 12: Inc 1 st in first st, k 8, inc 1 st in each of next 2 sts, k 14, inc 1 st in next st—30 sts. K 1 rnd.

Shape Breast: Rnd 14: K 18, k 2 tog, k 2, k 2 tog, k 6—28 sts.

Rnd 15: K 17, k 2 tog, k 2, k 2 tog, k 5—26 sts.

Rnd 16: K 16, k 2 tog, k 2, k 2 tog, k 4—24 sts.

Rnd 17: K 15, k 2 tog, k 2, k 2 tog, k 3—22 sts.

Rnd 18: K 14, k 2 tog, k 2, k 2 tog, k 2—20 sts.

Rnd 19: K 13, k 2 tog, k 2, k 2 tog, k 1—18 sts.

Rnd 20: K 1, k 2 tog, k 6, k 2 tog, k 1, k 2 tog, k 2, k 2 tog—14 sts. K 7 rnds.

Rnd 28: K 2 tog, k 3, (k 2 tog) twice, k 3, k 2 tog—10 sts. Bind off.

WINGS (make 2): With 2 dp needles, with raspberry, cast on 7 sts. K 6 rows.

Row 7: K 1, k 2 tog, k 4.

Row 8: K 1, k 2 tog, k 3.

Row 9: K 1, k 2 tog, k 2.

Row 10: K 1, k 2 tog, k 1.

Row 11: K 1, k 2 tog.

Row 12: K 2 tog. End off.

EARS (make 2): With 2 dp needles, with raspberry, cast on 3 sts. K 4 rows.

Row 5: K 1, k 2 tog—2 sts.

Row 6: K 2 tog. End off.

FINISHING: Stuff head and body firmly. Weave cast-on edge of body to tail; weave top of head tog. Sew cast-on edge of ears to top of head. Work yellow French knots for eyes and bill. Work rows of alternating white and navy French knots across top of head. Beg 1 row above tail, working in every other row, work 6 rows of alternating navy and white French knots across back. Weave wings in place. Attach a strand of yarn to back for hanging.

6: MOUSE: Beg at tail, with 2 dp needles and white, cast on 4 sts. Work back and forth in stockinette st (k 1 row, p 1 row) for 2″, end p row.

Body and Head: Next Row: Inc 1 st in each st across—8 sts. Divide sts on 3 dp needles.

Rnd 1: From right side, working with 4th dp needle, join; k 1 rnd, inc 2 sts evenly spaced—10 sts. Mark end of rnds.

Rnd 2: (Inc 1 st in next st, k 2, inc 1 st in next st, k 1) twice—14 sts. K 1 rnd.

Rnd 4: (Inc 1 st in next st, k 4, inc 1 st in next st, k 1) twice—18 sts. K 1 rnd.

Rnd 6: (Inc 1 st in next st, k 6, inc 1 st in next st, k 1) twice—22 sts. K 1 rnd.

Rnd 8: (Inc 1 st in next st, k 8, inc 1 st in next st, k 1) twice—26 sts. K 1 rnd.

Rnd 10: (Inc 1 st in next st, k 10, inc 1 st in next st, k 1) twice—30 sts. K 14 rnds. Stuff body firmly; continue to add stuffing every other rnd.

Rnd 25: (K 1, k 2 tog) 10 times—20 sts.

Rnd 26: K 3, k 2 tog, k 1, k 2 tog, k 12.

Rnd 27: K 2, k 2 tog, k 1, k 2 tog, k 11.

Rnd 28: K 1, k 2 tog, k 1, k 2 tog, k 10.

Rnd 29: K 2 tog, k 1, k 2 tog, k 9—12 sts.

Rnd 30: K 3, k 2 tog, k 5, k 2 tog—10 sts.

Rnd 31: K 3, k 2 tog, k 3, k 2 tog—8 sts.

Rnd 32: (K 2 tog) 4 times—4 sts. Cut yarn, leaving a long end; draw through sts; fasten securely.

EARS (make 2): With white and crochet hook, ch 6. End off, leaving end for sewing.

FINISHING: Sew tail seam. With orange, work French knot eyes. Beg 1 row above tail, following chart 3, work French knots across back. Attach ears to body. Attach a strand of yarn to back for hanging.

7: ROOSTER: Beg with legs, with maroon, cast on 8 sts; divide on 3 dp needles; join; k 6 rnds. Sl sts on a thread. Make 2nd leg the same; do not end off. Mark end of rnd. With free dp needle, k 5; with 2nd dp needle, k 3; k 2 sts of first leg; with 3rd dp needle, k remaining 6 sts of first leg—16 sts. K 2 rnds.

Next Rnd: (K 1, inc 1 st in next st) 8 times—24 sts. K 1 rnd.

Next Rnd: (K 2, inc 1 st in next st) 8 times—32 sts. K 1 rnd.

Next Rnd: (K 3, inc 1 st in next st) 8 times—40 sts. Cut maroon; join royal blue. K 6 rnds. Cut royal blue; join dark blue.

Next Rnd: (K 4, inc 1 st in next st) 8 times—48 sts. K 5 rnds. Cut dark blue; join yellow. K 6 rnds.

Shape Body: Bind off next 17 sts, k until 14 sts from bound-off sts, bind off next 17 sts. Divide these 14 sts on 3 dp needles; join; with dark green, k 16 rnds.

Shape Head: Next Rnd: K 4, inc 1 st in next st, k 3, inc 1 st in next st, k 5.

Next Rnd: K 4, inc 1 st in next st, k 5, inc 1 st in next st, k 5—18 sts.

Next Rnd: K 2 tog, k 2, inc 1 st in next st, k 7, inc 1 st in next st, k 3, k 2 tog. Bind off.

FEET: With red and crochet hook, ch 6, sl st in 4th ch from hook, sl st in next 2 ch, ch 3, sl st in last ch worked in; working across other side of starting ch, sl st in next ch, ch 3, sl st in next ch. End off, leaving a long end for sewing. Sew a foot to lower edge of each leg.

FINISHING: Stuff legs, body and head firmly. Weave upper edge of body and head tog. With red, work sc under beak and at top of head for wattle and comb. Work yellow French knot eyes. Spacing French knots in every 3rd st at center of each color, work knots around each stripe, as pictured. Knot assorted colors into seam at top of body for tail. Attach a strand of yarn to back for hanging.

8: BLUEBIRD: Beg at tail, working with 2 dp needles, with royal blue, cast on 7 sts. Work 10 rows in garter st.

Row 11: K 3, k 2 tog, k 2. K 1 row.

Row 13: (K 2 tog) 3 times—3 sts. Cast on 3 sts at end of last row—6 sts on needle.

Body and Head: Divide sts on 3 dp needles.

Rnd 1: From right side, working with 4th needle, join; (inc 1 st in each of next 2 sts, k 1) twice—10 sts. Mark end of rnds. K 9 rnds.

Rnd 11: Inc 1 st in next st, k 2, inc 1 st in next st, k 1, inc 1 st in next st, k 2, inc 1 st in next st, k 1—14 sts. K 1 rnd.

Rnd 13: (Inc 1 st in next st, k 4, inc 1 st in next st, k 1) twice—18 sts. K 1 rnd.

Rnd 15: (Inc 1 st in next st, k 6, inc 1 st in next st, k 1) twice—22 sts. K 1 rnd.

Rnd 17: (Inc 1 st in next st, k 8, inc 1 st in next st, k 1) twice—26 sts. K 1 rnd.

Rnd 19: Inc 1 st in next st, k 10, inc 1 st in next st, k 14—28 sts. K 6 rnds.

Rnd 26: K 1, k 2 tog, k 9, k 2 tog, k 14—26 sts.

Rnd 27: (K 1, k 2 tog, k 7, k 2 tog, k 1) twice—22 sts.

Rnd 28: (K 1, k 2 tog, k 5, k 2 tog, k 1) twice—18 sts.

Rnd 29: (K 1, k 2 tog, k 3, k 2 tog, k 1) twice—14 sts.

Rnd 30: (K 1, k 2 tog, k 1, k 2 tog, k 1) twice—10 sts. K 6 rnds. Stuff body; continue to stuff body every other rnd.

Shape Head: Rnd 37: (K, p, k) in next st for eye, k 3, (k, p, k) in next st, k 2 tog, k 1, k 2 tog—12 sts.

Rnd 38: K 7, k 2 tog, k 1, k 2 tog—10 sts.

Rnd 39: Sl 1, k 2 tog, psso, k 3, (sl 1, k 1, psso) twice—6 sts.

Rnd 40: (K 2 tog) 3 times—3 sts. K 1 rnd. Cut yarn, draw sts tog; fasten securely.

WINGS (make 2): Cast on 6 sts. Work back and forth in garter st for 10 rows. Dec 1 st each side every other row twice—2 sts. K 1 row. K 2 tog. End off.

FINISHING: Weave cast-on edge of body to tail. With raspberry, work French knots for eyes. Beg at first inc rnd on body, following chart 4, work French knots on back of bird. Sew on wings. Attach a strand of yarn to back for hanging.

9: GOLDFISH: Beg at tail, working with 2 dp needles, with orange, cast on 6 sts. K 12 rows, cast on 6 sts at end of last row—12 sts.

Body: Divide sts on 3 dp needles.

Rnd 1: From right side, working with 4th dp needle, join; k 1 rnd, inc 3 sts evenly spaced—15 sts. Mark end of rnds. K 9 rnds.

Rnd 11: Inc 1 st in next st, k 4, inc 1 st in next st, k 2, inc 1 st in next st, k 4, inc 1 st in next st, k 1—19 sts. K 1 rnd.

Rnd 13: Inc 1 st in next st, k 16, inc 1 st in next st, k 1—21 sts. K 1 rnd.

Rnd 15: Inc 1 st in next st, k 7, inc 1 st in next st, k 2, inc 1 st in next st, k 7, inc 1 st in next st, k 1—25 sts. K 5 rnds.

Rnd 21: K 1, k 2 tog, k to within last 3 sts, k 2 tog, k 1—23 sts.

Rnds 22-30: Repeat rnd 21, 9 times—5 sts.

Rnd 31: K 2 tog, k 1, k 2 tog—3 sts. K 1 rnd. End off; draw sts tog; fasten securely.

FIN: With 2 dp needles, cast on 9 sts. K 3 rows. Bind off.

FINISHING: Stuff body firmly. Weave cast-on sts of body to tail. With black, work French knot eyes. Sew cast-on edge of upper fin in place. Leaving 3 sts at upper and lower edge of body free, beg on rnd 11, work French knots in each st every other rnd on each side of body, working 5 raspberry knots, 6 raspberry knots, 7 pink knots, 9 royal blue knots, 10 aqua knots. Attach a strand of yarn to back for hanging.

10: ELF: BODY: Beg at lower edge, with white, cast on 16 sts; divide on 3 needles. Join; k 14 rnds.

Neck: Rnd 15: (K 2 tog) 8 times—8 sts.

Head: Rnd 16: K, inc 1 st in each st—16 sts. K 7 rnds.

Rnd 24: (K 2, k 2 tog) 4 times—12 sts.

Rnd 25: (K 1, k 2 tog) 4 times—8 sts.

Rnd 26: K 2 tog 4 times—4 sts. Cut yarn; draw sts tog; fasten securely. Stuff head and body firmly. Weave lower edge tog.

LEGS (make 2): Beg at upper edge, with white, cast on 8 sts; divide on 3 dp needles. Join; k 6 rnds.

Rnd 7: (K 2, k 2 tog) twice—6 sts. K 5 rnds.

Shape Heel: (K 3, turn; p 3, turn) twice, k around. K 5 rnds.

Shape Toe: K 2 tog 3 times—3 sts. K 3 tog. End off. Weave open sides of heels tog; stuff firmly. Sew to lower edge of body.

ARMS (make 2): Beg at upper edge, with white, cast on 8 sts; divide on 3 dp needles. Join; k 6 rnds.

Shape Thumb: (K 2, turn; p 2, turn) twice. Bind off these 2 sts. Work back and forth in stockinette st on remaining 6 sts for 5 rows. Bind off. Sew side of thumb tog; sew side and top of hand tog. Stuff firmly; sew to sides of body.

With blue, embroider eyes, nose and mouth. With yellow, ch 8″. End off. Tack chain to lower edge of chin for beard (see picture).

HAT: With 2 dp needles, with pink, cast on 20 sts. Work in ribbing of k 1, p 1 for 2 rows. Work in garter st for 12 rows. Bind off. Fold hat in half, sew back seam; roll ribbing to right side for front cuff; tack in place.

TUNIC: BACK: Beg at lower edge, with 2 dp needles, with maroon, cast on 12 sts. Work in stockinette st (k 1 row, p 1 row) for 8 rows, end p row.

Shape Armholes: Dec 1 st each side of next row, then every other row 3 times—6 sts. Work 4 rows even. Bind off.

FRONT: Work same as for back.

Sew side seams. Put tunic on figure; sew shoulder seams. Put hat on head; tack to neck. Attach a green tassel to top of hat. Attach a strand of yarn to back for hanging.

11: DUCK: Body: Beg at back with royal blue, cast on 9 sts; divide on 3 dp needles. Join; k 1 rnd. Mark end of rnds.

Rnd 2: Inc 1 st in each st—18 sts. K 1 rnd.

Rnd 4: (K 1, inc 1 st in next st) 9 times—27 sts. K 1 rnd.

Rnd 6: K around, inc 5 sts evenly spaced around—32 sts. K 10 rnds.

Shape Body and Head: Rnd 17: K 1, k 2 tog, k 26, k 2 tog, k 1—30 sts.

Rnd 18: K 1, k 2 tog, k 24, k 2 tog, k 1—28 sts.

Rnd 19: K 1, k 2 tog, k 22, k 2 tog, k 1—26 sts.

Rnd 20: K 1, k 2 tog, k 20, k 2 tog, k 1—24 sts.

Rnd 21: K 1, k 2 tog, k 18, k 2 tog, k 1—22 sts.

Rnd 22: K 1, k 2 tog, k 16, k 2 tog, k 1—20 sts. K 4 rnds.

Rnd 27: K 7, k 2 tog, k 2, k 2 tog, k 7—18 sts.

Rnd 28: K 5, k 3 tog, k 2, k 3 tog, k 5—14 sts.

Rnd 29: K 3, k 3 tog, k 2, k 3 tog, k 3—10 sts.

Rnd 30: K 1, k 3 tog, k 2 tog, k 3 tog, k 1—5 sts.

Rnd 31: K 2 tog, k 1, k 2 tog—3 sts. K 5 rnds. K 3 tog. End off.

WINGS (make 2): With 2 dp needles, with royal blue, cast on 7 sts. Work in garter st for 6 rows.

Row 7: K 2 tog, k across.

Row 8: K to within last 2 sts, k 2 tog.

Rows 9-11: Repeat rows 7, 8, 7—2 sts. K 2 tog. End off.

FINISHING: Stuff body and head firmly. Weave cast-on edge of body tog. Work yellow French knots for eyes. Following chart 4, work French knots across center back. Weave cast-on edge of wings to back. Attach a strand of yarn to hat for hanging.

TWELVE ORNAMENTS
Shown on pages 72 and 73

SIZE: 3″ to 5″ high.

MATERIALS: J. & P. Coats Knit-Cro-Sheen. 1 ball each of white (W), red (R), green (G), black (B), ecru (E). Steel crochet hook No. 7. Piece of 3″ thick foam rubber or other material for stuffing. Disposable plastic bottle.

GAUGE: 8 sts = 1″.

SANTA: BODY: Beg at top of head, with E, ch 6. Sl st in first ch to form ring. **Rnd 1:** Ch 1, 2 sc in each ch around.

Rnd 2: Sc in back lp of each sc around. **Note:** Work in back lp only of each st throughout.

Rnd 3: 2 sc in each sc around—24 sc.

Rnds 4-7: Work even in sc.

Rnd 8: (Sc in each of 3 sc, sk next sc) 6 times—18 sc. Work 1 rnd even. Cut E.

Rnd 10: With R, 2 sc in each sc—36 sc.

Rnds 11-13: Work even.

Rnd 14: (Sc in each of 5 sc, 2 sc in next sc) 6 times—42 sc. Work 3 rnds even. Drop R.

Rnd 18: With B, (sc in each of 6 sc, 2 sc in next sc) 6 times—48 sc.

Rnd 19: Sc in each sc. Cut B.

Rnds 20-22: With R, work even. Drop R.

Rnds 23 and 24: With W, work even. Cut W.

Rnd 25: With R, work even.

Rnd 26: (Sc in each of next 7 sc, sk next sc) 6 times—42 sc.

Rnd 27: (Sc in each of next 6 sc, sk next sc) 6 times—36 sc. Cut R.

Rnds 28-30: With B, work even.

Rnd 31: (Sc in each of next 5 sc, sk next sc) 6 times—30 sc.

Rnds 32-34: Work even. End off.

BOTTOM: With B, ch 6. Sl st in first ch to form ring. **Rnd 1:** 2 sc in each ch around—12 sc.

Rnd 2: 2 sc in each sc around—24 sc.

Rnd 3: (Sc in each of 3 sc, 2 sc in next sc) 6 times—30 sc. End off.

ARM (make 2): With R, ch 6. Sl st in first ch to form ring. **Rnd 1:** 2 sc in each ch around—12 sc.

Rnds 2-8: Sc in each sc around. Cut R.

Rnds 9 and 10: With W, work even. Cut W.

Rnds 11 and 12: With B, work even.

Rnd 13: (Sc in next sc, sk next sc) 6 times. End off.

BEARD: With W, ch 16.

Row 1: Sc in 2nd ch from hook and in each ch—15 sc. Ch 1, turn.

Row 2: (Sc in 3 sc, 2 sc in next sc) 3 times, sc in last 3 sc—18 sc. Ch 1, turn.

Row 3: (Sc in 4 sc, 2 sc in next sc) 3 times, sc in last 3 sc—21 sc. Ch 1, turn.

Row 4: Sc in each sc across. End off.

HAT: With W, ch 6. Sl st in first ch to form ring. **Rnd 1:** 2 sc in each ch around. Cut W.

Rnds 2-4: With R, sc in each sc around.

Rnd 5: (Sc in 2 sc, 2 sc in next sc) 4 times—16 sc.

Rnd 6: Sc in each sc around.

Rnd 7: (Sc in 3 sc, 2 sc in next sc) 4 times—20 sc.

Rnd 8: Sc in each sc around.

Rnd 9: (Sc in next sc, 2 sc in next sc) 10 times—30 sc.

Rnds 10 and 11: Sc in each sc around. Cut R.

Rnds 12-14: With W, work even.

FINISHING: Stuff head with 1″ ball of foam rubber. Cut a foam rubber block 2″ x 1½″ x 1½″ for body. Trim to barrel shape 2″ high, with ½″ diameter at top for neck, 1½″ diameter at center, and 1″ diameter at bottom. Stuff body. For legs, cut foam rubber in drum shape, 1″ diameter, ¾″ high. Stuff legs. Cut 1″ diameter disk from plastic bottle. Place at bottom of legs. Sew bottom to Santa over disk. Sew top of arms to sides of body. Sew beard to face in a curve. With B, embroider eyes ½″ apart. Turn up W cuff on hat; sew hat to head. Make hanging loop with double strand of R, drawn through center front of hat; knot ends tog.

SOLDIER: BODY: With E, work as for Santa through rnd 9. Work in back lp of each sc throughout. Work 1 more rnd of 18 sc. Cut E.
Rnd 11: With R, 2 sc in each sc around —36 sc.
Rnds 12-24: Sc in each sc around. Cut R.
Rnd 25: With B, (sc in next 5 sc, sk next sc) 6 times—30 sc.
Rnds 26-36: Sc in each sc around. End off.
BOTTOM: Same as for Santa.
ARM (make 2): With R, ch 6. Sl st in first ch to form ring. **Rnd 1:** 2 sc in each ch around—12 sc.
Rnds 2-10: Work even in sc. Cut R.
Rnds 11 and 12: With E, work even in sc.
Rnd 13: (Sk next sc, sc in next sc) 6 times. End off.
HAIR: With B, ch 6. Sl st in first ch to form ring. **Rnd 1:** 2 sc in each ch around—12 sc.
Rnd 2: Sc in each sc around.
Rnd 3: 2 sc in each sc around—24 sc.
Rnds 4-6: Sc in each sc around. End off.
BELT AND STRAPS: With W, ch 36. Sl st in first ch to form ring. Sc in each ch around. Sl st in first sc. * Ch 24 for shoulder strap, sl st in 19th sc of belt. Turn and work sc in each ch of strap. Repeat from * for 2nd strap. End off.
HAT: With B, work as for hair through rnd 4—24 sc.
Rnd 5: (Sc in each of 3 sc, 2 sc in next sc) 6 times—30 sc.
Rnds 6-8: Sc in each sc around.
Rnd 9: (Sk next sc, sc in each of next 4 sc) 6 times—24 sc.
Rnd 10: Sc in each sc around. Cut B.
Rnds 11 and 12: With R, sc in each sc around. End off.
PLUME: With W, ch 7. Sc in 2nd ch from hook and in each of next 4 ch, 5 sc in last ch. Working on opposite side of starting ch, sc in each of 5 ch. End off.
FINISHING: Stuff head with 1″ ball of

foam rubber. Stuff body with a drum-shaped piece 1½″ high and 1¼″ in diameter. Stuff legs with a drum-shaped piece 1½″ high and 1⅛″ in diameter. Cut a 1″ disk from plastic bottle. Place at bottom of legs. Sew bottom to soldier over disk. Sew an arm to each side of body at shoulders. Sew belt to soldier around waist; tack strap to each shoulder. Tack hand in place at each side. Embroider black eyes ½″ apart and red mouth on front of face. Sew hair to head, fitting it to rnd 3 of head at center front and rnd 9 of head at center back. Stuff hat with drum-shaped piece ¾″ high, 1″ diameter. Sew red band to head. Sew plume to center front of hat. Make hanging loop with double strand of B, drawn through top of hat; knot ends tog.

ANGEL: HEAD AND BODY: With E, ch 6. Sl st in first ch to form ring.
Rnd 1: 2 sc in each ch around—12 sc.
Rnd 2: Sc in back lp of each sc around.
Note: Work in back lp of each st throughout.
Rnd 3: 2 sc in each sc around—24 sc.
Rnds 4-7: Repeat rnd 2.
Rnd 8: (Sk next sc, sc in each of next 3 sc) 6 times—18 sc.
Rnd 9: Repeat rnd 2. Cut E.
Rnd 10: With W, (sc in next 2 sc, 2 sc in next sc) 6 times—24 sc.
Rnds 11 and 12: Sc in each sc around.
Rnd 13: (Sc in next 3 sc, 2 sc in next sc) 6 times—30 sc.
Rnds 14-16: Sc in each sc around.
Rnd 17: (Sc in next 4 sc, 2 sc in next sc) 6 times—36 sc.
Rnds 18-20: Sc in each sc around.
Rnd 21: (Sc in next 5 sc, 2 sc in next sc) 6 times—42 sc.
Rnds 22-24: Sc in each sc around.
Rnd 25: (Sc in next 6 sc, 2 sc in next sc) 6 times—48 sc.
Rnds 26-28: Sc in each sc around.
Rnd 29: Ch 2, dc in each sc around. Sl st in top of ch 2. End off.
BOTTOM: With W, ch 6. Sl st in first ch to form ring. **Rnd 1:** 2 sc in each ch around.
Rnd 2: (2 sc in next sc, sc in next sc) 6 times—18 sc.
Rnd 3: (2 sc in next sc, sc in each of next 2 sc) 6 times—24 sc.
Rnd 4: (2 sc in next sc, sc in each of next 3 sc) 6 times—30 sc.
Rnds 5-7: Continue to inc 6 sc each rnd—48 sc. End off.
ARM (make 2): With W, ch 6. Sl st in first ch to form ring. **Rnd 1:** 2 sc in each ch around—12 sc. Work even on 12 sc for 3 more rnds.
Rnd 5: (Sc in next 2 sc, 2 sc in next sc) 4 times—16 sc. Work even on 16 sc for 3 more rnds.
Rnd 9: Ch 2, dc in each sc around. Sl st in top of ch 2. End off.
HAND (make 2): With E, ch 5. Sl st

in first ch to form ring. **Rnd 1:** 2 sc in each ch around—10 sc. Work even on 10 sc for 2 more rnds.
Rnd 4: (Sk next sc, sc in next sc) 5 times. End off.
WING (make 2): With W, ch 6. Sl st in first ch to form ring. **Rnd 1:** 2 sc in each ch around—12 sc.
Rnd 2: (Sc in next sc, 2 sc in next sc) 6 times—18 sc.
Rnd 3: (Sc in next 2 sc, 2 sc in next sc) 6 times—24 sc.
Row 4: Ch 2, (dc in next sc, ch 1) 5 times, dc in next sc. Ch 2, turn.
Row 5: (Dc in next ch-1 sp, ch 1) 4 times, dc in next sp. Ch 2, turn.
Row 6: (Dc in next ch-1 sp, ch 1) 3 times, dc in next sp. Ch 2, turn.
Row 7: (Dc in next ch-1 sp, ch 1) twice, dc in next sp. Ch 2, turn.
Row 8: Dc in next ch-1 sp, ch 1, dc in next sp. Ch 1; work 1 rnd sc around outer edge of wing. Sl st in first sc. End off.
COLLAR: With W, ch 24. Sl st in first ch to form ring. Ch 2, dc in next ch, * ch 1, dc in next ch, repeat from * around, sl st in top of ch 2. End off.
HALO: With W, ch 24. Sl st in first ch to form ring. Ch 1, sc in each ch around. Sl st in first sc. End off.
FINISHING: Stuff head with 1″ ball of foam rubber. Stuff body with cone shape 2¾″ high, 2″ diameter at bottom and ¾″ diameter at top. Cut 1⅞″ diameter disk from plastic bottle. Place at bottom; sew bottom to angel over disk. Sew collar around neck. Sew arms to sides of body. Sew hands inside arms. For hair, cut 30 W strands 3″ long; tie tog tightly around center with another strand. Sew tied center on top of head. Sew halo over hair after spreading out hair. Sew wings tog at sides of circles; sew wings to back below collar. Make hanging loop with double strand of W, drawn through top of head; knot ends tog. Embroider black eyes ½″ apart and red mouth.

CHOIR BOY: HEAD AND BODY: Work as for Angel through Rnd 9. With G, work as for Angel through rnd 27. Cut G.
Rnd 28: With W, ch 2, dc in each sc around.
Rnd 29: Dc in each dc around. End off.
BOTTOM: Work as for bottom of Angel.
ARM (make 2): With G, work as for Angel's arm through rnd 5. Work even on 16 sc for 3 more rnds. Cut G.
Rnd 9: With W, ch 2, dc in each sc around. Sl st in top of ch 2. End off.
HAND (make 2): Same as Angel's Hand.
HAIR: With B, ch 6. Sl st in first ch to form ring. **Rnd 1:** 2 sc in each ch around—12 sc.

Rnd 2: Sc in each sc around.

Rnd 3: 2 sc in each sc around—24 sc.

Rnds 4-6: Sc in each sc around. End.

BOOK: With R, ch 7. **Row 1:** Sc in 2nd ch from hook and in each ch—6 sc. Ch 1, turn each row.

Rows 2-6: Sc in each sc. End off. Make another piece the same. Sc pieces tog along one long edge for binding. Sc all around outside of book.

COLLAR: With W, ch 23, 2 dc in 3rd ch from hook and in each of next 5 ch, dc in each of next 9 ch, 2 dc in each remaining ch. End off.

FINISHING: Stuff and finish bottom of Choir Boy as for Angel. Sew hands inside arms; sew top of arms to sides of body at first G row. Sew book to hands. Sew collar around neck. With R, ch 36. Tie into a bow; sew to front of collar. Sew hair in place on head. Embroider black eyes, red mouth. For hanging loop, run a double strand of B through top of head; knot ends tog.

SNOWMAN: HEAD AND BODY: With W, ch 6. Sl st in first ch to form ring. **Rnd 1:** 2 sc in each ch around.

Rnd 2: Sc in back lp of each sc around. **Note:** Work in back lp of each st throughout.

Rnd 3: 2 sc in each sc around—24 sc.

Rnds 4-7: Sc in each sc around.

Rnd 8: (Sc in 3 sc, sk next sc) 6 times.

Rnd 9: Sc in each sc around—18 sc.

Rnd 10: 2 sc in each sc around—36 sc.

Rnds 11-17: Sc in each sc around.

Rnd 18: (Sc in 2 sc, sk next sc) 12 times—24 sc.

Rnd 19: Sc in each sc around.

Rnd 20: 2 sc in each sc around—48 sc.

Rnd 21-28: Sc in each sc around.

Rnd 29: (Sc in 5 sc, sk next sc) 8 times—40 sc.

Rnd 30: Sc in each sc around.

Rnd 31: (Sc in 4 sc, sk next sc) 8 times—32 sc. End off.

BOTTOM: With W, ch 6. Sl st in first ch to form ring. **Rnd 1:** 2 sc in each ch—12 sc.

Rnd 2: (Sc in 2 sc, 2 sc in next sc) 4 times—16 sc.

Rnd 3: (Sc in next sc, 2 sc in next sc) 8 times—24 sc.

Rnd 4: (Sc in 2 sc, 2 sc in next sc) 8 times—32 sc. End off.

HAT: With B, ch 6. Sl st in first ch to form ring. **Rnd 1:** 2 sc in each ch around—12 sc.

Rnd 2: Sc in each sc around.

Rnd 3: 2 sc in each sc around—24 sc.

Rnds 4-9: Sc in each sc around.

Rnd 10: Repeat rnd 3—48 sc.

Rnd 11: Sc in each sc around. End off. With G, ch 28 for hatband. Place on hat; tack to hat at back.

SCARF: With R, ch 61. Work 60 sc on ch. End off.

FINISHING. Stuff head with 1″ ball of foam rubber. Stuff upper body with 1½″ ball and lower body with 2″ ball of foam rubber. Cut 1¼″ disk from plastic bottle: place at bottom, sew bottom to snowman over disk. Tie scarf around neck. Tack hat to head. Embroider black eyes ½″ apart. For hanging loop, run double strand of B through hat; knot ends tog.

SNOWLADY: HEAD AND BODY: Work as for Snowman through rnd 28. Work 2 more rnds of 48 sc. End off.

BOTTOM: With W, ch 6. Sl st in first ch to form ring. **Rnd 1:** 2 sc in each ch around—12 sc.

Rnd 2: 2 sc in each sc around—24 sc.

Rnd 3: Sc in each sc around.

Rnd 4: (Sc in next sc, 2 sc in next sc) 12 times—36 sc.

Rnd 5: Sc in each sc around.

Rnd 6: (Sc in next 2 sc, 2 sc in next sc) 12 times—48 sc. End off.

HAT: With R, ch 6. Sl st in first ch to form ring. **Rnd 1:** 2 sc in each ch around—12 sc.

Rnd 2: 2 sc in each sc around—24 sc.

Rnd 3: Sc in each sc around.

Row 4: Sc in 18 sc. Ch 1, turn.

Rows 5-8: Sc in each sc. Ch 1, turn each row.

Row 9: 2 sc in each sc—36 sc.

Rows 10 and 11: Sc in each sc. End off. With W, sc around edge of hat.

FINISHING: Stuff head and upper body as for Snowman. Cut a foam rubber drum-shaped piece 2″ high and 2″ in diameter. Round off top. Stuff lower body. Cut a disk from plastic bottle 1¾″ diameter. Place at bottom, sew bottom to figure over disk. Embroider eyes with B. Place hat on head. With G, make a ch 12″ long. Place behind brim of hat, tie under chin. For hanging loop, run a double strand of G through top of head through hat; knot ends tog.

DRUM: With W, ch 6. Sl st in first ch to form ring. **Rnd 1:** 2 sc in each ch around—12 sc. Work in back lp of each sc throughout.

Rnd 2: 2 sc in each sc around—24 sc.

Rnd 3: Sc in each sc around.

Rnd 4: Repeat rnd 2—48 sc.

Rnd 5: Repeat rnd 3. Cut W.

Rnds 6-11: With B, sc in each sc around. Cut B.

Rnds 12-27: With R, repeat rnd 6. Cut R.

Rnds 28-32: With B, repeat rnd 6. End off.

For bottom of drum, work first 5 rnds of drum. End off.

Side Strings: With G, make a ch 24″ long.

FINISHING: Cut two 2″ diameter disks from plastic bottle. Cut a drum-shaped piece of foam rubber 3″ high, 2″ diameter. Place one disk in top of drum, stuff drum with foam rubber piece. Sew bottom to drum over 2nd disk. Sew start of G ch to first R sc of rnd 12.

Using about 2″ of ch, bring it down to 5th sc of last R rnd; sew ch in place. Sew ch up and down around drum, skipping 8 sc at each end; end ch at starting point. For hanging loop, run double strand of B through one top edge of drum; knot ends tog.

STOCKING: Beg at toe, with W, ch 6. Sl st in first ch to form ring. **Rnd 1:** 2 sc in each ch around—12 sc. Work in back lp of each sc throughout.

Rnd 2: Sc in each sc around.

Rnd 3: 2 sc in each sc around—24 sc.

Rnd 4: (Sc in each of next 2 sc, 2 sc in next sc) 8 times—32 sc. Cut W.

Rnds 5-14: Work even with 4 rnds R, 1 rnd W, 1 rnd G, 1 rnd W, 3 rnds R.

Row 15: Sc in 24 sc. Drop R.

Heel: Row 1: With W, sc in next 16 sc. Ch 1, turn each row.

Rows 2-8: Work even on 16 sc. Cut W; leave 6″ end. Fold heel in half, right sides tog; sew back seam of heel. Turn heel to right side. Pick up R, work 16 sc across top of heel, sc in each sc around to center back of heel.

Leg: Work even on 32 sc, working 7 rnds R, 1 rnd W, 1 rnd G, 1 rnd W, 8 rnds R, 4 rnds W. End off.

Top: With W, ch 6. Sl st in first ch to form ring. **Rnd 1:** 2 sc in each ch around.

Rnd 2: (2 sc in next sc, sc in next sc) 6 times—18 sc.

Rnd 3: (Sc in each of 2 sc, 2 sc in next sc) 6 times—24 sc.

Rnd 4: (Sc in each of 2 sc, 2 sc in next sc) 8 times—32 sc. End off.

FINISHING: Cut 2 cylinders of foam rubber 2½″ high and 1¼″ in diameter. Round off one end of one cylinder; stuff foot. Stuff leg with other piece. Cut 1¼″ disk from plastic bottle, place at top of stocking, sew top over disk. For hanging loop, run double strand of W through top back of stocking; knot ends tog.

BELL: With G, ch 6. Sl st in first, ch to form ring. **Rnd 1:** 2 sc in each ch around—12 sc.

Rnd 2: 2 sc in back lp of each sc around—24 sc. **Note:** Work in back lp only of each st throughout. Work 2 rnds even.

Rnd 5: (Sc in 2 sc, 2 sc in next sc) 8 times—32 sc.

Rnd 6: (Sc in 3 sc, 2 sc in next sc) 8 times—40 sc. Work 1 rnd even.

Rnd 8: (Sc in 4 sc, 2 sc in next sc) 8 times—48 sc. Work 1 rnd even.

Rnds 10 and 11: With W, work even.

Rnd 12: With R, work even.

Rnds 13 and 14: With W, work even.

Rnd 15: With G, work even.

Rnd 16: (Sc in 5 sc, 2 sc in next sc) 8 times—56 sc. Work 1 rnd even.

Rnd 18: (Sc in 6 sc, 2 sc in next sc) 8 times—64 sc. Work 1 rnd even.

Rnd 20: (Sc in 7 sc, 2 sc in next sc) 8 times—72 sc. Work 1 rnd even.

Rnd 22: (Sc in 8 sc, 2 sc in next sc) 8 times—80 sc. Work 1 rnd even. Cut G. With W, work 2 rnds even. With R, work 1 rnd even. With W, work 1 rnd even. End off.

BOTTOM AND CLAPPER: With W, ch 6. Sl st in first ch to form ring. **Rnd 1:** 2 sc in each ch around—12 sc. Work 2 rnds even. Cut W. With G, work 1 rnd even.

Rnd 5: 2 sc in each sc around—24 sc.

Rnd 6: (Sc in next sc, 2 sc in next sc) 12 times—36 sc.

Rnd 7: (Sc in 2 sc, 2 sc in next sc) 12 times—48 sc.

Rnd 8: (Sc in 5 sc, 2 sc in next sc) 8 times—56 sc.

Rnd 9: (Sc in 6 sc, 2 sc in next sc) 8 times—64 sc.

Rnd 10: (Sc in 7 sc, 2 sc in next sc) 8 times—72 sc.

Rnd 11: (Sc in 8 sc, 2 sc in next sc) 8 times—80 sc. Work 1 rnd even. End off.

FINISHING: Cut a foam rubber cylinder 1½″ high, 2″ in diameter. Round off top; stuff top of bell. Cut another cylinder 1½″ high, 3″ in diameter. Trim sides toward top so that top is 2½″ in diameter. Stuff bottom of bell. Cut a 2¾″ diameter disk from plastic bottle. Sew bottom to bell over disk. For hanging loop, run double strand of red through top of bell; knot ends tog.

STRIPED BALL (make 2 pieces): With G, ch 6, sl st in first ch to form ring. **Rnd 1:** 2 sc in each ch around.

Rnd 2: Working in back lp of each sc only, sc in each sc around. **Note:** Work in back lp of each st throughout.

Rnd 3: 2 sc in each sc around—24 sc. With W, work 1 rnd even.

Rnd 5: With R, (sc in next sc, 2 sc in next sc) 12 times—36 sc. With W, work 1 rnd even.

Rnd 7: With G, (sc in 2 sc, 2 sc in next sc) 12 times—48 sc. Work 1 rnd.

Rnd 9: With W, (sc in 3 sc, 2 sc in next sc) 12 times—60 sc. With R, work 1 rnd even.

Rnd 11: With W, (sc in 4 sc, 2 sc in next sc) 12 times—72 sc. Working even, work 2 rnds G, 1 rnd W, 1 rnd R, 1 rnd W, 1 rnd G. End off.

FINISHING: Trim foam rubber piece to a 2½″ ball. Sew 2 halves of ball tog over foam rubber. For hanging loop, run double strand of G through top; knot ends tog.

STAR (make 2 pieces): With W, ch 6. Sl st in first ch to form ring. **Rnd 1:** 2 sc in each ch around—12 sc.

Rnd 2: Working in back lps only, (sc in next sc, 2 sc in next sc) 6 times—18 sc.

Rnd 3: (Sc in 2 sc, 2 sc in next sc) 6 times—24 sc.

Rnd 4: (Sc in 3 sc, 2 sc in next sc) 6 times—30 sc.

Rnd 5: Ch 2, (dc in next sc, ch 1) 30 times, sl st in first dc.

First Point: Row 1: Ch 2, (dc in next ch-1 sp, ch 1) 5 times, dc in next sp. Ch 2, turn.

Row 2: (Dc in next ch-1 sp, ch 1) 4 times, dc in next sp. Ch 2, turn. Continue in this manner until there are 2 dc with ch 1 between. End off. Join W in next ch-1 sp of rnd 5; work 2nd point as for first point. Work 3 more points the same.

FINISHING: Cut a disk of foam rubber ½″ thick, 1¾″ diameter. Sc 2 stars tog around 4 points, insert disk, finish joining last points. For hanging loop, run double strand through one point; knot ends tog.

DOVE: HEAD AND BODY: Beg at back of body, with W, ch 20. Sl st in first ch to form ring. **Rnd 1:** Ch 1, sc in each ch around.

Rnds 2-4: Working in back lps of sc only throughout, work even in sc.

Rnd 5: 2 sc in first sc, sc in 8 sc, 2 sc in next sc. Ch 1, turn. Working on inside, sc in 12 sc, then work 1 complete rnd of 22 sc. Ch 1, turn.

Rnd 6: 2 sc in first sc, sc in 10 sc, 2 sc in next sc, sc in 10 sc.

Rnd 7: Sc in 14 sc. Ch 1, turn. Working on inside, sc in 14 sc, then work 1 complete rnd of 24 sc. Ch 1, turn.

Rnd 8: 2 sc in first sc, sc in 12 sc, 2 sc in next sc, sc in 10 sc.

Rnd 9: Sc in 16 sc. Ch 1, turn. Working on inside, sc in 16 sc, then work 1 complete rnd of 26 sc. Ch 1, turn.

Rnd 10: Sk first sc, sc in 14 sc, sk 1 sc, sc in 10 sc.

Rnd 11: Sc in 14 sc. Ch 1, turn. Working on inside, sc in 14 sc, then work 1 complete rnd of 24 sc. Ch 1, turn.

Rnd 12: Sk first sc, sc in 12 sc, sk 1 sc, sc in 10 sc.

Rnd 13: Sc in 12 sc. Ch 1, turn. Working on inside, sc in 12 sc, then work 1 complete rnd of 22 sc. Ch 1, turn.

Rnd 14: Sk first sc, sc in 10 sc, sk 1 sc, sc in 10 sc.

Rnd 15: Sc in 10 sc. Ch 1, turn. Working on inside, sc in 10 sc, then work 1 complete rnd of 20 sc. Ch 1, turn.

Rnd 16: Sk first sc, sc in 8 sc, sk 1 sc, sc in 10 sc.

Rnd 17: (Sc in 8 sc, 2 sc in next sc) twice. Ch 1, turn.

Rnd 18: Sc in 12 sc. Ch 1, turn. Sc in 12 sc, then work 1 complete rnd of 20 sc. Ch 1, turn.

Rnd 19: Repeat rnd 18. Do not turn at end of rnd.

Rnd 20: (Sk 1 sc, sc in 4 sc) 4 times.

Rnd 21: (Sk 1 sc, sc in 3 sc) 4 times.

Rnd 22: (Sk 1 sc, sc in 2 sc) 4 times.

Rnd 23: (Sk 1 sc, sc in 1 sc) 4 times. End off.

WING (make 2): Work as for Angel's wings.

TAIL: With W, ch 9. Sc in 2nd ch from hook and in each remaining ch. Ch 2, turn.

Row 2: Dc in each sc—8 dc. Ch 2, turn.

Row 3: Dc in first sp between 2 sts, (ch 1, dc in next sp) 7 times. Ch 2, turn.

Row 4: (Dc in next ch-1 sp, ch 1) 7 times, dc in last sp. Ch 2, turn.

Row 5: (Dc, ch 1, dc) in each sp across. Work 1 rnd sc around tail. End off.

OLIVE BRANCH: With G, ch 9. Sl st in 5th ch from hook, (ch 6, sl st in next ch of ch 9) 3 times. End off.

FINISHING: Sew olive branch to front of head. Stuff head with ¾″ ball of foam rubber. Cut crescent shape of foam rubber 2½″ long and 1″ thick; stuff body. Sew beg of body flat; sew on tail. Sew a wing to each side. Embroider eyes with B. For hanging loop, run double strand of W through center back; knot ends tog.

ARAN STOCKING
Shown on page 73

SIZE: 14″ long.

MATERIALS: Coats & Clark Red Heart Fabulend, 4 ply, 3 ozs. Eggshell. Knitting needles No. 7. One cable needle. Two stitch holders.

GAUGE: 4 sts = 1″; 7 rows = 1″.

STOCKING: Beg at top, cast on 70 sts.

Row 1: K.

Row 2: Bind off 14 sts at beg of row for hanging loop, k remaining 56 sts.

Row 3 (wrong side): K 1, (p 1, k 1) twice, place a marker on needle, * k 1, p 6, k 1 for cable panel, place a marker on needle, k 1, (p 1, k 1) 5 times for popcorn panel, place a marker on needle, repeat from * once, k 1, p 6, k 1 for cable panel, place a marker on needle, (k 1, p 1) twice, k 1.

Row 4 (right side): K 1, (p 1, k 1) twice, sl marker, * p 1, sl next 2 sts to cable needle and hold in front of work, k next 2 sts, k 2 sts from cable needle (front cable twist made); k 2, p 1, sl marker, k 1, (p 1, k 1) twice; loosely k in front and back and front and back and front of next st (popcorn started); (k 1, p 1) twice, k 1, sl marker, repeat from * once, p 1, front cable twist over next 4 sts, k 2, p 1, sl marker, k 1, (p 1, k 1) twice. Sl markers each row.

Row 5: K 1, (p 1, k 1) twice, * k 1, p 6, k 1, (k 1, p 1) twice, k 1, p next 5 sts tog (popcorn made), k 1, (p 1, k 1) twice, repeat from * once, k 1, p 6, k 1, (k 1, p 1) twice, k 1.

Row 6: K 1, (p 1, k 1) twice, * p 1, k 2, sl next 2 sts to cable needle and hold in back of work, k next 2 sts, k 2 sts from cable needle (back cable twist made), p 1, (k 1, p 1) 5 times, k 1, repeat from * once, p 1, k 2, back cable twist over next 4 sts, p 1, (k 1, p 1) twice, k 1.

Row 7: Work as for row 3.

Row 8: K 1, (p 1, k 1) twice, * p 1, front cable twist over next 4 sts, k 2, p 1, k 1, p 1, start popcorn in next st, (p 1, k 1) twice, p 1, start popcorn in next st, p 1, k 1, repeat from * once, p 1, front cable twist over next 4 sts, k 2, p 1, (k 1, p 1) twice, k 1.

Row 9: K 1, (p 1, k 1) twice, * k 1, p 6, k 1; k 1, p 1, complete popcorn, (p 1, k 1) twice, p 1, complete popcorn, p 1, k 1, repeat from * once, k 1, p 6, k 1, (k 1, p 1) twice, k 1.

Row 10: Repeat row 6. Repeat rows 3-10 for pat until piece is 8″ long, end with row 9 of pat.

Sides and Instep: Row 1: Continue in pat, work across first 24 sts, cast 8 sts onto right-hand needle. Place next 8 sts from left-hand needle on a safety pin for instep and remaining 24 sts on a stitch holder.

Row 2: Working on 32 sts on needle, k 1, p 6, k 1, work in established pat across.

Row 3: Work in pat across, cast on 7 sts at end of row.

Row 4: K 1, (p 1, k 1) 3 times, work in pat across.

Row 5: Work in pat across, cast on 4 sts at end of row—43 sts.

Row 6: K 1, (p 1, k 1) 5 times, work in pat across.

Row 7: Work in pat across. Place these sts on a 2nd stitch holder.

From wrong side, sl 8 instep sts from safety pin onto needle. Continue in cable pat for 4″, end row 8 of cable pat. Place these sts on the 2nd stitch holder. From right side, work in pat across sts on first stitch holder. Work to correspond to other side, reversing shaping, end with a right side row.

Foot: Row 1: Work in pat across sts on needle, then work in pat across sts on 2nd stitch holder—94 sts. Work even in pat for 1″, end wrong side row. Mark p st on each side of center cable.

Next Row: Dec 1 st at beg of row, work in pat to 2 sts before marker, dec 1 st, work across to st after next marker, dec 1 st, work across to last 2 sts, dec 1 st.

Next Row: Work even. Repeat last 2 rows 8 more times—58 sts. Bind off in pat.

FINISHING: Sew instep edges to cast-on edges of sides. Sew center back and sole seam. Fold hanging loop in half; sew end to center back seam.

ARGYLE STOCKING
Shown on page 73

SIZE: 14″ long.
MATERIALS: Coats & Clark Red Heart Fabulend, 4 ply, 2 ozs. each of Devil Red (R), Eggshell (E) and Emerald Green (G). Knitting needles No. 7. 13 bobbins. Two stitch holders.
GAUGE: 9 sts = 2″; 6 rows = 1″.
STOCKING: Wind 3 R, 4 G and 6 E bobbins. Beg at top, with R, cast on 68 sts. **Row 1:** K.
Row 2: Bind off 13 sts at beg of row for hanging loop, k across remaining 55 sts.
Rows 3 and 4: K. At end of last row, cut R.
Note: When changing colors, twist dropped color around new color to prevent holes.
Diamond Pattern: Row 1: Joining a bobbin for each color change, * with G, k 1, drop G; with E, k 8, drop E; with R, k 1, drop R; with E, k 8, drop E; repeat from * across; with G, k last st.
Row 2: With G, p 2; * with E, p 6; with R, p 3; with E, p 6; with G, p 3; repeat from * across, end with G, p 2.
Row 3: With G, k 3; * with E, k 4; with R, k 5; with E, k 4; with G, k 5; repeat from * across, end with G, k 3.
Row 4: With G, p 4; * with E, p 2; with R, p 7; with E, p 2; with G, p 7; repeat from * across, end with G, p 4.
Row 5: With G, k 5; * with R, k 9; with G, k 9; repeat from * across, end with G, k 5.
Row 6: Repeat row 4.
Row 7: Repeat row 3.
Row 8: Repeat row 2.
Row 9: * With G, k 1; with E, k 8; with R, k 1; with E, k 8; repeat from * across, end with G, k 1. Repeat rows 2-9 for pat until piece is 8″ long, end row 8 of pat.
Sides and Instep: Row 1: Keeping to diamond pat throughout, k across 22 sts, cast 6 sts onto right-hand needle; place next 11 sts on a safety pin and remaining 22 sts on a stitch holder.
Row 2: P across 28 sts on needle.
Row 3: Continuing in diamond pat, cast on 6 sts at end of next row and every other row once more—40 sts. Place these sts on a 2nd stitch holder. Sl 11 sts from safety pin to needle, work even in diamond pat with R and E until 3 complete R diamonds have been made, then work another diamond until row 4 of pat has been completed.
Next Row: With G, k 1; with R, k 9;

with G, k 1. Sl these sts on 2nd stitch holder.

From wrong side, sl 22 sts from first holder to needle, join E at instep edge and cast on 6 sts.
Next Row: K across 28 sts on needle. Keeping to pat, cast on 6 sts at end of next row and every other row once more—40 sts. Work 1 row even.
Foot: Working in pat across all sts, p across sts on needle and p across sts on stitch holder. Work even in pat on 91 sts until row 6 of next diamond pat has been completed. Mark center st of last row.
Next Row: K 1, k 2 tog, k across to 5 sts before marked st, k 2 tog, k 3, k marked st, k 3, sl 1, k 1, psso, k across to last 3 sts, sl 1, k 1, passo, k 1.
Next Row: P. Repeat last 2 rows 4 more times—71 sts. Bind off with E.
FINISHING: Sew instep edges to cast-on edges of sides. Sew center back and sole seam. Fold hanging loop in half; sew end to center back seam.

STRIPED STOCKING
Shown on pages 72 and 73

SIZE: 14″ long.
MATERIALS: Coats & Clark Red Heart Fabulend, 4 ply, 2 ozs. each of Devil Red (R), Eggshell (E) and Emerald Green (G). Knitting needles No. 7. Two stitch holders.
GAUGE: 9 sts = 2″; 6 rows = 1″.
STOCKING: Beg at top, with R, cast on 67 sts. **Row 1:** K across.
Row 2: Bind off 13 sts at beg of row for hanging loop, k across remaining 54 sts.
Rows 3 and 4: K.
Rows 5-10: Work in stockinette st (k 1 row, p 1 row) for 6 rows. Cut R; join E.
Rows 11-16: With E, work even in stockinette st. Cut E; join G.
Rows 17-22: With G, work even in stockinette st. Cut G; join R.
Repeat rows 5-22 for stripe pat. Work even until piece is 8½″ long, end row 16 of pat.
Sides and Instep: Row 1: With G, k first 22 sts, cast 6 sts onto right-hand needle; place next 10 sts from left-hand needle on a safety pin for instep. Place remaining 22 sts on a stitch holder.
Row 2: P across 28 sts. Keeping to stripe pat, cast on 5 sts at end of next row and every other row once more—38 sts. Work 1 row even. Place these sts on a 2nd stitch holder.
Sl the 10 sts from safety pin onto needle. Beg with a k row, work even in pat until 2nd G stripe has been com-

pleted. Place these sts on the 2nd stitch holder.

From right side, k across 22 sts on first stitch holder. P back, cast on 6 sts at end of row—28 sts. Work 1 row even. Keeping to pat, cast on 5 sts at end of next row and every other row once more—38 sts. Leave sts on needle. Sl sts from 2nd stitch holder onto same needle—86 sts.

Foot: From right side, with R, k 37, k 2 tog, k 8, sl 1, k 1, psso, k remaining sts. Work even in R for 5 rows, placing a marker at center of last row.

Next Row: With E, k 1, k 2 tog, k to 4 sts before marker, k 2 tog, k 2, sl marker, k 2, sl 1, k 1, psso, k to last 3 sts, sl 1, k 1, psso, k 1.

Next Row: P across, slipping marker. Keeping to stripe pat, repeat last 2 rows 8 more times—48 sts. Bind off.

FINISHING: Sew instep edges to cast-on edges of sides. Sew center back and sole seam. Fold hanging loop in half; sew end to center back seam.

CROCHETED CRECHE
Shown on pages 74 and 75

SIZE: Figures from 8"-10".
MATERIALS: Knitting worsted weight yarn, 1 4-oz. skein each of medium brown, gray, white, light blue; 2 1-oz. skeins beige; 1 1-oz. skein each of black, royal blue, light green, turquoise, bright pink, purple, orange, yellow, emerald green, maroon, old gold, light orange; few yards dark brown, oxford gray; Crochet hook size D. Two 12" pipe cleaners. Foam rubber block 3" x 24" square for stuffing, or other stuffing material. Eight 3" plastic circles (cut from coffee can covers). Plastic rings, one 1", three 1¼". Gold metallic yarn.
GAUGE: 9 sc = 2"; 9 rnds = 2".
Note: When working in rnds, work in back lp only of each st. When working in rows (for shaping or for robes), work in front lp only of each st.

LAMB (make 2): Beg at nose, with black, ch 6. Join with sl st in first ch to form ring. **Rnd 1:** Sc in each ch.
Rnd 2: Sc in each sc (see Note). Change to white. **Rnd 3:** 2 sc in each sc.
Rnd 4: Sc in 8 sc; ch 1, turn. Sc in 5 sc; ch 1, turn; sc in 5 sc, sc in side of row, sc in next sc of rnd 3; ch 1, turn; sc in 7 sc, sc in side of row, sc in next sc of rnd 3; ch 1, turn; sc in 9 sc, sc in side of row, sc in next 3 sc.
Rnd 5: Sc in first 2 sc, sc in side of row, sc in 13 sc. **Rnd 6:** Sc in 16 sc.
Rnd 7: Sc in first 3 sc; ch 1, turn; sc in 3 sc, sc in next 4 sc of rnd 6; ch 1, turn; sc in 7 sc, 2 sc in side of row, sc in next sc of rnd 6; ch 1, turn; sc in 10 sc, 2 sc in side of row, sc in next sc of rnd 6; ch 1, turn; sc in 13 sc,

2 sc in side of row, sc in next 7 sc of rnd 6; 2 sc in side of row, sc in next 7 sc.
Rnds 8-12: Sc around—24 sc. Stuff head and body (see Finishing).
Rnd 13: (Sk 1 sc, sc in 3 sc) 6 times.
Rnd 14: (Sk 1 sc, sc in 2 sc) 6 times.
Rnd 15: (Sk 1 sc, sc in next sc) 6 times. Cut yarn; sew up end.
Legs (make 4): With black, ch 6. Join to form ring. **Rnd 1:** Sc in each ch.
Rnds 2-4: Sc in each sc. End off.
Ears (make 2): With black, ch 4. Sc in 2nd ch from hook and in next 2 ch. End off.
Tail: With white, ch 5. Sc in 2nd ch from hook and in next 3 ch. End off.

FINISHING: Cut 1¼" cube of foam rubber; trim to a ball; stuff head. Cut block 2" x 2" x 3" for body; trim to rounded shape; stuff body. Stuff legs. Sew on legs, ears, tail. Embroider black eyes.

COW: Beg at nose, with beige, ch 6. Join to form ring. **Rnd 1:** 2 sc in each ch. Change to brown.
Rnd 2: (Sc in next sc, 2 sc in next sc) 6 times (see Note).
Rnd 3: (Sk 1 sc, sc in next sc) 9 times.
Rnd 4: 2 sc in each of 3 sc, sc in each of 3 sc, 2 sc in each of 3 sc—15 sc.
Rnd 5: (2 sc in next sc, sc in next sc) twice, 2 sc in next sc, sc in next 5 sc, (2 sc in next sc, sc in next sc) twice, 2 sc in last sc—21 sc. **Rnd 6:** Sc in each sc around.
Rnd 7: Sc in 5 sc, 2 sc in next sc, sc in 9 sc, 2 sc in next sc; ch 1, turn; sc in 13 sc; ch 1, turn; sc in 13 sc, sc in side of row, sc in next 5 sc of rnd 6.
Rnd 8: Sc in 5 sc, sc in side of row, sc in each of next 19 sc.
Rnd 9: Sc in each sc around—25 sc.
Rnd 10: Sc in 17 sc; ch 1, turn; sc in 9 sc; ch 1, turn; sc in 9 sc, sc in side of row, sc in 8 sc of rnd 9.
Rnd 11: Sc in first sc, 2 sc in next sc, sc in next sc, 2 sc in next sc, sc in 4 sc, sc in side of row, sc in next 2 sc, sk 1 sc, sc in 3 sc, sk 1 sc, sc in 7 sc, (2 sc in next sc, sc in next sc) twice—29 sc.
Rnd 12: (Sc in next sc, 2 sc in next sc) twice, sc in 6 sc, sk 1 sc, sc in 7 sc, sk 1 sc, sc in 6 sc, (2 sc in next sc, sc in next sc) twice—31 sc.
Rnd 13: (Sc in next sc, 2 sc in next sc) twice, sc in 23 sc, (2 sc in next sc, sc in next sc) twice—35 sc.
Rnds 14-17: Sc in each sc around.
Rnd 18: (Sc in next sc, 2 sc in next sc) twice, sc in 27 sc, (2 sc in next sc, sc in next sc) twice.
Rnd 19: Sc in each sc around—39 sc.
Rnd 20: (Sc in next sc, 2 sc in next sc) twice, sc in 31 sc, (2 sc in next sc, sc in next sc) twice.
Rnds 21-30: Sc in each sc around—43 sc.

Rnd 31: Sc in first sc, sk next sc, sc in 39 sc, sk next sc, sc in last sc.
Rnd 32: Sc in each sc around—41 sc.
Rnd 33: Sc in first sc, sk next sc, sc in 37 sc, sk next sc, sc in last sc—39 sc.
Rnd 34: Sc in 15 sc, 3 sc in next sc, sc in 7 sc, 3 sc in next sc, sc in 15 sc.
Rnd 35: Sc in each sc around—43 sc.
Rnd 36: Sc in 15 sc, sk 1 sc, sc in next sc, sk 1 sc, sc in 7 sc, sk 1 sc, sc in next sc, sk 1 sc, sc in 15 sc. Stuff head and body (see Finishing).
Rnd 37: (Sk next sc, sc in each of 2 sc) 13 times.
Rnd 38: (Sc in 2 sc, sk 1 sc) 8 times, sc in 2 sc.
Rnd 39: (Sk 1 sc, sc in next sc) 11 or 12 times. End off. Sew up end.
Forelegs (make 2): With brown, ch 6. Join to form ring. **Rnd 1:** Sc in each ch around. **Rnd 2:** Sc in each sc around.
Rnd 3: 2 sc in first sc, sc in 4 sc, 2 sc in last sc. **Rnd 4:** Sc in each sc around—8 sc. **Rnd 5:** 2 sc in first sc, sc in 6 sc, 2 sc in last sc. **Rnd 6:** Sc in each sc around—10 sc. **Rnd 7:** Sc in 4 sc, 2 sc in each of next 2 sc, sc in 4 sc.
Rnds 8-10: Sc in each sc around—12 sc.
Rnd 11: Sc in 5 sc, 2 sc in each of next 2 sc, sc in 5 sc.
Rnd 12: Sc in each sc around—14 sc. End off.
Back Legs (make 2): Work as for forelegs through rnd 7.
Rnd 8: Sc in 5 sc, 2 sc in each of next 2 sc, sc in 5 sc.
Rnd 9: Sc in 6 sc, 2 sc in each of next 2 sc, sc in 6 sc.
Rnd 10: Sc in each sc around. End off.
Tail: With dark brown, ch 15. Sc in 2nd ch from hook and in each remaining ch. End off.
Ears (make 2): With brown, ch 6. Sc in 2nd ch from hook, sc in next 3 ch, 3 sc in last ch; working on opposite side of ch, sc in each of next 4 ch. End off.
Horns (make 2): With beige, ch 3. Join to form ring. End off.

FINISHING: Stuff scraps of foam rubber into nose. Cut 1¾" cube of foam rubber; trim to a ball; stuff head. Cut block 3" x 3" x 6"; trim to rounded shape, taking a little more off neck end; stuff body. Embroider dark brown eyes. Sew ears and horns to head. Make tassel for end of tail. Sew on tail. Stuff legs; sew on (ends of rnds are back of legs). Embroider dark brown lines on front of legs for hoofs.

DONKEY: With gray, beg at nose, ch 6. Join to form ring. **Rnd 1:** 2 sc in each ch.
Rnd 2: Sc in first sc, sk 1 sc, sc in 8 sc, sk 1 sc, sc in last sc (see Note).
Rnd 3: 2 sc in first 2 sc, sc in 6 sc, 2 sc in last 2 sc.
Rnd 4: 2 sc in first 2 sc, sc in 12 sc, 2 sc in last 2 sc.

Rnd 5: Sc in first 2 sc, 2 sc in next sc, sc in 10 sc, 2 sc in next sc, sc in last 2 sc.

Rnd 6: Sc in 13 sc; ch 1, turn; sc in 8 sc; ch 1, turn; sc in 8 sc, sc in side of row, sc in next sc of rnd 5; ch 1, turn; sc in 10 sc, sc in side of row, sc in next sc of rnd 5; ch 1, turn; sc in 12 sc, sc in side of row, sc in each of next 4 sc.

Rnd 7: 2 sc in first sc, sc in 3 sc, sc in side of row, sc in 16 sc, 2 sc in next sc—24 sc.

Rnd 8: Sc in 20 sc; ch 1, turn; sc in 16 sc; ch 1, turn; sc in 16 sc, sc in side of row, sc in next sc of rnd 7; ch 1, turn; sc in 18 sc, sc in side of row, sc in next sc of rnd 7; ch 1, turn; sc in 20 sc, sc in side of row, sc in next 3 sc—27 sc.

Rnd 9: Sc in first 3 sc, sc in side of row, sc in 24 sc.

Rnd 10: Sc in each sc around—28 sc.

Rnd 11: 2 sc in each of first 2 sc, sc in next 24 sc, 2 sc in each of last 2 sc.

Rnd 12: Sc in each sc around—32 sc.

Rnd 13: 2 sc in each of first 2 sc, sc in next 28 sc, 2 sc in each of last 2 sc.

Rnd 14: Sc in each sc around—36 sc.

Rnd 15: Sc in 9 sc; ch 1, turn; sc in 9 sc, sc in next 9 sc of rnd 14; ch 1, turn; sc in 18 sc, sc in side of row, sc in next 6 sc of rnd 14, sk 1 sc, sc in next 4 sc, sk 1 sc, sc in next 6 sc, sc in side of row, sc in next 9 sc—36 sc.

Rnd 16: 2 sc in each of first 2 sc, sc in 32 sc, 2 sc in each of last 2 sc.

Rnd 17: Sc in each sc around—40 sc.

Rnd 18: Sc in first 10 sc; ch 1, turn; sc in 10 sc, sc in 10 sc of rnd 17; ch 1, turn; sc in 20 sc, sc in side of row, sc in next 7 sc, sk 1 sc, sc in 4 sc, sk 1 sc, sc in 7 sc, sc in side of row, sc in last 10 sc.

Rnds 19-21: Sc in each sc around—40 sc.

Rnd 22: Sc in first sc, sk 1 sc, sc in 36 sc, sk 1 sc, sc in last sc.

Rnds 23-31: Sc in each sc around—38 sc. Stuff head and body (see Finishing).

Rnd 32: Sc in first sc, (sk 1 sc, sc in 5 sc) 6 times, sk last sc.

Rnd 33: (Sc in 5 sc, sk 1 sc) 5 times, sc in last sc.

Rnd 34: (Sk 1 sc, sc in 4 sc) 5 times, sk last sc.

Rnd 35: (Sc in 3 sc, sk 1 sc) 5 times.

Rnd 36: (Sc in next sc, sk 1 sc) 7 times, sc in last sc. End off. Sew up end.

Forelegs (make 2): With gray, ch 6. Join to form ring. **Rnd 1:** Sc in each ch around.

Rnd 2: 2 sc in first sc, sc in 4 sc, 2 sc in last sc. **Rnd 3:** 2 sc in first sc, sc in 6 sc, 2 sc in last sc.

Rnds 4-8: Sc in each sc around—10 sc.

Rnd 9: Sc in 4 sc, 2 sc in each of next 2 sc, sc in 4 sc.

Rnd 10: Sc in 5 sc, 2 sc in each of next 2 sc, sc in 5 sc. **Rnd 11:** Sc in each sc around—14 sc. End off.

Back Legs (make 2): With gray, ch 5. Join to form ring. **Rnd 1:** Sc in each ch.
Rnd 2: 2 sc in each sc.

Rnds 3-5: Sc in each sc around—10 sc.
Rnd 6: Sk first sc, sc in 3 sc, 2 sc in each of next 2 sc, sc in 3 sc, sk last sc.
Rnd 7: Sc in first sc, sk 1 sc, sc in next sc, 2 sc in each of 4 sc, sc in next sc, sk 1 sc, sc in last sc.
Rnd 8: 2 sc in first sc, sc in 4 sc, 2 sc in each of next 2 sc, sc in 4 sc, 2 sc in last sc. **Rnd 9:** Sc in each sc around—16 sc. End off.

Ears (make 2): With gray, ch 7. Sc in 2nd ch from hook and in next 4 ch, 3 sc in end ch. Working back on opposite side of ch, sc in 5 ch. End off.

FINISHING: With foam rubber, stuff body: scraps in nose and legs, 1½" cube trimmed to a ball in head, 2" x 2" x 3" block trimmed to a 3" long cylinder in neck, 2½" x 3" x 4½" block trimmed to a rounded shape in body. Sew on legs. Embroider black eyes. Sew on ears. With gray, knot 3 short fringes across head between ears. With oxford gray, knot longer fringes down back of neck; make 3" tassel for tail; sew on.

BABY JESUS: Head: With beige, ch 6. Join to form ring. **Rnd 1:** 2 sc in each ch—12 sc.

Rnds 2-4: Sc in each sc (see Note). Stuff head with 1" ball of foam rubber.

Rnd 5: (Sk 1 sc, sc in 2 sc) 4 times. End off.

Blanket: With light blue, ch 6. Join to form ring. **Rnd 1:** 2 sc in each ch. **Rnd 2:** (2 sc in next sc, sc in 2 sc) 4 times—16 sc.

Rnd 3: Sc in 10 sc, ch 1, turn; sc in 10 sc, ch 1, turn; sc in 10 sc, 2 sc in side of rows, sc in 6 sc of rnd 2, 2 sc in side of rows. Sew head inside blanket hood.

Rnd 4: Sc in 10 sc of blanket, sc in 3 sc on last rnd of head—13 sc.

Rnd 5: Sk first sc of rnd 4, sc in next 12 sc. **Rnd 6:** (2 sc in next sc, sc in 2 sc) 4 times—16 sc.

Rnd 7: (2 sc in next sc, sc in 3 sc) 4 times—20 sc. **Rnd 8:** (Sc in 3 sc, 2 sc in next sc) 5 times—25 sc.

Rnds 9 and 10: Sc in each sc around.
Rnd 11: (Sk 1 sc, sc in 4 sc) 5 times. Stuff blanket.

Rnd 12: (Sk 1 sc, sc in 4 sc) 4 times.

Rnd 13: (Sk 1 sc, sc in next sc) 8 times. End off.

FINISHING: Cut foam rubber block 2½" x 1½" x 1". Trim to egg shape; stuff blanket. Embroider brown eyes. Cover 1" ring with sc worked in metallic yarn. Sew to back of head.

MANGER (not shown): With brown, ch 15. **Rnd 1:** 2 sc in 2nd ch from hook, sc in next 12 ch, 4 sc in last ch; working back on opposite side of starting ch, sc in 12 ch, 2 sc in last ch.

Rnd 2: 2 sc in each of first 2 sc (see Note), sc in each of 12 sc, 2 sc in each of last 2 sc.

Rnd 3: Sc in each of first 2 sc, 3 sc in 3rd sc, sc in 14 sc, 3 sc in next sc, sc in 4 sc; 3 sc in next sc, sc in 14 sc, 3 sc in next sc, sc in last 2 sc.

Rnd 4: Sc in each of first 3 sc, 3 sc in next sc, sc in 16 sc, 3 sc in next sc, sc in 6 sc, 3 sc in next sc, sc in 16 sc, 3 sc in next sc, sc in last 3 sc.

Rnd 5: Ch 3, dc in each sc around, sl st in top of ch 3. **Rnd 6:** Ch 3, dc in each dc around, sl st in top of ch 3.

Rnd 7: Sc in each dc around, sl st in first sc. End off. Cut 1" pieces of white and yellow yarn for hay to fill manger.

MARY: Sleeves (make 2): With light blue, ch 6. Join to form ring. **Rnd 1:** 2 sc in each ch. **Rnds 2-5:** Sc in each sc around (see Note).

Rnd 6: Sc in 6 sc, ch 1, turn; sc in 6 sc, ch 1, turn; sc in 6 sc, sc in side of row, sc in next 6 sc.

Rnd 7: Sc in side of row, sc in next 13 sc.

Rnd 8: Sc in each sc around—14 sc.

Rnd 9: Sc in 3 sc, 2 sc in each of next 2 sc, sc in 9 sc—16 sc.

Rnd 10: Sc in first 5 sc; change to white, sc in each of next 16 sc. End off.

Hands (make 2): With beige, ch 4. Join to form ring. **Rnd 1:** 2 sc in each ch. **Rnds 2 and 3:** Sc in each sc around. **Collar:** With white, ch 18. Join to form ring. **Rnd 1:** Sc in 5 ch, 2 sc in next ch, sc in 6 ch, 2 sc in next ch, sc in 5 ch. End off.

Head and Body: With beige, ch 6. Join to form ring. **Rnd 1:** 2 sc in each ch.

Rnd 2: Sc in each sc around—12 sc.

Rnd 3: (2 sc in next 2 sc, sc in next sc) 4 times—20 sc.

Rnds 4-7: Sc in each sc around.

Rnd 8: (Sk next sc, sc in 3 sc) 5 times. Cut beige. **Rnds 9 and 10:** With blue, sc in each sc—15 sc.

Rnd 11: (Sc in next 2 sc, 2 sc in next sc) 5 times—20 sc.

Rnd 12: Sc in each sc around. See Finishing before going on with body.

Rnd 13: (Sc in 4 sc, 2 sc in next sc) 4 times. **Rnd 14:** Sc in each sc around—24 sc. **Rnd 15:** (Sk 1 sc, sc in next 5 sc) 4 times. **Rnds 16 and 17:** Sc in each sc around—20 sc. **Rnd 18:** (2 sc in next sc, sc in 4 sc) 4 times. **Rnd 19:** Sc in each sc around—24 sc. **Rnd 20:** (2 sc in next sc, sc in 3 sc) 6 times.

Rnds 21 and 22: Sc in each sc around—30 sc. **Rnd 23:** (2 sc in next sc, sc in 4 sc) 6 times.

Rnds 24-26: Sc in each sc around—36 sc. **Rnd 27:** (Sc in 5 sc, 2 sc in next sc) 6 times.

Rnds 28-30. Sc in each sc around—42 sc.

Rnd 31: (Sc in 6 sc, 2 sc in next sc) 6 times. Cut blue.

Rnds 32 and 33: With white, sc in each sc around—48 sc. End off.

Bottom Piece: With white, ch 6. Join to form ring. **Rnd 1:** 2 sc in each ch—12 sc.

Rnd 2: (Sc in next sc, 2 sc in next sc) 6 times—18 sc. **Rnd 3:** (Sc in 2 sc, 2 sc in next sc) 6 times—24 sc.

Rnd 4: (Sc in next sc, 2 sc in next sc) 12 times—36 sc. **Rnd 5:** (Sc in 2 sc, 2 sc in next sc) 12 times—48 sc. End off.

Sash: With white, ch 60. Add little tassel to each end.

Head Covering: With white, ch 6. Join to form ring. **Rnd 1:** 2 sc in each ch around—12 sc. **Rnd 2:** (Sc in next sc, ch 1) 12 times. Turn.

Row 3: Sc in first sc, (ch 1, sk next ch, sc in next sc) 7 times. Ch 1, turn.

Row 4: Repeat row 3.

Row 5: Sc in first sc, (ch 2, sk next ch, sc in next sc) 7 times. Ch 1, turn.

Rows 6-12: Repeat row 5. At end of row 12, do not turn; work ch 2, sc pat around front edge. End off.

FINISHING: After rnd 12 of head and body, embroider brown eyes on rnd 6 of head, pink mouth on rnd 7. Slip collar over head; sew to back of neck. Stuff head with 1½″ ball of foam rubber. Sew hands inside sleeve ends; sew sleeve openings closed. Sew top of sleeves to sides of body. Sew hands tog. Complete crocheting. For hair, cut 16 12″ strands of brown yarn; tie tightly tog at center with matching yarn. Sew to middle of forehead at rnd 2. Spread hair over sides and back of head, pull tog at back of neck; tie with blue yarn; trim ends. Sew head covering to top of head. Stuff upper body with foam rubber block, cut 2″ x 1½″ x 1½″, trimmed to rounded shape. Trim foam rubber block 3″ x 3″ x 5″ to a cone shape 5″ high, 3″ diameter at bottom, 1¼″ diameter at top. Stuff skirt. Sew bottom piece to skirt half way. Insert 3″ plastic disk; finish sewing. Tie sash around waist. Cover 1¼″ ring with sc worked in metallic yarn. Sew to back of head.

ANGEL: Work as for Mary, but use all white. Make blue eyes, yellow hair tied with white. Do not make head covering.

Wings (make 2): With white, ch 6. Join to form ring. **Rnd 1:** 2 sc in each ch—12 sc.

Rnd 2: (Sc in next sc, 2 sc in next sc) 6 times—18 sc. **Row 3:** 2 sc in each of first 6 sc. Ch 1, turn.

Row 4: Sk first sc, sc in next 11 sc. Ch 1, turn. **Row 5:** Sk first sc, sc in next 10 sc. Ch 1, turn.

Rows 6-14: Continue to dec 1 sc each row until 1 sc remains. Sc around entire wing. End off. Sew wings tog for ½″; sew to back below collar.

JOSEPH: Sleeves (make 2): With gray, ch 6. Join to form ring. **Rnd 1:** 2 sc in each ch around.

Rnds 2-9: Sc in each sc around. See Note. Cut gray.

Rnd 10: With light blue, (sc in 2 sc, 2 sc in next sc) 4 times—16 sc.

Rnd 11: Sc in each sc. End off.

Hands: Same as Mary's.

Head and Body: With beige, ch 6. Join to form ring. **Rnd 1:** 2 sc in each ch.

Rnd 2: Sc in each sc—12 sc.

Rnd 3: 2 sc in each sc—24 sc.

Rnds 4-7: Sc in each sc around.

Rnd 8: (Sk next sc, sc in next 3 sc) 6 times.

Rnd 9: Sc in each sc—18 sc. Cut beige.

Rnds 10 and 11: With light blue, repeat rnd 9. Cut light blue.

Rnd 12: With gray, (sc in 2 sc, 2 sc in next sc) 6 times.

Rnd 13: Sc in each sc—24 sc. **Rnd 14:** (Sc in 3 sc, 2 sc in next sc) 6 times.

Rnd 15: Sc in each sc—30 sc. See Finishing before going on.

Rnds 16 and 17: Repeat rnd 15.

Rnd 18: (Sc in 4 sc, 2 sc in next sc) 6 times. **Rnds 19-34:** Sc in each sc—36 sc. Cut gray.

Rnd 35: With light blue, (sc in 5 sc, 2 sc in next sc) 6 times—42 sc.

Rnd 36: (Sc in 6 sc, 2 sc in next sc) 6 times—48 sc. End off.

Bottom Piece: With light blue, work as for Mary.

Head Covering: With light blue, ch 6. Join to form ring. **Rnd 1:** 2 sc in each ch around.

Rnd 2: 2 sc in each sc—24 sc.

Rnd 3: Sc in each sc.

Row 4: Sc in each of 14 sc. Ch 1, turn each row. **Row 5:** Sc in first 2 sc, (2 sc in next sc, sc in 2 sc) 4 times—18 sc.

Rows 6-20: Work even on 18 sc. At end of row 20, sc up front edge, across top and down other front edge. End off.

Headband: With black, ch 30. Join to form ring. End off.

Hair and Beard: With dark brown, ch 30. Join to form ring. **Rnd 1:** Sc in each ch around. **Rnd 2:** Dc in first sc, (2 dc in next sc, dc in next sc) 3 times, 2 dc in next sc, sl st in next 2 sc. End off.

FINISHING: After rnd 15 of Head and Body, embroider dark brown eyes on head. Stuff head with foam rubber, cut 1½″ x 1½″ x 2″, trimmed to rounded shape. Sew hands inside sleeve ends; close sleeve openings. Sew sleeve tops to sides of body. Sew hands tog. After completing crochet, sew hair and beard to face. Sew on head covering and headband. Cut foam rubber block 3″ x 3″ x 6″, trim to a cylinder 6″ high with a little more off top for upper body and neck. Stuff body. Sew bottom piece to body half way. Insert 3″ plastic disk; finish sewing. Add halo as for Mary.

SHEPHERDS: Work as for Joseph, omitting headband, and with these color changes:

First Shepherd: Sleeves: Rnds 1-10: Gray. **Rnd 11:** Pink.

Head and Body: Rnd 10: Pink. **Rnds 11-32:** Gray. **Rnd 33:** Royal blue. **Rnd 34:** Pink. **Rnd 35:** Light blue. **Rnd 36:** Purple.

Bottom Piece: Gray.

Head Covering: Work 1 rnd or row of royal blue, pink, light blue, purple and gray and repeat. Edge with gray.

Hair and Beard: Medium brown.

Eyes: Dark brown.

Crook: With gray, cover pipe cleaner with sc. Bend to form crook. Sew to inside of left sleeve.

2nd Shepherd: Sleeves: Rnds 1-10: Medium brown. **Rnd 11:** Orange.

Head and Body: Rnd 10: Orange. **Rnds 11-32:** Medium brown. **Rnd 33:** Orange. **Rnd 34:** Turquoise. **Rnd 35:** Yellow: **Rnd 36:** Green.

Bottom Piece: Green.

Head Covering: Work 1 rnd or row of orange, turquoise, yellow, green and medium brown and repeat. Edge with medium brown.

Hair and Beard: Gray.

Eyes: Blue.

Crook: Medium brown.

FIRST KING: Work as for Joseph with these color changes:

Sleeves: Rnds 1-8: Yellow. **Rnd 9:** * 1 yellow sc, 1 orange sc, repeat from * around. **Rnds 10 and 11:** Orange.

Hands: Medium brown.

Head and Body: Rnds 1-9: Medium brown. **Rnds 10-27:** Yellow. **Rnd 28:** * 1 orange sc, 3 yellow sc, repeat from * around. **Rnd 29:** Orange. **Rnd 30:** Repeat rnd 28. **Rnd 31:** Orange. **Rnd 32:** * 3 orange sc, 1 yellow sc, repeat from * around. **Rnd 33:** Orange. **Rnd 34:** Repeat rnd 32. **Rnds 35 and 36:** Orange.

Bottom Piece: Orange.

Cape: With green, ch 19. **Row 1:** Sc in 2nd ch from hook and in each remaining ch—18 sc. Ch 1, turn each row.

Row 2: (Sc in 2 sc, 2 sc in next sc) 6 times—24 sc. **Row 3:** (Sc in 1 sc, 2 sc in next sc) 12 times—36 sc.

Row 4: Sc in each sc across. **Row 5:** (1 green sc, 1 orange sc) 18 times.

Row 6: With orange, sc across. **Row 7:** (1 orange sc, 1 green sc) 18 times.

Rows 8-10: With green, sc across.

Row 11: (Sc in 5 sc, 2 sc in next sc) 6 times—42 sc.

Rows 12-20: Sc in each sc. **Row 21:** (1 green sc, 1 orange sc) 21 times.

Row 22: With orange, sc across.

Row 23: Repeat row 21. Cut green.

Rows 24 and 25: With orange, sc across. With orange, work 1 row sc around edge of cape, working 2 sc in each corner. End off.

Tie: With green, ch 51. Pull tie through top corners of cape. Tie small green tassel to each end.

Hair and Beard: With black, ch 6. Join to form ring. **Rnd 1:** 2 sc in each ch—12 sc.

Rnd 2: 2 sc in each sc—24 sc.

Rnd 3: Sc in each sc around. **Rnd 4:** (Sc in 11 sc, 2 sc in next sc) twice—26 sc.

Rnds 5-7: Sc in each sc around. At end of rnd 7, ch 16, sk 9 sc, sl st in next sc, ch 2, turn. Dc in each of 16 ch. End off.

Crown: With orange, ch 30. Join to form ring. **Rnd 1:** With green, sc in each ch. **Rnd 2:** With orange, ch 2, dc in 15 sc, ch 4, sl st in last dc, dc in each of last 15 sc. End off.

Gift: With green, ch 7. **Row 1:** Sc in 2nd ch from hook and in each remaining ch. Ch 1, turn each row.

Rows 2-4: Sc in each sc. End off. Make another piece the same. Sc pieces tog with yellow, stuffing before last side is closed.

FINISHING: Finish as for Joseph. Make eyes black. Sew crown to hair. Sew gift to hands.

SECOND KING: Work as for Joseph with these color changes.

Sleeves: Rnds 1-7: Turquoise. **Rnd 8:** Light green. **Rnd 9:** Turquoise. **Rnds 10 and 11:** Light green.

Hands: Beige.

Head and Body: Rnds 1-9: Beige. **Rnds 10-27:** Turquoise. **Rnd 28:** Light green. **Rnd 29:** Turquoise. **Rnds 30 and 31:** Light green. **Rnds 32 and 33:** Turquoise. **Rnds 34-36:** Light green.

Bottom Piece: Light green.

Cape: Work as for cape of First King with these color changes: **Rows 1-4:** Royal blue. **Row 5:** Light green. **Row 6:** Royal blue. **Rows 7 and 8:** Light green. **Rows 9-17:** Royal blue. **Row 18:** Light green. **Row 19:** Royal blue. **Rows 20 and 21:** Light green. **Rows 22 and 23:** Royal blue. **Rows 24 and 25:** Light green. Work edging around cape in light green. Work tie in royal blue.

Hair and Beard: With white, ch 26. Join to form ring. **Rnd 1:** Sc in each ch around.

Rnd 2: Sc in each of 6 sc, sk 2 sc, 2 sc in each of next 2 sc, sc in each of 6 sc, 2 sc in each of next 2 sc, sc in each of next 2 sc, sk 2 sc, sc in each of next 6 sc—26 sc.

Rnd 3: Sc in each of 10 sc, 2 sc in next sc, sc in next sc, 2 sc in each of next 2 sc, sc in next sc, 2 sc in next sc, sc in each of next 10 sc—30 sc.

Rnd 4: Sc in each of 10 sc, 2 sc in next sc, sc in each of 3 sc, 2 sc in each of next 2 sc, sc in each of 3 sc, 2 sc in next sc, sc in each of next 10 sc—34 sc. End off.

Crown: With light green, ch 32. Join to form ring. **Rnd 1:** With royal blue, sc in each ch around. Cut royal blue.

Rnd 2: With light green, ch 2, dc in each sc around. Join with sl st to first dc.

Rnd 3: Ch 2, dc in first dc, * sk next dc, dc in next dc, repeat from * around, end sl st in top of first dc.

Rnd 4: Sc in first dc, * sk next dc, sc in next dc, repeat from * around, end sl st in first sc. End off.

With royal blue, ch 21. Sew one end of ch to front of crown at row 1, sew other end to back of crown at row 1. With royal blue, ch 14, sl st in 4th ch from hook, ch 11. Sew ends of ch to sides of crown. Tack chs tog where they cross to top of crown.

Gift: With royal blue, ch 6. Join to form ring. **Rnd 1:** 2 sc in each ch around.

Rnds 2-5: Sc in each sc around—12 sc. **Rnd 6:** (Sk next sc, sc in next sc) 6 times.

Rnds 7 and 8: Sc in each sc around—6 sc. End off.

FINISHING: Finish as for Joseph. Make eyes blue. Stuff and sew on crown after sewing hair and beard in place. Crown meets top of hair at back of head. Sew gift to hands.

THIRD KING: Work as for Joseph with these color changes:

Sleeves: Rnds 1-9: Light orange. **Rnds 10 and 11:** Maroon.

Hands : Beige.

Head and Body: Rows 1-9: Beige. **Rows 10-30:** Light orange. **Rows 31-36:** Maroon.

Bottom Piece: Maroon.

Cape: Work as for First King with these color changes.

Rows 1-4: Old gold. **Row 5:** * 1 old gold sc, 1 light orange sc, repeat from * across. Cut light orange. **Row 6:** Old gold. **Rows 7 and 8:** Maroon. **Rows 9-18:** Old gold. **Row 19:** Repeat row 5. **Row 20:** Old gold. **Rows 21-25:** Maroon. Work edging around cape in maroon. Work tie in maroon.

Hair and Beard: With gray, ch 24. Join to form ring. **Rnd 1:** Ch 2, dc in each ch around. Sl st in top of first dc. Turn.

Rnd 2: Sl st in each of next 5 dc, sc in each of next 3 dc, hdc in next dc, 2 dc in each of next 4 dc, hdc in next dc, sc in each of next 3 dc, sl st in each st to end of rnd. End off.

Crown: With old gold, ch 28. Join to form ring. **Rnd 1:** Sc in each of 13 ch, 3 sc in next ch, sc in each of next 14 ch. Cut old gold.

Rnd 2: With maroon, sc in 14 sc, 3 sc in next sc, sc in 15 sc. **Rnd 3:** Sc in 15 sc, 3 sc in next sc, sc in 16 sc.

Rnd 4: Sc in each sc around—34 sc.

Rnd 5: * Sc in next sc, sk next sc, repeat from * around. **Rnd 6:** * Sc in each of next 2 sc, sk 1 sc, repeat from * around, end sc in each of last 2 sc—12 sc.

Rnd 7: * Sk 1 sc, sc in next sc, repeat from * around. End off.

Gift: With old gold, ch 6. Join to form ring. **Rnd 1:** 2 sc in each ch around—12 sc. **Rnd 2:** (Sc in next sc, 2 sc in next sc) 6 times.

Rnd 3: Sc in each sc around—18 sc.

Rnd 4: (Sk next sc, sc in each of next 2 sc) 6 times—12 sc.

Rnd 5: (Sk next sc, sc in next sc) 6 times—6 sc. **Rnd 6:** 3 sc in each sc around—18 sc. End off.

FINISHING: Finish as for Joseph. Make eyes black. Sew hair and beard around head at top of rnd 7. Stuff crown; sew to head. Sew gift to hands.

KNIT STOCKINGS
Shown on page 76

BOY'S STOCKING: MATERIALS: Coats & Clark's Red Heart Wintuk Sport Yarn, one 2-oz. skein white; small amounts of green, blue, red and black. Knitting needles No. 5, 1 set dp needles No. 5. Four buttons. Two bells. Bobbins. Stitch holder. Tapestry needle. Crochet hook size F.

GAUGE: 6 sts = 1"; 8 rows = 1".

Notes: Name is embroidered in duplicate stitch when stocking is completed. When working chart, k from right to left on right side rows; p from left to right on wrong side rows. Use a separate bobbin of yarn for each color change. Always change colors on wrong side, picking up new strand from under dropped strand. Cut and join colors as needed.

STOCKING: Beg at upper edge with white, cast on 62 sts. Work in ribbing of k 1, p 1 for 5 rows. Do not break off white; join green.

Row 1: With green, * k 1, sl 1, repeat from * across.

Row 2: Purl. Cut green; pick up white. With white, repeat rows 1 and 2 once more. Starting with a k row work 10 rows in stockinette st.

Do not break off white; join green. With green, repeat rows 1 and 2. Cut green; pick up white, with white, repeat rows 1 and 2. K 1 row. P 1 row. Starting with row 21, follow chart to top, dec 1 st each side on rows 41, 47, 53, 59 and 65—52 sts. Work even in stockinette st until 82 rows of chart have been completed, end p row. Cut white.

Instep: Place first 13 sts on a holder; place last 13 sts on a holder. Attach white and work 16 rows even on 26 sts. Sl these sts to a holder. Cut yarn.

Heel: Place heel sts on needle, with back edges at center of needle. Join white; with right side of work facing you, work even in stockinette st for 13 rows on 26 sts, end k row.

Turn Heel: Row 1: P 15, p 2 tog, p 1, turn.

Row 2: Sl 1, k 5, sl 1, k 1, psso, k 1, turn.

Row 3: Sl 1, p 6, p 2 tog, p 1, turn.

Row 4: Sl 1, k 7, sl 1, k 1, psso, k 1, turn.

Row 5: Sl 1, p 8, p 2 tog, p 1, turn.

Row 6: Sl 1, k 9, sl 1, k 1, psso, k 1, turn.

Row 7: Sl 1, p 10, p 2 tog, p 1, turn.

Row 8: Sl 1, k 11, sl 1, k 1, psso, k 1, turn.

Row 9: Sl 1, p 12, p 2 tog, p 1, turn.

Row 10: Sl 1, k 13, sl 1, k 1, psso, k 1—16 sts. Cut white, sl st on a holder.

Shape Heel: From right side, with white, pick up and k 12 sts on side of heel, k across 16 heels sts, pick up and k 12 sts on other side of heel—40 sts.

Heel Gusset: Row 1: Purl.

Row 2: K 1, sl 1, k 1, psso, k to last 3 sts, k 2 tog, k 1. Repeat rows 1 and 2 until 26 sts remain, end k row.

Foot: Put 26 instep sts on a dp needle; divide heel sts on 2 dp needles (13 sts on each needle).

K across instep and first 13 sts of heel, center of heel is beg of each rnd. K 24 rnds even. Cut white. Join green.

Shape Toe: Rnd 1: On first needle, k to last 3 sts, k 2 tog, k 1; on 2nd needle, k 1, sl 1, k 1, psso, k to last 3 sts, k 2 tog, k 1; on 3rd needle, k 1, sl 1, k 1, psso, k to end of rnd.

Rnd 2: Knit.

Repeat these 2 rnds until there are 16 sts on needles, end with first needle. Slip 4 sts from 3rd needle to first needle (8 sts on each needle). Cut yarn leaving 12″ end. Hold the 2 needles parallel, each with 8 sts and with yarn coming from first stitch on back needle. Thread 12″ end into tapestry needle. Working from right to left, * pass needle through first st on front needle as if to k and sl st off needle, pass yarn through 2nd st on front needle as if to p but leave st on needle, pass yarn through first st on back needle as if to p and sl st off needle; pass yarn through 2nd st on back needle as if to k, but leave on needle. Repeat from * until all sts are worked.

FINISHING: Sew back seam and side seams of instep. For hanger, ch 14. Sew ends inside at back seam. Sew buttons in place on train. Make a red 8″ twisted cord, tie into a bow, sew to

BOY'S STOCKING

⊘ GREEN   ⊙ RED   ⊠ BLUE   ⊟ BLACK

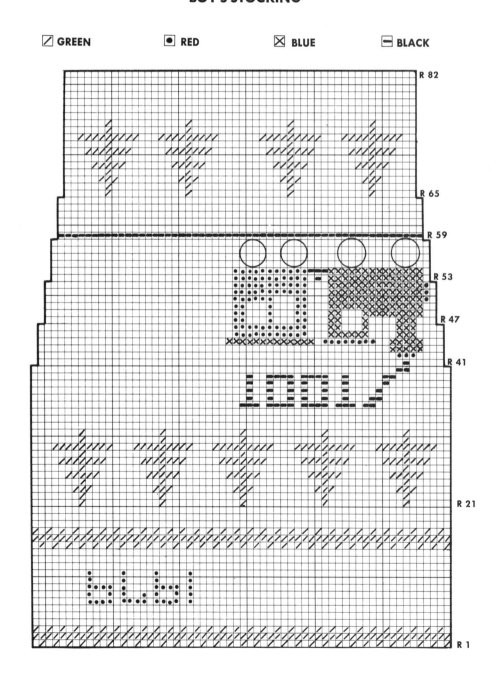

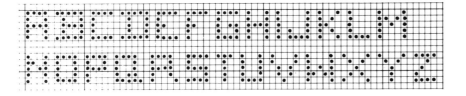

GIRL'S STOCKING

☑ GREEN   ⊡ RED   ☒ BLUE

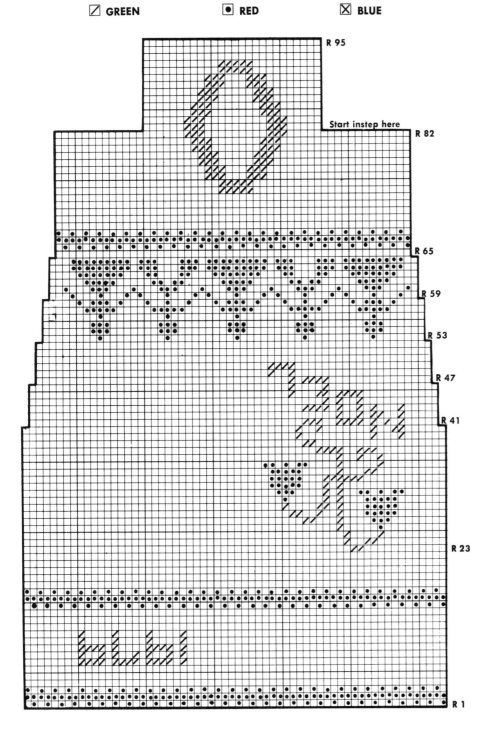

stocking (see illustration). Sew bells in same place.

Embroidery: With red, embroider name in duplicate st on white stripe at top of stocking.

GIRL'S STOCKING: MATERIALS: Coats and Clark's Red Heart Wintuk Sport Yarn, 1 2-oz. skein white; small amounts of green and red; knitting needles No. 5, 1 set dp needles No. 5, 20 small red beads. Two bells. Bobbins. Stitch holders. Tapestry needle.
GAUGE: 6 sts = 1"; 8 rows = 1".
Notes: Same as for boy's stocking.
STOCKING: Work as for boy's stocking, substituting red for green on Rows 1 and 2. Starting with row 23, follow chart to top and continue to follow the chart on the 26 instep stitches.
Shape Toe: With red work same as for boy's stocking.
FINISHING: Sew back seam and side seams of instep. Weave toe tog. Make a red 8" twisted cord, tie in a bow and sew to wreath as pictured. Sew beads to wreath and flowers. For hanger, ch 14. Sew ends inside at back seam. Sew bells at top of center back seam.
Embroidery: With green, embroider name in duplicate stitch on white stripe at top of stocking.

CROCHETED STOCKINGS
Shown on page 77

SIZE: 17" long.
MATERIALS: Knitting worsted weight yarn. For red stocking, 4 ozs. red, 1 oz. white. For green stocking, 5 ozs. green; small amounts of red and white. Afghan hook size J. Yarn needle.
GAUGE: 4 sts = 1"; 3 rows = 1".
STOCKING: First Half: Beg at top, with green or white, ch 26. **Row 1:** Pull up a lp in 2nd ch from hook and in each ch across, keeping all lps on hook.
To Work Lps Off: Yo hook, pull through first lp, * yo hook, pull through next 2 lps, repeat from * across until 1 lp remains. Lp that remains on hook always counts as first st of next row.
Row 2: Keeping all lps on hook, pull up a lp under 2nd vertical bar and under each vertical bar across. Work lps off as before. Repeat row 2 on 26 sts for 32 rows, changing to red on 9th row for red stocking.
Foot: Ch 18; pull up a lp in 2nd ch from hook and in each of next 16 ch, pull up a lp in each vertical bar across. Work even on 44 sts for 15 rows. Sl st in each vertical bar across. End off.
2nd Half: Work as for first half to foot.
Next Row: Pull up a lp in 2nd vertical bar and in each vertical bar across; drop yarn. Join a separate 1 yd. strand of main color to last st, ch 18. End off.

Pick up dropped yarn, pull up a lp in each of 18 ch. Complete foot as for first half.

FINISHING: Steam-press pieces lightly. Place pieces, right sides tog; sew seams with backstitch, rounding off top and bottom of toe and rounding off heel. Turn to right side.

Red Stocking: With red, work blanket stitch around top of stocking and around bottom row of white section.

Green Stocking: With white, work blanket stitch around top of stocking; work cross-stitch in every other st around 3rd and 7th rows. With red, work running stitch around 2nd and 8th rows; work cross-stitch in every other st around 5th row. Outline heel with white running stitch, working across 11th row from bottom and down 13th st in from back of heel. With red, work cross-stitches inside running stitches. With white, skip 1 row, work cross-stitches inside red stitches.

Hanger: With matching color, ch 30. Sc in 2nd ch from hook and in each remaining ch. End off. Sew both ends of hanger 1″ inside back of stocking.

SANTA STOCKING
Shown on page 78

MATERIALS: Knitting worsted, 2 ozs. green (G), 1 oz. each of red (R) and white (W); small amounts of black and pink. Knitting needles No. 8. Nine bobbins. Red and blue embroidery floss. Red twisted cord, 10″.

GAUGE: 5 sts = 1″.

Pattern Notes: On brick pat, carry color not being used loosely across back of work. Always change colors on wrong side: pick up R from under dropped W strand; pick up W over dropped strand. On Santa patterns, do not carry colors across back of work; use separate bobbins or balls for each color change. Twist strands tog to prevent holes.

STOCKING: Beg at lower edge of front and back, with W, cast on 104 sts. K 1 row. Join R. Work in brick pat as follows:

Row 1: * P 1 W, p 3 R, repeat from * across.

Row 2: * K 3 R, k 1 W, repeat from * across.

Row 3: P 1 row W.

Row 4: K 1 R, * k 1 W, k 3 R, repeat from * across, end k 2 R.

Row 5: P 2 R, * p 1 W, p 3 R, repeat from * across, end p 1 R.

Row 6: K 1 row W. Repeat these 6 rows twice, omitting last W row. Break off W and R. Join G, work 4 rows even.

Next Row: With G, k 33; with black, k 4; with a separate strand of G, k 3; with black, k 4; with a separate bobbin or ball of G, k 16; with another black bobbin, k 4; with a separate short strand of G, k 3; with black, k 4; with a separate bobbin or ball of G, k 33. Beg with row 2 of chart for Santa (p row), continue with two Santa patterns as established through row 6. Keeping to pattern, bind off 26 sts at beg of next 2 rows. Continue on 52 sts to top of chart. Work 4 rows G, ending with k row. Beg with row 3 of brick pat, work in pat for 19 rows, ending with p 1 row W. Break off R.

Eyelet Row: * Yo, k 2 tog, repeat from * across. P 1 row. Work in ribbing of k 1, p 1 for 3 rows. Bind off.

FINISHING: With blue floss, embroider eyes in satin stitch; with red floss, embroider nose in satin stitch on pink face. With red floss, make outline stitch mouth on beard. Run in yarn ends on wrong side. Steam-press piece. Fold stocking wrong side out, sew front and bottom seams, rounding off corners at toe and heel. Turn top edge to inside on eyelet row; sew in place. Sew ends of twisted cord inside stocking at back top edge.

JINGLE BELLS
Shown on page 78

SIZES: Small (3″) and large (4″).

MATERIALS: Small amounts of orlon yarn of knitting worsted weight in green, red and white. Knitting needles No. 6 for small bells, No. 8 for large bells. Jingle bell for each large bell. Crochet hook size H. Cotton balls for stuffing. Yarn needle.

SMALL BELL: Beg at lower edge, with No. 6 needles and white, cast on 25 sts. Work in garter st (k each row) for 28 rows (14 ridges).

Next Row: (K 3, k 2 tog) across—20 sts. K 1 row.

Next Row: K 2 tog across—10 sts. Cut yarn, leaving a 10″ end. Draw through sts, pull up and fasten. Sew seam.

LARGE BELL: Work as for small bell using No. 8 needles and double strand of white, green or red yarn.

FINISHING: With contrasting color, from wrong side, work 1 row single crochet around lower edge. Turn up one ridge at lower edge to right side.

For small bells, with double strand of yarn, work four red lazy daisy stitches (see page 3), two green lazy daisy stitches (for leaves) on front of bell. For large bell, with double strand of contrasting yarn, work eight lazy daisy stitches in a circle. Sew a jingle bell to center.

With two or three colors, make a chain 2″ long. Attach to top of knit bell for hanging loop, leaving an end same length as bell for attaching pompon.

Pompon "Clappers": For small bell, wind contrasting color 45 times around a 1½″ piece of cardboard. Remove cardboard; tie at center. Cut loops on both ends, trim into shape. Make pompon for large bell in same way using 2″ cardboard and winding yarn 60 times.

Attach pompon using yarn from hanging loop. Stuff bell with cotton balls; place pompon over stuffing to cover.

THREE SCANDINAVIAN STOCKINGS
Shown on page 79

MATERIALS: For stockings with knit-in designs: Knitting worsted, 1 4-oz. skein red (R) for Pattern 1 (with three trees), 1 skein blue (B) for Pattern 2

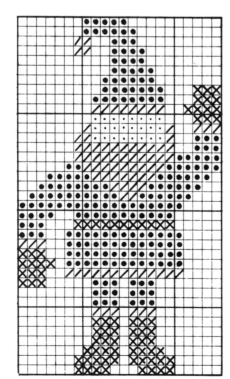

⊠ B

☑ W

⊡ P

⊡ R

☐ G

(with reindeer); 1 oz. white (W). Knitting needles No. 6. Two stitch holders. Six bobbins. For stocking with embroidery: Knitting worsted, 1 4-oz. skein red (R); small amounts of white (W) and green (G) for embroidery. Knitting needles No. 6. Two stitch holders. Tapestry needle.

GAUGE: 6 sts = 1″.

PATTERN 1 (at left in illustration): With R, cast on 66 sts. Work in stockinette st (k 1 row, p 1 row) for 6 rows.

Next Row: * Yo, k 2 tog, repeat from * across. Beg with p row, work 5 rows of stockinette st. Following Chart 1, work pattern with W, repeat chart once for other half of stocking. For border patterns, carry unused color across back of work. For tree pattern, join 6 bobbins of W, work each tree with separate bobbin. When top of chart is reached, cut off bobbins, work 11 rows of R stockinette st, then repeat 2 border patterns. Cut off W. Work 5 rows of R stockinette st.

Divide for Heel: Place first 16 sts and last 16 sts on 2 stitch holders.

Instep: Attach R at instep, k first 2 sts tog, k across to last 2 sts, k last 2 sts tog. Work 55 more rows in stockinette st on these 32 sts. Cut yarn.

Heel: Slip heel sts on one needle with back edges at center. Place instep sts on a holder.

Row 1 (wrong side): Sl 1, p across.

Row 2 (right side): * Sl 1, k 1, repeat from * across. Repeat last 2 rows until there are 27 rows, end wrong side.

Turn Heel: Row 1 (right side): K 18, k 2 tog, k 1, turn.

Row 2: Sl 1, p 5, p 2 tog, p 1, turn.

Row 3: Sl 1, k 6, k 2 tog, k 1, turn.

Row 4: Sl 1, p 7, p 2 tog, p 1, turn. Continue in this manner, working 1 more st between decreases until all sts have been worked and 18 sts remain, end p row.

Sole: From right side, pick up and k 16 sts along side of heel, k across 18 heel sts, pick up and k 16 sts on other side of heel.

Row 1: Purl.

Row 2: K 1, sl 1, k 1, psso, k to last 3 sts, k 2 tog, k 1. Repeat these 2 rows until 30 sts remain. Work even on 30 sts until sole measures same as instep, end p row.

Shape Toe: Row 1 (right side): K 1, sl 1, k 1, psso, k to last 3 sts, k 2 tog, k 1.

Row 2: Purl. Repeat last 2 rows until 10 sts remain. Place sts on stitch holder. Slip instep sts from holder to needle, shape toe as for sole. Weave toe sts tog with Kitchener st; see page 3.

FINISHING: Sew back and side seams. Turn down hem at eyelet edge; sew in place. Crochet a chain or make a braid 5″ long for hanger. Sew ends inside top back of stocking. Steam-press stocking.

PATTERN 2 (at center in illustration): With B, cast on 68 sts. Work in ribbing of k 1, p 1, for 14 rows. K 1 row, p 1 row. Working in stockinette st and following Chart 2, work pattern with W, repeat chart once for other half of stocking. For border pattern, carry unused color across back of work. For tree and reindeer patterns, join a separate bobbin of W for each motif. When top of chart is reached, work 2 rows B, then repeat double border pattern, trees, and single border pattern. Cut W. Work 4 rows B.

Divide for Heel: Place first 17 sts and last 17 sts on 2 stitch holders.

Instep: Attach B at instep, k first 2 sts tog, k across to last 2 sts, k last 2 sts tog. Work 55 more rows in stockinette st on these 32 sts. Cut yarn.

Heel: Slip heel sts on one needle with back edges at center. Place instep sts on a holder.

Row 1 (wrong side): Sl 1, p 2 tog, p across to last 2 sts, p 2 tog.

Row 2: * Sl 1, k 1, repeat from * across.

Row 3: Sl 1, p across. Repeat last 2 rows until there are 27 rows.

Turn Heel: Work as for Pattern 1.

Sole: Work as for Pattern 1.

Shape Toe: Work as for Pattern 1.

FINISHING: Sew back and side seams. Crochet a chain or make a braid 7″ long for hanger. Sew ends inside top back of stocking. Steam-press stocking.

EMBROIDERED STOCKING: With R, cast on 68 sts. Work in ribbing of k 1, p 1, for 14 rows. Work in stockinette st

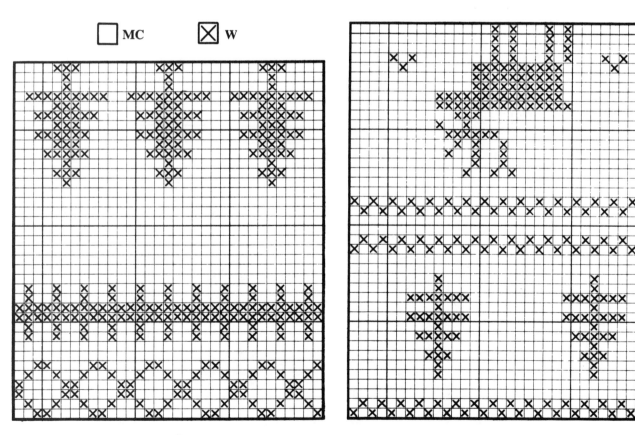

☐ MC   ☒ W

CHART 1   **CHART 2**

(k 1 row, p 1 row) for 78 rows. Cut yarn. Slip first 17 sts and last 17 sts on 2 stitch holders for heel. Join yarn at instep, dec 1 st each side of first row, work in stockinette st on 32 sts for 66 rows. Cut yarn.
Heel: Slip heel sts on one needle with back edges at center. Place instep sts on a holder.
Row 1 (wrong side): Sl 1, p 2 tog, p across to last 2 sts, p 2 tog.
Row 2: * Sl 1, k 1, repeat from * across.
Row 3: Sl 1, p across. Repeat last 2 rows until there are 27 rows.
Turn Heel: Work as for Pattern 1.
Sole: Work as for Pattern 1.
Shape Toe: Work as for Pattern 1.
FINISHING: Sew back and side seams. Crochet a chain or make a braid 6" long for hanger. Sew ends inside top back of stocking. Steam-press stocking.
Embroidery: See page 299 for stitches. With W, blanket st around top edge. With W, working below ribbing over 2 sts and 2 rows, make first half of cross-stitch; finish cross-stitches with G. Work 1 row of W chain stitch 2 rows below. Work 1 row of G chain stitch 2 rows below. Work 1 row of W chain stitch 2 rows below. Working over and under 2 sts, work 1 row of W running stitch 2 rows below. Fill in spaces with G running stitch. Work first half of cross-stitch with G 2 rows below. Scatter W "snowflakes" over one side of stocking. To

make snowflake, work 7 lazy daisy stitches in a circle; fill in spaces between with straight stitch. Make a French knot at end of each straight stitch.

SANTA'S HELPERS
Shown on page 80

SIZE: About 3" high.
MATERIALS: Red fingering yarn, 2 1-oz. skeins (for 20 elves); few yards white yarn for hair. Steel crochet hook No. 5. 40 six-inch pipe cleaners. 20 round wooden beads, ¾". Scraps of red, pink, green felt. Sewing thread to match felt. Blue and red felt markers. Small party favors and Christmas beads. All-purpose glue. Small amount of stuffing.
GAUGE: 7 sc = 1".
ELF: Bend one pipe cleaner in half for body. For arms, cut a pipe cleaner 4" long. Wind center of arms around body once ¾" down from folded end of body. Cut 2 pink hands and 2 green shoes from felt; see pattern. Fold in half, sew side edges, leaving short end open. Slip hands over arm ends, shoes over leg ends; sew tight.
HEAD: Cut hat from red felt; see pattern. Sew straight edges together. Glue short ends of white yarn inside front of hat for bangs; glue hat to wooden bead for head, having one hole of bead at

bottom of head for neck opening. With markers, make blue dots for eyes, red mouth and nose.
SUIT: Top: With red yarn, ch 23.
Row 1: Sc in 2nd ch from hook and in each remaining ch—22 sc. Ch 1, turn each row.
Rows 2–5: Sc in each sc across. End off. Make another piece the same.
Pants (make 2): With red yarn, ch 15.
Row 1: Sc in 2nd ch from hook and in each remaining ch—14 sc. Ch 1, turn each row.
Rows 2–13: Sc in each sc across. Join top and bottom edges; slip on legs. Gather lower edge, sew to feet. Stuff lightly. Gather top edge; sew together at waist.

Join pieces for top at shoulders, leaving small opening at center for neck; slip over neck. Sew to front and back of pants and under arms. Stuff sleeves lightly; gather at wrists; sew to hands. Glue neck into hole of head. Sew favors and trimmings to hands when elves are in place.

NOEL CUTOUTS
Shown on page 80

EQUIPMENT: Paper for patterns. Tracing paper. Pencil. Ruler. X-acto

knife or single-edge razor blade. Scissors. Masking tape.

MATERIALS: Foam core or any thick cardboard ³⁄₁₆″ thick. Small amount of thin cardboard. Felt: two pieces of white, each 9″ × 12″; scraps of green and yellow. Rubber cement. Six crocheted elves (see directions for Santa's Helpers). Length of embroidery floss, 18″. Small nail. Wire for hanging.

DIRECTIONS: Enlarge patterns for letters by copying on paper ruled in 1″ squares. Trace actual-size patterns for brush, paint can, and hammer. Tape letter patterns onto thick board, and, with knife or razor blade, carefully cut out letters. Cement letters to white felt; carefully trim away excess felt. Cut hammer, paint can, and paintbrush out of lightweight cardboard; cement to felt; trim away excess felt. Cement elves and other pieces to letters as shown.

To hang, shape a length of wire into small loop for each letter; tape ends of wire loop to back of letter.

KNITTED SANTA
Shown on page 81

SIZE: About 9″ high.
MATERIALS: Knitting worsted, 1 oz. red, small amount white. Double-pointed needles No. 5. Scraps of felt: white, black, red, blue, yellow. 6″ styrofoam cone. 2″ styrofoam ball, pink satin-covered. Cardboard roll from toilet tissue. Two 12″ chenille sticks. Fabric cement. Pink pearl bead.
COAT: With red, cast on 45 sts. Divide evenly on 3 needles; join, k 2 rnds.
Next Rnd: K 2 tog at beg of each needle—42 sts. K 2 rnds even. Repeat last 3 rnds until 18 sts remain. Bind off.
Sleeves: With red, cast on 12 sts. Divide evenly on 3 needles, join and k 27 rnds. Bind off.
HAT: With red, cast on 27 sts. Divide evenly on 3 needles, join and k 4 rnds.
Next Rnd: K 2 tog at beg of each needle—24 sts. K 1 rnd even. Repeat these 2 rnds until 15 sts remain. K 6 rnds even.
Next Rnd: K 2 tog at beg of each needle—12 sts. Repeat last 7 rnds twice —6 sts. K 3 rnds even. (K 2 tog) 3 times. K 1 rnd even; run yarn through sts, pull tight and fasten off.
LEGS: With red, cast on 18 sts. Divide on 3 needles, join and k 11 rnds. Bind off.
FINISHING: Measure 4″ up from bottom of 6″ cone, cut off tip (save tip for feet). Cover cone with knit coat, pulling to fit. Run yarn around edge; gather and cross yarn from side to side on cone bottom to hold coat taut. Glue a circle of red felt over bottom.

For arms, run a chenille stick through cone ½″ from top. Put on sleeves; sew in place. Cut 4 black mittens. Bend each end of "arm" so that ends of chenille stick will go into thumb of mitten and a small loop near end will be in palm of mitten. Glue 2 mittens over each end.

For head, run 3½″ piece of chenille stick through satin-covered ball. Bend over at one end; insert other end in top of cone.

For legs, cut 2½″ piece of toilet tissue roll; cover with knit piece about halfway. Cover lower half with black felt. Shape into oval. Glue to bottom of cone. For feet, cut ½″ point off cone tip, cut 1¼″ piece of cone top in half. Cover halves with black felt. Hold to legs with chenille stick pieces; bend pieces up inside cardboard roll to hold tight; glue feet to outside of roll.

For hair, cut 50 strands of white yarn 6″ long. Arrange crosswise, side by side, centering on a 4½″ strip of masking tape. Stitch down center of tape for hair part. Strip off tape, fold hair piece in half, glue together along stitching. Glue hair to head. Cut a few strands short at front. For beard, cut about 40 strands of white yarn 2″ long. Arrange ends of strands across 3½″ piece of masking tape. Stitch across ends of yarn on tape. Remove tape. Glue stitching line of beard to head. Trim hair and beard to shape. Pin hat to head. Cut strip of white felt; glue around hat and head to hold securely. Trim hat with small white pompon.

Trim jacket with strips of white felt, a black belt and yellow buckle. Glue thin strip of black felt to front and back of legs for separation. Cut blue eyes, dark blue pupils, red mouth, from felt. Glue in place. Pin on pink pearl for nose. Glue on white wool strand for moustache.

MRS. SANTA
Shown on page 81

SIZE: About 8½″ high.
MATERIALS: Knitting worsted, 1 oz. red, small amount gray. Double-pointed needles No. 5. Scraps of felt: white, red, green, blue, pink, black. 9″ styrofoam cone. 2″ styrofoam ball, pink satin-covered. Two 12″ chenille sticks. Fabric cement. Pink pearl bead.
DRESS: With red, cast on 57 sts. Divide evenly on 3 needles, join and k 2 rnds.
Next Rnd: K 2 tog at beg of each needle—54 sts. K 2 rnds even. Repeat last 3 rnds until 18 sts remain. K 4 rnds even. Run yarn through sts, gather sts until only a small hole remains; fasten off.
FINISHING: Cut off top of cone, leaving 6″. Pull dress over cone. Glue cast-on edge of dress around lower edge of cone. Cover botom of cone with red

felt circle. Make arms, sleeves and hands same as Santa's cutting hands from pink felt.

For feet, cut ½″ point off cone tip, cut 1″ piece of cone top in half. Cover halves with black felt. Hold to lower edge of cone with chenille stick pieces; glue inner edge of feet to dress.

Trim lower edge of dress and sleeves with white felt, upper edge cut with pinking shears. Using patterns and white felt, place dash line of apron skirt and bib on fold of felt piece. Cut out; glue skirt to bib. Cut 2 strips 5″ long for straps. Glue ends to apron, crossing straps at back. Cut 1″ pocket; glue on. Trim with holly leaves and berries.

Attach head as for Santa. For hair, cut 12 strands of gray yarn 12″ long. Put centers side by side over 2½″ strip of masking tape. Sew down center; remove tape. Glue to head along sewn line and at sides of face. Take back part of hair and twist into a bun. Pin to head. Wrap remaining hair around bun and rest of head to conceal pink ball; glue. If necessary, add extra strands of yarn. Cut blue eyes, dark blue pupils, red mouth; glue on. Pin on pink pearl for nose.

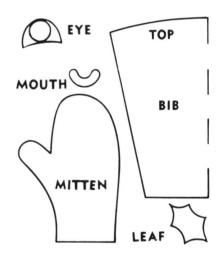

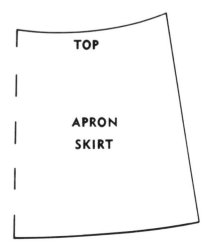

POCKETS FULL OF FUN

**Trim the tree with tiny surprises! Crocheted pockets
(4"–8") hold candy and small gifts.
Pocket Pals, page 44; Cornucopias, page 45.**

Cornucopia designs and photograph from Lindberg Press.

CHRISTMAS CHARACTERS

Knit this delightful candy-holder collection for small holiday visitors. Candy Caddies, page 45.

HOLIDAY GLITTER

Cotton pompons make a 14″ wreath and 19″ tree. Poinsettia Wreath and Christmas Tree, page 46.

POMPON TREE TRIMS

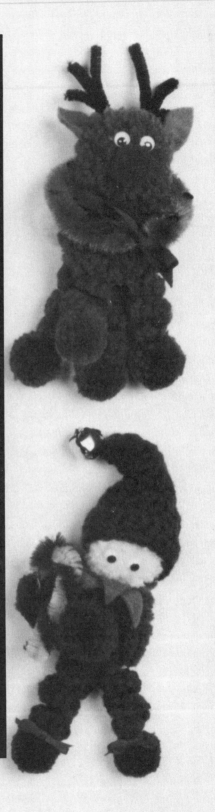

Plump little characters to hang on your tree are made on a Susan Bates Pompon Maker. Santa and his elf have crocheted caps and spiral legs. Directions, Pompon Ornaments, page 47. Opposite: charming gift box decorations to crochet include Santa, reindeer, angel, sheep, stocking, snowman, and wreath. See Package Trims, page 47.

GIFT

TRIMS

Designed by Jane Slovachek

Colorful critters to hang on
your tree are knitted of
fingering yarn. Peruvian
Ornaments, page 48. Tiny folk
and other Christmas
ornaments are crocheted of
cotton; Twelve Ornaments,
page 51. Three knit boots hold
little gifts and other goodies.
Directions for Aran Stocking,
page 54; Striped Stocking, page
55; Argyle Stocking, page 55.

TO KNIT AND CROCHET

A CRECHE TO CROCHET

The story of the Nativity is told here
in glowing colors. Three kings, an angel,
shepherds, and animals of the manger surround
the Holy Family and form part of the magical
scene. Figures, 8″ to 10″ high, are single
crocheted and softly stuffed. Directions on page 56.

TWO
STOCKINGS TO KNIT

Merry motifs are knit-in designs;
charts and directions, page 59.

EASY STOCKINGS

Embroidery accents these afghan stitch stockings.
Crocheted Stockings, page 61.

Santa
sends greetings
from a stockinette-
knit stocking with
"chimney" bands
(page 62). Jingle Bells
make "ap-pealing" gift
and tree trims;
garter-stitched
bells have pompon
clappers, embroidered
flowers (3"–4");
see page 62.

Three Scandinavian
Stockings come in
long, longer, longest
—one is just right
for each member of
the family.
Stockinette knit
in bright colors,
trim in white.
Tree and Reindeer
designs are knit-in;
Snowflakes are
embroidered.
Reindeer and Snow-
flake Stockings
have ribbed cuffs;
all have crocheted
chains for hanging.
Directions on page 62.

SANTA'S BUSY HELPERS

Put Santa's elves to work on your Christmas decorating! They love to trim gifts and stockings, the tree, a party table. Make the bendable bodies of pipe cleaners, with wooden bead heads; dress them in red easy-crochet suits, red felt hats and shoes. This tiny troupe stands 3″ tall. Directions for Elves and Noel Cutout on page 64.

Knitted Mr. & Mrs. Santa and red-harnessed reindeer admire a knitted tree decorated with felt gingerbread men and candles, while red and white bells ring overhead. Crochet bells in seven sizes. Directions for Santa, page 65. Directions for Mrs. Santa, page 65, for Christmas Bells, page 84. Directions for reindeer and tree, page 84.

81

Red candy-stripe sock, large and roomy, holds lots of goodies; page 86. Embroidered stocking has decorative stitches at cuff, heel, and toe; page 85. Crocheted Santa, made in rounds of single crochet, is 25″ tall without his hat; page 87. Dolls in stockings are charming toys with room in the sock foot for other small gifts; page 86.

STOCKINGS
AND
TOYS TO
MATCH

HI, SANTA!

Child-sized afghan alternates Santa motifs with plain squares in checkerboard fashion. Santas have button eyes and stand-away stocking caps, pompon-trimmed. Santa Afghan is on page 87. Matching 21″ Santa toy is crocheted in two identical pieces, sewn together and stuffed. Hair and beard are loops of yarn. Santa Toy, page 88.

CHRISTMAS BELLS
Shown on page 81

SIZES: ¾" to 2" high.
MATERIALS: 3-ply fingering yarn, 1 ounce white or red. 1 50-yard card gold or other metallic yarn. Steel crochet hook size 5. Stiff paper. All-purpose glue.
GAUGE: 8 sc = 1".
¾" BELL: Beg at center top, ch 2.
Rnd 1: 6 sc in 2nd ch from hook.
Rnd 2: * Sc in next sc, 2 sc in next sc, repeat from * around—9 sc.
Rnd 3: * Sc in each of next 2 sc, 2 sc in next sc, repeat from * around—12 sc.
Rnds 4-6: Sc in each sc around.
Rnd 7: * Sc in next sc, 2 sc in next sc, repeat from * around—18 sc. End off.
FINISHING: Turn piece inside out (wrong side is right side of bell). Insert hook through a st in rnd 1. Pull up a lp of metallic yarn to right side. * Insert hook in next st of same rnd, pull up a lp and draw through first lp on hook, repeat from * around. Work same chain trimming 3 rnds from bottom.
Picot Edging: Join gold yarn in any st on edge of bell. * Ch 3, sc in same st, sc in each of next 2 sts, repeat from * around. End off.

Roll a strip of stiff paper over outside of bell; trim strip to reach from rnd 3 to next to last rnd. Overlap ends of strip; glue ends together. Place glue over outside surface of paper; insert paper inside bell to shape and stiffen bell.
Hanger: With yarn, make a chain 3" long. Knot ends of chain together in a large knot. Insert hook through center top of bell and pull loop of chain through. (Knot should hold inside bell.) Place a bit of glue on knot.
⅞" BELL: Work as for ¾" bell through rnd 5.
Rnd 6: * Sc in next sc, 2 sc in next sc, repeat from * around—18 sc.
Rnd 7: * Sc in each of next 2 sc, 2 sc in next sc, repeat from * around—24 sc. End off. Finish as for ¾" bell.
1" BELL: Work as for ¾" bell through rnd 1.
Rnd 2: 2 sc in each sc around—12 sc.
Rnd 3: Sc in each sc around.
Rnd 4: * Sc in next sc, 2 sc in next sc, repeat from * around—18 sc.
Rnds 5 and 6: Sc in each sc around.
Rnd 7: * Sc in each of next 2 sc, 2 sc in next sc, repeat from * around—24 sc.
Rnd 8: Sc in each sc around, inc 4 sc in rnd—28 sc. End off. Finish as for ¾" bell.
1¼" BELL: Work as for 1" bell through rnd 8.
Rnd 9: Sc in each sc around. End off. Finish as for ¾" bell.
1½" BELL: Beg at center top, ch 2.

Rnd 1: 6 sc in 2nd ch from hook.
Rnd 2: 2 sc in each sc around—12 sc.
Rnd 3: * Sc in next sc, 2 sc in next sc, repeat from * around—18 sc.
Rnd 4: Sc in each sc around.
Rnd 5: * Sc in each of next 2 sc, 2 sc in next sc, repeat from * around—24 sc.
Rnds 6-10: Sc in each sc around.
Rnd 11: * Sc in each of next 3 sc, 2 sc in next sc, repeat from * around—30 sc.
Rnd 12: * Sc in each of next 4 sc, 2 sc in next sc, repeat from * around—36 sc.
Rnd 13: * Sc in each of next 3 sc, 2 sc in next sc, repeat from * around—45 sc. End off. Finish as for ¾" bell.
1¾" BELL: Work as for 1½" bell through rnd 13.
Rnd 14: Sc in each sc around, inc 3 sc in rnd. End off. Finish as for ¾" bell, making hanger 4" long.
2" BELL: Work as for 1½" bell through rnd 12.
Rnds 13-15: Sc in each sc.
Rnd 16: * Sc in each of next 2 sc, 2 sc in next sc, repeat from * around—48 sc. End off. Finish as for ¾" bell, making hanger 4" long instead of 3".

KNIT TREE
Shown on page 81

SIZE: 19" high.
MATERIALS: Knitting worsted, 1 oz. white; small amounts of gold, brown. Double-pointed needles, No. 5. 12" styrofoam cone. Scraps of felt: gold, brown, tan, olive, white. Empty tin can, such as tuna can, with one lid on, 4" diameter. Pipe cleaners. Fabric cement. Empty toilet tissue roll. White fabric paint.
DIRECTIONS: Beg at lower edge, cast

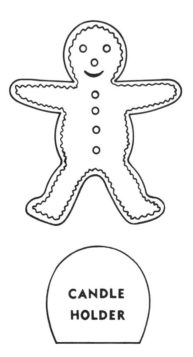

CANDLE HOLDER

on 60 sts. Divide evenly on 3 dp needles. Join: k 4 rnds.
Next Rnd: K 2 tog at beg of each needle—57 sts. Repeat these 5 rnds until 3 sts remain. Run yarn through sts, pull up tightly; fasten securely.
FINISHING: Stuff tip of knitted cone with yarn scraps. Cover cone with knit piece, pulling to fit. Run yarn around edge; gather and cross yarn from side to side on cone bottom to hold knitted piece taut. Glue a circle of white felt over bottom. Glue a piece of yarn around the base to conceal the joining.

Cut toilet tissue roll to about 2½". Cover with brown felt. Glue to center bottom of tree. Glue white felt around sides of tin can; cover lid with olive felt. Glue yarn around joining. Glue on 3 strips of brown felt ¾" x 2¼" evenly spaced around sides, being sure to cover the joining. Glue tree to stand; glue a piece of yarn around joining. Using patterns, from tan felt cut 11 gingerbread men. Following outline, with fabric paint put on "frosting." Let dry. Cut eight ⅝" tan ovals. Put a small hole in center. Cut 8 pieces of pipe cleaner, ¾" long; bend into "L" shape. Stick small part of "L" through oval; put glue on oval, then glue to back of man. When dry, push protruding part of cleaner into tree. Put 8 men on tree, glue the 3 flat men to stand between brown strips. Make 7 candles as follows: for each, cut olive felt into 1½" x 2" strip. Place a piece of gold yarn in middle of felt with ½" sticking out. Roll up felt tightly; glue. Cut 2 gold oval "flames" from felt, ½" long; glue over yarn. Using pattern, from gold felt, cut 2 candle holders for each candle. Glue piece of pipe cleaner between with small piece protruding. Glue candle to candle holder; stick pipe cleaner end into tree. Make a gold pompon for top of tree.

KNITTED REINDEER
Shown on page 81

SIZE: About 9" tall.
MATERIALS: Knitting worsted, 2 ozs. medium brown; about 2 feet red, for reins. Set of dp needles No. 5. Scraps of felt: red, pink, green, tan, brown, black. Cotton batting. Three jingle bells. Two pipe cleaners. Needle and thread. Yarn needle. Stitch holder. All-purpose glue.
GAUGE: 5 sts = 1".
BODY: Beg at lower neck edge, cast on 39 sts; divide on 3 dp needles. Join; work in stockinette st (k each rnd) for 39 rnds.
Rnd 40: (K 2 tog, k 11) 3 times—36 sts.
Rnds 41, 43, 45: K around.
Rnd 42: (K 2 tog, k 4) 6 times—30 sts.
Rnd 44: (K 2 tog, k 3) 6 times—24 sts.

Rnd 46: K 2 tog around—12 sts. Cut yarn, leaving 8″ end; thread yarn needle. Draw up sts, fasten securely. Stuff body firmly. Draw up cast-on sts tightly; fasten securely.

HEAD AND NECK: Working with 2 dp needles, cast on 3 sts. Beg on wrong side, with p row, work back and forth in stockinette st (p 1 row, k 1 row), inc 1 st each side every 4th row 3 times— 9 sts. Cast on 9 sts at end of next 2 rows—27 sts. Divide sts on 3 dp needles. Mark beg of rnd. Join; k 14 rnds.

Shape Head: K 8, sl next 11 sts on a holder. With 2 needles, work back and forth on remaining 16 sts in stockinette st for 10 rows. Sl sts from holder to dp needle. Divide 27 sts on 3 dp needles. Join; k 1 rnd.

Next Rnd: Inc 1 st in first st, k 9, inc 1 st in next st, finish rnd—29 sts.

Next Rnd: Inc 1 st in first st, k 11, inc 1 st in next st, finish rnd—31 sts. K 8 rnds.

Next Rnd: K 2 tog, k 11, k 2 tog, finish rnd.

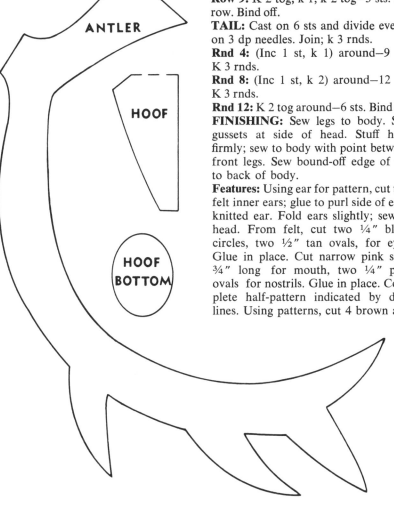

HOLLY

ANTLER

HOOF

HOOF BOTTOM

Next Rnd: K 2 tog, k 9, k 2 tog, finish rnd—27 sts.

Next Rnd: (K 2 tog, k 7) 3 times—24 sts. K 1 rnd.

Next Rnd: K 2 tog around—12 sts. Run yarn through sts, fasten securely.

BACK LEGS (make 2): Beg at top edge, cast on 18 sts and divide evenly on 3 dp needles. Join; k 12 rnds.

Shape Back Leg: K 6, sl next 12 sts on a holder. With 2 needles, work back and forth on remaining 6 sts in stockinette stitch for 3 more rows. Sl sts from holder to dp needle. Divide 18 sts on 3 dp needles. Join; k 2 rnds.

Next Rnd: (K 4, k 2 tog) 3 times—15 sts. K 12 rnds.

Next Rnd: * K 1, (k 2 tog) twice, repeat from * twice—9 sts. K 5 rnds. Run yarn through sts, fasten securely. Sew gusset. Stuff firmly. Sew across top.

FRONT LEGS (make 2): Beg at top edge, cast on 15 sts and divide evenly on 3 dp needles. Join; k 25 rnds.

Next Rnd: * K 1, (k 2 tog) twice, repeat from * twice—9 sts. K 5 rnds. Run yarn through sts, fasten securely. Stuff firmly. Sew across top.

EARS (make 2): Beg at lower edge, working with 2 dp needles, cast on 7 sts. Work in stockinette st for 6 rows.

Row 7: K 2 tog, k 3, k 2 tog. P 1 row.

Row 9: K 2 tog, k 1, k 2 tog—3 sts. P 1 row. Bind off.

TAIL: Cast on 6 sts and divide evenly on 3 dp needles. Join; k 3 rnds.

Rnd 4: (Inc 1 st, k 1) around—9 sts. K 3 rnds.

Rnd 8: (Inc 1 st, k 2) around—12 sts. K 3 rnds.

Rnd 12: K 2 tog around—6 sts. Bind off.

FINISHING: Sew legs to body. Sew gussets at side of head. Stuff head firmly; sew to body with point between front legs. Sew bound-off edge of tail to back of body.

Features: Using ear for pattern, cut two felt inner ears; glue to purl side of each knitted ear. Fold ears slightly; sew to head. From felt, cut two ¼″ black circles, two ½″ tan ovals, for eyes. Glue in place. Cut narrow pink strip ¾″ long for mouth, two ¼″ pink ovals for nostrils. Glue in place. Complete half-pattern indicated by dash lines. Using patterns, cut 4 brown ant-

lers, four black hooves and hoof bottoms, 4 green holly leaves. Glue hooves and hoof bottoms to legs. Run a 4″ piece of pipe cleaner through middle 3 sts between ears. Glue short ends of antlers to each side of pipe cleaner; glue short antlers tog, then glue pipe cleaner pieces between balance of antlers. Bend to desired shape.

Harness: Follow illustration on page 21. Cut three ½″ wide strips of red felt, 9″, 8″, and 6″ long. Cut a ¼″ strip, 5½″ long. Place 5½″ strip around mouth; glue or sew ends in place. Put 6½″ strip around neck, ends 1½″ apart at front neck; glue these ends, centered, to 8″ strip. Glue ends of 8″ strip to 9″ strip, 1¾″ from ends. Glue 9″ strip tog at bottom of body. Sew a jingle bell to each side of harness. Glue two holly leaves each side of neck. Cut tiny red felt circles; glue to holly. String a jingle bell on red yarn. Glue yarn ends to sides of mouth.

EMBROIDERED STOCKING
Shown on page 82

MATERIALS: Knitting worsted, 1 4-oz. skein green (G); small amounts white (W), red (R), yellow (Y), blue (B), and lime (L) for embroidery. Knitting needles No. 6. Steel crochet hook No. 00. Two stitch holders. Yarn needle.

GAUGE: 5 sts = 1″; 13 rows = 2″.

STOCKING: Beg at top, with G, cast on 68 sts. Work in ribbing of k 1, p 1, for 14 rows. Work in stockinette st (k 1 row, p 1 row) for 78 rows. Cut yarn. Slip first 17 sts and last 17 sts on 2 stitch holders for heel. Join yarn at instep, dec 1 st each side of first row, work in stockinette st on 32 sts for 66 rows, end p row. Cut yarn.

Heel: Slip heel sts on one needle with back edges at center. Place instep sts on a holder.

Row 1 (wrong side): Sl 1, p 2 tog, p across to last 2 sts, p 2 tog.

Row 2: * Sl 1, k 1, repeat from * across.

Row 3: Sl 1, p across. Repeat last 2 rows until there are 27 rows.

Turn Heel: Row 1 (right side): K 18, k 2 tog, k 1, turn.

Row 2: Sl 1, p 5, p 2 tog, p 1, turn.

Row 3: Sl 1, k 6, k 2 tog, k 1, turn.

Row 4: Sl 1, p 7, p 2 tog, p 1, turn. Continue in this manner, working 1 more st between decreases until all sts have been worked and 18 sts remain, end p row.

Sole: From right side, pick up and k 16 sts along side of heel, k across 18 heel sts, pick up and k 16 sts on other side of heel.

Row 1: Purl.

Row 2: K 1, sl 1, k 1, psso, k to last 3 sts, k 2 tog, k 1. Repeat these 2 rows until 30 sts remain. Work even on 30 sts until sole measures same as instep, end p row.

Shape Toe: Row 1 (right side): K 1, sl 1, k 1, psso, k to last 3 sts, k 2 tog, k 1.

Row 2: Purl. Repeat last 2 rows until 10

sts remain. Place sts on stitch holder. Slip instep sts from holder to needle, shape toe as for sole. Weave toe sts tog with Kitchener st.

FINISHING: Steam-press stocking. Sew back and side seams. Crochet or braid a 6″ chain with 1 strand each of R and W for hanger. Sew ends inside top back of stocking.

Embroidery: With 1 strand each of R and W, blanket st around top edge. With W, working below ribbing, work a row of coral sts; then, always working 2 rows below previous embroidery sts, work 1 row of R cross-sts, 1 row of Y chain sts. Working over and under 2 sts, work 1 row of W running st; fill in spaces with B running st. Work 1 row L chain sts, then 1 row R running st. With W, work a cluster of 4 lazy daisy sts over 5 G sts; skip 3 sts between each. Work 1 row Y running st, 1 row L chain sts. At start of toe shaping, work a row of R chain sts around toe. Working down and up toe along seam, work a row of Y chain sts; space rows of B and W, R and W running sts on sides of Y sts. Work clusters of 4 lazy daisy sts between sections. See illustration on page 82.

RED CANDY-STRIPED SOCK
Shown on page 82

MATERIALS: Knitting worsted, 1 4-oz. skein red (R), 1 oz. white (W). Knitting needles No. 6; set of dp needles No. 6. Two stitch holders. Yarn needle.

GAUGE: 5 sts = 1″.

Note: Top part of sock is worked back and forth; foot part is worked in the round on dp needles.

SOCK: Beg at upper edge, with regular needles, cast on 68 sts. Work in stockinette st (k 1 row, p 1 row) for 6 rows.

Next Row (eyelet row): * Yo, k 2 tog, repeat from * across. Beg with a p row, work in stockinette st until piece measures 14″ from eyelet row, end p row.

Divide for Heel: Place first 17 sts and last 17 sts on 2 stitch holders.

Instep: Join R at instep; k 2 tog, k across to last 2 sts, k 2 tog—32 sts. Working in stockinette st, work 21 rows, end p row.

Heel: Slip heel sts on one needle with back edges at center. Place instep sts on a holder. With wrong side facing, join W.

Row 1 (wrong side): With W, (p 2 tog, p 6) 4 times, p 2 tog—29 sts. Working in stockinette st, work 3 more rows W, (4 rows R, 4 rows W) twice, 1 row R, end p row. Cut W.

Turn Heel: Row 1 (right side): K 16, k 2 tog, k 1, turn.

Row 2: Sl 1, p 4, p 2 tog, p 1, turn.

Row 3: Sl 1, k 5, k 2 tog, k 1, turn.

Row 4: Sl 1, p 6, p 2 tog, p 1, turn. Continue in this manner, working 1 more st between decs until all sts have been worked and 17 sts remain, end p row.

From right side, with R, pick up and k 15 sts along side of heel, k across 17 heel

sts, pick up and k 15 sts on other side of heel—47 sts.

Row 1: Purl.

Row 2: K 1, sl 1, k 1, psso, k to last 3 sts, k 2 tog, k 1. Repeat last 2 rows until 29 sts remain. P 1 row, k 1 row.

FOOT: Place 29 heel sts and 32 instep sts on 3 dp needles. First heel st is beg of rnd. Work around in stockinette st (k each rnd) on 61 sts for 40 rnds, dec 1 st on last rnd—60 sts. Join W.

Shape Toe: Row 1: With W, (k 2 tog, k 26, k 2 tog) twice—56 sts. K 1 rnd W.

Rnd 3: With W, (k 2 tog, k 24, k 2 tog) twice—52 sts. K 1 rnd W. Repeat last 2 rnds, having 2 sts less between decs every other rnd until 20 sts remain; **at the same time,** work in following color sequence: (4 rnds R, 4 rnds W) twice. Weave toe sts tog in Kitchener st.

FINISHING: Steam-press sock. Sew back and gusset seams. Turn hem to wrong side on eyelet row; sew in place.

Hanger: With W, cast on 30 sts. K 1 row, p 1 row. Bind off. Sew to inside top back.

DOLLS IN STOCKINGS
Shown on page 82

SIZE: Each doll, about 6″ high plus hat.

MATERIALS: Knitting worsted, about 1½ ozs. main color (MC); small amounts other colors for trim (see individual directions for colors). Knitting needles No. 5. Two stitch holders. Cotton batting for stuffing. Yarn needle. All-purpose glue.

GAUGE: 5 sts = 1″, 7 rows = 1″.

GENERAL DIRECTIONS: STOCKING: Beg at top, with contrasting color (CC), cast on 24 sts. Work in garter st (k each row) for 7 rows. Change to MC and work in stockinette st (k 1 row, p 1 row) for 16 rows, end p row. Cut yarn.

Divide for Heel: Slip first 7 sts and last 7 sts on 2 stitch holders.

Instep: Join MC and work even in stockinette st on 10 sts for 20 rows, end p row.

Shape Toe: (For Snowman only, change to CC.) **Row 1:** K 1, sl 1, k1, psso, k to last 3 sts, k 2 tog, k 1.

Row 2: Purl. Repeat last 2 rows once.

Row 5: K 1, sl 1, k 1, psso, k 2 tog, k 1 —4 sts.

For Elf only, work on these 4 sts for 2¼″, end p row. K 2 tog twice; p 2 tog —1 st remains. End off.

Heel: From wrong side, slip heel sts on one needle with back edges at center. Place 4 instep sts on a holder. Join MC on right side (for Snowman only, join CC).

Row 1 (right side): * Sl 1, k 1, repeat from * across.

Row 2: Purl. Repeat these 2 rows until heel measures 1¼″, end p row.

Turn Heel: Row 1: K 8, k 2 tog, k 1, turn.

Row 2: Sl 1, p 3, p 2 tog, p 1, turn.

Row 3: Sl 1, k 3, k 2 tog, k 1, turn.

Row 4: Sl 1, p 3, p 2 tog, p 1, turn.

Row 5: Sl 1, k 4, k 2 tog, k 1, turn.

Row 6: Sl 1, p 5, p 2 tog, p 1—8 sts. Cut yarn.

Sole: From right side, join MC at top of heel, pick up and k 4 sts along side of heel, k across 8 heel sts, pick up and k 4 sts along other side of heel—16 sts.

Row 1: Purl.

Row 2: K, dec 1 st each side. Repeat last 2 rows until 10 sts remain. Work even until sole measures same as instep, end p row. Shape toe as for instep; work elf toe as for instep.

Weave toe sts tog with Kitchener st.

FINISHING: Steam-press stocking. Sew back and side seams. Attach a loop of CC to back seam for hanger.

DOLL: SANTA AND ELF (make 2 pieces): Beg at tip of hat with MC, cast on 2 sts. Work in stockinette st for 4 rows.

Row 5: K, inc 1 st. Work 3 rows even. Repeat last 4 rows once—4 sts.

Row 13: K, inc 1 st. P 1 row.

Row 15: K, inc 1 st—6 sts. Work 3 rows even. Repeat these 6 rows once —8 sts.

Face: Join pink. K 1 row, p 1 row, k 1 row.

Next Row: P, dec 1 st. Work 4 rows even.

Next Row: K, dec 1 st. P 1 row, then dec 1 st on next row—5 sts. Cut pink; join MC. * **Body:** P across, cast on 10 sts at end of row. K next row, cast on 10 sts at end of row—25 sts.

Arms: Work in stockinette st for 5 rows. Bind off 8 sts at beg of next 2 rows—9 sts. Work 5 rows even.

Next Row: P, dec 1 st at center of row —8 sts.

Legs: K 2, inc 1 st in each of next 2 sts, sl last 4 sts to a holder. Work even in stockinette st on 6 sts for 13 rows. Bind off. Sl 4 sts to needle. Join MC. Inc 1 st in each of first 2 sts, k 2. Work as for first leg. *

Belt: With CC, cast on 22 sts. K 3 rows. Bind off in K.

Hat Brim: With CC, cast on 17 sts and work as for belt.

Pompon: With CC, cast on 6 sts. K 7 rows. Bind off. Make 2 for elf.

SNOWMAN AND GINGERBREAD
BOY (make 2 pieces): With MC, cast on 4 sts. Work in stockinette st for 2 rows.

Row 3: Inc 1 st each side. P 1 row. Repeat last 2 rows once.

Row 7: Inc 1 st each side—10 sts. Work 3 rows even.

Row 12: Dec 1 st each side. P 1 row. Repeat last 2 rows once.

Row 16: Dec 1 st at center of row—5

sts. Beg at first * on Body, work as for Santa and Elf from * to *.

FINISHING: Steam-press pieces. Overcast body pieces tog, stuffing as you go.

GINGERBREAD BOY: Colors: Medium brown (MC), white (CC), black, and bright pink. Following General Directions, make stocking and doll. Embroider 3 groups of white lazy daisy sts with pink French knot centers on each side of stocking as shown. Outline one side of entire body with white chain sts; embroider 2 groups of white lazy daisy sts on body. Make small, white straight sts for eyes with black French knot pupils; 3 white straight sts form bangs, a single strand of pink forms mouth.

SANTA: Colors: Red (MC), white (CC), pink, blue, and black. Following General Directions, make stocking and body. Sew pompon to tip of hat, brim at bottom of hat, belt around body. Embroider white straight sts for hair and beard. Make eyes as for Gingerbread Boy using blue and black; make red straight st mouth.

ELF: Colors: Green (MC), white (CC), pink, yellow, red, and black. Following General Directions, make stocking and body. Sew one CC pompon to tip of stocking, then tack pompon to stocking as shown. Sew on trims as for Santa, embroidering white lazy daisy sts on front of body. Embroider yellow beard and hair, green and black eyes, red mouth.

SNOWMAN: Colors: White (MC), black (CC), lime, and red. Following General Directions, make stocking and body.

Scarf: With lime, cast on 4 sts. Work in garter st for 11″ or desired length. Bind off. Tack around neck.

Hat: Top: With CC, cast on 20 sts. K 13 rows. Bind off. Sew ends tog; sew top seam (bound-off edge).

Brim: With CC, cast on 22 sts. K 1 row.

Next Row: K, inc 1 st in each st. K 1 row. Bind off. Sew ends tog; sew cast-on edge to top. Sew hat to head.

Buttons: With CC, cast on 4 sts. K 3 rows. Bind off. Sew into a ball; sew to body.

Eyes: With CC, cast on 3 sts. K 2 rows. Bind off. Sew into a ball; sew to face.

CROCHETED SANTA
Shown on page 82

SIZE: About 26″ high.
MATERIALS: Knitting worsted, about 6 ozs. red, 2 ozs. each of black and white, 1 oz. pink. Crochet hook size G. Small pieces of red, blue and black felt. Stuffing. Yarn needle. Glue. Red marker.
GAUGE: 7 sc = 2″; 4 rnds = 1″.
SANTA: HEAD: Beg at top of head, with pink, ch 2.

Rnd 1: 6 sc in 2nd ch from hook. Do not join rnds; mark end of each rnd.
Rnd 2: 2 sc in each sc around—12 sc.
Rnd 3: * Sc in next sc, 2 sc in next sc, repeat from * around—18 sc.
Rnd 4: 2 sc in each sc around—36 sc.
Rnds 5-8: Sc in each sc around.
Rnd 9: * Sc in 5 sc, 2 sc in next sc, repeat from * around—42 sc.
Rnds 10-20: Sc in each sc around.
Rnd 21: * Pull up a lp in each of 2 sc, yo hook and through 3 lps on hook (1 dec), sc in 5 sc, repeat from * around—36 sc.
Rnd 22: * Sc in 4 sc, dec over next 2 sc, repeat from * around—30 sc.
Chin: Rnd 23: Sc in each sc around.
Rnd 24: Sc in 10 sc, (dec over next 2 sc) 5 times, sc in 10 sc—25 sc.
Neck; rnds 25-28: Sc evenly around.
BODY: Change to red. **Rnd 29:** Sc in 5 sc, 2 sc in next sc, ch 6 for shoulder, sc in 2nd ch from hook and in next 4 ch, sc in 6 sc, 2 sc in next sc, sc in 6 sc, 2 sc in next sc, ch 6, sc in 2nd ch from hook and in next 4 ch, sc in last 5 sc.
Rnd 30: Sc around, working on both sides of shoulder chains, inc 2 sc at end of each shoulder—52 sc. Work even on 52 sc for 37 rnds. End off.
Seat: With red, ch 20. **Row 1:** Sc in 2nd ch from hook and in next 18 ch—19 sc. Ch 1, turn each row.
Rows 2-8: Sc in each sc. End off. Stuff head and body firmly, sew seat in place to last rnd of body.
ARM (make 2): With black, ch 2.
Rnd 1: 6 sc in 2nd ch from hook.
Rnd 2: 2 sc in each sc around—12 sc.
Rnd 3: * Sc in 2 sc, 2 sc in next sc, repeat from * around—16 sc.
Rnds 4-13: Work even on 16 sc.
Rnd 14: Join red, dec 1 sc, sc in 14 sc.
Rnds 15-42: Work even on 15 sc. End off. Stuff arm leaving last few rnds unstuffed; gather top, sew to shoulder.
Thumb: With black, ch 2, 5 sc in 2nd ch from hook. Work 5 rnds even. End off. Stuff lightly; sew in place.
Nose: With pink, ch 2, 5 sc in 2nd ch from hook. Work 1 rnd of 5 sc. End off. Sew in place.
LEG (make 2): With black, ch 20, join with sl st to form ring. **Rnd 1:** Ch 1, sc in each ch around.
Rnds 2-11: Work even on 20 sc.
Rnd 12: Change to red, dec 2 sc evenly, work in sc—18 sc.
Rnds 13-42: Work even in sc. End off. Sew last rnd tog flat. Sew to lower front edge of body.
FOOT (make 2): With black, ch 2.
Rnd 1: 6 sc in 2nd ch from hook.
Rnd 2: 2 sc in each sc around—12 sc.
Rnd 3: * Sc in next sc, 2 sc in next sc, repeat from * around—18 sc.
Rnds 4-15: Work even on 18 sc. End off. Stuff; sew flat across back. Stuff leg; sew foot to bottom of leg, sewing instep of foot to front of leg to bring foot up in front.
LEG CUFF (make 2): With white, ch 20.

Sl st in first ch to form ring. Work 3 rnds of 20 sc. End off. Sew in place.
ARM CUFF (make 2): With white, ch 16. Work as for leg cuff.
BODY CUFF: With white, ch 52. Work 4 rnds as for leg cuff.
BUTTON (make 3): With white, ch 2.
Rnd 1: 6 sc in 2nd ch from hook.
Rnd 2: 2 sc in each sc.
Rnd 3: * Sc in next sc, 2 sc in next sc, repeat from * around. End off. Sew buttons in place.
BELT: With black, work 2 rnds as for body cuff.
COLLAR: With white, ch 45.
Row 1: Sc in 2nd ch from hook and in each ch across. End off. Do not turn.
Row 2: Join yarn in first st of last row, sc in each sc across. End off. Do not turn. Repeat row 2 twice. Fold ends under, hem to wrong side. Sew collar around neck.
FINISHING: For beard, thread white yarn double in needle, work 3 rows of knotted loops about 1½″ long around sides of face and chin. For moustache, glue 2 long loops of white yarn each side of face under nose. For hair, sew long loops of white yarn to top of head along the "part", slightly to one side of head. Glue some of the hair to sides and back of head. For eyes, cut blue crescents and black pupils from felt; glue in place. Glue on narrow strip of red felt 1″ long in curve for mouth. Add color to cheeks with red marker.
CAP: With red, beg at tip, ch 2.
Rnd 1: 3 sc in 2nd ch from hook.
Rnd 2: Sc in each sc around.
Rnd 3: 2 sc in next sc, sc in 2 sc.
Rnd 4: Sc in each sc around.
Rnd 5: 2 sc in next sc, sc in 3 sc.
Rnds 6 and 7: Sc in each sc around.
Rnds 8-34: Inc 1 sc on rnd 8 and every 3rd rnd, work 2 rnds even—13 sc.
Rnds 35-72: Inc 1 sc on rnd 35 and every other rnd, work 1 rnd even—32 sc.
Rnds 73-77: Inc 2 sc evenly each rnd—42 sc.
Rnds 78-84: Work 7 rnds even. Change to white. Turn work.
Rnd 85: Working around on wrong side of cap, inc 3 sc evenly around—45 sc. Work even for 4 rnds. End off. Turn up cuff; sew in place.
Pompon: With white, ch 10.
Row 1: Sc in 2nd ch from hook and in each remaining ch. Ch 1, turn each row.
Rows 2-9: Work even on 9 sc. End off. Gather edges and stuff piece, pulling into ball shape. Sew to tip of cap.

SANTA AFGHAN
Shown on page 83

SIZE: 36″ x 52″, plus fringe.
MATERIALS: Knitting worsted weight yarn, 4 4-oz. skeins white, 3 skeins red, 1 skein green; 2 ozs. pink. Crochet hook size G. 26 black shiny shank

type buttons, 7/16". White buttonhole twist. Yarn needle.

GAUGE: 7 sts = 2".

AFGHAN: SANTA MOTIF (make 13): With white, ch 13. **Row 1** (right side): Sc in 2nd ch from hook and in each remaining ch. Ch 1, turn each row.

Row 2: Loop st in each sc across. (To make loop st, insert hook in st, wrap yarn over right index finger, pull yarn through st, yo and through 2 lps on hook.)

Row 3: Sc in each loop st across.

Rows 4-10: Repeat rows 2 and 3, end with loop st row.

Row 11: Sc in first 2 loop sts. Working on 2 sts only, repeat rows 2 and 3 until there are 4 loop st rows, end loop st row. Sk 8 sts on row 10, work loop st in each of last 2 sts. Work as for other side of face.

Face: With pink, ch 9. Work even in sc on 8 sc for 8 rows. End off; leave end for sewing. Sew face into beard.

Hat: From right side, with white, sc across 12 sts of beard and face. Ch 1, turn. Work 1 more row of sc. Change to red, work 3 rows.

Next Row: Sc in back lp only of 7 sc. Ch 1, turn.

Next Row: Work 2 sc tog, sc to last sc, 2 sc in last sc.

Next Row: Sc to last 2 sc, work 2 sc tog. Repeat last 2 rows twice—4 sc. Work 3 rows even.

Next Row: Sc in 2 sc, work 2 sc tog. Work 2 rows even.

Next Row: Work 2 sc tog, sc in 1 sc. Work 2 rows even. Work 2 sc tog. End off.

Border: Rnd 1: From right side, join green in lower corner. Ch 1, 2 sc, ch 1, 2 sc in corner, sc in 10 sc across bottom of beard, 2 sc, ch 1, 2 sc in corner, 20 sc up side to next corner, 2 sc, ch 1, 2 sc in corner, 10 sc across hat (work in free lps at back of hat), 2 sc, ch 1, 2 sc in corner, 20 sc down last side. Sl st in first sc.

Rnd 2: Ch 3, dc in next sc, 2 dc, ch 2, 2 dc in corner sp, dc in each sc around, working 2 dc, ch 2, 2 dc in each corner sp. Sl st in top of ch 3. End off.

Rnd 3: With white, sc in each dc around, 2 sc, ch 2, 2 sc in each corner sp. Join. End off.

Rnd 4: With red, 2 sc, ch 1, 2 sc in corner sp, * ch 1, sk 1 st, sc in next st, repeat from * to next corner, ch 1, 2 sc, ch 1, 2 sc in corner sp, repeat from first * around. Join. End off.

Rnd 5: With white, 2 dc, ch 1, 2 dc in corner sp (ch 3 for first dc), * ch 1, dc in next ch-1 sp, repeat from * to next corner, ch 1, 2 dc, ch 1, 2 dc in corner sp, repeat from first * around. Join. End off; leave long end for sewing.

Steam-press lightly, pulling motif into shape, 7¼" x 10".

PLAIN MOTIF (make 12): With red, ch 14.

Row 1: Sc in 2nd ch from hook and in each remaining ch. Ch 4, turn.

Row 2: Sk first and next sc, dc in next sc, * ch 1, sk 1 sc, dc in next sc, repeat from * across. Ch 1, turn.

Row 3: (Sc in dc, sc in ch-1 sp) 5 times, sc in next dc, sc in end sp, sc in 3rd ch of ch 4. Ch 4, turn.

Rows 4-15: Repeat rows 2 and 3. At end of row 15, ch 1, do not turn.

Border: Rnd 1: Working down side of motif, * work 20 sc to next corner, 2 sc, ch 1, 2 sc in corner; work 10 sc across end, 2 sc, ch 1, 2 sc in corner; repeat from * once. Sl st in first sc.

Rnd 2: Ch 4, sk next sc, dc in next sc, * ch 1, sk next sc, dc in next sc, repeat from * to corner sp, 2 dc, ch 2, 2 dc in corner sp, repeat from first * around, end ch 1, sl st in 3rd ch of ch 4. End off.

Rnd 3: With green, work 2 sc, ch 1, 2 sc in each corner, sc in each dc and ch-1 sp around. Join. End off.

Rnd 4: With white, work 2 sc, ch 1, 2 sc in each corner, sc in each sc around. Join.

Rnd 5: 2 dc, ch 1, 2 dc in corner sp, * ch 1, sk 1 sc, dc in next sc, repeat from * to next corner, ch 1, 2 dc, ch 1, 2 dc in corner sp, repeat from first * around. Join. End off; leave long end for sewing. Steam-press to same shape as Santa motif.

FINISHING: SANTA: Make small loose white pompon for each Santa. Sew to cap tip; sew tip down on green border. Sew buttons on for eyes. For nose, with pink, ch 2, 4 sc in 2nd ch from hook. Sew into a ball; sew to center of face. For mustache, with 32" piece of white, wind end around finger 4 or 5 times, sew to side of face, take a st to just under nose, back to "curl," and back to under nose; take 3 sts to other side of face and make other end of mustache same as first. Embroider red mouth (split yarn and use 2 strands), in outline st.

Sew motifs tog, 5 x 5, alternating motifs, having Santas in all 4 corners.

Border: With green, work 3 dc, ch 2, 3 dc in each corner sp of afghan, (ch 1, dc in next sp) repeated around.

Fringe: Cut red, white and green into 12" strands. Using 4 strands of same color tog, knot a fringe in every 3rd or 4th sp along top and bottom edges.

SANTA TOY
Shown on page 83

SIZE: 21" tall.

MATERIALS: Knitting worsted weight yarn, 4 ozs. red, 2 ozs. black, 1 oz. white. Crochet hook size G. Polyester stuffing. Two black ½" shank-type buttons. Yarn needle.

GAUGE: 4 sc = 1".

SANTA (make 2 pieces): With black, ch 21.

Row 1: Sc in 2nd ch from hook and in each remaining ch—20 sc. Work in sc throughout. Ch 1, turn each row.

Rows 2 and 3: Inc 1 sc each side.

Row 4: Work even—24 sc.

Rows 5-10: Dec 1 sc each side—12 sc.

Rows 11-20: Work even.

Row 21: Change to white; inc 1 sc each side.

Rows 22-24: Work even—14 sc.

Row 25: Change to red; inc 1 sc each side.

Rows 26-28: Work even—16 sc.

Row 29: Inc 1 sc each side.

Row 30: Work even—18 sc.

Rows 31-38: Repeat rows 29 and 30, 4 times—26 sc.

Row 39: Change to white; inc 1 sc each side.

Rows 40 and 41: Work even—28 sc.

Row 42: Inc 1 sc each side—30 sc.

Rows 43-50: Change to red, work even for 8 rows.

Rows 51-54: Change to black, work even for 4 rows.

Rows 55-58: Change to red, work even for 4 rows.

Row 59: Dec 1 sc each side.

Rows 60 and 61: Work even—28 sc.

Row 62: Dec 1 sc each side.

Row 63: Work even—26 sc.

Rows 64-71: Repeat rows 62 and 63, 4 times—18 sc.

Rows 72 and 73: Dec 1 sc each side—14 sc.

Rows 74 and 75: Change to pink, work even.

Row 76: Inc 1 sc each side.

Rows 77-81: Work even—16 sc.

Row 82: Inc 1 sc each side.

Rows 83-88: Work even—18 sc.

Row 89: Dec 1 sc each side.

Rows 90-92: Change to white, work 3 rows even—16 sc.

Rows 93 and 94: Change to red, work 2 rows even.

Row 95: Dec 1 sc each side.

Row 96: Work even—14 sc.

Rows 97 and 98: Repeat rows 95 and 96.

Row 99: Dec 1 sc each side—10 sc. End off.

Arm: Join red in 5th row below pink face, ch 15. **Row 1:** Sc in 2nd ch from hook and in remaining 13 ch, sl st in next row of body. Turn (do not ch 1).

Row 2: Sc in each of 14 sc. Ch 1, turn.

Row 3: Sc in 14 sc, sl st in next row of body. Turn.

Row 4: Repeat row 2.

Row 5: Sc in 12 sc, work 2 sc tog, sl st in next row of body. Turn. Work 3 more rows on 13 sc, joining to body as before. End off.

With white, work 8 sc across end of arm. Work 1 row even. Change to black, work 7 rows even. Dec 1 sc each side of next 2 rows. Work 1 row even. End off. On upper edge of mitten, join black in 2nd black row from wrist, work 3 sc along edge toward tip. Work 2 rows even. Dec 1 sc on next row. On last row, work 2 sc tog. End off.

FINISHING: Sew 2 body pieces tog, right sides out, stuffing as you go.

Cap Tip: With red, ch 11. **Row 1:** Sc in 2nd ch from hook and in each remaining ch.

Row 2: Work even—10 sc.

Row 3: Dec 1 sc, sc across.

Row 4: Sc across to last 2 sc, work 2 sc tog.

Row 5: Work even—8 sc.

Row 6: Dec 1 sc each side.

Row 7: Work even—6 sc.

Row 8: Dec 1 sc each side.

Rows 9-15: Work 7 rows even—4 sc.

Row 16: Dec 1 sc.

Rows 17-20: Work 4 rows even—3 sc.

Row 21: Dec 1 sc.

Rows 22-24: Work 3 rows even—2 sc.

Row 25: Work 2 sc tog.

Row 26: Work even. End off. Sew to first red row on side of cap. Make a white pompon; sew to tip.

Nose: With pink, ch 2. Work 6 sc in 2nd ch from hook. Shape into a ball; sew to face.

Beard and Hair: Wind white yarn around 1 or 2 fingers 3 or more times; sew "curls" all over back, sides and lower front of head, one curl at center of forehead. Make curls for each end of mustache; make long straight sts under nose joining ends of mustache.

Embroider red mouth in outline st. Sew button eyes on securely, or embroider eyes. For buckle, make white ch about 5″ long. Sew to belt in buckle shape. With white, embroider division between legs in backstitch.

GRANNY PATCH STOCKINGS
Shown on page 105

SIZE: 18″ long.
MATERIALS: Knitting worsted, 3 ozs. white, 1 oz. each of red and green for white stocking; 3 ozs. green, 1 oz. each of red and white for green stocking; 4 ozs. red, 1 oz. white for red stocking. Crochet hook size G. Yarn needle.
GAUGE: Large square = 4″; small square = 2″.
WHITE SQUARE: With red, ch 5. Sl st in first ch to form ring. **Rnd 1:** Ch 3, 2 dc in ring, ch 2, (3 dc in ring, ch 2) 3 times, sl st in top of ch 3.
Rnd 2: Join green in ch-2 sp, ch 3, 2 dc,

ch 1, 3 dc in ch-2 sp, (ch 2, 3 dc, ch 1, 3 dc in next sp) 3 times, ch 2, sl st in top of ch 3. End off.
Rnd 3: Join white in ch-2 sp, ch 3, 2 dc in same sp, * ch 2, 3 dc, ch 1, 3 dc in corner ch-1 sp, ch 2, 3 dc in next sp, repeat from * around, end ch 2, sl st in top of ch 3.
Rnd 4: Sl st in each of next 2 dc, sl st in ch-2 sp, ch 3, 2 dc in same sp, * ch 2, 3 dc, ch 1, 3 dc in corner ch-1 sp, (ch 2, 3 dc in next sp) twice, repeat from * around, end ch 2, sl st in top of ch 3. End off; leave end for sewing.

RED SQUARE: Work as for white square for 2 rnds making rnd 1 white, rnd 2 red.

GREEN SQUARE: Work as for white square through rnd 3, making rnds 1 and 2 green, rnd 3 white.
Rnd 4: Join red in any corner sp, ch 1, * 3 sc in corner sp, (sc in each of next 3 dc, sc in next sp) twice, sc in each of next 3 dc, repeat from * around, end sl st in first sc. End off.
Rnd 5: Join green in 2nd sc at any corner, ch 4, hdc in same sc, * hdc in each sc to next corner, hdc, ch 2, hdc in corner sc, repeat from * around, end sl st in 2nd ch of ch 4. End off.

WHITE STOCKING: Make 8 white squares. Sew 3 tog in a row for each side, sewing through back lps.
Heel (make 2): With white, ch 4.
Row 1: 3 dc in 4th ch from hook. Ch 2, turn.
Row 2: Dc in each of 3 dc, dc in top of ch 4. Ch 2, turn each row.
Row 3: Dc in first dc, dc in each dc across, 2 dc in top of turning ch.
Rows 4 and 5: Repeat row 3.
Row 6: Dc in first dc, dc in 4 dc, 2 dc in next dc, dc in each remaining dc, 2 dc in top of turning ch—12 dc. Ch 1, turn.
Row 7: Sc in first dc, hdc in next dc, dc in each of next 2 dc, tr in each of next 4 dc, dc in each of next 2 dc, hdc in next dc, sc in last dc. Ch 1, turn.
Row 8: Sc in sc, hdc in hdc, dc in each of next 2 dc, tr in next tr, 2 tr in each of next 2 tr, tr in next tr, dc in each of next 2 dc, hdc in hdc, sc in sc. Change to red, ch 1, turn.
Row 9: Sc in sc, hdc in hdc, dc in each of 2 dc, tr in each of 6 tr, dc in each of 2 dc, hdc in hdc, sc in sc. Ch 1, turn.
Row 10: * Sc in next st, 2 sc in next st, repeat from * across. End off.

Sew one edge of heel to end of side-strip. Sew other edge of heel to one side of single square.
Toe (make 2): **Row 1:** Working on opposite side of white square just joined to heel, join white in corner, ch 3, dc in each dc and sp across—16 dc. Ch 1, turn.
Row 2: Pull up a lp in each of first 2

dc, yo hook and through 3 lps on hook (1 dec), hdc in next dc, dc in each of 2 dc, tr in each of 6 dc, dc in each of 2 dc, hdc in next dc, dec 1 sc over last 2 sts. Ch 1, turn.
Row 3: Working in each st, work 1 sc dec, hdc, 2 dc, 4 tr, 2 dc, hdc, 1 sc dec. Change to red. Ch 1, turn.
Row 4: With red, work 1 sc dec, hdc, dc, 4 tr, dc, hdc, 1 sc dec. End off.
Top: Row 1: Join white in corner at top of side strip, ch 3, dc in each dc and sp across to next corner. Ch 3, turn.
Row 2: Working in dc across, inc 1 dc each end and 1 dc at center. Ch 3, turn.
Row 3: Dc in each dc across. End off.
Boxing Strip: Beg at top edge, with white, ch 8. Dc in 3rd ch from hook and in each ch across—6 dc. Ch 2, turn each row. Work even on 6 dc until strip reaches as far as bottom seam of top square, dec 1 dc at center. Work even on 5 dc until strip reaches top of heel, change to red. Dec 1 dc at center, work even on 4 dc for length of heel, change to white. Work even to start of red on toe, change to red. Work even to start of white on instep, change to white. Work even to start of leg, inc 1 dc at center. Work even to bottom seam of top square, inc 1 dc at center. Work even on 6 dc to top. End off.

Sew boxing strip around stocking.
FINISHING: With red, work 1 rnd dc around top of stocking. With white, make a ch 8″ long for hanger. Work 1 sc in each ch. Sew ends inside center back.
GREEN STOCKING: Make 8 green squares. Sew 3 tog in a row for each side, sewing through back lps. Work as for white stocking, substituting green for white.
RED STOCKING: Make 32 red squares. Sew 12 tog in a strip, 2 by 6, for each side, sewing through back lps. Sew 4 tog in a square for each side of foot. Work as for white stocking, substituting red for white and white for red.

GRANNY APPLIQUE STOCKING
Shown on page 105

SIZE: 18″ long.
MATERIALS: Knitting worsted, 1 4-oz. skein green; small amounts of red and white. Crochet hook size H.
GAUGE: 1 pat = 1″; 3 rnds = 2″.
STOCKING: LEG: Beg at top, with green, ch 48 loosely. Sl st in first ch to form ring.
Rnd 1: Ch 3, * sk 2 ch, 3 dc in next ch, repeat from * around, sl st in top of ch 3—15 pats.
Rnd 2: Ch 3, dc in same ch as sl st, * 3 dc in next sp between pats, repeat from * around, dc in same ch as first dc of rnd. Sl st in top of ch 3.

Rnd 3: Ch 3, * 3 dc in next sp between pats, repeat from * around; do not work in last sp—14 pats. Sl st in top of ch 3.
Rnd 4: Repeat rnd 2.
Rnd 5: Repeat rnd 3—13 pats.
Rnd 6: Repeat rnd 2.
Rnd 7: Ch 3, * 3 dc in next sp, repeat around, end 2 dc in last sp. Sl st in top of ch 3—13 pats.
Rnd 8: Sl st in next sp, ch 3, 2 dc in same sp, work in pat around, sl st in top of ch 3—13 pats.
Rnd 9: Repeat rnd 3—12 pats.
Rnd 10: Ch 3, * 3 dc in next sp between pats, repeat from * around, end 3 dc in sp before ch 3—12 pats. Sl st in top of ch 3.
Rnd 11: Ch 3, 2 dc in sp before first pat, * 3 dc in next sp, repeat from * around—12 pats. Sl st in top of ch 3.
Rnd 12: Repeat rnd 10.
Rnd 13: Repeat rnd 3—11 pats.
Rnds 14-21: Work even on 11 pats. End off.
FOOT: Beg at toe, with green, ch 6. Sl st in first ch to form ring. **Rnd 1:** Ch 1, 11 sc in ring. Sl st in first sc.
Rnd 2: Ch 3, 3 dc in each sc around. Sl st in top of ch 3.
Rnds 3-10: Work even on 11 pats. Join each rnd. End off. Mark center pat for top of foot.
Heel: Row 1: Join yarn in sp after marked pat, ch 3, * 3 dc in next sp, repeat from * 9 times. Ch 3, turn.
Row 2: * 3 dc in next sp, repeat from * 9 times. Ch 3, turn.
Rows 3-7: Repeat row 2. End off. Sew or crochet back seam of heel from wrong side.
FINISHING: Sew foot opening to lower edge of leg. With double strand of red, make a 25″ chain. Run through last rnd of leg. Tie in a bow at front.
Granny Square: With green, ch 3, sl st in first ch to form ring. **Rnd 1:** Ch 3, 2 dc in ring, (ch 1, 3 dc in ring) 3 times, ch 1, sl st in top of ch 3. End off.
Rnd 2: Join white in any ch-1 sp, ch 3, 2 dc, ch 1, 3 dc in same sp, (3 dc, ch 1, 3 dc in next sp) 3 times, sl st in top of ch 3. End off.
Rnd 3: Join red in any ch-1 sp, ch 3, 2 dc, ch 1, 3 dc in same sp, 3 dc in next sp, (3 dc, ch 1, 3 dc in next ch-1 sp, 3 dc in next sp) 3 times, sl st in top of ch 3. End off. Sew square to one side of leg as shown in ilustration.
Picot Edging: Join red in sp at top edge of stocking. Sc in sp, * ch 3, sc in 3rd ch from hook, sc in next sp, repeat from * around. Join. End off.

WEE ELF
Shown on page 106

SIZE: 12″ high.
MATERIALS: Knitting worsted weight yarn, 1 oz. green, ½ oz. pink and red, few yards yellow. Crochet hook size E. Four 12″ chenille sticks. Cotton batting. Scraps of felt. Glue.
GAUGE: 5 sc = 1″; 6 rows = 1″.
ELF: BODY: Beg at top edge of back, with green, ch 10.
Row 1: Sc in 2nd ch from hook and in each remaining ch—9 sc. Ch 1, turn each row.
Rows 2-30: Sc in each sc across. End off. Last row is top edge of front.
SIDE, LEG AND FOOT (make 2): Beg at top edge of side, with green, ch 4.
Row 1: Sc in 2nd ch from hook and in each remaining ch—3 sc. Ch 1, turn each row.
Rows 2-13: Sc in each sc across. At end of row 13, ch 4, turn (beg of leg).
Row 14: Sc in 2nd ch from hook, sc in each of next 2 ch, sc in each of 3 sc, ch 4, turn.
Row 15: Sc in 2nd ch from hook, sc in each of next 2 ch, sc in each of 6 sc—9 sc. Ch 1, turn.
Rows 16-25: Sc in each sc across.
Row 26: Dec 1 sc at beg and end of row. To dec, pull up a lp in each of 2 sts, yo and through 3 lps on hook.
Rows 27-29: Sc in each sc across—7 sc.
Row 30: Repeat row 26—5 sc.
Row 31: Sc in each sc across.
Row 32: Repeat row 26—3 sc.
Row 33: Sc in each sc across.
Row 34: Dec 1 sc. Work 5 rows of 2 sc. End off.
SHOULDER, ARM AND HAND (make 2): Beg at neck edge, with green, ch 4.
Row 1: Sc in 2nd ch from hook and in each remaining ch—3 sc. Ch 1, turn each row.
Rows 2 and 3: Sc in each sc across.
Row 4: Sc in each sc, ch 3, turn (beg of arm).
Row 5: Sc in 2nd ch from hook and in next ch, sc in 3 sc, ch 3, turn.
Row 6: Sc in 2nd ch from hook and in next ch, sc in 5 sc—7 sc.
Rows 7-18: Sc in each sc across.
Row 19: Dec 1 sc at beg and end of row—5 sc. Cut green. Join red.
Rows 20-23: Sc in each sc across.
Row 24: Dec 1 sc in row—4 sc.
Row 25: Sc in each sc. End off.
HEAD: Beg at top of head, with pink, ch 2.
Rnd 1: 6 sc in 2nd ch from hook.
Rnd 2: * Sc in next sc, 2 sc in next sc, repeat from * around—9 sc.
Rnd 3: 2 sc in each sc around—18 sc.
Rnd 4: * 2 sc in next sc, sc in next sc, repeat from * around—27 sc.
Rnds 5-10: Sc in each sc around.
Rnd 11: Sc around, dec 3 sc in rnd.
Rnd 12: Sc in each sc around—24 sc.
Rnd 13: * Sc in next sc, dec 1 sc in next 2 sc, repeat from * around—16 sc.
Rnds 14-18: Sc in each sc around. End off.
CAP: With green, ch 30.
Row 1: Sc in 2nd ch from hook and in each ch across. Ch 1, turn each row.

Rows 2 and 3: Sc in each sc across—29 sc.
Row 4: Dec 4 sc evenly spaced across.
Row 5: Sc in each sc across—25 sc.
Row 6: Repeat row 4—21 sc.
Rows 7 and 8: Sc in each sc across.
Row 9: Repeat row 4—17 sc.
Rows 10 and 11: Sc in each sc across.
Row 12: Dec 3 sc evenly spaced across.
Rows 13-16: Sc in each sc across—14 sc.
Row 17: Repeat row 12—11 sc.
Rows 18-20: Sc in each sc across.
Row 21: Repeat row 12—8 sc.
Rows 22-25: Sc in each sc across.
Row 26: Repeat row 12—5 sc.
Rows 27-29: Sc in each sc across.
Row 30: Dec 2 sc in row—3 sc.
Rows 31 and 32: Sc in each sc across.
Pompon: With red, ch 5.
Row 1: Sc in 2nd ch from hook and in each remaining ch—4 sc. Work even for 4 more rows. End off. Gather edges of square, stuff with cotton and pull into a ball. Sew to tip of cap.
Cap Cuff: With red, ch 30. Work 2 rows of 29 sc. Sew around bottom edge of cap.
ASSEMBLE BODY: Fold body in half. Sew side between front and back edges of body with leg at fold. There will be a slight opening. Sew shoulder to front and back of body at top leaving an opening for neck. Twist 2 chenille sticks tog for arms. Insert through holes under shoulders. Stuff around stick with cotton and sew up arm seams. Twist 2 sticks tog for legs. Insert through holes at bottom of sides. Stuff around stick with cotton and sew up leg seams. Stuff body. Sew tops of legs and arms to body at holes. Stuff head; sew to neck opening.
EARS: With pink, ch 6. **Row 1:** Sc in 2nd ch from hook and in each remaining ch— 5 sc. Ch 1, turn.
Row 2: Sc in each of first 4 sc; turn.
Row 3: Sk first sc, sc in each of next 3 sc. End off. Sew to head.
FINISHING: Arm Cuffs: With red, ch 9. Work 2 rows of 8 sc. Sew to sleeves.
Leg Cuffs: With red, ch 10. Work as for arm cuffs on 9 sc. Sew to legs.
Thumbs: With red, ch 4. Sc in 2nd ch from hook and in each of 2 ch. End off. Sew in place.
Hair: Thread yellow double in needle. Take long straight sts from top of head, down around back of head, some shorter sts in front.
Features: Cut green eyes, black pupils, red mouth from felt. Glue in place.
Scarf: With red, ch 51. Work 3 rows of 50 sc. End off. Add fringe on both ends.

LOOPY STOCKINGS
Shown on page 106

SIZES: Santa, 14″ long; Elf, 12″ long.
MATERIALS: Knitting worsted, 5 ozs. white, 2 ozs. pink, 1 oz. red, for Santa; 3 ozs. red, 2 ozs. pink, 1 oz. green for Elf. Crochet hook size I. Felt scraps, red, blue, green. Clear buttons with black center,

for eyes, 2 for each stocking. Light cardboard. Chenille stick for Elf.

GAUGE: 4 sc = 1"; 5 rows = 1".

STOCKINGS: Directions are for Santa. Any changes for Elf are in parentheses. Cut pieces of cardboard 4" long; ⅝" wide for eyebrows and Santa's moustache, ¾" wide for Elf's beard, hair and moustache, ⅞" wide for Santa's beard and hair.

FRONT: Beg at lower edge with white (red) ch 31 (27).

Row 1: Sc in 2nd ch from hook and in each ch across—30 (26) sc. Ch 1, turn each row.

Row 2: Hold cardboard in back of work, even with top of work. Bring yarn down between work and cardboard and up in back, work sc in first sc (1 loop st made). Work another loop st in first sc, work 1 loop st in each sc across to last sc, work 2 loop sts in last sc—32 (28) loop sts.

Row 3: 2 sc in first st, sc in each st across, 2 sc in last st—34 (30) sc.

Row 4: Repeat row 2—36 (32) sts.

Row 5: Sc in each st across to last st, 2 sc in last st—1 inc at toe edge.

Row 6: Inc 1 loop st in first sc, loop st in each sc across.

Row 7: Repeat row 5—39 (35) sc.

Rows 8-14 (10): Work even for 7 (3) rows.

Row 15 (11): Sc in each st across to last 2 sts, pull up a lp in each of last 2 sts, yo and through 3 lps on hook—1 dec at toe edge.

Rows 16 (12)-23 (19): Dec 1 st at toe edge every row—30 (26) sc. End off. Turn. Sk 7 sc, join pink in next sc; ch 1, sc in same sc and in each of next 15 (12) sc. Join white (red) in next sc, work loop st in same sc and in each of last 6 (5) sc. Working pink face in sc and white (red) hair in loop st, work even for 28 (24) rows; when changing colors, work last sc of one color until there are 2 lps on hook, complete sc with next color. Change to white (green) only, ch 2. Sc in 2nd ch from hook, sc in each st across, ch 2, turn. Sc in 2nd ch from hook, sc in each sc across—25 (21) sc. Work 4 (2) rows even. End off.

BACK: Work as for Front, reversing shaping; toe edge is at beg of row 5.

Hat: Sk first sc on last row, join red (green) in next sc. Ch 1, sc in same sc and in each of next 22 (18) sc. Ch 1, turn. Work 2 rows even—23 (19) sc.

Next Row: Dec 1 st each side.

Next Row: Work even—21 (17) sc. Repeat last 2 rows 4 times—13 (9) sc. Work 10 (7) rows.

Next Row: Dec 1 st each side. Work 3 rows even. Repeat last 4 rows once—9 (5) sc.

Next Row: Dec 1 st each side. Work 7 rows even—7 (3) sc.

Next Row: Dec 1 st each side. Work 10 (7) rows even.

For Elf Only: Dec 1 st, work 1 sc. Work 1 row even. Dec to 1 sc. End off.

For Santa Only: Next Row: Dec 1 st each side. Work 5 rows even.

Next Row: Dec 1 st each side. Work 10 rows even. Dec 1 st, work 1 sc. Work 1 row even. Dec to 1 sc. End off.

FINISHING: Make a white (red) pompon; sew to tip of cap. Sew front and back tog. Make a red (green) ch 6" long for hanger. Sew ends to top at back seam

SANTA'S NOSE (make 2 pieces): With pink, ch 2.

Rnd 1: 6 sc in 2nd ch from hook.

Rnd 2: 2 sc in each sc around. Sew pieces tog, stuffing with yarn scraps. Sew to front edge of face.

ELF'S NOSE: With pink, ch 4.

Row 1: Sc in 2nd ch from hook and in next 2 ch. Ch 1, turn.

Row 2: Sc in each sc. Ch 6.

Row 3: Sc in 2nd ch from hook and in next 4 ch, sc in each of 3 sc. Ch 1, turn. Work 2 rows even. End off. Bend chenille stick in half and lay on nose; cut to fit. Stuff around with yarn scraps, sew up seam. Sew wide part to front edge of face.

ELF'S EAR (make 2): With pink, ch 4.

Row 1: Sc in 2nd ch from hook and in next 2 ch. Ch 1, turn each row.

Row 2: Work even—3 sc.

Row 3: Inc 1 sc at one end (back edge).

Rows 4-7: Work even—4 sc.

Row 8: Inc 1 sc at back edge, dec 1 sc at front edge.

Row 9: Work even.

Rows 10 and 11: Repeat rows 8 and 9.

Row 12: Work 2 sts tog twice—2 sc.

Row 13: Work even.

Row 14: Work 2 sts tog—1 sc.

Row 15: Work 1 sc. End off. Sew front edge to head at a slant so some hair shows between ear and face.

BROWS: With white (red), ch 10 (8). Work 1 row of loop st. End off.

SANTA'S MOUSTACHE: With white, ch 51. Loop st in 2nd ch from hook and in each ch across. Do not turn. Cut yarn; join in 12th st from beg of row, work another row of loop sts, end 12 sts from other end. Tack center to front seam. Sew to face with ends in a curve.

ELF'S MOUSTACHE: With red, ch 29. Work 1 row loop st. Sew on as for Santa.

Cut red felt strips for mouth; sew or glue on. Cut blue (green) felt eyes. Sew button to felt eye; sew or glue to face.

NORTH POLE TOTES
Shown on page 106

SIZE: 14" long.

MATERIALS: Knitting worsted, 3 ozs. white, 2 ozs. pink, 1 oz. red for Santa; 3 ozs. red, 2 ozs. pink, 2 ozs. green for Elf. Crochet hook size G. Felt scraps, red, blue, green. Shank-type buttons for eyes. Light cardboard. 6" chenille stick for Elf.

GAUGE: 4 sc = 1"; 5 rows = 1".

TOTES: Directions are for Santa; any changes for Elf are in parentheses. Cut cardboard strip 4" long and ⅝" wide.

FRONT: Beg at lower edge, with white (red), ch 15.

Row 1: Sc in 2nd ch from hook and in each remaining ch. Ch 1, turn each row.

Row 2: Hold cardboard strip in back of work, even with top of work. Bring yarn down between work and cardboard and up in back, work sc in first sc (1 loop st made). Work another loop st in first sc, work 1 loop st in each sc across to last sc, work 2 loop sts in last sc—16 loop sts.

Row 3: 2 sc in first st, sc in each st across, 2 sc in last st—18 sc.

Rows 4-6: Repeat row 2, 3 and 2—24 loop sts.

Rows 7-10: Work even.

Row 11: Sc in each of 10 sts. Turn.

Row 12: Sk 1 sc, loop st in 9 sc. Ch 1, turn.

Row 13: Sc in each of 8 sts. Turn.

Row 14: Sk 1 sc, loop st in 7 sc. Ch 1, turn. Continue in this way until 4 sts remain. Work 15 more rows on remaining 4 sts. End off. Sk 4 sts on last long row, join yarn with sc in next st, sc in each remaining 9 sts. Ch 1, turn. Work 2nd side to correspond to first side.

FACE: With pink, ch 5. Sc in 2nd ch from hook and in each remaining ch—4 sc. Working in sc, inc 1 st each side each row until there are 16 sc. Work 16 rows even. End off. Sew face into beard.

HAT: With white (green), sc in each of 24 sts across top. Work 5 more rows even in sc. For Santa only, change to red. Work 1 more row even. Dec 1 sc each side each row until there are 16 sc. Work 4 rows even.

Next Row: Dec 1 sc each side—14 sc. Work 4 rows even.

Next Row: Dec 1 sc each side—12 sc. Work 2 rows even. Repeat last 3 rows—10 sc.

Next Row: Dec 1 sc each side—8 sc. Work 1 row even. Repeat last 2 rows 3 times.

BACK: Work as for front through row 10. Continue to work in loop st pat on 24 sts until back measures same as front to top of face. Work hat same as for front.

FINISHING: Sew front and back tog below hat. Sew hat points tog at top.

Pompon: With white (red), ch 13. Sc in 2nd ch from hook and in each ch across. Work 11 more rows on 12 sc. Gather piece around edges, stuffing with yarn scraps; pull up into a ball; sew to hat tip.

Brows: With white (red), ch 8. Work 1 row of loop st using slightly narrower cardboard. Sew to face.

Santa's Moustache: With white, ch 22. Work as for brows.

Santa's Nose: With pink, ch 2. Work 6 sc in 2nd ch from hook. Work 2 sc in each sc around—12 sc. Gather edge, pull up into a ball; sew on.

Elf's Nose: With pink, ch 9. Sc in 2nd ch from hook and each remaining ch. Ch 1, turn. Work 1 row even. On next row, work 4 sc only. End off. Roll piece around a piece of chenille stick; sew up long seam, stuffing nose with yarn scraps. Cut chenille stick longer than nose, turn under end to fit inside wide end of nose; sew nose to face.

Sew buttons to felt eyes; sew or glue eyes to face. Sew on red felt mouth.

BEANBAG ELF
Shown on page 107

SIZE: About 10″ tall.
MATERIALS: Knitting worsted, 1 oz. green (MC), small amounts pink, red, white, brown, black. Double-pointed needles No. 5. Large dried beans, ½ to ¾ cup. Cotton for stuffing.
GAUGE: 11 sts = 2″.
ELF: BODY, FACE AND HAT: With MC, cast on 36 sts; divide evenly on 3 dp needles. Join; k 8 rnds.
Rnd 9: K, dec 1 st at beg of each needle, k 4 rnds even. Repeat last 5 rnds twice—27 sts.
Rnd 24: Repeat rnd 9—24 sts. Cut MC.
Rnds 25-34: With pink, k around. Cut pink.
Rnd 35: With MC, k 1 rnd. Change to striped pat of 3 rnds white, 2 rnds red, 2 rnds white, 1 rnd MC. Repeat these 8 rnds.
Rnd 36: K around.
Rnd 37: Dec 1 st at beg of each needle. K 3 rnds even—21 sts.
Rnd 41: Repeat rnd 37—18 sts. K 4 rnds.
Rnd 46: Repeat rnd 37—15 sts. K 3 rnds. Repeat last 4 rnds 3 times—6 sts.
Next Rnd: K 2 tog 3 times. Cut yarn, draw through sts, pull up and fasten.
ARMS: With white, cast on 9 sts; divide on 3 needles. Join, k around in striped pat for 16 rnds. Change to pink, k 4 rnds.
Next Rnd: Dec 1 st at beg of each needle. Cut yarn, draw through sts, pull up and fasten.
LEGS: With white, cast on 12 sts; divide evenly on 3 needles. Join, work in striped pat for 19 rnds. Change to red. K 2 rnds.
Heel: Rnd 22: (K 6, turn; p 6, turn) twice. Working on all sts, k 7 rnds.
Dec Rnd: Dec 1 st at beg of each needle. Work 1 rnd even. Repeat last 2 rnds once. Repeat dec rnd. Work 5 rnds even—3 sts. Cut yarn, run through sts, pull up. Sew tip over to front of foot.
RIGHT EAR: With pink and two needles, cast on 5 sts. K 1 row, p 1 row.
Row 3: Inc 1 st in first st, k across. P 1 row. Repeat row 3. Bind off.
LEFT EAR: Work as for right ear, inc at end of rows.

Sew cast-on edge of ear to side of face.
BEARD: Thread long piece of brown yarn in needle. Beg at hat in front of ear, * wind yarn 3 times around two

fingers tightly. Take st in face going through loops on finger; knot yarn around loops. Take st in face bringing needle up ⅜″ away. Repeat from * around face and chin.

Embroider green eyes, black pupils, red nose and mouth.
Pompon: Wind red yarn around index finger 50 times. Tie one end; cut other end. Trim; sew to hat.

STOCKING TRIO
Shown on page 107

SIZE: About 17″ long.
MATERIALS: Knitting worsted weight yarn: 2 ozs. white, 2 ozs. red, small amounts of black and green for Snowman Stocking; 2 ozs. white, 2 ozs. green, small amounts of red, black and pink for Santa Stocking; 4 ozs. white, 1 oz. brown, small amount of black for Gingerbread Boy Stocking. Crochet hook size I. Scrap of red felt. Glue.
GAUGE: 4 sc = 1″; 5 rows = 1″.
STOCKING (make 2 pieces): Beg at bottom, with white, ch 36.
Row 1: Sc in 2nd ch from hook and in each ch across—35 sc. Ch 1, turn each row.
Row 2: 2 sc in first sc, sc in each sc across to last st, 2 sc in last sc—37 sc.
Rows 3 and 4: Repeat row 2—41 sc.
Row 5: 2 sc in first sc (toe), sc in each sc across—42 sc.
Row 6: Sc in each sc to last sc, 2 sc in last sc—43 sc.
Row 7: Repeat row 5—44 sc.
Rows 8-14: Work even.
Rows 15-23: Dec 1 st at toe end every row (to dec, pull up a lp in each of 2 sc, yo and through 3 lps on hook)—35 sc.
Row 24: Sc in each of 23 sc. Ch 1, turn.
Row 25: Work even on 23 sc. For Snowman Stocking, change to red; for Santa stocking, change to green; Work even for 53 rows. End off.
SNOWMAN: Head: With white, ch 2.
Rnd 1: 6 sc in 2nd ch from hook.
Rnd 2: 2 sc in each sc—12 sc.
Rnd 3: * Sc in next sc, 2 sc in next sc, repeat from * around—18 sc.
Rnd 4: Sc in each sc around. End off.
Body: With white, ch 5.
Rnd 1: Sc in 2nd ch from hook, sc in each of next 2 ch, 3 sc in last ch. Working along opposite side of ch, sc in each of next 2 ch, 2 sc in next ch.
Rnd 2: 2 sc in first sc, sc in each of next 3 sc, 3 sc in next sc, sc in each of next 4 sc, 2 sc in last sc.
Rnd 3: 2 sc in first sc, sc in each of 5 sc, 2 sc in each of next 2 sc, sc in each of 5 sc, 2 sc in last sc.
Rnd 4: (3 sc in next sc, sc in each of 8 sc) twice—22 sc.
Rnd 5: (2 sc in each of 3 sc, sc in each of 8 sc) twice. Work sc in each of next 5 sc

for neck edge; ch 1, turn; work sc in 4 sc. End off.
ARMS: Work as for Body through rnd 1. End off.

Sew pieces to front stocking piece, wrong side out, padding lightly with yarn or cotton.
SCARF: With green, ch 8.
Row 1: Sc in 2nd ch from hook and in each remaining ch. Ch 4, turn.
Row 2: Sc in 2nd ch from hook and in next 2 ch, sc in 7 sc. End off. Sew narrow part to neck. Fringe end.
HAT: Brim: With black, ch 11. Work 1 row of 10 sc. End off.
Top: With black, ch 7. Work 4 rows of 6 sc. End off. Sew above head, padding with yarn scraps; sew brim in place.
EYES: With black, ch 2. Sc in 2nd ch from hook. Sew into round shape, run the 2 loose ends through appliqué and tie securely to wrong side of stocking.

Make nose same as eyes.

Make 2 buttons like eyes but work 2 sc in 2nd ch from hook. Glue on red felt mouth.
FINISHING: Sew front and back of stocking tog. Join white at top back, work 3 rnds of sc around top. For hanger, ch 25. Work 1 row sc in ch. Sew ends inside at back seam.

SANTA: BODY: With white, ch 11.
Row 1: Sc in 2nd ch from hook and in each ch across—10 sc. Change to red.
Row 2: Sc in first 2 sc, dec 1 sc (to dec, pull up a lp in each of 2 sc, yo and through 3 lps on hook), sc in each sc across—9 sc. Ch 1, turn each row.
Row 3: Repeat row 2—8 sc.
Rows 4 and 5: Work even.
Row 6: Dec 1 sc each side—6 sc. Work 5 rows even. End off.
HEAD AND HAT: With pink, ch 5. Sc in 2nd ch from hook and in each remaining ch. Work 5 more rows of 4 sc. Change to white, work 2 rows even. Change to red, work 1 row even. Dec 1 sc on next row; work 3 rows even. Dec 1 sc on next row; work 5 rows even. Dec to 1 sc. Work 1 row. End off.
Pompon: With white, ch 2. Work 4 sc in 2nd ch from hook. Sew into a ball, sew to tip of hat.
LEGS: With black, ch 5, sc in 2nd ch from hook and in each remaining ch. Ch 1, turn. Sc in 2 sc; ch 1, turn each row. Work 1 row even; change to white. Work 2 rows even; change to red. Work 3 rows even. End off. For 2nd leg, work as for first leg through first row. Turn. Sl st in each of 2 sc, sc in each of last 2 sc. Ch 1, turn. Sc in 2 sc. Ch 1, turn. Finish as for first leg.
ARMS: With black, ch 3. Work 2 rows on 2 sc. Change to white, work 2 rows even. Change to red, work 7 rows even.
FINISHING: Sew pieces to front piece of stocking, padding head, body, arms and legs lightly. Have tops of legs under body. Leave cap and mittens free. Sew

white straight sts for hair and moustache, loops for beard. Glue on felt mouth. Embroider black eyes, or glue on felt pieces. Finish stocking as for Snowman Stocking.

GINGERBREAD BOY: HEAD: With brown, ch 2.

Rnd 1: 6 sc in 2nd ch from hook.

Rnd 2: 2 sc in each sc around.

Rnd 3: Sc in each sc—12 sc.

Rnd 4: 2 sc in each sc around.

Rnd 5: Sc in each sc—24 sc. End off.

BODY: With brown, ch 7.

Rnd 1: Sc in 2nd ch from hook and in next 4 ch, 3 sc in last ch. Working on opposite side of starting ch, sc in 4 ch, 2 sc in same ch with first sc. Work around in sc for 4 more rnds, inc 3 sc evenly spaced at each end each rnd—38 sc. End off.

LEGS AND ARMS: With brown, ch 5. Work around as for body, inc 3 sc each rnd for 2 rnds. End off.

FEET: Work as for leg for 1 rnd. End off.

FINISHING: Sew pieces of Gingerbread Boy, wrong side out, to stocking, padding lightly. Work white chain st around figures. Make eyes, nose, buttons same as for Snowman. Glue on red felt strip for mouth. Sew front and back of stocking tog. Join brown at top back, work 5 rnds of sc around top, white chain st around center of cuff.

GRANNY STOCKING
Shown on page 107

SIZE: 20″ long.

MATERIALS: Knitting worsted, 4 ozs. green, 2 ozs. red, 1 oz. white. Crochet hook size I or J.

GAUGE: Each motif is 4″ square.

FRONT: MOTIF (make 7): With green, ch 4. Sl st in first ch to form ring.

Rnd 1: Ch 3 (counts as 1 dc), 2 dc in ring, ch 1, (3 dc in ring, ch 1) 3 times. Join to top of ch 3 with sl st. End off.

Rnd 2: Join white in any ch-1 sp, ch 3, 2 dc in sp, ch 1, 3 dc in same sp, (3 dc, ch 1, 3 dc in next sp) 3 times. Join to top of ch 3. End off.

Rnd 3: Join red in any ch-1 sp, ch 3, 2 dc in sp, ch 1, 3 dc in same sp, (3 dc in next sp between groups of 3 dc, 3 dc, ch 1, 3 dc in next ch-1 sp) 3 times, 3 dc in next sp between groups of 3 dc. Join to top of ch 3. End off.

Sew 5 motifs tog in a row, sewing through back lps of dc's. Sew last 2 motifs in a row and to side of last motif to form foot.

BORDER: Join green in ch-1 sp at top left corner, ch 3, 2 dc in sp, ch 1, 3 dc in same sp; working down back edge * (3 dc in next sp) twice, 3 dc in seam between motifs, repeat from * 3 times, (3 dc in next sp) twice, work corner as before in heel, work as for border on back across bottom of foot, 3 dc in ch-1 sp at corner,

(3 dc in next sp) twice, 3 dc in ch-1 sp at top corner of toe, work as for border on back across foot motifs to inner corner, work 1 dc in inner corner, work as for border on back up front, work corner at top, work across top; join to top of ch 3. End off.

Next Row: Join green in sp after 3 dc in corner at top of toe, sc in same sp, (3 dc in next sp) 4 times, dc in dc at inner corner, (3 dc in next sp) 5 times, (3 tr in next sp) 6 times, 3 tr, ch 1, 3 dc in top corner, (3 dc in next sp) 3 times, 3 dc, ch 1, 3 tr in next corner, (3 tr in next sp) 6 times, (3 dc in next sp) 6 times, sc in next sp. End off.

BACK: Work as for front, reversing position of foot motifs and working border to correspond to front.

FINISHING: With red, ch 8 for hanger; working through both thicknesses, with front piece toward you, sc front and back of stocking tog down back, around foot and up front, working 1 sc in each st; end at top of front edge. End off. Sew end of hanger in place.

MR. & MRS. SANTA
Shown on pages 108 and 109

SIZES: 10″, 18″, 35″ tall.

MR. & MRS. SANTA (10″ tall).

MATERIALS: Cardinal red knitting worsted, 8 ozs. winter white sport yarn, 1 oz. White bulky orlon yarn for beard and hair, 1 oz. Knitting needles: 1 pr. No. 5; 1 set dp needles No. 5. White fake fur, 18″ x 6″. Small pieces of black felt. 2″ styrofoam ball for each head. Red and brown embroidery floss. Stuffing. Fine wire for glasses. Stiff wire for standing figures. Metal brush.

GAUGE: 5 sts = 1″.

SANTA HEAD: With white sport yarn and dp needles, cast on 5 sts; divide on 3 needles. Join; k 1 rnd.

Rnd 2: Inc 1 st in each st—10 sts. K 1 rnd.

Rnd 4: Inc 1 st in each st—20 sts. K 2 rnds.

Rnd 7: (K 4, inc 1 st in next st) 4 times —24 sts. K 10 rnds or long enough to fit over 2″ styrofoam ball. Bind off (neck edge). Put on ball; gather sts tog tightly; fasten off.

HAT: With red, cast on 21 sts; divide on 3 dp needles. Join; k even for 1″.

First Dec Rnd: (K 5, k 2 tog) 3 times.

Rnds 2-5: K.

Rnd 6: (K 4, k 2 tog) 3 times.

Rnds 7-10: K.

Rnd 11: (K 3, k 2 tog) 3 times.

Rnds 12-15: K.

Rnd 16: (K 2, k 2 tog) 3 times.

Rnds 17-20: K

Rnd 21: (K 1, k 2 tog) 3 times.

Rnds 22-25: K.

Rnd 26: (K 2 tog) 3 times.

Rnds 27 and 28: K. Draw remaining sts tog tightly; fasten off.

BODY: BACK: With red and 2 needles, cast on 13 sts. Work in stockinette st (k 1 row, p 1 row) for 10 rows. Dec 1 st each side of next row. P 1 row. Cast on 10 sts at end of next 2 rows—33 sts. Work even for 5 rows. Bind off 10 sts at beg of next 2 rows, 2 sts at beg of next 2 rows. Work 2 rows even. Bind off 9 sts for back of neck.

FRONT: Work as for back but cast on and bind off 7 sts each side for arms, instead of 10 sts.

PANTS: LEFT LEG: With red, cast on 10 sts. Beg with p row, work even for 11 rows. Mark last row for crotch.

Row 12: Dec 1 st at end of row (front edge).

Row 13: P.

Shape Back: Row 14: K 5, turn.

Row 15: Sl 1, p to end.

Row 16: K 4, turn.

Row 17: Repeat row 15.

Row 18: K 3, turn.

Row 19: Repeat row 15.

Row 20: K 2, turn.

Row 21: Repeat row 15. Work even on all 9 sts for 4 rows. Bind off.

RIGHT LEG: Work as for left leg, beg with a k row. Wherever directions say "k", p; wherever directions say "p", k.

FINISHING: Embroider brown eyes and nose, red mouth. Take a few short strands of bulky yarn, tie securely at center, brush out and attach over mouth for mustache. Thread needle with bulky yarn. Attach strands to face and around lower part of head. Brush and trim to form beard and hair. Add eyebrows. Rouge cheeks under eyes. Sew hat firmly in place. Trim hat with ½″ strips of fur; sew ball of fur to end of hat.

Sew front and back of body tog, leaving top and bottom open. Stuff firmly. Sew each leg to marker, then sew back and front seams to make pants. Stuff. Sew top and bottom tog, stuffing as you sew parts tog to make body firm. Cut 4 boot pieces and 4 mitten pieces from felt, using patterns. Sew boot pieces tog, turn. Stuff firmly to 1″ from top. Pull boots on legs; sew on. Trim with ½″ fur strips. Sew mitten pieces tog; do not turn. Stuff; sew to end of arm. Trim with fur. Trim front and bottom of "jacket" with 1″ strips of fur. Attach head, adding stuffing to make neck firm.

Attach 9″ piece of wire, shaped into horseshoe to bottom of boots to help figure stand.

MRS. SANTA: HEAD: Same as Santa.

HAT: With red and dp needles, cast on 18 sts; divide on 3 needles. Join; k 2 rnds.

Rnd 3: (K 2, inc in next st) 6 times.

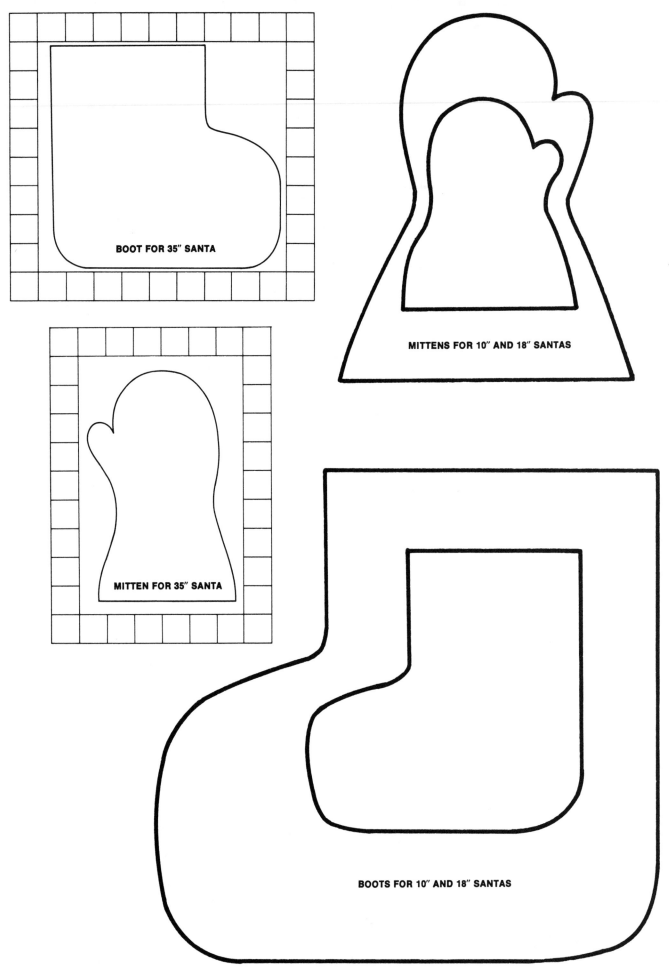

BOOT FOR 35" SANTA

MITTENS FOR 10" AND 18" SANTAS

MITTEN FOR 35" SANTA

BOOTS FOR 10" AND 18" SANTAS

Rnd 4: P.

Rnd 5: K.

Rnd 6: (K 4, k 2 tog) 4 times.

Rnd 7: K.

Rnd 8: (K 3, k 2 tog) 4 times.

Rnd 9: (K 2, k 2 tog) 4 times.

Rnd 10: (K 1, k 2 tog) 4 times.

Rnd 11: (K 2 tog) 4 times; draw remaining sts tog; end off.

BODY: BACK: With red and 2 needles, cast on 12 sts. Work even in stockinette st for 14 rows. Dec 1 st each side of next row. Work 1 row even. Cast on 10 sts at end of next 2 rows. Work 5 rows even. Bind off 10 sts at beg of next 2 rows, 2 sts at beg of next 2 rows. Work on remaining 6 sts for 2 rows. Bind off for back of neck.

FRONT: With red and 2 needles, cast on 8 sts. Work even for 12 rows.

Row 13: (K 2, inc in next st) twice, k 2.

Row 14: P.

Row 15: K 2 tog, inc in next 2 sts, k 2, inc in next 2 sts, k 2 tog.

Row 16: P. Cast on 7 sts at end of next 2 rows for arms. Work even for 5 rows. Bind off 7 sts at beg of next 2 rows, 2 sts at beg of next 2 rows. Work on remaining sts for neck for 2 rows. Bind off.

SKIRT: With red and 2 needles, cast on 60 sts. Work in stockinette st for 3½″. Bind off.

FINISHING: Embroider features as for Santa. For hair, wind bulky yarn around 2″ width of 4″ length of cardboard. Wind smoothly. Slip off cardboard; stitch down center of windings to a piece of ribbon. Cut loops each side; brush out. Sew to center of head. Shape into hair style. Use combings from brushing out "hair" to twist into rope to wind into bun for back of head. Tack hair in place with thread where needed. Rouge cheeks. Make glasses out of fine wire. Put ball of fur on top of hat; sew hat to head.

Sew back and front tog, leaving open only at top. Stuff firmly. Make mittens, sew on and trim as for Santa. Sew skirt seam. Run gathering yarn around top. Sew 1″ strip of fur to bottom edge. Gather skirt; sew to body. Sew narrow strip of fur around waist over seam and around neck for collar. Sew small round fur pieces to front for buttons.

Make a stand of wire: a ring to fit around waist under skirt, a larger ring for bottom of stand and a straight piece each side, connecting rings. Or, use a cardboard cone.

MR. & MRS. SANTA (18″ tall).

MATERIALS: Cardinal red knitting worsted, 12 ozs. Winter white sport yarn, 2 ozs. White bulky orlon yarn for beard and hair, 2 ozs. Knitting nee-

dles: 1 pr. No. 5; 1 set dp needles No. 5. White fake fur, 36″ wide, ¼ yd. Black felt, ⅛ yd. 3″ styrofoam ball for each head. Red and brown embroidery floss. Stuffing. Fine wire for glasses. Stiff wire for standing Mrs. Santa. Metal brush.

GAUGE: 5 sts = 1″.

SANTA: HEAD: With white sport yarn and dp needles, cast on 9 sts; divide on 3 needles. Join, k 1 rnd.

Rnd 2: Inc 1 st in each st around. K 1 rnd.

Rnd 4: Repeat rnd 2—36 sts. K 2 rnds.

Rnd 7: (K 5, inc 1 st in next st) 6 times —42 sts. K 15 rnds. Put on 3″ styrofoam ball, draw all sts tog tightly; fasten off.

HAT: With red and dp needles, cast on 36 sts. Divide on 3 needles. Join, work even for 2″.

First Dec Rnd: (K 7, k 2 tog) 4 times.

Rnds 2-6: K.

Rnd 7: (K 6, k 2 tog) 4 times.

Rnds 8-12: K.

Rnd 13: (K 5, k 2 tog) 4 times.

Rnds 14-18: K.

Rnd 19: (K 4, k 2 tog) 4 times.

Rnds 20-24: K.

Rnd 25: (K 3, k 2 tog) 4 times.

Rnds 26-28: K.

Rnd 29: (K 2, k 2 tog) 4 times.

Rnds 30-34: K.

Rnd 35: (K 1, k 2 tog) 4 times.

Rnds 36-40: K.

Rnd 41: (K 2 tog) 4 times.

Rnds 42-44: K. Draw remaining sts tog; fasten off.

BODY: BACK: With red and 2 needles, cast on 25 sts. Work in stockinette st for 20 rows. Dec 1 st each side every other row twice. Cast on 15 sts at end of next 2 rows for arms. Work even for 9 rows. Bind off 15 sts at beg of next 2 rows, 5 sts at beg of next 2 rows. Work remaining sts for neck for 3 rows. Bind off.

FRONT: Work as for back, but cast on and bind off 11 sts for arms.

PANTS: LEFT LEG: With red, cast on 20 sts. Work in stockinette st for 22 rows. Mark last row for crotch.

Row 23: Dec 1 st at end of row (front edge).

Row 24: P.

Row 25: Repeat row 23. Work even for 3 rows.

Shape Back: Row 29: K 9, turn.

Row 30: Sl 1, p to end.

Row 31: K 8, turn.

Row 32: Sl 1, p to end.

Row 33: K 7, turn.

Row 34: Sl 1, p to end.

Row 35: K 6, turn.

Row 36: Sl 1, p to end.

Row 37: K 5, turn.

Row 38: Sl 1, p to end.

Row 39: K 4, turn.

Row 40: P across. Work 6 rows even. Bind off.

RIGHT LEG: Work as for left leg, reversing shaping; dec 1 st at beg of row 23 for front edge. In shaping back, substitute "k" for "p" and "p" for "k".

FINISHING: Finish as for 10″ Santa with these exceptions: Trim hat with 1″ strip of fur, boots and cuffs with 1½″ strips of fur, suit with 2″ strips of fur.

MRS. SANTA: HEAD: Same as Santa.

HAT: With red and dp needles, cast on 36 sts; divide on 3 needles. Join, k 3 rnds.

Rnd 4: (K 2, inc in next st) 12 times.

Rnd 5: P.

Rnds 6 and 7: K.

Rnd 8: (K 6, k 2 tog) 6 times.

Rnd 9: K.

Rnd 10: (K 5, k 2 tog) 6 times.

Rnd 11: K.

Rnd 12: (K 4, k 2 tog) 6 times.

Rnd 13: K.

Rnd 14: (K 3, k 2 tog) 6 times.

Rnd 15: (K 2, k 2 tog) 6 times.

Rnd 16: (K 1, k 2 tog) 6 times.

Rnd 17: (K 2 tog) 6 times. Draw remaining sts tog; fasten off.

BODY: BACK: With red and 2 needles, cast on 16 sts. Work in stockinette st for 16 rows.

Row 17: Inc 1 st each side.

Row 18: P.

Row 19: Inc 1 st each side.

Rows 20-24: Work even.

Row 25: Dec 1 st each side.

Row 26: P. Cast on 15 sts at end of next 2 rows for arms. Work even for 9 rows. Bind off 15 sts at beg of next 2 rows, 5 sts at beg of next 2 rows. Work even on remaining neck sts for 3 rows. Bind off.

FRONT: Work as for back through row 16.

Row 17: K 5, inc in next st, k 4, inc in next st, k 5.

Row 18 and All Even Rows: P.

Row 19: K 5, inc in next 2 sts, k 4, inc in next 2 sts, k 5.

Row 21: K 2 tog, k 3, inc in next st, k 2, inc in next st, k 4, inc in next st, k 2, inc in next st, k 3, k 2 tog.

Rows 23 and 25: Dec 1 st each side.

Row 26: P. Cast on 11 sts at end of next 2 rows for arms. Work even for 9 rows. Bind off 11 sts at beg of next 2 rows, 5 sts at beg of next 2 rows. Work on remaining neck sts for 3 rows. Bind off.

SKIRT: With red and 2 needles, cast on 115 sts. Work even in stockinette st for 5½″. Bind off.

FINISHING: Finish as for 10″ Mrs. Santa with these exceptions: For hair, wind bulky yarn around 3″ width of 5″ length of cardboard. Sew 2″ strip of fur to bottom edge of skirt.

MR. & MRS. SANTA (35″ tall).

MATERIALS: Cardinal red knitting worsted, 8 4-oz. skeins. Winter white sport yarn, 6 ozs. White bulky orlon yarn for beard and hair, 4 ozs. Knitting needles: 1 pr. No. 5; 1 set dp needles No. 5. White fake fur, 36″ wide, ½ yd. Black felt, 18″ x 36″. 6″ styrofoam ball for each head. Red and brown embroidery floss. Stuffing. Fine wire for glasses. Metal stand for Santa. Plastic or cardboard cone-shaped stand for Mrs. Santa, about 14″ high, 6″ diameter at top. Metal brush.

GAUGE: 5 sts = 1″.

SANTA: HEAD: With white sport yarn and dp needles, cast on 18 sts; divide on 3 needles. Join; k 1 rnd.

Rnd 2: Inc 1 st in each st.

Rnds 3 and 4: K around.

Rnd 5: Inc 1 st in each st.

Rnds 6-9: K around—72 sts.

Rnd 10: (K 5, inc 1 st in next st) 12 times—84 sts. K 28 rnds even. Put on 6″ styrofoam ball; draw sts tog tightly; fasten off.

HAT: With red, cast on 70 sts. Divide on 3 dp needles. Join; k around for 3½″.

First Dec Rnd: (K 5, k 2 tog) 10 times. K 16 rnds even.

2nd Dec Rnd: (K 4, k 2 tog) 10 times. K 16 rnds even.

3rd Dec Rnd: (K 3, k 2 tog) 10 times. K 16 rnds even.

4th Dec Rnd: (K 2, k 2 tog) 10 times. K 16 rnds even.

5th Dec Rnd: (K 1, k 2 tog) 10 times. K 8 rnds even. (K 2 tog) 10 times. K 8 rnds. (K 2 tog) 5 times. Draw remaining sts tog; fasten off.

BODY: BACK: With red and 2 needles, cast on 50 sts. Work in stockinette st for 42 rows. Dec 1 st each side of next row. Work 1 row even. Repeat last 2 rows 3 times more—42 sts. Cast on 30 sts at end of next 2 rows for arms. Work even on 102 sts for 19 rows. Bind off 30 sts at beg of next 2 rows, 10 sts at beg of next 2 rows. Work remaining 22 sts for neck for 4 rows. Bind off.

FRONT: Work as for back, but cast on and bind off 22 sts for arms.

PANTS: LEFT LEG: With red, cast on 35 sts. Work even in stockinette st for 6″, end p row. Mark last row for crotch. Dec 1 st at end of next row (front edge). P 1 row. Repeat dec row once—33 sts. Work even for 3½″ from marker; end p row.

Shape Back: Row 1: K 25, turn.

Row 2: Sl 1, p to end.

Row 3: K 22, turn.

Row 4: Sl 1, p to end.

Row 5: K 19, turn.

Row 6: Sl 1, p to end.

Row 7: K 15, turn.

Row 8: Sl 1, p to end.

Row 9: K 10, turn.

Row 10: Sl 1, p to end.

Row 11: K 6, turn.

Row 12: Sl 1, p to end. Work 6 rows even on all sts. Bind off.

RIGHT LEG: Work as for left leg, reversing shaping: dec 1 st at beg of k rows twice for front edge. In shaping back substitute "k" for "p" and "p" for "k".

FINISHING: Finish as for 10″ Santa with these exceptions: Trim hat with 2″ strip of fur. Enlarge patterns for boots and mittens by copying on paper ruled in 1″ squares. Trim boots and cuffs with 2½″ strips of fur; suit with 4″ strips of fur.

MRS. SANTA: HEAD: Same as Santa.

HAT: With red and dp needles, cast on 72 sts; divide on 3 needles. Join, work in k 1, p 1 ribbing for 5 rows.

Rnd 6: (K 2, inc 1 st in next st) 24 times.

Rnds 7-9: K around, inc 2 sts in last rnd.

Rnd 10: P around—98 sts.

Rnd 11: (K 12, k 2 tog) 7 times.

Rnd 12: K.

Rnd 13: (K 11, k 2 tog) 7 times.

Rnd 14: K.

Rnd 15: (K 10, k 2 tog) 7 times.

Rnd 16: K.

Rnd 17: (K 9, k 2 tog) 7 times.

Rnd 18: K.

Rnd 19: (K 8, k 2 tog) 7 times.

Rnd 20: (K 7, k 2 tog) 7 times.

Rnd 21: (K 6, k 2 tog) 7 times.

Rnd 22: (K 5, k 2 tog) 7 times.

Rnd 23: (K 4, k 2 tog) 7 times.

Rnd 24: (K 3, k 2 tog) 7 times.

Rnd 25: (K 2, k 2 tog) 7 times.

Rnd 26: (K 1, k 2 tog) 7 times.

Rnd 27: (K 2 tog) 7 times. Draw remaining sts tog tightly; fasten off.

BODY: BACK: With red and 2 needles, cast on 32 sts. Work even for 34 rows. Inc 1 st each side of next row. Work 1 row even. Repeat last 2 rows 3 more times. Dec 1 st each side of next row. Work 1 row even. Repeat last 2 rows 3 more times. Cast on 30 sts at end of next 2 rows. Work even for 19 rows. Bind off 30 sts at beg of next 2 rows, 10 sts at beg of next 2 rows. Work even on remaining 12 sts for neck for 6 rows. Bind off.

FRONT: Work as for back through row 34.

Row 35: K 10, put marker on needle, inc in next 2 sts, put marker on needle, k 8, put marker on needle, inc in next 2 sts, put marker on needle, k 10.

Row 36 and All Even Rows: P.

Row 37: K 10, sl marker, inc in next st, k across to next marker, inc in st before marker, sl marker, k 8, sl marker, inc in next st, k to next marker, inc in st before marker, sl marker, k 10.

Rows 39 and 41: Repeat row 37.

Row 43: K 2 tog, k 8, inc after and before markers, k 8, inc after and before markers, k 8, k 2 tog.

Row 45: K 2 tog, k 7, inc after and before markers, k 8, inc after and before markers, k 7, k 2 tog.

Row 47: K 2 tog, k to last 2 sts, k 2 tog.

Row 49: Repeat row 47.

Row 50: P. Cast on 22 sts at end of next 2 rows for arms. Work even for 19 rows. Bind off 22 sts at beg of next 2 rows, 10 sts at beg of next 2 rows. Work even on remaining sts for 6 rows. Bind off.

SKIRT: With red and 2 needles, cast on 230 sts. Work even in stockinette st for 11½″. Bind off.

FINISHING: Finish as for 10″ Mrs. Santa with these exceptions: For hair, wind bulky yarn around 6″ width of 9″ length of cardboard. Sew 4″ strip of fur around bottom edge of skirt. Sew 2″ strips of fur around waist and sleeve ends. Make collar from 1½″ strip.

CROCHETED CRECHE
Shown on pages 110 and 111

SIZE: Figures about 7″ high.

MATERIALS: Knitting worsted in various colors for clothes, hair, sheep. Knitting and crochet cotton, ecru, and brown for heads and arms only. Steel crochet hook No. 4. Aluminum or plastic crochet hook size E. Chenille sticks 12″ long. Cotton for stuffing. Embroidery floss for features. Beads from old jewelry. Fabric paint. Black glass headed pins. All-purpose glue. Sheet of Styrofoam® ½″ thick. Gold paper.

GAUGE: 6 sc = 1″ (knitting and crochet cotton, double); 4 sc = 1″ (knitting worsted).

FIGURES (all figures except the Baby):

HEAD: Using knitting and crochet cotton double and No. 4 hook, ch 2. **Rnd 1:** 6 sc in 2nd ch from hook.

Rnd 2: 2 sc in each sc around.

Rnd 3: * Sc in next sc, 2 sc in next sc, repeat from * around—18 sc.

Rnd 4: Sc in each sc around.

Rnd 5: * Sc in each of 2 sc, 2 sc in next sc, repeat from * around—24 sc.

Rnds 6-11: Sc in each sc around.

Rnd 12: * Sc in each of 4 sc, pull up a lp in each of next 2 sc, yo and through 3 lps on hook (1 dec), repeat from * around—20 sc.

Rnd 13: Sc in each of 6 sc, dec 1 sc 4 times, sc in 6 sc—16 sc.

Rnd 14: Dec 1 sc, sc in each of 12 sc, dec 1 sc.

Rnd 15: Sc in each sc around. End off.

ARM AND HAND (make 2): Using cotton double and No. 4 hook, ch 6, sl st in first ch to form ring.

Rnds 1-5: Sc in each ch around, then sc in each sc around.

Rnd 6: (Sc in each of next 2 sc, 2 sc in next sc) twice—8 sc.

Rnds 7-11: Sc in each sc around.

Rnd 12: (Dec over next 2 sc) 4 times. End off.

ROBE: With knitting worsted and size E hook, ch 33, sl st in first ch to form ring.

Rnds 1-3: Sc in each ch around, then sc in each sc around—33 sc.

Rnd 4: Dec 3 sc evenly spaced—30 sc.

Rnds 5-7: Sc in each sc around.

Rnd 8: Dec 5 sc evenly spaced—25 sc.

Rnds 9-11: Sc in each sc around.

Rnd 12: Dec 5 sc evenly spaced—20 sc.

Rnds 13-17: Sc in each sc around.

Rnd 18: Dec 5 sc evenly spaced—15 sc.

Rnds 19-21: Sc in each sc around.

Rnd 22: Dec 5 sc evenly spaced—10 sc.

Rnd 23: Sc in each sc around. End off.

SLEEVES AND SHOULDERS: With knitting worsted and size E hook, ch 10, sl st in first ch to form ring.

Rnds 1-10: Sc in each ch around, then sc in each sc around.

Rnd 11: Dec 2 sc in rnd.

Rnds 12 and 13: Sc in each sc around (end of one sleeve). At end of rnd 13, ch 1, turn.

Row 14: Sc in 3 sc, ch 1, turn.

Rows 15-19: Repeat row 14. At end of row 19, ch 5, sl st to beg of row 19.

Rnd 20: Sc in each sc and ch around—8 sc. Work 1 rnd even. On next rnd, inc to 10 sc. Work 10 rnds even. End off.

TO VARY FIGURES: All figures have bands of crochet on bottom of robes. Use sc or dc bands of same color as robe or different colors to decorate robes and vary heights of figures. Sleeves can have edges or tops of different colors.

TO ASSEMBLE FIGURES: Fold 12″ chenille stick in half, insert fold end in head. Stuff head. Sew head to center of shoulders. Slip robe over chenille stick; sew around sleeves and shoulders, attaching to robe. For arms, cut 9″ piece of chenille stick; run through sleeves. Turn over ends to desired length. Slip hands over ends. Stuff figures lightly with cotton.

To make figures kneel, bend body wire. For standing figures, cut oval of styrofoam to fit bottom of robe, stretch bottom of robe over oval.

Trim robes with simple embroidery, beads, braids, etc. Halos for Holy Family and angel are circles cut from gold paper, pinned to head.

HAIR: Use worsted yarn. Comb out strands of yarn. Glue on for hair and beards.

ANGEL WINGS (make 2): With yellow yarn, ch 9.

Row 1: Dc in 4th ch from hook and in each ch across. Ch 3, turn.

Row 2: Sk first dc, dc in each of next 4 dc, 2 dc in next dc, 2 dc in top of ch 3. Ch 3, turn.

Row 3: Sk first dc, dc in each dc across—9 dc. Ch 3, turn.

Row 4: Sk first dc, dc in each of next 6 dc, 2 dc in next dc, 2 dc in top of turning ch. Ch 3, turn.

Row 5: Dc in first dc, 2 dc in next dc, dc in each dc across, dc in top of turning ch. End off. Inc edge is top of wing. Gather bottom of wing a bit. Sew wings tog part way up; sew to back of angel.

CAPE (black and gray-haired kings): Ch 14. Repeat row 1 of Angel's Wings. Work even on 12 dc for 2 more rows, inc 1 dc each side of next row. Work 2 rows even, inc 1 dc each side of next row. Work even for desired length.

HEAD CAPE (white-haired king): Ch 10. Repeat row 1 of Angel's Wings. Work 2 rows even. On next row, inc 1 dc at center; work 1 row even. Repeat last 2 rows until there are 12 dc. End off.

CROWNS: Gray-Haired King: Ch 15, sl st in first ch to form ring. Sc in each ch around. On next rnd, sc in first sc, dc in next sc, 3 tr in next sc, dc in next sc, sc in each sc to end. Join; end off. Sew to head.

Black-Haired King: Work as for gray-haired king, but make 3 points around ring; sew points tog at tips.

White-Haired King: Ch 12, sl st in first ch to form ring. Sc in each ch around. * Sc in next sc, ch 4, sk 1 sc, repeat from * around; sl st in first sc. For center of crown, ch 2, 6 sc in 2nd ch from hook. Work 2 sc in each sc around—12 sc. Work 2 rnds of 12 sc. End off. Sew into center of crown. Sew cape to crown; sew crown to head. For top ornament, press a pearl-headed pin through beads and through crown and head.

MARY'S MANTLE: Ch 59; work 1 row sc, 1 row dc, 1 row sc, 1 row dc. End off. With same color, ch 28; work 1 row dc. Ch 2, turn. Work first 15 sts in dc, last sts in sc. Sc around tip of piece to starting ch. Work sc in each ch to last 15 sts, dc in each of last 15 ch. End off. (This piece is for center back of mantle.) Fold mantel in half, insert center back piece, with narrower end at fold. Sew center back piece to back edges of mantle, forming a cap for head at top fold. Make a ch of white to fit around face; work 1 row sc. Sew to front of mantle to frame face. Sew mantle to head.

SHEPHERD'S HEADCLOTHS: Ch 16. Work 6 rows of 14 dc. End off. Fold over a bit at top to fit head; sew sides. Gather and sew to head. Tie a ch of yarn around head.

SHEPHERD'S CROOKS: Cut chenille sticks to desired lengths; turn ends over. Make ch same length as stick; sc 1 row in ch. Sew piece over stick; bend stick into shape.

MANGER: Cut a chenille stick in fourths; cover same as for crooks. Sew 2 pairs tog in crosses.

Sides (make 2): Ch 19. Work 6 rows of 18 sc. End off. Sew sides tog on one long edge. Set into top V's of crosses; sew in place. Place straw-colored yarn in manger.

BABY: HEAD: Using cotton double, ch 2.

Rnd 1: 6 sc in 2nd ch from hook.

Rnd 2: 2 sc in each sc around.

Rnd 3: Sc in each sc around—12 sc.

Rnd 4: * Sc in each of 2 sc, 2 sc in next sc, repeat from * around—16 sc.

Rnds 5-7: Work even.

Rnd 8: (Pull up a lp in each of 2 sc, yo and through 3 lps on hook) 4 times, sc in each of 8 sc—12 sc.

Rnd 9: Work 6 dec's as in rnd 8—6 sc.

Rnd 10: Work even. End off.

HAND: Using cotton double, ch 4. Sc in 2nd ch from hook and in next 2 ch. Work 2 more rows of 3 sc. End off. Sew into shape.

SLEEVES: With yarn, ch 6. Work 4 rows of 5 sc. End off. Sew edges tog. Slip on 4″ chenille stick; slip hands on ends.

BODY: With yarn, ch 12. Sl st in first ch to form ring. Work even on 12 sc until piece is 2″ long. End off. Sew starting edge closed in flat seam. Stuff body, sew top over neck edge and to top of sleeves.

FACES: All faces except Mary's and Baby's have embroidered eyes and mouth. Mary's and Baby's are paint. Eyes are outlined in paint, brows and noses are paint.

SHEEP: BODY: Ch 13. **Note:** Directions are for small sheep. For larger sheep, inc 1 or more sts on body and head.

Row 1: Insert hook in 2nd ch from hook, catch strand of yarn at back of left index finger, pull through st, dropping lp from index finger, leaving small loop at back of work; complete sc—1 loop st made. Work loop st in each ch across. Ch 1, turn.

Row 2: Sc in each st across. Ch 1, turn.

Row 3: Loop st in each sc across. Ch 1, turn. Work sc and loop st rows alternately until there are 4 loop st rows. End off.

BODY ENDS (make 2): Ch 4. Repeat rows 1-3 of Body—3 loop sts.

TAIL: Work as for Body End for 4 rows.

HEAD-NECK: Ch 9. Work 1 row of 8 loop sts. Turn. Sl st to 3rd st, ch 1, sc in 3rd st, 2 sc in next st, sc in each of next 2 sts—5 sc. Ch 1, turn. Work 3 more rows of 5 sts as for body.

Next Row. Work in sc, dec 1 st. Work 1 row of 4 loop sts. End off.

FACE: Ch 2; 4 sc in 2nd ch from hook. On next rnd, 2 sc in each sc. Work 2 rnds even on 8 sc. End off.

EARS: Ch 2, sc in 2nd ch from hook. End off. Sew into ear shape. For larger ears, ch 3; sc in 2nd and 3rd ch.

TO ASSEMBLE SHEEP: Cut chenille stick in fourths (thirds for large sheep). Form 2 pieces in U shape. Sew up bottom body seam. Stick one U through back end, one through front end, forming 4 legs. Stuff body. Sew ends over openings (loops down on ends, toward back on body). Sew bottom of neck tog forming a circle. Stuff back of head and neck. Gather top of head a little, stuff face and sew in. Roll tail; sew up seam; sew on. Sew on ears. Cover legs as for shepherd's crook. Nose and mouth are straight sts; eyes, black glass-headed pins.

CRECHE
Shown on page 112

SIZE: 11″-12″ tall.
MATERIALS: Knitting worsted weight yarn, 1 oz. each of white, brown, tan, dark blue, light blue, old gold; smaller amounts of yellow, pink, gray. Knitting needles No. 4. Crochet hook size G. Polyester stuffing. White felt, 9″ × 12″. Scraps of black and blue felt. Glue. Three gold tinsel sticks. Stick for Joseph's staff.
GAUGE: 5 sts = 1″; 7 rows = 1″.
LARGE FIGURES: FRONT: Beg at top of head, with pink, cast on 7 sts. Work even in stockinette st (k 1 row, p 1 row) for 2 rows.
Row 3: Inc 1 st each side.
Rows 4-10: Work even.
Row 11: Dec 1 st each side.
Rows 12-14: Work even.
Row 15: Dec 1 st at center.
Row 16: Work even.
Row 17: Change to robe color (white for angel, light blue for Mary, tan for Joseph). Knit across, cast on 3 sts.
Row 18: P across, cast on 3 sts.
Rows 19-25: Work even on 12 sts.
Row 26: Inc 1 st each side.
Rows 27-31: Work even on 14 sts.
Row 32: Inc 1 st each side.
Rows 33-43: Work even on 16 sts.
Row 44: Inc 1 st each side.
Rows 45-49: Work even on 18 sts.
Row 50: Inc 1 st each side.
Rows 51-58: Work even on 20 sts.
Row 59: Inc 1 st each side.
Rows 60-67: Work even on 22 sts. Bind off.
BACK: Work as for front, changing to dark blue for Mary, brown for Joseph on row 17. Steam-press pieces lightly. Sew back to front, right sides out, leaving bottom open. Cut oval of white felt same size as bottom opening. Stuff figure; sew felt to bottom edge.
MARY'S HOOD: With dark blue, cast on 15 sts. Work even in stockinette st for 44 rows. Bind off. Fold in half with

cast-on and bound-off edges tog. Sew back seam, rounding off seam near fold to make hood round at top.
MARY'S ROBE (make 2 pieces for front): With dark blue, cast on 5 sts. Work even in stockinette st for 7 rows.
Row 8: Inc 1 st each side.
Rows 9-18: Work even on 9 sts.
Row 19: Inc 1 st each side.
Rows 20-31: Work even on 11 sts.
Row 32: Inc 1 st each side.
Rows 33-43: Work even on 13 sts.
Row 44: Inc 1 st each side.
Rows 45-55: Work even on 15 sts.
Row 56: Inc 1 st each side.
Rows 57-60: Work even on 17 sts. Bind off. Steam press. Sew a piece to each side seam, leaving free at top, bottom and front edges. Sew hood to top of robe, gathering hood at back.
SLEEVES: Cast on 16 sts (white for angel, dark blue for Mary, brown for Joseph). Work even in stockinette st for 10 rows.
Row 11: Dec 2 sts evenly across.
Rows 12-16: Work even on 14 sts.
Row 17: Repeat row 11.
Rows 18-22: Work even on 12 sts.
Row 23: Repeat row 11.
Rows 24 and 25: Work even on 10 sts. Bind off. Sew side seam; sew flat across top. Sew top to shoulder.
HANDS: With pink, cast on 6 sts. Work even for 10 rows.
Next Row: (K 2 tog) 3 times. Remove sts from needle, run yarn through sts, pull up and fasten. Sew side seam; tuck ends of yarn inside. Stuff sleeves at top, position hands and glue hands inside sleeves. Mary's hands are glued tog in prayer. Joseph's hands are glued to stick, angel has one arm raised a bit.
ANGEL'S WINGS: With old gold, cast on 10 sts. Work in garter st (k each row) for 3 rows.
Row 4: Inc 1 st each side.
Rows 5 and 6: Work even on 12 sts.
Row 7: Bind off 4 sts, k across.
Rows 8 and 9: Work even on 8 sts.
Row 10: K across, cast on 6 sts.
Row 11: K across 14 sts.
Rows 12-16: Work even.
Row 17: Bind off 4 sts, k across.
Rows 18 and 19: Work even on 10 sts.
Row 20: K across, cast on 8 sts.
Row 21: K across 18 sts.
Rows 22-26: Work even. Bind off. Make another piece the same. Work 1 row sc around edge. Sew to angel's back.
MANGER: With brown, cast on 16 sts. Work in garter st for 40 rows. Bind off. This is bottom piece. For short sides, cast on 16 sts. Work even for 10 rows. Bind off. For long sides, cast on 24 sts. Work even for 10 rows. Bind off. Sew 4 sides around bottom piece; join 4 sides at corner. Fill manger with pieces of yellow or gold yarn.
BABY: Back: With pink, cast on 4 sts. Work in stockinette st for 2 rows.
Row 3: Inc 1 st in row.

Rows 4-7: Work even on 5 sts.
Row 8: Dec 1 st in row. Cut pink.
Row 9: With white, cast on 6 sts, k across, cast on 6 sts.
Row 10: P across—16 sts.
Rows 11-14: Work even.
Rows 15 and 16: Bind off 5 sts at beg of each row.
Rows 17 and 18: Work even on 6 sts.
Row 19: Inc 1 st each side.
Rows 20-28: Work even on 8 sts. Bind off.
Front: Work as for back through row 8.
Row 9: With white, cast on 2 sts, k across neck sts, cast on 2 sts. Work even on 8 sts until piece is same length as back. Bind off. Fold arms, sew edges tog for 4 sts from outer edge. Sew back and front tog, stuffing as you go. Sew over ends of arms with pink for hands.

Embroider hair with straight sts and a few French knots at front. See Contents for Stitch Details.

FINISHING: Cut back felt circles for eyes, tiny blue circles for Baby's eyes. Glue in place. Embroider mouths with red. For hair, place strands down back of head from top of head. Sew down at top of head. Place strands over these from side to side. Sew down center. Trim to desired length. Loop some front strands of angel's hair into curls; tack in place. Loop some strands of yarn for Joseph's beard; sew loops across chin.

Make halos from tinsel sticks. Sew to back of head. Make ties for Mary's cape from strands of dark blue yarn. Run light blue yarn around angel's neck; tie into bow at front. If desired, trim front edges of Mary's cape with lace edging. Sew flower sequins to front of Mary's robe. Sew gold leaves to bottom of Joseph's robe. Sew gold flower sequins to front of angel's robe and wings. Sew gold rickrack around manger and tiny star sequins to front of Baby's robe.

SANTA AND ELF
Shown on page 127

SIZE: About 27″ tall.
MATERIALS: Knitting worsted. For Santa, 4 ozs. red (R), 1½ ozs. white (W), 1 oz. black (B). For elf, 3 ozs. green (G), 2 ozs. white (W), 1½ ozs. each red (R) and pink (P). Set of dp needles No. 5. Scraps of felt (see individual directions). Cellophane tape. All-purpose glue. For elf, two pipe cleaners, three jingle bells.
GAUGE: 5 sts = 1″.
Inc Note: K in front and back of st.
SANTA: HEAD: Beg at top of head, with P, cast on 9 sts and divide evenly on 3 dp needles. Join; k 1 rnd.
Rnd 2: Inc 1 st (see inc Note) in each st around—18 sts. K 2 rnds even.
Rnd 5: (K 1, inc 1 st in next st) 9 times —27 sts. K 2 rnds even.

Rnd 8: (K 2, inc 1 st in next st) 9 times—36 sts. K 2 rnds even.

Rnd 11: (K 1, inc 1 st in next st) 18 times—54 sts. K 30 rnds even.

Next Rnd: (K 1, k 2 tog) 18 times—36 sts. K 1 rnd even.

Next Rnd: K 2 tog around—18 sts. K 8 rnds even. Bind off.

NOSE: With P, cast on 12 sts and divide evenly on 3 dp needles. Join; k 3 rnds.

Rnd 4: (K 2 tog, k 2) 3 times— 9 sts. K 1 rnd.

Rnd 6: (K 2 tog, k 1) 3 times—6 sts. K 1 rnd. Run yarn through sts, pull up, fasten.

BODY: With 2 dp needles (or 2 straight needles), and R, cast on 84 sts. Work back and forth in stockinette st (k 1 row, p 1 row) for 54 rows. Cut R; join W. Work 7 rows more. Bind off.

BOTTOM BOXING STRIP: With 2 dp needles and R, cast on 30 sts. Work in stockinette st for 9 rows. Bind off.

ARMS (make 2): Beg at top edge, with R, cast on 18 sts and divide evenly on 3 dp needles. Join; k 57 rnds. Cut R; join W. K 7 rnds more. Bind off. Sew top edge straight across.

MITTENS (make 2): Beg at top edge, with B, cast on 15 sts and divide evenly on 3 dp needles. K 7 rnds.

Rnd 8: (K 4, inc 1 st in next st) 3 times —18 sts. K 2 rnds even.

Rnd 11: (K 5, inc 1 st in next st) 3 times—21sts. K 14 rnds even.

Rnd 26: K 2 tog, k around—20 sts.

Rnd 27: (K 2 tog, k 8) twice.

Rnd 28: (K 2 tog, k 7) twice.

Rnd 29: (K 2 tog, k 6) twice—14 sts. K 2 tog around. Run yarn through sts; pull up, fasten.

Thumbs (make 2): With 2 dp needles and B, cast on 5 sts.

Row 1: K across. Do not turn; push sts to other end of needle. With yarn taut at back of work, repeat row 1 for 1½". K 2 tog, k 1, k 2 tog. Run yarn through sts; pull up, fasten.

LEGS (make 2): Beg at top edge, with R, cast on 21 sts and divide evenly on 3 dp needles. Join; k 58 rnds. Cut R; join W. K 7 rnds more. Bind off loosely.

BOOTS (make 2): Beg at top edge, with B, cast on 18 sts and divide evenly on 3 dp needles. Join; k 25 rnds. Mark end of rnd (back of boot).

Shape Foot: K 5, sl next 8 sts on a safety pin. With 2 dp needles, work back and forth in stockinette st on 10 sts for 8 rows. Divide 18 sts evenly on 3 dp needles. K 12 rnds.

Next Rnd: (K 2 tog, k 1) around—12 sts. K 1 rnd. Repeat last 2 rnds once—8 sts. K 2 tog around—4 sts. Run yarn through sts, pull up, fasten.

HAT: Beg at lower edge, with W, cast on 54 sts and divide evenly on 3 dp

needles. Join; k 7 rnds. Cut W; join R; k 10 rnds.

Rnd 18: (K 16, k 2 tog) 3 times—51 sts. K 4 rnds even.

Rnd 23: (K 15, k 2 tog) 3 times—48 sts. K 4 rnds even. Continue in this manner, dec 3 sts every 5th rnd having 1 st less between decs, until 3 sts remain. Run yarn through sts, pull up, fasten.

HAIR: Loop W back and forth on sticky side of cellophane tape, making loops about 12" long (6" on each side of tape). Machine stitch down center of tape. Carefully remove tape.

BEARD (make 3): Loop W back and forth on 6"-7" piece of tape making loops 1½" long, having top loops on tape. Machine stitch ⅛" down from top. Remove tape. Make moustache in same way on 1" piece.

FINISHING: Steam-press flat pieces. Weave side edges of body piece for front of body. Turn up W trim at bottom; sew in place. Pin boxing strip in place at bottom of body; sew. Stuff body. Sew top of head; stuff firmly, including neck. Insert neck about ¼" into center of body. Sew neck to body; weave shoulder seams. Stuff arms up to W cuff; turn up cuff. Stuff mitten; sew on thumb. Sew mitten to arm under cuff. Sew arms to top of body (they should swing freely). Sew and stuff legs as for arms. Stuff boots; sew up gusset. Insert into leg; sew in place. Sew legs to body at front, ½" each side of center seams. Cut ¾"wide strip of black felt long enough to fit around body. Glue on 2½" from W trim.

For features, from felt, cut blue oval outer eyes, 1" x 1⅜". Cut off top quarter as shown. Cut two black ¾" circles for pupils. Cut thin red strip for mouth. Glue on features. Stuff nose; sew in place at center of face. Sew hair, moustache and beard in place. See illustration, page 15. For eyebrows, thread needle with 16" piece of W. Beg at other end, run needle in and out of yarn every ½". Pull needle and yarn through, pull up and sew to face over eyes.

On hat, turn up W brim; sew in place. For pompon, wind W 70 times around a 2" piece of cardboard. Slip loops off, tie at center, cut loops on both ends; trim. Sew to hat.

ELF: HEAD: Work as for Santa.
BODY: With G, work as for Santa for 54 rows. Bind off.

BOTTOM BOXING STRIP: With G, work as for Santa.

NOSE: With P, cast on 9 sts and divide evenly on 3 dp needles. Join; k 3 rnds.
Rnd 4: (K 2 tog) twice, k 5—7 sts. K 5 rnds even.
Rnd 10: (K 2 tog) twice, k 3—5 sts. K

5 rnds even. Run yarn through sts, pull up, fasten (tip).

RIGHT EAR: Beg at inner edge, with P and 2 dp needles, cast on 6 sts. K 1 row, p 1 row.

Row 3: K, inc 1 st each side. P 1 row.

Row 5: K, inc 1 st in first st, k across. P 1 row. Repeat last 2 rows once—10 sts.

Row 9: Inc 1 st in each of first 2 sts, k across—12 sts. P 1 row.

Row 11: Dec 1 st each side. Bind off in p.

LEFT EAR: Work same as for right ear, reversing shaping (inc at end of rows 5, 7 and 9).

ARMS: With G only, work same as Santa for 64 rnds. Bind off; finish as for Santa.

MITTENS: Working as for Santa, with W, cast on and work first 7 rnds. Drop W; join G. Work rnds 8-10. Drop G.

Rnd 11: With W, (k 5, inc 1 st in next st) 3 times—21 sts. Work 3 rnds even. Drop W, join R. K 2 rnds. Cut R; with W, k 5 rnds.

Next Rnd: K 2 tog, k around—20 sts. Cut W. With G, finish as for Santa from rnd 27.

Thumb: With W, work as for Santa.

LEGS (make 2): Beg at top edge, with W, cast on 18 sts and divide evenly on 3 dp needles. * (K 7 rnds W, 3 rnds G, 4 rnds W, 2 rnds R) 5 times, end k 7 rnds W, 3 rnds G. * Mark end of rnd (back of foot). With G only, work as follows:

Shape Foot: K 5, sl next 8 sts on a safety pin. With 2 dp needles, work back and forth in stockinette st on 10 sts for 8 rows. Divide 18 sts evenly on 3 dp needles; k 12 rnds even.

Next Rnd: (K 2 tog, k 4) 3 times—15 sts. K 1 rnd even.

Next Rnd: (K 2 tog, k 3) 3 times—12 sts. K 1 rnd even. Continue in this manner, dec 3 sts every other rnd having 1 st less between decs, until 6 sts remain. K 11 rnds.

Next Rnd: (K 2 tog) 3 times. Run yarn through sts, pull up, fasten.

DICKEY: Beg at top edge, with 2 dp needles and W, cast on 24 sts. Working in stockinette st, work 2 rows even. Work in stripe pat as follows: 2 rows R, 4 rows W, 3 rows G, 4 rows W, 2 rows R, 4 rows W; **at the same time,** dec 1 st each side every k row—4 sts. Run yarn through sts, pull up, fasten.

HAT: Beg at lower edge, with G, cast on 54 sts and divide evenly on 3 dp needles. Join; work in ribbing of k 1, p 1 for 7 rnds. Beg at *, work stripe pat same as for legs from * to *; **at the same time,** dec 3 sts evenly spaced every 5th row (as on Santa's hat), until 3 sts remain. Run yarn through sts, pull up, fasten.

BEARD AND HAIR: With R, make 3

strips as for Santa's beard. Make hair same as beard, having strip 9″ long.

FINISHING: Steam-press flat pieces. Weave side edges of body piece for front of body for 5″ beg at bottom edge (bound-off edge). Insert dickey. Sew 7 sts on each side of dickey to 7 sts on back of body, leaving center 10 sts free on both. Sew dickey to front. Pin boxing strip in place at bottom of body; sew. Stuff body. Sew top of head; stuff firmly, including neck. Insert neck about ¼″ into center opening. Sew neck in place. Weave remainder of shoulder seams. Turn up last 7 rows of arms for cuffs. Stuff arms. Stuff mitten; sew on thumb; sew mitten to arm under cuff. Sew arms to body. Stuff foot, inserting a double piece of pipe cleaner at tips. Bend into shape. Sew up gussets. Stuff leg; sew to body as for Santa. Stuff nose, inserting a small double piece of pipe cleaner. Bend into shape. Sew nose to center of face. Sew ears to head in line with nose, knit side to front.

For features, cut green outer eyes, black pupils, red mouth as for Santa, leaving outer eyes complete ovals. Glue in place. Sew on beard. Sew hair strip at back and sides. Sew a jingle bell to top of hat, one to each foot.

TISSUE-HOLDER MITTENS
Shown on page 127

SIZES: Directions for 3 years. Changes for 4-5 and 6-7 years are in parentheses.
MATERIALS: For Santa, 2 ozs. red (R) knitting worsted, small amount pink (P). White moss fringe, about 8″. Two white ball fringe pompons. Four black, two pink shank buttons. For clown, ½ oz. white (W) knitting worsted, ¼ oz. each blue (B), red (R), green (G). Six ball fringe pompons. Knitting needles Nos. 6 and 8. Two stitch holders. Yarn needle.
GAUGE: 4 sts = 1″; 6 rows = 1″.
Note: Mittens are worked with a double strand of yarn throughout.
GENERAL DIRECTIONS: RIGHT MITTEN: With No. 6 needles and double strand of yarn (see Note), cast on 22 (22-24) sts. Work in ribbing of k 1, p 1 for 11 (13-15) rows. Change to No. 8 needles. Beg with a p row, work in stockinette st (k 1 row, p 1 row) for 5 (7-7) rows.
Inc for Thumb: K 12 (12-13), cast on 1 st, k 1, cast on 1 st, k 9 (9-10). P 1 row.
Next Row: K 12 (12-13), cast on 1 st, k 3, cast on 1 st, k 9 (9-10). P 1 row.
Next Row: K 12 (12-13), cast on 1 st, k 5, cast on 1 st, k 9 (9-10). P 1 row.
Divide for Thumb: K 12 (12-13), sl these sts on a holder (back of hand),

inc 1 st in next st, k 6, sl remaining 9 (9-10) sts on a holder (palm).
Thumb: Work in stockinette st on 8 sts for 5 (7-8) rows.
Next Row: Work 2 tog across—4 sts. Cut yarn leaving an end for sewing; draw through remaining sts. Pull up tightly, sew seam.
Hand: From right side, sl sts from first holder (back of hand) to needle; join yarn, pick up 1 st at base of thumb, k sts from 2nd holder (palm)—22 (22-24) sts. Work in stockinette st for 11 (13-15) rows, end p row, dec 0 (0-2) sts on last row—22 sts.
Shape Top: Row 1: (K 2 tog, k 9) twice —20 sts.
Rows 2 and 4: Purl.
Row 3: (K 2 tog, k 3) 4 times—16 sts.
Row 5: K 2 tog across—8 sts. Finish as for thumb.
LEFT MITTEN: Work as for right mitten, having 9 (9-10) sts (palm) before thumb, 12 (12-13) sts (back) after thumb on k rows.
FACE: With one strand and No. 8 needles, cast on 12 sts. Work in stockinette st for 2″ (2½″-3″). Bind off. After completing features, sew to back of mitten on 3 sides, leaving bottom open for tissue.
SANTA MITTENS: Following general directions, with R, make mittens; with P, make face. For hair, cut one tuft from moss fringe; for moustache, cut one tuft, spread open; for beard, cut strip of tuft. Sew in place. Sew on black button eyes, pink button nose. With R, embroider mouth in outline stitch. See illustration on page 15. Sew a white pompon to top.
CLOWN MITTEN: Following general directions, with W, work ribbing. On right mitten, work 12 (14-14) rows G (work thumb with G); work 6 (8-10) rows R; finish mitten with B. On left mitten, the color sequence is B (work thumb with B), R, G. With W, make face. Embroider green diamond eyes, blue French knot pupils, blue cheeks, red outline st mouth. Sew on small red tassels to sides of face for hair. See illustration, page 15. Sew on pompons as shown.

CHRISTMAS TREE STOCKING
Shown on page 127

MATERIALS: Knitting worsted, 2 1-oz. balls each of white (W) and green (G). Small amounts of red (R), brown (B) and yellow (Y). Knitting needles No. 8. Seven bobbins. Yarn needle.
GAUGE: 5 sts = 1″.
Pattern Notes: On border pat at bottom and top, carry unused color loosely across back of work. On tree pats, do not carry unused colors across back of

work; use separate balls or bobbins for each color change. Twist strands tog to prevent holes when changing colors.
STOCKING: Beg at lower edge of front and back, with G, cast on 104 sts. Work in stockinette st (k 1 row, p 1 row) for 2 rows. Join W; following Chart 1, work border for 10 rows, repeat from A to B across on k rows and B to A on p rows. When top of chart is reached, work 2 rows G. End off G.

With W, work 2 rows. Wind 2 bobbins each of R, B and G, one bobbin W.
Next Row: K 35 W; join R, k 8; join bobbin of W, k 18 W; join another R bobbin, k 8; join 2nd ball of W, k 35 W. Beg with row 2 of Chart 2 (p row), continue with tree patterns as established through row 10. Bind off 26 sts at beg of next 2 rows—52 sts. Work even on 52 sts to top of chart. Work 2 rows W, 3 rows G. Repeat 10 rows of border pat, then work 2 rows G.
Eyelet Row: With G, * yo, k 2 tog, repeat from * across. P 1 row. Work in ribbing of k 1, p 1 for 3 rows. Bind off.

CHART 1

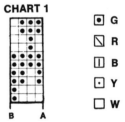

- ⊙ G
- ◨ R
- ▥ B
- ⊡ Y
- ☐ W

CHART 2

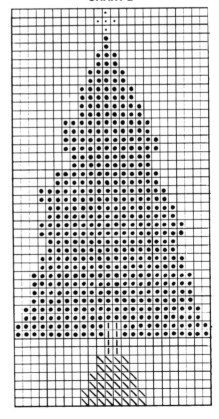

FINISHING: Run in yarn ends on wrong side. Steam-press piece. Fold stocking wrong side out, sew front and bottom seams, rounding off corners at toe and heel. Turn top edge to inside on eyelet row; sew in place. Make twisted cord hanger 10″ long from 2 strands of G. Sew ends of cord inside stocking at back top edge.

RED STOCKING
Shown on page 127

MATERIALS: Knitting worsted, 3 ozs. red (R); ¼ oz. each green (G) and white (W). Knitting needles No. 8. Yarn needle.

GAUGE: 5 sts = 1″.

Pattern Notes: Always change colors on wrong side; pick up one color from under dropped strand; pick up other color over dropped strand to prevent holes. Carry color not being used loosely across back of work. Cut and join colors when necessary.

STOCKING: Beg at lower edge of front and back, with R, cast on 100 sts. Work in stockinette st (k 1 row, p 1 row) for 4 rows. Drop R; join G and W. Following Chart 1, work from A to B on k rows and B to A on p rows, repeating chart across. When top of chart is reached, break off G and W. With R,

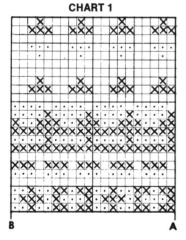

☒ G   ☐ W   ☐ R

CHART 1

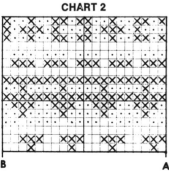

CHART 2

B   A

p 1 row, k 1 row. Bind off 25 sts at beg of next 2 rows—50 sts. Work even in stockinette st until piece is 6″ from last pat row, end p row.

Top Border: Following Chart 2, work top border. On row 11, repeat from A to B across, k last 2 sts in G. On row 12, p first 2 sts in W, work from B to A across. When top of chart is reached, break off G and W. With R, p 1 row.

Eyelet Row: * Yo, k 2 tog, repeat from * across. P 1 row. Work in ribbing of k 1, p 1 for 3 rows. Bind off.

FINISHING: Same as for Christmas Tree Stocking. Make twisted cord hanger from 1 strand each of R and G.

SANTA AND HELPER
Shown on page 128

SIZE: 14″ high.

MATERIALS: Knitting worsted, 3 ozs. red, 2 ozs. pink, 1 oz. white, few yards of black, for Santa; 3 ozs. green, 2 ozs. red, 2 ozs. pink, few yards of black and yellow for helper. Crochet hook size F. Dacron stuffing. Scraps of black, red, yellow and blue felt.

GAUGE: 4 sc = 1″.

SANTA: With red, beg at top, ch 2.

Rnd 1: 6 sc in 2nd ch from hook. Mark end of rnds.

Rnd 2: 2 sc in each sc around.

Rnds 3 and 4: Work even on 12 sc.

Rnd 5: (Sc in next sc, 2 sc in next sc) 6 times.

Rnd 6: Work even on 18 sc.

Rnd 7: (Sc in next 2 sc, 2 sc in next sc) 6 times.

Rnd 8: Work even on 24 sc.

Rnd 9: (Sc in next 3 sc, 2 sc in next sc) 6 times.

Rnd 10: Work even on 30 sc.

Rnd 11: (Sc in next 4 sc, 2 sc in next sc) 6 times.

Rnd 12: Work even on 36 sc. Change to pink.

Rnds 13-21: Continue to inc 6 sc evenly around every other rnd 3 times more. Work 4 rnds even on 54 sc. Change to red.

Rnds 22-27: Work 6 rnds even. Change to black.

Rnds 28 and 29: Work 2 rnds even. Change to red.

Rnds 30 and 31: Work 2 rnds even.

Rnds 32-38: Dec 6 sc evenly around each rnd until 12 sc remain. (To dec 1 sc, pull up a lp in each of 2 sts, yo hook and through 3 lps on hook.) Before opening is too small, stuff body firmly. Gather remaining sts tog; sew opening closed.

Arms (make 2): With pink, ch 2. **Rnd 1:** 6 sc in 2nd ch from hook.

Rnd 2: 2 sc in each sc around.

Rnd 3: (Sc in 3 sc, 2 sc in next sc) 3

times. **Rnds 4-6:** Work even on 15 sc. Change to white.

Rnds 7 and 8: Work even. Change to red.

Rnds 9-17: Work even. End off. Stuff arms. Flatten top edge; sew opening closed; sew arms to sides above belt.

Legs (make 2): With black, ch 2. **Rnd 1:** 6 sc in 2nd ch from hook.

Rnd 2: 2 sc in each sc around.

Rnd 3: (Sc in next sc, 2 sc in next sc) 6 times.

Rnds 4-6: Work even on 18 sc. Change to red.

Rnds 7-22: Work even. End off. Stuff legs. Flatten top edge; sew opening closed; sew legs to body.

FINISHING: Make a 1″ white pompon; sew to top of hat. With white, work 1 row of sc around lower edge of hat. For beard, thread double strand of white in yarn needle, work 2 rows of knotted loop st down each side and across lower edge of face. For mustache, wind yarn 30 times around 2 fingers. Tie tog at center, sew to face. From felt, cut 2 blue crescent eyes, red circular nose, yellow rectangular belt buckle. Glue in place.

HELPER: With green, work as for Santa through rnd 12. Do not change to pink.

Rnd 13: (Sc in next 5 sc, 2 sc in next sc) 6 times.

Rnd 14: Work even on 42 sc.

Rnd 15: (Sc in next 6 sc, 2 sc in next sc) 6 times. Change to pink.

Rnds 16 and 17: Work even on 48 sc.

Rnds 18-23: Inc 6 sc evenly around on rnd 18. Work 5 rnds even on 54 sc. Change to red.

Rnds 24-29: Work 6 rnds even. Change to black.

Rnds 30 and 31: Work 2 rnds even. Change to green.

Rnds 32 and 33: Work 2 rnds even.

Rnds 34-40: Work and finish as for rnds 32-38 of Santa.

Arms: Work as for Santa, working rnds 1-6 in pink, 7-17 in red.

Legs: Work as for Santa, using green throughout.

Shoes (make 2): With green, ch 2. **Rnd 1:** 6 sc in 2nd ch from hook.

Rnds 2 and 3: Work even.

Rnd 4: 2 sc in each sc around.

Rnds 5-8: Work even on 12 sc. End off. Stuff shoes lightly. Sew to bottom front of legs.

FINISHING: Make a 1″ red pompon; sew to top of hat. With red, work 1 row of sc around lower edge of hat. For hair, cut 15 2″ strands of yellow; tie tog at center; sew to center front under hat. From felt, cut 2 black crescent eyes, red circular nose and crescent mouth, yellow rectangular belt buckle. Glue in place.

LITTLE MISS

Shown on page 128

SIZE: 13″ tall.

MATERIALS: Knitting worsted, 2 ozs. pink or other color for doll. Sport yarn, 2 ozs. white, 1 oz. blue, 1 oz. red, for clothes, ½ oz. brown for hair. Knitting needles, one set of dp needles No. 4, 1 pair needles No. 2. Six-strand embroidery floss: black, dark blue, light blue, rose, red. Seven small pearl buttons. Three small snaps. Scrap of brown felt. Two yards narrow red ribbon or bulky yarn. Polyester fiberfill for stuffing.

GAUGE: 11 sts = 2″; 8 rows = 1″ (No. 4 needles, knitting worsted). 7 sts = 1″; 10 rows = 1″ (No. 2 needles, sport yarn).

DOLL: BODY: Beg at lower edge, with pink and No. 4 needles, cast on 36 sts. Divide evenly on 3 needles. Mark beg of rnd. Work even (k each rnd) for 16 rnds.

Next Rnd: K 2 tog around for waistline—18 sts. K 1 rnd even.

Next Rnd: Inc 1 st in each st around—36 sts. Work 18 rnds even.

Shape Shoulders: Bind off 5 sts, k to end of first needle; k 1 on 2nd needle, bind off next 10 sts; k 7 on 3rd needle, bind off last 5 sts—16 sts remain. Cut yarn.

Neck: Rearrange 16 sts—5 on first, 6 on 2nd, 5 on 3rd needle. Join yarn at beg of first needle, k 4 rnds, pulling sts tightly tog.

Next Rnd: (K 3, inc 1 st in next st) 4 times.

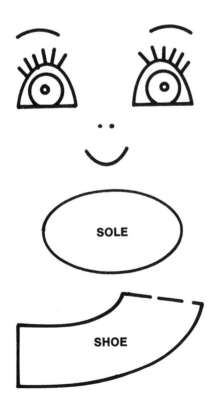

Next Rnd: Inc 1 st in each st around—40 sts. K even for 20 rnds. K 2 tog around for 2 rnds—10 sts. Cut yarn, leave end for sewing. Draw end through remaining sts, pull up tight; sew top of head closed.

Legs: Cast on 15 sts; divide on 3 needles. Join, k 16 rnds.

First Dec Rnd: (K 3, k 2 tog) 3 times. K 12 rnds even.

2nd Dec Rnd: (K 2, k 2 tog) 3 times. K 6 rnds even.

3rd Dec Rnd: K 3, k 2 tog, k 2, k 2 tog—7 sts. K 2 rnds even.

Heel: Working back and forth on 3 sts of first needle, k 1 row, p 1 row, k 1 row, p 1 row, k 1 row. With free needle, pick up and k 2 sts along side of heel piece just made, k 2 sts from 2nd needle. With free needle, k 2 from 3rd needle, pick up and k 2 sts along other side of heel—11 sts.

Foot: K 3, (k 2 tog) 4 times—7 sts. K 5 rnds even. K 1, (k 2 tog) 3 times—4 sts. Cut yarn; draw end through remaining sts, sew toe closed.

Arms: Cast on 12 sts; divide on 3 needles. Join, k 10 rnds.

First Dec Rnd: (K 2, k 2 tog) 3 times. K 10 rnds even.

2nd Dec Rnd: (K 1, k 2 tog) 3 times. K 2 rnds even.

Next Rnd: (K 1, inc 1 st in next st) 3 times. K 1 rnd even.

Hand: K 3, inc 1 st in each of next 3 sts, k 3—12 sts. K 2 rnds even.

Next Rnd: K 3, (k 2 tog) 3 times, k 3. K 2 rnds even.

Next Rnd: (K 1, k 2 tog) 3 times. Cut yarn, draw through remaining sts, sew tip closed.

FINISHING: Sew shoulder seams. Stuff head, neck and body very firmly. Fold lower edge of body flat, sew closed. Stuff feet and legs firmly; stuff last ¼″ at top lightly. Fold top edge flat; sew closed. Sew to body. Stuff arms in same way; sew to sides of body at ends of shoulder seams. Trace pattern for face on tissue paper. Pin pattern on head, embroider face through paper, using 3 strands of floss: black eyebrows and eye outlines in outline st, lashes in straight st; dark blue eyes in satin st, light blue dot at center; rose dots for nose; red mouth in outline st. For hair, wind brown yarn around 11″ cardboard 40 times. Do not cut; remove from cardboard. Arrange evenly across top and back of head; pin in place. With matching thread, sew hair to head with back st from center front to back. Gather hair to each side; sew down just above neck. Tie with ribbon or yarn bows. For bangs, wind yarn 12 times around 2 fingers. Sew loops across forehead, tucking top of loops under hair.

CLOTHES: PANTIES (make 2 pieces): With white and No. 2 needles, cast on 22 sts. Work in ribbing of k 1, p 1 for 2 rows. Work in stockinette st (k 1 row, p 1 row) for 6 rows. Dec 1 st at beg and end of next 9 rows—4 sts. Bind off. Sew side and crotch seams.

SHIRT: Front: With white and No. 2 needles, cast on 32 sts. K 1 row, p 1 row. Drop white, tie in red, p 2 rows. Drop red; with white, k 1 row, p 1 row. Drop white; with red, p 2 rows. Cut red. With white, work even in stockinette st (k 1 row, p 1 row) for 6 rows. Bind off 3 sts at beg of next 2 rows. Work even for 8 rows. Dec 1 st at each end of next row—24 sts. Work even for 9 rows. Bind off.

Back: Right Half: With white and No. 2 needles, cast on 16 sts. Work as for front through red pat. Cut red. With white, work even in stockinette st for 6 rows. Place sts on a holder.

Left Half: Work as for right half.

Next Row: Bind off 3 sts, k across, k sts from holder. On next row, bind off 3 sts, p across. Finish as for front. Sew side and underarm seams. Sew shoulders from armhole edge for 1″ toward neck. Sew snap on back opening.

JUMPER: Back: With blue and No. 2 needles, cast on 32 sts. Work in garter st (k each row) for 40 rows (20 ridges). Dec 1 st each end of next row—30 sts.

Next Row: (K 2, k 2 tog) 7 times, k 2—23 sts. Dec 1 st each end of next row—21 sts. Work in k 1, p 1 ribbing for 4 rows. Bind off in ribbing. Make another piece the same for front. Sew side seams.

Bib: With blue and No. 2 needles, cast on 16 sts. Work in garter st for 14 rows. Work in k 1, p 1 ribbing for 4 rows. Bind off in ribbing. Sew to center front of jumper.

Straps (make 2): With blue and No. 2 needles, cast on 40 sts. K 2 rows. Bind off loosely. Sew one end of each strap to back waistline ¾″ in from sides. Cross in back; sew tog. Sew snaps to underside of each strap end and at top front bib. Sew a button to front end of each strap.

SOCKS: With white and No. 2 needles, cast on 18 sts. Work in ribbing of k 1, p 1 for 2 rows. Work in stockinette for 8 rows.

Next Row: K 3, (k 2 tog, k 3) 3 times. Work even for 11 rows.

Next Row: (K 3, k 2 tog) 3 times—12 sts. P 1 row.

Shape Foot: Row 1: K 9, turn.

Row 2: Sl 1, p 5, turn.

Row 3: Sl 1, k 5, turn. Repeat rows 2 and 3 twice more, repeat row 2 once.

Next Row: K 6, pick up and k 5 sts along side of instep, k to end. P back;

102

pick up and k 5 sts along other side of instep, p to end—22 sts.

Next Row: K 2 tog, k 7, (k 2 tog) twice, k 7, k 2 tog—18 sts. P back. Bind off. Sew seam along bottom of foot and back of leg.

Shoes: Trace patterns for shoes. Using patterns, cut shoes from brown felt. Sew back seam. Sew shoe to sole, gathering in around toe edge. Turn shoe to right side.

CARDIGAN: Beg at neckline, with red and No. 2 needles, cast on 44 sts. Work in ribbing of k 1, p 1 for 2 rows Drop red.

Buttonhole Row (wrong side): Join white; k 1, p 1, yo, p 2 tog, work in ribbing across. Work in ribbing for 1 row more. Cut white. With red, rib 4, p to last 4 sts, rib 4.

Shape Raglan: Row 1: Rib 4 (front band), k 5, inc 1 st in next st, place marker on needle, inc 1 st in next st, k 4, inc 1 st in next st, place marker on needle, inc 1 st in next st, k 10, inc 1 st in next st, place marker on needle, inc 1 st in next st, k 4, inc 1 st in next st, place marker on needle, inc 1 st in next st, k 5, rib 4 (front band).

Row 2: Rib 4, p across to last 4 sts, rib 4.

Row 3: Keeping first and last 4 sts in ribbing, k across, inc 1 st before and after each marker, slipping markers. Repeat last 2 rows, making buttonhole on row 6, until there are 92 sts on needle, end p row 14.

Divide for Sleeves and Body: Rib 4, k 12, sl next 18 sts on a holder; cast on 2 sts, k next 24 sts, sl next 18 sts on a holder; cast on 2 sts, k 12, rib 4—60 sts. Working buttonhole on next row and 9th row, work even for 15 rows. Drop red. Join white; work in ribbing of k 1, p 1 for 2 rows, working buttonhole on 2nd row. Cut white; pick up red, work 2 rows of ribbing. Bind off loosely in ribbing.

Sleeves: Sl 18 sts from holder to needle. Join red; beg with a k row, inc 1 st at beg and end of first row, work even on 20 sts for 9 more rows. * K 2 tog at beg and end of next row. Work 3 rows even. Repeat from * once— 16 sts. Work 2 more rows even. Drop red; join white; work in ribbing for 2 rows. Cut white. With red, work in ribbing for 2 rows. Bind off loosely in ribbing. Sew sleeve seams. Sew on buttons.

CAP: With white and No. 2 needles, cast on 60 sts. Work in ribbing of k 1, p 1 for 3 rows.

Row 1: (K 4, inc 1 st in next st) 12 times.

Row 2 and All Even Rows: P.

Row 3: (K 5, inc 1 st in next st) 12 times.

Row 5: (K 6, inc 1 st in next st) 12 times.

Row 7: (K 7, inc 1 st in next st) 12 times.

Row 9: (K 8, inc 1 st in next st) 12 times—120 sts.

Row 10: P.

Row 11: (K 8, k 2 tog) 12 times.

Row 13: (K 7, k 2 tog) 12 times. Continue to dec in this manner until 24 sts remain. (K 2 tog) 12 times. Cut yarn; leave end for sewing. Draw end through remaining 12 sts, pull tight and fasten. Sew back seam.

Pompon: With red and white strands tog, wind yarn around 3 fingers 16 times. Lay strands flat; tie tog at center with double strand of yarn. Cut loops at both ends. Sew to cap.

CHOCOLATE MOOSE
Shown on page 128

SIZE: 12″ long.

MATERIALS: Knitting worsted, 1 4-oz. skein brown, small amount of black, 1 yard red. Crochet hook size G. Felt, 2 pieces brown, 6″ x 12″; scrap of tan. Two 12″ chenille sticks. Polyester stuffing. Two black shank buttons for eyes. Yarn needle.

GAUGE: 4 sc = 1″.

MOOSE: BODY: With brown, beg at bottom, ch 2. **Rnd 1:** 6 sc in 2nd ch from hook.

Rnd 2: 2 sc in each sc around.

Rnd 3: (Sc in next sc, 2 sc in next sc) 6 times—18 sc.

Rnd 4: (Sc in each of 2 sc, 2 sc in next sc) 6 times—24 sc.

Rnd 5: (Sc in each of 2 sc, 2 sc in next sc) 8 times—32 sc.

Rnd 6: (Sc in each of 3 sc, 2 sc in next sc) 8 times—40 sc.

Rnd 7: (2 sc in next sc, sc in each of 4 sc) 8 times—48 sc.

Rnds 8-22: Work even for 15 rnds.

Rnd 23: (Work 2 sc tog, sc in each of 6 sc) 6 times—42 sc.

Rnds 24-29: Work even for 6 rnds.

Rnd 30: (Sc in each of 5 sc, work 2 sc tog) 6 times—36 sc.

Rnds 31 and 32: Work even.

Rnd 33: (Work 2 sc tog, sc in each of 4 sc) 6 times—30 sc.

Rnds 34 and 35: Work even.

Rnd 36: (Sc in each of 3 sc, work 2 sc tog) 6 times—24 sc.

Rnds 37 and 38: Work even. End off. Stuff body firmly; do not sew up hole.

HEAD: With brown, beg at back, work as for body through rnd 6. Work 8 rnds even.

Rnd 15: (Work 2 sc tog) 6 times, sc in each remaining sc—34 sc.

Rnd 16: Work even.

Rnd 17: (Work 2 sc tog) 4 times, sc in each remaining sc—30 sc. Work 1 rnd even.

Rnd 19: (Work 2 sc tog, sc in each of 4 sc) 5 times—25 sc. Work 4 rnds even.

Rnd 24: (Sc in 3 sc, work 2 sc tog) 5 times. Work 2 rnds even.

Rnd 27: Sc in 15 sc, 3 sc in each of 2 sc, sc in 3 sc. Work 1 rnd even.

Rnd 29: (Sc in 2 sc, work 2 sc tog) 6 times—18 sc.

Rnd 30: (Sc in next sc, work 2 sc tog) 6 times. Work 1 rnd even. Stuff head. Work 2 sc tog around. Sew up. Sew to body.

EAR (make 2): With brown, ch 8. Sc in 2nd ch from hook and in each of next 5 ch, 3 sc in last ch. Working on opposite side of ch, sc in each of next 6 ch. Ch 1, turn. Sc in each of next 8 sc (tip of ear). End off.

FORELEG (make 2): With brown, ch 12. Sl st in first ch to form ring. Ch 1, sc in each ch around. Work 10 rnds even on 12 sc. Change to black, work 3 rnds even. (Work 2 sc tog) 6 times. Work 1 rnd even. Sew up hole. Stuff legs to ½″ of top. Sew top flat; sew to side of body. Catch inside of legs to body.

BACK LEG (make 2): With brown, ch 14. Sl st in first ch to form ring. Ch 1, sc in each ch around. Work 11 rnds even. Change to black, work 3 rnds even. (Work 2 sc tog) 7 times. Work 1 rnd even. Sew up hole. Finish as for forelegs.

TAIL: With brown, ch 8. Sl st in first ch to form ring. Ch 1, sc in each ch around. Work 1 rnd even.

Rnd 3: (Sc in 3 sc, 2 sc in next sc) twice. Work 2 rnds even.

Rnd 6: (Sc in 3 sc, work 2 sc tog) twice. Work 1 rnd even.

Rnd 8: (Sc in 2 sc, work 2 sc tog) twice.

Rnd 9: Work 2 sc tog around. Sew up tip. Sew tail flat to lower back.

HEADPIECE: With brown, ch 5. Sc in 2nd ch from hook and in next 3 ch. Ch 1, turn. Work 5 more rows of 4 sc. End off.

FINISHING: Enlarge half-pattern for antlers on paper ruled in 1″ squares. Cut out pattern. Double one piece of felt. Place dash line of pattern on fold of felt, cut out one antler piece. Pin to 2nd felt piece, machine-stitch around

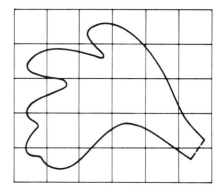

close to edge, leaving an opening at center of antler. Cut out 2nd felt piece around edge of first piece. Bend chenille sticks in U shape. Hold ends of one stick tog, push into wide part of one side of antler. Repeat on other side of antler. Place antlers on head, straighter edge toward front, cover center with headpiece; sew down tightly. Sew ears behind headpiece. Bend chenille sticks up at back. Split red yarn into 2 strands; embroider mouth in outline st, nostrils in satin st. Cut 2 tan felt circles ¾" diameter. Cut a slit in center of each. Slip shank of buttons through slits. Using long needle and heavy thread, sew one eye to head, come out where other eye should be. String on eye, bring needle through to top of head; knot under antlers.

MR. & MRS. SANTA, ANGEL PUPPETS
Shown on page 128

SIZE: 9½" high.
MATERIALS: Knitting worsted weight yarn, for santa and elf: 1½ oz. red, 1 oz. pink; for angel: 1 oz. white and 1 oz. pink; small amounts of white and yellow. Felt scraps in blue, pink, white and red. Three 4" gold paper doilies. Three ½" buttons. Knitting needles No. 5. Yarn needle.
GAUGE: 5 sts = 1"; 7 rows = 1".
MR. SANTA: BODY: Front: Starting at top of head with pink, cast on 10 sts. Work 2 rows even in stockinette st (k 1 row, p 1 row).
Row 3: K across, inc 1 st at beg and end of row—12 sts.
Rows 4-6: Continuing in stockinette st, work even.
Row 7: Repeat row 3—14 sts.
Rows 8-17: Work even.
Rows 18: Dec 1 st at beg and end of row—12 sts.
Rows 19 and 20: Work even.
Row 21: Repeat row 18—10 sts.
Row 22: Work even. Cut pink; join red and cast on 12 sts for arm.
Row 23: With red, work across 22 sts, cast on 12 sts for second arm—34 sts.
Row 24: Work even across all 34 sts.
Rows 25-27: Work even.
Rows 28 and 29: Work across, dec 1 st at end of each row—32 sts.
Rows 30-34: Dec 1 st at beg and end of each row—22 sts.

Rows 35-40: Work even.
Row 41: Inc 1 st at beg and end of row —24 sts.
Rows 42-49: Work even.
Row 50: Inc 1 st at beg and end of row —26 sts. Work 15 rows even. Bind off.
BACK: Work same as front.
Sew back and front tog with matching yarn, leaving lower edge open.
Hand (make 2): With pink, cast on 6 sts. Work 7 rows even in stockinette st.
Row 8: Dec 1 st at beg and end of row—4 sts.
Row 9: Work 2 tog twice. End off. Sew hand to arm, overlapping ½".
Features: From felt cut 2 small blue circles for eyes, 1 small pink circle for nose and 1 red crescent for mouth. Glue features to face.
FINISHING: Hat: Front: Starting at tip of hat with red, cast on on 3 sts. Work 6 rows even in stockinette st.
Row 7: Work across, inc 1 st in center of row—4 sts. Work 5 rows even. **Next Row:** Work across, inc 1 st in center of row—5 sts. Inc 1 st every 5th row 5 times more—10 sts. Work 6 rows even. Bind off. Work back same as front.

Sew hat sections to top of head sections.
Trim: With white, cast on 3 sts. Work even in garter st to length desired to fit around hat and wrist edges. Bind off. Sew in place.
With white make a 1" pompon. Sew to tip of hat.
Buttons (make 3): With white, cast on 4 sts, work 5 rows in garter st. Bind off.
Gather cast-on and bound-off edges slightly. Sew to center front.
Beard: Cut a 5" strip of scotch tape. Place on a flat surface with sticky side up. Loop a strand of white yarn over it. See illustration. Sew in place. Fold top section down and press in place. Remove tape. Sew to face.
MRS. SANTA: Work same as for santa. Sew trim around neck.
Hair: Wind yarn 3 times around fingers to make a curl of hair, sew curls to head. Sew 3 buttons to center front of body.
ANGEL: Work same as santa, using white for dress.
Hair: Cut yellow yarn into 10" strands. With yellow, sew across center of all strands for part, about 1½" long. Glue ends of strands to head. Trim sides.

SLEIGH RIDE
Shown on page 129

Size: Larger sleigh is 7" long, 5" high.
MATERIALS: Knitting worsted, 1 4-oz. skein red for sleighs; small amounts of light brown, dark brown, black, white, natural, green, orange, blue, dark green for trimmings and figures. Coats & Clark's Speed-Cro-Sheen, 1 ball ecru for each horse. Cotton stuffing for figures. Foam rubber stuffing for sleighs. Two dozen 1" chenille sticks. Crochet hook size G. Steel crochet hook No. 00. Yarn needle. Sewing needles and threads.
GAUGE: 4 sc = 1" (size G hook, knitting worsted). 5 sc = 1" (No. 00 hook. Speed-Cro-Sheen).
Note: Use size G hook unless otherwise instructed.
LARGE SLEIGH: SIDES (make 2): With red, ch 18. **Row 1:** Sc in 2nd ch from hook and in each ch across—17 sc. Ch 1, turn each row.
Row 2: 2 sc in first sc, sc in each sc across, 2 sc in last sc.
Row 3: 2 sc in first sc, sc across.
Row 4: Repeat row 2—22 sc.
Row 5: Sc in each sc across.
Row 6: 2 sc in first sc, sc in next 20 sc.
Row 7: Sk first sc, sc in 21 sc.
Row 8: 2 sc in first sc, sc in next 10 sc.

DIAGRAM

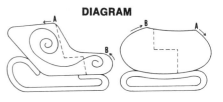

Row 9: Sk first sc, sc in next 11 sc.
Row 10: Repeat row 8.
Row 11: Repeat row 9.
Row 12: Repeat row 8.
Row 13: Repeat row 9.
Row 14: Repeat row 8.
Row 15: Repeat row 9. End off.
BODY: With red, ch 17. **Row 1:** Sc in 2nd ch from hook and in each ch across. Ch 1, turn each row.
Rows 2-60: Work even on 16 sc. Mark sides of row 60. Cut red.
Rows 61-80: With brown, work even on 16 sc. End off.
RUNNERS (make 2): With red, ch 41. **Rows 1-4:** Work even on 40 sc. End off.
FINISHING: Pin upper front corner of side to marked row (row 60) of body (A on diagram). Sew side and red section of body tog from A to B with overhand stitch. Sew 2nd side to body in same way. Stuff sleigh in section behind brown bench. Attach bench to side (dash lines on diag.).

Continued on page 113

←2"→

FOR STUFFING WITH GOODIES

Four stockings for Santa to stuff with good things are crocheted. Two top designs in granny squares, red and white stocking in mini-grannies, are made with heel and toe insets. Green sock has double crochet pattern, granny applique and picot trim. Directions for Granny Patch Stockings, page 89. Granny Applique Stocking, page 89.

A tiny elf to perch on a branch is all single crochet, with bendable arms and legs. Wee Elf, page 90. Profile stockings have loopy crocheted beards that form the feet. See Loopy Stockings, page 90. Elf and Santa faces are handy totes with pointed hats to form handles. North Pole Totes, page 91. Opposite: Knitted elf is a beanbag; page 92. Granny squares make a quick-crochet stocking to hold goodies, page 93. Padded appliques trim a trio of stockings with Snowman, Santa, gingerbread cookie (see page 92).

HOLIDAY
GIFT
TOTES

Mr. & Mrs. Claus, big, little, and middle-sized, are ready to greet you in the hallway, on the mantel or table. All three couples are knitted, have fake fur trim. Directions for Mr. & Mrs. Santa, 35", 18", 10" tall, begin on page 93.

CHRISTMAS CRECHE

All the charming figures of the Christmas story are here, worked in easy crochet stitches. Styrofoam bases provide sturdy stands for the figures; chenille sticks make bendable arms and shepherds' crooks. Figures, about 7″ tall. Directions for Crocheted Creche, page 96.

THE FIRST NOEL

The story of the first Christmas is told in a sweet four-piece creche. Soft knitted figures are trimmed in bits of gold and lace. Mary and Joseph stand 11″ high. Directions on page 98.

Creche by Jane Slovachek.
Photography by Arthur Klonsky.

SLEIGH RIDE

Continued from page 104.

With brown, work 2 rnds sc around opening of sleigh. Using outline stitch, embroider scroll design on sides.

Runners (make 2): Braid 3 chenille sticks tog. Cover with crocheted runners, whipping edges tog. Sew runners securely to bottom of sleigh close to sides in position shown on diagram.

SMALL SLEIGH: SIDES (make 2): With red, ch 15. **Row 1:** Sc in 2nd ch from hook and in each ch across—14 sc. Ch 1, turn each row.

Row 2: 2 sc in first sc, sc in each sc across, 2 sc in last sc.

Rows 3 and 4: Repeat row 2—20 sc.

Row 5: Sk first sc, sc across to last sc, do not work in last sc.

Rows 6-8: Repeat row 5—12 sc. End off.

BODY: With red, ch 17. Work even on 16 sc for 44 rows. End off.

BENCH: With brown, ch 15. Work even on 14 sc for 16 rows. End off.

RUNNERS (make 2): With red, ch 41. Work even on 40 sc for 4 rows. End off.

FINISHING: Sew sides to body from A to B in the direction shown on diagram, using an overhand stitch. Stuffing behind bench, sew bench inside sleigh in position shown by dash lines on diagram.

With brown, work 1 rnd sc around top of sleigh. With red, work sc in each brown sc around. End off.

With brown, ch 20. With matching sewing thread, sew ch, right side down, in a curve, to side of sleigh to simulate door. Repeat on other side.

With brown, make ch long enough to fit around side of sleigh from A to B. Sew ch, right side up, to edge of side. Repeat on other side.

Finish runners as for large sleigh and sew as shown in diagram.

HORSE: Use Speed-Cro-Sheen and No. 00 hook.

SIDES (make 2): Beg at top, ch 34.

Row 1: Sc in 2nd ch from hook and in next 2 ch, (sk 1 ch, sc in next ch) twice, sk 1 ch, sc in next 10 ch, 3 sc in next ch, sc in next 7 ch, sk 2 ch (mark these 2 ch with a safety pin), sc in next 5 ch. Ch 1, turn each row.

Row 2: Sc in 5 sc, sk next sc, sc in 24 sc.

Row 3: Sc in 15 sc, (2 sc in next sc) 4 times, sc in 5 sc, sk next sc, sc in 4 sc.

Row 4: Sk first sc, sc in next 2 sc, sk next sc, sc in 5 sc, (3 sc in next sc) 4 times, sc in 13 sc, (sk 1 sc, sc in 2 sc) twice.

Row 5: Sk first sc, sc in next 27 sc.

Row 6: Sk first sc, sc in next 22 sc, sk 1 sc, sc in next 3 sc.

Row 7: Sk first sc, sc in next sc, sk next sc, sc in next sc, sk next sc, sc in 6 sc, (sk next sc, sc in next sc) 5 times, sk next sc, sc in 3 sc.

Row 8: Sk first sc, sc in 12 sc, sk next sc, sc in 2 sc.

Row 9: Sk first sc, sc in 13 sc.

Row 10: Sk first sc, sc in 12 sc. End off.

Ears: Make lp on hook; work 4 sc in ch-2 sp marked with safety pin. End off. Knot the 2 ends tog to outside of head; bring ends to inside through hole at bottom of ear. On 2nd piece, work ear from opposite side.

BACK STRIP: Ch 31. Sc in 2nd ch from hook and in each ch across. End off.

BACK LEG (make 2): Ch 17. **Row 1:** Sc in 2nd ch from hook and in each ch across. Ch 1, turn each row.

Row 2: (Sk 1 sc, sc in next sc) 8 times.

Row 3: Sc in each sc—8 sc.

Row 4: Sc in 2 sc, (sk 1 sc, sc in next 2 sc) twice.

Rows 5-10: Sc in 6 sc.

Row 11: 2 sc in each of 6 sc. End off.

FRONT LEG (make 2): Ch 11. **Row 1:** Sc in 2nd ch from hook and in each ch across. Ch 1, turn each row.

Row 2: Sc in first sc, sk 1 sc, sc in next sc, sk 1 sc, sc in next 2 sc, (sk 1 sc, sc in next sc) twice.

Rows 3-10: Sc in 6 sc.

Row 11: 2 sc in each of 6 sc. End off.

HARNESS: With brown wool, leaving 5″ end, ch 60. End off, leaving 5″ end. With brown wool, ch 10 in same way.

FINISHING: Beg at tip of nose (beg of starting ch for side of horse), overcast top of horse to one edge of back strip, being sure to keep ear to outside. Strip will not extend entire length of horse. Attach other side of horse to other edge of back strip in same way. Sew front, bottom and back edges of horse tog, stuffing firmly.

Cut 3 pieces of chenille stick the length of leg, twist tog, wrap with cotton. Cover with crocheted leg; sew side edges of leg tog. Make sure legs are fully stuffed. Sew legs to body.

Cut 30 pieces of cotton yarn 3″ long for mane. Fold in half and knot singly or 2 strands tog down back of neck. For tail, cut 20 pieces 4½″ long. Knot 2 strands tog to top back of horse.

With black yarn, embroider eyes, nose and mouth in satin stitch. For bridle and reins, thread 30″ length of brown yarn in sharp needle. Make a knot 12″ from end. Insert needle from one side to other side of head just behind mouth, pull yarn through to knot (12″ length is one side of reins). Bring yarn to back of head under ear, through part of mane, under other ear and go through head again in same place as before. Now, bring yarn over top of face and through head in same

place as before, then bring yarn under face and through head for the 4th time. Cut remaining end same length as first rein.

Attach one end of 60″ harness ch to front of sleigh ½″ to one side of center. Bring ch around front of horse and attach other end to front of sleigh ½″ to other side of center. Place 10″ ch over back of horse; sew to horse each side, catching in harness.

FIGURES: HEAD (same for all figures): With white and No. 00 hook, ch 3. **Rnd 1:** 3 sc in 3rd ch from hook, 3 sc in each of next 2 ch—9 sc. Work 3 rnds of 9 sc. (Sk 1 sc, sc in next sc) twice. Sl st in next st; end off. Push yarn end into head.

Note: All other parts of figures are worked with size G hook.

SLEEVES (make 2 for each figure): With color of sweater or dress, ch 9. Work 2 rows of 8 sc. End off.

PANTS LEGS (make 2 for each man): With color of pants, ch 11. Work 4 rows of 10 sc. End off.

DRESS: With color of skirt, ch 20. Sl st in first ch to form ring. **Rnd 1:** Sc in each ch around—20 sc.

Rnds 2-8: Sc in each sc around.

Rnd 9: (Sk 1 sc, sc in 3 sc) 5 times.

Rnd 10: Sc in each sc around—15 sc.

Rnd 11: (Sk 1 sc, sc in 2 sc) 5 times.

Rnd 12: Sc in each sc around—10 sc.

Note: For different color top, change colors here.

Rnd 13: 2 sc in each sc around—20 sc.

Rnd 14: (Sk 1 sc, sc in next sc) 10 times.

Rnd 15: Sc in each sc around.

Rnd 16: (Sk 1 sc, sc in next sc) 5 times. End off.

MAN'S SWEATER: Ch 10. Sl st in first ch to form ring. **Rnd 1:** Sc in each ch around.

Rnds 2-5: Sc in each sc around.

Rnd 6: (Sk 1 sc, sc in next sc) 5 times—5 sc. (Sk 1 sc, sc in next sc) twice. Sl st in next sc. End off.

FINISHING: Use matching sewing thread to sew figures. For arms, cut 6″ piece of chenille stick. Fold back ¼″ on one end. Cover this end with one sleeve; sew edges tog (sleeve seam). Push other end of stick through top of dress or sweater. Tack top of sleeve to dress or sweater. Finish 2nd arm and sleeve the same. Tack head in place. Stuff top of dresses and sweaters.

Cut 6″ piece of chenille stick for each leg. Fold in half. Sew pants leg over each leg. Insert stick ends into bottom of sweater. Tack in place.

Scarf: Ch 31. Work 1 row of 30 sc.

Shawl: Ch 25. Work 2 rows of 24 sc.

Brimmed Hat: Ch 4. **Rnd 1:** 2 dc in 4th ch from hook, 2 dc in each of next 3 ch.

Rnd 2: Dc in each dc around—8 dc.

Rnd 3: 3 sc in each dc around.

Rnd 4: Sc in each sc around. End off.

Cap: Work as for brimmed hat through rnd 2. Work 1 more rnd of 8 dc. End off. Tack accessories to figures.

PINCUSHION CHAIR
Shown on page 130

MATERIALS: Knitting worsted, 4-ply, 1 oz. each of green, white and red. Crochet hook size I (5½ mm). Two 1″ plastic rings. One empty tuna fish can and cover. Polyester filling.

GAUGE: 4 sc = 1″; 4 rnds = 1″.

CHAIR: BACK: Beg at center with green, ch 4. Join with a sl st in first ch.

Rnd 1: Ch 1, work 12 sc in rnd. Do not join; mark end of each rnd.

Rnd 2: (Sc in next sc, 2 sc in next sc) 6 times—18 sc.

Rnd 3: (Sc in each of next 2 sc, 2 sc in next sc) 6 times—24 sc.

Rnd 4: (Sc in each of next 3 sc, 2 sc in next sc) 6 times—30 sc.

Rnd 5: (Sc in each of next 4 sc, 2 sc in next sc) 6 times—36 sc.

Rnd 6: (Sc in each of next 5 sc, 2 sc in next sc) 6 times—42 sc. End off.

FRONT OF BACK: Beg with white, work same as for back, working 4 rnds white, 2 rnds green. End off. Padding front slightly, place can cover between the two pieces. With front facing you, with red, sc back and front tog. Join with a sl st in first sc; end off.

SEAT: Work same as for front of back; do not end off. With green, work 2 rnds even (no incs). With red, work even until piece fits snugly over top and sides of can.

BOTTOM: Work same as for back, working 4 rnds green, 2 rnds white. Stuff can. Slip seat over can; with white, sew seat and bottom tog.

FRINGE: With green, make chain to fit snugly around can. Join with a sl st in first ch, being careful not to twist ch.

Rnd 1: Loop st in each ch around. (To make loop st, insert hook in ch, wrap yarn over right index finger, pull yarn through ch, yo and through 2 lps on hook.) Join with a sl st in first st. End off, leaving a 15″ end for sewing. Sew fringe around lower edge of can.

ARMS (make 2): With white, sc closely around plastic ring. Join; with red, sc in each sc around. Join; end off, leaving a long end for sewing. Sew back to seat as pictured; sew arms to back and seat. With red, make 8″ chain; end off. Tie into bow; tack to center of back.

SNOWBABY HANGER
Shown on page 130

SIZE: 10″ long.

MATERIALS: Worsted weight yarn, 1 oz. red, smaller amounts of white, green, black. Crochet hook size E. Wire hanger (type with cardboard roll in which ends of wire are hooked). Yarn needle. Cotton batting.

HANGER: Remove roll from hanger. Bend wire ends up and toward hook 5″ from center. Place cotton batting around hanger and wrap with yarn to secure.

Cover: With red, ch 11. Sc in 2nd ch from hook and in each remaining ch. Ch 1, turn. Work even on 10 sc until cover is as long as hanger, about 10″. End off. Fold cover in half both ways to find center. Push hook of hanger through center, fold piece around hanger and sew shut.

Hook Cover: With red, ch 4. Sc in 2nd ch from hook and in each remaining ch. Ch 1, turn. Work even on 3 sc until same length as hook. Sew to hanger cover and around hook. Sew top end well.

SNOWBABY: For body, with white, ch 2. Work 6 sc in 2nd ch from hook.

Rnd 2: 2 sc in each sc around. **Rnd 3:** (Sc in next sc, sc in next sc) 6 times.

Rnd 4: (2 sc in next sc, sc in each of 2 sc) 6 times. End off. Make another piece the same. For head, work 2 pieces as for body, end rnd 3—18 sc.

For arms and legs, with white, ch 5. Sc in 2nd ch from hook and in each remaining ch. Ch 1, turn. Sc in each of 4 sc. End off. Sew 2 pieces tog for each arm or leg, stuffing lightly.

Sew bottom of body to hanger, one piece to front, one to back. Sew upper parts tog, stuffing between. Sew heads tog over hook and to body at neck. Sew on arms and legs. Make green scarf 2 sc wide and 6″ long. Sew to neck. Make black french knots for eyes, nose, buttons, red straight st for mouth. Embroider white snowflakes on hanger, one large cross st on top of another.

SANTA HAND PUPPET
Shown on page 130

SIZE: 9″ high.

MATERIALS: Knitting worsted, 2 ozs. red, 1 oz. white; small amounts of peach, gold and black. Crochet hook size F or 5 (4 mm). Blue and red felt scraps.

GAUGE: 4 sts = 1″.

PUPPET: Beg at lower edge, with red, ch 48. **Rnd 1:** Hdc in first ch (forming ring), hdc in each ch around.

Rnds 2-6: Hdc in each hdc around.

Rnd 7: Sc in first 12 hdc, ch 9 for arm; sc in 2nd ch from hook and in next 7 ch, sc in next 24 hdc (front), ch 9 for arm; sc in 2nd ch from hook and in next 7 ch, sc in next 12 hdc.

Rnd 8: Sc in 12 sc; working on opposite side of arm ch, sc in 8 ch, sc in each sc of arm and front to next arm ch, work 2nd arm as for first arm, sc to center back.

Rnds 9-13: Work even in sc. End at center back.

Rnd 14 (neck): Work 5 sc for back of neck. Fold piece flat with arms at sides; sc in corresponding sc on front and in next 9 sc for front of neck, sc in corresponding 5 sc on back of neck to center back. Cut red. Change to peach.

Rnd 15: With peach, sc in each sc around neck, inc 1 sc each side—22 sc.

Rnds 16 and 17: Sc around, inc 4 sc each—30 sc.

Rnds 18-20: Work even in sc.

Rnds 21-24: Dec 6 sc evenly spaced each rnd—6 sc.

Rnd 25: (Work 2 sc tog) 3 times. End off. Sew shoulder seams.

HANDS (make 2): With peach, ch 16; sl st in first ch to form ring. **Rnd 1:** Sc in each ch around.

Rnd 2: Sc in each sc around.

Rnds 3-5: Work in sc, dec 4 sc each rnd. Cut yarn. Thread end in needle; sew up opening. Sew a hand over each arm end.

HAT: With red, ch 2; 4 sc in 2nd ch from hook. Work around in sc for 20 rnds, inc 1 sc each rnd, then work 3 more rnds, inc 3 sc evenly spaced each rnd. End off. Sew hat around 6th peach rnd of head. Make a 1″ white pompon; sew to tip of cap.

LOOP TRIM: Cut cardboard strip ¾″ wide. With white, make ch required length. Hold strip in back of work.

Row 1: Insert hook in 2nd ch from hook, wind yarn down back of strip and up front, work sc in ch. Work sc in each ch across, winding yarn around strip for each loop st. Ch 1, turn.

Row 2: Sc in each loop st across. Ch 1, turn.

Row 3: Loop st in each sc across. End off. For edge of Santa's suit, ch 60. For each wrist edge, ch 20. For cap, ch 40. Sew on trim.

HAIR: With white, ch 21. Work 4 rows of sc, dec 1 sc at each end of each row—12 sc. Sew ch edge to loop trim across back of head.

BEARD: With white, ch 24. **Row 1:** Sc in 2nd ch from hook and in each ch across. Ch 1, turn.

Row 2: Sk first st, sl st in next st, ch 1, sc in next 19 sc, sl st in next st. Ch 1, turn.

Row 3: Sk sl st, sl st in next 3 sts, ch 1, sc in 3 sc, dec 1 sc over next 2 sc, sc in 2 sc, dec 1 sc, sc in 3 sc, sl st in next 5 sts. Ch 1, turn.

Row 4: Sk first sl st, sl st in next 5 sts, dec 1 sc, sc in 3 sc, dec 1 sc, sl st in next 5 sts. Ch 1, turn.

Row 5: Sk first sl st, sl st in 5 sts, sc in next st, ch 5, sk 3 sts, sc in next st, sl st in 5 sts. End off. Sew beard to face. Ch 5 of row 5 is mustache.

Cut blue felt circles for eyes, red circle for nose. Sew on.

BELT: With black, ch 59. Work 2 rows of 58 sc. Sew around puppet. At center front, with gold, make straight sts over belt for buckle.

SACK: With gold, ch 2. **Rnd 1:** 6 sc in 2nd ch from hook.

Rnd 2: 2 sc in each sc around—12 sc.

Rnd 3: (Sc in next sc, 2 sc in next sc) 6 times.

Rnds 4 and 5: Work even on 18 sc.

Rnd 6: Dec 2 sc evenly spaced.

Rnd 7: Work even.

Rnds 8 and 9: Repeat rnds 6 and 7.

Rnd 10: Dec 4 sc evenly spaced—10 sc. Stuff sack.

Rnd 11: Dec 2 sc evenly spaced—8 sc.

Rnd 12: 2 sc in each sc. Work 1 rnd even. End off. Make a 10″ ch; weave through rnd 11. Tie ends tog; attach to left shoulder and hand.

SANTA BEANBAG
Shown on page 130

MATERIALS: Worsted weight yarn, small amounts of pink, red, white, black. Crochet hook size F. Yarn needle. Dry beans.

BACK: With white, beg at bottom, ch 5.

Row 1: Loop st in 2nd ch from hook and in each remaining ch. (To make loop st, cut strip of cardboard ½″ wide. Hold in back of work; wind yarn down back of strip and up front of strip, work sc in st.) Ch 1, turn.

Row 2: 2 sc in first sc, sc across, 2 sc in last sc—6 sc. Ch 1, turn.

Row 3: Loop st in each st. Ch 1, turn. Repeat rows 2 and 3 until there are 18 sc. Work even in pat until there are 5 rows of 18 loop sts. Work 2 rows of 18 sc. Change to red, work 2 rows of 18 sc. Dec 1 sc each side of next row and every other row until there are 10 sc. End off.

FRONT: Work as for back until there are 18 sc. Working on 4 end sts only, work even for 10 rows (5 loop-st rows, 5 sc rows). End off. Work same on last 4 sts. For face, with pink, ch 11. Work even on 10 sc for 10 rows. End off. Sew face into beard. Working across top, with white, work 2 rows of 18 sc. Change to red and finish as for back. Embroider black eyes, white eyebrows and mustache, red nose and mouth on face. Sew front and back tog, filling with beans before sewing top closed.

POINSETTIA POT HOLDER
Shown on page 131

SIZE: 7″ wide.

MATERIALS: Acrylic yarn of knitting worsted weight, 1 oz. each of white (W), red (R), and green (G). Small amount of yellow (Y). Crochet hook size G (4½ mm). Plastic ring.

GAUGE: 9 sts = 2″.

FRONT: With Y, ch 4, join with sl st to form ring.

Rnd 1: Ch 1, 12 sc in ring. Sl st in first sc. Cut Y.

Rnd 2: Join R in any sc, ch 8, * sc in 2nd ch from hook, hdc in next ch, dc in next 2 ch, hdc in next ch, sc in next sc, ch 7, repeat from * 10 times, sc in 2nd ch from hook, hdc in next ch, dc in next 2 ch, hdc in next ch, sc in last ch, sl st in first ch of first petal. Cut yarn.

Rnd 3: Join G in any sc between petals; ch 5; * working in back of petals, dc in next sc between petals, ch 2, repeat from * around, sl st in 3rd ch of ch 5.

Rnd 4: Ch 9, * sc in 2nd ch from hook, hdc in next ch, dc in next ch, tr in next ch, dc in next ch, hdc in next ch, sc in next ch, 2 sc in ch-2 sp, sc in dc, ch 8, repeat from * 10 times, work last ch 8 as before, 2 sc in ch-2 sp, sl st in first ch of first leaf. Cut yarn.

Rnd 5: With W, sc in each of 3 sc between leaves, * ch 1; working behind leaves, sc in each of next 3 sc, repeat from * around, end ch 1, sl st in first sc.

Rnd 6: Ch 1, sc in first sc, sc in next sc, * insert hook in sc at tip of red petal and into next sc of rnd 5 at same time, draw yarn through, complete sc, 2 sc in next ch-1 sp, sc in each of next 2 sc, repeat from * around, end 2 sc in last ch-1 sp, sl st in first sc.

Rnd 7: Ch 3 (counts as 1 dc), dc in each of next 3 sc, * ch 2, sk 1 sc, dc in each of next 4 sc, repeat from * around, end ch 2, sl st in top of ch 3.

Rnd 8: Ch 3, dc in each of next 3 dc, * dc in ch-2 sp, sc in sc at tip of leaf, dc in each of next 4 dc, repeat from * around, end dc in ch-2 sp, sc in tip of last leaf, sl st in top of ch 3.

Rnd 9: Ch 1, sc in each of first 5 dc, * sc in sc at tip of leaf, sc in each of next 2 dc, 3 dc in next dc (corner), sc in each of next 2 dc, sc in sc at tip of leaf, sc in each of next 5 dc, repeat from * around (6 corners), and sc in each of last 2 dc, sc in sc at tip of leaf, sl st in first sc. End off.

BACK: With W, ch 4, join with sl st to form ring. **Rnd 1:** Ch 1, 12 sc in ring. Sl st in first sc.

Rnd 2: Ch 3, dc in same sc with sl st, 2 dc in each sc around—24 dc. Sl st in top of ch 3.

Rnd 3: Ch 3, dc in same place as sl st, 2 dc in each dc around—48 dc. Sl st in top of ch 3.

Rnd 4: Ch 3, dc in each of next 3 dc, (ch 1, dc in each of next 4 dc) 11 times, ch 1, sl st in top of ch 3.

Rnd 5: Ch 3, dc in each of next 3 dc, (ch 2, dc in each of next 4 dc) 11 times, ch 2, sl st in top of ch 3.

Rnd 6: Ch 3, dc in each of next 3 dc, (2 dc in ch-2 sp, dc in each of next 4 dc) 11 times, 2 dc in last ch-2 sp, sl st in top of ch 3.

Rnd 7: Ch 1, sc in same ch as sl st, sc in each of next 7 dc, (3 dc in next dc, sc in each of next 11 dc) 5 times, 3 dc in next dc, sc in each of last 3 dc, sl st in first sc. End off.

FINISHING: Place front and back tog. From right side, sc pieces tog with W, working sc in each sc, 2 sc in center dc at each corner; at one corner, place plastic ring between front and back, work 12 sc over ring, sk center dc at corner and continue to sc pieces tog.

SANTA DOOR KNOB COVER
Shown on page 131

MATERIALS: Knitting worsted weight yarn, 1 oz. each of white and red. Crochet hook size H. Tapestry needle. Two plastic eyes. Two jingle bells.

GAUGE: 7 sts = 2″.

HEAD: With white, ch 3. Sl st in first ch to form ring. **Rnd 1:** 6 sc in ring.

Rnd 2: 2 sc in each sc around.

Rnd 3: (Sc in next sc, 2 sc in next sc) 6 times.

Rnd 4: (Sc in 2 sc, 2 sc in next sc) 6 times.

Rnd 5: (Sc in 3 sc, 2 sc in next sc) 6 times.

Rnd 6: (Sc in 4 sc, 2 sc in next sc) 6 times.

Rnds 7 and 8: Sc in each sc around—36 sc.

Rnd 9: (Sc in next sc, work next 2 sc tog) 12 times.

Rnd 10: (Sc in next sc, work next 2 sc tog) 8 times. Sl st in next st. End off.

BEARD: Thread white yarn in needle. Working under sts of rnd 4, bring yarn to right side at top of st, * insert needle down in same place and pull through, leaving ½″ loop; bring needle up at bottom of same st, insert needle down in same place and pull through, leaving ½″ loop; bring needle up at top of next st, repeat from * two-thirds of the way around rnd 4. Work loops in same way at top and bottom of sts of rnds 5-7.

HAT: With red, ch 3. Sl st in first ch to form ring. **Rnd 1:** 6 sc in ring.

Rnd 2: 2 sc in each sc—12 sc.

Rnds 3-13: Work around in sc, inc 1 sc each rnd. End off. Tack hat to head on section without loops. Sew a white pompon to top of hat.

FINISHING: Sew eyes to face. Embroider red nose and mouth. Make red ch 10″ long. Sew a bell to each end. Sew center of ch to side back of cover.

SANTA RATTLE
Shown on page 131

SIZE: 8″.

MATERIALS: Worsted weight yarn, 1 oz. red; small amounts of white, black, pink, gold. Crochet hook size F (4 mm). Red and blue felt scraps. L'eggs® egg. Jingle bell. Stuffing.

GAUGE: 4 sc = 1″.
BODY: With red, ch 2. **Rnd 1:** 6 sc in 2nd ch from hook.
Rnd 2: 2 sc in each sc around—12 sc.
Rnd 3: (Sc in next sc, 2 sc in next sc) 6 times.
Rnd 4: (Sc in 2 sc, 2 sc in next sc) 6 times.
Rnds 5-9: Work even on 24 sc.
Rnd 10: (Sc in 3 sc, 2 sc in next sc) 6 times.
Rnds 11-14: Work even on 30 sc. Cut red. With pink, work 1 rnd even.
Rnd 16: Dec 6 sc evenly spaced around. Work 1 rnd even on 24 sc. Place egg containing bell inside.
Rnd 18: Repeat rnd 16. Work 1 rnd even on 18 sc.
Rnd 20: Repeat rnd 16. Work 1 rnd even on 12 sc.
Rnd 22: Repeat rnd 16. Cut yarn. Gather last 6 sts tog. Close opening.
Leg (make 2): With black, ch 2.
Rnd 1: 5 sc in 2nd ch from hook.
Rnd 2: 2 sc in each sc around.
Rnds 3-5: Work even on 10 sc. Cut black.
Rnds 6-7: With white, work even. Cut white.
Rnds 8-10: With red, work even. End off. Stuff legs; sew to body.
Arm (make 2): With pink, ch 2.
Rnd 1: 4 sc in 2nd ch from hook.
Rnd 2: 2 sc in each sc around.
Rnds 3 and 4: Work even on 8 sc. Cut pink.
Rnds 5 and 6: With white, work even. Cut white.
Rnds 7-10: With red, work even. End off. Stuff arms. Sew top of arm flat across; sew to side of body on rnd 15. Tack to body 3 rows below.
SACK: With gold, work as for body through rnd 3.
Rnds 4 and 5: Work even on 18 sc.
Rnd 6: Dec 2 sc evenly spaced.
Rnd 7: Work even on 16 sc.
Rnds 8 and 9: Repeat rnds 6 and 7.
Rnd 10: Dec 4 sc evenly spaced—10 sc. Stuff sack.
Rnd 11: Dec 2 sc evenly spaced—8 sc.
Rnd 12: 2 sc in each sc. Work 1 rnd even. End off. Make a 10″ ch; weave through rnd 11. Tie ends tog; attach to left shoulder and hand.
BELT: With black, ch 37. Sc in 2nd and in each ch across. End off; leave long end. Sew ends of belt tog; sew to body.
HAT: With red, ch 2. **Rnd 1:** 3 sc in 2nd ch from hook.
Rnds 2 and 3: Inc 2 sc each rnd.
Rnd 4: Work even—7 sc.
Rnds 5-10: Repeat rnds 3 and 4—13 sc.
Rnd 11: Work even.
Rnd 12: Inc 2 sc in rnd—15 sc.
Rnd 13: Work even.
Rnds 14-19: Inc 2 sc in each rnd—27 sc.
Rnd 20: Work even. Cut red.
Rnds 21-23: With white, work even.

End off. Sew hat to head. Fold point to left. Sew white pompon to tip of hat. Sew tip to side of head.
BEARD: With white, ch 24. **Row 1:** Sc in 2nd ch from hook and in each ch across. Ch 1, turn.
Row 2: Sk first st, sl st in next st, ch 1, sc in next 19 sc, sl st in next st. Ch 1, turn.
Row 3: Sk sl st, sl st in next 3 sts, ch 1, sc in 3 sc, dec 1 sc over next 2 sc, sc in 2 sc, dec 1 sc, sc in 3 sc, sl st in next 5 sts. Ch 1, turn.
Row 4: Sk first sl st, sl st in next 5 sts, dec 1 sc, sc in 3 sc, dec 1 sc, sl st in next 5 sts. Ch 1, turn.
Row 5: Sk first sl st, sl st in 5 sts, sc in next st, ch 5, sk 3 sts, sc in next st, sl st in 5 sts. End off. Sew beard to face. Ch 5 of row 5 is mustache.

Cut ½″ blue felt circles for eyes, ¼″ red circle for nose. Glue on.

SNOWFLAKE MITT
Shown on page 133

SIZE: 8″ × 6″.
MATERIALS: Coats & Clark's Speed-Cro-Sheen, 2 balls red, 1 ball navy. J.&P. Coats Six Strand Floss, 2 skeins white. Steel crochet hook No. 0. Large-eyed embroidery needle. Lining material, 13″ × 9″.
GAUGE: 11 sc = 2″; 13 rows = 2″.
MITT: BACK: With red, ch 37.
Row 1: Sc in 2nd ch from hook and in each ch—36 sc. Ch 1, turn each row. Work even on 36 sc for 30 rows. End off.
FRONT: Work as for back for 6 rows. * Change to navy, work even for 6 rows. Change to red, work even for 6 rows. Repeat from * once. End off.
FINISHING: Work 2 rows sc with navy around each piece, working 2 sc in each corner. On 2nd row of edging on front, work ch 14 loop for hanger at center of center red stripe. Embroider navy stripes with cross-stitch following chart, using 12 strands of floss. Embroider cross-stitch in every other st around 2nd row of edging on front. Sew front to back along 3 sides, leaving side with hanger open. Fold lining material in half, right sides tog; stitch one side and ends tog, taking ½″ seams, to form piece 6″ × 8½″. Insert in pot holder. Turn under raw edges; hem to inside of pot holder.

PENNSYLVANIA DUTCH POT HOLDER
Shown on page 132

SIZE: 6½″ × 7½″.
MATERIALS: Coats & Clark's Speed-Cro-Sheen, 1 ball each of white and green. J.&P. Coats Six Strand Floss, 1 skein each of red, blue, green, yellow, and brown. Steel crochet hook No. 0. Large-eyed embroidery needle.
GAUGE: 11 sc = 2″; 13 rows = 2″.
POT HOLDER: FRONT: With white, ch 37. **Row 1:** Sc in 2nd ch from hook and in each ch across. Ch 1, turn each row. Work even on 36 sc for 40 rows. End off. With green, work 2 rows sc around piece, working 3 sc in each corner.
BACK: With green, ch 41. Work as for front on 40 sc for 44 rows. End off.

● Red	☑ Green
◹ Blue	⠭ Yellow
■ Brown	

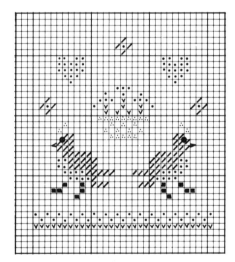

EMBROIDERY: Use 12 strands of floss for cross-stitch design, except for birds' feet; use only 6 strands for feet. Following chart, embroider front of pot holder. Make birds' eyes with brown French knots, beaks with brown straight stitch. See Contents for Stitch Details.
FINISHING: Sew back to front with green, picking up back lp of each sc on front border. With green, ch 14 for hanger; sl st in each ch across. Sew to top corner.

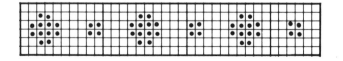

HOLIDAY POT HOLDERS
Shown on pages 132 and 133

SIZE: 7″ square.
MATERIALS: American Thread's Giant Mercerized Crochet Cotton, 1 (550-yd.) ball each of green, red and white. Crochet hook size E. Star Six Strand Embroidery Cotton, 4 skeins white, 2 skeins red, 2 skeins black, 2 skeins green, 1 skein pink. Embroidery needle.
GAUGE: 11 sc = 2″.
Note: Use double strand of cotton throughout.
SQUARE (make 2 green, 2 red, 2 white): With double strand of cotton, ch 41.
Row 1: Sc in 2nd ch from hook and in each ch across. Ch 1, turn each row.
Rows 2-44: Work even on 40 sc. End off.
EMBROIDERY: Using 6 strands of embroidery floss, following charts, embroider squares.
EDGING: Place 2 green squares wrong sides tog. Join double strand of green cotton to upper left corner of pot holder. Working through both pieces, sc, * ch 4, sc in 3rd ch for picot, ch 1, sk 2 sts, sc in 3 sts, repeat from * around square, end sc in first corner, ch 12, sl st in same st. End off.

Work same edging with red for red pot holder, with white for white pot holder. White pot holder may need a

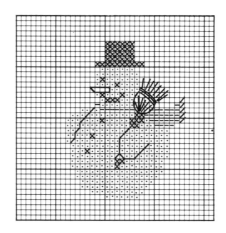

· **White**   ⊠ **Black**   ⊟ **Green**

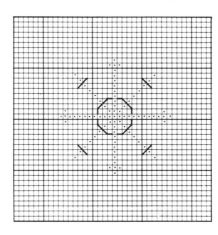

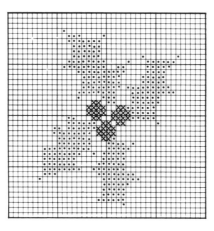

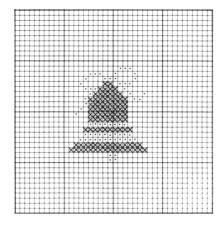

· **White**   Ⓢ **Pink**   ⊠ **Red**

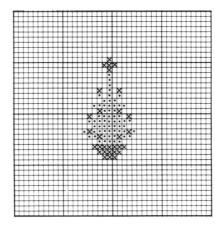

⊠ **Red**   · **Green**

piece of white felt or other material inserted between squares, if cross-stitches show through.

PLAY BOLSTER
Shown on page 134

SIZE: 30″ long.
MATERIALS: Dawn Sayelle, 3 4-oz. skeins white, main color (MC), 1 skein flame, contrasting color (CC). Dawn Wintuk Sport Yarn, 1 2-oz. skein each of white (W), flame (F), blue (B), pink (P), yellow (Y), burnt orange (O). Crochet hooks sizes I or 9 (5½ mm) and G or 6 (4½ mm). Polyester fiberfill, 2 packages. Yarn needle.
GAUGE: 3 sts = 1″ (Sayelle, size I hook); 4 sc = 1″ (sport yarn, size G hook).
BOLSTER: Beg at one end, with MC, ch 91. **Row 1:** Dc in 3rd ch from hook and in each ch—90 dc. Ch 2, turn.
Row 2: Sc in first dc; * with CC, working over MC strand, dc in next dc; with MC, working over CC strand, sc in next dc, repeat from * across, end CC dc in top of turning ch. With MC, ch 1, turn.
Row 3: With MC, sc in each st across. Ch 2, turn.
Row 4: Sk first sc, dc in next sc and in each sc across. Ch 2, turn. Repeat rows 2-4 for pat until piece is 30″ long, end row 4. Sew side edges of piece tog. Thread a double strand of MC in yarn needle, run through ch sts at beg of piece, gather sts tog tightly and secure. Stuff bolster. Gather sts at open end of bolster and secure.
LARGE POCKET #1: With CC, ch 2; * with MC, ch 1; cut this MC strand to 1 yard length; with CC, ch 6, repeat from * twice, end last repeat with CC, ch 3. **Row 1:** With CC, sc in 2nd ch from hook and in next ch; * with MC, sc in MC ch; with CC, sc in 6 CC ch, repeat from * across, end with CC, sc in last 2 ch. Ch 1, turn.
Rows 2-5: Work in sc, working CC in CC, MC in MC. Ch 1, turn each row.
Row 6: With MC, sc across.
Rows 7-14: Work in sc, working 2 CC, 1 MC, 6 CC, 1 MC, 6 CC, 1 MC, 2 CC.
Row 15: Repeat row 6.
Rows 16-18: Repeat row 7. End off.
Flap: With MC, ch 20. **Row 1:** Sc in 2nd ch from hook and in each ch across. Ch 1, turn each row.
Rows 2-15: Working in sc, work 2 rows CC, 2 rows MC alternately. End off. Sew last row to last row of pocket, wrong side of flap to right side of pocket. Fold flap in half to right side. Sew pocket in place near one end of bolster.
LARGE POCKET #2: With MC, ch 2. **Row 1:** Sc in 2nd ch from hook. Ch 1, turn each row.
Row 2: 2 sc in sc.

Row 3: 2 sc in each sc.

Row 4: 2 sc in first sc, sc in each sc to last sc, 2 sc in last sc—6 sc.

Rows 5 and 6: With CC, repeat row 4. Cut CC.

Rows 7-12: With MC, repeat row 4.

Rows 13 and 14: Repeat rows 5 and 6.

Row 15: With MC, repeat row 4.

Row 16: With MC, sc in each sc.

Rows 17 and 18: With CC, sc across, dec 1 sc at beg and end of row.

Rows 19-24: With MC, repeat row 17.

Rows 25 and 26: Repeat rows 17 and 18.

Rows 27-30: With MC, repeat row 17 until 1 st is left. End off.

Flap: With CC, ch 21. Reversing colors, work rows 1-5 of bolster pat. End off. Sew wrong side of row 5 to top of pocket. Fold flap down to right side. Sew pocket in place at center of bolster at same level as first pocket.

LARGE POCKET #3: With CC, ch 16. Work in sc on 15 sc for 25 rows, working 3 rows CC, 2 rows MC, 15 rows CC, 2 rows MC, 3 rows CC. Sl st in each st across. End off. Work flap as for first pocket. Sew pocket in place near end of bolster.

SMALL POCKETS (make 2): With F and G hook, ch 13. Work in sc on 12 sc, 2 rows F, 2 rows W, until piece is square. Sew pockets between large pockets.

UMBRELLAS (make 2): With F and G hook, ch 16. Work in sc on 15 sc for 5 rows. Gather one edge of piece, sew to bolster above small pocket. Embroider shaft of umbrella down into pocket.

DOLL'S PILLOW: With W and G hook, ch 10. Work in sc on 9 sc for 7 rows. Make another piece the same. Sew tog with stuffing between. With F, work 1 rnd of dc around pillow, working 3 dc in each corner.

DOLL: Head: With P and G hook, ch 2.

Rnd 1: 6 sc in 2nd ch from hook.

Rnd 2: 2 sc in each sc around.

Rnd 3: (Sc in next sc, 2 sc in next sc) 6 times—18 sc.

Rnds 4-6: Work even.

Rnd 7: (Work 2 sc tog) 9 times.

Rnd 8: Sc in each sc around. Stuff head.

Rnd 9: Dec 2 sc in rnd.

Rnd 10: Work even on 7 sc. End off.

Body (make 2 pieces): With P and G hook, ch 25. Work in sc on 24 sc for 3 rows. Sl st in first 8 sc, sc in next 8 sc. Ch 1, turn. Working on center 8 sc, work even for 8 rows. Sc in 4 sc for first leg. Ch 1, turn. Work even on 4 sc for 9 rows. Cut P. With O (or any shoe color), sc in 4 sc. Ch 1, turn. Sc in first sc, 2 sc in 2 sc, sc in last sc. End off. Work 2nd leg the same. Sew 2 body pieces tog, stuffing as you go. Stuff neck, sew head to body.

Hair: Cut 4″ strands of Y or O. With 2 strands tog, fold strands in half, knot folded ends around top of head. Draw half of ends to each side of head, tie ends tog with a yarn bow.

Embroider eyes in French knots, mouth in outline stitch.

Blue Dress: With B and G hook, ch 15. Work in sc on 14 sc for 7 rows. Ch 2, turn. Work in dc for 2 rows. Work 3 dc in each dc across. End off. Make another piece the same. Sew pieces tog for 3 sts on each shoulder. Leave 4 rows open at sides for armholes, sew side seams. Run W around waistline for belt; tie in a bow.

Yellow Dress: With Y and G hook, ch 20. Dc in 3rd ch from hook and in each ch across. Ch 2, turn. Work 3 dc in each dc across for 2 rows. End off. Sew back seam. Working across center front on starting ch, sc in 7 ch. Ch 1, turn. Work even on 7 sc for 2 rows. Dec 1 sc each side of next row. Work 2 rows even on 5 sc. Make ch long enough to reach over shoulder to center back of dress. Sew end of ch in place. Make another ch the same at beg of last row.

SNOWMAN SCENE
Shown on page 135

SIZES: Snowman, 7″; boy and girl, 7″; bird and bunny, 2″.

MATERIALS: Knitting worsted, small amounts of white, black, red, blue, gray, pink, brown, orange, green, yellow, dark rose and light rose. Crochet hook size F. Polyester fiberfill for stuffing. Scrap of red felt. Glue. Box of glass head pins. Two small sticks. Plastic foam forms needed:

For Snowman: 1½″ ball, 2″ ball, 2½″ ball.

For Boy: 1½″ ball, 2″ egg.

For Girl: 1½″ ball, 2″ egg.

For Bird: 1″ egg.

For Bunny: ¾″ ball, 1″ egg.

Note: These patterns are worked in continuous rounds. Do not chain and turn, unless otherwise indicated. Always use both loops of each st, unless otherwise directed.

GAUGE: 4 to 5 sts = 1″.

SNOWMAN: HEAD AND BODY: With white, ch 4, sl st in first ch to form ring.

Rnds 1 and 2: 2 sc in each st around.

Rnd 3: * Sc in each of next 3 sts, 2 sc in next st, repeat from * around.

Rnds 4-7: Sc in each st around—20 sc. Slip 1½″ ball into head.

Rnds 8 and 9: * Sc in each of next 2 sts, sk next st, sc in next st, repeat from * around.

Rnd 10: 2 sc in each st around—24 sc.

Rnds 11-17: Sc in each st around. Slip 2″ ball into first section of body.

Rnd 18: * Sc in next st, sk next st, sc in next st, repeat from * around.

Rnd 19: 2 sc in each st around—32 sc.

Rnds 20-26: Sc in each st around. Slip 2½″ ball into lower section of body.

Rnd 27: * Sc in each of next 2 sts, sk next st, sc in next st, repeat from * around—24 sc. Enlarge last lp, drop yarn.

Rnd 28: With black, working in front lps, * sc, hdc in next st, 2 dc in each of next 2 sts, hdc, sc in next st, sc in each of next 2 sts, repeat from * to complete 2nd foot. End off. Go back to enlarged white lp; working in back lps, sc in each of next 10 sts; working in both lps, work sc in each st around—24 sc.

Rnd 29: Sc in every other st around—12 sc.

Rnds 30 and 31: Sl st in every other st around, to close. End off. Use glass head pins for the face and buttons.

SCARF: With red, ch 41.

Row 1: Sc in each st. End off, weaving in ends. Tie scarf around snowman's neck.

HAT: With white, ch 4; sl st in first ch to form ring.

Rnd 1: Sc in each st around. End off.

Rnd 2: With red, 2 sc in each st around.

Rnd 3: Sc in each st around.

Rnd 4: 2 sc in each st around.

Rnds 5-7: Sc in each st around.

Rnd 8: * Sc in next st, 2 sc in next st, repeat from * around—24 sc.

Rnd 9: Sc in each st around. End off. Slip hat onto head, and shape. Hat can either be sewn or pinned to head. Insert two small sticks for arms.

BOY: HEAD AND BODY: With pink, ch 4; sl st in first ch to form ring.

Rnds 1 and 2: 2 sc in each st around.

Rnd 3: * Sc in each of next 3 sts, 2 sc in next st, repeat from * around.

Rnds 4-8: Sc in each st around—20 sc. Slip 1½″ ball into head.

Rnd 9: Sc in every other st around—10 sc. End off.

Rnd 10: With green, * sc in next st, 2 sc in next st, repeat from * around.

Rnd 11: * Sc in each of next 2 sts, 2 sc in next st, repeat from * around.

Rnds 12 and 13: Sc in each st around—20 sc.

Rnd 14: * Sc in each of next 4 sts, 2 sc in next st, repeat from * around.

Rnd 15: Sc in each st around—24 sc.

Rnd 16: * Sc in each of next 3 sts, 2 sc in next st, repeat from * around.

Rnds 17 and 18: Sc in each st around—30 sc. Slip 2″ egg into body.

Rnd 19: * Sc in next st, sk next st, sc in next st, repeat from * around—20 sc.

Rnd 20: Sc in every other st around—10 sc.

Rnds 21 and 22: Sl st in every other st around, to close. End off.

ARMS AND MITTENS (make 2): With green, leaving an 8″ end, ch 8; sl st in first ch to form ring.

Rnds 1-10: Sc in each st around. End off.

Rnd 11: With yellow, sc in each st around.

Rnd 12: Working in front lp of next st, sc, ch 2, sc in same st; working in both lps, sc in each st around.

Rnd 14: Sl st in every other st around. End off. Using starting chain end, sew arm to side of body.

LEGS AND BOOTS (make 2): With green, leaving an 8″ end, ch 8; sl st in first ch to form ring.

Rnds 1-3: Sc in each st around. End off.

Rnds 4-6: With black, sc in each st around.

Rnd 7: Sc, hdc, dc in same st, 3 dc in next st, dc, hdc, sc in next st, sl st to join. End off; weave in end. Sew other end of leg onto bottom side of body. With stuffing or several cotton balls, stuff leg. Use glass head pins for eyes, nose and buttons. Cut a small felt mouth and glue on.

SCARF: With yellow, ch 41.

Row 1: Sc in each st. End off. Tie scarf around boy's neck.

HAT: With yellow, ch 4; sl st in first ch to form ring.

Rnds 1 and 2: 2 sc in each st around.

Rnd 3: * Sc in next st, 2 sc in next st, repeat from * around—24 sc.

Rnds 4 and 5: Sc in each st around. Drop yellow.

Rnd 6: With green, sc in each st around.

Rnd 7: With yellow, sc in each st around.

Rnd 8: With green, sc in each st around.

Rnd 9: With yellow, sc in each st around. End off. Slip hat onto head.

GIRL: HEAD AND BODY: Work as for Boy through rnd 9.

Rnd 10: With light rose, working in front lps, sc, dc in same st, 2 dc in each of next 8 sts, dc, sc in last st (to complete collar). End off.

Rnd 11: With dark rose, working in back loops, * sc in next st, 2 sc in next st, repeat from * around—15 sc.

Rnd 12: * Sc in each of next 2 sts, 2 sc in next st, repeat from * around.

Rnds 13 and 14: Sc in each st around—20 sc.

Rnd 15: * Sc in each of next 4 sts, 2 sc in next st, repeat from * around.

Rnd 16: Sc in each st around—24 sc.

Rnd 17: * Sc in each of next 3 sts, 2 sc in next st, repeat from * around.

Rnds 18 and 19: Sc in each st around—30 sc. Slip 2″ egg into body.

Rnd 20: * Sc in 2 sts, sk next st, sc in next st, repeat from * around—20 sc.

Rnd 21: Sc in every other st around—10 sc.

Rnds 22 and 23: Sl st in every other st around, to close. End off.

ARMS AND MITTENS (make 2): With dark rose, leaving an 8″ end, ch 8; sl st in first ch to form ring.

Rnds 1-10: Sc in each st around. End off.

Rnd 11: With light rose, sc in each st around.

Rnd 12: Working in front lp of next st, sc, ch 2 in same st; working in both lps, sc in each st around.

Rnd 14: Sl st in every other st around. End off. Using starting ch end, sew arm to side of body.

LEGS AND BOOTS (make 2): With dark rose, leaving an 8″ end, ch 8; sl st in first ch to form ring.

Rnds 1-3: Sc in each st around. End off.

Rnds 4-6: With black, sc in each st around.

Rnd 7: Sc, hdc, dc in same st, 3 dc in next st, dc, hdc, sc in next st, sl st to join. End off; weave in end. Sew other end of leg onto bottom side of body. With stuffing or several cotton balls, stuff leg. Use glass head pins for eyes, nose and buttons. Cut a small felt mouth and glue on.

HAT: With light rose, ch 4; sl st in first ch to form ring.

Rnd 1: Sc in each st around. End off.

Rnds 2 and 3: With dark rose, 2 sc in each st around.

Rnd 4: * Sc in next st, 2 sc in next st, repeat from * around.

Rnds 5-9: Sc in each st around—24 sc. End off.

Rnd 10: With light rose, sc in each st around. Enlarge lp, drop yarn.

Rnd 11 (hair): With brown, working in back lps, 2 lp sts in each of next 8 sts, sc in each of next 8 sts, 2 lp sts in each of next 8 sts.

To Make Lp St: * Insert hook in st, pass yarn round middle finger of left hand, yo hook, draw through 1 lp, yo hook, draw through 2 lps, drop lp off finger; repeat from * twice in each of required sts.

Rnds 12 and 13: Working in front lps, pick up enlarged lp of dropped color, sc in each st around—24 sc. End off. Slip hat and hair onto head, shape and arrange hair.

BIRD: HEAD AND BODY: With blue, ch 4; sl st in first ch to form ring.

Rnd 1: Sc in each st around.

Rnd 2: 2 sc in each st around.

Rnd 3: * Sc in next st, 2 sc in next st, repeat from * around—12 sc. Enlarge lp, drop yarn.

Rnd 4: Working in front lp of next st, with orange, sc, ch 2, sc in same st. End off orange. Pick up enlarged lp; sc in back lp of next st; working in both lps, sc in each st around.

Rnd 5: Sc in each of next 3 sts; * working in front lp of next st, work sc, ch 3, 2 tr in same st; ch 4, sc in same st; working in both lps, sc in each of next 4 sts, repeat from * in next st to complete second wing; continue working in both lps, sc in each of next 3 sts.

Rnd 6: Sc in each of next 3 sts, sc in back lp of next st, sc in each of next 4 sts, sc in back lp of next st, continue sc in each st around.

Rnd 7: Sc in each st around—12 sc.

Rnd 8: Sc in each of next 5 sts; working in front lp of next st, ch 3, tr; working in both lps, sc in each st; working in front lp of next st, tr, ch 3, sc in same st; working in both lps, continue sc in each of next 5 sts. Slip egg into head and body.

Rnd 9: * Working in back lps, sc in each of next 2 sts, sk next st, sc in next st, repeat from * around.

Rnd 10: Sl st in every other st around, to close. End off, tucking in ends and shaping wings and tail. Use glass head pins for eyes.

BUNNY: HEAD AND BODY: With gray, ch 4; sl st in first ch to form ring.

Rnd 1: 2 sc in each st around.

Rnd 2: * Sc in next st, 2 sc in next st, repeat from * around.

Rnd 3: Sc in each st around—12 sc.

Rnd 4: * Working in front lp, sc, ch 3, tr, ch 3, sc in same st; working in both lps, sc in next st, repeat from * once, continue to work sc in each st around. Slip ¾″ ball into head.

Rnd 5: Sc in back lp of next st, sc in both lps of next st, sc in back lp of next st; sc in both lps of each st around.

Rnd 6: Sc in each st around—12 sc.

Rnd 7: Sc in every other st around—6 sc.

Rnd 8: 2 sc in each st around—12 sc.

Rnd 9: Sc in each st around.

Rnd 10: Sc in each of next 7 sts; working in front lp, sc, ch 2, sc in same st; working in both lps, sc in next st; working in front lps, sc in next st, ch 2, sc in same st; working in both lps, sc in each of next 2 sts.

Rnd 11: Sc in each of 7 sts, sc in back lp of next st, sc in both lps of next st, sc in back lp of next st, sc in both lps around.

Rnd 12: Sc in each st around—12 sc.

Rnd 13: Repeat rnd 10, to complete the back feet.

Rnd 14: Repeat rnd 11. Slip 1″ egg into body.

Rnds 15 and 16: Sl st every other st around, to close. End off. Use glass head pins for eyes and nose. Fringe whiskers into head on either side of bunny's nose. Make one ½″ pompon for tail and tie on.

NORTH POLE ELVES
Shown on page 135

SIZE: About 10″ high.

MATERIALS: Worsted weight yarn, 3 ozs. red, 1 oz. each of pink, white, and black. Knitting needles No. 5. Set of dp needles No. 4.

GAUGE: 11 sts = 2″.

HEAD AND BODY: With red, cast on 16 sts. Work even in stockinette st (k 1 row, p 1 row) for 3½″ (front of body). Change to pink, work even for 4¾″. Change to red, work even for 3½″ (back of body). Bind off. Fold piece in half, wrong side out, matching red sections. Sew side seams, curving seams at top fold to make head round. Turn piece to right side; stuff firmly, shaping head round. Tie string tightly around neck.

NOSE: With pink, cast on 6 sts. Work in stockinette st for 5 rows. Bind off. Shape nose around stuffing; sew to face.

Embroider eyes and mouth. Color nose and cheeks lightly with red crayon. For beard, wind white wool around a strip of cardboard. Sew chain stitches along edge of cardboard. Remove loops from cardboard. Sew to face.

ARMS: With pink, cast on 10 sts. Work ½" stockinette st. Change to red, work 2½". Bind off. Sew seams, padding firmly. Sew to body.

LEGS: With black, cast on 12 sts. Work ¾" stockinette st. Change to red, work 2¾". Bind off. Sew seams, padding firmly. Sew to body.

CAP: With No. 4 needles, cast on 36 sts. Divide on 3 dp needles, work in k 1, p 1 ribbing for 2 rnds. Work in stockinette st (k each rnd) for 3".

Next Rnd: * K 2 tog, k 4, repeat from * around. Work 6 rnds even.

Next Rnd: * K 2 tog, k 3, repeat from * around. Work 6 rnds even.

Next Rnd: * K 2 tog, k 2, repeat from * around. Work 4 rnds even.

Next Rnd: * K 2 tog, k 1, repeat from * around. Work 4 rnds even.

Next Rnd: K 2 tog around. Cut yarn, draw through remaining sts. Make a small tassel, sew to end of cap.

KNITTED CAT, KITTENS
Shown on page 145

SIZES: Cat: About 15" high. Kittens: About 10" high.

MATERIALS: Mohair yarn, 2 ozs. for cat, 1½ ozs. for each kitten. Fingering yarn, 1 oz. for cat, ½ oz. for each kitten. Small amount of knitting worsted for mittens. Set of dp needles No. 5. Cotton batting for stuffing. Black buttonhole twist for whiskers. Carpet thread. Small piece gingham, matching sewing thread, and red iron-on tape for apron. Scraps of felt: black, blue, gold, pink, green, white, brown. All-purpose glue. Pipe cleaners. Stitch holder. Two ½" buttons for attaching arms to each pet. Tapestry needle.

GAUGE: 5 sts = 1" (using 1 strand each mohair and fingering yarn).

Note: Cat and kittens are knit using 1 strand each of mohair and fingering yarn throughout.

CAT: BODY: Beg at neck edge, with 2 strands (see Note), cast on 12 sts; divide on 3 dp needles. Join; work in stockinette st (k each rnd) for 2 rnds.

Rnd 3: Inc 1 st in each st—24 sts. K 4 rnds.

Rnd 8: Inc 1 st in each st—48 sts. K 2 rnds.

Rnd 11: (K 3, inc 1 st in next st) 12 times—60 sts. K 28 rnds.

Next Rnd: (K 3, k 2 tog) 12 times—48 sts. K 1 rnd.

Next Rnd: (K 2, k 2 tog) 12 times—36 sts. K 1 rnd.

Divide for Legs: Sl next 18 sts on a holder (one leg); divide remaining 18 sts on 3 dp needles (2nd leg). Join; k 11 rnds.

Next Rnd: (K 2 tog, k 4) 3 times—15 sts. K 9 rnds.

Shape Heel: Sl front 7 sts on a safety pin; with 2 dp needles, work back and forth on remaining 8 sts in stockinette st (p 1 row, k 1 row) for 6 rows. Sl front 7 sts on a dp needle. Divide the 15 sts on 3 dp needles. Join; k 9 rnds. Bind off.

Sl the 18 sts from holder to 3 dp needles. Work other leg the same.

HEAD: Beg at top of head, cast on 9 sts and divide evenly on 3 dp needles. Join; k 2 rnds.

Rnd 3: Inc 1 st in each st around—36 sts. K 1 rnd.

Rnd 5: Inc 1 st in each st around—36 sts. K 1 rnd.

Rnd 7: (Inc 1 st in next st, k 2) 12 times—48 sts.

Rnd 8: * Inc 1 st in each of 2 sts, k 22, repeat from * once—52 sts. K 7 rnds.

Rnd 16: * Inc 1 st in each of 2 sts, k 24, repeat from * once—56 sts. K 7 rnds.

Rnd 24: * (K 2 tog) twice, k 24, repeat from * once—52 sts. K 1 rnd.

Rnd 26: * (K 2 tog) twice, k 22, repeat from * once—48 sts. K 2 rnds.

Rnd 29: K 2 tog around—24 sts. K 1 rnd.

Rnd 31: (K 1, k 2 tog) 8 times—16 sts. K 4 rnds. Bind off.

ARMS (make 2): Beg at upper edge, cast on 15 sts; divide on 3 needles. Join; k 17 rnds.

Shape Elbow: Sl next 8 sts on a holder. With 2 needles, work back and forth on remaining 7 sts in stockinette st for 4 rows. Sl sts from holder to dp needle. Divide 15 sts on 3 dp needles. Join; k 2 rnds.

Next Rnd: (K 3, k 2 tog) 3 times—12 sts. K 12 rnds.

Shape Paw: (K 3, inc 1 st in next st) 3 times—15 sts. K 1 rnd.

Next Rnd: (K 4, inc 1 st in next st) 3 times—18 sts. K 7 rnds.

Next Rnd: (K 2 tog, k 1) 6 times—12 sts. Bind off.

FACE: With 2 needles, cast on 14 sts. Work back and forth in stockinette st (k 1 row, p 1 row) for 12 rows. Bind off.

TAIL: Cast on 12 sts; divide on 3 dp needles. Join; k 16 rnds.

Next Rnd: Dec 3 sts evenly spaced—9 sts. Work for 12" or desired length.

Next Rnd: (K 1, k 2 tog) 3 times—6 sts. Cut yarn, leaving 8" end; thread needle. Draw up sts; fasten securely.

EARS (make 2): Beg at lower edge, with 2 needles, cast on 11 sts. Work back and forth in stockinette st, dec 1 st each side every 3rd row 4 times—3 sts. Work 1 row. Cut yarn, leaving 8" end. Draw through sts; fasten securely.

KITTEN: BODY: Work as for Cat for 5 rnds.

Rnd 6: Inc 1 st in each st—48 sts. K 21 rnds.

Next Rnd: (K 2, k 2 tog) 12 times—36 sts.

Divide for Legs: Sl next 18 sts on a holder (one leg); divide remaining 18 sts on 3 dp needles (2nd leg). Join; k 8 rnds.

Next Rnd: (K 2 tog, k 4) 3 times—15 sts. K 6 rnds.

Shape Heel: Sl front 7 sts on a safety pin; with 2 dp needles, work back and forth on remaining 8 sts in stockinette st (p 1 row, k 1 row) for 6 rows. Sl front 7 sts on a dp needle. Divide the 15 sts on 3 dp needles. Join; k 6 rnds. Bind off.

Sl the 18 sts from holder to 3 dp needles. Work other leg the same.

HEAD: Work as for Cat for 4 rnds.

Rnd 5: Inc 1 st in each st around—36 sts. K 2 rnds.

Rnd 8: * Inc 1 st in each of 2 sts, k 16, repeat from * once—40 sts. K 5 rnds.

Rnd 14: * Inc 1 st in each of 2 sts, k 18, repeat from * once—44 sts. K 5 rnds.

MOUTH

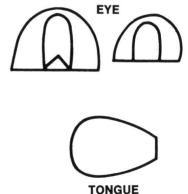

EYE

TONGUE

Rnd 20: * (K 2 tog) twice, k 18, re-peat from * once—40 sts.

Rnd 21: * (K 2 tog) twice, k 16, re-peat from * once—36 sts. K 1 rnd.

Rnd 23: K 2 tog around—18 sts. K 1 rnd.

Rnd 25: (K 1, k 2 tog) 6 times—12 sts. K 3 rnds. Bind off.

ARMS (make 2): Beg at upper edge, cast on 12 sts; divide on 3 dp needles. Join; k 12 rnds.

Shape Elbow: Sl next 6 sts on a holder. With 2 needles, work back and forth on remaining 6 sts in stock-inette st for 4 rows. Sl sts from holder to dp needle. Divide 12 sts on 3 dp needles. Join; k 2 rnds.

Next Rnd: (K 2, k 2 tog) 3 times—9 sts. K 9 rnds.

Shape Paw: (K 2, inc 1 st in next st) 3 times—12 sts. K 1 rnd.

Next Rnd: (K 3, inc 1 st in next st) 3 times—15 sts. K 5 rnd.

Next Rnd: (K 2 tog, k 1) 5 times—10 sts. Bind off.

FACE: With 2 needles, cast on 10 sts. Work back and forth in stock-inette st for 8 rows. Bind off.

TAIL: Cast on 9 sts; divide on 3 dp needles. Join; k 13 rnds.

Next Rnd: Dec 2 sts evenly spaced—7 sts. Work for 12″ or desired length.

Next Rnd: (K 2 tog) 3 times, k 1—4 sts. Cut yarn, leaving 8″ end; thread needle. Draw up sts; fasten securely.

EARS (make 2): Beg at lower edge, with 2 needles, cast on 7 sts. Work back and forth in stockinette st, dec 1 st each side every 4th row twice—1 st. End off.

MITTENS (make 2): With single strand of knitting worsted, cast on 12 sts; divide on 3 needles. Join; work in rib-bing of k 2, p 2 for 6 rnds.

Next Rnd: (K 3, inc 1 st in next st) 3 times—15 sts. K 9 rnds.

Next Rnd: (K 2 tog, k 1) 5 times—10 sts. K 1 rnd.

Next Rnd: K 2 tog around—5 sts. Cut yarn, leaving 8″ end. Draw up sts; fasten securely.

Thumb: With 2 dp needles and single strand of knitting worsted, cast on 4 sts. Work in stockinette st for 6 rows.

Next Row: K 2 tog twice. Cut yarn, leaving 8″ end. Draw up sts, sew side. Sew thumb to side of mitten.

FINISHING: Sew heel to foot, elbow to arm. Weave front of foot; weave front of paws. Stuff lower body and legs firmly. Stuff lower arms. Using carpet thread, sew arms in place by sewing through body and inner arm, through button eyes and back through arm and body. Fasten securely. Finish stuffing arms and body. Sew top of head; stuff firmly; sew to body. Stuff face; sew to head as shown. Using ear

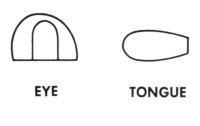

EYE   **TONGUE**

MOUTH

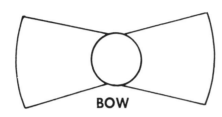

BOW

for pat, cut pink felt; glue to p side of ears. Sew ears to head. Run a few strands (loops) of mohair through top of head for hair. Trace all patterns. Small eye and small nose patterns are for kittens; large pats are for cat. Using patterns, cut black felt nose, mouth and pupils, pink tongue. Cut felt bows and outer eyes in colors to match mit-tens as pictured, page 30, attach bows to kittens with a strand of matching knitting worsted. Glue features in place as shown. Run buttonhole twist through face for whiskers; stiffen with glue. Glue 1″ oval felt pads to soles of legs, and paws. With buttonhole thread, embroider toes as shown. Insert che-nille stick in tail; sew tail to back of pets.

For apron, cut gingham 5½″ x 9½″. Sew side seams (shorter edges) turning in material ½″; make 1″ hem. Gather top to measure 5½″. Cut belt 2″ x 28″. Fold in half; turn in ¼″ seams; sew to apron. Cut pocket 2½″ x 2½″; turn in ¼″ seams; sew to apron. From iron-on tape, cut four small hearts, ½″ x ¾″, one large heart, 1″ x 1″. Press smaller hearts on front of belt, large heart on pocket.

SUNNY PETS
Shown on page 146

SIZE: About 6″ long.

MATERIALS: Knitting worsted, 1 oz. main color (MC), small amounts of other colors. Crochet hook size E. Scraps of felt, black, white, beige. Cotton batting. Glue. Rust embroidery cotton for mouths. White paint.

GAUGE: 5 sc = 1″.

BODY: With MC (brown for dog, gray for bunny, gold for lion, burnt orange for tiger, yellow for leopard), ch 2. Work 6 sc in 2nd ch from hook.

Rnd 2: 2 sc in each sc around.

Rnd 3: * Sc in next sc, 2 sc in next sc, repeat from * around—18 sc. Work even for 1 rnd.

Rnd 5: Repeat rnd 3—27 sc. Work even for 15 rnds. For tiger, leopard and bunny, change to white.

Rnds 21 and 22: * Sc in next sc, work 2 sc tog, repeat from * around—12 sc. Work 2 sc tog around. Stuff body; sew up opening.

HEAD: With MC for lion, white for tiger, leopard and bunny, beige for dog, ch 2. Work 6 sc in 2nd ch from hook.

Rnd 2: 2 sc in each sc around. For tiger and leopard, change to MC.

Rnd 3: * Sc in each of next 2 sc, 2 sc in next sc, repeat from * around—16 sc. Work even for 2 rnds. For bunny and dog, change to MC.

Rnd 6: * Sc in next sc, 2 sc in next sc, repeat from * around—24 sc. Work 4 rnds even.

Rnd 11: * Sc in 2 sc, work next 2 sc tog, repeat from * around—18 sc.

Rnd 12: * Sc in next sc, work 2 sc tog, repeat from * around—12 sc. Repeat rnd 12. End off. Stuff head; sew up opening. Sew head to body.

FRONT LEG (make 2): With MC, ch 6. Sl st in first ch to form ring. Work even in 6 sc for 8 rnds (6 rnds for bunny). End off. Stuff. Sew back and front openings flat.

BACK LEG (make 2): Work as for front leg for 4 rnds only.

PAW (make 4): With MC for tiger and lion, white for leopard and bunny, beige for dog, ch 2. Work 6 sc in 2nd ch from hook.

Next Rnd: (Sc in next sc, 2 sc in next sc) 3 times. End off. Sew to front of leg. Cut white or beige felt in shape of paws. Sew to bottom of paws stuffing with cotton.

HAUNCH (make 2): With MC, work as for body for 3 rnds. End off. Sew to side of body near back end, stuffing as you go. Sew back leg under haunch. Sew front legs close tog under front of body.

TAILS: For bunny, make a 1½″ white pompon; sew on. For tiger, lion and leopard, with MC, ch 4. Sc in 2nd ch from hook and each remaining ch. Ch 1, turn. Work even on 3 sc until piece is same length as body, changing to white for leopard for last inch. Sew up side seam. Add MC loops to end of lion's tail. Sew on tail. For dog, work tail only 2″ long.

EARS: For lion, tiger and leopard, with MC, ch 3. Sc in 2nd ch from hook and in next ch, sc in each ch on other side of starting ch—5 sc. Ch 1, turn. Sc in 2 sc, 2 sc in next sc, sc in 2 sc. End off. Sew to head, cupping slightly.

For dog, ch 4. Sc in 2nd ch from hook and in next 2 ch. Ch 1, turn each row. Work 2 rows even. Inc 1 sc on next row—4 sc. Work 4 rows even. Work 2 sc tog twice. End off. Sew starting ch of ear to head.

For bunny, ch 14. Sc in 2nd ch from hook and in each ch across. Ch 1, sc in each ch on opposite side of starting ch. Ch 1, turn. Sc in each sc to tip, sc in ch at tip, ch 3; sc in 2nd ch from hook and in next ch, sc in first sc on other side of ear. End off. Sew to head.

FINISHING: For eyes, cut ¼″ black felt circles. Glue on. Paint a white dot on each eye for highlight. Work mouth in straight sts. Glue black felt nose over top of mouth, circles for dog and bunny, triangles for other animals. For leopard's spots, work 1 or 2 rnds of sc with black, sew on. For tiger's stripes, embroider black straight sts of different lengths. For lion's mane, form MC loops over finger, sew to head in groups of 3 or 4 loops.

MOUSE FAMILY
Shown on page 147

SIZE: 6″ to 8¼″ high, including ears.
MATERIALS: Knitting worsted, 1 4-oz. skein gray. Crochet hook size G. Dacron or cotton stuffing. Glue. Gray felt, 6″ square. Pink felt or velour, 6″ square. Blue and black felt scraps. 6″ piece of 4″ wide eyelet trimming. Heavy waxed gray thread. Six-strand embroidery floss, bright pink. One small button. Two small gold safety pins. Scraps of cotton materials. Narrow white ribbon, 1 yard. Tracing paper.
GAUGE: 4 sc = 1″.
MOTHER MOUSE: BODY: Beg at bottom, ch 2.
Rnd 1: 6 sc in 2nd ch from hook. Do not join rnds; mark end of rnds.
Rnd 2: 2 sc in each sc.
Rnd 3: (Sc in next sc, 2 sc in next sc) 6 times—18 sc.
Rnd 4: (Sc in next sc, 2 sc in next sc) 9 times—27 sc.
Rnd 5: (Sc in each of 2 sc, 2 sc in next sc) 9 times—36 sc.
Rnds 6-11: Work even in sc.
Rnd 12: (2 sc in next sc, sc in each of next 3 sc) 9 times—45 sc.
Rnds 13-17: Work even in sc.
Rnd 18: (Sc in each of 3 sc, work next 2 sc tog) 9 times—36 sc.
Rnds 19-23: Work even in sc.
Rnd 24: (Sc in each of 4 sc, work next 2 sc tog) 6 times—30 sc.
Rnd 25: Work even in sc.

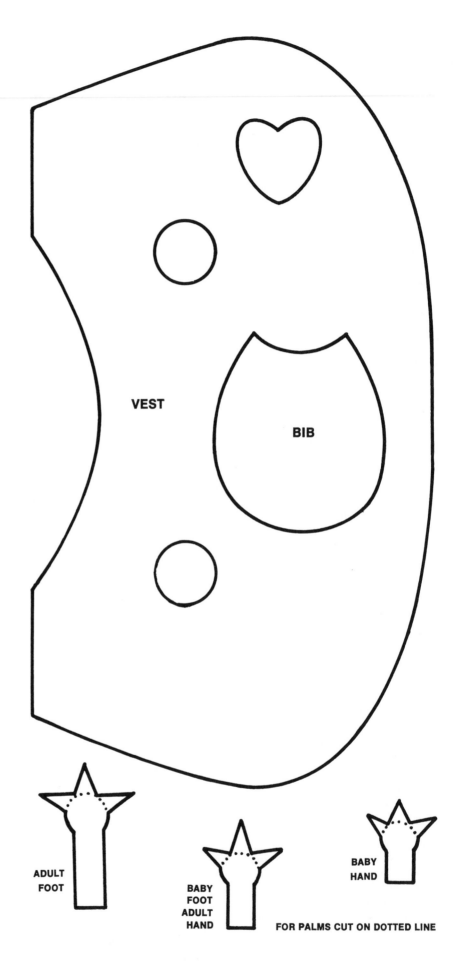

VEST

BIB

ADULT FOOT

BABY FOOT ADULT HAND

BABY HAND

FOR PALMS CUT ON DOTTED LINE

Rnd 26: (Sc in each of 3 sc, work next 2 sc tog) 6 times—24 sc.

Rnd 27: Work even in sc.

Rnd 28: (Sc in each of 2 sc, work next 2 sc tog) 6 times—18 sc.

Rnd 29: Work even in sc.

Rnd 30: (Sc in next sc, work next 2 sc tog) 6 times—12 sc.

Rnds 31 and 32: Work even in sc. End off. Stuff; leave neck open.

TAIL: Ch 6; sc in 2nd ch from hook and in each remaining ch—5 sc. Ch 1, turn each row. Work 4 rows even. Dec 1 st on next row. Work 4 rows even—4 sc. Dec 1 st on next row. Work 16 rows even—3 sc. Dec 1 st on next row. Work 10 rows even—2 sc. Work 2 sts tog. Work 5 rows even—1 sc. End off. Roll tail; sew edges tog. Sew tail to rear of body over rnds 6 and 7.

HEAD: Beg at tip of nose, ch 2.

Rnd 1: 4 sc in 2nd ch from hook.

Rnd 2: 2 sc in each sc around.

Rnd 3: Work even in sc—8 sc.

Rnd 4: (Sc in next sc, 2 sc in next sc) 4 times—12 sc.

Rnd 5: Work even in sc.

Rnd 6: (Sc in next sc, 2 sc in next sc) 6 times—18 sc.

Rnd 7: Work even in sc.

Rnd 8: (Sc in next sc, 2 sc in next sc) 9 times—27 sc.

Rnds 9-14: Work even in sc.

Rnd 15: (Sc in next sc, work next 2 sc tog) 9 times—18 sc.

Rnd 16: Work even in sc.

Rnd 17: Work 2 sc tog around. Stuff head; sew up opening. Sew head to neck.

Ear (make 2): Ch 7.

Row 1: Sc in 2nd ch from hook and in each remaining ch—6 sc. Ch 1, turn each row.

Row 2: 2 sc in first sc, sc across, 2 sc in last sc—8 sc.

Rows 3 and 4: Work even in sc.

Rows 5 and 6: Work 2 sc tog, sc across to last 2 sc, work last 2 sc tog—4 sc.

Row 7: Work even in sc. End off (upper edge of ear).

Cut pink felt same shape as ear. If velour is used, add ¼″ all around for turning under. Sew ear lining to ear. Sew ears to head, cupping slightly.

HAUNCH AND LEG: Beg at center of haunch, ch 2.

Rnd 1: 6 sc in 2nd ch from hook.

Rnd 2: 2 sc in each sc around.

Rnd 3: (Sc in next sc, 2 sc in next sc) —18 sc.

Rnd 4: Work even in sc.

Rnd 5: (Sc in next sc, 2 sc in next sc) 9 times—27 sc.

Rnd 6: Work even in sc. Ch 6 for leg. Sc in 2nd ch from hook and in each of next 4 ch, sc in 4 sc on edge of haunch. Ch 1, turn. Work 3 more rows on these 9 sc. End off.

For other leg, after finishing haunch, ch 1, turn. Work 4 sc on haunch, ch 6, for leg. Work as for first leg. Stuff haunch; roll leg, stuff and sew up, leaving toe end open. Sew to body, leg sticking out to front.

ARM (make 2): Ch 7, sl st in first ch to form ring. Ch 1, sc in each ch around. Work 2 more rnds even on 7 sc. Dec 1 sc on next rnd. Work 1 rnd even—6 sc. Dec 1 sc on next rnd—5 sc.

Form Elbow: Sc in first 2 sc. Ch 1, turn. Work 1 row even on 2 sc. Ch 1, turn.

Next Row: Sc in 2 sc, sc in each of 3 sc on rnd. Work 4 rnds even on 5 sc. End off. Stuff; sew to toy, leaving wrist end open.

FINISHING: Trace patterns for hands, feet and palms. Cut out paper patterns. Using patterns, from gray felt, cut 2 hands, 2 feet and 4 palms. Glue palms to feet and hands, stuffing lightly with yarn scraps. Insert in leg and arm openings; sew securely. For eyes, cut 2 blue circles ½″ diameter. Cut 3 black felt circles ¼″ diameter for pupils and nose. Glue in place. For mouth, take one long stitch with embroidery floss. For whiskers, thread needle with waxed thread; run needle back and forth through nose several times, leaving long loops each side and taking small stitches at side of nose to secure whiskers. Cut through loops.

Clothes: Cut fabric for dress: one piece, 18″ x 5″, for skirt; one piece 5½″ x 2¼″ for top. Stitch ends of skirt together for back seam. Gather top edge. Fit on toy up under arms; mark hem. Hem bottom edge. Adjust gathers on top edge; sew skirt to toy at underarms. Fold each long edge of top piece to center; press. Make a narrow hem on each short end. Put around neck bringing short ends together at front. Sew ends to skirt top at front, sew back to skirt top at back.

For cap, cut circle of fabric 3½″ diameter, with pinking shears. Gather ¾″ in from edge, pull up, stuff center and sew to head.

For apron, hem sides of 6″ piece of eyelet trimming. Gather top raw edge to 2″, sew to center of 20″ piece of ribbon. Tie ribbon ends into bow at back.

FATHER MOUSE: Make as for Mother Mouse.

Clothes: Trace pattern for vest, cut out paper pattern. Place pattern on toy; adjust to fit. Place pattern on vest fabric, draw around outline. Cut out vest ¼″ outside marked line. Cut another piece in same way from lining material. Cut out armholes on lining material. Stitch vest to lining, right sides together, taking ¼″ seam, leav-ing opening at bottom. Turn to right side; press. Close opening. Make 4 slashes in each armhole from center to outer edge of armhole. Turn fabric to inside of vest over lining. Trim to ⅛″ and hem down. Place vest on toy, turn back lapels. Sew button to both fronts below lapels. For dickey, cut 2″ square of fabric. Turn under one edge; gather slightly; sew to neck. Tuck dickey inside vest. For tie, cut 2 pieces of fabric 2½″ x 1¾″. Stitch, right sides together, around edge leaving opening for turning. Turn to right side; press. Cut another piece ¾″ square. Fold back two opposite sides of piece; wind folded strip around center of tie to form bow tie; sew ends together. Sew tie to dickey.

BABY MOUSE: BODY: Work as for Mother Mouse through rnd 4.

Rnds 5-10: Work even in sc.

Rnd 11: (Sc in each of 7 sc, work 2 sc tog) 3 times—24 sc.

Rnd 12: Work even.

Rnd 13: (Sc in each of 4 sc, work 2 sc tog) 4 times—20 sc.

Rnd 14: Work even.

Rnd 15: (Sc in each of 2 sc, work 2 sc tog) 5 times—15 sc.

Rnd 16: Work even.

Rnd 17: (Sc in next sc, work 2 sc tog) 5 times—10 sc. **Rnd 18:** Work even.

Rnd 19: Work 2 sc tog around. End off. Stuff; leave neck open.

HEAD: Beg at tip of nose, ch 2.

Rnd 1: 5 sc in 2nd ch from hook.

Rnd 2: Work even.

Rnd 3: 2 sc in each sc around.

Rnd 4: Work even.

Rnd 5: (Sc in next sc, 2 sc in next sc) 5 times—15 sc.

Rnds 6 and 7: Work even.

Rnd 8: (Sc in each of 2 sc, 2 sc in next sc) 5 times—20 sc.

Rnds 9-11: Work even.

Rnd 12: (Sc in each of 2 sc, work 2 sc tog) 5 times—15 sc.

Rnd 13: Work even. Stuff.

Rnd 14: Sc in next sc, (work 2 sc tog) 7 times. End off. Sew up opening. Sew head to neck.

Ear (make 2): Ch 5.

Row 1: Sc in 2nd ch from hook and in each remaining ch—4 sc. Ch 1, turn each row.

Row 2: 2 sc in first sc, sc in 2 sc, 2 sc in last sc. **Rows 3 and 4:** Work even.

Rows 5 and 6: Work first 2 and last 2 sc tog each row. End off. Line ears as for Mother Mouse. Sew on.

LEG (make 2): Ch 6.

Row 1: Sc in 2nd ch from hook and in each remaining ch. Ch 1, turn each row.

Rows 2 and 3: Sc in each sc. End off. Roll up; sew long edges tog. Sew to body.

ARM (make 2): Work as for leg working only 2 rows.

TAIL: Make a ch about 6″ long. Sew to lower back of body.

FINISHING: Finish as for Mother Mouse, cutting features slightly smaller.

CLOTHES: Cut piece 6″ x 3½″ for diaper. Narrow it slightly at center. Pin on each side with safety pin; for bib, using pattern, cut 2 pieces. Stitch, right sides together, leaving top open. Turn to right side, press. Turn in open edges; sew opening closed. Sew top of bib to center of 15″ piece of ribbon. Cut out heart-shaped piece of plain fabric. Glue to bib. Tie bib on baby.

THREE PIGS AND WOLF
Shown on page 146

SIZE: Pig, 12″ high. Wolf, 16″ high.
MATERIALS: Knitting worsted, 4 ozs. main color (MC) for each pig; small amounts of pink and black; bright colors for shirts. For wolf, 6 ozs. gray, 2 ozs. red. Crochet hook size E. Stuffing. Black shank buttons for eyes.

GAUGE: 5 sc = 1″.
PIG: Beg at top of head, ch 2 MC.
Rnd 1: 6 sc in 2nd ch from hook.
Rnd 2: 2 sc in each sc.
Rnd 3: (Sc in next sc, 2 sc in next sc) 6 times—18 sc.
Rnd 4: (2 sc in each of next 2 sc, sc in 7 sc) twice—22 sc. Work even for 1 rnd.
Rnd 6: (2 sc in next sc, sc in next sc) 11 times—33 sc.
Rnd 7: 2 sc in each of 2 sc, sc in 14 sc, 2 sc in each of 2 sc, sc in 15 sc—37 sc.
Rnd 8: Inc 1 sc in rnd.
Rnds 9-16: Work even—8 sc.
Rnd 17: (Work 2 sc tog twice, sc in 15 sc) twice.
Rnd 18: (Work 2 sc tog twice, sc in 13 sc) twice. Work 1 rnd even—30 sc.
Rnd 20: Work 2 sc tog around. Work even for 1 rnd—15 sc.
Form Arms: Rnd 22: Sc in first sc, * ch 21; sc in 2nd ch from hook and in each ch, sc in 7 sc on neck, repeat from * once.
Rnd 23: Work around, * working 20 sc on opposite side of arm ch, 20 sc on other side of arm, 7 sc across neck, repeat from * once. Mark end of rnd.
Rnds 24-27: Work even. Sc in each sc to 16th sc from end of arm. End off. Sew up arms each side, joining 15 sc on back to 15 sc on front of arm. Stuff arms.
Body: Join MC at underarm, sc around, inc 1 sc each side of each arm. Mark end of rnd.
Rnds 2 and 3: Work even—37 sc.
Rnd 4: Inc 3 sc evenly spaced on front

of pig (choose whichever side you want).
Rnds 5-8: Work even—40 sc.
Rnd 9: (Sc in 7 sc, 2 sc in next sc) 5 times—45 sc.
Rnds 10-16: Work even.
Rnd 17: (Sc in 8 sc, 2 sc in next sc) 5 times—50 sc.
Rnds 18 and 19: Work even.
Rnd 20: Work 2 sc tog around—25 sc.
Rnd 21: Work even. Stuff head and most of body.
Form Legs: Sc to center front of body, ch 5, join to center back; work around on one leg, working in each of the 5 ch—17 sc. Mark end of rnd.
Rnds 2-6: Work even.
Rnd 7: Dec 2 sc evenly spaced.
Rnds 8-12: Work even.
Rnd 13: Dec 3 sc evenly spaced.
Rnds 14-16: Work even—12 sc.
Rnds 17-19: Change to black, work even for 3 rnds. End off. Work other leg to correspond. Finish stuffing toy.
Sole: With black, ch 2. Work 6 sc in 2nd ch from hook. Work 2 sc in each sc around. Sew to bottom of leg.
Hoof: With black, ch 7. Sc in 2nd ch from hook and in next 2 ch. Ch 1, turn. Work 2 sc tog, sc in last sc. Ch 1, turn. Work 2 sc tog. Work other half of ch in same way. Sew ch edge across top front of foot.
Tail: With MC, ch 15. Work * 3 sc in 1 ch, 2 sc in next ch, repeat from * to end. Sew on tail.
Snout: With MC, ch 2. Work 6 sc in 2nd ch from hook.
Rnd 2: 2 sc in each sc around.
Rnd 3: * Sc in each of 4 sc, 2 sc in each of 2 sc, repeat from * once—16 sc. Work 1 rnd even.
Rnd 5: (Sc in next sc, 2 sc in next sc) 8 times. Work 1 rnd even. End off. Stuff; sew to center front of head.
Nose: Work as for snout through rnd 3. Sew wrong side out, to snout. For nostrils, with pink, ch 2. Work 4 sc in 2nd ch from hook. Sew into a circle. Sew two to nose. For mouth, with pink, make long st on snout under nose.
Ears: With MC, ch 7. Work 2 rows of 6 sc. Sk first sc on next 5 rows. End off. Sew ch edge to head.

Sew on button eyes securely.

BLUE SHIRT: With dark blue (DB), ch 3. Sl st in first ch to form ring.
Rnd 1: Ch 3, 2 dc in ring, (ch 2, 3 dc in ring) 3 times, ch 2. Sl st in top of ch 3. End off.
Rnd 2: Join light blue (LB) in any ch-2 sp; ch 3, 2 dc in same sp, ch 2, 3 dc in same sp, (ch 1, 3 dc, ch 2, 3 dc in next sp) 3 times, ch 1, sl st in top of ch 3. End off.
Rnd 3: Join DB in any corner ch-2 sp; ch 3, 2 dc in same sp, ch 2, 3 dc in same sp, (ch 1, 3 dc in ch-1 sp, ch 1, 3 dc,

ch 2, 3 dc in corner sp) 3 times, ch 1, 3 dc in next sp, ch 1, sl st in top of ch 3. End off.
Rnd 4: Join LB in any corner sp; work as for rnd 3, working 1 more group of 3 dc on each side of square. End off.

Make another square the same. Sew the top corner sts of squares tog for shoulders. For sleeve, join LB in side center sp of one square; ch 2, work dc in each st to shoulder and to side center sp of other square—19 dc. Work 2 more rows of dc. Work in 1 row DB sc. Sew sleeve seam to underarm.

For side gusset, join LB at underarm; working down to bottom edge, make 2 sc, 2 hdc, 4 dc, ch 2; turn. Work 4 dc, 2 hdc, 2 sc to underarm. End off. Sew underarm seam. Repeat sleeve and gusset on other side. With DB, work 1 rnd sc around neck and lower edges.

Work pink shirt the same, beg with lighter pink.

GREEN SHIRT: Work 2 squares as for blue shirt having rnds 1 and 2 in dark green, rnd 3 in light green. End off. For sleeves, work 4 squares of 2 rnds; rnd 1 dark, rnd 2 light green. Sew 2 squares tog forming a tube for each sleeve. Slip sleeves on arms of pig having seams at top and bottom of arm. Beg ½″ down from top seam of each sleeve, sew sleeve to large square each side for about 5 sts. Repeat on back. Work 3 rows of dark green dc on each free side edge of large front square. Sew to free side edges of back square and to underarm of sleeves. Work 1 rnd dark green sc around bottom, sleeve and neck edges.

WOLF: Beg at top of head, with gray, work as for pig through rnd 7—37 sc.
Rnd 8: 2 sc in each of 3 sc, sc in 16 sc, 2 sc in each of next 2 sc, sc in 16 sc—42 sc. Work even for 1 rnd.
Rnd 10: (2 sc in each of 2 sc, sc in 19 sc) twice—46 sc. Work even for 10 rnds.
Rnd 21: (Work 2 sc tog twice, sc in 19 sc) twice—42 sc.
Rnd 22: (Work 2 sc tog twice, sc in 17 sc) twice—38 sc. Work even for 1 rnd.
Rnd 24: (Work 2 sc tog twice, sc in 15 sc) twice—34 sc. Work even for 1 rnd.
Rnd 26: Work 2 sc tog around—17 sc. Work even for 1 rnd.
Form Arms: Rnd 28: * Ch 29; sc in 2nd ch from hook and in each ch, sc in next 8 sc of neck, repeat from * once.
Rnd 29: * Work 28 sc on opposite side of arm ch, 28 sc on other side of arm, 8 sc across neck, repeat from * once—128 sc. Work even for 5 rnds, then sc to 23rd sc from end of arm. Cut yarn; sew bottom arm seam, 22 sc of

front and back arm sewn tog. Repeat on other arm. Stuff head and arms.

Body: Join yarn at underarm, work around in sc, inc 2 sc at each underarm—44 sc. Mark end of rnd. Work 12 rnds even.

Rnd 14: Dec 2 sc each side. Work 1 rnd even.

Rnd 16: (Work 2 sc tog, sc in 8 sc) 4 times. Work 1 rnd even.

Rnd 18: (Sc in 7 sc, work 2 sc tog) 4 times. Work 8 rnds even—32 sc. Fold body to find center, sc to center front, ch 6, join to center back; work around on one leg, working 6 sc in ch, 16 sc on body—22 sc. Work 2 rnds even.

Rnd 4: Dec 1 sc each side of leg. Work 1 rnd even.

Rnd 6: Repeat rnd 4. Work 8 rnds even.

Rnd 15: (Work 2 sc tog, sc in 4 sc) 3 times. Work 8 rnds even—15 sc. Sc to center front, ch 7; sc in 2nd ch from hook and in each ch, sc around leg, sc in 6 ch on other side of ch. Work 6 rnds even. End off. Stuff body; make other leg to correspond. Stuff legs; sew up soles.

SNOUT: Ch 2. Work 6 sc in 2nd ch from hook.

Rnd 2: 2 sc in each sc around. Work 1 rnd even. Repeat rnd 2—24 sc. Work 9 rnds even. End off. Stuff and sew on.

Nose: With black, ch 2. Work 6 sc in 2nd ch from hook. Gather edge to round shape; sew on.

EARS: Ch 9. Sc in 2nd ch from hook and in each ch. Ch 1, turn each row. Work 1 row even—8 sc. Dec 1 sc each side of next row. Repeat last 2 rows—4 sc. Work 1 row even. Work 2 sc tog twice. Work 1 row even. Work 2 sc tog. End off. Sew ears to head.

With red, embroider mouth in outline st. Sew on button eyes.

TAIL: Ch 4. Work loop st in 2nd ch from hook and in next 2 ch. To make loop st, insert hook in st, catch yarn underneath left index finger and draw through st; drop loop from index finger, draw up yarn until loop at back of work is ½″ long, yo hook and through 2 lps on hook. Ch 1, turn each row. Sc in each st, inc 1 sc each side. Alternating loop st and sc rows, inc 1 sc each side of each sc row until there are 13 sts. Work even for 37 rows. Sew up; sew to wolf.

Work hair on chest in same way as tail until there are 11 sts. End off. Sew to chest, point down.

Hair on top of head is 2 rows of 5 loops.

SHIRT: BACK: With red, ch 51. Dc in 3rd ch from hook and each ch across. Ch 2, turn each row. Work 4 more rows even. End off. Turn. Join yarn in 14th st from end, ch 2, work in

dc to 14th st from other end. Work 5 more rows even.

FRONT (make 2): With red, ch 27. Work in rows of dc as for back for 5 rows. Work in dc on next row to 14th st from end. Ch 2, turn. Work 5 rows even. Sew fronts to back at shoulders and top of sleeves leaving 14 sts free for back of neck. Sew sleeve and side seams. Sew fronts tog for 5 rows from bottom. Work 1 rnd of sc around bottom edge, working each 2 sts tog to draw in edge.

CATERPILLAR
Shown on page 148

SIZE: 52″ long.
MATERIALS: Aunt Lydia's Rug Yarn, 4 70-yd. skeins each of Cerise, Coral, Yellow, Spring Green, Lt. Blue, and Turquoise Icing. Crochet hook size I. Polyester fiberfill. Rug needle.
GAUGE: 7 sts = 2″; 7 rnds = 2″.
CATERPILLAR: SEGMENT (make one of each color): Ch 6, sl st in first ch to form ring. **Rnd 1:** Ch 1, 10 sc in ring. Join with sl st in first sc. Mark end of each rnd.

Rnds 2 and 3: Ch 1, * sc in next sc, 2 sc in next sc, repeat from * around. Join—22 sc on last rnd.

Rnd 4: Ch 1, * sc in 2 sc, 2 sc in next sc, repeat from * around—29 sc. Join each rnd.

Rnd 5: Ch 1, * sc in last 3 sc, 2 sc in next sc, repeat from * around—36 sc.

Rnd 6: Ch 1, sc in each sc around.

Rnd 7: Repeat rnd 5—45 sc.

Rnd 8: Ch 1, * sc in 8 sc, 2 sc in next sc, repeat from * around—50 sc.

Rnd 9: Ch 1, * sc in 5 sc, 2 sc in next sc, repeat from * around—58 sc.

Rnd 10: Repeat rnd 6.

Rnds 11 and 12: Repeat rnd 8—71 sc on last rnd.

Rnd 13: Repeat rnd 9—82 sc.

Rnds 14-32: Repeat rnd 6.

Rnd 33: Ch 1, * sc in 5 sc, dec 1 sc (to dec, pull up a lp in each of 2 sc, yo and through all 3 lps on hook), repeat from * around—71 sc.

Rnds 34 and 35: Ch 1, * sc in 8 sc, dec 1 sc, repeat from * around—58 sc on last rnd.

Rnd 36: Repeat rnd 6.

Rnd 37: Repeat rnd 33—50 sc.

Rnd 38: Repeat rnd 34—45 sc.

Rnd 39: Ch 1, * sc in 3 sc, dec 1 sc, repeat from * around—36 sc.

Rnd 40: Repeat rnd 6.

Rnd 41: Repeat rnd 39—29 sc.

Rnd 42: Ch 1, * sc in 2 sc, dec 1 sc, repeat from * around—22 sc. Now fill segment with fiberfill before completing segment.

Rnds 43 and 44: Ch 1, * sc in 1 sc, dec 1 sc, repeat from * around—10 sc on last rnd.

Rnd 45: Ch 1, (dec 1 sc) 5 times. End off.

FINISHING: With Turquoise Icing, embroider round eyes about 1″ in diameter on yellow segment, using chain stitch in a continuous line from center of eye out to outer edge. With green, embroider chain stitch nose around rnd 1. With Cerise, embroider big crescent for mouth using chain stitch. For antennae, with blue, ch 20 tightly. Make two. Sew to head above eyes. Sew segments tog, joining 7th rnd of a segment to the 7th rnd of next segment.

ARMADILLO
Shown on page 148

SIZE: 64″ long, including tail.
MATERIALS: Aunt Lydia's Rug Yarn, 2 70-yd. skeins each of Spring Green, Grass Green, Tangerine, Phantom Red, Turquoise and Light Jade; 3 skeins Forest Green; 6 skeins Peach. Crochet hook size I. 6 lbs. polyester fiberfill for stuffing. Rug needle.
GAUGE: 5 sc = 2″.
Note: When working in rnds, work in back lp only of each sc throughout.
ARMADILLO: BODY: Beg at tail end, with Light Jade, ch 6. Sl st in first ch to form ring. **Rnd 1:** Ch 1, 12 sc in ring. Join with sl st in ch 1. Join each rnd in this way. Ch 1 at beg of each rnd.

Rnd 2: 2 sc in back lp (see Note) of each sc around—24 sc.

Rnd 3: (Sc in 2 sc, 2 sc in next sc) 8 times—32 sc.

Rnd 4: (Sc in 4 sc, 2 sc in next sc) 6 times, sc in 2 sc—38 sc.

Rnd 5: (Sc in 6 sc, 2 sc in next sc) 5 times, sc in 3 sc—43 sc. Sl st in ch 1. End off.

Rnd 6: With Turquoise, (sc in 4 sc, 2 sc in next sc) 8 times, sc in 3 sc—51 sc.

Rnd 7: (Sc in 5 sc, 2 sc in next sc) 8 times, sc in 3 sc—59 sc. End off.

Rnd 8: With Forest Green, (sc in 4 sc, 2 sc in next sc) 11 times, sc in 4 sc—70 sc. End off.

Rnd 9: With Tangerine, 2 sc in first sc, sc in 11 sc, 2 sc in next sc, sc in 35 sc, 2 sc in next sc, sc in 11 sc, 2 sc in next sc, sc in 9 sc—74 sc.

Rnd 10: Sc in 18 sc, 2 sc in next sc, sc in 36 sc, 2 sc in next sc, sc in 18 sc—76 sc. End off.

Rnds 11-22: Inc 2 sc each rnd, having incs over incs of previous rnd, working in the following colors: 2 rnds Phantom Red, 1 rnd Forest Green, 2 rnds Spring Green, 2 rnds Grass Green, 1 rnd Forest Green, 2 rnds Light Jade, 2 rnds Turquoise—100 sc at end of rnd 22.

Rnds 23-67: Sc evenly around in the following colors: 1 rnd Forest Green, 2 rnds Tangerine, 2 rnds Phantom Red, 1 rnd Forest Green, 3 rnds Spring Green, 4 rnds Grass Green, 2 rnds Forest Green, 3 rnds Light Jade, 4 rnds Turquoise, 2 rnds Forest Green, 3 rnds Tangerine, 4 rnds Phantom Red, 2 rnds Forest Green, 3 rnds Spring Green, 4 rnds Grass Green, 1 rnd Forest Green, 2 rnds Light Jade, 2 rnds Turquoise.

Rnd 68: With Forest Green, sc in 24 sc, dec over next 2 sts (to dec, pull up a lp in each of next 2 sts, yo and through all 3 lps on hook), sc in 48 sc, dec, sc in 24 sc.

Rnds 69-85: Dec 2 sc each rnd, having decs over decs of previous rnd, working in the following colors: 2 rnds Tangerine, 2 rnds Phantom Red, 1 rnd Forest Green, 2 rnds Spring Green, 2 rnds Grass Green, 1 rnd Forest Green, 2 rnds Light Jade, 2 rnds Turquoise, 1 rnd Forest Green, 2 rnds Tangerine. Stuff body.

Rnd 86: With Tangerine (sc in 4 sc, dec) 10 times, sc in 4 sc—54 sc.

Rnd 87: (Sc in 2 sc, dec) 13 times, sc in 2 sc—41 sc.

Rnds 88 and 89: Dec over each 2 sc around for 2 rnds. End off.

HEAD: With Peach, ch 5. Join to form ring.

Rnd 1: Ch 1, 10 sc in ring. Sl st in ch 1. Join each rnd this way. Ch 1 at beg of each rnd.

Rnd 2: 2 sc in each sc—20 sc.

Rnds 3-12: Sc in each sc around.

Rnd 13: Sc in 7 sc, (2 sc in next sc, sc in 2 sc) twice, 2 sc in next sc, sc in 6 sc—23 sc.

Rnd 14: Sc in 7 sc (2 sc in next sc, sc in 3 sc) twice, 2 sc in next sc, sc in 7 sc—26 sc.

Rnd 15: Sc in 8 sc, (2 sc in next sc, sc in 4 sc) twice, 2 sc in next sc, sc in 7 sc—29 sc.

Rnds 16-20: Repeat rnd 3.

Rnd 21: Sc in 10 sc, (2 sc in next sc, sc in 2 sc) 3 times, 2 sc in next sc, sc in 9 sc—33 sc.

Rnd 22: Sc in 10 sc, (2 sc in next sc, sc in 3 sc) 3 times, 2 sc in next sc, sc in 10 sc—37 sc.

Rnd 23: Sc in 11 sc, (2 sc in next sc, sc in 4 sc) 3 times, 2 sc in next sc, sc in 10 sc—41 sc.

Rnd 24: Sc in 11 sc, (2 sc in next sc, sc in 5 sc) 3 times, 2 sc in next sc, sc in 11 sc—45 sc.

Rnds 25-35: Repeat rnd 3.

Rnds 36-38: (Sc in 6 sc, dec over next 2 sc) around for 3 rnds—30 sc. Stuff head firmly.

Rnd 39: (Sc in 2 sc, dec) 7 times, sc in 2 sc—23 sc.

Rnd 40: Dec in each 2 sc around. End off.

EARS (make 2): With Peach, beg at tip of ear, ch 4.

Row 1: Sc in 2nd ch from hook and in next 2 ch. Ch 1, turn each row.

Row 2: Sc in first sc (work in both lps throughout ears), 2 sc in next sc, sc in last sc—4 sc.

Row 3: 2 sc in first sc, sc to last sc, 2 sc in last sc—6 sc.

Row 4: Sc in each sc.

Rows 5-10: Repeat rows 3 and 4, 3 times—12 sc.

Rows 11 and 12: Repeat row 4.

Rows 13-15: Dec 1 sc at beg and end of each row—6 sc.

Row 16: Repeat row 4. End off.

With Forest Green, work 1 row of sc along sides and tip of ear.

TAIL: With Peach, beg at tip of tail, ch 5. Join to form ring.

Rnd 1: Ch 1, 6 sc in ring. Join each rnd in ch 1. Work in back lps only.

Rnds 2-4: Sc in each sc.

Rnd 5: (Sc in 2 sc, 2 sc in next sc) around—8 sc. Drop Peach. Carry dropped colors on inside of tail.

Rnd 6: With Forest Green, work even.

Rnd 7: With Peach, repeat rnd 5—10 sc.

Rnds 8 and 9: Work even.

Rnd 10: With Forest Green, work even.

Rnd 11: With Peach, repeat rnd 5—13 sc.

Rnds 12 and 13: Work even.

Rnd 14: With Forest Green, work even.

Rnds 15-18: Repeat rnds 11-14—17 sc.

Rnd 19: With Peach, repeat rnd 5—22 sc.

Rnd 20: Work even.

Rnd 21: (Sc in 4 sc, 2 sc in next sc) around—26 sc.

Rnd 22: With Forest Green, work even.

Rnds 23-25: With Peach, work even.

Rnd 26: With Forest Green, work even.

Rnds 27-34: Repeat rnds 23-26 twice.

Rnd 35: With Peach, (sc in 5 sc, dec over next 2 sc) around—23 sc.

Rnds 36 and 37: Work even.

Rnd 38: With Forest Green, work even. End off Green.

Rnds 39-42: With Peach, work even.

Rnd 43: Repeat rnd 35—20 sc. Stuff tail.

Rnd 44: (Sc in 4 sc, dec) around—17 sc. Dec over each 2 sc until 9 sc remain. End off.

FEET (make 4): With Peach, ch 16. Join to form ring.

Rnd 1: Sc in each ch around.

Rnd 2: (Sc in 2 sc, 2 sc in next sc) around—21 sc.

Rnd 3: (Sc in 3 sc, 2 sc in next sc) around—26 sc.

Rnds 4-9: Work even.

Rnds 10 and 11: (Sc in 4 sc, 2 sc in next sc) around—37 sc.

Rnd 12: Work even.

Rnd 13: (Sc in 5 sc, 2 sc in next sc) around—43 sc.

Rnds 14-17: Work even. End off.

TOES: With Spring green, sc in first 5 sc. Ch 1, turn.

Rows 2-5: Sc in each sc. Ch 1, turn each row.

Row 6: Dec 1 sc at beg and end of row—3 sc.

Row 7: Sc in 3 sc. End off. With Spring Green, sc in next 5 sc on last rnd of foot, ch 1, turn. Complete as for first toe.

Sk 1 sc on last rnd. With Tangerine, sc in next 5 sc. Complete as for first toe. Work 3 more Tangerine toes on next 15 sc of foot. Sk 1 sc, work 2 more Spring Green toes on next 10 sc. With Tangerine on top and green on bottom, buttonhole st top and bottom toes tog with Forest Green. Stuff feet and toes. Sew rnd 1 tog flat with beg of rnd at center bottom of foot.

FINISHING: With Turquoise, embroider oval eyes on head with chain stitch, outline with Forest Green. Make Forest Green French knot for pupil. Embroider nose with Light Jade, crescent mouth with Tangerine chain stitch.

Sew head and tail to body. Sew ears to head above eyes. Sew feet to side of body so body is balanced by them.

PRINCELY FROG
Shown on page 149

SIZE: 20".

MATERIALS: Knitting worsted weight yarn, 3 ozs. green (G), 1 oz. lime (L); scraps of bright pink (P) and white (W). Crochet hook size G. Stuffing. Black felt scrap. Yarn needle.

GAUGE: 5 sc = 1".

BODY: Front: Beg at top, with L, ch 7. **Row 1:** Sc in 2nd ch from hook and in each ch. Ch 1, turn each row. **Rows 2 and 3:** Work even—6 sc. **Row 4:** 2 sc in each sc—12 sc. **Row 5:** Inc 1 sc each side—14 sc. **Row 6:** Work even. **Row 7:** Repeat row 5—16 sc. **Rows 8-19:** Work even. **Row 20:** Dec 1 sc each side—14 sc. **Row 21:** Work even. **Rows 22-25:** Repeat rows 20 and 21 twice. **Rows 26-30:** Work even. End off. **Back:** With G, work as for front, but ch 9 instead of 7 to begin. Sew to front leaving neck and bottom open. **Bottom:** With L, ch 10. Work 6 rows of 9 sc. Sew over opening at bottom.

HEAD: Lower Section: Beg at back, with L, ch 9.

Row 1: Sc in 2nd ch from hook and in each ch. Ch 1, turn each row. **Row 2:** Inc 1 sc each side—10 sc. **Row 3:** Work even. **Rows 4-7:** Repeat rows 2 and 3 twice. **Rows 8-12:** Work even—14 sc. **Row 13:** Dec 1 sc each side. **Row 14:** Work even—12 sc. **Rows 15-19:** Repeat rows 13 and 14—6 sc. **Row 20:** Work 2 sc tog across. End off.

Top: With G, ch 9. **Row 1:** Sc in 2nd ch from hook and in each ch—8 sc. **Row 2:** Inc in every other st—12 sc. **Row 3:** Work even. **Rows 4-7:** Inc 1 sc each side—20 sc. **Rows 8-11:** Work even—20 sc. **Row 12:** Dec 1 sc each side—18 sc. **Row 13:** Work even. **Rows 14-17:** Repeat rows 12 and 13 twice. **Row 18:** Dec 1 sc each side, 1 sc at center. **Rows 19 and 20:** Work even—11 sc. **Row 21:** Repeat row 12—9 sc. **Row 22:** Work 2 tog across. End off. Sew head sections tog and stuff. Em-

Continued on page 136

Big floppy
Santa and
helper are
delightful
knitted toys.
Legs and arms
are skinny
tubes that twist
and bend. Big
Santa, Elf,
page 98.

KNIT A BIG OR LITTLE GIFT

Gift mittens have
faces that form
pockets!
Directions for
Tissue-Holder
Mittens, page
100; Christmas
Tree Stocking,
page 100; Red
Stocking,
page 101.

PLAYTHINGS

Little Miss with her all-knit wardrobe—shirt, jumper, panties, tam, cardigan, socks—is sure to be a favorite (page 102). Humpty Dumpty and Santa can stand or sit. Make them as toys for the kids or as bright decorations (page 101). Chocolate Moose is single crochet, 12″ long (page 103). Floating angel is a hand puppet with paper-doily wings, crown (page 104). Mr. & Mrs. Claus are easy-knit hand puppets; garter-stitch trim, felt features, curly hair are finishing touches (page 104). Toy-size sleighs (7″ long), little people and prancing horses dash through the snow. Directions for Sleigh Ride, all in single crochet, are on page 104.

TO KNIT AND CROCHET

QUICK GIFTS

Santa
Hand Puppet,
page 114.

Santa
Beanbag,
page 115.

Pincushion
Chair,
page 114.

Snowbaby
Hanger,
page 114.

easy on your budget.

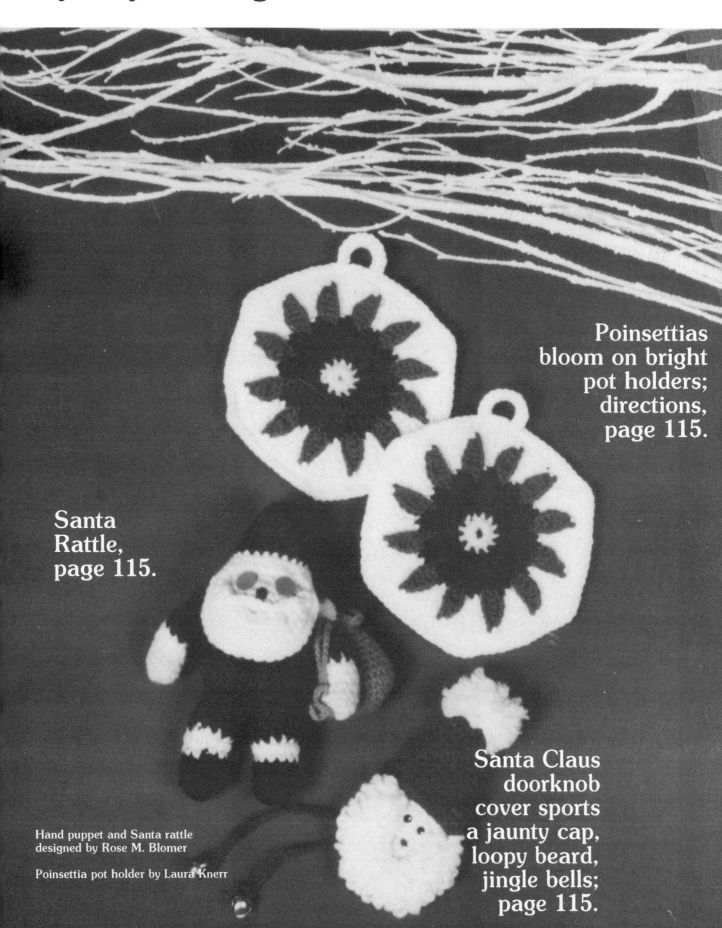

Poinsettias
bloom on bright
pot holders;
directions,
page 115.

Santa
Rattle,
page 115.

Santa Claus
doorknob
cover sports
a jaunty cap,
loopy beard,
jingle bells;
page 115.

Hand puppet and Santa rattle
designed by Rose M. Blomer

Poinsettia pot holder by Laura Knerr

CHRISTMAS STITCHIN'
FOR THE KITCHEN

Pot holders make ideal gifts for Christmas—the kitchen's busiest season! Crochet them in washable cotton, two layers thick to really beat the heat. Cross-stitch bright motifs in embroidery floss. Three picot-edged Holiday Pot Holders, by American Thread, page 117; Pennsylvania Dutch design, page 116; Snowflake Mitt, by Coats & Clark, page 116.

Photography by Sal Corbo.

A PLAY PILLOW

Candy-striped bolster, crocheted of Dawn Sayelle, has pockets for little toys; page 117.

Snowman
Scene, page
118; knitted
North Pole
Elves, page
119. Dolls
stand about 6"
tall.

North Pole Elves from
Stampa Italiana Associata.

Snowman scene by Sue Penrod.
Photography by Arthur Klonsky.

PRINCELY FROG

Continued from page 126.

broider with pink in outline st. Sew head to neck.

EYES (make 2): With G, ch 2. Work 6 sc in 2nd ch from hook, then 2 sc in each sc around. Work 2 rnds even. End off. With W, ch 2. Work 6 sc in 2nd ch from hook, then 2 sc in each sc around. End off. Sew to eye opening after stuffing eye. Glue on black felt pupils. Highlight pupils with white dots of paint. Sew eyes to head.

ARMS (make 2): **Top:** With G, ch 8. Work 15 rows of 7 sc. Dec 2 sc on next row. Work 1 row even. End off. Sew up and stuff. **Bottom:** With G, ch 7. Work 10 rows of 6 sc. End off. Sew up and stuff. Sew to top. Sew arm to shoulder so it swings freely. **Hand:** With G, ch 3. Sc in 2nd ch from hook and in next ch. Ch 1, turn. Inc 1 sc in next row, work 1 row even. Inc 1 sc in next row, ch 4. Sc in 2nd ch from hook and in next 2 ch, sc in next sc, work next 2 sc tog, ch 5. Work 4 sc across ch, sc in last sc worked in on hand and next sc, ch 4. Work 3 sc across ch. Sl st in last sc worked in on hand. End off. With L, work another piece the same. Sew pieces tog, tucking yarn ends inside. Sew hand to arm.

LEGS (make 2): **Top:** With G, ch 13. Work 18 rows of 12 sc. Dec 4 sc evenly across next row, work 1 row even. End off. Sew up and stuff. **Center:** Ch 9 and work as for top on 8 sc for 16 rows. Dec 2 sc on next row, work 1 row even. End off. Sew up and stuff. Sew to top at an angle. **Bottom:** Ch 7 and work 5 rows even on 6 sc. Sew up, stuff and sew to center at an angle. **Foot:** With G, ch 3. Sc in 2nd ch from hook and in next ch. Inc 1 sc in each of next 2 rows. Work even on 4 sc for 2 rows. Inc 1 sc each side of next row—6 sc. Form toes: Sc in first 2 sc. * Ch 1, turn. Sc in 2 sc. Work 2 sc tog. Work 2 rows of 1 sc. Sl st down side of toe, sc in next 2 sc. Repeat from * for next 2 toes, working 1 extra row of 2 sc for middle toe. End off. Make another piece the same. Sew pieces tog, stuffing lightly. Sew to bottom of legs. Sew legs to sides of body so they swing freely.

DYNAMIC DRAGON

Shown on page 149

SIZE: 24″ long.

MATERIALS: Knitting worsted weight yarn, 4 ozs. red (R), 1 oz. gold (G), few yards of black (B). Crochet hook size G. Stuffing. Light cardboard. Yarn needle.

GAUGE: 5 sc = 1″.

BODY: With R, ch 3.

Row 1: Sc in 2nd ch from hook and in next ch. Ch 1, turn each row. **Row 2:** Work even. **Rows 3-35:** Inc 1 sc on next row and every 3rd row until there are 13 sc. Work 2 rows even. **Rows 36-56:** Inc 1 sc each side of next row and every 4th row until there are 25 sc. **Rows 57-66:** Work even. **Row 67:** Inc in every 5th st—30 sc. **Row 68:** Work even. **Row 69:** Repeat row 67—36 sc. **Rows 70-91:** Work even. **Row 92:** Dec 6 sts evenly across—30 sc. **Row 93:** Work even. **Row 94:** Dec 6 sts evenly across—24 sc. **Row 95:** Work even. **Row 96:** Work 2 sc tog across—12 sc. **Row 97:** Work even. **Rows 98 and 99:** Repeat row 96—3 sc. End off. Sew sides of rows 97-99 tog.

UNDERBODY: With G, ch 3.

Rows 1-3: Repeat rows 1 and 2 of body. **Row 4:** Inc 1 sc—3 sc. **Rows 5 and 6:** Work even. **Row 7:** Inc 1 sc each side—5 sc. **Row 8:** Work even. **Rows 9-14:** Repeat rows 7 and 8, 3 times. **Row 15:** Repeat row 7—13 sc. **Rows 16-24:** Work even. **Row 25:** Dec 2 sc each side—9 sc. **Row 26:** Work even. **Rows 27 and 28:** Repeat rows 25 and 26—5 sc. **Row 29:** Dec 1 sc each side—3 sc. Work 3 sc tog. End off. This end goes toward head. Sew up tail for 60 rows (30 ridges). Sew underbody to body opening, stuffing as you go.

BACK LEG (make 2): With R, ch 15. Work 3 rows of 14 sc. Dec 2 sc evenly spaced across next row. Work 2 rows even. Sew side seam. Stuff; sew larger end to body. **Foot:** With R, ch 2. Work 6 sc in 2nd ch from hook. Working around, 2 sc in each sc—12 sc. Ch 1, turn. Sc in 6 sc. Ch 1, turn. * Sc in 2 sc for toe. Ch 1, turn. Work 2 sc tog, ch 3, turn. Sc in 2nd ch from hook and next ch, sl st down side of toe. Repeat from * twice for toes, but ch 4 for middle toe.

With G, work underfoot same as foot. Sew tog; sew to end of leg.

FRONT LEG (make 2): Work as for back leg, but work 4 rows even.

NECK: With R, ch 2.

Row 1: Sc in 2nd ch from hook. Ch 1, turn each row. **Row 2:** Inc 1 sc. **Row 3:** Work even—2 sc. **Row 4:** Repeat row 2 —3 sc. **Row 5:** Inc 1 sc each side—5 sc. **Row 6:** Work even. **Rows 7 and 8:** Repeat rows 5 and 6—7 sc. Ch 10. **Row 9:** Sc in 2nd ch from hook and in each ch, sc in 7 sc. Ch 10. **Row 10:** Sc in 2nd ch from hook and in each ch, sc across —25 sc. Work 10 rows even. Sew up back seam. Sew triangular piece over front of body. Stuff neck; sew on.

HEAD: With R, ch 5.

Row 1: Sc in 2nd ch from hook and in each ch. **Row 2:** 2 sc in each sc. **Row 3:** Work even—8 sc. **Rows 4 and 5:** Repeat rows 2 and 3—16 sc. **Row 6:** Inc in every other st—24 sc. **Rows 7-14:** Work even. Ch 6 at end of row 14, sl st in first sc of row 14. Turn. **Row 15** (lower jaw): Sc in each of 6 ch, sc in next 4 sc. Ch 1, turn. **Row 16:** Sc in 10 sc of row 15, sc in next 4 sc—14 sc for lower jaw. Ch 1, turn. **Row 17:** Work even. **Row 18:** Dec 1 st each side. **Row 19:** Work even—12 sc. **Row 20:** (Work 2 sc tog, sc in next st) 4 times—8 sc. **Rows 21-24:** Work even. **Row 25:** (Work 2 sc tog, sc in 2 sc) twice—6 sc. **Rows 26 and 27:** Work even. **Row 28:** Work 2 sc tog across. **Row 29:** Work 2 sc tog, sc in last st. End off.

Upper Jaw: Row 1: Join R, sc in each of remaining 16 sc of Row 14. Ch 1, turn. **Row 2:** (Work 2 sc tog, sc in 2 sc) 4 times. **Rows 3-5:** Work even—12 sc. **Row 6:** (Work 2 sc tog, sc in 2 sc) 3 times. **Rows 7-9:** Work even—9 sc. **Row 10:** (Work 2 sc tog, sc in next sc) 3 times. **Rows 11-13:** Work even—6 sc. **Rows 14 and 15:** Repeat rows 28 and 29 of lower jaw. Stuff head; sew to neck.

MOUTH (make 2): With G, ch 10. Work 2 rows of 9 sc. Dec 1 sc at center of next row; work 1 row even. Dec 1 sc each side of next row, work 5 rows even. Dec 1 sc at center of next row; work 1 row even. Dec 1 sc each side of next row; work 1 row even. Work 2 sc tog, 1 sc. Cut 2 cardboard pieces same size and shape as mouth. Place 1 under mouth for lower jaw; sew mouth in, stuffing under cardboard. Sew mouth pieces tog at back of mouth. Sew other mouth piece to top jaw in same way.

TONGUE: With R, ch 2. Sc in 2nd ch from hook. Ch 1, turn. Work in rows of 1 sc until tongue is 3″ long; ch 6; sc in 2nd ch from hook and in each ch, sc in base sc, ch 6 for other side of fork; finish in same way. Sew inside mouth.

Embroider black nostrils.

EYE (make 2): Work as for alligator's eye, working back with R and front with G.

TRIANGLES: With R or G, ch 2. Sc in 2nd ch from hook. Ch 1, turn. Inc 1 sc each row until 4 sc. End off. Sew to back, alternating R and G, with starting point up. Work last 4 triangles with 3 sc.

ROYAL ALLIGATOR

Shown on page 149

SIZE: 26″ long.

MATERIALS: Knitting worsted weight yarn, 4 ozs. green (G); small amounts of pink (P), lime (L) and black (B). Crochet hook size G. Stuffing. Light cardboard. Yarn needle.

GAUGE: 5 sc = 1″.

BODY: Beg at tail, with G, ch 3.

Row 1: Sc in 2nd ch from hook and in next ch. Ch 1, turn each row. **Rows 2-4:** Work even. **Row 5:** Inc 1 sc in row. **Rows 6-9:** Work even. **Row 10:** Inc 1 sc in row. **Rows 11 and 12:** Work even. **Row 13:** Inc 1 sc in row—5 sc. **Row 14:** Work even. **Rows 15-44:** Repeat rows 13 and 14—20 sc. **Rows 45-64:** Work even. **Row 65:** * Sc in each of 3 sc, 2 sc in next sc, repeat from * across. **Rows 66 and 67:** Work even—25 sc. **Row 68:** * Sc in each of 4 sc, 2 sc in next sc, repeat from * across. **Rows 69 and 70:** Work even—30 sc. **Rows 71-73:** Repeat rows 68-70—36 sc. **Row 74:** * Sc in each of 5 sc, 2 sc in next sc, repeat from * across. **Rows 75-82:** Work even —42 sc. **Row 83:** * Sc in each of 6 sc, 2 sc in next sc, repeat from * across. **Rows 84-98:** Work even—48 sc. **Row 99:** * Sc in each of 4 sc, work 2 sc tog, repeat from * across—40 sc. **Rows 100-102:** Work even. **Row 103:** * Sc in each of 8 sc, work 2 sc tog, repeat from * across—36 sc. **Rows 104 and 105:** Work even. **Row 106:** Sc in 8 sc, 2 sc in next sc, sc in next sc, 2 sc in next sc, sc in 14 sc, 2 sc in next sc, sc in next sc, 2 sc in next sc, sc in 8 sc. **Rows 107-110:** Work even—40 sc. **Row 111:** Sc in 10 sc, (2 sc in next sc, sc in 3 sc) 5 times, sc in 10 sc. **Row 112:** Work even—45 sc. End off. **Bottom Jaw: Row 1:** Beg 10 sts from edge, sc in 10 sts to edge, sc in 10 sts on other side, joining opening. Ch 1, turn. **Row 2:** Sc in 8 sc, work 2 sc tog twice, sc in 8 sc—18 sc. **Row 3:** Sc in 7 sc, work 2 sc tog twice, sc in 7 sc—16 sc. **Row 4:** Work even. **Row 5:** (Work 2 sc tog, sc in 2 sc) 4 times. **Rows 6-11:** Work even—12 sc. **Row 12:** (Work 2 sc tog, sc in 2 sc) 3 times. **Rows 13-16:** Work even—9 sc. **Row 17:** (Sc in 1 sc, work 2 sc tog) 3 times. **Row 18:** Work 2 sc tog each end. End. **Top Jaw: Row 1:** Join yarn at side of bottom jaw, sc in 25 sc. **Row 2:** Dec 1 sc each side of row. **Rows 3-5:** Work even —23 sc. **Row 6:** Repeat row 2—21 sc. **Row 7:** (Sc in 1 sc, work 2 sc tog) 7 times. **Rows 8 and 9:** Work even—14 sc. **Row 10:** Repeat row 2—12 sc. **Rows 11 and 12:** Work even. **Row 13:** (Work 2 sc tog, sc in 2 sc) 3 times. **Rows 14-19:** Repeat rows 13-18 of bottom jaw. Work 1 row even. End off.

LEGS (make 4): **Top:** With G, ch 13. Work 6 rows of 12 sc. Sew up sides (ridges, go around leg); stuff. **Bottom:** With G, ch 10. Work 6 rows of 9 sc. Sew first and last rows tog; sew up one end; stuff. Sew closed end to top of leg. **Foot:** With G, ch 5. Sc in 2nd ch from hook and in each ch—4 sc. Inc 1 sc in each of next 2 rows—6 sc. Work 1 row even. For toe, work 2 sc, ch 1, turn. Work 1 row of 2 sc. Work 2 sc tog. Work 1 sc. End off. Middle toe is worked with 2 rows even of 2 sc. Third toe is same as first. Make another foot the same. Sew 2 feet tog, tucking yarn ends inside. Sew to end of leg.

UPPER MOUTH: With P, ch 17. Work 3 rows of 16 sc. * Dec 1 sc each side of next row. Work 2 rows even. Repeat from * once—12 sc. Dec 4 sc across next row, work 5 rows even—8 sc. Dec 1 sc on next row, work 3 rows even. Dec 1 sc on next row, work 1 row

even. Dec 1 sc on next row, work 3 rows even—5 sc. Work 2 sc tog, sc in next st, work 2 sc tog. End off.
LOWER MOUTH: With P, ch 17. Work 1 row of 16 sc. Dec 1 sc each side of next 2 rows. Work 2 rows even— 12 sc. Dec 1 sc each side of next row. Work 6 rows even—10 sc. Dec 1 sc each side of next row. Work 3 rows even—8 sc. Dec 1 sc each side of next 2 rows—4 sc. Work 2 sc tog twice. End off.

Cut cardboard pieces to fit inside lower jaw and upper jaw. Sew upper and lower mouths inside head with cardboard in place, stuffing as you go. Sew mouth pieces tog at back. Sew up body, stuffing as you go. Sew on legs. Decorate back and toes with L lazy daisy sts. Embroider pink nostrils.
EYES: BACK: With G, ch 2. Work 4 sc in 2nd ch from hook. Ch 1, turn. 2 sc in each sc. Work 2 rows even—8 sc. End off. **Front:** With L, work as for back for 2 rows. Sew to back around last row. Stuff. Sew to head. **Pupil:** With B, ch 2. Work 5 sc in 2nd ch from hook. Sew to front of eye.

SNOWMAN
Shown on page 150

SIZE: 12″ tall.
MATERIALS: Acrylic, cotton or rayon rug yarn, 3 ozs. white, 1 oz. black, small amount red. Set of dp needles No. 10. Crochet hook size H. Four white buttons. Two black buttons for eyes. Orange chenille stick. Scrap of red felt.
GAUGE: 3 sts = 1″.
SNOWMAN: BODY: Beg at lower edge, with white, cast on 20 sts. Divide sts on 3 needles. Join, k 2 rnds.
Rnd 3: Inc 4 sts evenly around. K 2 rnds even.
Rnd 6: Inc 4 sts evenly around. K 2 rnds even.
Rnd 9: Inc 4 sts evenly around. K 14 rnds even—32 sts.
Rnd 24: Dec 4 sts evenly. K 2 rnds even.
Rnd 27: Dec 4 sts evenly. K 2 rnds even.
Rnd 30: (K 2 tog) 12 times. K 1 rnd.
Rnd 32: Inc 1 st in each st. K 1 rnd— 24 sts.
Rnd 34: Inc 4 sts evenly. K 1 rnd.
Rnd 36: Inc 4 sts evenly. K 8 rnds even— 32 sts.
Rnd 43: Dec 4 sts evenly. K 1 rnd.
Rnd 45: Dec 4 sts evenly. K 1 rnd.
Rnd 47: Dec 4 sts evenly. Cut yarn, weave top of head tog with Kitchener st.
LEG (make 2): Beg at lower edge, with white, cast on 20 sts. K 5 rnds.
Rnd 6: K 6, k 2 tog, k 4, sl 1, k 1, psso, k 6.
Rnd 7: K 5, k 2 tog, k 4, sl 1, k 1, psso, k 5. K 20 rnds on 16 sts.
Rnd 28: Dec 4 sts evenly around. K 1 rnd. Cut yarn, weave top of leg tog.

ARM (make 2): Beg at top edge, with white, cast on 14 sts. K 17 rnds.
Rnd 18: Inc 2 sts in rnd. K 5 rnds even.
Rnd 24: Dec 4 sts in rnd. K 1 rnd. Cut yarn; weave end of hand tog.
FINISHING: Stuff body, arms and legs. Sew openings tog. Sew buttons on arms and legs through body so arms and legs will move. Sew on button eyes. Form a coil with chenille stick; sew one end to face for nose. Cut crescent mouth from red felt; sew or glue on. Make 3 black "buttons": ch 2; 6 sc in 2nd ch from hook. Sew to front of body.
SCARF: With red and 2 needles, cast on 4 sts. Knit each row until scarf is 16″ long. Fringe ends.
HAT: With black, ch 2.
Rnd 1: 6 sc in 2nd ch from hook.
Rnd 2: 2 sc in each sc around.
Rnd 3: (Sc in next sc, 2 sc in next sc) 6 times.
Rnds 4-7: Sc in each sc around—18 sc.
Rnd 8: (Sc in 2 sc, 2 sc in next sc) 6 times.
Rnd 9: (Sc in 3 sc, 2 sc in next sc) 6 times.
Rnd 10: (Sc in 4 sc, 2 sc in next sc) 6 times. Sl st in first sc of rnd. End off.

BLONDIE AND BUTCH
Shown on pages 150 and 151

SIZE: 20″ tall.
MATERIALS: Rug yarn, 4-oz. skeins, 3 skeins red (A), 2 skeins each white (B) and eggshell (C), 1 skein each blue (D), yellow (E), black (F) and brown (G). Susan Bates or Marcia Lynn crochet hooks sizes H-8 and K-10½. Susan Bates 5 in 1 Pompon-Maker. Susan Bates Adjustable "Trim-Tool" for hair. Six packages 1″ "bone" rings. Two ⅞″ "bone" rings. Polyester or cotton stuffing. Four ⅝″ movable eyes. Two 1″ white buttons. Two ½″ black half-ball buttons. Scrap of black felt.

GAUGE: 1 circle = 2½″ diameter (size K hook); 3 sc = 1″ (size H hook).

CIRCLE PATTERN: With size K hook, work 12 sc in 1″ ring. Mark beg of each rnd.
Rnd 2: Work 2 sc in each sc.
Rnd 3: Sl st in each sc. End off.

BOY: HEAD: Beg at top, with size H hook and C, work 10 sc in ⅞″ ring. Mark beg of each rnd.
Rnd 1: Work 2 sc in each sc—20 sc.
Rnd 2: * Sc in next sc, 2 sc in next sc; repeat from *.
Rnd 3: * Sc in next 2 sc, 2 sc in next sc; repeat from *.
Rnd 4: * Sc in next 3 sc, 2 sc in next sc; repeat from *.
Rnds 5-11: Sc in each sc—50 sc.
Rnd 12: * Sc in next 3 sc, dec 1 st; repeat from *.
Rnds 13 and 14: Repeat rnd 5—40 sc.

Rnd 15: * Sc in next 2 sc, dec 1 st; repeat from *.

Rnds 16 and 17: Repeat rnd 5—30 sc.

Rnd 18: * Sc in next sc, dec 1 st; repeat from *.

Rnd 19: Repeat rnd 5—20 sc. Stuff.

Rnds 20 and 21: * Dec 1 st; repeat from *. End off, leaving a long tail for sewing.

BODY: With size H hook and A, ch 36; join with a sl st in first ch. Mark beg of each rnd.

Rnd 1: Sc in each st—36 sc. Work rnd 1, 13 times. With D, work rnd 1, 19 times. End off. Flatten piece. Sew tog along last D row. Stuff. Sew top edge tog. Sew head to body.

LEGS (make 2): With F, make a 3″ pompon, leaving a long tail for threading. Make 6 D, 3 C, 4 A, and 3 B circles, following the circle pattern. Thread tail of pompon through center of circles in following manner: A and B alternately, beg with A, 3 C and 6 D. Attach to bottom of body.

ARMS (make 2): Thread 5 C, then 6 A circles onto 2½″ C pompon. Attach to shoulder. Sew last circle to shoulder on top.

STRAPS (make 2): With D and size H hook, ch 34. Sc in 2nd ch from hook and in each ch across, ch 2, sc in each st on other side of foundation ch. End off. Sew one end to first D row on back. Crisscross strap and bring to front. Sew to first D row with button.

HAIR: With "Trim-Tool" and G, cut 3″ fringe. Beg in 14th rnd from bottom at back of head, insert hook under sc, fold 2 strands in half and pull through, then pull ends through lp. Continue in this manner, leaving face open, for 5 rnds towards top of head, then fill in remainder of rnds, forming bangs.

FINISHING: Sew on eyes. Cut eyelashes from felt, using pattern, then glue under eyes. Sew on button for nose. With A, make couching st for mouth (see Contents for Stitch Details).

 EYELASH

GIRL: Make head same as for boy.

With B, make body same as for boy. Make legs same as for boy, but alternate 4 A and 3 B circles, then 9 C. Make arms same as for boy, but thread 5 C, then 6 B circles.

HAIR: With E and size K hook, ch 50. Work 2 sc in each ch across. End off. Insert hook under top ring. Pull ends of curl through, forming lp, then pull ends through lp. Make 12 curls in same manner and attach to head. Line up curls around head and tack approximately 3½″ from top. Cut strands to measure 8″. Using 2 strands at once, form bangs by pulling through 2nd sc rnd.

SKIRT: With size H hook and A, ch 38; join with a sl st in first ch. Mark beg of each rnd.

Rnd 1: Sc in each st around.

Rnds 2 and 4: Dc in each st around.

Rnd 3: Dc in each dc, inc 8 sts evenly spaced. Repeat rnds 3 and 4 two more times, join with a sl st.

Next Rnd: Working from left to right, with size K hook, * ch 1, sk 1 sc, sc in next sc; repeat from * around, join. End off.

BIB: Sc in front 9 sc of first rnd, ch 1 to turn all rows.

Rows 2–7: Sc in each sc. End off.

ARMBANDS: With D, work 7 sc along side of bib, ch 30.

Row 1: Dc in 2nd ch from hook and in each st of ch, then in 7 sc; ch 2, turn.

Row 2: Dc in each dc; ch 4, turn.

Rows 3 and 4: Dc in first dc, * ch 2, dc in next dc; repeat from *; ch 4 to turn. End off. Sew side edge of band to top edge of skirt, leaving last 2 rows of band free. Work other side the same. Put skirt on doll. Sew ends of bands tog at back, then tack bands to skirt, pulling bands to fit. Form remaining sections of bands in bow. Tack in place. Complete face same as for boy.

HUMPTY DUMPTY RATTLE
Shown on page 150

SIZE: 6″ high.

MATERIALS: Worsted weight yarn, small amounts of white, red, blue, and yellow. Crochet hook size G. L'eggs® container. Pink, rose and red embroidery floss. Small amount of stuffing. Bell, pebbles or beans for rattle. Glue.

GAUGE: 4 sc = 1″.

HUMPTY DUMPTY: BODY: With white, ch 2.

Rnd 1: 6 sc in 2nd ch from hook.

Rnd 2: 2 sc in each sc around.

Rnd 3: (2 sc in next sc, sc in next sc) 6 times.

Rnd 4: (Sc in 5 sc, 2 sc in next sc) 3 times—21 sc.

Rnd 5: (Sc in 6 sc, 2 sc in next sc) 3 times—24 sc.

Rnd 6: (Sc in 7 sc, 2 sc in next sc) 3 times—27 sc.

Rnds 7-10: Continue to inc 3 sc each rnd—39 sc.

Rnds 11 and 12: Work even on 39 sc for 2 rnds. Sl st in next sc. End off.

Rnds 13-15: Join red with sc in sc before sl st, sc in each sc around for 3 rnds. Sl st in next sc. End off.

Rnd 16: Join blue, (sc in 11 sc, work next 2 sc tog) 3 times—36 sc.

Rnd 17: (Sc in 10 sc, work 2 sc tog) 3 times—33 sc.

Rnds 18-21: Continue to dec 3 sc each rnd, slipping plastic egg in pointed end first (containing rattle material and glued shut), after rnd 18.

Rnd 22: Work 2 sc tog around until 5 sc remain, sl st in next sc. End off; sew opening closed with yarn end.

ARMS (make 2): With red, ch 2; 6 sc in 2nd ch from hook. Work in sc, inc 3 sc in next rnd, then work even on 9 sc for 4 rnds. End off; leave end for sewing. Stuff arms, sew to red body on opposite sides, slightly toward front.

LEGS (make 2): With blue, ch 2; 6 sc in 2nd ch from hook. Work 2 sc in each sc around, then work even on 12 sc for 7 rnds. End off. Stuff legs; sew to front of body so egg will sit up.

HAT: With yellow, ch 2.

Rnd 1: 6 sc in 2nd ch from hook.

Rnd 2: 2 sc in each sc around.

Rnd 3: (2 sc in next sc, sc in next sc) 6 times.

Rnd 4: Sc in back lp of each sc around. Drop yellow.

Rnd 5: With blue, sc in each sc around. End off.

Rnds 6 and 7: With yellow, inc 4 sc in rnd—26 sc.

Rnd 8: Sc in each sc around. End off; leave end for sewing hat to head.

FINISHING: Sew 1″ loops of gold or brown yarn to forehead for hair. Sew hat in place over loops, stuffing hat first. Make black French knots for eyes. Embroider oval nose with rose floss in satin stitch. Embroider long smiling mouth with red floss in outline stitch. With pink floss, embroider lazy daisy flower at each side of mouth.

DISK DOLL
Shown on page 150

SIZE: 22″ tall.

MATERIALS: Knitting worsted, 12 ozs. of assorted colors, including 3 ozs. dark pink and 1 oz. dark red. Crochet hook size G. Tapestry needle. Polyester fiberfill.

GAUGE: 4 sts = 1″.

DOLL: BODY: With dark pink, ch 20.

Rnd 1: Dc in 4th ch from hook, dc in each ch to last ch, 3 dc in last ch. Working on opposite side of starting ch, dc in each ch, dc in same ch with first dc—36 dc. Sl st in top of ch 3.

Rnd 2: Ch 3, dc in same ch with sl st, dc in each of next 17 dc, 3 dc in end dc, dc in each of next 17 dc, dc in same ch with first dc—40 dc. Sl st in top of ch 3.

Rnd 3: Ch 3, dc in next dc and in each dc around. Join. Repeat rnd 3 until piece is 6″ from start. Cut yarn, leaving long end for sewing. Sew first 6 sts each side of last st tog for shoulder. Leaving next 8 sts free each side for neck, sew last 6 sts each side tog for shoulder. Stuff body.

HEAD: With dark pink, ch 16. Sl st in first ch to form ring.

Rnd 1: Ch 1, sc in each ch around—16 sc. Join each rnd.

Rnd 2: Ch 1; working in back lp of each sc throughout head, work 2 sc in first sc, sc in 7 sc, 2 sc in next sc, sc in 7 sc—18 sc.

Rnd 3: Ch 1; 2 sc in first sc, sc in 7 sc, 2 sc in each of next 2 sc, sc in 7 sc, in last sc—22 sc.

Rnds 4-8: Continue to work in sc, inc 3 sts each side of head each rnd—52 sc.

Rnds 9 and 10: Work even.

Rnds 11-16: Dec 3 sts each side each rnd. End off. Sew top edges tog. Stuff head.

With white, embroider eyes in satin stitch; make brown pupils. Outline eyes and make lashes with black. Make 2 black sts for nose. Embroider mouth with red. (See Contents for Stitch Details.)

For hair, thread double strand of dark red in tapestry needle. Stitching through head and leaving 1″ loops each stitch, make loops all over head.

Sew head to neck, adding more stuffing before closing seam.

ARMS: With pink, ch 2.

Rnd 1: 6 sc in 2nd ch from hook.

Rnd 2: 2 sc in each sc around.

Rnd 3: (Sc in next sc, 2 sc in next sc) 6 times.

Rnds 4-6: Work even on 18 sc.

Rnd 7: (Sc in next 2 sc, sk next sc) 6 times. Stuff hand firmly.

Rnd 8: (Sc in next sc, sk next sc) 6 times. Sc in every other sc to close hole. Make a ch 8″ long. End off, leaving long end for sewing.

Disks (make 26 for each sleeve): With any color, ch 5. Sl st in first ch to form ring. Ch 3, work 16 dc in ring. Join; end off. Run in yarn ends.

SUIT (make 18 disks): With any color, ch 40. Sl st in first ch to form ring. Ch 2, hdc in each ch around. Join. Change color; ch 4 for first tr, * 2 tr in next st, tr in next st, repeat from * around, changing color as desired. Join; end off. Place 3 disks around neck; tack to body and shoulders as necessary to hold in place. Make a black ch 8″ long; form bow; tack to center front of top disk.

String 26 small disks for sleeves on each arm chain. Sew top of arm chains firmly to shoulders.

Place remaining suit disks around body. Tack in place at sides. Lowest one should be tacked all around.

LEGS: With double strand of black, work as for arms. Make ch 10″ long. End off, leaving long end for sewing.

Disks (make 30 for each leg): With any color, ch 5. Sl st in first ch to form ring. Ch 4, work 16 tr in ring. Join; end off. Run in yarn ends. String disks on leg chains. Sew top of leg chains to each side of body at lower edge.

MARTY MOUSE
Shown on page 151

SIZE: 6″ plus tail.

MATERIALS: Knitting worsted, 1 oz. each of main color (MC) and contrasting color (CC). Crochet hook size J. Stuffing. Scraps of black felt. Glue.

GAUGE: 3 sc = 1″.

MOUSE: BODY: Beg at nose, with MC, ch 4. Sl st in first ch to form ring.

Rnd 1: 2 sc in each ch around.

Rnds 2-7: Working in back lps only (throughout), * sc in 2 sts, 2 sc in next st, repeat from * for 6 rnds or until there are 50 sc in rnd.

Rnds 8-11: Work even on 50 sc for 4 rnds. Stuff.

Rnds 12-17: * Sc in 3 sts, sk next st, repeat from * until there are 10 sc in rnd.

Rnd 18: Sl st in every other st until body opening is closed. End off.

TAIL: With CC, work 4 sc around end of mouse, work 15 rounds of 4 sc. End off. Close end of tail.

FEET: Join CC between rnds 8 and 9 on underside of body, work sc, hdc, 3 dc, hdc and sc all in the same st. End off. Tie two ends tog; tuck ends inside body. Repeat for other front foot on other side of the body. Work two back feet the same, making feet between rnds 13 and 14.

EARS: Join CC with sc in st on rnd 8, sc in each of next 8 sts, ch 1, turn. Working in back lps, * sc in next st, 2 sc in next st, repeat from * across. Turn. Working in free lps of original 8 sc, repeat from * to * across—24 sc.

Rnds 2 and 3: Sc in each sc around.

Rnds 4-6: Sl st in every other st until ear is closed. End off. Repeat ear on other side of head.

WHISKERS: Cut 4 pieces of CC 3″ long. Fold 2 strands in half, knot fringe through st on one side of nose. Repeat on other side of nose.

FINISHING: Tuck in all ends. Cut eyes and mouth from black felt; glue on.

Eye

Mouth

Actual-Size Patterns

PINAFORE PATTIE
Shown on page 151

SIZE: 25″ tall.

MATERIALS: Worsted weight yarn, 4

ozs. light green, 3 ozs. pink, 2 ozs. white, 1 oz. brown. Scrap of red. Crochet hook size F-5. Polyester fiberfill for stuffing. Two green shank-type buttons. Yarn needle. Long sewing needle. Thread.

DOLL: HEAD AND BODY: With pink, beg at top of head, ch 2.

Rnd 1: 6 sc in 2nd ch from hook.

Rnd 2: 2 sc in each sc around.

Rnd 3: (Sc in next sc, 2 sc in next sc) 6 times.

Rnd 4: Work even on 18 sc.

Rnd 5: (Sc in 2 sc, 2 sc in next sc) 6 times.

Rnd 6: (Sc in 2 sc, 2 sc in next sc) 8 times.

Rnd 7: Work even on 32 sc.

Rnd 8: (Sc in 3 sc, 2 sc in next sc) 8 times.

Rnds 9-17: Work even on 40 sc.

Rnd 18: (Sc in 8 sc, work 2 sc tog) 4 times.

Rnds 19 and 20: Work even on 36 sc.

Rnd 21: (Work 2 sc tog) 8 times, sc in each remaining sc.

Rnd 22: Work even on 28 sc.

Rnd 23: (Work 2 sc tog) 4 times, sc in each remaining sc.

Rnd 24: Work even on 24 sc. Work sc in next sc.

Rnd 25: Ch 1, turn; sc in 5 sc; ch 1, turn; sc in 13 sc, (work 2 sc tog) 4 times, sc in each of next 20 sts. End off. Fold head to find center back.

Body: Join white in center back st, sc in 5 sc, ch 4 (shoulder); sc in 2nd ch from hook and in next 2 ch, sc in 10 sc, ch 4 (shoulder); sc in 2nd ch from hook and in next 2 ch, sc in 5 sc. Mark end of rnd.

Rnd 2: Sc in 5 sc, 3 sc in each ch, 3 sc on shoulder, sc in 10 sc, 3 sc in each ch, 3 sc on shoulder, sc in 5 sc—32 sc.

Rnd 3: Sc around, inc 1 st at end of each shoulder.

Rnd 4: Work even—34 sc.

Rnd 5: Sc around, inc 1 st at each shoulder and 2 at front center, evenly spaced.

Rnd 6: Work even—38 sc.

Rnd 7: Inc 1 st at back and front center.

Rnds 8 and 9: Work even on 40 sc.

Rnd 10: Inc 2 sts in back and 2 sts in front.

Rnds 11 and 12: Work even on 44 sc.

Rnd 13: Repeat rnd 10.

Rnds 14-26: Work even on 48 sc. Cut white.

Rnds 27-29: With green, work even on 48 sc.

Rnd 30: (Sc in 6 sc, work 2 sc tog) 6 times.

Rnd 31: Work even on 42 sc.

Rnd 32: (Sc in 5 sc, work 2 sc tog) 6 times.

Rnds 33-36: Work even on 36 sc. End off. Stuff.

BOTTOM: Beg at back edge, with green, ch 11.

Row 1: Sc in 2nd ch from hook and in each ch. Ch 1, turn each row.

Row 2: Working in sc, inc 1 sc each side.

Row 3: Work even—12 sc.
Rows 4-7: Repeat rows 2 and 3 twice—16 sc.
Row 8: Dec 1 sc each side.
Row 9: Work even.
Rows 10-12: Repeat rows 8, 9, 8. End off. Sew bottom to doll.
LEGS: Thigh: With pink, ch 20. Sl st in first ch to form ring.
Rnds 1-8: Work even on 20 sc.
Rnd 9: (Sc in 8 sc, work 2 sc tog) twice.
Rnds 10-17: Work even on 18 sc.
Rnd 18: Dec 1 sc in rnd.
Rnds 19-22: Work even on 17 sc. End off.
Lower Leg: With pink, ch 16. Sl st in first ch to form ring.
Rnds 1-14: Work even on 16 sc. Cut pink.
Rnds 15-20: With white, work even.
Rnd 21: Dec 1 sc, work to end.
Rnd 22: Ch 5, sc in 2nd ch from hook and in next 3 ch, sc in 15 sc around.
Rnd 23: Sc in 4 ch, 2 sc in next sc, sc in each sc around. Cut white.
Rnd 24: With brown, work around, inc 1 sc at front of foot.
Rnds 25-28: Work even.
Rnd 29: Dec 1 sc at toe and 1 sc at heel. End off. Sew legs flat across; stuff before sewing last seam. Sew thigh to lower leg. Sew up slit at bottom of shoe.
Shoe Strap (make 2): With brown, ch 11. Work 1 row of 10 sc. Sew on.
Button: With white, ch 2; 2 sc in 2nd ch from hook; sew into a ball; sew to shoe.
Cuff of Sock: With white, ch 21. Work 1 row of 20 sc. Sew on.
Knee: With pink, ch 2.
Rnd 1: 5 sc in 2nd ch from hook.
Rnd 2: Work 2 sc in each sc around. End off. Stuff with yarn end; sew, wrong side out, over knee joint.
Panty Legs: With green, ch 22. Sl st in first ch to form ring. Work 3 rnds even on 22 sc. Slip over leg and sew to panties.
ARMS: Upper Arm: With white, ch 16. Sl st in first ch to form ring. Work 12 rnds even on 16 sc. Cut white.
Rnds 13-18: With pink, work even.
Rnd 19: Dec 1 sc. End off. Stuff and sew top of arm flat across. Sew elbow end flat across in the opposite direction.
Lower Arm: With pink, ch 15. Sl st in first ch to form ring.
Rnds 1-4: Work even on 15 sc.
Rnd 5: Dec 1 sc in rnd.
Rnds 6-12: Work even on 14 sc.
Rnds 13 and 14: Dec 1 sc in each rnd.
Rnd 15: Work even on 12 sc.
Rnd 16: (2 sc in next sc, sc in 2 sc) 4 times.
Rnd 17: Work even on 16 sc.
Rnd 18: (Sc in 7 sc, 2 sc in next sc) twice.
Rnds 19 and 20: Work even on 18 sc.
Rnd 21: (Work 2 tog, sc in 7 sc) twice.
Rnd 22: (Work 2 tog) 8 times.
Rnd 23: Work even. End off. Run yarn

through sts. Stuff arm.

Place arm on flat surface so hand is flat. Sew arm flat across at elbow. Sew to upper arm. Make trim for sleeve as for sock cuff. Make elbow same as knee. Sew arms to shoulders.

PINAFORE: Bib: With green, ch 12.
Row 1: Sc in 2nd ch from hook and in each ch across. Ch 3, turn.
Row 2: Dc in 2nd st and in each sc across. Ch 1, turn.
Row 3: Sc in each st across. Ch 3, turn.
Rows 4-9: Repeat rows 2 and 3. End off.
Skirt: With green, ch 50. Sc in 2nd ch from hook and in each ch across. Ch 1, turn each sc row.
Rows 2 and 3: Work even in sc. At end of row 3, ch 2, turn.
Row 4: Dc across. Ch 1 turn.
Row 5: Sc across, inc 1 sc in every 4th st. Ch 2, turn.
Row 6: Work even in dc. Ch 1, turn.
Rows 7 and 8: Repeat rows 5 and 6.
Rows 9-12: Work even, alternating sc and dc rows.
Row 13: Sc across, inc 12 sts evenly spaced across.
Row 14: Work even in dc.
Row 15: Work even in sc. End off.
RUFFLE (make 2): With green, ch 25.
Row 1: 2 sc in 2nd ch from hook and in each ch to end. Ch 2, turn.
Row 2: 2 dc in each sc. Ch 1, turn.
Row 3: Sc in each dc across.
STRAP (make 2): With green, ch 5. Work in rows of 4 sc until strap is long enough to go from top of bib to back of skirt.
FINISHING: Sew bib to skirt; sew back skirt seam; sew on straps; sew ruffles to straps.

Hair is made by winding yarn around pencil. Place end of yarn up pencil ½", then start winding over pencil. Cut yarn, leaving 8". Thread needle with end, run needle through yarn, up pencil. Slide windings off pencil, pull up a bit, adjust curl, sew to head. For top curls, pull up more. Tie bow in hair.

Press face in a bit, about half way down; sew on button eyes. Make pink nose like shoe button, or embroider dots for nose. Embroider mouth with red, lashes with brown.

SCHOOL BUS
Shown on page 152

SIZE: 18" long, 8" high, 5" wide.

MATERIALS: Aunt Lydia's Heavy Rug Yarn, 4 70-yard skeins Sunset (orange), 2 skeins Flax (beige) and 1 skein Black. Crochet hook size K. Two ⅞" shiny flat buttons for headlights. Polyester filling, 12 ozs. Felt, 3" square each of red and white.

GAUGE: 5 sc = 2"; 3 rows = 1".
Notes: Entire bus is worked in sc. Ch 1 to turn all rows unless otherwise specified. To change colors, work

last st of old color to last 2 lps, then with new color work off last 2 lps. Markers are placed on several rows to aid in assembling pieces.

BUS: LEFT SIDE: Beg at lower edge with Sunset, ch 46.
Row 1: Sc in 2nd ch from hook and in each ch across—45 sc.
Rows 2-10: Work even on 45 sc. At end of row 10, change to Flax; cut Sunset. Place marker at beg of row 10.
Row 11: Sc in each of first 37 sts; leave last 8 sts unworked.
Rows 12-24: Work even on 37 sc. End off. Place marker at beg and end of row 24.

RIGHT SIDE: Beg at lower edge with Sunset, ch 46. Work as for left side through row 10. At end of row 10, cut Sunset; do not change to Flax. Turn work.
Row 11: Sk first 8 sts; join Flax in next st, sc in same st and in each st across—37 sc. Work rows 12-24 as for left side.

BACK, TOP AND FRONT SECTION: Beg at back bottom edge, with Sunset, ch 13.
Row 1: Sc in 2nd ch from hook and in each ch across—12 sc.
Rows 2-10: Work even on 12 sc. At end of row 10, change to Flax; cut Sunset.
Rows 11-24: With Flax, work even. At end of row 24, change to Sunset; cut Flax. Mark both ends of row 24.
Rows 25-68: With Sunset, work even. At end of row 68, change to Flax; cut Sunset.
Rows 69-82: With Flax, work even; mark both ends of row 69. At end of row 82, change to Sunset; cut Flax.
Rows 83-101: With Sunset, work even; mark both ends of row 92. End off.

BOTTOM: With Sunset, ch 13.
Row 1: Sc in 2nd ch from hook and in each ch across—12 sc.
Rows 2-54: Work even on 12 sc. End off.

WHEELS (make 4): With Black, ch 4; sl st in first ch to form ring.
Rnd 1: Ch 3, 13 dc in ring, sl st in top of ch 3.
Rnd 2: Sl st in each st around. End off. (Note: For white wall tires, work rnd 2 with white.)

FINISHING: Weave in loose ends on wrong side. Steam pieces lightly. Place wrong sides of left side and back, top and front section tog, matching markers and colors. Beg at back bottom edge and working through both thicknesses, with Sunset, sc left side to back, top windshield, top of hood, and front of bus. End off.

Beg at front bottom edge, attach right side in same way.

To outline windshield, place Black inside bus. Insert hook ½″ in from side edge in st at right inner corner of hood, pull up a lp; * insert hook in next row above, pull up another lp and pull through first lp on hook, repeat from * up side edge of windshield. Continue to work sl sts across roof edge, down other side edge of windshield and across hood to first st. End off.

In same way, outline windows on sides of bus; work 5 vertical lines evenly spaced, to make 6 windows. On back, work 2 windows in same way.

Sew buttons to front for headlights. Stuff bus. Sew bottom in place. Sew two wheels to each side of bus. Using pattern, cut octagonal piece of white felt. Cut red felt slightly smaller. Cut away letters from red piece so that white felt shows through, being careful to preserve centers of "O" and "P". Glue red piece to white piece. Tack sign loosely to side of bus.

MAIL TRUCK
Shown on page 152

SIZE: 10″ long, 8″ high, 5″ wide.
MATERIALS: Aunt Lydia's Heavy Rug Yarn, 2 70-yard skeins each of National Blue and White, 1 skein each of Black and Red. Crochet hook size K. Two ⅞″ shiny flat buttons for headlights. Polyester filling, 6 ozs.
GAUGE: 5 sc = 2″; 3 rows = 1″.
Notes: Entire bus is worked in sc. Ch 1 to turn all rows unless otherwise specified. To change colors, work last st of old color to last 2 lps, then with new color work off last 2 lps. Carry colors not in use loosely along side of work unless otherwise specified. Markers are placed on several rows to aid in assembling pieces.

TRUCK: LEFT SIDE: Beg at lower edge with blue, ch 26.
Row 1: Sc in 2nd ch from hook and in each ch across—25 sc.
Rows 2-9: Sc in each sc—25 sc.
Row 10: Work even, change to white at end of row; cut blue. Place a marker at beg of row 10.
Row 11: Sc in each of first 20 sts, change to red; drop white. Leave last 5 sts unworked.
Rows 12 and 13: With red, sc in each st across. At end of row 13, change to white; cut red.
Row 14-24: Work even with white; place a marker at beg and end of last row. End off.

RIGHT SIDE: Beg at lower edge with blue, ch 26.
Rows 1-10: Work as for left side, but do not change to white at end of row 10; cut blue. Mark end of row 10.
Row 11: Sk first 5 sts, pull up a lp of white in next st, ch 1, sc in same st and in each st across; change to red. Drop white.
Rows 12-24: Work as for left side.

BACK, TOP AND FRONT SECTION: Beg at back bottom edge, with blue, ch 13.
Row 1: Sc in 2nd ch from hook and in each ch across—12 sc.
Rows 2-10: Work even. At end of row 10, change to white; cut blue.
Row 11: Work even. At end of row, change to red; drop white.
Rows 12 and 13: With red, work even. At end of row 13, change to white. Cut red.
Rows 14-62: With white, work even; mark each end of rows 24 and 49. At end of row 62, change to blue; cut white.
Rows 63-77: With blue, work even. Mark each end of row 68. End off.

BOTTOM: With blue, ch 13.

Row 1: Sc in 2nd ch from hook and in each ch across—12 sc.
Rows 2-30: Work even. End off.
WHEELS (make 4): With black, ch 4; sl st in first ch to form ring.
Rnd 1: Ch 3, 13 dc in ring, sl st in top of ch 3.
Rnd 2: Sl st in each st around. End off.
FINISHING: Weave in loose ends on wrong side. Steam pieces lightly. Place wrong sides of left side and back, top and front section tog, matching markers and colors. Beg at back bottom edge and working through both thicknesses, with blue, sc left side to back to white section. Matching colors of pieces, continue to sc left side to back, top, windshield, top of hood and front of truck. End off.

Beg at front bottom edge, attach right side in same way.

To outline windshield, place black inside truck. Insert hook ½″ in from side edge in st at right inner corner of hood, pull up a lp; * insert hook in next row above, pull up another lp and pull through first lp on hook, repeat from * up side edge of windshield. Continue to work sl sts across roof edge, down other side edge of windshield and across hood to first st. End off.

Sew buttons to front for headlights. Stuff truck. Sew bottom in place. Sew two wheels to each side of bus.

DELIGHTFUL DOLLS
Shown on page 153

SIZE: About 28″ tall.
MATERIALS: Knitting worsted or yarn of similar weight. For each: 4 ozs. pink (P) for body. For Yellow-Haired Doll: 3 ozs. white (W) for dress, 1 oz. yellow (Y) for hair, 1 oz. black (B) for boots. Yellow satin ribbon, ⅝″ wide, 1½ yards. For Black-Haired Doll: 2 ozs. each of red (R) and navy (N) for sweater, pants, boots, 1 oz. black for hair. Small amount round elastic thread. Knitting needles No. 8; set of dp needles. No. 5. Crochet hook size F or G. Stitch holder. Scraps of black or blue and red felt. All-purpose glue.
GAUGE: 5 sts = 1″ (stockinette st, No. 5 needles). 4 sts = 1″; 1 pat (4 rows) = ¾″ (No. 8 needles).
Notes: To inc 1 st, k in front and back of same st. Sl all sl sts as if to knit.
DOLL: BODY: Body directions are for Yellow-Haired Doll; any changes for other doll are in parentheses.

Beg at lower chest, with P and No. 5 needles, cast on 60 sts and divide evenly on 3 dp needles. Join, being careful not to twist sts. Work in ribbing of k 1, p 1 for 2½". Mark end of rnds.

Dec Rnd: * (K 1, p 1) 3 times, k 2 tog, p 2 tog, repeat from * around—48 sts. Work 1 rnd in ribbing.

Shape Neck: * K 6, k 2 tog, repeat from * around—42 sts. K 2 rnds even.

Shape Head: First Inc Rnd: K 20, inc 1 st in each of next 2 sts (see Notes), k 20—44 sts.

2nd Inc Rnd: K 20, inc 1 st, k 2, inc 1 st, k 20—46 sts.

3rd Inc Rnd: K 20, inc 1 st, k 4, inc 1 st, k 20—48 sts. Continue to inc in this manner until there are 12 sts between inc (chin and mouth)—56 sts on all 3 needles. K around for 3".

Shape Top: First Dec Rnd: (K 6, sl 1, k 1, psso) 7 times—49 sts.

2nd Dec Rnd: (K 5, sl 1, k 1, psso) 7 times—42 sts. Continue to dec in this manner having 1 st less between decs until there are 14 sts. Cut yarn leaving 12" end. Run yarn through remaining sts. Pull up, fasten securely.

Bottom and Legs: With P and No. 5 needles, cast on 54 sts and divide on 3 dp needles. Join, being careful not to twist sts. Mark end of rnd for middle of body. Work in stockinette st (k each rnd) for 6".

Divide for Legs: Bind off first 2 sts for crotch, k until 25 sts from bound-off sts, sl remaining 27 sts on a holder (2nd leg). Divide 25 sts of first leg on 3 dp needles. K around for 7½" (12¾"). Cut P; join B (R). With B (R), k around for 5½" (¼").

Shape Foot: K 18, put a marker on needle, (inc 1 st in next st) twice, put a marker on needle, finish rnd.

Next Rnd: K to first marker, sl marker, inc 1 st in next st, k to 1 st before 2nd marker, inc 1 st in next st, sl marker, finish rnd. Repeat this rnd until there are 10 sts between markers. K 2 rnds even. Bind off.

Sl the 27 sts from holder to 3 dp needles. Join P; bind off first 2 sts for crotch, finish rnd. Work 2nd leg same as first leg to foot shaping.

Shape Foot: K 5, put a marker on needle, (inc 1 st in next st) twice, put a marker on needle, finish rnd. Complete as for first foot.

Soles (make 2): With B (R) and 2 dp needles, cast on 2 sts. Work back and forth in garter st (k each row) as follows:

Row 1: K, inc 1 st in last st. Repeat this row twice—5 sts. Work even for 2".

Next Row: K, dec 1 st at end of row. Repeat this row twice—2 sts. Bind off.

Arms (make 2): With P and 2 dp needles cast on 18 sts. Work back and

forth in stockinette st (k 1 row, p 1 row) for 9".

Next Row: * K 1, sl 1, k 1, psso, repeat from * across—12 sts. Work even for 1" more, end p row. Cut yarn leaving about 30" end. Thread needle, draw through remaining sts; sew arm seam.

FINISHING: With matching yarn, sew soles to feet. Sew crotch seam. Stuff both body pieces; sew body pieces tog. Tie double strand of P around neck (beg of stockinette st section). Tie double strand of P around waist, 1½" down from ribbing. Stuff arms. Sew to body with seam as inner arm. From felt, cut ⅞" circles for eyes, ½" oval for nose. Glue on. With yarn, sew imitation lacing on sides of black boots. Make bow at top.

Hair: Cut 100 strands of Y (B), each 16" long. Arrange crosswise on a 5" strip of cellophane tape having strands 6" on one side of tape, 10" on the other. Machine stitch down center of tape for hair part. Carefully remove tape. Backstitch hair to side of head along machine stitching. Apply glue to head and press hair in place. Trim ends. Hold side hair in place with ribbon bow or barrette as shown.

CLOTHING: PATTERN: Row 1: * K 1, wrap yarn twice around needle, repeat from * across, end k 1.

Row 2: Knit, dropping wraps off left-hand needle. Pull sts down forming long sts.

Row 3: Knit.

Row 4: Purl. Repeat these 4 rows for pat.

DRESS: Front: Beg at lower edge, with W and No. 8 needles, cast on 35 sts. K 3 rows, then work 4 rows of pattern 10 times. Check gauge; piece should measure about 6" wide, 8" from start.

Shape Sleeves: Work rows 1-4 of pat, casting on 25 sts at end of rows 2 and 3 for sleeves—85 sts, 11 pats from start. Work pat 3 more times, then work rows 1 and 2.

Shape Neck Opening: K 30, bind off next 25 sts, finish row.

Next Row: P, cast on 25 sts over bound-off sts.

Back: Work pat 3 times more, then work rows 1 and 2. Bind off 25 sts at beg of next 2 rows—35 sts. Work 4 rows of pat 11 times. K 2 rows. Bind off loosely in k.

FINISHING: Sew side and sleeve seams. With crochet hook, make 2 chains, each 12" long, for ties at neck opening. Insert in 5th st from neck opening on each side. Draw satin ribbon through sts at waistline (11th pat).

SWEATER: Front: Beg at lower edge, with R and No. 8 needles, cast on 35

sts. K 3 rows. Work 4 rows of pattern 3 times.

Shape Sleeves: Work rows 1-4 of pat, casting on 25 sts at end of rows 2 and 3 for sleeves—85 sts, 4 pats from start. Work pat 3 more times, then work rows 1 and 2.

Shape Neck Opening: K 30, bind off next 25 sts, finish row. **Next Row:** P, cast on 25 sts over bound-off sts.

Back: Work pat 3 times more, then work rows 1 and 2. Bind off 25 sts at beg of next 2 rows—35 sts. Work 4 rows of pat 4 times. K 2 rows. Bind off loosely in k.

FINISHING: Finish as for dress. Crochet a chain about 1 yard long for belt.

PANTS: Beg at waistline, with N and No. 8 needles, cast on 54 sts. (K 1 row, p 1 row) twice, then work the 4 rows of pat 3 times. Work rows 1 and 2.

Divide for Legs: K 2 tog, k 23, k 2 tog—25 sts. Sl remaining 27 sts on a holder for 2nd leg. P 1 row, then work the 4 rows of pat 12 times. K 3 rows. Bind off.

Sl 27 sts from holder to No. 8 needles. Join N. Complete as for first leg.

FINISHING: Sew back and leg seams. Sew elastic thread through top to draw waistline in to desired fit; fasten securely.

LOVABLE LION
Shown on page 154

SIZE: 14" high.

MATERIALS: Rug yarn, 3 180-yard skeins gold, 1 skein yellow. Knitting worsted, 1 oz. light gold. Crochet hook size I. Stuffing. Two black buttons. Black embroidery floss. Two pipe cleaners.

Note: For smaller lion, use knitting worsted and size F hook.

GAUGE: 3 sc = 1".

HEAD: Beg at mouth, ch 2.

Rnd 1: 6 sc in 2nd ch from hook. Mark ends of rnds for bottom of head.

Rnd 2: 2 sc in each sc around—12 sc.

Rnds 3 and 4: Work in sc, inc 6 sc each rnd—24 sc.

Rnd 5: 2 sc in each sc around—48 sc.

Rnd 6: Sc in every other sc—24 sc.

Rnd 7: (Sc in next sc, 2 sc in next sc) 3 times, sc in 12 sc, (2 sc in next sc, sc in next sc) 3 times—30 sc.

Rnd 8: Work even.

Rnd 9: (Sc in next 2 sc; 2 sc in next sc) 3 times, sc in 12 sc, (2 sc in next sc, sc in next 2 sc) 3 times—36 sc.

Rnds 10 and 11: Work even.

Rnd 12: (Sc in 5 sc, 2 sc in next sc) twice, sc in 12 sc, (2 sc in next sc, sc in 5 sc) twice—40 sc.

Rnd 13: Work even.

Rnd 14: Sc in 3 sc, 2 sc in next sc, sc in 6 sc, 2 sc in next sc, sc in 18 sc, 2 sc in next sc, sc in 6 sc, 2 sc in next sc, sc in 3 sc.

Rnds 15 and 16: Work even—44 sc.

Rnd 17: Sc in 13 sc, 2 sc in next sc, sc in next sc, 2 sc in next sc, sc in 12 sc, 2 sc in next sc, sc in next sc, 2 sc in next sc, sc in 13 sc—48 sc.

Rnds 18-21: Work even.

Rnd 22: (Sc in 6 sc, work 2 sc tog) 6 times—42 sc.

Rnd 23: (Sc in 5 sc, work 2 sc tog) 6 times—36 sc.

Rnd 24: (Sc in 4 sc, work 2 sc tog) 6 times—30 sc.

Rnd 25: (Sc in 3 sc, work 2 sc tog) 6 times—24 sc.

Rnd 26: (Sc in 2 sc, work 2 sc tog) 6 times—18 sc.

Rnds 27 and 28: Dec 6 sc each rnd, stuffing head before last rnd. End off.

BODY: Beg at neck, ch 8. Sl st in first ch to form ring. Mark ends of rnds for back of body.

Rnd 1: 2 sc in each ch around.

Rnds 2 and 3: Work even—16 sc.

Rnds 4 and 5: Inc 4 sc evenly around.

Rnd 6: Work even—24 sc.

Rnd 7: Inc 4 sc evenly around—28 sc.

Rnd 8: Sc in 3 sc, 2 sc in next sc, sc in 20 sc, 2 sc in next sc, sc in 3 sc—30 sc.

Rnd 9: (Sc in next sc, 2 sc in next sc) 3 times, sc in 18 sc, (2 sc in next sc, sc in next sc) 3 times.

Rnd 10: (Sc in 2 sc, 2 sc in next sc) twice, sc in 24 sc, (2 sc in next sc, sc in 2 sc) twice.

Rnd 11: Work even—40 sc.

Rnd 12: (Sc in 2 sc, 2 sc in next sc) twice, sc in 28 sc, (2 sc in next sc, sc in 2 sc) twice.

Rnd 13: Work even—44 sc.

Rnd 14: (Sc in 2 sc, 2 sc in next sc) twice, sc in 32 sc, (2 sc in next sc, sc in 2 sc) twice.

Rnd 15: Work even—48 sc.

Rnd 16: (Sc in 2 sc, 2 sc in next sc) twice, sc in 36 sc, (2 sc in next sc, sc in 2 sc) twice.

Rnd 17: Work even—52 sc.

Rnd 18: (Sc in 2 sc, 2 sc in next sc) twice, sc in 13 sc, (work next 2 sc tog, sc in 2 sc) 3 times, work next 2 sc tog, sc in 13 sc, (2 sc in next sc, sc in 2 sc) twice.

Rnd 19: Work even—52 sc.

Rnd 20: (Sc in 2 sc, 2 sc in next sc) twice, sc in 15 sc, (work next 2 sc tog) twice, sc in 2 sc, (work next 2 sc tog) twice, sc in 15 sc, (2 sc in next sc, sc in 2 sc) twice.

Rnd 21: Work even—52 sc.

Rnd 22: Sc in 22 sc, (work next 2 sc tog) 4 times, sc in 22 sc—48 sc.

Rnd 23: Sc in 22 sc, (work next 2 sc tog) twice, sc in 22 sc—46 sc.

Rnd 24: Sc in 21 sc, (2 sc in next sc) 4 times, sc in 21 sc—50 sc.

Rnd 25: Work even.

Rnd 26: Sc in 23 sc, (work next 2 sc tog) twice, sc in 23 sc.

Rnd 27: Sc in 22 sc, (work next 2 sc tog) twice, sc in 22 sc—46 sc.

Rnd 28: Sc in next sc, work next 2 sc tog, sc in 2 sc, work next 2 sc tog, sc in next 32 sc, work next 2 sc tog, sc in 2 sc, work next 2 sc tog, sc in next sc.

Rnd 29: Sc in next sc, work next 2 sc tog, sc in 2 sc, work next 2 sc tog, sc in next 28 sc, work next 2 sc tog, sc in 2 sc, work next 2 sc tog, sc in 2 sc, work next 2 sc tog, sc in next sc.

Rnd 30: Sc in 10 sc, (work next 2 sc tog, sc in 6 sc) twice, work next 2 sc tog, sc in 10 sc—34 sc.

Rnd 31: Sc in 5 sc, work next 2 sc tog) 5 times. Stuff and continue decreasing as in rnd 31 until there are 16 sc remaining. Work 2 sc tog around until hole is closed. Sew underside of head to top front of body.

HAUNCH (make 2): Beg at front end of haunch, ch 2.

Rnd 1: 6 sc in 2nd ch from hook.

Rnd 2: 2 sc in each sc around.

Rnd 3: (Sc in next sc, 2 sc in next sc) 6 times—18 sc.

Rnds 4-10: Work even.

Rnd 11: (Sc in 2 sc, 2 sc in next sc) twice, sc in next 6 sc, (2 sc in next sc, sc in 2 sc) twice—22 sc.

Rnd 12: (Sc in 2 sc, 2 sc in next sc) twice, sc in next 10 sc, (2 sc in next sc, sc in 2 sc) twice—26 sc. Work 1 rnd even.

Rnd 14: Work as for rnd 12, but make 14 sc between incs—30 sc. Work 1 rnd even.

Rnd 16: Work as for rnd 12, but make 18 sc between incs—34 sc. Work 1 rnd even.

Rnd 18: Work as for rnd 12, but make 22 sc between incs—38 sc.

Rnd 19: (Work next 2 sc tog, sc in 2 sc) 3 times, work next 2 sc tog, sc in 10 sc, (work next 2 sc tog, sc in 2 sc) 3 times, work last 2 sc tog—30 sc.

Rnd 20: (Work next 2 sc tog) twice, (sc in next sc, work 2 sc tog) twice, sc in 10 sc, (work 2 sc tog, sc in next sc) twice, (work 2 sc tog) twice—22 sc.

Rnd 21: Work next 2 sc tog, sc in 2 sc, work next 2 sc tog, sc in 10 sc, work next 2 sc tog, sc in 2 sc, work last 2 sc tog. Stuff.

Rnd 22: (Work 2 sc tog) twice, sc in 10 sc, (work 2 sc tog) twice. Work 2 sc tog around until opening is closed. Sew to side of body toward bottom, sewing around sections that touch.

FORELEG (make 2): Work as for haunch through rnd 2.

Rnd 3: (2 sc in next sc, sc in 2 sc) 4 times.

Rnds 4-15: Work even—16 sc.

Rnd 16: (Sc in 3 sc, 2 sc in next sc) 4 times—20 sc.

Rnd 17: (2 sc in next sc, sc in 4 sc) 4 times—24 sc.

Rnd 18: Ch 12, sk 12 sc, sc in next 12 sc.

Rnd 19: Sc in each of 12 skipped sc, sc in next 12 sc. (Do not work in ch.)

Rnd 20: Ch 12, sk 12 sc, sc in next 2 sc, work next 2 sc tog, sc in 4 sc, work next 2 sc tog, sc in 2 sc.

Rnd 21: Sl st in 12 skipped sc, sc in 10 sc. Sl st in next st. End off. Stuff. Sew foreleg to lower chest of body along 12 sl sts. Sew top of foreleg to body toward top and side of body.

EARS: With front of head toward you, join yarn in rnd 21 of head about 8 sts to right of center; sc in 5 sc. Ch 1, turn. Sc in 5 sc. Ch 1, turn. Sk first sc, sc in 2 sc, sk 1 sc, sc in next sc. Ch 1, turn. Sk first sc, sc in next sc, sl st in next sc. End off. Sk 5 center front sc on rnd 21. Work 2nd ear the same.

FINISHING: For mane, cut rug yarn and knitting worsted in 4″ lengths. Using 1 strand of each tog, fold in half, knot fringe all over top, back and sides of head and down front of chest. Sew on button eyes separately, then with some strong thread, draw eyes tog slightly to indent face. Embroider nose in satin stitch, mouth with three straight stitches, using black floss. For tail, insert 2 pipe cleaners in lower back. Bend ends up for 1″ to 2″, catching 4 4″ strands each of rug yarn and knitting worsted. Twist tightly to hold strands. Wind tail with rug yarn or cover with sc.

RED SQUIRREL
Shown on page 154

SIZE: 8″ high.

MATERIALS: Knitting worsted weight yarn, 1 4-oz. skein red. Crochet hook size G. Stuffing. Craft glue. Black embroidery floss. Two black shank-type buttons. Scrap of rust felt.

GAUGE: 4 sc = 1″.

BODY: Beg at bottom, ch 2.

Rnd 1: 6 sc in 2nd ch from hook.

Rnd 2: 2 sc in each sc around.

Rnd 3: * Sc in next sc, 2 sc in next sc, repeat from * around—18 sc.

Rnd 4: Repeat rnd 3—27 sc.

Rnd 5: * 2 sc in next sc, sc in each of next 2 sc, repeat from * around—36 sc.

Rnds 6-10: Work even.

Rnd 11: * Sc in each of 3 sc, 2 sc in next sc, repeat from * around—45 sc.

Rnds 12-16: Work even.

Rnd 17: * Sc in each of 3 sc, work next 2 sc tog, repeat from * around—36 sc.

Rnds 18-23: Work even.

Rnd 24: * Sc in each of 7 sc, work next 2 sc tog, repeat from * around—32 sc.

Rnd 25: Work even.

Rnd 26: * Sc in each of 6 sc, work 2 sc tog, repeat from * around—28 sc.

Rnd 27: Work even.

Rnd 28: * Sc in each of 2 sc, work 2 sc tog, repeat from * around—21 sc.

Rnd 29: Work even.

Rnd 30: * Sc in next sc, work 2 sc tog, repeat from * around—14 sc.

Rnds 31 and 32: Work even. End off. Stuff body very firmly. Do not close neck.

HEAD: Ch 2.

Rnd 1: 6 sc in 2nd ch from hook.

Rnd 2: * Sc in next sc, 2 sc in next sc, repeat from * around—9 sc.

Rnd 3: Work even.

Rnd 4: * Sc in each of 2 sc, 2 sc in next sc, repeat from * around—12 sc.

Rnd 5: Repeat rnd 2—18 sc.

Rnds 6 and 7: Work even.

Rnd 8: Repeat rnd 2—27 sc.

Rnds 9-12: Work even.

Rnd 13: * Sc in each of 8 sc, 2 sc in next sc, repeat from * around—30 sc.

Rnds 14-16: Work even.

Rnd 17: Work 2 sc tog around—15 sc.

Rnd 18: Work even.

Rnd 19: Sc in next sc, * work next 2 sc tog, repeat from * around—8 sc. End off. Stuff; sew up hole (back of head). Sew head to neck.

HAUNCH AND FOOT: Ch 2.

Rnd 1: 6 sc in 2nd ch from hook.

Rnd 2: 2 sc in each sc.

Rnd 3: * Sc in next sc, 2 sc in next sc, repeat from * around—18 sc.

Rnd 4: Work even.

Rnd 5: Repeat rnd 3—27 sc.

Rnd 6: Work even. Ch 8 for foot. Sc in 2nd ch from hook and in each ch, sc in 5 sc on edge of haunch. Ch 1, turn. Work 4 rows even on these 12 sc. End off.

For 2nd foot, at end of rnd 6, ch 1, turn. Sc in 5 sc on haunch, ch 8. Sc in 2nd ch from hook and in each ch, sc in 5 sc on haunch. Work 4 rows even on these 12 sc. Roll foot and stuff. Fold back of foot in half and sew up to form heel. Stuff haunch. Sew toy so foot is level with bottom of toy.

ARM (make 2): Beg at top, ch 7. Sl st in first ch to form ring.

Rnd 1: Sc in each ch around.

Rnds 2-4: Sc in each sc.

Form Elbow: Rnd 5: Ch 1, turn, sc in 3 sc, ch 1, turn, sc in 3 sc and continue around on next 4 sc.

Rnd 6: Work even on 7 sc.

Rnd 7: Dec 1 sc in rnd.

Rnd 8: Work even.

Rnds 9 and 10: Repeat rnds 7 and 8. End off. Stuff; sew top of arm flat across. Leave lower arm open. Sew body.

EAR (make 2): Ch 4.

Row 1: 2 sc in 2nd ch from hook, sc in next ch, 2 sc in last ch. Ch 1, turn each row.

Row 2: Work 2 sc tog, sc in 1 sc, work 2 sc tog.

Row 3: Work 2 sc tog, sc in last sc.

Row 4: Work 2 sc tog. Cup a bit; sew to side of head toward back.

TAIL (make 2 pieces): Beg at bottom ch 3.

Row 1: Sc in 2nd ch from hook and in next ch. Ch 1, turn each row—2 sc.

Row 2: Work even.

Row 3: Inc 1 sc in last st.

Row 4: Work even.

Rows 5-14: Repeat rows 3 and 4, 5 times.

Row 15: Repeat row 3—9 sc.

Rows 16-18: Work even.

Row 19: Repeat row 3—10 sc.

Rows 20 and 21: Work even. At end of row 21, ch 4.

Row 22: Sc in 2nd ch from hook and in next 2 ch, sc in 8 sc, work last 2 sc tog.

Row 23: Repeat row 3—13 sc.

Row 24: Sc across, work last 2 sc tog.

Row 25: Repeat row 3.

Row 26: Work even.

Row 27: Repeat row 3.

Rows 28 and 29: Work even.

Row 30: Sc across, work last 2 sc tog.

Row 31: Dec 1 sc each side.

Rows 32 and 33: Repeat row 31. Cut yarn in 3″ lengths. Fold in half, knot or sew pieces separately to both pieces of tail, being sure to fringe opposite sides, having ends pointing up. Sew pieces tog; stuff. Sew to toy.

FINISHING: Cut 2 hands and 2 palms from felt. Glue palms to hands, stuffing with yarn or a strip of felt to make firmer. Push wrists into arm openings; sew in place. Cut ¾″ long felt ovals for eyes, sew on button eyes through felt. Cut felt linings for ears; glue on. Embroider nose and mouth.

KANGAROO PAIR
Shown on page 154

SIZE: Mother, 10″ high.

MATERIALS: Knitting worsted, 1 4-oz. skein gold. Crochet hook size G. Dacron stuffing. Scraps of black and gold felt. Scrap of gold print fabric. Six-strand embroidery floss, black and red. Craft glue. Yarn needle.

GAUGE: 4 sc=1″.

MOTHER: BODY: Beg at bottom, ch 2.

Rnd 1: 6 sc in 2nd ch from hook.

Rnd 2: 2 sc in each sc—12 sc.

Rnd 3: * Sc in next sc, 2 sc in next sc, repeat from * around—18 sc.

Rnd 4: Repeat rnd 3—27 sc.

Rnd 5: * Sc in 2 sc, 2 sc in next sc, repeat from * around—36 sc.

Rnd 6: Repeat rnd 5—48 sc.

Rnds 7-9: Work even.

Rnd 10: * Sc in 5 sc, 2 sc in next sc, repeat from * around—56 sc.

Rnds 11-24: Work even.

Rnd 25: * Sc in 5 sc, work 2 sc tog, repeat from * around—48 sc.

Rnds 26-28: Work even.

Rnd 29: * Sc in 4 sc, work 2 sc tog, repeat from * around—40 sc.

Rnds 30-32: Work even.

Rnd 33: * Sc in 3 sc, work 2 sc tog, repeat from * around—32 sc.

Rnds 34-36: Work even.

Rnd 37: * Sc in 6 sc, work 2 sc tog, repeat from * around—28 sc.

Rnds 38 and 39: Work even.

Rnd 40: * Sc in 2 sc, work 2 sc tog, repeat from * around—21 sc.

Rnds 41 and 42: Work even.

Rnd 43: * Sc in next sc, work 2 sc tog, repeat from * around—14 sc.

Rnds 44 and 45: Work even. End off. Stuff; leave neck open.

TAIL: Ch 2. Work 4 sc in 2nd ch from hook. Work 1 rnd even. Inc 1 sc in next rnd. Repeat last 2 rnds until there are 18 sc. Work 10 rnds even. Inc 2 sc on next rnd—20 sc. Work 10 rnds even. End off. Stuff; sew in place.

HEAD: Beg at nose, ch 2.

Rnd 1: 6 sc in 2nd ch from hook.

Rnd 2: Work even.

Rnd 3: 2 sc in each sc around.

Rnd 4: Work even—12 sc.

Rnd 5: * Sc in next sc, 2 sc in next sc, repeat from * around.

Rnds 6-9: Work even—18 sc.

Rnd 10: Repeat rnd 5—27 sc.

Rnds 11-18: Work even.

Rnd 19: * Sc in next sc, work 2 sc tog, repeat from * around—18 sc.

Rnd 20: Work even.

Rnd 21: Repeat rnd 19—12 sc. Stuff head. Work 1 rnd even; sew up hole; sew to neck.

EAR (make 2): Ch 5. Sc in 2nd ch from hook and in next 3 ch. Ch 1, turn each row. Work 4 more rows of 4 sc. Dec 2 sc on next row. Work 2 sc tog. End off. Line ears with print fabric if desired. Sew on ears.

POUCH: Ch 11. Sc in 2nd ch from hook and in next 9 ch. Work 1 row even. Inc 1 st each side of next row and each row until there are 22 sc. Work 2 rows even. Inc 1 st each side of next row. Work 8 rows even. End off. Line pouch if desired. Sew to front of toy leaving room at top for baby to fit in.

ARM (make 2): Beg at top, ch 7, sl st in first ch to form ring. Work 4 rnds of 7 sc. Dec 2 sc in next rnd—5 sc.

Form Elbow: Sc in 3 sc; ch 1, turn; sc in same 3 sc, ch 1, turn; sc in same 3 sc and continue around other sts. Work 3 rnds even on 5 sc. Inc 3 sc in next rnd. Work 1 rnd even. Work 2 sc tog around. End off. Stuff; sew up; sew to toy.

HAUNCH (make 2): Work as for body through rnd 3.

Rnd 4: Work even.

Rnd 5: Repeat rnd 3—27 sc.

Rnd 6: Work even.

Rnd 7: * Sc in 2 sc, 2 sc in next sc, repeat from * around—36 sc.

Rnds 8 and 9: Work even. At end of rnd 9, ch 1, turn. Sc in each of 10 sc. Ch 1, turn. Sc in each of 10 sc. End off (bottom of haunch). Stuff; sew to body, leaving front open for 1″ above bottom edge.

LEG (make 2): Ch 2. Work 6 sc in 2nd ch from hook. Work 2 sc in each sc

Continued on page 161

ANIMAL PETS
TO KNIT AND CROCHET

Three kittens, all knitted of fluffy mohair
and fingering yarn on double-pointed needles,
show mom the mittens they have found.
Felt features are glued on; mother wears
a gingham apron. Knitted Cat and Kittens,
page 120.

A PARADE OF

PETS FROM FANTASYLAND

Merry menagerie at rest in the noonday sun:
bunny, dog, tiger, leopard, lion, all are single
crochet, have felt and embroidered features.
Each animal is about 6″ long. See Sunny
Pets on page 121. Three little pigs meet the
not-so-bad wolf. All four are in single crochet,
wear removable sweaters. Pigs have curly tails;
wolf has loop-stitch "fur." Pigs are 12″ high;
wolf, 16″. Of knitting worsted. Three Pigs and Wolf,
page 124. Mouse family is ready for a favorite snack!
In rounds of single crochet, mice are
easy to make and dress up in Sunday-best clothes.
Mom, Dad, 8½″; baby, 6″; page 122.

CREATURE CUSHIONS TO CROCHET

Crocheted cushions in wild colors make tame
toys for tots! Stitch in rounds of easy crochet;
stuff with fiberfill. Caterpillar and Armadillo, page 125.

MORE CRITTERS TO CROCHET

for a child's favorite toy.
Princely Frog, page 126;
Dynamic Dragon in red,
page 136; Royal
Alligator, 26″
long, page
136.

DOLLS SIT PRETTY

When it comes to children's gifts, huggable dolls can't be beat. Knitted Snowman, page 137; crocheted Blondie, page 137; Disk Doll, page 138; Humpty Dumpty, page 138.

In this chair: Blondie's twin brother, Butch, crocheted with disk arms and legs, pompon shoes, standing 21″ tall (page 137); a chubby, easy-crochet Marty Mouse (page 139); and long-legged Pinafore Pattie, 25″ tall, with bendable knees and elbows, her yarn hair wound in ringlets (page 139).

Snowman by Marjorie Bowen; Disk Doll by Catherine Rhoades;
Humpty Dumpty by Barbara Shillinger; Marty Mouse by Sue Penrod;
Pinafore Pattie by Jane Slovachek. Photography by Sal Corbo.

TOYS ON WHEELS
School bus and mail truck are quick to crochet
of rug yarn; sides are crocheted to the
strip that forms back, top, windshield and
hood. Directions, pages 140 and 141.

A pair of tall charmers have knitted bodies, worked around on double-pointed needles. Removable outfits are in quick and easy drop-stitch pattern. Dolls, 28″ tall, are made of knitting worsted. Laced-up boots on blonde blue-eyed doll and red slippers on brunette beauty are knitted in. See Delightful Dolls, page 141.

KNIT A DOLL

VISITORS FROM TOYLAND

Lovable lion has courage—and a great big heart! In bulky yarn, he sits 14″ high, has twinkling button eyes; page 142.
Kangaroo mama and her little joey are a friendly pair. Polka-dot fabric lines joey's "home," mama's ears; page 144.
Bright-eyed squirrel, with arms open wide, has a bushy fringed tail as tall as he is (8″); page 143.
Mother bear hostess and her cub entertain guests from a stuffed crocheted chair. Loopy Bears, page 162; Chair, page 161. Crocheted guests—mouse, panda, bear, and cat—have movable arms and legs, plastic button eyes, bright neckties; directions, page 161.

TEN FRIENDLY TOYS

Amusing tippable toys, each made with two Styrofoam balls, are covered with knitting. A fishing sinker inserted in bottom ball keeps toy standing. Top-hatted snowman, red bird, bewhiskered mouse are 5½″ tall. Smiling panda, friendly dog and cat, roly-poly boy, girl, and clown are 7″ tall. Of knitting worsted, with felt features, fashion accessories. Tippable Toys, page 163. Playful Pup knits up fast in garter stitch. His long, floppy ears, felt eyes, and tongue make his 25″ irresistible! Sew a colorful calico coat and a bone for him, too. Directions, page 164.

DOLLS FROM A MAGIC WORLD

Topsy-turvy dolls from story-book land! Cinderella, Dorothy, Goldilocks and Alice, knitted in garter stitch. Turn the crocheted skirts over and Fairy Godmother, Cowardly Lion, Baby Bear and White Rabbit appear! 11" tall; Flipover Dolls, page 165.

Lovable hand and finger puppets for your youngster are of simple crochet stitches. Shaggy dog is in loop stitch; baby joey in mother's pouch is a finger puppet. Directions for Puppet Friends, page 167.

FUN WITH FELT AND YARN

Bits of yarn and felt make tiny pals. For a child's holiday party, favors with personality! Knit caddies cover cardboard rolls. Trim with felt and fill with goodies. They make "sweet" tree ornaments too; page 169.

KANGAROO PAIR
Continued from page 144.

around. Work 11 rnds even on 12 sc. End off. Stuff; insert in opening of haunch and sew in place.

Embroider nose in black satin stitch; mouth is red straight stitch. Cut black felt circles for eyes, gold crescent eyelids. Glue in place.

BABY: BODY: Ch 16. Sl st in first ch to form ring. Work 4 rnds of 16 sc. On 5th rnd (sc in 2 sc, work next 2 sc tog) 4 times. Work 2 rnds even. On 8th rnd (sc in next sc, work 2 sc tog) 4 times. Work 2 rnds even—8 sc. End off (neck edge). Sew bottom edge tog flat. Stuff.

HEAD: Ch 2. Work 4 sc in 2nd ch from hook. Work 1 rnd even. On next rnd, inc in every other st—6 sc. Work 1 rnd even. Repeat last 2 rnds—9 sc. On next rnd inc in every 3rd st—12 sc. Work 1 rnd even. On next rnd (sc in next sc, work 2 sc tog) 4 times—8 sc. Stuff head. (Work 2 sc tog) 4 times. Sew up opening. Sew head to body.

FOOT (make 2): Ch 5. Sc in 2nd ch from hook and in each ch. Ch 1, turn. Sc in each sc. Sew last row to beg ch. Sew one end to front of body toward side and bottom.

ARM (make 2): Ch 4. Work as for foot. Sew to upper body.

TAIL: Ch 6. Sc in 2nd ch from hook and in each ch. Work 3 more rows of 5 sc. Dec 1 sc on next row. Work 2 rows even. Dec 1 sc on next row. Work 1 row even. Dec 1 sc on next row. End off. Sew long sides tog. Do not stuff. Sew to body.

EAR (make 2): Ch 3. Sc in 2nd ch from hook and in next ch. Work 1 row even. Work 2 sc tog. End off. Sew to head. Line ear, if desired. Glue on small black felt circles for eyes. Embroider black nose, red mouth.

BROWN ARMCHAIR
Shown on page 155

SIZE: 9″ wide; 7½″ high.

MATERIALS: Rug yarn, 2 180-yd. skeins. Crochet hook size I. Polyester fiberfill, 1 lb.

GAUGE: 3 sc = 1″; 4 rows = 1″.

CHAIR: Beg at lower front edge, ch 27.

Row 1 (right side): Sc in 2nd ch from hook and in each remaining ch—26 sc. Ch 1, turn each row.

Rows 2-10: Sc in each sc across.

Front of Arm: Row 11: Sc in each of 5 sc. Ch 1, turn.

Rows 12-15: Sc in each of 5 sc.

Row 16: Sl st in each of 5 sc.

Top of Arm: Row 17: Working in back lp of each sl st, sc in 5 sts.

Rows 18-31: Sc in each of 5 sc.

Row 32: Sl st in each of 5 sc. End off. Mark this edge for edge A.

Sk 16 sc on row 10, work rows 11-32 for 2nd arm of chair.

Seat: Row 1: Sl st in each of 16 free sc of row 10 of chair front. Ch 1, turn.

Row 2: Working in front lp of each sc of row 10 (do not work in sl sts), sc in 16 sc. Ch 1, turn each row.

Rows 3-16: Work even in sc.

Row 17: Sl st in each sc.

Row 18: Working in back lp of each sl st, sc across.

Rows 19-22: Work even in sc. End off. Turn work.

Chair Back: Row 1: Working across marked edge A, working in front lps of sc only, sc in each of 5 sc, sc in each of 16 sc on seat extension, sc in front lps only of 5 sc on 2nd arm piece—26 sc.

Rows 2-10: Work even in sc.

Top of Chair: Row 1: Sl st in each sc across.

Row 2: Working in front lps of sc only, sc in each sc across.

Rows 3-6: Sc in each sc.

Row 7: Sl st in each sc across.

Back of Chair: Row 1 (wrong side): Working in front lps of sc only, sc in each sc across.

Rows 2-24: Work even in sc.

Row 25 (wrong side): Sl st in each sc across.

Bottom of Chair: Working in back lp of each sl st, sc in each sl st across. Work 19 more rows of sc, end wrong side. End off. Pin last row to starting ch of chair.

Chair Side: Beg at lower edge, ch 21. Work 15 rows of 20 sc. At end of row 15, do not ch 1; drop lp off hook.

Join Chair Side to Top of Arm: Insert hook in end st at front outer edge of first arm top, draw dropped lp through. Working through both thicknesses, sc the 15 rows of arm top to 15 sc on chair side. Working on remaining 5 sc of chair side, work 10 rows of 5 sc. End off.

Join Chair Side to Chair: Join yarn at back of arm; sc chair side in place, joining to chair back, across top, down back of chair, across bottom, and up front to arm. End off.

2nd Chair Side: Beg at lower edge, ch 21. Work 15 rows of 20 sc. Working on first 5 sc only, work 10 rows of sc. Drop lp from hook. Turn. Insert hook in back edge of chair top, draw lp through; sc chair side in place.

Inner Arm Piece (make 2): Ch 16. Work 4 rows of 5 sc. End off. Sc top and front edges to chair. Turn chair to wrong side. Sew back and seat edges to chair.

Stuff chair. Sc lower front and bottom front edges closed.

CROCHETED GUESTS
Shown on page 155

SIZE: About 6″ high.

MATERIALS: Knitting worsted, about 2 oz. for each animal. Crochet hook size G. Stuffing. Four buttons to match toy for attaching arms and legs. For eyes, buttons, plastic eyes (from hobby shop), felt scraps or embroidery thread. Black embroidery floss. Button and carpet thread. Narrow ribbon.

GAUGE: 5 sc = 1″. **Note:** Toys can be made smaller with sport yarn and size E hook, or larger with bulky yarn and size J hook, or furry with mohair yarn.

BEAR: Head and Body: Beg at top of head, ch 2.

Rnd 1: 6 sc in 2nd ch from hook.

Rnd 2: 2 sc in each sc around.

Rnd 3: (Sc in next sc, 2 sc in next sc) 6 times—18 sc.

Rnd 4: (Sc in each of next 2 sc, 2 sc in next sc) 6 times—24 sc.

Rnds 5-10: Work even for 6 rnds.

Rnd 11: (Sc in each of next 2 sc, work next 2 sc tog) 6 times—18 sc.

Rnd 12: (Sc in next sc, work next 2 sc tog) 6 times—12 sc.

Rnd 13: Work even.

Rnds 14 and 15: Repeat rnds 3 and 4— 24 sc.

Rnds 16-24: Work even for 9 rnds.

Rnd 25: Repeat rnd 11.

Rnd 26: Work even. End off.

Leg (make 2): Ch 7.

Rnd 1: Sc in 2nd ch from hook and in each of next 4 ch, 5 sc in end ch; working on opposite side of ch, sc in each of next 4 ch, 2 sc in last ch.

Rnds 2 and 3: Work even on 16 sc.

Rnd 4: Sc in each of 6 sc, (work next 2 sc tog) twice, sc in each of 6 sc.

Rnds 5-12: Work 8 rnds even—14 sc. End off.

Arm (make 2): Ch 2.

Rnd 1: 6 sc in 2nd ch from hook.

Rnd 2: 2 sc in each sc. Work even on 12 sc for 11 more rnds. End off.

Ear (make 2): Ch 2.

Rnd 1: 8 sc in 2nd ch from hook.

Rnd 2: 2 sc in each sc.

Rnds 3 and 4: Work even—16 sc.

Rnd 5: (Work 2 sc tog) 8 times. End off.

Finishing: Stuff head and body, arms and legs. Sew up bottom of body and tops of arms and legs. Attach legs to body with button and carpet thread: * through body, right leg, button, right leg, body, left leg, button, left leg, repeat from * once. Fasten securely. Attach arms in same way. Sew ears to head. Sew on button or plastic eyes (some plastic eyes are not safe for small children); or make eyes from felt or embroidery floss. Embroider nose and mouth: triangle in satin stitch for nose, 2 straight lines for a mouth. Tie 12″ piece of ribbon around neck into bow.

PANDA: Head and Body: With white, work as for Bear through rnd 4.

Rnd 5: Join black and carry unused color along wrong side of work. Working in sc, work 2 white, 2 black, 3 white, 2 black, 15 white.

Rnd 6: 2 white, 3 black, 2 white, 3 black, 14 white.

Rnd 7: 2 white, 4 black, 1 white, 4 black, 13 white.

Rnd 8: 3 white, 3 black, 2 white, 3 black, 13 white. Cut black. With white, finish as for Bear.

Work arms, legs and ears with black as for Bear. Finish as for Bear.

MOUSE: Head and Body: Work as for Bear through rnd 4.

Rnd 5: Sc in each of 9 sc, 2 sc in next sc, sc in each of 4 sc, 2 sc in next sc, sc in each of 9 sc—26 sc.

Rnd 6: Sc in each of 11 sc, 2 sc in next sc, sc in each of 2 sc, 2 sc in next sc, sc in each of 11 sc—28 sc.

Rnd 7: Sc in each of 13 sc, 2 sc in each of next 2 sc, sc in each of 13 sc—30 sc.

Rnd 8: Work even.

Rnd 9: Sc in each of 11 sc, (work next 2 sc tog) 4 times, sc in each of 11 sc.

Rnd 10: Sc in each of 11 sc, (work next 2 sc tog) twice, sc in each of 11 sc.

Rnds 11-26: Work as for Bear.

Leg (make 2): Ch 9.

Rnd 1: Sc in 2nd ch from hook and in each of next 6 ch, 5 sc in end ch; working on opposite side of ch, sc in each of next 6 ch, 2 sc in last ch—20 sc.

Rnds 2 and 3: Work even.

Rnd 4: Sc in each of 6 sc, (work next 2 sc tog) 4 times, sc in each of 6 sc.

Rnd 5: Sc in each of 6 sc, (work next 2 sc tog) twice, sc in each of 6 sc.

Rnds 6 and 7: Work even—14 sc.

Rnd 8: Sc in each of 5 sc, 2 sc in next sc, sc in 2 sc, 2 sc in next sc, sc in each of 5 sc.

Rnds 9-11: Work even—16 sc.

Rnd 12: (Sc in each of 2 sc, work next 2 sc tog) 4 times. End off.

Arm: Same as for Bear.

Ear: Same as for Bear.

Tail: Ch 2. Work 4 sc in 2nd ch from hook. Work 18 rnds of 4 sc. End off. Sew to lower back. Finish as for Bear. Make straight stitch whiskers with white thread each side of nose.

CAT: Head and Body: Work as for Bear through rnd 4.

Rnd 5: Sc in each of 10 sc, 2 sc in next sc, sc in 2 sc, 2 sc in next sc, sc in each of 10 sc.

Rnd 6: Sc in each of 12 sc, 2 sc in each of next 2 sc, sc in each of 12 sc.

Rnd 7: Work even—28 sc.

Rnd 8: Sc in each of 12 sc, (work next 2 sc tog) twice, sc in each of 12 sc.

Rnd 9: Sc in each of 10 sc, work next 2 sc tog, sc in 2 sc, work next 2 sc tog, sc in each of 10 sc.

Rnds 10-26: Work as for Bear.

Leg: Work as for Mouse.

Arm: Work as for Bear.

Ear (make 2): With main color, ch 7.

Row 1: Sc in 2nd ch from hook and in each remaining ch. Ch 1, turn each row.

Row 2: Sc in each sc.

Row 3: Work first 2 sc tog, sc in 2 sc, work last 2 sc tog.

Row 4: Sc in each sc.

Row 5: (Work 2 sc tog) twice.

Row 6: Sc in 2 sc. End off.

Ear Lining (make 2): With white, ch 5.

Rows 1 and 2: Work as for ear.

Row 3: (Work 2 sc tog) twice.

Row 4: Sc in each sc.

Row 5: Work 2 sc tog.

Row 6: Work 1 sc. End off. Sew inside ear.

Tail: Ch 2. Work 6 sc in 2nd ch from hook, then work 18 rnds on 6 sc. End off. Sew to lower back. Finish as for Bear. Make straight stitch whiskers with white thread each side of nose.

LOOPY BEARS
Shown on page 155

SIZE: Mama bear, 12″ high; baby bear, 7″ high.

MATERIALS: Mohair or loopy mohair, 3 ozs. gold. Small amount of beige. Small amounts of mohair or other novelty yarns for apron and pants. Crochet hook size G. Knitting needles No. 7. Stuffing. Brown six-strand embroidery floss. Two buttons to match pants.

GAUGE: 4 sts = 1″.

BABY BEAR: HEAD: Beg at tip of nose with gold, ch 2.

Rnd 1: 6 sc in 2nd ch from hook. Mark end of rnds.

Rnd 2: (Sc in next sc, 2 sc in next sc) 3 times. Work 1 rnd even—9 sc.

Rnd 4: (2 sc in next sc, sc in 2 sc) 3 times. Work 1 rnd even—12 sc.

Rnd 6: 2 sc in each of next 8 sc, sc in 4 sc—20 sc.

Rnd 7: Sc in 6 sc, 2 sc in each of 4 sc, sc in 10 sc—24 sc. Work 2 rnds even.

Rnd 10: (Sc in 5 sc, 2 sc in next sc) 4 times. Work 1 rnd even—28 sc.

Rnd 12: (Sc in 5 sc, sk 1 st) 4 times. Work 1 rnd even—24 sc.

Rnd 14: (Sc in 4 sc, sk 1 st) 4 times.

Rnd 15: (Sc in 3 sc, sk 1 st) 4 times. Stuff.

Rnd 16: (Sc in 2 sc, sk 1 st) 4 times.

Rnd 17: (Sc in next sc, sk 1 st) 4 times. End off.

Ears: Working on rnd 10 of head, beg 6 sc to right of center top, work sc in 4 sc. Ch 1, turn. Sc in 4 sc. Ch 1, turn. (Sc 2 sts tog) twice. Ch 1, turn. Sl st in 2nd st. End off. Sk 4 sc from first ear, make 2nd ear the same.

BODY: Beg at neck, ch 8. Sl st in first ch to form ring.

Rnd 1: 12 sc in ring.

Rnd 2: (Sc in 2 sc, 2 sc in next sc) 4 times—16 sc.

Rnd 3: Sc in next sc, (2 sc in next sc, sc in 3 sc) 3 times, 2 sc in next sc, sc in 2 sc—20 sc. Work 1 rnd even.

Rnd 5: (Sc in 4 sc, 2 sc in next sc) 4 times. Work 4 rnds even—24 sc.

Rnd 10: Sc in 12 sc, ch 12, sk 12 sc.

Rnd 11: Sc in 12 sc, ch 12, sk the same 12 sc.

Rnd 12: Sc in 12 sc, sc in the 12 skipped sc of rnd 10 (front edge), sc in first 12 sc of rnd (back edge). Stuff. Sc front and back edges tog with 12 sc.

LEGS (make 2): Beg at foot, ch 2.

Rnd 1: 6 sc in 2nd ch from hook.

Rnd 2: 2 sc in each sc—12 sc.

Rnd 3: (Sc in 5 sc, 2 sc in next sc) twice.

Rnds 4-10: Work even—14 sc. End off. Stuff. Crochet legs to body, having seam at back of bear, closing top of legs at same time.

ARMS (make 2): Work as for legs through rnd 2. Work 7 rnds even on 12 sc. Stuff. Fold in half; sew top tog flat; sew to sides of body with seam at back.

PANTS: With novelty yarn and knitting needles, beg at back, cast on 16 sts. K 4 rows. Working in garter st (k each row), k 2 tog at beg and end of every other row until 4 sts remain. K 2 rows. Inc 1 st each side every other row until there are 16 sts. K 2 rows. Bind off. Sew side seams.

Straps: Join yarn to back edge a little to one side of center, * ch 20; sl st in 6th ch from hook and in each remaining ch *, sl st across center back to other side of center, repeat from * to * for 2nd strap. End off. Sew buttons to front.

MAMA BEAR: HEAD: Beg at tip of nose with beige, ch 2.

Rnd 1: 6 sc in 2nd ch from hook.

Rnd 2: 2 sc in each sc around.

Rnd 3: Work even—12 sc.

Rnd 4: (Sc in next sc, 2 sc in next sc) 6 times.

Rnds 5 and 6: Work even—18 sc.

Rnd 7: (Sc in 5 sc, 2 sc in next sc) 3 times—21 sc. Cut yarn.

Rnd 8: With gold, 2 sc in each of next 14 sc, sc in 7 sc—35 sc.

Rnd 9: Sc in 7 sc, (2 sc in next sc, sc in next sc) 7 times, sc in 14 sc.

Rnds 10-13: Work even—42 sc.

Rnd 14: (Sc in 6 sc, 2 sc in next sc) 6 times.

Rnds 15-19: Work even—48 sc.

Rnd 20: (Sc in 6 sc, sk 1 st) 6 times.

Rnd 21: (Sc in 5 sc, sk 1 st) 6 times.

Rnd 22: Work even—36 sc.

Rnd 23: (Sc in 4 sc, sk 1 st) 6 times. Stuff.

Rnd 24: (Sc in 3 sc, sk 1 st) 6 times.

Rnd 25: (Sc in 2 sc, sk 1 st) 6 times.

Rnd 26: (Sc in next st, sk 1 st) 6 times. (Work 2 sc tog) 3 times. End off.

Ears: Working on 18th rnd of head, sc in 6 sc. Ch 1, turn each row. Work 2 more rows of 6 sc. Sk first sc, sc in 3 sc, sk next sc, sc in last sc. Sk first sc, sc in next sc, sk 1 sc, sc in last sc. End off.

BODY: Beg at neck, ch 12. Sl st in first ch to form ring.

Rnd 1: 18 sc in ring.

Rnd 2: Sc in each sc around.

Rnd 3: (Sc in 2 sc, 2 sc in next sc) 6 times.

Rnd 4: Work even—24 sc.

Rnd 5: (Sc in 3 sc, 2 sc in next sc) 6 times.

Rnd 6: Work even—30 sc.

Rnd 7: (Sc in 4 sc, 2 sc in next sc) 6 times.

Rnd 8: Work even—36 sc.

Rnd 9: (Sc in 5 sc, 2 sc in next sc) 6 times.

Rnds 10-15: Work even—42 sc.

Rnd 16: (Sc in 5 sc, sk 1 st) 6 times.

Shape bottom: Sc in 10 sc. Ch 1, turn each row. Work 4 rows on these sts, inc 1 st each end each row—18 sc. End off. Stuff. Sew side edges of flap to rnd 16 along 7 sts each side, leaving 18 sts of front body and 18 sts of flap open. Sew head to body.

LEGS (make 2): Beg at foot, ch 2.

Rnd 1: 6 sc in 2nd ch from hook.

Rnd 2: 2 sc in each sc around.

Rnd 3: (Sc in next sc, 2 sc in next sc) 6 times.

Rnds 4-18: Work even—18 sc. End off. Stuff. Crochet top tog flat. Crochet legs to body with seam in back, closing body opening.

ARMS (make 2): Work as for legs through rnd 2.

Rnd 3: Work even—12 sc.

Rnd 4: (Sc in next sc, 2 sc in next sc) 6 times.

Rnds 5-16: Work even—18 sc. End off. Crochet top of arm tog flat. Sew to sides of body.

APRON: With mohair and knitting needles, cast on 17 sts.

Row 1: K 17.

Row 2: Inc 1 st in first st, k across, inc 1 st in last st.

Row 3: K 19.

Row 4: Repeat row 2.

Row 5: K 21.

Row 6: Repeat row 2.

Row 7: K 5, p 13, k 5.

Row 8: K 23.

Rows 9-24: Repeat last 2 rows.

Row 25: K 5, (p 2 tog) 3 times, p 1, (p 2 tog) 3 times, k 5.

Row 26: K 17.

Row 27: K 2 tog, k 4, p 5, k 4, k 2 tog.

Row 28: K 15.

Strap: Row 29: K 5, turn. Work 34 rows of garter st on these sts. Bind off. Bind off 5 sts along top edge, k last 5 sts. Finish 2nd strap as for first. Sew ends to sides of apron, crossing straps in back.

FACES: Embroider faces with brown floss, using 3 strands. Work square-shaped eyes in satin stitch, then outline top and inner edges of eyes with long straight stitches. Embroider triangular noses in satin stitch. Mouths are straight stitches, one short stitch down from nose, one long stitch slanting down to each side.

TIPPABLE TOYS
Shown on page 156

SIZES: Larger toys, 7″ high. Smaller toys, 5½″ high.

MATERIALS: Knitting worsted: 1 oz. white for snowman; 1 oz. white and ½ oz. black for panda; 1 oz. red for bird; 1½ ozs. brown for dog; 1 oz. gray for mouse; 1½ ozs. orange for cat; ½ oz. each pink, blue and white, small amount of brown for boy; 1 oz. red, ½ oz. each pink and yellow for girl; ½ oz. pink, small amounts of six different colors and yellow for clown. Set of double-pointed needles No. 5. Scraps of felt. Styrofoam balls: 4″ diameter for bodies of larger toys, 3″ diameter for heads of larger toys and bodies of smaller toys. 2½″ diameter for heads of smaller toys. Lead fishing sinkers, bell type, 4 oz. for larger toys, 3 oz. for smaller toys. Adhesive tape. All-purpose glue. Chenille pipe cleaner for snowman. Jingle bell for cat. Heavy duty black thread for mouse and cat. Tapestry needle. For patterns: paper, ruler, pencil, scissors. Compass.

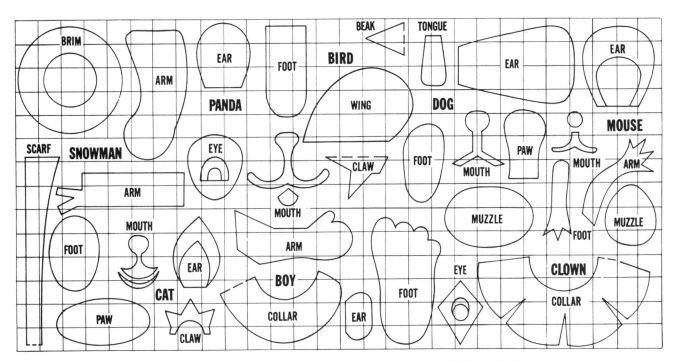

PATTERNS FOR TIPPABLE TOYS—ENLARGE ON PAPER RULED IN ½″ SQUARES

163

GENERAL DIRECTIONS: 4″ BALL COVER: Cast on 9 sts; divide on 3 needles.

Rnd 1: Join; knit around.

Rnd 2: K, inc 1 st in each st—18 sts.

Rnd 3: Knit even.

Rnd 4: K, inc 1 st in each st—36 sts.

Rnd 5: Knit even.

Rnd 6: * K 2, inc 1 st in next st, repeat from * around—48 sts.

Rnd 7: Knit even.

Rnd 8: K 7, inc 1 st in next st, repeat from * around—54 sts.

Rnds 9-30: Knit even for 22 rnds.

Rnd 31: * K 2 tog, k 7, repeat from * around—48 sts.

Rnds 32-34: Knit even. Cut yarn, leaving 14″ end. Thread end in tapestry needle, run end through sts on needles, removing needles.

3″ BALL COVER: Work as for 4″ ball cover until there are 36 sts. K 2 rnds even.

Next Rnd: * K 5, inc 1 st in next st, repeat from * around—42 sts. Work even for 19 rnds. Cut yarn, leaving 12″ end. Run end through sts.

2½″ BALL COVER: Work as for 4″ ball cover until there are 36 sts. Work even for 15 rnds. Cut yarn, leaving 10″ end. Run end through sts.

FINISHING: Press sinker into bottom ball (larger one, for body), hollowing out foam if necessary. Have sinker flush with bottom of ball. Cover with adhesive tape to hold sinker in place. Stretch larger knitted cover over bottom ball, cast-on sts of cover at bottom. Be sure sinker is centered at bottom hole of cover. Sew up bottom hole. Draw up sts at top; fasten yarn. Sew up top hole if necessary. Stretch smaller cover over top ball in same way. Center top ball over bottom ball; sew tog through covers. A toothpick can be used to hold them tog as you sew. Cut out felt pieces using patterns below. Toys will tilt slightly in one direction. Using this slant as a backward tilt, glue felt pieces in place.

TO MAKE PATTERNS: Rule up a sheet of paper into ½″ squares. Enlarge patterns below to actual size by copying them on ruled paper. Cut out patterns.

TO USE PATTERNS: Place patterns on felt. Place any edges with dash lines on fold of felt. Cut out felt pieces. See individual directions for color and numbers of pieces to be cut.

SNOWMAN: Make 3″ and 2½″ covers in white. Cut 2 brown arms, green scarf, black hat brim, using patterns. Cut black felt rectangle 5″ x 2″, for sides of hat. Glue rectangle to black construction paper or Pellon, cut slightly smaller than felt piece. Form

into tube for hat; glue ends tog. Glue brim in place. Trim hat with narrow red band. Cut pipe cleaner in half; insert ends into sides of snowman for arms. Glue brown arms over pipe cleaners. Trim ends of scarf with brown wool fringe. Cut 6 black circles, ¼″ in diameter. Glue on 3 for buttons, one for nose. Cut wedges out of two, glue on for eyes. Glue on red mouth.

PANDA: Make 4″ cover for panda, working 9 rnds black, 11 rnds white, remaining rnds black. Make 3″ cover in white for head. Cut 2 black ears, arms, feet and eyes, using patterns. Glue in place. Inner eyes are white half-ovals, then small black half-ovals. Cut dark pink mouth (2 patterns). Glue in place, small piece first. Cut 1″ yellow felt strip for scarf 11″ long; taper to ½″ at center. Trim ends with red wool fringe.

BIRD: Make 3″ and 2½″ covers in red. Cut 2 yellow claws, yellow beak and 2 white wings, using patterns. Slash straight edge of wings to simulate feathers. Glue on pieces. Cut a few narrow white strips about 1″ long. Glue to top of head and front of body. Cut 1″ red triangle for tail; glue one edge to lower back, top point free. Cut small black circles for eyes; cut out wedges; glue eyes in place. Cut 1″ strip of green felt, 10″ long, for scarf. Slash ends for fringe.

DOG: Make 4″ and 3″ covers in brown. Cut 2 tan ears, front paws and feet, using patterns. Glue in place. Cut beige muzzle, black mouth, red tongue, using patterns. Glue in place. Eyes are beige semicircles with brown pupils. Glue a few narrow tan strips to top of head for bangs. Add brown wool bangs. Cut yellow collar ½″ wide, 7″ long. Glue around neck, one end extending at side. Glue on black "buckle." Cut a brown tail. Trim one end with tan felt strips or yarn. Glue on tail.

MOUSE: Make 3″ and 2½″ covers in gray. Cut gray and pink ears, white arms, feet and muzzle, dark pink mouth, black nose and eyes, using patterns. Glue in place. Cut long thin tapered gray tail; glue on. Stitch loops of gray wool on front of body and top of head. Glue on black thread whiskers stiffened with glue under nose.

CAT: Make 4″ and 3″ covers in orange. Cut 2 yellow feet, paws and outer ears; 4 white claws, 2 pink inner ears, red and black mouth, using patterns. Glue in place. Cut green almond-shaped eyes, black pupils. Make collar and bow of white felt strips ½″ wide. Sew on bell. Make black thread whiskers.

BOY: Make 4″ cover white to rnd 20, blue to top; make 3″ cover pink. Cut white collar, pink ears and arms, using patterns. Cut black shoes using foot pattern for dog. Glue in place. Add red bow, white buttons. Cut blue oval 1″ long; cut in half for eyes. Add black pupils. Cut red V-shaped mouth, semicircular nose. Glue in place. Glue on strands of brown yarn for hair.

GIRL (not shown): Make 4″ red cover, 3″ pink cover. Cut collar, arms, shoes and features as for boy. Add blue bow to collar, tiny red bows to shoes. Glue on strands of yellow wool for hair, first placing strands from front to back, then from side to side. Glue on red bow.

CLOWN: Make 4″ cover of 6 colors, 3″ pink cover. Cut pink feet, arms (same as boy's) and ears, white collar and eyes, using patterns. Center of eyes are blue with black pupils. Make ¾″ circles for buttons, ¼″ red circle for nose, ½″ red circles for cheeks, red crescent for mouth. Glue in place. Draw yellow wool strands through front and sides of head to make tufts of hair.

PLAYFUL PUP
Shown on page 157

SIZE: 15″ long, plus tail.

MATERIALS: Knitting worsted, 1 4-oz. skein red-brown, main color (MC), 1 oz. white, contrasting color (CC). Knitting needles No. 6. Yarn needle. Stitch holder. Fiberloft polyester stuffing. Scraps of felt: red, white, black. For dog coat, ¼ yd. each of two contrasting calico prints.

GAUGE: 4 sts = 1″.

SIDE SECTION (make 2): Beg at top of head, with MC, cast on 10 sts. **Row 1:** Knit. Work in garter st (k every row) throughout.

Row 2: Inc 1 st at beg and end of row —12 sts.

Row 3: Knit.

Row 4: Inc 1 st at beg of row (mark for front of head), k across, cast on 2 sts (back).

Rows 5-12: Repeat rows 3 and 4, 4 times—27 sts.

Rows 13-18: Inc 1 st at back edge every other row 3 times—30 sts.

Row 19: Knit.

Row 20: K across, cast on 32 sts at back edge—62 sts.

Rows 21-28: Dec 1 st at front edge and inc 1 st at back edge every other row 4 times—62 sts.

Rows 29-37: Work even, end at front edge.

Shape Head: K 15; turn. Working on these sts only, dec 1 st at beg of next row (neck edge) and every other row twice more—12 sts. Bind off 1 st at beg of next 6 rows. Bind off remaining 6 sts.

Shape Body: Join yarn at neck edge, k across 47 sts on needle. Inc 1 st at neck edge of next row, then work even on 48 sts for 13 rows, ending at back edge—16 ridges from cast-on sts at top edge.

Back Leg: K 13; turn. Dec 1 st at front edge on next row and every other row twice more—10 sts. K across to front edge (this is for left side of toy; when making 2nd piece for right side of toy, end at back edge). Change to CC. Dec 1 st at front edge every other row twice. Work even on 8 sts until there are 7 ridges for back leg. Bind off.

Front Leg: Join MC at beg of back leg, bind off 6 sts, k across. K 1 row. Bind off 6 sts at beg of next row, k across. K 1 row. Bind off 10 sts at beg of next row, k across—13 sts. K 2 rows, end at front edge. (When making 2nd piece, k 3 rows, end at back edge.) Change to CC. Dec 1 st at back edge on next row and every other row twice more—10 sts. Work even until there are 4 CC ridges. Bind off.

UNDERBODY (make 2): With CC, cast on 8 sts for back leg. K 6 rows (3 ridges). Inc 1 st at beg of next row (front edge) and every other row twice more—11 sts. K to front edge; place sts on holder. With CC, cast on 10 sts for front leg. K 4 rows (2 ridges). Inc 1 st at end of next row (back edge) and every other row once more—12 sts. K 2 rows, end back edge. Cast on 10 sts at back edge. K across—22 sts. Cast on 6 sts at back edge every other row twice—34 sts. When last sts are cast on, drop yarn. Sl sts from holder to free needle, then, with same needle, k 34 sts to front edge. K 9 rows on 45 sts, end back edge.

Next Row: K 11, bind off 22 sts, finish row. Working on front leg sts only, dec 1 st at back edge every other row until 2 sts remain. Bind off. Join yarn at front edge of back leg, k across. Dec 1 st at front edge every other row until 1 st remains. End off.

FACE: Beg at neck edge, with CC, cast on 4 sts. Work even for 14 rows (7 ridges). Inc 1 st each side of next row. Work even on 6 sts for 25 rows (20 ridges from start). Inc 1 st each side of next row. Work even on 8 sts for 7 rows (24 ridges from start). Dec 1 st each side every other row 3 times. K 2 tog. End off.

EARS (make 2): With MC, cast on 12 sts. Work even for 24 ridges. Bind off.

TAIL: With MC, cast on 12 sts. Work even for 16 ridges. Cut MC; join CC. With CC, work 8 ridges. Dec 1 st each side of next row and every 4th row 4 times more. Bind off remaining 2 sts.

FINISHING: Sew an underbody to each side section from neck edge to tail end, using MC except for feet. Sew feet with CC. With CC, sew underbodies tog, leaving a few inches open at center for stuffing. Sew face in place, beg at neck edge. Sew side sections tog. Stuff dog firmly; close opening. Gather cast-on edge of ears; sew to head. Sew tail tog lengthwise, stuffing as you go. Sew on tail. From felt, using patterns, cut white eyes, black pupils and nose, red tongue. Glue or sew in place.

For coat, cut fabric piece 8″ x 6½″. Curve corners. From contrasting fabric, cut 1½″ bias strips. Bind edges with bias strips. For ties, cut 1″ wide strips on straight of fabric, one 10″ long, one 15″ long. Turn in raw edges, fold strips in half lengthwise; stitch closed. Sew to ends of coat. Cut letters for dog's name; glue or sew to coat.

BONE: Make paper pattern for bone, using ¼ pattern given. Cut 2 pieces from fabric, adding ¼″ seam allowance all around. Stitch pieces together right sides facing, leaving opening for turning. Turn to right side. Stuff firmly. Close opening.

FLIP-OVER DOLLS
Shown on page 158

SIZE: About 10″ tall.
Notes: Dolls are knitted in garter st (k each row). When changing colors, al-ways tie in colors at same side of work; leave 12″ end for sewing doll tog.

DOROTHY AND COWARDLY LION

MATERIALS: Knitting worsted weight yarn, 3 ozs. turquoise, 1 oz. each light pink, brown and dark gold. Red embroidery floss. Polyester filling. Knitting needles No. 4. Crochet hook size D. Yarn needle.

GAUGE: 4 sts = 1″.

DOROTHY: Beg at waist, with turquoise, cast on 10 sts. K 16 rows. Cut turquoise, tie in pink. With pink, k 12 rows. Cut pink, tie in brown. With brown, k 24 rows. Cut brown, tie in turquoise. With turquoise, k 16 rows. Cut turquoise, tie in gold.

LION: With gold, k 68 rows. Bind off.
Dorothy's Arms (make 2): With pink, cast on 8 sts. K 4 rows. Cut pink, tie in turquoise. With turquoise, k 14 rows. Bind off.

Lion's Arms (make 2): With gold, cast on 8 sts. K 18 rows. Bind off.

Lion's Ears and Snout (make 3 pieces): With gold, ch 2; 4 sc in 2nd ch from hook, sl st in first sc. Ch 1, turn. Work 2 sc in each sc around. Sl st in first sc. End off.

Skirt: With turquoise, ch 23. **Row 1:** Sc in 2nd ch from hook and in each ch across—22 sc. Ch 3, turn.
Row 2: Dc in first sc, 2 dc in each sc across—44 dc. Ch 3, turn.
Row 3: Dc in first dc, dc in next dc, * 2 dc in next dc, dc in each of next 2 dc, repeat from * across, end dc in top of turning ch. Ch 3, turn.
Row 4: Dc in first dc, dc in next dc, * 2 dc in next dc, dc in each of next 3 dc, repeat from * across, end dc in top of turning ch. Ch 3, turn.

Work 9 more rows of dc, without increasing. End off.

FINISHING: Sew cast-on and bound-off edges tog. Sew up side edges on wrong side, rounding off corners slightly at each end to shape heads. Leave opening at one side of lion's body for turning and stuffing. Turn to right side; stuff firmly; sew up side.

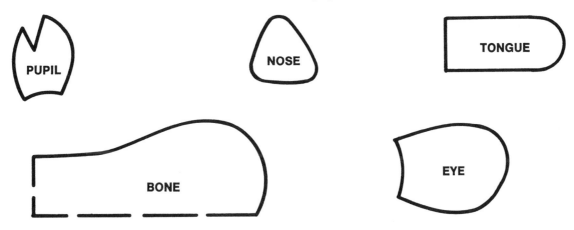

Gather top row of Dorothy's blouse with matching yarn to form neck. Fasten yarn securely. With gold yarn, indent lion's neck in same way.

Fold arms lengthwise, sew up hands and sides; leave top open. Stuff and sew to sides of body ¼" below neck. Pull arms slightly toward front and catch to front of body. Finish lion's arms the same.

Dorothy's Hair: For each braid, cut 12 7" lengths of brown yarn, tie strands firmly tog at center. Fold strands at tie and braid ends for 1¼" below tie. Fasten securely. Sew top of braid to hairline, sew braid to side of face. Tie yarn bows around braids. Embroider bangs in straight sts across forehead.

Dorothy's Face: With red floss, embroider tiny mouth in straight st. With black yarn or floss, embroider eyes: 1 lazy daisy st for each eye.

Lion's Mane: With brown yarn in yarn needle, working around oval of face, pull double strand of yarn through knitted st leaving 1" loop; take a small st through same st to fasten loop. Cut through loops; trim mane.

Lion's Face: Sew ears below mane at top of face. Sew snout to lower center of face. Embroider nose triangle with brown yarn, using satin st. Embroider eyes as for Dorothy.

Place skirt on doll; sew up back seam. Sew skirt to doll at waistline.

GOLDILOCKS AND BEAR

MATERIALS: Knitting worsted weight yarn, 3 ozs. red, 2 ozs. brown, 1 oz. each of yellow and pink. Polyester filling. Knitting needles No. 4. Crochet hook size D. Yarn needle.
GAUGE: 4 sts = 1".
GOLDILOCKS: Beg at waist, with red, cast on 10 sts. K 16 rows. Cut red, tie in pink. With pink, k 12 rows. Cut pink, tie in yellow. With yellow, k 24 rows. Cut yellow, tie in red. With red, k 16 rows. Cut red, tie in brown.
BEAR: With brown, k 68 rows. Bind off.
Goldilocks' Arms (make 2): With pink, cast on 8 sts. K 4 rows. Cut pink, tie in red. With red, k 14 rows. Bind off.
Bear's Arms (make 2): With brown, cast on 8 sts. K 18 rows. Bind off.
Bear's Ears and Snout (make 3 pieces):

With brown, work as for Lion's ears and snout.
Skirt: With red, work as for Dorothy's skirt through row 4. At end of row 4, sl st in top of ch 3 at beg of row to join work. Ch 3; do not turn. Work 9 rnds of dc from right side without increasing, sl st in top of ch 3 to join each rnd. End off.
FINISHING: Sew up and stuff doll as for Dorothy and Lion.
Goldilocks' Hair: Cut 10 3" strands of yellow for each tufts. Tie strands tog at center with matching yarn. Sew a tuft to each side of head at hairline. Tie red yarn bows to hair.
Goldilocks' Face: With red, embroider small mouth in straight st. With blue yarn or floss, embroider eyes in lazy daisy st.
Bear's Face: Sew ears to top of head. Sew snout to lower center of face. Embroider nose triangle with pink, using satin st. Embroider eyes as for Goldilocks.

Place skirt on doll. Sew up back opening. Sew skirt to doll at waistline.

ALICE AND WHITE RABBIT

MATERIALS: Knitting worsted weight yarn, 3 ozs. purple, 2 ozs. white, 1 oz. each pink and yellow. Polyester filling. Knitting needles No. 4. Crochet hook size D. Yarn needle.
GAUGE: 4 sts = 1".
ALICE: Beg at waist, with purple, cast on 10 sts. K 16 rows. Cut purple, tie in pink. With pink, k 12 rows. Cut pink, tie in yellow. With yellow, k 24 rows. Cut yellow, tie in purple. With purple, k 16 rows. Cut purple, tie in white.
RABBIT: With white, k 68 rows. Bind off.
Alice's Arms (make 2): With pink, cast on 8 sts. K 4 rows. Cut pink, tie in purple. With purple, k 14 rows. Bind off.
Rabbit's Arms (make 2): With white, cast on 8 sts. K 18 rows. Bind off.
Rabbit's Ears (make 2): With white, ch 5. **Row 1:** Sc in 2nd ch from hook and in each of next 3 ch. Ch 1, turn.
Rows 2-5: Sc in each sc. Ch 1, turn each row.
Row 6: Sc in first st; pull up a lp in each of next 2 sts, yo and through 3 lps on hook, sc in last sc. Ch 1, turn.
Row 7: Pull up a lp in each of first and

2nd sts, yo and through 3 lps on hook, sc in last sc. Ch 1, turn.
Row 8: Dec as before over last 2 sc. End off.
Skirt: With purple, work as for Dorothy's skirt, making rows 8 and 10 in white.

FINISHING: Sew up and stuff doll as for Dorothy and Lion.
Alice's Hair: Wind yellow yarn around 2" cardboard 8 times. Tie strands tightly tog at one edge; cut through strands at opposite edge. Sew tied ends to side of head at hairline. Trim hair with bows.
Alice's Face: With red, embroider small mouth in straight st. With blue yarn or floss, embroider eyes in lazy daisy st.
Rabbit's Face: Sew ears to head. With pink yarn or floss, embroider triangle for nose. Make eyes as for Alice's eyes.

Place skirt on doll; sew up back seam. Sew skirt to doll at waistline.

CINDERELLA AND FAIRY GODMOTHER

MATERIALS: Knitting worsted weight yarn, 3 ozs. yellow, 1 oz. each brown, pink, dark gold. Red embroidery floss. Polyester filling. Knitting needles No. 4. Crochet hook size D. Yarn needle. 5" sequin braid.
GAUGE: 4 sts = 1".

FAIRY GODMOTHER: Beg at waist, with yellow, cast on 10 sts. K 16 rows. Cut yellow, tie in pink. With pink, k 12 rows. Cut pink, tie in brown. With brown, k 24 rows. Cut brown, tie in yellow. With yellow, k 16 rows. Cut yellow, tie in brown.

CINDERELLA: With brown, k 16 rows. Cut brown, tie in yellow. With yellow, k 24 rows. Cut yellow, tie in pink. With pink, k 12 rows. Cut pink, tie in brown. With brown, k 16 rows. Bind off.
Fairy Godmother's Arms (make 2): With pink, cast on 8 sts. K 4 rows. Cut pink, tie in yellow. With yellow, k 14 rows. Bind off.
Cinderella's Arms: Work as for Fairy Godmother's arms, using brown instead of yellow.
Skirt: With yellow, ch 23. **Row 1:** Sc in

STRAIGHT STITCH

SATIN STITCH

LAZY DAISY STITCH

2nd ch from hook and in each ch across—22 sc. Ch 3, turn.

Row 2: Dc in first sc, 2 dc in each sc across—44 dc. Ch 3, turn.

Row 3: Dc in first dc, dc in next dc, * 2 dc in next dc, dc in each of next 2 dc, repeat from * across, end dc in top of turning ch. Ch 3, turn.

Row 4: Dc in first dc, dc in next dc, * 2 dc in next dc, dc in each of next 3 dc, repeat from * across, end dc in top of turning ch. Sl st in top of ch 3 at beg of row to join work. Ch 3; do not turn. Work 9 rnds of dc without increasing, sl st in top of ch 3 to join each rnd. End off.

Apron: With gold, ch 7. **Row 1:** Sc in 2nd ch from hook and in each remaining ch—6 sc. Ch 3, turn each row.

Row 2: 2 dc in each sc across.

Row 3: * Dc in each of next 2 dc, 2 dc in next dc, repeat from * across.

Row 4: * Dc in each of 3 dc, 2 dc in next dc, repeat from * across. Work 3 more rows of dc without increasing. End off.

Make 2 gold chains about 6″ long. Sew to top ends of apron for ties.

FINISHING: Sew up and stuff doll as for Dorothy and Lion.

Cinderella's Hair: Same as Alice's hair. Tack hair ends tog at sides of face.

Cinderella's Face: Same as Alice's face.

Fairy Godmother's Face: Same as Alice's face.

Fairy Godmother's Hair: With brown, embroider lazy daisy sts all around face. Form crown from sequin braid, sew to head.

Place skirt on doll; sew up back seam. Sew skirt to doll at waistline. Sew apron to front of skirt on Cinderella side. Tie ends at back.

PUPPET FRIENDS
Shown on page 159

BEAR: SIZE: 10″ high.

MATERIALS: Chenille, 3 ozs. brown; or knitting worsted (use double), 1 4-oz skein. Small amount black and off-white knitting worsted. Crochet hook size G. Two buttons.

GAUGE: 3 sc = 1″.

BODY: With chenille or double strand of knitting worsted, ch 34. Join with sl st to form ring.

Rnd 1: Ch 1, sc in each ch around. Sl st in first sc.

Rnd 2: Ch 7 for first leg, sc in 2nd ch from hook and in next 5 ch, sc in next 12 sc for front, ch 7 for 2nd leg, sc in 2nd ch from hook and in next 5 ch, sc in each remaining sc for back.

Rnd 3: Sc in 6 ch of first leg, sc in 6 sc of first leg, sc across to 2nd leg, sc in 6 ch and 6 sc of 2nd leg, sc across back.

Rnds 4-8: Sc around first leg, front, 2nd leg and back.

Rnd 9: Sk 12 sc of first leg, sc in 12 sc for front, sk 12 sc of 2nd leg, sc in 22 sc for back.

Rnd 10: Sc around, dec 7 sc across back (to dec, pull up a lp in 2 sc, yo and through 3 lps)—27 sc.

Rnd 11: Sc around 25 sc.

Rnd 12: Ch 6 for first arm, sc in 2nd ch from hook and in next 4 ch, sc in next 12 sc of front, ch 6 for 2nd arm, sc in 2nd ch from hook and in next 4 ch, sc in 15 sc of back.

Rnd 13: Work as for rnd 3 around first arm, front, 2nd arm, and back.

Rnds 14-18: Sc around first arm, front, 2nd arm and back, dec 3 sc across back on rnd 18. Sl st in first sc of rnd. End off.

Sew arm and shoulder seams leaving 8 sts on front and 8 sts on back open for neck. Sew leg seams.

HEAD: Front: With black yarn, ch 2. **Rnd 1:** 6 sc in 2nd ch from hook, changing to white yarn to complete last sc. Cut black. With white, sl st in first sc.

Rnd 2: With white, 2 sc in each sc around.

Rnds 3 and 4: Sc around. Finish last sc with brown. Cut white.

Rnd 5: 2 sc in each sc around—24 sc.

Rnds 6-8: Work even.

Rnd 9: 2 sc in each sc around—48 sc. Sl st in first sc. End off.

Back: With brown, ch 2.

Rnd 1: 6 sc in 2nd ch from hook.

Rnd 2: 2 sc in each sc around—12 sc.

Rnd 3: Repeat rnd 2—24 sc.

Rnd 4: * Sc in next sc, 2 sc in next sc, repeat from * around—36 sc.

Rnd 5: * 2 sc in next sc, sc in each of 2 sc, repeat from * around—48 sc. Sl st in first sc. End off.

With right sides tog, crochet or sew front and back of head tog, leaving 8 sts open on each piece for neck opening. Sew head to body around neck sts.

EARS (make 2): Work as for back of head through rnd 2.

Rnd 3: Work as for rnd 4—18 sc. Sl st in next sc. End off. Sew ears to head. Sew on button eyes.

MOUSE: SIZE: 9″ high.

MATERIALS: Knitting worsted weight yarn in beige heather, 3 ozs. Dark yarn for whiskers. Crochet hook size G. Two buttons for eyes, one for nose.

GAUGE: 7 sc = 2″.

BODY: Ch 34; join with sl st to form ring.

Rnd 1: Ch 1, sc in each ch around.

Rnds 2-10: Sc in each sc around.

Rnd 11: Dec 1 sc at beg of rnd (to dec 1 sc, pull up a lp in each of 2 sc, yo and through 3 lps), sc in 15 sc, dec 1 sc, sc in last 15 sc.

Rnd 12: Work even—32 sc.

Rnd 13: Dec 1 sc at beg and center of rnd—30 sc.

Rnd 14: Repeat rnd 13—28 sc.

Rnds 15 and 16: Work even.

ARMS: Rnd 1: Ch 7 for first arm; sc in 2nd ch from hook and in each ch, sc in next 14 sc (front), ch 7 for 2nd arm; sc in 2nd ch from hook and in each ch, sc in next 14 sc (back).

Rnd 2: 6 sc in opposite side of ch for first arm, sc in tip of ch, sc in 6 sc of arm, sc across front, 6 sc in opposite side of ch for 2nd arm, sc in tip of ch, sc in 6 sc of arm, sc across back.

Rnds 3-6: Work even in sc. Sl st in first sc. End off.

Sew arm and shoulder seams leaving 7 sts on front and 7 sts on back open for neck.

HEAD: Front: Ch 2.

Rnd 1: 6 sc in 2nd ch from hook.

Rnd 2: Sc around, inc 2 sc in rnd—8 sc.

Rnd 3: Repeat rnd 2—10 sc.

Rnd 4: Inc 5 sc in rnd—15 sc.

Rnd 5: Repeat rnd 4—20 sc.

Rnd 6: Inc 10 sc in rnd—30 sc.

Rnds 7 and 8: Work even in sc—30 sc.

Rnd 9: Inc 10 sc in rnd—40 sc.

Rnd 10: Sc in each of 33 sc, sl st in next sc. End off. Mark next 7 sts for neck edge.

Back: Ch 2.

Rnd 1: 6 sc in 2nd ch from hook.

Rnd 2: 2 sc in each sc around—12 sc.

Rnd 3: Inc 10 sc in rnd—22 sc.

Rnd 4: Inc 6 sc in rnd—28 sc.

Rnd 5: Work even in sc.

Rnd 6: Inc 12 sc in rnd—40 sc. Sl st in first sc. End off.

With right sides tog, sew front and back of head tog leaving 7 sts open on each piece for neck opening. From right side, sew head to neck opening.

EARS (make 2): Work as for back of head through rnd 3. End off. Sew ears in place. Sew on button eyes and nose. Fringe each side of nose with dark yarn cut 4″ long, folded in half and knotted in place.

KANGAROO WITH JOEY: SIZE: 12″ high, plus tail.

MATERIALS: Knitting worsted weight yarn in gray heather, 6 ozs. Crochet hook size G. Two large, two small buttons for eyes.

GAUGE: 7 hdc = 2″; 5 rnds = 2″.

BODY: Ch 36; sl st in first ch to form ring.

Rnd 1: Ch 1, hdc in each ch around. Sl st in first hdc.

Rnds 2-9: Ch 1, hdc in each hdc around. Join each rnd.

Rnd 10: Ch 1, sk first hdc, hdc in each of 17 hdc, sk next hdc, hdc in each of 17 hdc—34 hdc. Join.

Rnds 11 and 12: Work as for rnd 10, dec 1 st each side each rnd—30 hdc.

Rnd 13: Work even.

ARMS: Rnd 14: Ch 9 for first arm; hdc in 2nd ch from hook and in each remaining ch, hdc in 15 hdc for front of body; ch 9 for 2nd arm; hdc in 2nd ch from hook and in each remaining ch, hdc in 15 hdc for back of body.

Rnd 15: Hdc in 8 ch on opposite side of first arm, hdc in 8 hdc of arm, hdc across front, hdc in 8 ch on opposite side of 2nd arm, hdc in 8 hdc of arm, hdc across back.

Rnds 16-18: Work even in hdc.

From tip of arm, sc front and back of first arm tog for 11 sc; sc across front of neck for 9 sts; sc front and back of 2nd arm tog.

POUCH: Holding body upside down, join yarn in front of body 1 st in from left side edge. Ch 1, hdc in each of 16 ch. Ch 1, turn. Work back and forth on 16 hdc for 10 rows. End off. Sew sides of pouch to body, slanting sides in a little towards top to form pouch.

TAIL: Ch 24; sl st in first ch to form ring.

Rnd 1: Ch 1, hdc in each ch around.

Rnds 2-4: Hdc in each hdc around.

Rnd 5: Dec 1 st each side—22 hdc.

Rnd 6: Work even.

Rnd 7: Repeat rnd 5—20 hdc.

Rnds 8-10: Work even.

Rnds 11-14: Repeat rnd 5—12 hdc.

Rnds 15-17: Work even. End off. Sew bottom opening tog. Flatten tail; sew both edges at beg of tail to center back edge of body. Tack upper surface of tail to back of body 1″ above seam.

HEAD: Front: Ch 2.

Rnd 1: 6 hdc in 2nd ch from hook.

Rnd 2: 2 hdc in each hdc around—12 hdc.

Rnd 3: Inc 1 hdc in every other st.

Rnd 4: Work even.

Rnd 5: (2 hdc in next st, hdc in next st) 3 times, 2 hdc in each of next 6 sts, (hdc in next st, 2 hdc in next st) 3 times—30 hdc (center section of rnd forms forehead).

Rnd 6: Work even. Sl st in first st. End off.

Back: Ch 2.

Rnd 1: 6 hdc in 2nd ch from hook.

Rnd 2: 2 hdc in each st around—12 hdc.

Rnds 3 and 4: Repeat rnd 2—48 hdc. Sew front and back of head tog from wrong side, leaving 8 sts free on front and 8 sts free on back for neck, gathering in extra back sts to fit. Sew head to neck opening.

EARS (make 2): Ch 9; hdc in 2nd ch from hook and in each of 6 ch, 3 hdc in last ch; working back on opposite side of ch, hdc in each of 6 ch, 2 hdc in next ch. Work 1 more rnd of hdc, working 2 hdc in 1 st at each end. End off. Sew in place. Sew on button eyes.

JOEY: Ch 14. Sl st in first ch to form ring.

Rnd 1: Ch 1, hdc in each ch around.

Rnds 2-6: Hdc in each hdc around.

Rnd 7: Ch 6 for first arm; hdc in 3rd ch from hook and in next 3 ch, sk 1 hdc, hdc in next 6 hdc for front, ch 6 for 2nd arm; hdc in 3rd ch from hook and in next 3 ch, sk 1 hdc, hdc in last 6 hdc for back.

Rnd 8: Work around arms and body as for kangaroo. Beg at tip of first arm, sc front and back of first arm tog; sl st across 4 sts at front neck edge, leaving 4 sts free at back neck edge; sc front and back of 2nd arm tog.

HEAD: Front: Ch 2.

Rnd 1: 6 hdc in 2nd ch from hook.

Rnd 2: Hdc around, inc 2 sts—8 hdc.

Rnd 3: Hdc around, inc 4 sts—12 hdc.

Rnd 4: Hdc around, inc 3 sts—15 hdc. End off.

Back: Ch 2.

Rnd 1: 6 hdc in 2nd ch from hook.

Rnd 2: 2 hdc in each st around—12 hdc. End off. Sew back and front tog, leaving 4 sts open on front and 4 sts open on back for neck. Sew head to neck opening.

EARS (make 2): Ch 5. Hdc in 2nd ch from hook and in next 2 ch, 3 hdc in last ch; working back on opposite side of ch, hdc in each of next 2 ch, 2 hdc in next ch. Join; end off. Sew ears to head.

TAIL: Ch 12. Sl st in first ch to form ring.

Rnd 1: Ch 1, hdc in each ch around.

Rnd 2: Hdc in each st around.

Rnds 3-8: Hdc around, dec gradually to a point. End off. Flatten tail; sew to back of body. Sew button eyes to head. Tuck Joey into pouch.

SHAGGY PUP: SIZE: 10″ high.

MATERIALS: Knitting worsted weight yarn, 1 4-oz. skein each of charcoal and white. Crochet hook size G. Two buttons for eyes.

GAUGE: 3 sts = 1″.

BODY: With double strand of charcoal (use yarn double throughout), ch 32. Sl st in first ch to form ring.

Rnd 1: Ch 1, sc in each ch around. Join each rnd with sl st.

Rnd 2: Ch 1, loop st in each sc around. Join. To make loop st, insert hook in st, wind yarn from front to back over right index finger, catch strand under finger with hook and draw through st, drop loop from finger, yo and through 2 lps on hook.

Rnds 3-12: Ch 1, loop st in each st around. Join each rnd.

Rnd 13: Ch 8 for first arm; sc in 3rd ch from hook and in each of 5 ch, loop st across next 14 sts (front of body), ch 8 for 2nd arm; sc in 3rd ch from hook and in each of 5 ch, loop st in each st to end of rnd.

Rnd 14: Loop st in each of 6 ch of arm, loop st in tip of ch, loop st in each of 6 sc of arm, loop st across front, work

2nd arm as for first arm, loop st across back.

Rnds 15-18: Loop st in each loop st around. End off. Sew top of arms tog, leaving center 6 sts free on front and center 10 sts free on back for neck opening.

HEAD: Front: With double strand of white, ch 2.

Rnd 1: 6 sc in 2nd ch from hook.

Rnd 2: 2 sc in each sc around.

Rnd 3: Repeat rnd 2—24 sc.

Rnd 4: Sc in each sc around.

Rnds 5-11: Work even in loop st. End off.

Back: With double strand of white, ch 2.

Rnd 1: 6 sc in 2nd ch from hook.

Rnd 2: 2 loop sts in each sc around.

Rnd 3: Repeat rnd 2—24 loop sts.

Rnd 4: Work even in loop st. End off. Sew front and back of head tog, leaving 8 sts on front and 8 sts on back free for neck opening. Sew head in place.

EARS (make 2): With double strand of white, ch 9.

Row 1: Sc in 2nd ch from hook and in each of next 7 ch. Ch 1, turn each row.

Row 2: Work in loop st, inc 2 sts in row—10 loop sts.

Row 3: Work even in loop st.

Row 4: Repeat row 2—12 loop sts.

Row 5: Work even in loop st.

Row 6: Working in loop st, dec 2 sts in row—10 loop sts.

Row 7: Work even in loop st.

Row 8: Repeat row 6—8 loop sts.

Row 9: Work even in loop st.

Row 10: Repeat row 6—6 loop sts.

Row 11: Work even in loop st. End off. Sew ear in place, taking a tuck at top of ear. Sew button eyes in place. Embroider nose with charcoal yarn.

RACCOON: SIZE: 9″ high.

MATERIALS: Knitting worsted weight yarn, 3 ozs. light gray or brown heather, 1 oz. charcoal. Crochet hook size G. Two silver buttons for eyes; one black button for nose. Small piece of black felt.

GAUGE: 7 hdc = 2″.

BODY: With gray, ch 30. Sl st in first ch to form ring.

Rnd 1: Ch 1, hdc in each ch around.

Rnds 2-10: Hdc in each hdc around.

Rnd 11: Ch 8 for first arm; hdc in 3rd ch from hook and in each remaining ch, hdc in 14 hdc for front, ch 8 for 2nd arm; hdc in 3rd ch from hook and in each remaining ch, hdc in 16 hdc for back.

Rnd 12: Work 6 hdc in opposite side of arm ch, hdc in tip of ch, hdc in each hdc across arm and front, work 6 hdc in opposite side of 2nd arm ch, hdc in tip of ch, hdc in each hdc across arm and back.

Rnds 13-16: Work even in hdc. End off. Beg at tip of arm, sc front and back edges tog; leave center 8 sts of front and center 10 sts of back open for neck. Sl st across 8 center front sts, sc front and back edges of 2nd arm tog.

HEAD: Front: With gray, ch 2.

Rnd 1: 6 hdc in 2nd ch from hook.

Rnd 2: 2 hdc in each hdc around.

Rnd 3: Work even in hdc.

Rnd 4: Hdc around, inc 1 hdc in every other st—18 hdc.

Rnd 5: Repeat rnd 4—27 hdc.

Rnd 6: Hdc around, inc 1 hdc in every 3rd st—36 hdc.

Rnd 7: Hdc around, inc 4 hdc in rnd.

Rnd 8: Work even on 32 hdc, sl st in next st. End off. Last unworked 8 sts of rnd are for neck.

Back: With gray, ch 2.

Rnd 1: 6 hdc in 2nd ch from hook.

Rnds 2 and 3: 2 hdc in each st around —24 hdc.

Rnd 4: Hdc around, inc 1 hdc in every 3rd st—32 hdc.

Rnd 5: Hdc around, inc in every 4th st —40 hdc. End off. Sew head pieces tog, leaving neck opening. Sew head to body around neck opening.

EARS (make 2): With gray, ch 2.

Rnds 1 and 2: Work as for back of head.

Rnd 3: Hdc around, inc in every other st—18 hdc. End off. Join charcoal in same st with last hdc, 2 hdc in same st, hdc in each of next 11 hdc, 2 hdc in next st. End off. Sew ears in place.

TAIL: With gray, ch 22. Sl st in first ch to form ring.

Rnd 1: Ch 1, hdc in each ch around.

Rnd 2: Hdc in each hdc around. Change to charcoal.

Rnds 3-5: With charcoal, work even. Change to gray.

Rnds 6 and 7: With gray, work even. Change to charcoal.

Rnds 8 and 9: With charcoal, dec 2 hdc evenly each rnd—18 hdc. Change to gray.

Rnd 10: With gray, dec 2 hdc in rnd. Work 1 rnd even. Change to charcoal.

Rnds 12-16: With charcoal, dec 2 hdc each rnd. End off. Flatten tail, sew to back edge of body.

FINISHING: Cut 2 eye-shaped pieces about 1½" long from black felt. Sew to face above nose for mask. Sew silver buttons on mask for eyes. Cut 8 strands of charcoal yarn for whiskers. Sew nose button to tip of face catching in whiskers at center.

CANDY CADDIES
Shown on page 160

SIZE: 8" long.

MATERIALS: Small amounts knitting worsted (colors given in individual directions). Set of dp needles No 5. Chenille sticks, 12" long. Cardboard rolls from toilet tissue, 1 for each caddy. Scraps of felt. All-purpose glue.

GAUGE: 5 sts = 1".

Notes: Stockinette St: K each rnd. Garter St: K 1 rnd, p 1 rnd. Cut and join colors as needed.

SANTA, ELF, CLOWN: GENERAL DIRECTIONS: Body: Beg at top edge, cast on 18 sts and divide evenly on 3 needles. Work 4 rnds garter st, 32 rnds stockinette st (see Notes), 7 rnds garter st.

Rnd 44: K 2 tog around—9 sts. Cut yarn, draw through sts, pull up and fasten securely (bottom).

Legs: Beg at top edge, cast on 9 sts and divide evenly on 3 needles. Work 10 rnds stockinette st, 4 rnds garter st, 13 rnds stockinette st.

Rnd 28: (K 2 tog, k 1) 3 times—6 sts. Cut yarn, draw through sts, pull up and fasten.

Arms: Beg at top edge, cast on 6 sts and divide evenly on 3 needles. Work 11 rnds stockinette st, 4 rnds garter st, 3 rnds stockinette st.

Rnd 19: K 2 tog around—3 sts. Finish as for legs.

FINISHING: Pull body over tissue roll, centering the pulled-up sts at bottom. Cover should come to top of roll (1 or 2 rows may extend beyond top). Sew a piece of yarn to each side of body for hanger. Cut a chenille stick in half and twist into a loop at one end. Insert into leg with loop at front. Stuff very lightly with yarn scraps. Sew top of leg closed; sew to bottom of body. Bend into desired position. Insert a 3" piece of chenille stick into each arm. Complete as for leg.

PATTERNS: Patterns are given actual size. Complete quarter and half patterns indicated by dash lines. Cut from felt; glue in place as shown.

SANTA: Body: Following General Directions, work 4 rnds white, 9 rnds pink, 23 rnds red, 7 rnds white (43 rnds).

Legs: Following General Directions, use red, white, black.

Arms: Following general directions, use red, white, black.

Hat: With red, cast on and divide 18 sts evenly on 3 needles. Join; k 5 rnds.

Rnd 6: Dec 1 st at beg of each needle. Repeat last 6 rnds once—12 sts. K 10 rnds, then repeat rnd 6. Repeat last 11 rnds once—6 sts. K 5 rnds even.

Next Rnd: K 2 tog around. Cut yarn, draw through sts, pull up and fasten.

Sew a small white pompon to top of hat. Sew bottom of hat closed flat. Glue to inside front center of tissue roll.

Features: Cut blue and black eyes, red nose, mouth. Glue on white yarn loops for beard, white yarn strand for mustache.

ELF: Body: Following General Directions, work 4 rnds red, 9 rnds pink, 23 rnds green, 7 rnds red (43 rnds).

Legs: Following General Directions, work 18 rnds green, 4 rnds red (garter st), then k 5 rnds red.

Next Rnd: (K 2 tog, k 1) 3 times. K 1 rnd even. K 2 tog around—3 sts. K 2 rnds even. Finish, following General Directions.

Arms: Following General Directions, use green and red.

Hat: With green, cast on and divide 18 sts evenly on 3 needles. Join; k 5 rnds.

Rnd 6: Dec 1 st at beg of each needle. Repeat last 6 rnds 3 times more—6 sts. K 5 rnds even. K 2 tog around. Finish as for Santa's hat, using a red pompon.

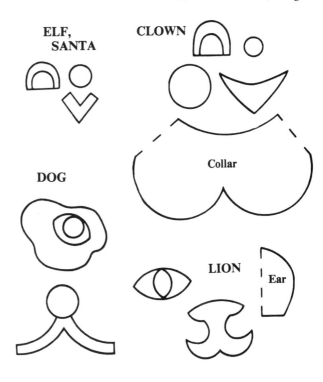

ELF, SANTA

CLOWN

Collar

DOG

LION   Ear

Features: Cut green and black eyes, red nose, mouth. Glue on yellow loops for beard.

CLOWN: Body: Following General Directions, work 4 rnds lime, 11 rnds pink, 21 rnds blue, 7 rnds lime (43 rnds).

Legs: Following General Directions, work 18 rnds blue, 4 rnds lime (garter st), 5 rnds white (27 rnds).

Arms: Following General Directions, use blue, lime, pink.

Hat: Work as for elf, using blue, with a lime pompon.

Features: Cut lime and black eyes, red nose, mouth, blue cheeks, white collar.

LION, DOG: GENERAL DIRECTIONS: Body, Legs, Arms: Work same as for other caddies, working completely in stockinette st (k each rnd).

LION: Following General Directions, make body, arms, legs in gold.

Tail: With 2 needles, cast on 4 sts. Work back and forth in stockinette st (k 1 row, p 1 row) for 4½″ or desired length. Cut yarn leaving 12″ end; draw through sts, pull up and fasten. Sew seam with same yarn. Insert a piece of chenille stick and sew a few loops of yarn to tip of tail. Sew other end in place.

Features: Cut lime and black eyes, black nose, gold ears. Glue loops of gold yarn around face for mane.

DOG: Following General Directions, make body in tan; arms, legs in brown (start one leg with tan).

Ears: With 2 needles and brown, cast on 4 sts. Work back and forth in stockinette st for 4 rows.

Next Row: K, inc 1 st each side. Work 5 rows even, then dec 1 st each side. Work 2 rows even. Bind off. Press lightly. Cut pink felt lining. Glue lining to purl side of ear. Sew in place.

Tail: With 2 needles, cast on 4 sts. Work back and forth in stockinette st for 1½″ or desired length. Bind off leaving an end for sewing. Sew seam. Insert a piece of chenille stick. Sew to body.

Features: Cut white and black eyes, brown spots, black nose, red mouth. Cut red felt belt, ½″ wide, 6″ long with point at one end. Cut ½″ yellow felt square; cut out center for buckle. Glue belt to body, glue buckle over belt, as shown. Glue few strands of brown yarn to inside front, for hair.

CHILDREN'S HANGERS
Shown on page 186

EQUIPMENT: Pliers. Scissors. Knitting needles No. 5.

MATERIALS: For Each: Knitting worsted, ½ oz. for hanger cover, ¼ oz. for hat. Wire hanger. Scraps of felt. Cotton batting. Powder puff. 2¼″ diameter. All-purpose glue.

GENERAL DIRECTIONS: Cover: Cast on 16 sts. K in garter st (k each row) for about 76 rows (38 ridges). Bind off. With pliers, bend each end of hanger under and together 5½″

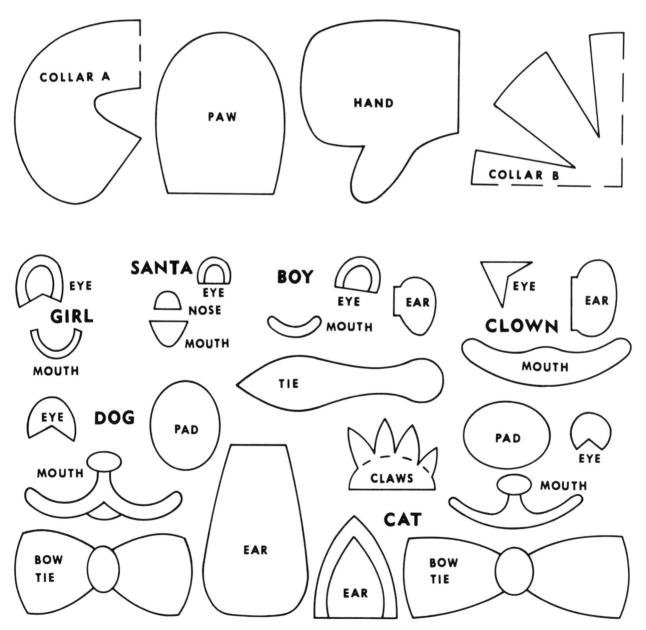

170

from center. Put a piece of cotton batting over top of arms almost to end; wind yarn around cotton and tie to hold in place. Put hanger hook through exact center of cover. Sew bottom edges of cover together. Cut 4 hand or paw pieces; stitch 2 pieces together around curved edges for each hand, leaving open at straight edge. Slip over arm ends; stuff with cotton; sew or glue inside knitted piece.

Head: Open powder puff seam a bit on opposite edges for top and bottom of head. Run hanger hook through holes. Stuff head with cotton. Sew to cover to keep head from turning. Glue top shut. Cut felt features, using patterns; glue in place.

DOG: Knit cover of light blue for boy or pink for girl. From felt, cut light blue paws and ears, dark blue pads, bow tie and eyes, dark blue pads, bow tie and eyes, black nose, coral mouth. Wind a little yarn around fingers, loop over hanger hook, glue to top of head.

CAT: Work as for dog with these exceptions: Cut white felt claws; glue beneath pads. Cut coral inner ears and nose. Add whiskers of blue thread.

GIRL: Knit cover of green. From felt, cut white collar A, rust-brown eyes, black pupils, red oval nose and mouth, pink hands. For hair, cut 21 strands of brown yarn 24″ long. Lay strands side by side across a 3″ piece of masking tape to a width of 2¼″. Stitch across center of strands to make hair part. Glue short pieces of yarn across front of head for bangs. Glue hair to top and back of head. Tie around hair each side where braids will start. Braid hair; tie around each braid with cover color. Glue on collar.

BOY: Knit cover of blue. From felt, cut white collar A, pink hands and ears, blue eyes, black pupils, red nose, mouth and tie. For hair, cut about 30 strands of yarn 5″ long. Lay strands, off center, side by side, across a 3″ piece of masking tape, to a width of 2¼″. Stitch across strands for side part. Glue to head. Trim hair as desired. Glue on collar and tie.

SANTA: Knit cover, hat of red.

Hat: Cast on 24 sts. K 4 rows.

First Dec Row: (K 2 tog, k 4) 4 times —20 sts. K 6 rows even.

2nd Dec Row: (K 2 tog, k 3) 4 times— 16 sts. K 6 rows even.

3rd Dec Row: (K 2 tog, k 2) 4 times— 12 sts. K 8 rows even.

4th Dec Row: (K 2 tog, k 1) 4 times— 8 sts. K 8 rows even.

5th Dec Row: (K 2 tog, k 1) twice, k 2 tog—5 sts. K 6 rows.

6th Dec Row: K 2 tog, k 1, k 2 tog. K 2 rows even. Run yarn through sts, tighten and fasten off. Sew back seam.

From felt, cut black mittens and pupils, blue eyes, red nose and mouth. Cut

white felt strips ⅝″ wide for hatband and cuffs and 2 circles ¾″ diameter for trim on tip of hat. Glue features to head. Cut short lengths of white yarn, glue around head for hair and beard; glue 3 pieces under nose for moustache.

Run hook through front of hat, glue to head. Glue on white trim. Tack point of hat to back.

CLOWN: Knit cover and hat (same as Santa's hat) of white. From felt, cut white hands and ears, light blue collar B, dark blue eyes, red nose and ¼″ circle for mouth. Cut ⅝″ circles in various colors for trimming arms and hat.

Put collar over hook before adding head. Glue on features and trimming. Run hook through side of hat, glue on.

HAPPY HANGERS
Shown on page 187

MATERIALS: Knitting worsted, ½ oz. brown, ¼ oz. black, for Indian; ¾ oz. shaded greens, 1 yard yellow, for elf; a few yards of 6 to 10 colors, for clown. Knitting needles No. 5. Wire hangers. Scraps of felt. Cotton batting. Powder puffs, 2¼″ diameter,

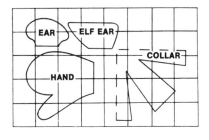

peach for Indian and elf, white for clown. Glue.

GENERAL DIRECTIONS: COVER: Cast on 16 sts. K in garter st (k each row) for about 76 rows (38 ridges). Bind off. With pliers, bend each end of hanger under and together 5½″ from center. Put a piece of cotton batting over top of arms almost to end; wind yarn around cotton and tie to hold in place. Put hanger hook through exact center of cover. Sew bottom edges of cover together. Enlarge patterns below on paper ruled in ½″ squares. Complete quarter-pattern indicated by dash lines. Cut 4 hand pieces from felt (see pattern); stitch 2 pieces together around curved edges for each hand, leaving open at straight edge. Slip over arm ends; stuff; sew or glue inside knitted piece.

Head: Open powder puff seam a bit on opposite edges for top and bottom of head. Run hanger hook through holes. Stuff head with cotton. Sew to cover to keep head from turning. Glue top shut. Cut felt features; glue on.

INDIAN: Knit cover of brown. Using pat, cut peach hands; cut ½″ x ¾″ brown ovals for eyes (cut in half), ¼″ black circles for pupils ¼″ red circle for nose (cut off bottom), ½″ red crescent for mouth, ⅝″ x 2″ yellow, rust, red feathers. Cut ½″ strips of brown felt to trim arms. Fringe strips; glue on. Cut 1″ strip of brown felt, 4″ long, for collar. Fringe strip; glue around neck. For hair, cut 21 strands of black yarn 24″ long. Lay strands side by side across 3″ piece of masking tape to a width of 2¼″. Stitch across center of strands to make hair part. Glue hair to top and back of head. Tie around hair where braids will start. Braid hair; tie around each braid. Glue strips of red felt around bottom of braid. Cut red felt band ¼″ wide; glue around head over feather ends.

ELF: Knit cover and hat of shaded greens.

Hat: Cast on 24 sts. K 4 rows.

First Dec Row: (K 2 tog, k 4) 4 times —20 sts. K 6 rows even.

2nd Dec Row: (K 2 tog, k 3) 4 times— 16 sts. K 6 rows even.

3rd Dec Row: (K 2 tog, k 2) 4 times— 12 sts. K 8 rows even.

4th Dec Row: (K 2 tog, k 1) 4 times— 8 sts. K 8 rows even.

5th Dec Row: (K 2 tog, k 1) twice, k 2 tog—5 sts. K 6 rows even.

6th Dec Row: K 2 tog, k 1, k 2 tog. K 2 rows even. Run yarn through sts, tighten and fasten off. Sew back seam.

Cut red hands, nose and mouth, blue eyes, black pupils as for Indian, pink ears using pat. Trim neck with narrow red felt strip. Trim tip of hat with red felt circles, glued together over tip. Glue a few strands of yellow yarn to front, sides and across back of head, for hair. Run hook through front of hat; glue to head.

CLOWN: Knit cover in stripes of various colors and widths, having an even number of rows in each stripe. Cut white hands, collar, ears using pat. Cut ⅜″ red circle for nose; ½″ wide blue triangles for eyes, ¾″ yellow triangles for "cheeks," 1¾″ wide red triangle for mouth; cut out as shown in picture. Slip collar over hook before putting on head. Make yellow yarn loops for hair; glue on.

PLASTIC EGG TOYS
Shown on page 187

SIZE: About 6″ high.

MATERIALS: Knitting worsted, ½ oz. of main color (MC), ¼ oz. of contrasting color (CC) for each toy. Steel crochet hook No. 0. Scraps of white, black, red, yellow, orange felt. Two plastic eggs, 2¾″ long, for each toy. Cotton batting. A few buttons.

GAUGE: 5 sts = 1″.

GENERAL DIRECTIONS: Body and Head Pieces (make 8): With MC, ch 2.
Row 1: 2 sc in 2nd ch from hook. Ch 1, turn each row.
Row 2: 2 sc in each of 2 sc.
Row 3: Sc in each sc—4 sc.
Row 4: 2 sc in first sc, sc in each of next 2 sc, 2 sc in last sc.
Row 5: Sc in each sc—6 sc.
Row 6: 2 sc in first sc, sc in each of next 4 sc, 2 sc in last sc.
Rows 7 and 8: Sc in each sc—8 sc.
Rows 9-15: Dec 1 st at beg of each row until 1 sc remains. Sew 4 pieces tog for body and 4 for head, with last row of pieces tog for narrow end of egg (neck edge). Add features (see individual directions) before closing last seam. Insert eggs with buttons in them for rattle (or stuff pieces with cotton batting). Close last seam.
Arms (make 2): With MC, ch 10.
Row 1: Sc in 2nd ch from hook and in each ch across—9 sc. Ch 1, turn each row.
Rows 2-6: Sc in each sc. End off. Sew side edges tog for underarm seam.
Legs (make 2): With MC, ch 13. Work as for arms on 12 sc for 8 rows.
Patterns: Enlarge pats on paper ruled in ½″ squares.

SANTA: Make body, head, arms and legs in red. Using the patterns, from white felt, cut whiskers, moustache, outer eyes, nose, and hands; from black felt, cut pupils. From black felt, cut 4 shoe pieces (see pattern); cut a ¼″ strip for belt, long enough to go around body, and rectangular buckle. Sew features in place, sewing around inner edge of whiskers only. Insert eggs in head and body pieces; close seams. Sew points of eggs tog for neck, going around 3 times. Stuff arms and legs; sew to body, legs in sitting position.
Hatband: With white, ch 40. Sc in 2nd ch from hook and in each ch across. End off. Sew around head over top edge of whiskers.
Coat Band: Make as for hatband. Sew around body across top edge of legs.
Coat Trim: With white, ch 25. End off. Sew chain around neck and down front. Ch 10 for each wrist trim. Sew on, inserting hands. Ch 16 for each ankle trim. Sew on. Sew on belt and buckle.
Feet: Sew one shoe piece to bottom of each leg. Whip second shoe piece to first piece, stuffing lightly with cotton.
Pompon: Lay a strand of white yarn along pencil, wind yarn 50 times around pencil. Tie windings tog, cut loops, trim. Sew to top of head.

CLOWN: Make body, head, arms and legs in white. From red felt, cut ¼″ circle for nose and crescent for mouth.

Using pats, cut white felt ears, 2 orange hands, 4 orange shoe pieces; cut ¼″ circles for buttons. Sew features in place on head. With black cotton, embroider crosses for eyes. Insert eggs in head and body pieces, close seams. Sew points of eggs tog for neck, going around 3 times. For hair, cut strip of orange felt 1″ x 7½″. Fold in half. Cut one long edge into ragged ends curving away from fold. At fold, cut away some hair, leaving narrow strip at top for bangs. Sew hair around head. Sew 2 buttons to front of body. Stuff arms and legs; sew to body, legs in sitting position.
Brim: With rainbow yarn, ch 35.
Row 1: Sc in 2nd ch from hook and in each ch across. Ch 1, turn.
Row 2: * Sc in each of 2 sc, 2 sc in next sc, repeat from * across. End off. Sew around head over top of hair, so that brim turns up.
Collar: With rainbow yarn, ch 20.
Row 1: Sc in 2nd ch from hook and in each ch across. Ch 1, turn.
Row 2: Sc in first sc, * ch 2, sc in next sc, repeat from * across. Ch 3, turn.

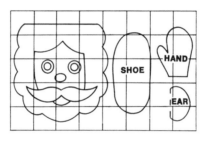

Row 3: Sc in first ch-2 lp, ch 2, sc in same lp, * ch 2, sc in next lp, ch 2, sc in same lp, repeat from * across. End off. Sew collar around neck.
Trim: With rainbow yarn, ch 10 for each wrist trim. Sew on, inserting hands. Ch 16 for each ankle trim. Sew on.
Feet: Sew one shoe piece to bottom of each leg. Whip second shoe piece to first piece, stuffing lightly with cotton.

With rainbow yarn, make pompon as for Santa's pompon. Sew to top of head.

BOY: Make body, head, arms and legs in white. From black felt, cut 2 small circles for eyes. From yellow felt, cut strip 1¼″ x 7½″, for hair. Cut one long edge into fringe; at center, cut short bangs. From red felt, cut hands and 4 shoe pieces (see pattern); cut 2 round buttons. Sew eyes in place. Embroider red mouth. Insert eggs in head and body pieces; close seams. Sew points of eggs together for neck, going around 3 times. Stuff arms and legs; sew to body in sitting position. Sew

hair around head. Sew buttons to front of body.
Brim: With red yarn, ch 35.
Row 1: Sc in 2nd ch from hook and in each ch across. Ch 1, turn.
Row 2: Sc in each sc across. End off. Sew brim around head over top edge of hair.
Scarf: With red yarn, ch 31. Sc in 2nd ch from hook and in each ch across. End off. Sew scarf around neck, crossing ends at left shoulder.

Insert hands in arms; sew opening closed.
Feet: Sew one shoe piece to bottom of each leg. Whip second shoe piece to first piece, stuffing lightly with cotton.

With red yarn, make pompon as for Santa's pompon. Sew to top of head.

KNITTED LION FAMILY
Shown on page 188

SIZES: Father, 15″ tall; mother, 14″ tall; cubs, 11″ tall.
MATERIALS: Knitting worsted, 6 ozs. gold, 4 ozs. green, 1 oz. brown. Set of double-pointed (dp) needles No. 5. Scraps of gold, green, brown, pink, white felt. Stitch holder. Cotton batting. All-purpose glue.
GAUGE: 5 sts = 1″.
ADULT LIONS: Directions are for mother; changes for father in parentheses.
BODY: Note: Top of body is worked in rnds of k for mother, in rnds of p for father. Beg at neck edge, with green, cast on and divide 15 sts on 3 dp needles. Join; k (p) 3 rnds (see Note).
Rnd 4: Inc 1 st in each st around—30 sts. Work 2 rnds even.
Rnd 7: Inc 1 st in every other st around—45 sts. Work 2 rnds even.
For Mother: Rnd 10: (Inc 1 st in next st, k 4) 9 times—54 sts. K 24 rnds even. Change to gold.
For Father: Rnd 10: (Inc 1 st in next st, p 2) 15 times—60 sts. P 26 rnds even. Change to gold and k following rnds.
Rnd 35 (37): * K 4, k 2 tog, repeat from * around—45 (50) sts. K 7 (8) rnds even.
Rnd 43 (46): * K 1, k 2 tog, repeat from * 4 (7) times, place these 10 (16) sts on one needle (back of toy), k to end of rnd—40 (42) sts. K 2 rnds even.
Divide for Legs: Take 5 (8) sts from back of toy needle (mark for heel) and 15 (13) sts from needle next to it. Sl the remaining 20 (21) sts on a holder. Divide the 20 (21) sts on 3 needles. K 14 (15) rnds.
Next Rnd: K 0 (1), * k 2 tog, k 2, repeat from * around—15 (16) sts. K 4 rnds even.
Shape Heel: Working on 7 sts centered at back only, work back and forth in stockinette st (k 1 row, p 1 row) for 8 rows. Leave these sts on one needle

for heel. Join with other sts; k 3 rnds even.

Shape Foot: Inc 1 st at beg of first foot needle and 1 st at end of 2nd foot needle (do not inc on heel needle). K 1 rnd. Repeat last 2 rnds twice—21 (22) sts. K 2 rnds even. Bind off.

Sl 20 (21) sts from holder to 3 dp needles. Work other leg the same.

HEAD: Beg at top of head, with gold, cast on and divide 12 sts on 3 dp needles. Join.

Rnds 1, 3, 5, 7 and 9: Knit around.

Rnd 2: * K 1, inc 1 st in next st, repeat from * around—18 sts.

Rnd 4: Inc 1 st in each st around—36 sts.

Rnd 6: Repeat rnd 2—54 sts.

Rnd 8: * K 24, inc 1 st in each of next 3 sts, repeat from * once—60 sts.

Rnd 10: * K 24, (k 1, inc 1 st in next st) 3 times, repeat from * once—66 sts.

Rnds 11-24: Knit around.

Rnd 25: * K 24, (k 1, k 2 tog) 3 times, repeat from * once—60 sts. K 1 rnd even.

Rnd 27: * K 24, (k 2 tog) 3 times, repeat from * once—54 sts. K 1 rnd even.

Rnd 29: K 2 tog around—27 sts. K 1 rnd.

Rnd 31: * K 1, k 2 tog, repeat from * around—18 sts. K 2 rnds even. Bind off (neck edge).

TAIL: With gold and 2 dp needles, cast on 8 sts. Beg with a p row, work in stockinette st for 21 (25) rows. Dec 1 st on next row. Work 10 rows even. Repeat last 11 rows once. Dec 1 st on next row. Work 5 rows even. Repeat last 6 rows once—4 sts. Break yarn, draw through sts, pull up and fasten.

ARM (make 2): **Note:** Arm is worked in rnds of k for mother, in rnds of p for father. For mother, k first 14 rnds in green, 7 rnds in gold. Beg at top, with green, cast on and divide 15 sts on 3 dp needles. Join; work around for 21 (22) rnds (see Note).

Shape Elbow: Work back and forth in stockinette st on first 7 sts for 4 rows. Join work; k (p) 12 (13) rnds more. (For father, change to gold and k.)

Shape Wrist: * K 2 tog, k 3, repeat from * around—10 sts. K 3 rnds even.

Shape Hand: Rnd 1: (Inc 1 st in next st, k 4) twice—12 sts. K 1 rnd even.

Rnd 3: (Inc 1 st in next st, k 5) twice—14 sts. K 2 rnds even.

Rnd 6: (Inc 1 st in next st, k 6) twice—16 sts. K 3 rnds even.

Rnd 10: (K 2 tog, k 6) twice. K 1 rnd even. Bind off.

EAR (make 2): With gold and 2 dp needles, cast on 8 sts. Work back and forth in stockinette st for 6 rows.

Row 7: Dec 1 st each side. Work 1 row even. Repeat last 2 rows once—4 sts. Break yarn, draw through sts, pull up and fasten.

PATTERNS: Patterns are given actual size. Complete half-patterns indicated by dash lines.

FINISHING: Sew top of head closed; stuff head. Sew spaces in body and legs together; sew foot closed. Stuff firmly; sew head to body. Sew space at elbow and hand closed. Stuff arms, leaving top 1″ unstuffed. Sew arms straight across at top of body. With brown yarn and straight sts, embroider claws on hands and feet, as shown. Steampress ear. Using ear as pattern, cut and line purl side with gold felt. Sew cast-on edge to head. Sew tail seam; stuff and sew tail to body below green section. Wind gold or brown yarn 25 times around 3 fingers. Tie one end and sew this end to tip of tail. Sew bunches of brown yarn around face for father's name. Cut features from felt using patterns: cut green pupils, white eyes, gold eyelids and snout, brown nose, pink mouth. Glue on as shown, having strands of gold yarn under nose. Sew a few strands of gold yarn at top of mother's head. Tie a strand of green yarn around mother's neck.

Clothing Details: Mother's Skirt: With green and 2 dp needles, cast on 100 sts. Work in stockinette st for 8 rows.

Row 9: (K 3, k 2 tog) across—80 sts. Break yarn, leaving long end. Draw through sts and gather to fit at last green row on body. Sew to body with opening at back; sew back seam.

Father's Cuffs: For Sleeves (make 2): With green and 2 dp needles, cast on 18 sts. Work in ribbing of k 1, p 1 for 6 rows. Bind off in ribbing. Sew to bottom of green section on arm.

For Lower Edge: With green, cast on 62 sts and work as for sleeve cuff for 8 rows. Bind off. Sew to bottom of green section on body with opening at back; sew back seam.

Turtleneck: Cast on 38 sts and work as for sleeve cuff. Sew around neck.

CUBS: BODY: Beg at neck edge, with gold, cast on and divide 12 sts on 3 dp needles. Join; k 2 rnds.

Rnd 3: Inc 1 st in each st around—24 sts. K 2 rnds even.

Rnd 6: * K 2, inc 1 st in next st, repeat from * around—32 sts. K 1 rnd.

Rnd 8: * K 3, inc 1 st in next st, repeat from * around—40 sts.

Rnds 9-26: Knit around. For boy cub only, change to green at end of rnd 26.

Rnd 27: * K 8, k 2 tog, repeat from * around—36 sts.

Rnds 28-35: Knit around.

Rnd 36: * K 2 tog, k 2, repeat from * 3 times; put these 12 sts on one needle (back of toy), k to end of rnd—32 sts. K 2 rnds even.

Divide for Legs: Take 6 sts from back of toy needle and 10 sts from needle next to it. Sl remaining 16 sts on a

holder. Divide 16 sts on 3 dp needles. K 13 rnds even, changing to gold after 4th rnd for boy cub.

Next Rnd: * K 2 tog, k 2, repeat from * around—12 sts. K 3 rnds even.

Shape Heel: Working on 5 sts centered at back only, work back and forth in stockinette st for 6 rows. Leave these sts on one needle for heel. Join with other sts; k around for 3 rnds.

Shape Foot: Inc 1 st at beg of first foot needle and at end of 2nd foot needle (do not inc on heel needle). K 1 rnd even. Repeat last 2 rnds twice more—18 sts. K 1 more rnd. Bind off.

Sl 16 sts from holder to dp needles. Work other leg the same.

HEAD: Beg at top of head, with gold, cast on and divide 12 sts on 3 dp needles. Join; k 2 rnds even.

Rnd 3: * K 1, inc 1 st in next st, repeat from * around—18 sts.

Rnds 4, 6 and 8: Knit around.

Rnd 5: Inc 1 st in each st around—36 sts.

Rnd 7: * K 3, inc 1 st in next st, repeat from * around—45 sts.

Rnd 9: K 20, inc 1 st in each of next 3 sts, k 19, inc 1 st in each of last 3 sts—51 sts.

Rnds 10-21: Knit around.

Rnd 22: K 20, k 2 tog 3 times, k 19, k 2 tog 3 times—45 sts. K 1 rnd even.

Rnd 24: * K 2 tog, k 3, repeat from * around—36 sts. K 1 rnd even.

Rnd 26: K 2 tog around—18 sts. K 2 rnds even. Bind off.

ARM (make 2): Beg at top, with gold, cast on and divide 12 sts on 3 dp needles. Join; k around for 16 sts.

Shape Elbow: Work back and forth on first 5 sts for 4 rows. Join; k 10 rnds.

Shape Wrist: * K 2 tog, k 2, repeat from * around—9 sts. K 2 rnds.

Shape Hand: Inc 1 st in first st, k 3, inc 1 st in next st, k 4—11 sts. K 1 rnd even. Continue to inc 2 sts every other rnd, having 1 st more between incs, until there are 15 sts all around. K 2 rnds.

Next Rnd: K 2 tog, k 5, k 2 tog, k 6—13 sts. K 1 rnd even. Bind off.

TAIL: With 2 needles and gold, cast on 7 sts. Work in stockinette st for 17 rows. Dec 1 st on next row. Work 8 more rows in stockinette st. Dec 1 st on next row. Work 12 more rows. Dec 1 st on next row—4 sts. Work 10 more rows. Break yarn, draw through remaining sts, pull up and fasten.

EAR (make 2): With gold and 2 needles, cast on 7 sts. Work in stockinette st for 5 rows. Dec 1 st each side of next row. Work 1 row even. Dec 1 st each side of next row—3 sts. Break yarn; draw through remaining sts, pull up and fasten.

FINISHING: Sew, stuff and finish as for mother lion.

Clothing Details: Girl's Skirt: With

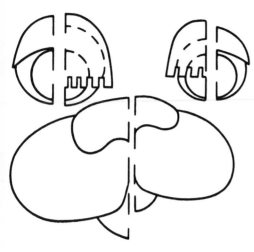

green and 2 needles, cast on 80 sts. Work in stockinette st for 12 rows.

Next Row: (K 2, k 2 tog) across—60 sts. Break yarn, draw through sts, gather to fit body about 3¼″ down from neck. Sew on, having tail between back edges. Tack top and bottom of back seam.

Straps (make 2): With green and 2 needles, cast on 40 sts. K 2 rows (garter st). Bind off in k. Sew to front of skirt; cross in back, sew to back of skirt.

Boy's Pants Cuff (make 2): With green and 2 needles, cast on 18 sts. K 4 rows (garter st). Bind off in k. Sew on at last green row on legs.

Waistband: Work as for cuffs on 44 sts. Sew on.

Straps: Work as for girl's straps. Sew on in same way.

DRESSED-UP ANIMALS
Shown on page 189

MATERIALS: Knitting worsted, about 1½ ozs. main color (MC) for each ani-
mal: tan for bear, gray for mouse, turquoise for rabbit and black for panda; small amounts of contrasting color (CC); beige for bear, white for rabbit and panda. Crochet hook size G. Pieces of felt for clothes and features: purple, yellow, green, black, pink, orange, white, red, dark blue, light blue, gray. Cotton batting. All-purpose glue. Tapestry needle.

GAUGE: 9 sc = 2″.

BODY: Beg at neck, with MC, ch 2.

Rnd 1: 6 sc in 2nd ch from hook. Do not join rnds. Mark end of rnds.

Rnd 2: 2 sc in each sc around.

Rnd 3: * Sc in next sc, 2 sc in next sc, repeat from * around—18 sc.

Rnd 4: * Sc in each of 2 sc, 2 sc in next sc, repeat from * around—24 sc.

Rnds 5-14: Work even for 10 rnds; **for panda only,** change to CC on rnd 9.

Rnd 15: * Sc in each of 5 sc, 2 sc in next sc, repeat from * around—28 sc.

Rnds 16-19: Work even for 4 rnds; **for panda only,** change to MC on rnd 18.

Rnd 20: * Sc in each of 6 sc, 2 sc in next sc, repeat from * around—32 sc.

Rnds 21-24: Work even. End off.

BASE: With MC, ch 7. **Rnd 1:** Sc in 2nd ch from hook and in each of next 4 ch, 3 sc in last ch. Working on other side of ch, sc in each of 5 ch, 3 sc in last ch—16 sc.

Rnd 2: Sc in each sc around.

Rnds 3 and 4: Work in sc, inc 3 sc at each end each rnd. End off.

LEG (for bear, rabbit, panda): With MC, beg at front of foot, ch 2. **Rnd 1:** 5 sc in 2nd ch from hook.

Rnd 2: Sc in each sc around.

Rnd 3: Inc 3 sc in rnd—8 sc.

Rnds 4-7: Work even. **For rabbit only,** work 1 more rnd.

Next Rnd: Ch 9; sc in 2nd ch from hook and in next 7 ch, sc around foot, sc in each ch on opposite side of ch—24 sc. Work 3 more rnds, inc 1 sc at top of each rnd. End off. Stuff foot; sew up back seam of leg; stuff leg.

LEG (for mouse): Ch 13.

Row 1: Sc in 2nd ch from hook and in each ch across. Ch 1, turn each row.

Rows 2-5: Sc in each sc. End off. Sew long edges tog over stuffing.

Stuff body. Sew on base, sewing tops of legs in at front.

ARM (for bear, rabbit, panda): With MC, beg at front of paw, ch 5.

Row 1: Sc in 2nd ch from hook and in each of last 3 ch. Ch 1, turn.

Row 2: Sc in each sc. Ch 1, turn.

Row 3: Sc in each sc. Ch 7.

Row 4: Sc in 2nd ch from hook and in each of next 5 ch, sc in each of next 4 sc. Ch 1, turn.

Rows 5-8: Work 4 rows even—10 sc. Ch 1, turn each row.

Row 9: Sc in each of 4 sc. Ch 1, turn.

Rows 10 and 11: Work even on 4 sc. End off. Fold piece in half, stuff and sew up. Sew to body.

ARM (for mouse): Ch 9. Work as for mouse legs for 4 rows. Sew long edges tog over stuffing. Sew to body.

HEAD (for rabbit, mouse): With MC, ch 2.

Rnd 1: 5 sc in 2nd ch from hook.

Rnd 2: 2 sc in each sc around.

Rnd 3: * Sc in next sc, 2 sc in next sc, repeat from * around—15 sc.

Rnd 4: Sc in each sc around.

Rnd 5: * Sc in each of next 2 sc, 2 sc in next sc, repeat from * around—20 sc.

Rnd 6: Sc in each sc around.

Rnd 7: * Sc in each of 3 sc, 2 sc in next

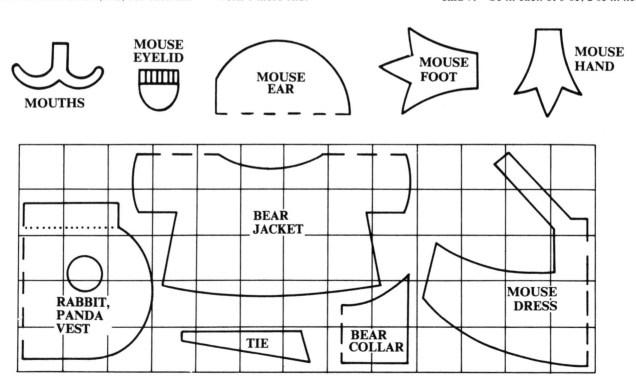

MOUTHS

MOUSE EYELID

MOUSE EAR

MOUSE FOOT

MOUSE HAND

RABBIT, PANDA VEST

BEAR JACKET

MOUSE DRESS

TIE

BEAR COLLAR

sc, repeat from * around—25 sc.

Rnd 8: Sc in each sc around.

Rnd 9: * Sc in each of 4 sc, 2 sc in next sc, repeat from * around—30 sc.

Rnds 10-13: Sc in each sc around.

Rnd 14: * Sc in next sc, pull up a lp in each of next 2 sc, yo hook and through 3 lps (dec), repeat from * around—20 sc.

Rnd 15: Sc in each sc around.

Rnd 16: Dec over each 2 sc—10 sc.

Rnd 17: Sc in each sc around. Stuff head.

Rnd 18: Dec over each 2 sc—5 sc. Sew opening closed. Sew head to body.

HEAD (for bear, panda): With CC, ch 2.

Rnd 1: 5 sc in 2nd ch from hook.

Rnd 2: 2 sc in each sc around.

Rnd 3: * Sc in next sc, 2 sc in next sc, repeat from * around—15 sc.

Rnd 4: * Sc in each of next 2 sc, 2 sc in next sc, repeat from * around—20 sc.

Rnd 5: * Sc in each of next 3 sc, 2 sc in next sc, repeat from * around—25 sc.

Rnd 6: Change to MC for bear. Sc in each sc around.

Rnd 7: * Sc in each of next 4 sc, 2 sc in next sc, repeat from * around—30 sc.

Rnds 8 and 9: Sc in each sc around.

Rnd 10: * Sc in 9 sc, 2 sc in next sc, repeat from * around—33 sc.

Rnd 11: Sc in each sc around.

Rnd 12: * Sc in next sc, pull up a lp in each of next 2 sc, yo hook and through 3 lps (dec), repeat from * around—22 sc.

Rnd 13: Sc in each sc around.

Rnd 14: Dec over each 2 sc—11 sc. Stuff head.

Rnd 15: Dec 5 sc in rnd. Sew opening closed (back of head). Sew head to body.

EAR (for bear and panda): With MC, ch 2.

Rnd 1: 5 sc in 2nd ch from hook.

Rnd 2: 2 sc in each sc around.

Rnd 3: Sc in each sc around. Sew to head.

EAR (for rabbit): With MC, ch 14. **Row 1:** Sc in 2nd ch from hook and each remaining ch. Ch 1, turn.

Row 2: Sc in each of 12 sc, 2 sc in last sc, 2 sc in next ch; sc in each ch on opposite side of starting ch. Ch 1, turn.

Row 3: Sc in each sc around, inc 2 sc at ear tip. End off. Cut pink felt a bit smaller than ear; glue to inside. Fold base of ear in half to cup ear; sew to head.

TAIL (for rabbit): Make a 2" CC pompon; sew to lower back.

TAIL (for mouse): With MC, ch 7.

Row 1: Sc in 2nd ch from hook and in next 5 ch. Ch 1, turn each row. Work 2 more rows of 6 sc.

* **Next Row:** Sc across, dec 1 sc. Work 10 more rows of 5 sc. Repeat from * twice more, working 1 less sc after each dec.

Next Row: Dec 1 sc. Work 1 row of 2 sc. End off. Sew long edges tog (no stuffing). Sew to lower back.

FELT FEATURES, CLOTHES: Patterns for features are given actual size; enlarge patterns for clothes by copying on paper ruled in 1" squares. Cut out patterns on outlines. Mark broken lines on patterns' "fold." In cutting pieces, place these edges on fold of felt.

RABBIT: Cut light blue vest. Fold top of vest down on dotted line for collar, run black yarn under collar; tie into bow at front. Cut pink mouth; glue on. Glue on small black circle for nose, blue ½" circles for eyes, smaller black circles for pupils.

PANDA: Cut red vest. Fold top of vest down on dotted line for collar, run blue yarn under collar; tie into bow at front. Cut pink mouth like rabbit's; glue on. Glue on small black circle for nose, 1" irregular "patches" to go under eyes, white ovals for eyes, small black circles for pupils.

BEAR: Cut dark blue jacket and collar, 2 red ties. Glue or stitch underarm and side seams. Slit jacket down center front. Glue curved edge of collar to back neck edge of jacket, catching in ends of ties at front. For hat, cut dark blue 2" circle and ½"-wide strip 4" long. Glue ends of strip together for hatband. Glue or sew to head; glue on circle. Cut red "ribbon" for hat somewhat smaller than tie; glue end to underside of hat. Cut pink mouth like rabbit's, small black circles for nose and eyes; glue on.

MOUSE: Cut gray feet and hands; glue into openings of legs and arms. Cut gray ears, pink ear linings slightly smaller. Glue linings to ears. Fold ears in half at bottom to cup them; sew to head. Cut light blue dress; glue or snap edges together at back. Cut a little pocket; glue on. Trim dress and pocket edges with white scalloped strips. Glue on 2 tiny white circles at neck for buttons as shown. Cut a pink mouth, black nose, black eyes and gray eyelids. Slash straight edge of eyelids for ¼" in, for lashes. Place a line of glue along top edge of lashes, fold up lashes and press down so lashes will stay up. Glue on features, covering top of eyes with eyelids. Run a few pieces of white thread through face for whiskers.

BASSET HOUND
Shown on page 190

SIZE: 10" all.

MATERIALS: Knitting worsted, 3 ozs. each of white (W) and tile (T). Knitting needles No. 8. Yarn needle. Stitch holder. Crochet hook. Scraps of white, black, yellow and red felt. Matching sewing thread. Cotton batting for stuffing.

GAUGE: 7 sts = 2"; 7 rows = 1" (garter st, double strand of yarn).

Note: Toy is worked in garter st (k each row).

FIRST HALF: Front Leg: Beg at lower edge, with a strand of W and T held together, cast on 9 sts.

Row 1: With yarn in front of work, slip first st as if to purl, k 8. Repeat row 1 until piece measures 2". Place these sts on a stitch holder. Cut yarn.

Hind Leg: Beg at lower edge, with a strand of W and T held together, cast on 10 sts.

Row 1: Slip first st as before, inc 1 st in next st (**to inc,** k in front and back of same st), k 8—11 sts.

Row 2: Slip 1, k across. Repeat rows 1 and 2 until there are 15 sts. Then repeat row 2 until piece measures 2", end at inc edge (back edge).

Next Row: Slip 1, k across; on same needle, cast on 2 sts, k across sts on holder—26 sts. Work 1 row even.

Back Shaping: Row 1: K 2 tog (1 st decreased at back edge), k across.

Row 2: Slip 1, k across. Repeat these 2 rows 10 times more—15 sts.

Neck: Dec 1 st at each end of next 3 rows—9 sts. Cut yarn; place sts on a holder.

Head: Beg at lower edge, with a strand of W and T, cast on 10 sts. Work 4 rows in garter st, slipping first st of each row.

Row 5: Slip 1, inc 1 st in next st (front edge), k across, cast on 2 sts; place sts from holder on free needle, slipping back edge on first; k across these sts.

Row 6: Slip 1, k across—22 sts.

Row 7: Slip 1, inc in next st, k across. Slipping first st of each row, work even on 23 sts until piece measures 1¾" from cast-on sts of head. Keeping back edge straight and slipping first st at back edge, dec 1 st at front edge on every other row until 15 sts remain, then dec 1 st at both edges on every row until 9 sts remain. Bind off.

SECOND HALF: Work as for First Half.

EAR (make 2): Beg at side edge with single strand of T, cast on 19 sts.

Row 1: Slip 1 as before (lower edge), k across.

Row 2: K all sts. Repeat rows 1 and 2 until piece measures 2¾". Bind off.

TAIL: With single strand of T, cast on 9 sts. K each row for 2". Bind off. Fold in half, sew one end together, sew cast-on and bound-off edges together, stuffing lightly.

FINISHING: Sew halves together, sewing through back loops of end sts (front loops will form ridges), leaving a large opening. Stuff firmly; sew opening. Gather top edge of each ear; sew an ear to each side of head. Sew tail in place.

Cut 24 strands of T, 3″ long. Insert crochet hook through corner st of front leg; double one strand of T, pull loop through st; draw ends through loop; tighten knot. Knot 6 strands in this manner on front and hind legs each side.

For eyes, cut two ovals of white felt, 2″ x 1½″, and two ovals of black felt, 1″ x ¾″. Sew eyes in place. For nose, cut a strip of black felt, ⅜″ x 1½″. Sew in place over front edge.

Cut tongue of red felt; sew in place. Cut ¾″ wide strip of yellow felt about 24″ long; tie around neck. If desired, make leash of braided string. Make loop by gluing felt around string. Attach leash with brass ring.

PETEY PUPPY
Shown on page 191

SIZE: 9″ long, 6″ high.
MATERIALS: Knitting worsted, 4 ply, 1 oz. each of dark turquoise (T), green (G), orange (O) and white (W). Aluminum crochet hook size G. Two jet buttons. Cotton batting for stuffing. Black embroidery floss. Embroidery and yarn needles.
GAUGE: 4 sc = 1″; 4 rnds = 1″.
Note: Wrong side of work is used for right side of puppy.
PUPPY: HEAD: Front: Beg at tip of nose, with W, ch 2.
Rnd 1: 7 sc in 2nd ch from hook. Do not join; mark end of each rnd.
Rnd 2: 2 sc in each sc around—14 sc.
Rnd 3: (2 sc in next sc, sc in next sc) 7 times—21 sc.
Rnds 4 and 5: Sc in each sc around.
Rnd 6: Dec 1 sc (**to dec,** pull up a lp in each of 2 sc, yo and through 3 lps on hook), sc in each of 2 sc, 2 sc in each of 15 sc, sc in each of 2 sc—35 sc.
Rnd 7: Sc in each of 12 sc, (2 sc in next sc, sc in each of 4 sc) twice, 2 sc in next sc, sc in each of 12 sc—38 sc.
Rnd 8: Sc in each of 4 sc, * 2 sc in next sc, sc in next sc, repeat from * around —55 sc.
Rnd 9: Sc in each sc. Cut W; join G.
Rnd 10: With G, * dec 1 sc, sc in each of 6 sc, repeat from * around, end last repeat sc in each of 5 sc—48 sc.
Rnds 11 and 12: Sc in each sc around. Drop yarn. Do not end off.
Back: Beg at center back, with T, ch 2.
Rnd 1: 7 sc in 2nd ch from hook. Do not join; mark end of each rnd.
Rnd 2: 2 sc in each sc around—14 sc.
Rnd 3: (Sc in next sc, 2 sc in next sc) 7 times—21 sc.
Rnd 4: (Sc in each of 2 sc, 2 sc in next sc) 7 times—28 sc.

Rnd 5: (Sc in each of 3 sc, 2 sc in next sc) 7 times—35 sc.
Rnd 6: Sc in each sc around.
Rnd 7: Inc 7 sc evenly around—42 sc.
Rnd 8: Repeat rnd 7—49 sc.
Rnd 9: Sc in each sc around.
Rnd 10: Repeat rnd 7—56 sc.
Rnd 11: (Sc in each of 5 sc, dec 1 sc) 8 times—48 sc. End off.

With right sides tog, with G, sc halves of head tog, stuffing firmly before closing opening. End off.
BODY: Front: Beg at front of body, with T, ch 2.
Rnd 1: 7 sc in 2nd ch from hook. Do not join; mark end of each rnd.
Rnd 2: 2 sc in each sc around—14 sc.
Rnd 3: 2 sc in each sc around—28 sc.
Rnd 4: * Sc in next sc, 2 sc in next sc, repeat from * around—42 sc.
Rnds 5 and 6: Sc in each sc around.
Rnd 7: (Sc in each of 5 sc, dec 1 sc) 6 times—36 sc. Work 4 rnds even. Cut T; join G. With G, work 11 rnds even. End off.
Back: Beg at center back, with O, work as for front of body through rnd 7—36 sc. With right sides tog, with O, sc back and front body tog, stuffing firmly before closing opening. End off.
LEGS (make 4): Beg at toe, with W, ch 2.
Rnd 1: 4 sc in 2nd ch from hook. Do not join; mark end of rnds.
Rnd 2: 2 sc in each sc around—8 sc.
Rnd 3: (Sc in next sc, 2 sc in next sc) 4 times—12 sc. Work 3 rnds even. End off, leaving a long end. Turn wrong side out. Stuff firmly and sew to body.
EARS (make 2): With O, ch 9.
Row 1: Sc in 2nd ch from hook and in each of 5 ch, 2 sc in next ch, 5 sc in last ch; working on opposite side of ch, work 2 sc in next ch, sc in each of 6 sc —21 sc. Ch 1, turn.
Row 2 (wrong side): Sc in front lp of each sc around—21 sc. Ch 1, turn.
Row 3: Working in back lp, sc in each of 6 sc, 2 sc in each of 9 sc, sc in each of 6 sc—30 sc. Ch 1, turn.
Row 4: Repeat row 2. End off, leaving a long end.
BOTTLE STRAP: With W, ch 21.
Row 1: Sc in 2nd ch from hook and in each ch across—20 sc. Ch 1, turn. Work 2 rows even. End off. Sew ends to each side of G section on top of body.
TAIL: Beg at tip, with T, ch 2.
Rnd 1: 4 sc in 2nd ch from hook.
Rnd 2: 2 sc in each sc around—8 sc. Work even for 5 rnds. End off, leaving a long end. Turn wrong side out. Stuff firmly and sew to back of body. Sew eyes to head, shaping sides of head at same time. Embroider mouth as pictured with short sts. Sew head to body. Gather straight edge of ears, sew to sides of head.

DINA DACHSHUND
Shown on page 191

SIZE: 14″ long; 6″ high.
MATERIALS: Knitting worsted, 4 ply, 2 ozs. each of purple (P), dark turquoise (T) and green (G); 1 oz. orange (O). Aluminum crochet hook size G. Two jet buttons. Cotton batting. Yarn needle.
GAUGE: 4 sc = 1″; 4 rnds = 1″.
Note: Wrong side of work is right side of dachshund.
DACHSHUND: HEAD: Front: With T, work as for puppy back of head through rnd 11—48 sc. End off.
Back: Beg at center back, with T, ch 2.
Rnd 1: 7 sc in 2nd ch from hook. Do not join; mark end of each rnd.
Rnd 2: 2 sc in each sc around—14 sc.
Rnd 3: (Sc in next sc, 2 sc in next sc) 7 times—21 sc.
Rnd 4: (Sc in each of 2 sc, 2 sc in next sc) 7 times—28 sc.
Rnd 5: (Sc in next sc, 2 sc in next sc) 14 times—42 sc.
Rnd 6: Sc in each sc around.
Rnd 7: (Sc in each of 6 sc, 2 sc in next sc) 6 times—48 sc.
Rnd 8: (Sc in each of 3 sc, 2 sc in next sc) 12 times—60 sc.
Rnd 9: Sc in each sc around.
Rnd 10: (Sc in each of 3 sc, dec 1 sc) 12 times—48 sc.
Rnds 11 and 12: Sc in each sc around. Do not end off. With right sides tog, sc front and back of head tog, stuffing firmly before opening becomes too small. End off.
SNOUT: Beg at tip, with T, ch 2.
Rnd 1: 4 sc in 2nd ch from hook. Do not join; mark end of each rnd.
Rnd 2: 2 sc in each sc around—8 sc.
Rnd 3: (Sc in next sc, 2 sc in next sc) 4 times—12 sc.
Rnd 4: (Sc in each of 2 sc, 2 sc in next sc) 4 times—16 sc.
Rnd 5: (Sc in each of 3 sc, 2 sc in next sc) 4 times—20 sc.
Rnds 6-10: Sc in each sc around. End off, leaving a long end. Turn wrong side out; stuff firmly. Sew to front of head.
NOSE: Beg at tip, with O, ch 2. Work as for snout through rnd 2—8 sc.
Rnd 3: Sc in each sc around.
Rnd 4: (Dec 1 sc) 4 times—4 sc. End off, leaving a long end. Turn wrong side out, stuff lightly and sew to tip of snout.
BODY: Front: Beg at front of body, with G, work same as for puppy body through rnd 11—36 sc. End off.
Back: Work as for front body. End off.
Center section: With P, ch 36. Join with a sl st forming a ring.
Rnd 1: Sc in each ch around—36 sc.
Rnds 2-10: Sc in each sc around. End off. Make 2nd P section, make one T section. With right sides tog, with O, sc one P section to front body, T section

to P section, 2nd P section to T section, and back to P section, stuffing body firmly before opening becomes too small.

LEGS (make 4): Beg at toe, with P, ch 2.

Rnd 1: 7 sc in 2nd ch from hook. Do not join; mark end of each rnd.

Rnd 2: 2 sc in each sc around—14 sc.

Rnds 3-7: Sc in each sc around. End off, leaving a long end. Turn wrong side out; stuff firmly. Sew to body.

EARS (make 2): With G, ch 9.

Row 1: Sc in 2nd ch from hook and in each of 5 ch, 2 sc in next ch, 5 sc in last ch; working on opposite side of ch, work 2 sc in next ch, sc in each of 6 sc —21 sc. Ch 1, turn.

Row 2: * Insert hook in next sc, wrap yarn over first finger of left hand to form 1″ lp, pull yarn under finger through sc, remove finger, hold lp in back, then yo and through 2 lps on hook (loop st made), repeat from * around. Ch 1, turn.

Row 3: Sc in each of 6 sts, 2 sc in each of 9 sts, sc in each of 6 sts—30 sc. Cut G; join O. Ch 1, turn.

Row 4: With O, repeat row 2. End off.

TAIL: Beg at tip, with T, ch 2.

Rnd 1: 4 sc in 2nd ch from hook.

Rnd 2: 2 sc in each sc around—8 sc.

Rnds 3-18: Sc in each sc around. End off, leaving a long end. Turn wrong side out; stuff firmly, sew to back of body. Sew head to body; sew ears to head. Sew buttons in place for eyes.

LOOPY PUPPY
Shown on page 192

SIZE: 14″ long.

MATERIALS: Coats & Clark Red Heart Knitting Worsted, 4-oz. skeins, 2 skeins white, few yards each black and coral. Crochet hook size G. Polyester fiberfill for stuffing. Two buttons for eyes.

GAUGE: 4 sts = 1″; 4 rows = 1″.

LOOP STITCH: * With yarn over left index finger, insert hook in next sc, draw free end through sc making a ¾″ loop for muff and hat (1″ loop for dog), drop loop off, hold in back, yo and through 2 lps on hook, repeat from * across row.

DOG: BACK OF HEAD: Beg at center with white, ch 4, join to form ring.

Rnd 1 (right side): Ch 1, 12 sc in ring. Join with sl st in first sc. Ch 1, turn.

Rnd 2 and All Even Rnds: Work loop st (see Loop St) in each sc around. Join in first st. Ch 1, turn.

Rnd 3: 2 sc in each loop st around—24 sc. Join. Ch 1, turn each rnd.

Rnd 5: Ch 1, * sc in next st, 2 sc in next st, repeat from * around—36 sc.

Rnd 7: Sc in each of 2 sts, 2 sc in next st, repeat from * around—48 sc.

Rnd 9: Sc in each loop st around.

Rnd 10: Repeat rnd 2. Join. End off.

FRONT OF HEAD: Work as for back of head to end of rnd 2—12 loop sts. Join. Ch 1, turn each rnd.

Rnd 3: Sc in each loop st around.

Rnd 4 and All Even Rnds: Loop st in each sc around.

Rnd 5: 2 sc in each of 6 loop sts (mark these 6 sc for forehead), sc in each of 6 sts—18 sc.

Rnd 7: 2 sc in each of 12 sts (forehead), sc in each of 6 sts—30 sc.

Rnd 9: Sc in each of 3 sts, 2 sc in each of 18 sts, sc in each of 9 sts—48 sc.

Rnds 10-14: Repeat rnds 4 and 3 alternately, ending with rnd 4. Join. End off. Sew last rnds of front and back of head tog, stuffing firmly before opening is entirely closed. With black, embroider nose over ⅓ of sts on rnd 1 of front.

TONGUE: With coral, ch 4. Sc in 2nd ch from hook, sc in next ch, 3 sc in last ch; on opposite side of starting ch, sc in each of 2 ch. End off. Sew straight end to face. Sew on buttons for eyes.

EAR (make 2): With white, ch 9.

Row 1: Sc in 2nd ch from hook, sc in each of 5 ch, 2 sc in next ch, 5 sc in last ch (tip); working on opposite ch of starting ch, 2 sc in next ch, sc in each of 6 ch—21 sc. Ch 1, turn.

Row 2: Loop st in each sc. Ch 1, turn.

Row 3: Sc in each of 6 loop sts, 2 sc in each of 9 sts, sc in each of 6 sts—30 sc. Ch 1, turn.

Row 4: Repeat row 2. End off. Sew straight edge of ears to head.

BODY: Beg at center of bottom, work as for back of head until end of rnd 8—48 loop sts. Join. Ch 1, turn.

Rnd 9: * 2 sc in next st, sc in each of 3 sts, repeat from * around—60 sc. Join. Ch 1, turn.

Rnds 10-24: Work 1 rnd loop st, 1 rnd sc alternately (no incs). Join. Ch 1, turn each rnd.

Rnd 25: * Sc in each of 8 loop sts, dec 1 sc, repeat from * around—54 sc. Join. Ch 1, turn.

Rnds 26-28: Work 1 rnd loop st, 1 rnd sc, 1 rnd loop st (no decs).

Rnd 29: * Sc in each of 7 sts, dec 1 sc, repeat from * around—48 sc. Join. Ch 1, turn.

Rnds 30-41: Repeat rnds 26-29 three times, having 1 st less between decs after each dec rnd—30 sc.

Rnd 42: Work sc in each sc around. Join. End off. Stuff body firmly; sew to head as pictured.

FORELEG (make 2): Beg at paw, work as for back of head to end of rnd 1—12 sc.

Rnds 2-7: Sc in each sc around. Join. Ch 1, turn each rnd.

Rnds 8-20: Work 1 rnd loop st, 1 rnd sc alternately, ending with loop st rnd.

Rnd 21: * 2 sc in next st, sc in next st, repeat from * around—18 sc. Join. Ch 1, turn.

Rnds 22-24: Work 1 rnd loop st, 1 rnd sc, 1 rnd loop st. Join. End off. Stuff legs firmly; sew to top of body.

HIND LEG (make 2): Work as for fore leg to end of rnd 14—12 loop sts.

Rnd 15: Repeat rnd 21 of foreleg.

Rnd 16: Loop st in each sc around—18 loop sts. Join. Ch 1, turn.

Rnds 17-22: Repeat last 2 rnds alternately, having 1 st more between incs after each inc rnd—36 loop sts.

Rnds 23-28: Work 1 rnd sc, 1 rnd loop st. Join. End off. Stuff legs firmly; sew to lower edge of body as pictured.

TAIL: Beg at tip, ch 4.

Row 1: Sc in 2nd ch from hook, sc in each of 2 ch—3 sc. Ch 1, turn.

Rows 2-7: Work loop st in each st on each row. Ch 1, turn each row.

Rows 8 and 9: 2 loop sts in first st, loop st to end of row—5 loop sts.

Rows 10 and 11: Loop st in each st on each row. End off. Sew tail to body.

HAND PUPPETS
Shown on page 193

MATERIALS: Wintuk sock and sweater yarn, 3 ply, 1 2-oz. skein pink for elephant, green for frog, yellow for duck, tan for lion. Knitting worsted, 1 ounce brown, for lion. Steel crochet hook No. 3. Small pieces of felt: white, black, light blue, dark blue, green, orange, red. Cotton for stuffing. Pellon, 2″ × 7″ strip for each puppet. Sewing threads to match yarn and felt. ½ yard elastic thread or round elastic. Two black buttons with shaft, two 1″ white pompons, for frog. Small bunch of artificial flowers, narrow blue ribbon, for duck. Small black pompon for lion.

GAUGE: 15 sc = 2″; 8 rows = 1″.

ELEPHANT FRONT: Beg at lower edge, ch 41.

Row 1: Sc in 2nd ch from hook and in each ch across—40 sc. Ch 1, turn each row.

Rows 2-14: Sc in each sc across. At end of row 14, ch 12.

Row 15: Sc in 2nd ch from hook and in each of next 10 ch, sc in each sc across. Ch 12.

Row 16: Sc in 2nd ch from hook and in each of next 10 ch, sc in each sc across— 62 sc.

Rows 17-29: Sc in each sc across.

Row 30: Sc in each of 51 sc. Ch 1, turn.

Rows 31-39: Sc in each of 40 sc. Ch 1, turn.

Row 40: Repeat row 14.

Row 41: Repeat row 15.

Row 42: Repeat row 16.

Rows 43-55: Repeat rows 14-29.

Row 56: Sc in each of 40 sc. Ch 1, turn.

Row 57: Sc in each of 18 sc. Ch 1, turn.

Working on center 18 sts only for head, work 66 rows. End off.

BACK: Work as for front through row 55. End off.

HEAD SIDES (make 2): Ch 4, sl st in first ch to form ring.

Rnd 1: Ch 1, 8 sc in ring. Do not join rnds with sl st; mark end of rnds.

Rnd 2: 2 sc in each sc—16 sc.

Rnd 3: * Sc in next sc, 2 sc in next sc, repeat from * around—24 sc.

Rnd 4: * Sc in each of 2 sc, 2 sc in next sc, repeat from * around—32 sc.

Rnd 5: * Sc in each of 3 sc, 2 sc in next sc, repeat from * around—40 sc.

Rnds 6-13: Work around in sc, inc 8 sc evenly each rnd. End off.

TRUNK: Ch 25.

Row 1: Sc in 2nd ch from hook and in each ch across—24 sc. Ch 1, turn each row.

Rows 2-10: Sc in each sc across.

Rows 11-18: Sk first sc, sc in each sc across—16 sc. End off.

FINISHING: Sew front and back of body tog at shoulders and sides including top and bottom edges of legs. Sew end of head strip to center top of back of body. Fit in head sides; sew to strip.

* Stuff head ⅓ full. Roll Pellon strip to make tube 1″ in diameter. Stitch edges of tube to secure. Insert tube into head and push stuffing all around it, holding tube in center of head until head is firmly stuffed. Then, holding one finger in tube, take a few stitches at each side of neck, catching tube to crochet.

From light blue felt, cut 4 circles 1½″ diameter for feet. Using patterns, cut 2 ears and 1 mouth. Cut 2 white ovals ⅝″

long for eyes, 2 small black circles for pupils.

Sew felt feet in place. Stuff ends of legs. With thread to match elephant, stitch loosely back and forth through stuffing and legs.

Weave elastic through first row at bottom of body. Pull to fit hand; secure ends.

Sew sides of trunk tog; stuff. Sew small blue felt circle to small end. With seam at top, make fold in trunk and tack to turn trunk up. Sew trunk to head with mouth behind trunk, point of mouth extending down. Sew eyes in place. With black thread, make small stitches for eyebrows. Pleat inner edge of each ear. Sew to head.

FROG: FRONT: Work as for elephant through row 55.

Row 56: Sc in each of 41 sc. Ch 1, turn.

Row 57: Sc in each of 20 sc. Ch 1, turn.

Rows 58-69: Working on center sts only, inc 1 sc at beg of each row—32 sc.

Rows 70-75: Work even in sc.

Rows 76-81: Sk first sc, sc in each sc across—26 sc. End off.

BACK: Work as for front.

MOUTH: Upper Lip: Ch 21.

Row 1: Sc in 2nd ch from hook and in each ch across—20 sc. Ch 1, turn each row.

Rows 2 and 3: Sc in each sc across. End off.

Lower Lip: Ch 41.

Row 1: Work as for upper lip—40 sc.

Rows 2-4: Work as for row 2 of upper lip. End off.

FINISHING: Sew front and back tog, leaving open at ends of legs and bottom

of body. Stuff head and insert tube as for elephant; see Finishing for elephant, beginning at *.

From green felt, cut 8 feet and 2 eyelids, using patterns. From red felt, cut 1 tongue.

Whipstitch 2 pieces tog for each foot, leaving bottom open; stuff. Sew open edges of feet to open edge of legs. Stuff legs for ½″. With matching thread, stitch back and forth loosely through stuffing and legs.

Join notch edges of each eyelid with whipstitch. Sew buttons to white pompons. Sew pompons to head for eyes; sew eyelids to head over eyes. Tack inner edge of tongue to lower lip at center and ends of tongue. Sew lower lip to head at ends and lower edge. Sew one edge of upper lip to head in curved line; fold each end up and tack in place.

Weave elastic through first row at bottom of body. Pull to fit hand; secure ends.

DUCK: FRONT: Beg at lower edge, ch 41.

Row 1: Sc in 2nd ch from hook and in each ch across—40 sc. Ch 1, turn each row.

Rows 2-40: Sc in each sc. At end of row 40, ch 13.

Row 41: Sc in 2nd ch from hook and in each of 11 ch, sc in each sc across. Ch 13.

Row 42: Sc in 2nd ch from hook and in each of 11 ch, sc in each sc across—64 sc.

Rows 43-55: Sc in each sc across.

Row 56: Sc in each of 41 sc. Ch 1, turn.

Row 57: Sc in each of 18 sc. Ch 1, turn.

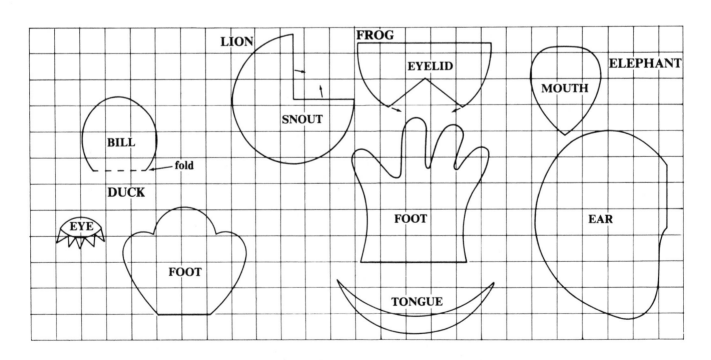

Patterns for Hand Puppets: To enlarge to actual size, copy patterns on paper ruled in ½″ squares.

Working on center 18 sts only for head, work even for 28 rows. End off.

BACK: Work as for front.

HEAD SIDES (make 2): Ch 6.

Rnd 1: 3 sc in 2nd ch from hook, sc in each of next 3 ch, 3 sc in last ch. Working on opposite side of ch, sc in each of next 3 ch—12 sc. Do not join rnds with sl st.

Rnd 2: * 2 sc in each of next 3 sc, sc in each of 3 sc, repeat from * once—18 sc.

Rnds 3-7: Work in sc, inc 3 or 4 sc around curve at each end each rnd. End off.

FINISHING: Sew front and back of body tog at sides, around wings, across shoulders and up neck for 1″. Join top of head. Pin, then sew head sides in place.

Wing Edging: Row 1: Work sc around 3 sides of wing. Ch 1, turn.

Row 2: Sc in first sc, * ch 3, sc in same sc, sc in next sc, repeat from * around. End off.

Stuff head and insert tube as for elephant; see Finishing for elephant, beginning at *.

Stuff wings half full. With matching thread, stitch loosely back and forth through stuffing and wings to hold stuffing in place.

Wind yarn 50 times around 3 fingers; slip off and tie tightly around center. Cut loops and trim. Fluff up pompon; sew to top of head. Tie ribbon with flowers around pompon.

Using patterns, from orange felt, cut 1 piece for bill, 4 pieces for feet. From black, cut eyelashes. From dark blue, cut eyes. Sew eyes with eyelashes below to head. Make straight stitches with black thread for eyebrows. Fold bill in half. Fold the folded edge through center to pleat bill; sew to head. Whip 2 pieces tog for each foot, stuffing lightly. Sew feet to 12th row of body.

Weave elastic through first row at bottom of body. Pull to fit hand; secure ends.

LION: FRONT: Work as for elephant through row 55.

Row 56: Sc in each of 38 sc. Ch 1, turn.

Row 57: Sc in each of 14 sc. Ch 1, turn. Working on center 14 sc only, for head, work 64 rows. End off.

BACK: Work as for front through row 55. End off.

HEAD SIDES (make 2): Work as for elephant through rnd 10. End off.

EARS (make 2): Ch 10.

Row 1: Sc in 2nd ch from hook and in each ch across—9 sc. Ch 1, turn each row.

Row 2: Sc in each sc across.

Rows 3-10: Sk first sc, sc in each sc across—1 sc remains. End off.

FINISHING: Sew front and back tog at shoulders and sides, including top and bottom edges of legs. Sew end of head strip to center top of back of body. Fit in head sides; sew to strip.

Stuff head and insert tube as for elephant; see Finishing for elephant, beginning at *.

From white felt, cut 4 circles 1½″ diameter, for feet. Using pattern, cut 1 snout. Cut 2 white ovals ⅝″ long for eyes, 2 small black circles for pupils. Cut 1 red circle ½″ diameter for tongue; cut 2 sides to form a point for top of tongue.

Sew felt feet in place. Stuff ends of legs. With thread to match lion, stitch loosely back and forth through stuffing and legs.

Weave elastic through first row at bottom of body. Pull to fit hand; secure ends.

Whipstitch straight edges of snout tog. Stuff lightly; sew to face with seam at top, stuffing more as you sew. Tack point of tongue to snout. Sew pompon to top of snout. Sew on eyes. Make straight stitches with black thread for eyebrows. Sew ears to head.

For mane, cut 4″ lengths of knitting worsted. Insert hook through st on head, pull loop of yarn through; draw ends through loop; tighten knot. Cover head with mane, leaving face free.

LOBSTER
Shown at bottom, page 194

SIZE: 18″ long.

MATERIALS: Rayon and cotton rug yarn, 4 70-yard skeins bright pink (P), 1 skein orange (O); small amount of black (B). Aluminum crochet hook size G. Cotton for stuffing. Rug needle.

GAUGE: 7 sc = 2″; 3 rows = 1″.

HEAD: With P, ch 4; sl st in first ch to form ring.

Rnd 1: Ch 1, 5 sc in ring. Do not join rnds with sl st; mark end of rnds.

Rnd 2: 2 sc in each sc—10 sc.

Rnd 3: * Sc in next sc, 2 sc in next sc, repeat from * around—15 sc.

Rnd 4: (2 sc in next sc, sc in next sc) 7 times, 2 sc in last sc—23 sc.

Rnd 5: (Sc in next sc, 2 sc in next sc) 11 times, sc in last sc—34 sc.

Rnds 6-11: Sc around, inc 6 sc in each rnd—70 sc.

Rnds 12 and 13: Work even in sc. At end of rnd 13, sl st in next st. Fold piece in half, sc across end. End off.

With O, sc around head, joining open edges and stuffing with cotton. Work 1 more rnd O around head. End off.

Eyes (make 2): With B, ch 4; sl st in first ch to form ring.

Rnd 1: Ch 1, 6 sc in ring. Join in first sc.

Rnd 2: Ch 1, 2 sc in each sc around—12 sc. Join each rnd.

Rnd 3: Ch 1, * sc in next sc, 2 sc in next sc, repeat from * around—18 sc. End off B; join O.

Rnd 4: With O, ch 1, * 2 sc in next sc, sc in each of next 2 sc, repeat from * around—24 sc. End off.

Sew eyes to head with matching thread.

BODY: With P, ch 17.

Row 1: Sc in 2nd ch from hook and in each remaining ch—16 sc. Ch 1, turn.

Rows 2-84: Sc in each sc across. Ch 1, turn each row. Fold piece in half, sc around all 4 sides, including folded edge, stuffing body. Cut P; join O. With O, sc around body, joining head to body (with back of head toward you), at one end.

Cut three 20″ strands of P; double one strand. Tie doubled strand tightly around body ¼ way down from head; tuck ends into body. Repeat twice more ½ and ¾ way down.

ARMS: Cut 16 P strands and 8 O strands 30″ long for each arm. Draw 8 P strands through 1 sc of joining at back of neck, 2 sts in from end; pull to make 16 even ends. Repeat with 8 O strands in next st and 8 P strands in following st. Braid ends; tie ends tog with separate P strand 2″ from bottom. Make other arm the same.

SHIVERS
Shown on pages 194 and 195

SIZE: 36″ long uncoiled.

MATERIALS: Rayon and cotton rug yarn, 2 70-yard skeins black (B), 1 skein each white (W) and orange (O). Aluminum crochet hook size G. Two black buttons. Heavy-duty sewing thread, black and white. One large snap fastener.

GAUGE: 7 sc = 2″; 3 rows = 1″.

HEAD AND BODY: With B, ch 250.

Row 1: Sc in 2nd ch from hook and in each remaining ch—249 sc. Ch 1, turn.

Rows 2-4: Sc in each sc across. Ch 1, turn each row. Fold piece in half crosswise. Sc short ends tog, sc sides tog, sc across folded end, sc 2nd long edges tog to within 30 sts of end. Keep hook in work.

Turn open end wrong side out and flatten point that forms at end (this is top of head). Fold end under to last sc made on side. Leaving point for top of head free, insert hook through top and bottom edges of head, sc 2 thicknesses of head tog to fold (front edge of head), sc across folded edge, sc opposite side of head tog to beg of head. End off. Join W to top edge of body where body comes out from under head. Sc around body and around head. End off. Join O in first st of W edging and repeat.

FACE: With W, ch 8.

Row 1: Sc in 2nd ch from hook and in each remaining ch—7 sc. Ch 1, turn.

Rows 2-4: Sc in each sc. Ch 1, turn each row. Work 1 rnd sc around piece. End off. Sew black buttons to face, sew face to head with white thread.

Roll up body to meet head. Sew one part of snap fastener to body near head;

sew other part to last coil so body snaps together.

GADBERRY
Shown at top left, page 195

SIZE: 22″ long.
MATERIALS: Rayon and cotton rug yarn, 2 70-yard skeins orange (O), 1 skein each black (B) and white (W). Aluminum crochet hook size G. Cotton for stuffing. Two black buttons. Heavy-duty sewing thread, black and white.
GAUGE: 7 sc = 2″; 3 rows = 1″.
HEAD (make 4 pieces): With B, ch 4; sl st in first ch to form ring.
Rnd 1: Ch 1, 5 sc in ring. Do not join rnds with sl st; mark end of rnds.
Rnd 2: 2 sc in each sc around—10 sc.
Rnd 3: * 2 sc in next sc, sc in next sc, repeat from * around—15 sc.
Rnd 4: * 2 sc in next sc, sc in each of next 2 sc, repeat from * around—20 sc.
Rnd 5: * Sc in each of 3 sc, 2 sc in next sc, repeat from * around—25 sc.
Rnd 6: * Sc in each of 4 sc, 2 sc in next sc, repeat from * around—30 sc.
Rnd 7: Repeat rnd 4—40 sc.
Rnd 8: * Sc in each of 9 sc, 2 sc in next sc, repeat from * around—44 sc. Sl st in next st; end off.
With W, sc 2 circles tog across 11 sts. End off. Repeat with other 2 circles. Put 2 pieces tog for back and front of head, stuff and sc pieces tog around outer edges with W.
EYES (make 2): With O, ch 4; sl st in first ch to form ring. Repeat rnds 1-3 of head. Change to W, repeat rnd 4. End off. Sew buttons to sides of eyes. Sew on eyes with white thread.
UPPER BODY (make 2 pieces): With O, ch 20.
Row 1: Sc in 2nd ch from hook and in each remaining ch—19 sc. Ch 1, turn.
Rows 2-16: Sc in each sc across. Ch 1, turn each row.
Row 17: Sk first st, sc across to 2 sts from end, sk next st, sc in last st. Ch 1, turn. Repeat row 17 4 more times—9 sts. End off. With O, sc 2 body pieces tog, stuffing with cotton.
BOTTOM OF BODY: With O, ch 10.
Row 1: Sc in 2nd ch from hook and in each remaining ch—9 sc. Ch 1, turn.
Rows 2-20: Sc in each sc across. Ch 1, turn each row. Fold piece in half crosswise, stuff with cotton, sc around all sides including folded edge. With rows running vertically, sc piece to lower edge of upper body. With B, sc all around body. With W, sc all around body, joining head to top of body. End off.
LEGS (make 2): Cut 12 strands B 24″ long for each leg. Draw 4 strands through W sc 2 sts in from lower corner on bottom of body. Pull strands to make 8 even ends. Repeat in each of next 2 sts. Braid ends. Tie around braid ends; trim.

FEET (make 2): With O, ch 16.
Row 1: Sc in 2nd ch from hook and in each remaining ch—15 sc. Ch 1, turn.
Rows 2-8: Sc in each sc across. Ch 1, turn each row. End off.
With B, sc around piece. Join; end off. With W, sc around piece. Join; end off. Fold foot in half crosswise. With W, beg at fold, sc side edges tog, slip end of leg inside, sc top edges tog to leg, sc across front edge past leg, sc top and other side edges tog. End off. Secure feet by sewing through feet and legs with white thread.

POW WOW
Shown at bottom left, page 195

SIZE: 25″ long.
MATERIALS: Rayon and cotton rug yarn, 2 70-yard skeins black (B), 1 skein each white (W) and orange (O). Aluminum crochet hook, size G. Cotton for stuffing. Two black buttons. Three large snap fasteners. White, black and orange sewing threads.
GAUGE: 7 sc = 2″; 3 rows = 1″.
HEAD (make 2 pieces): With B, ch 31.
Row 1: Sc in 2nd ch from hook and in each remaining ch—30 sc. Ch 1, turn.
Rows 2-18: Sc in each sc across. Ch 1, turn each row.
Row 19: Sk first st, sc across to 2 sts from end, sk next st, sc in last st—28 sc. Ch 1, turn.
Rows 20-28: Repeat row 19—10 sc. End off. With B, sc 2 head pieces tog all around, stuffing head with cotton.
FACE: With W, ch 19.
Row 1: Repeat row 1 of head—18 sc.
Rows 2-12: Sc in each sc across. Ch 1, turn each row.
Rows 13-17: Repeat row 19 of head—8 sc. With white thread, sew face to head.
EYES (make 2): With W, ch 4. Sl st in first ch to form ring.
Rnd 1: Ch 1, 5 sc in ring. Do not join rnds; mark end of rnds.
Rnd 2: 2 sc in each sc around—10 sc.
Rnd 3: * 2 sc in next sc, sc in next sc, repeat from * around, 2 sc in first sc, sl st in next sc. End off. Sew a button to each eye. Sew eyes to head above face.
FEATHER: With O, ch 11.
Row 1: Repeat row 1 of head—10 sc.
Rows 2-10: Sc in each sc across. Ch 1, turn each row. Ch 1, sc around 4 sides; join to first sc. Ch 1, insert hook in opposite corner of square, sl st 2 sides tog to form point. Flatten piece with seam at center. Sew half of a snap fastener to point over seam. Sew other half to center top of head at back.
BODY (make 2 pieces): With O, ch 15.
Row 1: Repeat row 1 of head—14 sc.
Rows 2-27: Sc in each sc across. Ch 1, turn each row.
Rows 28-31: Repeat row 19 of head—6 sc. Ch 1, sc around all sides. Join in

first sc. End off. With B, sc 2 body pieces tog, stuffing body. With B, sc body to bottom of head across center 11 sts.
FEET (make 2): With B, make feet same as feather. Snap to front of body 2 rows from bottom.

HANNIBAL
Shown at top right, page 195

SIZE: 13″ long, plus legs.
MATERIALS: Rayon and cotton rug yarn, 4 70-yard skeins black (B), 2 skeins orange (O) and 1 skein white (W). Aluminum crochet hook size G. Cotton for stuffing. Two black buttons. Heavy-duty sewing thread, white, black and orange.
GAUGE: 7 sc = 2″; 3 rows = 1″.
BODY (make 2 pieces): With B, ch 26.
Row 1: Sc in 2nd ch from hook and in each remaining ch—25 sc. Ch 1, turn.
Rows 2-34: Sc in each sc across. Ch 1, turn each row.
Row 35: Sk first st, sc across to 2 sts from end, sk next st, sc in last st—23 sc. Ch 1, turn. Repeat last row 5 more times—13 sc. End off.
Sc 2 body pieces tog, stuffing with cotton.
FACE: With W, ch 16.
Row 1: Repeat row 1 of body—15 sc.
Rows 2-22: Repeat row 2 of body.
Row 23: Repeat row 35 of body—13 sc. Repeat last row 3 more times—7 sc. Sc around face; join; end off.
EYES: With O, ch 9.
Row 1: Repeat row 1 of body—8 sc.
Rows 2-4: Repeat row 2 of body. Sc around eyes; join; end off. Sew black buttons to eyes. With orange thread, sew eyes to face. With white thread, sew face to body.
LEGS (make 2): Cut 21 strands O 36″ long for each leg. Pull 7 strands through each of 3 sts at bottom of body to left of center. Pull strands to make 14 even ends from each st. Braid ends. Tie a separate strand O around braid 2″ from bottom. Repeat to right of center for 2nd leg.

MIZER
Shown at top, page 194

SIZE: 12″ long, plus 8″ legs.
MATERIALS: Rayon and cotton rug yarn, 2 70-yard skeins black (B), 1 skein each white (W) and orange (O). Aluminum crochet hook size G. Cotton for stuffing. Two black buttons. Rug needle.
GAUGE: 7 sc = 2″; 3 rows = 1″.
HEAD (make 2 pieces): With B, ch 25.
Row 1: Sc in 2nd ch from hook and in each remaining ch—24 sc. Ch 1, turn.
Rows 2-21: Sc in each sc across. Ch 1, turn.
Row 22: Sk first st, sc across to next to

last st, sk 1 st, sc in last st. Ch 1, turn. Repeat row 22 until 12 sc remain. Work 1 row of sc all around head, working 2 sc in each bottom corner. Join to first sc. End off.

FACE: With W, ch 15.

Row 1: Sc in 2nd ch from hook and in each remaining ch—14 sc. Ch 1, turn.

Rows 2-12: Sc in each sc across. Ch 1, turn.

Row 13: Repeat row 22 of head—12 sc. Repeat this row twice more—8 sc. Work row of sc around entire face. End off.

NOSE: With O, ch 8.

Row 1: Sc in 2nd ch from hook and in each remaining ch—7 sc. Ch 1, turn.

Rows 2-5: Sc in each sc across. Ch 1, turn. Work row of sc around nose. End off.

With O, sew nose to center of face, leaving open at top to make penny pocket. With W, sew face to one head piece 9 rows down from top.

EYES (make 2): With O, ch 4; sl st in first ch to form ring.

Rnd 1: Ch 1, 5 sc in ring. Sl st in ch 1.

Rnd 2: Ch 1, 2 sc in each sc around. Cut O. Insert hook in next st, pull W through st and lp on hook.

Rnd 3: With W, ch 1, * sc in next st, 2 sc in next st, repeat from * around. Join; end off. Sew buttons on eyes; sew eyes to head.

With O, sc head pieces tog, stuffing head before closing last edge. Join; cut O. With W, sc around edge. Join; end off.

BODY: With O, ch 26. Work in sc on 25 sts for 6 rows.

Fold piece in half (12 sts each half), sc all around folded piece, including fold edge, joining sides. End off. With B, sc around piece. End off. With W, sc around piece. End off. Center body below head. With W, sc body to head.

LEGS: Cut 8 strands of B, W and O 22″ long. Mark off 3 center W sts at bottom of body. Draw 4 W strands through next st to the left; pull to make 8 even ends. Repeat with 4 O strands in next st to left; repeat with 4 B strands in next st. Braid ends; tie ends tog with separate B strand 2″ from bottom. Make other leg the same.

O'MALLEY
Shown on page 195

SIZE: 13″ long, plus legs.

MATERIALS: Rayon and cotton rug yarn, 4 70-yard skeins orange (O), 1 skein each white (W) and black (B). Aluminum crochet hook, size G. Cotton for stuffing. Two black buttons.

GAUGE: 7 sc = 2″; 3 rows = 1″.

BODY (make 2 pieces): With O, ch 25.

Row 1: Sc in 2nd ch from hook and in each remaining ch—24 sc. Ch 1, turn.

Rows 2-24: Sc in each sc across. Ch 1, turn each row.

Rows 25-34: Sk first st, sc in each st to 2 sts from end, sk next st, sc in next st. Ch 1, turn each row. When 4 sts remain, ch 1, sc all around piece. Join to first sc. End off.

With W, sc 2 body pieces tog, stuffing with cotton. With B, sc all around body.

WING (make 2): With O, ch 4. Sl st in first ch to form ring.

Rnd 1: 6 sc in ring. Do not join rnds with sl st; mark end of rnds.

Rnd 2: 2 sc in each sc around—12 sc.

Rnd 3: * 2 sc in next sc, sc in next sc, repeat from * around—18 sc.

Rnd 4: * Sc in each of next 2 sc, 2 sc in next sc, repeat from * around—24 sc.

Rnd 5: * Sc in each of next 5 sc, 2 sc in next sc, repeat from * around—28 sc.

Rnd 6: * Sc in each of next 6 sc, 2 sc in next sc, repeat from * around—32 sc.

Rnd 7: * 2 sc in next sc, sc in each of next 3 sc, repeat from * around—40 sc.

Rnd 8: * 2 sc in next sc, sc in each of next 9 sc, repeat from * around—44 sc.

Rnd 9: * Sc in each of next 10 sc, 2 sc in next sc, repeat from * around—48 sc. Sl st in next sc. Ch 1. Fold piece in half, sc edges of half circle tog, sc across folded edge. Sl st in first sc. End off.

With W, sc in each st around. With B, sc in each st around. With B, sc folded edge of wings to body, having wings meet at center top.

EYES: With W, ch 4. Sl st in first ch to form ring.

Rnd 1: Ch 1, 6 sc in ring. Join each rnd with sl st.

Rnd 2: Ch 1, 2 sc in each sc around—12 sc.

Rnd 3: Ch 1, * sc in next sc, 2 sc in next sc, repeat from * around—18 sc.

Rnd 4: Ch 1, * sc in each of 2 sc, 2 sc in next sc, repeat from * around—24 sc. End off. Make 3 more pieces the same. With W, sc 2 pieces tog for each eye.

With O, sc around each eye. With B, sc around each eye. With B, sl st eyes to top of head. Sew a button to center of each eye.

LEGS: Cut 15 strands of O, 26″ long for each leg. Pull 5 strands through 1 st at bottom of body 8 sts in from side; pull strands to make 10 even ends. Repeat in each of next 2 sts. Braid ends; tie strand near bottom.

RED RIDING HOOD
Shown on page 196

MATERIALS: Knitting worsted, 4 ply, 2 ozs. red (R), 1 oz. each of pink (P) and white (W); small amounts of black (B) and yellow (Y). Set of dp needles No. 5. Two stitch holders. Scraps of blue, pink, red, black felt. Two buttons;

one snap. Glue. Yarn needle. Small piece of gingham for tablecloth. Small straw basket. Compass.

GAUGE: 5 sts = 1″.

BODY: Beg at neck edge, with W, cast on 12 sts and divide evenly on 3 dp needles. Join; work in stockinette st (k each rnd) for 2 rnds.

Rnd 3: Inc 1 st (k in front and back of st) in each st around—24 sts. K 4 rnds.

Rnd 8: (K 1, inc 1 st in next st) 12 times—36 sts. K 20 rnds.

Next Rnd: (K 4, k 2 tog) 6 times—30 sts. K 1 rnd.

Next Rnd: (K 3, k 2 tog) 6 times—24 sts. K 1 rnd.

Divide for Legs: Sl next 12 sts on a holder (one leg); divide remaining 12 sts on 3 dp needles (2nd leg). Join; k 2 rnds. Cut W; join P. With P, k 8 rnds.

Next Rnd: (K 2 tog, k 4) twice—10 sts. K 4 rnds. Cut P; join W. K 6 rnds. Cut W; join B.

Shoe: Shape Heel: Sl front 5 sts on a holder; with 2 dp needles, work back and forth on remaining 5 sts in stockinette st (p 1 row, k 1 row) for 8 rows. Sl front 5 sts on a dp needle. Divide the 10 sts on 3 dp needles. Join; k 8 rnds.

Next Rnd: (K 2 tog, k 1) 3 times, k 1–7 sts. K 1 rnd.

Next Rnd: (K 2 tog) 3 times, k 1—4 sts. Break yarn, leaving a long end. Draw end through sts and fasten securely. Sl the 12 sts from holder to 3 dp needles. Work 2nd leg same as first leg.

HEAD: Beg at top of head, with P, cast on 9 sts and divide evenly on 3 dp needles. Join; k 2 rnds.

Rnd 3: Inc 1 st in each st around—18 sts. K 2 rnds.

Rnd 6: (K 1, inc 1 st in next st) 9 times—27 sts. K 18 rnds.

Divide for Chin: Sl next 9 sts on a holder (chin); divide remaining 18 sts on 3 dp needles (neck). Join; k 4 rnds. Bind off.

Chin: Sl 9 sts from holder to dp needle. From right side, join P.

Rows 1-3: With 2 dp needles, work in stockinette st, dec 1 st each side every row—3 sts. Work 2 rows even. Break yarn, leaving a long end. Draw end through sts and fasten. Sew chin in opening.

NOSE: Working with 2 dp needles, with P, cast on 3 sts. Work in stockinette st for 4 rows. Break yarn, leaving a long end. Draw end through sts and around all edges; pull end tightly forming a ball.

ARMS (make 2): Beg at upper edge, with W, cast on 9 sts and divide evenly on 3 dp needles. Join; k 9 rnds. Cut W, join P.

Next Rnd: K 2 tog, k 2, k 2 tog, k 3—7 sts. K 4 rnds.

Shape Elbow: Sl next 3 sts on a holder. With 2 needles, work back and forth in stockinette st on remaining 4 sts for 6 rows. Sl 3 sts from holder on dp needle. Divide 7 sts on 3 dp needles. Join; k 10 rnds.

Next Rnd: K 2 tog, k 1, k 2 tog, k 2 tog—4 sts. K 1 rnd.

Hand: Next Rnd: Inc 1 st in each st around—8 sts. K 4 rnds.

Next Rnd: (K 2 tog, k 2) twice—6 sts. Break yarn, leaving a long end. Stuff hand. Draw end through sts and fasten.

SKIRT: Beg at waistline, working with 2 dp needles, with R, cast on 40 sts. Work in ribbing of k 2, p 2 for 4 rows.

Row 5: Bind off 2 sts, k across—38 sts. P 1 row.

Row 7: (Inc 1 st in next st, k 18) twice—40 sts. Divide sts on 3 dp needles; join, k 7 rnds.

Next Rnd: (K 3, inc 1 st in next st) 10 times—50 sts. K 7 rnds. P 1 rnd, k 1 rnd, p 1 rnd. Bind off in k.

STRAPS (make 2): Working with 2 dp needles, with R, cast on 3 sts. Work in garter st (k each row) for 5 ″.

Next Row (buttonhole row): K 1, yo, k 2 tog. K 1 row. Bind off. Close back of skirt with a snap. Sew buttons to front waistline 2″ apart. Button straps; cross in back and sew ends to back waistline 1″ on each side of opening.

CAPE: Beg at lower edge, with 2 dp needles and R, cast on 66 sts. Work in stockinette st for 22 rows, end p row.

Arm Opening: K 13, bind off next 4 sts, k until 32 sts from bound-off sts, bind off next 4 sts, finish row.

Next Row: P, cast on 4 sts over bound-off sts. Work 8 rows, end p row.

Next Row: (K 4, k 2 tog) 11 times—55 sts. Work 3 rows even.

Next Row: (K 3, k 2 tog) 11 times—44 sts. P 1 row.

Shape Neck: Bind off 10 sts at beg of next 2 rows—24 sts.

Hood: Work in stockinette st for 26 rows. Bind off. Fold bound-off edge in half; weave top for top of hood. Run a piece of yarn around hood and neck for tie.

FINISHING: Sew heel to foot, elbow to arm. Stuff arms; sew top of arm. Stuff body and legs firmly. Sew arms to body. Sew top of head; stuff firmly and sew to body. Sew on nose. Cut 32 strands of Y 6″ long; glue down back of head, forming bangs at front. Cut 22 strands of Y 8″ long. Sew across top of head. From white felt, cut a 2½″-diameter circle. Slit to center; cut out a 1½″ circle from center; cut strip in half; glue in place for collar. Glue a white felt strip 2″ × ½″ on each arm. From felt, cut pink circles for cheeks, red crescent for mouth; glue. Cut a blue star ½″ diameter; cut in half; glue in place for eyes; glue on a black circle for pupil. Pink edge of gingham for tablecloth; put in basket.

GRANDMA
Shown on page 196

MATERIALS: Knitting worsted, 4 ply, 1½ ozs. pink (P), 1 oz. white (W) and small amount of gray. Set of dp needles No. 5. Steel crochet hook No. 1. Two stitch holders. Cotton batting. Scraps of dark pink, red, blue, yellow, black, green felt. Cotton flannel, ⅓ yard. Cotton eyelet edging, 1¾ yards 1″ wide. Pipe cleaners. Yarn needle. Glue. Snap fastener. Matching sewing thread. Round elastic. Lightweight cardboard.

GAUGE: 5 sts = 1″.

BODY: Beg at neck edge, with W, cast on 15 sts and divide evenly on 3 dp needles. Join; work in stockinette st (k each rnd) for 3 rnds.

Rnd 4: Inc 1 st (k in front and back of st) in each st around—30 sts. K 3 rnds.

Rnd 8: (K 1, inc 1 st in next st) 15 times—45 sts. K 3 rnds.

Rnd 12: (K 1, inc 1 st in next st) 7 times, k 31—52 sts. K 9 rnds.

Rnd 22: (K 1, k 2 tog) 7 times, k 31—45 sts. K 8 rnds.

Rnd 31: (K 2 tog, k 7) 5 times—40 sts. K 2 rnds.

Rnd 34: (K 4, inc 1 st in next st) 8 times—48 sts. K 8 rnds.

Rnd 43: (K 2 tog, k 4) 8 times—40 sts. K 1 rnd.

Rnd 45: (K 2 tog, k 8) 4 times—36 sts.

Divide for Legs: Sl next 18 sts on a holder (one leg); divide remaining 18 sts on 3 dp needles (2nd leg). Join; k 2 rnds. Cut W; join P. With P, k 10 rnds.

Next Rnd: (K 2 tog, k 1) 6 times—12 sts. K 11 rnds.

Shape Heel: Sl front 6 sts on a holder; with 2 dp needles, work back and forth on remaining 6 sts in stockinette st (p 1 row, k 1 row) for 8 rows. Sl front 6 sts on a dp needle. Divide the 12 sts on 3 dp needles. Join; k 10 rnds. Bind off. Sl the 18 sts from holder to 3 dp needles. Join W; work same as first leg.

HEAD: Beg at top of head, with P, cast on 9 sts and divide evenly on 3 dp needles. Join; k 2 rnds.

Rnd 3: Inc 1 st in each st around—18 sts. K 2 rnds.

Rnd 6: Inc 1 st in each st around—36 sts. K 2 rnds.

Rnd 9: (K 5, inc 1 st in next st) 6 times—42 sts. K 16 rnds.

Divide for Chin: Sl next 14 sts on a holder (chin); divide remaining 28 sts on 3 dp needles (neck). Join; k 5 rnds. Bind off.

Chin: Sl 14 sts from holder to dp needle. From right side, join P. With 2 dp needles, work in stockinette st, dec 1 st each side every row for 5 rows—4 sts. Work 1 row. Break yarn leaving an end; draw through sts; fasten. Sew chin in opening.

NOSE: Working with 2 dp needles, with P, cast on 4 sts. Work in stockinette st for 5 rows. Break yarn leaving a 12″ end. Draw end through sts and around all edges; pull end tightly forming a ball.

EARS (make 2): Working with 2 dp needles, with P, cast on 6 sts. Work in stockinette st for 4 rows, end p row.

Next Row: K 2 tog, k 2, k 2 tog—3 sts. P 1 row. Break yarn, leaving a 12″ end. Draw end through sts.

ARMS (make 2): Beg at upper edge, with P, cast on 15 sts and divide evenly on 3 dp needles. Join; k 18 rnds.

Shape Elbow: Sl next 7 sts on a holder. With 2 needles, work back and forth in stockinette st on remaining 8 sts for 4 rows. Sl 7 sts from holder to dp needle. Divide 15 sts on 3 dp needles. Join; k 2 rnds.

Next Rnd: (K 2 tog, k 3) 3 times—12 sts. K 11 rnds.

Next Rnd: (K 2 tog, k 1) 4 times—8 sts. K 2 rnds.

Hand: Next Rnd: (K 1, inc 1 st in next st) 4 times—12 sts. K 4 rnds.

Next Rnd: (K 2 tog, k 4) twice—10 sts. K 4 rnds. Bind off. Stuff hand; sew lower edge straight across.

FINISHING: Sew heel to foot; elbow to arm. Stuff arms; sew top of arms. Stuff legs and body firmly; weave front of foot. Sew top of head. Stuff head; sew to body. With knit side facing front of head, sew ears to head. Sew on nose. Cut about fifty 10″ strands of gray. With crochet hook, insert hook in a st at center front hairline, catch center of a strand, pull lp through st, pull ends of strand through lp; tighten knot. Repeat along hairline as shown. Twist into a bun at back of head; tack in place. Glue a short strand over front ear seam. From felt, cut black ¼″ half circles for pupils, blue ½″ half circles for eyes, red ½″ crescent for mouth. Glue in place. Form glasses from pipe cleaners. Using sole of foot for pattern, cut cardboard for slipper sole. Cut four pieces of dark pink felt same size, for soles and inner soles. Cut two pink strips 1″ × 2½″ for tops. Cover cardboard with felt; glue tops between inner sole and cardboard. Cover edges with ⅛″ yellow strip. Cut yellow flowers, pink centers and green leaves; glue to top of slippers.

GOWN: Cut flannel 8½″ × 24″ for skirt. Cut top 12″ × 9″. Fold top in half lengthwise. Make 3″ slit across center top for head opening; slit down center of one half for back opening. Make a wedge on each side for sleeves as follows: at lower edge, measure 2″ in; mark. Measure ¾″ up side edge; mark, then draw a line in for 3″; mark. Draw a line from 3″ mark to 2″ mark; cut out shape. Hem back slit and neck edge. Sew sleeve seams. Sew back of skirt up for 5″ from lower edge; gather; sew to top. Adjust length. Sew slightly gathered eyelet to neck, sleeve, and lower edges. Close back neck with a snap fastener.

CAP: Cut a 3½″ flannel circle. Hem edge to wrong side over round elastic. Sew gathered eyelet around circle.

WOLF
Shown on page 196

SIZE: About 14″ tall.
MATERIALS: Knitting worsted, 4 ply,

2½ ozs. dark gray (G), 1¼ ozs. blue (B). Set of dp needles No. 5. Steel crochet hook No. 1. Two stitch holders. Two buttons. Scraps of red, white, black, pink felt. Cotton batting. Pipe cleaner. Yarn needle. Red sewing thread.

GAUGE: 5 sts = 1".

BODY: Beg at neck edge, with G, cast on 15 sts and divide evenly on 3 dp needles. Join; work in stockinette st (k each rnd) for 3 rnds.

Rnd 4: Inc 1 st (k in front and back of st) in each st around—30 sts. K 3 rnds.

Rnd 8: (K 1, inc 1 st in next st) 15 times—45 sts. K 3 rnds.

Rnd 12: (K 4, inc 1 st in next st) 9 times—54 sts. K 18 rnds.

Next Rnd: (K 2 tog, k 4) 9 times—45 sts. K 10 rnds.

Next Rnd: (K 7, k 2 tog) 5 times—40 sts. K 2 rnds.

Divide for Legs: Sl next 20 sts on a holder (one leg); divide remaining 20 sts on 3 dp needles (2nd leg). Join; k 12 rnds.

Next Rnd: (K 2, k 2 tog) 5 times—15 sts. K 10 rnds.

Shape Heel: Sl front 7 sts on a holder; with 2 dp needles, work back and forth on remaining 8 sts in stockinette st (p 1 row, k 1 row) for 8 rows. Sl front 7 sts on a dp needle. Divide 15 sts on 3 needles. Join; k 4 rnds.

Next Rnd: Inc 1 st in first st, k 5, inc 1 st in next st, k 8—17 sts. K 11 rnds. Bind off.

Sl the 20 sts from holder to 3 dp needles. Work 2nd leg same as first leg.

HEAD: Beg at top of head, with G, cast on 9 sts and divide evenly on 3 dp needles. Join; k 2 rnds.

Rnd 3: Inc 1 st in each st around—18 sts. K 2 rnds.

Rnd 6: Inc 1 st in each st around—36 sts. K 2 rnds.

Rnd 9: (K 5, inc 1 st in next st) 6 times—42 sts. K 18 rnds.

Next Rnd: K 2 tog around—21 sts. K 4 rnds. Bind off.

MUZZLE: Beg at base, with G, cast on 24 sts and divide evenly on 3 dp needles. Join; k 4 rnds.

Divide Work: Sl next 14 sts on a holder (top); with 2 dp needles, work back and forth in stockinette st on remaining 10 sts (bottom) for 7 rows.

Next Row: Dec 1 st each side—8 sts. Work 2 rows. Repeat last 3 rows—6 sts. Bind off.

Sl the 14 sts to dp needle. Join G; work back and forth in stockinette st for 7 rows.

Next Row: Dec 1 st each side—12 sts. Work 2 rows. Repeat last 3 rows—10 sts.

Next Row: Dec 1 st each side—8 sts. Work 1 row. Bind off.

ARMS (make 2): Beg at upper edge, with G, cast on 15 sts and divide evenly on 3 dp needles. Join; k 20 rnds.

Shape Elbow: Sl next 7 sts on a holder. With 2 needles, work back and forth on

remaining 8 sts in stockinette st for 4 rows. Sl 7 sts from holder to dp needle. Divide 15 sts on 3 needles. Join; k 2 rnds.

Next Rnd: (K 2 tog, k 3) 3 times—12 sts. K 11 rnds.

Next Rnd: (K 2 tog, k 1) 4 times—8 sts. K 1 rnd.

Hand: Next Rnd: Inc 1 st in each st around—16 sts. K 4 rnds.

Next Rnd: (K 2 tog, k 2) 4 times—12 sts. K 4 rnds. Bind off.

Stuff hands. Cut two ¾"-square pieces of white felt. On each, make one edge jagged, for claws. Insert straight edge in tip of hand. Sew across.

EARS (make 2): Working with 2 dp needles, with G, cast on 9 sts. Work in stockinette st for 4 rows.

Next Row: Dec 1 st each side—7 sts. Work 3 rows.

Next Row: Dec 1 st each side. Work 1 row.

Next Row: Dec 1 st each side—3 sts. Work 1 row. Break yarn, leaving a long end. Draw end through sts; fasten securely.

TAIL: With G, cast on 9 sts and divide evenly on 3 dp needles. Join; work in stockinette st for 9" or desired length.

Next Rnd: (K 2 tog, k 1) 3 times—6 sts. K 1 rnd.

Next Rnd: K 2 tog around—3 sts. Break yarn, leaving a long end. Draw end through sts; fasten securely.

PANTS: Beg at waistline, with B, cast on 48 sts and divide on 3 dp needles. Join; (k 1 rnd, p 1 rnd) 3 times. K 13 rnds.

Next Rnd: (K 2 tog, k 4) 8 times—40 sts. K 1 rnd.

Divide for Legs: Sl next 20 sts on a holder (one leg); divide remaining 20 sts on 3 dp needles (2nd leg). Join; k 18 rnds. P 1 rnd, k 1 rnd, p 1 rnd. Bind off in k.

Sl the 20 sts from holder to 3 dp needles. Join B; work same as first leg.

STRAPS (make 2): Working with 2 dp needles, with B, cast on 6 sts. Work in garter st (k each row) for 10".

Next Row (buttonhole row): K 2, bind off next 2 sts, finish row.

Next Row: Cast on 2 sts over bound-off sts. K 2 rows. Bind off.

FINISHING: Sew heel to foot; elbow to arm. Stuff arms. Sew top of arm. From white felt, make foot claws in same manner as hand claws, cutting felt 1½" × ¾". Insert in tip of foot; sew across. Stuff body and legs firmly; sew arms to body. Sew top of head; stuff firmly and sew to body. For inner mouth, cut red felt and cardboard ovals 3¾" long × 1½" wide. Fold widthwise so that one part is slightly shorter (lower mouth). Glue felt to cardboard. Open knitted muzzle and sew felt inner mouth to muzzle. Stuff muzzle and sew to face. Cut red felt tongue 2" × ½". Round one end; glue other end to back of mouth. From felt, cut ¾" white circle; cut in

half for eyes. Cut two ¼" black felt ovals for pupils. Cut ½" black half-circle for nose. Using ear for pat, cut two pink inner ears. Cut white felt 1¼" long, ⅝" wide; make fangs on long edge. Glue features in place; glue pink felt to wrong side of ears. Sew ears in place. Sew two buttons at waistline of pants, 2" apart. Put pants on wolf. Button straps; cross in back, sew ends to back waistline 2" apart. Wind G evenly around a 1¼" × 20" piece of thin cardboard. Machine-stitch across top; remove cardboard. Insert pipe cleaner in tail. Wind and sew loop-strip around tail. Cut bottom loops and trim. Sew tail to back above pants. Wind G around a 1" × 6" piece of cardboard. Machine-stitch as for tail; cut in half and sew in an inverted "V" on each side of face for whiskers. With crochet hook, knot several strands of G to head between ears, and to chest as for Grandma's hair.

PLAY OUTFIT
Shown on page 197

SIZE: Fits 15"-17" toddler doll.

MATERIALS: Knitting worsted, 1½ ozs. light pink, 1 oz. dark pink. Knitting needles No. 4. Steel crochet hook No. 0. Three snap fasteners.

GAUGE: 11 sts = 2"; 8 rows = 1" (stockinette st).

TOP: FRONT: Beg at lower edge, with light pink, cast on 50 sts.

Rows 1-4: Knit.

Row 5 (wrong side): Purl.

Row 6: Knit.

Rows 7-18: Repeat rows 1-6 twice.

Rows 19-23: Repeat rows 1-5.

Shape Armholes: Bind off 4 sts, k until 3 sts from bound-off sts, (k 2 tog) 18 times, k 7.

Next Row: Bind off 5 sts, p across to last 2 sts, p 2 tog—22 sts. Work in stockinette st (k 1 row, p 1 row) for 10 rows, end p side.

Shape Neck: K 9 sts, join another ball of yarn, bind off next 4 sts, finish row —9 sts each side. Working on both sides at once, p 1 row. **Next Row:** K, dec 1 st at each neck edge. Work even for 6 rows. Bind off.

RIGHT BACK: With light pink, cast on 25 sts. Work rows 1-23 same as for front, end wrong side.

Shape Armholes: Bind off 4 sts, work until 3 sts from bound-off sts, (k 2 tog) 9 times—12 sts.

Next Row: P, dec 1 st at arm side— 11 sts. Work even in stockinette st for 13 rows, end neck edge. (**Note:** Work 1 row less on left back.)

Next Row: Bind off 2 sts, finish row. Dec 1 st at neck edge on next row—8 sts. Work even for 5 rows. Bind off.

LEFT BACK: Cast on, work rows 1-23 same as for right back.

Row 24: (K 2 tog) 9 times, k 7—16 sts.

Row 25: Bind off 5 sts, finish row— 11 sts. Complete as for right back.

Sew shoulder seams.

Sleeves: From right side, pick up and k 28 sts around armhole. Work in stockinette st for 11 rows. Bind off.

FINISHING: Steam-press piece lightly. Use steam iron, or damp cloth and dry iron. Sew side and sleeve seams. From right side, with light pink, work 1 row sc around back opening, neck edge, and sleeve edges. Close back opening with 3 evenly spaced snap fasteners.

PANTS: FIRST SIDE: Starting at waistband, with dark pink, cast on 28 sts. Work in k 1, p 1 ribbing for 4 rows, inc 1 st each side on last row—30 sts. Work 9 rows even in stockinette st (k 1 row, p 1 row).

Next Row: * Inc 1 st each side. Work 6 rows even. Repeat from * once—34 sts.

Shape Crotch: Cast on 3 sts at the beg of the next 2 rows—40 sts. Work in stockinette st, dec 1 st each side every 3rd row 5 times—30 sts. Bind off. Make other side same way.

FINISHING: Steam-press pieces lightly. Sew leg seams. Sew center front and back seams. With light pink, work 2 rows sc around each leg edge.

GARTER STITCH CAT
Shown on page 197

SIZE: About 12″ high.

MATERIALS: Medium weight mohair, 3 40-gram balls. Knitting needles No. 6. Tapestry needle. Cotton batting for stuffing. Six-strand embroidery floss, 1 skein black. Scraps of white, black, pink and yellow felt. Sewing thread to match felt. Two black buttons, ⅝″. Ribbon, ¾ yard.

GAUGE: 5 sts = 1″; 10 rows (5 ridges) = 1″.

CAT: HEAD: Front: Beg at neck, cast on 9 sts. **Rows 1 and 2:** Knit.

Row 3: Inc 1 st (k in front and back of same st) in each st across—18 sts.

Row 4: Inc 1 st in each of first 2 sts, k to last 3 sts, inc 1 st in each of last 3 sts—23 sts. Work even in garter st (k each row) for 28 rows (14 ridges).

Next Row: K, dec 1 st each side—21 sts. K 1 row even. Repeat last 2 rows twice more—17 sts. Bind off.

Back: Work as for front; do not bind off.

Shape Ears: K 5, join another ball of yarn, bind off next 7 sts, finish row—5 sts each side. Working on both sides at once, k 5 rows.

Next Row: K, dec 1 st each side—3 sts. K 2 rows even. K 3 tog. End off.

Cut 2 yellow pieces of felt slightly larger than ears. Make crease in center of each to fit ears. With matching thread, sew to front of each ear. Sew top of head tog, catching felt slightly. Leave neck edge open.

BODY: Side Section: Beg at top of neck, cast on 12 sts. Work in garter st for 12 rows (6 ridges). Cast on 4 sts at beg of next row for back. Cast on 4 sts at beg of rows at back edge 3 times more—28 sts. Work even for 32 rows (16 ridges) above last cast-on sts.

Shape Legs: Work first 9 sts, join another ball of yarn, bind off center 10 sts, finish row. Work even on both sides at once for 3 rows.

Dec Row: Dec 1 st at beg of row on first leg (outside edge); dec 1 st at end of row on 2nd leg (outside edge). Work even on 8 sts of each leg for 6 rows. Repeat dec row once more. Work even on 7 sts of each leg for 8 rows. Bind off. Make another side section in same way. Sew sides of neck and top of back tog. Sew head to body.

INNER FORELEG SECTION: Beg at lower edge, cast on 10 sts. Work in garter st, inc 1 st at beg of every 8th row (outside edge) twice. Work even on 12 sts for 6 rows, ending at even edge (inside edge).

Shape Top: Dec 1 st at beg of next row (inside edge), then dec 1 st at same edge every other row until 3 sts remain. Bind off. Make another piece in same way. Sew tog top dec edges of inner hind legs. Sew inner legs to body forelegs, easing in extra rows of inner legs, with top point ending 9 ridge rows above legs at front edge of body. Sew front seam of body tog above forelegs; leave lower edges of legs open.

INNER HIND LEG SECTION: Work as for inner foreleg section to top shaping.

Shape Top: Bind off 2 sts at beg of each row at inside edge 6 times. End off. Make another piece in same way. Sew tog top bound-off edges of inner hind legs. Sew inner legs to body hind legs, easing in extra rows of inner legs, with top point ending 5 ridge rows above legs on back edge of body. Sew back seam of body tog above hind legs.

Stuff head, body forelegs and hind legs firmly; sew bottom of body tog.

TAIL: Beg at larger end, cast on 11 sts. Work in garter st, dec 1 st each side every 1½″ twice—7 sts. Work even until piece measures 7″ from start. Bind off (tip). Fold tail over a tapered roll of stuffing and sew long edges of tail tog. Sew larger end of tail to body.

FINISHING: Cut four pink felt circles the size of a quarter; with matching sewing thread, sew over opening at bottom of feet for soles. Cut two white felt ovals, ¾″ x 1½″, for eyes. Sew a black button in center of each, for pupils. Sew eyes in place as shown with buttonhole st. From black felt, cut ⅝″ triangle, for nose. Sew in place with matching thread. With embroidery floss, embroider black mouth under nose, using outline st. From pink felt, cut ½″ teardrop shape, for tongue. Sew pointed end at mouth, slightly off center. Tack three 2″ pieces of black floss each side of nose for whiskers; stiffen with glue. Tie ribbon bow around neck.

WEE FOLK
Shown on pages 198 and 199

SIZE: About 8″ tall, excluding hat.

MATERIALS: Knitting worsted, small amounts: red and white for Santa; brown, tan and orange, green, red and yellow for the two elves; white and yellow for pixie; turquoise and yellow for sailor; red and black for soldier; green and orange for leprechaun; blue, orange, yellow, green, red, white for clown. Knitting needles No. 3. Rayon-covered pink styrofoam balls (with hole in center), 1½″ diameter. 12″ pipe cleaners or chenille sticks. Scraps of felt (see individual directions). Fabric glue. Pink "pearl" and straight pin for nose (Santa, clown, leprechaun). Cotton batting. Thread to match felt. Lightweight cardboard. Yarn needle. Compass.

GAUGE: 11 sts = 2″.

GENERAL DIRECTIONS: BODY: Cast on 32 sts. Work in garter st (k each row) for 18 rows. Bind off. Fold piece in half widthwise. Weave side seams. Stuff lightly. Weave top seam.

LEG: Cast on 18 sts. K 10 rows. Bind off. Weave cast-on and bound-off edges tog.

ARM: Cast on 16 sts. K 8 rows. Bind off. Finish as for leg.

POINTED CAP (for Santa, elves, clown): Cast on 23 sts. K 4 rows.

Row 5: K 10, k 2 tog, k 11—22 sts.

Row 6: (K 2 tog, k 9) twice—20 sts. K 2 rows even.

Row 9: (K 2 tog, k 8) twice—18 sts.

Rows 10, 12, 14, and 16: Knit.

Row 11: (K 2 tog, k 7) twice—16 sts.

Row 13: (K 2 tog, k 6) twice—14 sts.

Row 15: (K 2 tog, k 5) twice—12 sts.

Row 17: (K 2 tog, k 4) twice—10 sts. K 9 rows even.

Row 27: (K 2 tog, k 3) twice—8 sts. K 3 rows even.

Row 31: (K 2 tog, k 2) twice—6 sts. K 3 rows even.

Row 35: (K 2 tog, k 1) twice—4 sts. K 9 rows even.

Next Row: K 2 tog twice. K 2 rows even. Break yarn; run through remaining 2 sts; pull up tightly; fasten. Weave seam.

SOLDIER HAT: Cast on 23 sts. K 30 rows. **Next Row:** K 10, k 2 tog, k 11. **Next Row:** K 2 tog across—11 sts. K 2 rows even.

Next Row: K 1, (k 2 tog) 5 times—6 sts. K 1 row even. Break yarn, run through sts; pull up tightly, fasten. Weave seam.

FINISHING: Fold a 12" pipe cleaner in half. Insert through hole in styrofoam ball, bending looped piece at top to hold in place. Put ends through top center of body; bring one end out at each side, ¼" below top. Pull so that the stick does not show under head. Place a knitted arm on each extension. Sew to body. Run a pipe cleaner through bottom of body having ends extend at each seam slightly to front. Place a knitted leg on each extension; sew to body.

Felt Pieces: Where indicated, cut pieces from felt using pats. Enlarge pats by copying on paper ruled in ½" squares. Complete half-patterns indicated by dash lines. For shoes, slit the two tops only; two bottom pieces are cut without the slit. Sew mitts and slippers tog with matching sewing thread, using an overcast stitch. Features and details are of felt unless otherwise noted.

SANTA: With red yarn, make body, arms, legs and pointed cap. Cut two ¼" dark blue circles for pupils (blunt at bottom end), two ⅜" wide light blue half-ovals for outer eyes. Glue to head. Glue on a small red crescent mouth. Put straight pin through hole in "pearl"; insert above mouth. Glue 2" and 3" strands of white yarn around bottom of face for beard. Cut ten 3" strands of white yarn; glue to head for hair, bringing 3 strands forward; trim for bangs. Glue on cap. Using white: cut a ⅜" wide strip to fit around bottom of cap; glue. Glue two ¾" circles tog at tip of cap; glue two ½" circles to body below head. Cut ⅜" wide strip to fit around bottom of body; glue. Cut ¼" wide black strip to fit around body; glue in place as shown with yellow belt buckle. From pats, cut four black mitts and shoes. Overcast edges of two mitts tog. Place mitts over cleaner extensions looping ends if necessary for correct length. Glue mitt to arm at wrist. Glue a ⅜" wide white strip above mitt. Cut a piece of cardboard to fit between shoe pieces, glue to bottom. With cleaner on top of cardboard, pulling up knitted leg piece if necessary, glue top to bottom (slit goes around cleaner). For shoe top, glue a ¾" wide black strip above shoe, a ⅜" wide white strip above black strip.

BROWN (GREEN) ELF: With brown (green) yarn, make body, legs, arms and pointed cap. Glue a few strands tan (yellow) yarn to front of cap for hair. Glue cap to head. Make small red

yarn ball; attach to top of cap. Glue on eyes as for Santa using dark brown and light tan (black and lime green), and red crescent mouth. Glue on two ⅜" dark pink circles for cheeks. From pats, cut two light pink ears; from tan (green), cut one collar, four mitts, two slipper tops and bottoms. Glue ears to side of head. Glue collar around neck. For brown elf, make a small orange bow; glue to collar. For green elf, knot a strand of red yarn; tack to front as shown. Assemble mitts as for Santa. On slippers, sew A to B on both sides of bottom. With long triangular sections meeting, sew top to bottom. Place a small piece of cardboard on slipper bottom; put slipper over cleaner, pulling back knitted leg piece, if necessary, to have cleaner nearly reach slipper tip. Stuff lightly; glue top to leg.

PIXIE: With white yarn, make body, legs and arms. Cut and glue face features, including ears, as for elves, using dark and light blue for eyes. Cut 18 strands of yellow yarn, 3" long. Glue over back of head, bringing strands to one side at front for bangs, as shown. From pats and white, cut collar, two slipper tops and bottoms, four mitts. Glue collar around neck. Knot a strand of narrow pink ribbon; tack to front. Assemble mitts and slippers as for elves. For skirt, cut a 4" diameter circle from white. Slit to center; cut out a 1¼" diameter circle from center. For waistline, tie a piece of white yarn tightly around body about 1¼" from bottom. Glue on skirt at waistline; overlap and glue at back.

SAILOR: With turquoise yarn, make body, legs and arms. Cut and glue felt features as for elves. For ears, cut two ⅜" light pink ovals; glue to head. From turquoise, cut a strip ½" x 4¾" and a 1½" diameter circle. Glue ends of strip tog; glue circle to strip to form hat. Glue four ½" strands of yellow yarn to inside of hat for hair; glue hat

to head. Cut a ¼" x 4" strip of red; fold in half; glue to back of hat. From pats, cut turquoise collar, red bow, four light pink hands and black shoes. Glue collar around neck; glue bow over collar at front; glue a small red circle in center of bow. Glue hands over cleaner extension. Glue shoes as for Santa.

SOLDIER: With red yarn, make body and arms; with black yarn, make legs and hat. Cut and glue felt features, including ears, as for sailor. From black, cut narrow 4" long strip; place around head in front of ears; glue at top for hat strip. Cut 1" diameter circle, cut in half; glue one half to front of hat for visor. Glue hat to head. For plumes, cut ½" x 1¼" red oval, ½" x ¾" gold oval; blunt one end; glue to hat as shown. From gold, cut four ¼" circles; from black, cut two narrow 1¼" long strips, a ¼" wide strip to fit around body; glue in place as shown. From pats, cut four white hands and black shoes. Glue on as for sailor. Cut red collar slightly smaller than collar pat; glue on around neck.

LEPRECHAUN: With green yarn, make body, legs and arms. Cut felt features as for Santa, using dark and light green for eyes. Make nose as for Santa. For hair, wind orange yarn 18 times around a ¾" piece of lightweight cardboard. Machine stitch across top; remove cardboard. Glue to chin for beard; tack a strand on each side of face for sideburns and a few loops at top of head for bangs. Cut a 2¾" diameter circle from green. Cut out a 1½" diameter circle from center. Use outer circle for brim, inner circle for hat top. Cut 1¼" x 5¼" wide strip of green for side of hat; overlap ¼"; glue. Glue top of hat to sides; sew hat to brim. Cut narrow black strip; glue over seam line. Glue on yellow buckle at front, as shown. Glue hat on head. From pats, cut two light pink ears;

Continued on page 212

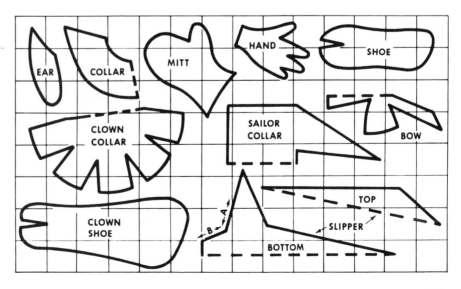

185

Children's hangers make delightful, useful gifts. "Arms" of wire hangers are padded, then covered with garter stitch piece. Powder puff heads have knit caps, yarn hair, felt features. Directions, page 170.

Happy hangers are knitted, with powder puff faces;
page 171. Plastic egg toys are crocheted,
double as rattles; page 171.

LION FAMILY

Lovable lions sport festive green outfits.
Directions, page 172.

CROCHET A MINIATURE MENAGERIE

Charming animals, stitched in simple single crochet, measure about 8″ tall, perfect stocking stuffers. To make Dressed-Up Animals, including Gray Mouse in a blue pinafore, Brown Bear in sailor's suit, Turquoise Rabbit and Black-and-White Panda in vests, just follow our complete directions on page 174.

189

Bright-eyed Basset Pup is easy to knit; page 175.

DOGGY GIFTS

Dina Dachshund, a huggable striped sausage, is in easy crochet, as is Petey Puppy. Carrying strap on pup can hold a mealtime bottle; page 176.

ADORABLE ANIMALS

We've got a case of puppy love! You see, we just couldn't resist those floppy ears and those big shiny black button eyes looking out from under all that shaggy loop-stitch hair! Delight your child on Christmas day with this easy-crochet cuddly canine; directions, page 177.

Crochet puppets with felt and pompon details; stuff head and legs with cotton. Easy to make! Green Frog, Pink Elephant, Tan Lion, Yellow Duck; directions on page 177.

WARM FUZZIES

Slightly strange and absolutely adorable, our Fuzzies make warm friends for children of all ages! This far-fetched family includes (clockwise from top far right) Hannibal (20"), O'Malley, lounging Pow Wow, skinny Shivers (36"), Lobster, Mizer, Gadberry. Single crochet, in wild orange, black and white! To make the whole Fuzzies family, turn to pages 179–181.

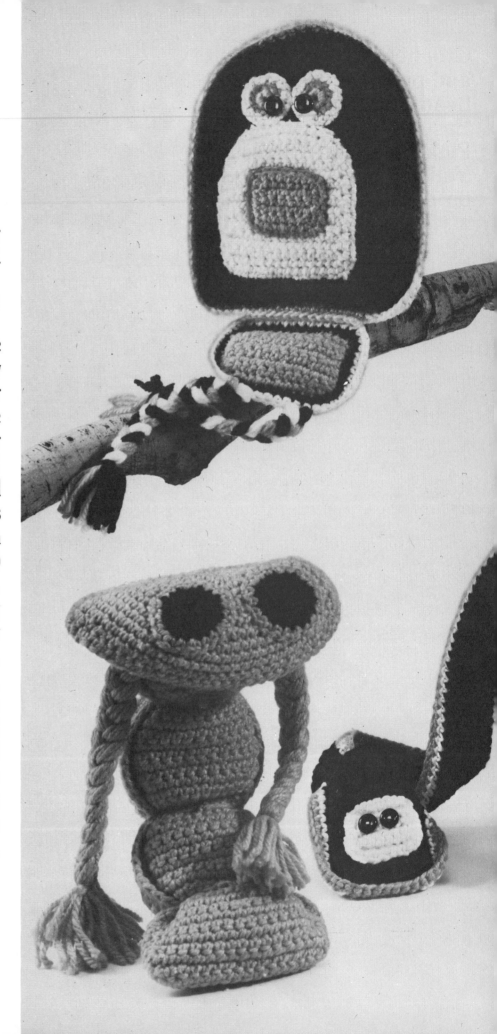

RED RIDING HOOD

Stitch a story! Knit gray Wolf in blue
overalls (14″), Red Riding Hood and Grandma;
stuff with fiberfill. Grandma's
nightgown, cap and pipe-cleaner glasses fit
Wolf, too! Directions begin on page 181.

KNITS FOR BABY DOLLS

Play separates —flared over-blouse with pattern stripes and pants— are knitted in two pinks for a toddler doll 15" to 17". Directions for Play Outfit on page 183. Her pet cat, knitted in garter stitch of mohair, has button eyes and felt paws, ears and tongue. Garter-Stitch Cat, page 184.

MILK

WEE KNIT FOLK SAY "HI"

Santa, elves and other captivating characters are easy-to-knit toys or original tree trimmings. Heads are rayon-covered Styrofoam balls; features and other details are cut from felt. Insert pipe cleaners in arms and legs for bendability. Wee Folk, page 184.

SEW A DOLL,

then knit and crochet summer and winter wardrobes for her, add sporty and dress-up shoes; Fabric Dolls, pages 212–213.

Party-time dress, (page 214); At-Home Set for 16"–17" doll, page 213.

Lace-knit cardigans
are for 22″ dolls.
Pink Lace, Powder Blue
Stripes, pages 214, 215.

DOLLS DRESS UP

Crochet a pretty
picot-edged
jacket, cap
and coverlet
in variegated
yarn; page 215.

Knit a cute three-piece
pompon-trimmed snow-
suit in pink and
white sport yarn.
Turn to page 216.

Photography by Sal Corbo.
Large Doll from Eugene Doll and Novelty Co., New York City.

Baby-doll cardigan is dainty,
with pink blossoms embroidered
at front and hem edges; page 216.

Boy doll sports a four-piece suit in stockinette stitch; his sister wears a sacque and bonnet trimmed with floral embroidery; pages 217, 218.

Baby doll bunting in garter stitch is designed for 9", 12" and 17" dolls, has zippered closing trimmed with a tassel; directions on page 218. Seed-stitch coverlet, 16", 19" or 24" square, has crocheted edging; directions, page 218.

DOLLS ON VACATION

Stitch fashion doll clothes for a fun-filled winter vacation!

For skating, knit bulky his-and-hers pullovers with "fisherman knit" mock cables; use white knitting worsted yarn. Directions for these sweaters, and the other fashions, on page 219.

For relaxing, knit a robe in winter white fingering yarn, trimmed at hem with an elegant band of gold. Crochet lounging pajamas with pull-on pants, wrap top.

Knit two pants sets for active days. Cardigan, slim slacks and hat in fingering yarn are well-suited for sightseeing. Skiers love pullover, pants and hat, in sport yarn.

WEDDING ENSEMBLES

Bride's gown and crown, page 221. Bridesmaid's set, page 221. Pink shell-stitch set, page 222. Pastel honeymoon beach outfit, page 222.

Slim knitted dress is patterned with cable bands; top with crocheted shawl.

Spaghetti-strap evening gown, crocheted in elegant scallop pattern, is worn with a lovely white shoulder cape.

Super knitted suit— sleeveless wide-rib sweater, worn over so-slim pants!

Photography by Sal Corbo.

A MINI

Carefree crocheted jumpsuit—terrific to team with a tam! Make all these fashion doll clothes with directions beginning on page 222.

Chic crocheted bateau-neck dress is caught at the waist with a colorful braided cord accent!

Crocheted top opens down the back—turn it around for a vest! Add pull-on pants and tote.

FASHION REVIEW

WEE FOLK
Continued from page 185.

glue on; cut green collar; glue around neck. Cut narrow green strip to fit around body and down front; glue on as shown. Cut four narrow triangles, ⅝" wide at base, 2" long, for coattails. Glue a 1¾" piece of cleaner between two pieces; glue to back at belt. From pats and green, cut and assemble mitts and slippers as for elves.

CLOWN: Beg with white yarn, work body, making 3 rows white, 4 rows green, 4 rows orange, 2 rows yellow, 2 rows blue, 3 rows red. Bind off in red. Make one arm with 4 rows each orange and blue, other arm 4 rows each red and white. Make legs with 3 different colors on each leg. Make pointed cap starting with 6 rows green, 6 rows yellow, 4 rows red, then vary colors and rows as desired. For eyes, cut two white diamond shapes ¾" long, ½" wide. Cut two tiny dark blue pupils. Cut two ½" red circles for cheeks, a narrow red strip for mouth. Glue features as shown. Use "pearl" and straight pin for nose. Glue a few loops of yarn to front of cap for hair; glue cap to head. Cut six white ½" circles. Glue two to cap and two to body as shown. From pats, cut white collar, four white mitts and four clown feet. Put collar around neck; sew seam. Assemble mitts and feet as for Santa. Glue a white circle at tip of each shoe.

FABRIC DOLLS
Shown on pages 200 and 201

EQUIPMENT: Paper. Pencil. Ruler. Scissors. Needle. Piece of cardboard 9" wide. Pointed dowel stick or knitting needle. Carbon paper.

MATERIALS: Cotton fabric, brown or pink, 10" x 18" for each. Sewing thread to match. Yarn for hair, black or yellow knitting worsted, ¼ ounce. Six-strand embroidery floss: black, white, and peach, or blue and pink. Kapok for stuffing.

DIRECTIONS: Enlarge patterns for body by copying on paper ruled in 1" squares; complete half-pattern indicated by dash line.

For each doll, cut two body pieces of brown or pink fabric. Trace features on head with carbon paper. Using full six strands of floss in needle, embroider eyes in satin stitch using black for brown doll and blue for pink doll; embroider back stitch in white around black eyes. Embroider nose and mouth in outline stitch, using peach for brown doll, pink for pink doll.

Place body pieces together, right sides facing, and stitch around with ¼" seams, leaving open across top of head. Clip into seams around curves and turn

right side out. Stuff dolls with kapok, using dowel stick to push stuffing into feet, legs, and arms; stuff body and head firmly. Turn in open edges across head and slip-stitch closed. Cut a strip of fabric ¾" x 3½". Turn in ¼" on each long edge. Wrap folded strip firmly around neck, overlapping ends on back; turn in end and sew in place.

For bangs, cut a 9" length of yarn; fold into several loops and tack to center front of head. For hair, wrap remainder of yarn (save a piece for tying) around the 9" piece of cardboard. Remove cardboard and tie all strands together at center with a piece of yarn. Tie strands together 1" from each end with two more pieces of yarn; do not cut end loops. Place hair over head with center tie across top of head; tack in place securely. Arrange hair to cover sides of face and back of head; tack in place around bottom of head at sides and back.

SHOE

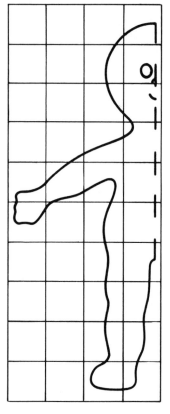

SHOES: MATERIALS: Small amount of simulated leather or felt. Strong sewing thread.

DIRECTIONS: Using actual-size pattern, below, cut 4 pieces, reversing pattern for 2 pieces. For Mary Janes, cut away striped section. Whip curved edges of 2 pieces together for each shoe.

STRIPED DRESS
Shown on page 200

MATERIALS: Wool or orlon yarn, 3 ply, ½ oz. rose. Small amounts of 4 other colors. Steel crochet hook No. 3. Two snap fasteners.

GAUGE: 5 dc = 1".

DRESS: BACK: With rose, ch 25.

Row 1: Dc in 4th ch from hook (counts as 2 dc), dc in each of next 21 ch. Ch 3, turn each row.

Row 2: Dec 1 dc over 2nd and 3rd sts.

To dec 1 dc, (yo hook, pull up a lp in next st, yo hook and through 2 lps on hook) twice, yo and through 3 lps on hook. Dc in each dc across to last 3 sts, dec 1 st over next 2 sts, dc in top of turning ch—21 dc.

Rows 3-7: Repeat row 2—11 dc.

Rows 8-10: Work even in dc. Work even on 3 sts for 2 rows for shoulder strap. End off. Join yarn in 3rd st from end. Ch 3, dc in each of last 2 sts. Work 1 more row on 3 sts; end off.

FRONT: Work as for back, beg with rose and working 1 row each of 4 colors; repeat color sequence. To change colors, work last dc of each row until there are 2 lps on hook, finish dc with new color, ch 3, turn. Make rose shoulder straps.

FINISHING: Steam-press. Sew side seams through row 8. Close straps with snaps.

CABLE-RIB SWEATER SET
Shown on page 201

MATERIALS: Fingering yarn, 3 ply, ½ oz. Knitting needles No. 2. Tapestry needle.

GAUGE: 7½ sts = 1".

PULLOVER: BACK: Beg at lower edge, cast on 25 sts loosely.

Row 1 (wrong side): * K 1, p 2, repeat from * across, end k 1.

Row 2: * P 1; make mock cable on next 2 sts (k 2 sts tog but do not slip off left needle; k in front of first of the 2 sts; slip sts off left needle); repeat from * across, end p 1.

Row 3: Repeat row 1.

Row 4: * P 1, k 2, repeat from * across end p 1.

Row 5: Repeat row 1.

Row 6: Repeat row 2.

Row 7: Repeat row 1. Beg with k row, work in stockinette st for 10 rows. Bind off 1 st at beg of next 2 rows for underarms. Work even on 23 sts for 10 rows.

Bind off 2 sts at beg of next 2 rows for shoulders—19 sts. Work collar as follows:

Row 1: * K 1, p 2, repeat from * across, end k 1.

Row 2: * P 1, k 2, repeat from * across, end p 1.

Row 3: Repeat row 1.

Row 4: * P 1, make cable on next 2 sts, repeat from * across, end p 1. Repeat rows 1-4 twice more. Repeat row 1 once more. Bind off very loosely.

FRONT: Work as for back. Weave shoulder and collar seams.

Sleeves: From right side, pick up and k 19 sts around armhole (1 st in each bound-off st, 17 sts across shoulder). Work in stockinette st for 12 rows, end with k row. Work wrist as for bottom border. Bind off.

FINISHING: Steam-press stockinette st only. Weave side and sleeve seams.

HAT: Cast on 46 sts.

Rows 1-7: Work as for Pullover Back.

Row 8: Repeat row 4. Beg with k row, work in stockinette st for 10 rows.

First Dec Row: K 1, * k 2 tog, k 4, repeat from * 7 times, k 1—38 sts. Work 5 rows even.

2nd Dec Row: K 1, * k 2 tog, k 3, repeat from * 7 times, k 1—30 sts. Work 3 rows even.

Next Row: * K 2 tog, repeat from * across. Break yarn, leaving 10″ end.

FINISHING: Steam-press. Thread end in needle, draw through remaining 15 sts. Slip off needle. Gather sts and fasten securely. Weave back seam. Turn up cuff. Make tiny pompon; sew to top of hat.

PARTY DRESS
Shown on page 201

MATERIALS: Baby yarn, 3 ply, ½ oz. pastel green. Knitting needles Nos. 2, 4, 10½. Steel crochet hook No. 7. 3″ strip ¼″ satin ribbon. Scraps of wool for flowers. 3 small snap fasteners.

GAUGE: 9 sts = 1″; 11 rows = 1″ (No. 2 needles).

GOWN: Bodice: Beg at neck edge with No. 2 needles, cast on 46 sts.

Row 1 (right side): * K 1, sl 1 as if to p, repeat from * across.

Rows 2 and 4: Purl.

Row 3: K 2, * yo, k 2 tog, repeat from * to last 2 sts, k 2.

Row 5: Knit.

Shape Armholes: Row 6: P 6, bind off next 9 sts, finish row.

Row 7: K 6, cast on 3 sts, k 16, cast on 3 sts, k 6—34 sts. P 1 row, k 1 row, p 1 row.

Shape Bodice: Row 11: K 7, put a marker on needle, k 2 tog, k 16, k 2 tog, put a marker on needle, k 7—32 sts.

Row 12: Purl, slipping markers.

Row 13: K to marker, sl marker, k 2

tog, k to within 2 sts of next marker, k 2 tog, sl marker, k to end of row—30 sts. P 1 row.

Row 15: Repeat row 13—28 sts. P 1 row, k 1 row, p 1 row.

Row 19: * K 1, sl 1 as if to p, repeat from * across. Change to No. 4 needles.

Row 20: Purl.

Inc Row: Row 21: K 1, * inc 1 st in each st to within 1 st of end (**to inc,** k in front and back of same st), end k 1—54 sts.

Row 22: P 1, inc 1 st in each st to within 1 st of end (**to inc,** p in front, k in back of same st), end p 1—106 sts.

Skirt: Row 23: With No. 10½ needles, knit.

Row 24: With No. 4 needles, knit. Repeat last 2 rows 4 times, end wrong side. With No. 4 needles, k 1 row. With No. 4 needles, bind off loosely in k.

FINISHING: Steam-press lightly, pulling down long sts on skirt. Sew back seam up for 1″ from lower edge. Work 2 rows sc around back opening. Close back opening with 3 snap fasteners. Cut notches at both ends of two 1½″ pieces of ribbon. Sew to waistline as pictured; sew lps of colored yarn to ribbon to form tiny flowers.

DOLL'S BATHING SUIT
Shown on page 201

MATERIALS: Wool or orlon 3-ply yarn, ½ oz. dark rose. Knitting needles No. 1. Steel crochet hook No. 7. One snap fastener.

GAUGE: 9 sts = 1″; 12 rows = 1″.

BATHING SUIT: Legs: Beg at lower edge of one leg, cast on 20 sts. K 3 rows. Break yarn. Leave sts on needle. On 2nd needle cast on 20 sts, work other leg piece the same.

Body: At beg of last leg made, cast on 2 sts.

Row 1: * K 4, p 4, repeat from * across leg, end p 2, cast on 4 sts, k 2 on 2nd leg piece; beg with p 4, work in pat across, end p 2, cast on 2 sts—48 sts.

Row 2: K 3, * p 4, k 4, repeat from * across, end k 1. **Row 3:** P 2, * k 4, p 4, repeat from * across, end p 2.

Row 4: K 1, * p 4, k 4, repeat from * across, end k 3.

Row 5: * P 4, k 4, repeat from * across.

Row 6: P 3, * k 4, p 4, repeat from * across, end p 1. **Row 7:** K 2, * p 4, k 4, repeat from * across, end k 2.

Row 8: P 1, * k 4, p 4, repeat from * across, end p 3. **Row 9:** * K 4, p 4, repeat from * across. Repeat rows 2-9 once, then repeat rows 2-8—24 rows.

Row 25: Bind off 15 sts, work in pat row 9 across. **Row 26:** Bind off 15 sts, k next 3 sts, work in pat across, end k 2.

Row 27 (right side): K 1, p 1; beg with p 1, work in pat to last 2 sts, p 1, k 1.

Row 28: P 1, k 1; beg with p 4, work in

pat to last 2 sts, k 1, p 1. Keeping 2 sts in ribbing each side, work in pat until bib is 1½″ long, end wrong side. K 1, p 1, k 1 for strap, bind off 12 sts, work last 3 sts for strap. Work in ribbing on strap sts for about 24 rows. Bind off. Make other strap to match.

FINISHING: Steam-press. Sew leg and crotch seam. Sew back seam for 1″. Work 1 row sc along waist edge and back opening. Sew ends of straps each side of back opening. Close back opening with snap.

RIBBED SKIRT
Shown on page 201

MATERIALS: Fingering yarn, 3 ply, ⅛ oz. Knitting needles No. 3. Small amount elastic thread.

GAUGE: 8 sts = 1″.

SKIRT: Beg at waistband, cast on 40 sts. Work in ribbing of k 1, p 1 for ½″.

Next Row: * K 1, inc 1 st in next st, repeat from * across—60 sts.

Pattern: Row 1 (right side): * K 4, p 2, repeat from * across.

Row 2: * K 2, p 4, repeat from * across. Repeat last 2 rows until piece measures 2½″ from start, end row 2. Bind off in pat.

FINISHING: Steam-press lightly. Weave back seam. Run elastic thread around inside top of skirt, drawing in to fit; fasten.

AT-HOME SET
Shown on page 202

SIZE: Fits 16″ toddler doll.

MATERIALS: Wintuk sport yarn, ½ oz. cherry red (C), 1¼ oz. white (W). Knitting needles No. 4. Steel crochet hook No. 0. Seven snap fasteners.

GAUGE: 6 sts = 1″.

SWEATER: FRONT: With C, cast on 35 sts. **Row 1** (wrong side): * P 2, k 1, repeat from * across, p 2.

Row 2: * K 2, p 1, repeat from * across, k 2. Repeat these 2 rows for ribbing pat. Work 5 more rows of C, end wrong side. Keeping to ribbing pat, work 6 rows W, 4 rows C, 6 rows W, 8 rows C.

Shape Armhole: With W, keeping to pat, bind off 4 sts at beg of next 2 rows. K 2 sts tog each side every other row 4 times, changing to C after 6 rows of W—19 sts. Work 4th row of C. Cut C. With W, work 5 sts in pat, place center 9 sts on a holder; with another strand of W, work last 5 sts in pat. Working on both sides at once, work 5 more rows. Bind off.

RIGHT BACK: With C, cast on 20 sts. Work in pat as for front to armhole.

Shape Armhole: With W, bind off 3 sts

213

at beg of row, then k 2 sts tog at same edge every other row 4 times, changing to C after 6 rows of W—13 sts. Work 4th row of C, change to W. With W, k 6 rows. Bind off 5 sts at beg of armhole edge, place remaining 8 sts on a holder.

LEFT BACK: Work as for right back, reversing shaping.

SLEEVES: With C, cast on 20 sts. With W, work in ribbing pat as for front for 6 rows. Continue in ribbing pat, work 4 rows C, 6 rows W, 8 rows C. Working 6 rows W and 4 rows C, bind off 3 sts at beg of next 2 rows, dec 1 st each side every other row 4 times. Bind off remaining sts.

FINISHING: Sew shoulder seams. Sew in sleeves, sew side and sleeve seams.

Neck Ribbing: With C, work across 8 sts of left back in k 1, p 1 ribbing, pick up and k 5 sts along left front shoulder, work in p 1, k 1 ribbing across 9 front neck sts, pick up and k 5 sts along right front shoulder, work in p 1, k 1 ribbing across 8 sts of right back—35 sts. Work in ribbing as established for 5 rows. Bind off in ribbing. Close back with 5 snap fasteners.

SLACKS: RIGHT LEG: Beg at lower edge, with W, cast on 35 sts. Work even in stockinette st (k 1 row, p 1 row) for 4½", end p row. Sl sts on holder. Work left leg the same.

Join Legs: K 35 sts of left leg, place marker on needle, k 35 sts of right leg. P 1 row—70 sts.

Next Row: K 1, sl 1, k 1, psso, k to 2 sts before marker, k 2 tog, sl marker, k 1, sl 1, k 1, psso, k to last 3 sts, k 2 tog, k 1. Work even in stockinette st for 5 rows. Repeat last 6 rows twice more. Repeat dec row once more; p 1 row. Bind off loosely.

FINISHING: Steam-press. Sew leg seams. Sew back seam; leave 1½" open at top. Beg at bottom of back opening, work 1 row sc up left side of opening around top of slacks and down right side of opening. Continue up left side of opening to top, working sc in sc. End off. Work 1 row sc around bottom of each leg. Sew 2 snap fasteners to back opening.

PARTY-TIME DRESS
Shown on page 202

SIZE: Fits 16" toddler doll.
MATERIALS: Baby Wintuk, 1 oz. pink. Knitting needles Nos. 4 and 2. Steel crochet hook No. 0. 3" zipper.
GAUGE: 6 sts = 1"; 8 rows = 1".
PUFF ST PAT: Row 1 (right side): K in front and back of st, turn; p 2, turn; k same 2 sts; with left-hand needle, pass 2nd st on right-hand needle over and off needle.

BACK: With No. 4 needles, cast on 45 sts. K 1 row, p 1 row.
Row 3 (hemline): K 2, * yo, k 2 tog, repeat from * across, end k 1.
Rows 4-10: Beg with p row, work even in stockinette st, end p row.
Row 11: K 5, * p 1, puff st in next st, p 1, k 5, repeat from * across.
Rows 12-14: P 1 row, k 1 row, p 1 row.
Row 15: K 1, * p 1, puff st in next st, p 1, k 5, repeat from * across, end p 1, k 1.
Row 16: P, dec 1 st each side—43 sts.
Rows 17 and 18: K 1 row, p 1 row.
Row 19: K 4, * p 1, puff st in next st, p 1, k 5, repeat from * across, end last repeat k 4.
Rows 20-27: Work even.
Row 28: Dec 1 st each side.
Rows 29-46: Change to No. 2 needles, dec 1 st each side on rows 36, 40 and 44—35 sts.
Divide for Back Opening: Row 47: K 17, drop yarn. Join another ball of yarn, bind off center st, finish row. Working on both sides, with separate balls of yarn, work even for 4 rows.
Row 52: Bind off 2 sts for armhole, p across.
Row 53: Bind off 2 sts, k across.
Rows 54-69: Dec 1 st at arm side of each p row 4 times, then work even on 11 sts each side.
Row 70: P 11. On right half, bind off 6 sts, finish row.
Row 71: K 5. Bind off 6 sts at neck edge of left half, finish row. Work even on 5 sts each side for 5 rows. Bind off.
FRONT: Work same as for back through row 51 but do not divide for back opening.
Rows 52 and 53: Bind off 2 sts at beg of each row.
Row 54: P 2 tog at beg and end of row—29 sts.
Row 55: K 13, p 1, puff st in next st, p 1, k 13.
Row 56: Repeat row 54—27 sts.
Row 57: K 11, k 2 tog; join another ball of yarn, bind off center st, k 2 tog, k 11.
Row 58: Repeat row 54—11 sts each side.
Row 59: K 9, k 2 tog; k 2 tog, k 9.
Row 60: Repeat row 54—9 sts each side.
Row 61: K 5, p 1, puff st in next st, k 2 tog; k 2 tog, puff st in next st, p 1, k 5. Work even on 8 sts each side for 1 row.
Row 63: K 6, k 2 tog; k 2 tog, k 6. Work even on 7 sts each side for 1 row.
Row 65: K 5, k 2 tog; k 2 tog, k 5. Work even on 6 sts each side for 1 row.
Row 67: K 3, p 1, puff st in next st, k 1; k 1, puff st in next st, p 1, k 3. Work even for 5 rows.

Row 73: Repeat row 67. Work even for 1 row. Bind off.
FINISHING: Steam-press, avoiding puff sts. Sew side and shoulder seams. Turn up hem. Sc around armhole, working 1 sc in every other st or row, sl st in first sc. * Ch 3, sk 1 sc, sl st in next sc, repeat from * around.
Neck Edge: From wrong side, sc around neck edge, work 1 sc in every other st or row. Ch 3, turn. Work as for armhole edge. Sew zipper in opening.

SHELL PINK LACE
Shown on page 203

SIZE: Fits 22" doll.
MATERIALS: Fingering yarn, 2 1-oz. skeins. Knitting needles No. 4. Three small buttons. Five stitch holders.
GAUGE: 8 sts = 1" (pattern stitch).
PATTERN STITCH (worked on a multiple of 3 sts): **Note:** Sl all sl sts as if to purl.
Row 1 (right side): K 2, * yo, sl 1, k 2, psso last 2 sts, repeat from * across, end k 1.
Row 2: Purl.
Row 3: K 1, * sl 1, k 2, psso last 2 sts, yo, repeat from * across, end k 2.
Row 4: Purl. Repeat these 4 rows for pat.
To Dec: When decreasing, k any sts of broken pats on right side, keeping to correct number of sts.
SLEEVES (make 2): Cast on 36 sts.
Seed Stitch Border: Row 1: * K 1, p 1, repeat from * across.
Row 2: * P 1, k 1, repeat from * across. Repeat these 2 rows for seed st pat, having a k 1 over a p st and p 1 over a k st, for 9 rows.
Next Row: Purl.
Next Row: K 3, work next 30 sts in row 1 of pat, k 3. Keeping first and last 3 sts in stockinette st (k 1 row, p 1 row), work in pat until sleeve measures about 5" from start, end pat row 1.
Shape Armholes: Keeping to pat, bind off 3 sts at beg of next 2 rows—30 sts. Sl these sts on a holder.
LEFT FRONT: Cast on 36 sts. Work as for sleeves for 9 rows.
Next Row: Work first 6 sts in seed st, purl across.
Next Row: Work first 3 sts in stockinette st, next 27 sts in pat, last 6 sts in seed st. Work as established until piece measures about 5" from start, end pat row 2.
Shape Armhole: Bind off first 3 sts (1 st on right-hand needle), k 3, repeat from * on pat row 3 across to last 6 sts, work last 6 sts in seed st—33 sts. Sl sts on a holder.
RIGHT FRONT: Work as for left front for 9 rows.
Next Row: P to last 6 sts, work last 6 sts in seed st.

Next Row: Work first 6 sts in seed st, next 27 sts in pattern, last 3 sts in stockinette st. Work as established until piece measures about 5″, end pat row 1.

Next Row: Bind off 3 sts, work across.

Next Row: Work first 6 sts in seed st, work pat across to last 5 sts, end with yo, k 5—33 sts. Sl sts on a holder.

BACK: Cast on 63 sts.

Row 1: * K 1, p 1, repeat from * across, end k 1. Repeat this row for seed st for 9 rows.

Next Row: Keeping first and last 3 sts in stockinette st, work in pat until piece measures about 5″ from start, end pat row 1.

Shape Armholes: Bind off 3 sts, purl across.

Next Row: Bind off 3 sts (1 st on right-hand needle), k 3, repeat from * on row 3 across to last 5 sts, end with yo, k 5—57 sts. Sl sts on a holder.

Yoke: From right side, sl sts of right front, one sleeve, back, 2nd front, left front on needle.

Joining Row (wrong side): Join yarn at left front edge. Keeping first and last 6 sts in seed st, work across—183 sts. Work yoke as follows:

Row 1: Work first 6 sts in seed st, (work in pat across next 24 sts, put a marker on needle, k 4, put a marker on needle, k 2) twice, work in pat across next 51 sts, (put a marker on needle, k 4, put a marker on needle, k 2, work in pat across next 24 sts) twice, work in seed st on last 6 sts.

Row 2: Keeping first and last 6 sts in seed st, p across, slipping markers.

Row 3: Repeat row 1, slipping markers.

Rows 4 and 5: Repeat rows 2 and 3.

Row 6: Repeat row 2.

Row 7 (buttonhole and dec row): K 1, p 1, k 2 tog, yo, k 1, p 1, * work across to 2 sts before marker, k 2 tog, sl marker, k 4, sl marker, sl 1, k 1, psso, repeat from * 3 times, finish row.

Row 8: Repeat row 2.

Row 9: Repeat row 7, omitting buttonhole.

Rows 10-32: Repeat rows 8 and 9, working a buttonhole on row 23.

Row 33: Work decs before first marker, after 4th marker, before 5th marker, and after 8th marker—4 decs-75 sts.

Row 34: Repeat row 2, removing markers.

Neckband: Work in seed st for 10 rows, working a buttonhole at the beg of the 5th row. Bind off in seed st.

FINISHING: Steam-press pieces lightly. Sew side and sleeve seams. Sew on 3 buttons opposite buttonholes.

POWDER BLUE STRIPES
Shown on page 203

SIZE: Fits 22″ doll.
MATERIALS: Fingering yarn, 2 1-oz.

skeins. Knitting needles Nos. 3 and 4. Seven small buttons. Five stitch holders.

GAUGE: 7 sts = 1″ (stockinette st, No. 4 needles).

PATTERN: Row 1 (right side): K 2, * yo, sl next 2 sts as if to k; from left to right insert left needle into fronts of these two sts and k them tog, repeat from * across, end k 2.

Row 2: P 2, repeat from * on row 1, end p 2. **Rows 3-8:** Repeat rows 1 and 2, 3 times.

Rows 9-12: Work in stockinette st (k 1 row, p 1 row). Repeat these 12 rows for pat.

SWEATER: BACK: Beg at lower edge, with No. 3 needle, cast on 64 sts. Work in ribbing of k 1, p 1 for 9 rows. Change to No. 4 needle. Work pat rows 1-12 twice, then work pat rows 1-8.

Shape Armholes: Bind off 3 sts at beg of next 2 rows. K 1 row, p 1 row.

Shape Raglan: Row 1: K 2, k 2 tog through back lps, work in pat across, end k 1, k 2 tog, k 2.

Row 2: P 4, work in pat across, end p 4.

Row 3: K 2, k 2 tog through back lps, k 2, work in pat across, end k 2, k 2 tog, k 2.

Row 4: P 5, work in pat across, end p 5.

Rows 5-8: Repeat rows 1-4.

Row 9: K 2, k 2 tog through back lps, k across, end k 2 tog, k 2. **Row 10:** Purl.

Row 11: Repeat row 9. **Row 12:** Repeat row 10. Repeat rows 1-12 once, then repeat rows 1-8—26 sts.

Row 33: Knit. Place sts on a holder for back neckband.

RIGHT FRONT: Beg at lower edge, with No. 3 needle, cast on 40 sts. Work as for back for 9 rows. Change to No. 4 needles.

Pattern: Work first 8 sts in ribbing, work 32 sts in pat. Keeping 8 sts at center front in ribbing, work as for back to end of row 32.

Shape Armholes: Next Row: Work first 8 sts in ribbing, k across.

Next Row: Bind off 3 sts at beg of row, work across. Work 2 rows even.

Shape Raglan: Row 1: Work center band and pat to last 5 sts, end k 1, k 2 tog, k 2.

Row 2: P 4, work across as established. Continue to work armhole decs as for left armhole on back to end of row 32 —21 sts. **Row 33:** Work first 8 sts in ribbing, k across. Place these sts on a holder for right front neckband.

LEFT FRONT: Work same as for right front, making the following changes: Center band is at end of right side rows; work buttonhole at beg of row 6 as follows: (K 1, p 1) twice, k 2 tog, yo, k 1, p 1, work across. Work 5 more buttonholes, one at every stockinette st band (7th buttonhole is made in neckband).

At armhole, bind off 3 sts, work across. Work 3 rows even, then shape raglan armhole as for right back armhole.

SLEEVES (make 2): Beg at lower edge, with No. 3 needles, cast on 36 sts. Work as for back through row 32.

Shape Armholes: Bind off 3 sts at beg of next 2 rows—30 sts. Work 2 rows stockinette st.

Shape Raglan: Rows 1-8: Work raglan decs as for back. **Rows 9-12:** Work even in stockinette st. **Rows 13-24:** Repeat rows 1-12 once—14 sts.

Rows 25-32: Work pat rows 1-8 without decs, working first and last 3 sts in stockinette st.

Row 33: K across. Place 14 sts on a holder.

FINISHING: Steam-press pieces lightly. Sew sleeves to armholes of back and fronts.

Neckband: From right side, sl sts of right front, one sleeve, back, 2nd sleeve, left front on No. 3 needle—96 sts. Join yarn at left front. Work in ribbing of k 1, p 1 for 4 rows. Work buttonhole on row 5. Work 4 more rows in ribbing. Bind off in ribbing.

Sew side and sleeve seams. Sew on button opposite buttonholes.

VARIEGATED BABY DOLL SET
Shown on pages 204 and 205

SIZE: Infants' size. Coverlet for baby doll, 13″ × 15″.
MATERIALS: Coats & Clark Baby Pompadour, 3 1¾-oz. balls Lullaby for sacque and cap, 1 ball for coverlet. Crochet hooks C and E. ¾ yard narrow ribbon for sacque. One yard 1″-wide ribbon for cap.
GAUGE: 5 sts = 1″; 7 rows = 3″ (pat).
SACQUE: Beg at neck, with C hook, ch 66.

Row 1: Sc in 2nd ch from hook and in each ch across—65 sc. Ch 1, turn each row.

Row 2: * Sc in 2 sc, 2 sc next sc, repeat from * across, end sc in last 2 sc—86 sc.

Rows 3-5: Sc in each sc.

Row 6: * Sc in 4 sc, 2 sc in next sc, repeat from * across, sc in last sc—103 sc.

Rows 7 and 8: Sc in each sc.

Row 9: * Sc in 6 sc, 2 sc in next sc, repeat from * across, sc in last 5 sc—117 sc.

Rows 10 and 11: Sc in each sc.

Row 12: * Sc in 6 sc, 2 sc in next sc, repeat from * across, sc in 5 sc—133 sc.

Rows 13 and 14: Sc in each sc.

Row 15: * Sc in 5 sc, 2 sc in next sc, repeat from * across, sc in last sc—155 sc.

Row 16: Sc in each sc. Change to E hook, ch 3, turn.

Pattern: Row 1 (wrong side): Sk first sc, 2 dc in next sc, * sk next sc, 2 dc in next sc, repeat from * across, end dc in last sc. Ch 3, turn.

Row 2 (right side): Dc in next dc, dc around post of dc just made, * sk next dc, dc in next dc, dc around post of dc just made, repeat from * across, end dc in turning ch. Do not turn. Drop yarn. Count off 13 pat groups on back. Join strand of yarn in 2nd dc of 13th pat group, ch 5, sk next 13 pat groups for sleeve, sl st in 2nd dc of next pat group. End off. Count off 23 pat groups on back. Join yarn in 2nd dc of 23rd pat group, ch 5, sk next 13 pat groups for sleeve, sl st in 2nd dc of next pat group. End off.

Row 3 (wrong side): Pick up dropped yarn, ch 3, turn; 2 dc in next dc, * sk next dc, 2 dc in next dc, repeat from * across, working 2 pat groups on each underarm ch, end dc in top of turning ch. Ch 3, turn.

Row 4: Dc in next dc, dc around post of dc just made, * sk next dc, dc in next dc, dc around post of dc just made, repeat from * across, end dc in turning ch. Ch 3, turn.

Row 5: 2 dc in next dc, * sk next dc, 2 dc in next dc, repeat from * across, end dc in top of turning ch, ch 3, turn. Repeat rows 4 and 5 until there are 17 pat rows altogether, end pat row 5. Ch 1, turn. Sc in each dc across. End off.

Sleeves: Beg on wrong side at underarm, work in pat across sleeve, making 2 pat groups on underarm ch. Work in pat for 14 more rows. Change to C hook. Ch 1, turn. Sc across, dec 4 sts in row. Work even in sc for 5 more rows. End off.

FINISHING; Sew sleeve seams. From right side, join yarn at front neck edge; ch 5, sk 2 sc, dc in next sc, * ch 2, sk 2 sc, dc in next sc, repeat from * across neck edge. End off.

From right side, join yarn at lower edge of right front. Working up front edge, * work 3 sc in edge, ch 3, sc in 3rd ch from hook for picot, repeat from * to neck edge, work same picot edging across neck edge and down left front. End off. Run ribbon through beading row at neck.

CAP: Beg at center of crown, with C hook, ch 3; sl st in first ch to form ring.

Rnd 1: 6 sc in ring.

Rnd 2: 2 sc in each sc around.

Rnd 3: (Sc in next sc, 2 sc in next sc) 6 times.

Rnd 4: (Sc in 2 sc, 2 sc in next sc) 6 times.

Rnd 5: (Sc in 3 sc, 2 sc in next sc) 6 times—30 sc.

Rnds 6-12: Continue to inc 6 sc evenly spaced around—72 sc.

Rnds 13 and 14: Work even in sc. At end of rnd 14, ch 3, turn. Change to E hook.

Pattern: Row 1 (wrong side): Sk first sc,

2 dc in next sc, * sk next sc, 2 dc in next sc, repeat from * until there are 30 pats, dc in next sc. Ch 3, turn.

Row 2 (right side): Dc in next dc, dc around post of dc just made, * sk next dc, dc in next dc, dc around post of dc just made, repeat from * across, end dc in turning ch. Ch 3, turn. Work even in pat (rows 5 and 4 of sacque pat) until there are 6 rows of pat. Ch 1, turn. Sc in each sc across. Ch 1, turn.

Picot Edging: * Sc in 2 sc, ch 3, sc in 3rd ch from hook, repeat from * across, end sc in last sc. Do not end off. Sc across sides and back of cap, skipping every other st across back edge to pull in back. End off. Fold cap at top of 5th pat row. From right side, work picot edging across row.

Gather one end of 18″ length of 1″ ribbon into rosette; sew to side of cap at front. Repeat on other side.

DOLL'S COVERLET: With E hook, ch 75.

Row 1: 2 dc in 4th ch from hook, * sk 1 ch, 2 dc in next ch, repeat from * across, dc in last ch. Ch 3, turn.

Row 2: * Sk next dc, dc in next dc, dc around post of dc just made, repeat from * across, end dc in top of turning ch. Ch 3, turn.

Row 3: * Sk next dc, 2 dc in next dc, repeat from * across, end dc in top of turning ch. Ch 3, turn. Repeat rows 2 and 3 until there are 37 rows of pat.

Picot Edging: Working down side of coverlet, * work 2 sc, ch 3, sc in 3rd ch from hook, repeat from * to bottom edge, then repeat edging on 3 remaining sides.

DOLL'S SNOW SUIT
Shown on page 204

SIZE: 15″-16″ doll with 10″ chest.
MATERIALS: Sport yarn, 2 ozs. pink, 1 oz. white. Knitting needles No. 6. Steel crochet hook No. 00. Four small buttons. Round elastic, ¼ yd.
GAUGE: 5 sts = 1″.
SUIT: PANTS: FRONT: Beg at waist, with pink, cast on 28 sts. Work in ribbing of k 1, p 1 for 1″, inc 10 sts evenly across last row. Work in stockinette st (k 1 row, p 1 row) on 38 sts until piece is 3¼″ from start, end p row. Inc 1 st each side of next 2 rows—42 sts. Work even for 4 rows.

Shape Legs: K 21 sts; join another ball of yarn, k last 21 sts. Working on both legs at once, work even for 3½″ or 1″ less than desired length to foot, end p row.

Next Row: K 1, (k 2 tog) 9 times, k 2. Work in ribbing of k 1, p 1 on 12 sts for 1″. Work in garter st (k each row) for 10 rows. Bind off.

BACK: Work as for front.
FINISHING: Sew side, leg and foot seams. Trim front of feet with white

pompons. Run elastic through waist ribbing. Sew ends tog securely.

JACKET: Beg at lower edge of back, with pink, cast on 32 sts. Work in ribbing of k 1, p 1 for 6 rows. Work in stockinette st until piece is 2½″ from start.

Sleeves: Cast on 18 sts at beg of next 2 rows. Work even on 68 sts until sleeves measure 2½″ from cast-on edge, end p row.

Shape Neck: K 27; join another ball of yarn, bind off center 14 sts, finish row. Working on both sides at once, work even for 4 rows.

Fronts: Cast on 10 sts at each center edge—37 sts each front. Keeping 3 sts at each center edge in garter st, remaining sts in stockinette st, form buttonhole at beg of right front border on next row and every 1″ 3 times more as follows: k 1, yo, k 2 tog. When sleeves measure 4″ in all, bind off 18 sts at beg of each sleeve edge. Work even on 19 sts of each front for 2″. Work in ribbing on 16 sts, keeping center band in garter st for 6 rows. Bind off.

FINISHING: From wrong side, with white, pick up and k 30 sts around neck edge, inside center bands, for collar. Work in garter st for 8 rows. Bind off loosely. From right side, with white, pick up and k 20 sts on sleeve edge. Work in k 1, p 1 ribbing for 6 rows. Bind off in ribbing.

Sew side and sleeve seams. Sew on buttons.

HAT: With pink, beg at one neck edge, cast on 24 sts. Work in stockinette st for 8½″. Bind off (other neck edge).

Cuff: From wrong side, with white, pick up and k 52 sts along one side edge. Work in ribbing of k 1, p 1 for 1″. Bind off in ribbing.

FINISHING: Fold piece in half, sew back seam. From right side, with pink, work 1 row sc on bound off edge of cuff. Turn back cuff; tack each side edge. Trim top of hat with small white pompon. From right side, with pink, work 1 row sc on neck edge, ch 2, turn.

Beading Row: * Sc in next sc, ch 1, sk 1 sc, repeat from * across, end sc. Make a 20″ pink ch, draw through beading; trim each end with small pompon.

PINK BLOSSOMS CARDIGAN
Shown on page 205

SIZE: Fits 16″ toddler doll.
MATERIALS: Baby Wintuk, 1 oz. Few yards of pink angora for embroidery. Knitting needles Nos. 2 and 4. Crochet hook No. 0. Tapestry needle. One button. Fifteen small pink sequins and crystal beads (optional).
GAUGE: 6 sts = 1″; 8 rows = 1″ (size 4 needles).
SWEATER: BACK: With No. 4 needles, cast on 35 sts. P 1 row, k 1 row, p 1 row.

Pattern: Row 1: K 1, * yo, k 2 tog, repeat from * across, end yo, k 2.
Row 2: Purl.
Row 3: K 5, * yo, k 2 tog, k 6, repeat from * across, end yo, k 2 tog, k 4.
Row 4: Purl.
Rows 5-10: Repeat rows 3 and 4.
Rows 11-29: Repeat rows 1-10 once, rows 1-9 once.
Shape Raglan Armholes: Keeping to pat, bind off 2 sts at beg of next 2 rows. Then dec 1 st each side every p row as follows: P 1, p 2 tog, p to last 3 sts, p 2 tog, p 1. Repeat decs until 13 sts remain. Sl sts on a holder.
LEFT FRONT: Cast on 21 sts. P 1 row, k 1 row, p 1 row.
Pattern: Row 1: K 1, * yo, k 2 tog, repeat from * across.
Row 2: Purl.
Row 3: K 5, yo, k 2 tog, k 6, yo, k 2 tog, k 6.
Row 4: Purl.
Rows 5-10: Repeat rows 3 and 4. Repeat rows 1-10 twice.
Shape Raglan Armhole and Neck: Keeping to pat, bind off 2 sts at beg of next k row. Dec 1 st every p row at armhole edge 9 times; **at the same time,** when row 10 of 4th pat is worked, work row 1 of next pat, repeat to last 4 sts; put 4 sts on a holder for neckband. Continue in pat, dec 1 st at arm side every p row until 6 sts remain. P 2 tog at neck edge and dec 1 st at armhole edge—4 sts. K 2 tog, at neck edge. P 3 tog. End off.
RIGHT FRONT: Cast on 21 sts. P 1 row, k 1 row, p 1 row.
Pattern: Row 1: K 2, * yo, k 2 tog, repeat from * across, end yo, k 2 tog, k 1.
Row 2: Purl.
Row 3: K 6, yo, k 2 tog, k 6, yo, k 2 tog, k 5.
Row 4: Purl.
Rows 5-10. Repeat rows 3 and 4. Repeat rows 1-10 once, rows 1-9 once.
Shape Raglan Armhole and Neck: Keeping to pat, bind off 2 sts at beg of p row. Dec 1 st every p row (p 1, p 2 tog) 9 times; **at the same time,** when row 10 of 4th pat is worked, k 4 sts at neck edge, place on a holder; k 2, * yo, k 2 tog, repeat from * across, end k 1. Continue in pat, dec 1 st at arm side every p row until 6 sts remain. K 2 tog at neck edge on next row. Dec 1 st at armhole edge on p row. K 2 tog, k 2. P 3 tog. End off.
SLEEVES: Cast on 21 sts. P 1 row, k 1 row, p 1 row.
Row 4: K 1, * yo, k 2 tog, repeat from * across.
Row 5: Purl.
Rows 6-14: Work even in stockinette st (k 1 row, p 1 row).
Row 15: P, inc 1 st each side.
Rows 16-24: Work even—23 sts.
Row 25: Repeat row 15.
Rows 26-28: Work even—25 sts.
Shape Raglan Armholes: Bind off 2 sts

at beg of next 2 rows. Dec 1 st each side each p row, as for back, until 3 sts remain. K 3 sts tog. End off.
FINISHING: Steam-press pieces lightly. Sew side and sleeve seams. Sew in sleeves.

With No. 2 needles, k 4 sts from right front holder, pick up and k 10 sts on right front neck edge, k 13 sts from back neck holder, pick up and k 9 sts on left front neck edge, k 4 sts from left front holder—40 sts. Work in ribbing of k 2, p 2 for 4 rows. Bind off in ribbing.

Work 1 row sc on each front edge, working ch 4 button loop on right front at start of ribbing. Work over loop with buttonhole stitch; see Contents for Stitch Details.

With pink angora, work 8-petaled flower in lazy daisy stitch in each square down center fronts and around lower edge. Sew sequin and bead in center of each flower. Sew button opposite button loop. Turn up 3 rows at bottom of sweater and sleeves. Hem in place.

BABY DOLL SET
Shown on page 206

SIZE: Directions for 9″ doll. Changes for 12″ and 17″ dolls are in parentheses.
MATERIALS: Sport yarn, 1 (1-2) 1-oz. skeins. Knitting needles No. 4. Steel crochet hook No. 2. Six-strand embroidery floss, 1 skein each pink and green. One hook and eye. One stitch holder. Embroidery needle.
GAUGE: 7 sts = 1″; 9 rows = 1″.
CARDIGAN: BACK: Beg at lower edge, cast on 19 (29-39) sts.
Border: Row 1: K 1, * p 1, k 1, repeat from * across. Repeat this row for seed st border 2 (4-4) times more, end wrong side. Work in stockinette st (k 1 row, p 1 row) for 7 (9-13) rows, end right side.
Shape Sleeves: Cast on 8 (10-12) sts at end of next 2 rows—35 (49-63) sts.
Row 1 (wrong side): K 1, p 1, k 1 for seed st border, p to last 3 sts, end k 1, p 1, k 1 for seed st border.
Row 2: K 1, p 1, k 1 for border, k across to last 3 sts, end k 1, p 1, k 1. Repeat these two rows 3 (4-7) times more, then work row 1, end wrong side.
Neck Border: Row 1: K 1, p 1, k 1, k 6 (11-17), k 1, * p 1, k 1, repeat from * to last 9 (14-20) sts, k 6 (11-17), k 1, p 1, k 1.
Row 2: K 1, p 1, k 1, p 6 (11-17), k 1, * p 1, k 1, repeat from * to last 9 (14-20) sts, p 6 (11-17), k 1, p 1, k 1.
Row 3: Repeat row 1, end right side.
Neck Shaping: * K 1, p 1, k 1, p 6 (11-17), k 1, p 1, k 1, place these 12 (17-23) sts on a holder for left front, bind off next 11 (15-17) sts in pat for

neck, p 1, k 1, p 6 (11-17), k 1, p 1, k 1 —12 (17-23) sts remain for right front.
Right Front: Work even in pat as established for 5 (9-13) rows, end right side at front edge. With free needle and separate strand of yarn, cast on 6 (6-8) sts. Beg with a p 1, work these sts in seed st onto right-hand needle— 18 (23-31) sts.
Next Row (wrong side): Work 9 (9-11) sts in seed st, p 6 (11-17), work last 3 sts in seed st.
Next Row: Work 3 sts in seed st, k 6 (11-17), work 9 (9-11) sts in seed st.
Next Row: Working first and last 3 sts in seed st, p across. Continue in stockinette st, working first and last 3 sts in seed st, for 6 (6-10) more rows, end wrong side at sleeve edge.
Shape Sleeve: Bind off 8 (10-12) sts at beg of next row, work across. Keeping 3 sts at front edge in seed st, work even for 7 (9-13) rows.
Border: Work in seed st for 3 (5-5) rows. Bind off in pat.
Left Front: From wrong side, sl sts from holder to needle. From right side, join yarn at neck edge. Work to correspond to right front for 4 (8-12) rows; cast on 6 (6-8) sts at end of last row for neck. Complete as for right front, reversing shaping.

FINISHING: Steam-press lightly. Sew side and sleeve seams. From right side, beg at lower right front edge, work 1 row sc around front and neck edges, keeping work flat. End off. Work 1 rnd sc around lower sleeve edges; join with a slip st. End off.

EMBROIDERY: Use full 6 strands of floss for flower, 3 strands for leaves. Work flower petals and leaves in lazy daisy stitch around front yoke as shown. Work flower centers in French knots.

BONNET: Beg at front edge, cast on 31 (49-71) sts. Work same as for cardigan back until 14 (16-24) rows above seed st border, end wrong side. Bind off 10 (16-23) sts at beg of next 2 rows—11 (17-25) sts. Work even on these sts for 12 (18-26) rows. Leave these sts on needle.

FINISHING: Sew back edges to side edges.
Neckband: From right side, with free needle, pick up and k 6 (10-12) sts along left front edge to back seam; k 2 tog 5 (8-12) times, k 1 across sts on needle, pick up and k 7 (10-12) sts along right front edge—19 (29-37) sts. Work 3 (4-5) rows in seed st. Bind off in pat.

From right side, work 1 row sc across front edge, keeping work flat.
TIES (make 2): Join yarn in neckband, 3 (5-6) sts from front edge. Ch 25

(35-45). Sc in 2nd ch from hook and in each ch across. End off.

Embroider cap same as for cardigan, as shown.

DOLL'S COVERLET
Shown on page 206

SIZE: About 16″ (19″-24″) square.
MATERIALS: Knitting worsted, 1 (2-2) 4-oz. skeins. Knitting needles No. 10½. Crochet hook size G.
GAUGE: 4 sts = 1″; 6 rows = 1″.
COVERLET: Cast on 65 (77-95) sts.
Row 1: K 1, * p 1, k 1, repeat from * across. Repeat this row for seed st pat until piece measures about 16″ (19″-24″) from start; do not end off.
Border: Rnd 1: Keeping work flat, work 1 row sc around entire blanket. Join with sl st in first sc; do not turn.
Rnd 2: * Ch 1, sl st in next st, repeat from * around. Join; end off.
FINISHING: Steam-press lightly.

FOUR-PIECE SUIT
Shown on page 206

SIZE: Directions for 9″ doll. Changes for 12″ and 17″ dolls are in parentheses.
MATERIALS: Sport yarn, 1 (1-2) 1-oz. skeins main color (A); 1 of contrasting color (B). Knitting needles No. 4. Steel crochet hook No. 2. Five ⅜″ diameter buttons. Small amount of elastic thread. Five stitch holders. Tapestry needle.
GAUGE: 7 sts = 1″; 9 rows = 1″.
CARDIGAN: BODY: Beg at lower edge, with A, cast on 42 (64-84) sts. Work in ribbing of k 1, p 1 for 3 rows, end wrong side.
Next Row (buttonhole row): Work in ribbing to last 3 sts, yo, k 2 tog, p 1. Work 0 (1-3) more rows of ribbing. Beg with a p (k-k) row, work in stockinette st (k 1 row, p 1 row) for 5 (8-10) rows.
2nd Buttonhole Row: K to last 3 sts, yo, k 2 tog, k 1. Continue in stockinette st, repeating buttonhole row every 6th (10th-14th) row until 13 (21-29) rows above ribbing, end k row. Mark for underarm.
Next Row (dividing row): P 11 (16-22), sl these sts on a holder for left front, bind off 1 (2-2) sts for left underarm, p until 18 (28-36) sts from bound-off sts and slip on holder for back, bind off 1 (2-2) sts for right underarm, finish row—11 (16-22) sts on needle.
Right Front: Shape Raglan: K to last 3 sts, k 2 tog, k 1—10 (15-21) sts. P 1 row. Drop A; join B. (**Note:** Carry color not being used loosely up side of work.) Repeating last 2 rows, work in striped pat as follows: With B, work 2 (4-6) rows, with A, work 2 (2-4) rows, with

B, work 2 (4-6) rows. Cut B. With A, work 2 (4-4) rows, end wrong side—6 (8-11) sts. Sl sts on a holder for neckband.
Back: From wrong side, sl 18 (28-36) sts to needle. From right side, join A.
Shape Raglan: K 1, sl 1, k 1, psso, k to last 3 sts, k 2 tog, k 1—16 (26-34) sts. P 1 row. Drop A, join B. Repeating last 2 rows, work in striped pat as for right front, end wrong side—8 (12-14) sts. Sl sts to a holder.
Left Front: From wrong side, sl 11 (16-22) sts to needle. From right side join A at underarm.
Shape Raglan: K 1, sl 1, k 1, psso, k across. P 1 row. Finish to correspond to right front, working a buttonhole on the first A stripe.
SLEEVES (make 2): Beg at lower edge, with A, cast on 10 (16-20) sts. Work in ribbing for 3 (5-7) rows, end wrong side.
Next Row (inc row): K, inc 5 (6-9) sts evenly spaced—15 (22-29) sts. Work in stockinette st for 15 (19-27) rows.
Shape Armholes: Bind off 1 st at beg of next 2 rows—13 (20-27) sts.
Shape Raglan: Work raglan decs as for back; work in striped pat as for back—3 (4-5) sts. Sl sts to a holder.
FINISHING: Sew sleeve and raglan seams, matching stripes.
Neckband: From wrong side, sl 6 (8-11) sts of left front, 3 (4-5) sts of one sleeve, 8 (12-14) sts of back, 3 (4-5) sts of 2nd sleeve, 6 (8-11) sts of right front to needle—26 (36-46) sts.
Dec and Buttonhole Row (right side): With A, k across, dec 4 (8-10) sts evenly spaced, to last 3 sts, end yo, k 2 tog, k 1. Work 2 (2-3) rows in k 1, p 1 ribbing. Bind off in ribbing.
Edging: With A, work 1 row sc along each front edge, keeping work flat. Steam sweater lightly. Sew on buttons opposite buttonholes.
PANTS: Beg at waist, with A, cast on 20 (28-38) sts. Work in ribbing of k 1, p 1 for 3 (5-7) rows, end wrong side. Work in stockinette st (k 1 row, p 1 row) for 12 (18-26) rows. Bind off 7 (10-14) sts at beg of next 2 rows for legs. K 1 row, p 1 row. Cast on 7 (10-14) sts at beg of next 2 rows. Work even in stockinette st for 12 (18-26) rows. Work in ribbing of k 1, p 1 for 3 (5-7) rows. Bind off in ribbing.
Legs: From right side, beg at side edge, with A, pick up and k 14 (22-28) sts on bound-off and cast-on edges. Work in ribbing for 3 (3-5) rows. Bind off in ribbing. Work other leg in same way.
FINISHING: Steam-press lightly. Sew side seams. Run elastic thread through waistband ribbing to tighten.

CAP: Beg at front edge, with A cast on 36 (48-68) sts. Work in ribbing of

k 1, p 1 for 3 (5-7) rows, end wrong side. Work in stockinette st for 4 rows. Drop A; join B. With B, work even for 2 (4-6) rows; cut B. With A, work even for 4 (4-6) rows.
Shape Top: K, dec 12 (12-20) sts evenly spaced across—24 (36-48) sts. Work in ribbing for 5 (7-9) rows.
Next Row: K 2 tog across—12 (18-24) sts. Cut yarn, leaving a 12″ end. Thread end through sts, pull up and fasten securely. Sew back seam. Steam.
Pompon: With A and B held tog, make pompon as shown. Sew pompon to top of hat.
SOCKS (make 2): Beg at cuff, with A, cast on 14 (18-28) sts. Work in ribbing of k 1, p 1 for 7 (9-11) rows, end wrong side. Work in stockinette st for 8 (12-16) rows.
Next Row: K 2 tog across—7 (9-14) sts. P 1 row. Cut yarn, leaving a 10″ end. Run end through sts; pull up and fasten securely. Sew back seam. Steam lightly.

DOLL'S BUNTING
Shown on page 206

SIZE: Directions for 9″ doll. Changes for 12″ and 17″ dolls are in parentheses.
MATERIALS: Knitting worsted weight yarn, 1 (2-3) 2-oz skeins. Knitting needles No. 8. 4″(6″-7″) zipper. Two stitch holders.
GAUGE: 5 sts = 1″; 10 rows = 1″.
BUNTING: Note: Bunting is made in one piece in garter stitch (k each row). Mark first row for wrong side. Beg at lower edge of back, cast on 30 (46-60) sts. Work in garter st for 21 (41-81) rows, end wrong side (see Note).
First Dec Row: Dec 1 st at beg and end of row—28 (44-58) sts. Repeat dec row every 14th row 1 (2-2) times—26 (40-54) sts. Work even for 29 (15-15) rows, end wrong side. Piece should be about 6½″ (8½″-12½″) from start. Mark for beg of sleeves.
SLEEVES: Cast on 9 (12-24) sts at end of each of next 2 rows—44 (64-102) sts. Work even for 18 (20-30) rows, end wrong side. Mark for top of sleeve.
Shape Neck: K 19 (28-46), place these sts on a holder for right front, bind off next 6 (8-10) sts for neck, finish row—19 (28-46) sts on needle.
Left Front: Work even for 6 (8-10) rows, end right side at sleeve edge. Cast on 3 (4-5) sts at end of next row for front of neck—22 (32-51) sts. Work even for 9 (11-19) rows more, end right side at sleeve edge. Bind off 9 (12-24) sts at beg of next row—13 (20-27) sts.
For 9″ Doll Only: Work even on 13 sts for 26 rows, end wrong side at front edge. Sl these 13 sts on a holder.

For 12″ and 17″ Dolls: Work even on 20 (27) sts for 16 rows, end wrong side at front edge. Inc 1 st at end of next row, then every 14th row twice more —23 (30) sts. Work 3 rows even after last inc, end wrong side at front edge. Sl these 23 (30) sts on a holder.

Right Front: From right side, sl 19 (28-46) sts to needle. Join yarn at neck edge. Work even for 6 (8-10) rows, end right side at front edge. Loop 3 (4-5) sts on right-hand needle—22 (32-51) sts. Work even for 11 (13-21) rows, end wrong side at sleeve edge. Bind off 9 (12-24) sts at beg of next row—13 (20-27) sts. Work to correspond to left front, reversing shaping, until same length as left front, end wrong side at side edge.

Joining Row: K 13 (23-30) sts of right front, k across 13 (23-30) sts of left front—26 (46-60) sts.

For 9″ Doll Only: Work even for 3 rows, end wrong side. Inc 1 st each side of next row. Work even for 13 rows, then repeat inc row—30 sts.

For All Sizes: Work even for 21 (37-77) rows. Bind off.

HOOD: Beg at front edge, cast on 33 (45-61) sts. Work in garter st for 26 (32-46) rows. Bind off.

Fold hood in half and sew bound-off edges tog for back seam. From right side, pick up and k 27 (45-49) sts at neck edge of hood.

Row 1: P 1, * k 1, p 1, repeat from * across.

Row 2: K 1, * p 1, k 1, repeat from * across.

Row 3: Repeat row 1. Bind off in ribbing.

FINISHING: Steam pieces lightly. Fold bunting in half at top of sleeve marker. Sew sleeves and side seams; sew lower edges tog. Pin hood to neck edge of bunting with seam at center back; sew in place. Sew zipper in front opening. If desired, make tassel as shown. Thread tapestry needle with a piece of yarn and run through last garter st ridge on sleeve edge; draw up tightly to close sleeve. Fasten securely.

BARBIE'S CARDIGAN AND PANTS
Shown on page 207

SIZE: Fits 11½″ fashion doll.
MATERIALS: Fingering yarn, ½ oz. gray (G), small amount red (R). Knitting needles No. 1. Markers. Steel crochet hook No. 6. Four small buttons. Stitch holder.
GAUGE: 10 sts = 1″; 12 rows = 1″.
Inc Note: K in front and back of same st.
PANTS: Beg at waistline of front and back, with G, cast on 40 sts. Work in ribbing of k 1, p 1 for 6 rows.

Next Row: K 20, place a marker on needle, k 20. P 1 row, slipping marker. Working in stockinette st (k 1 row, p 1 row), inc 1 st (see Inc Note) each side of marker every k row until there are 60 sts on needle, end p row.

Divide for Legs: K 30, sl remaining 30 sts on a holder for left leg. Working in stockinette st, dec 1 st each side of next row, then every 4th row 4 times more— 20 sts. Work even until leg measures 4¼″ from crotch. Work in ribbing of k 1, p 1 for 4 rows. Bind off in ribbing.

Left Leg: Sl sts from holder to No. 1 needle. From right side, join G. Work as for right leg.

FINISHING: Steam-press lightly. Sew back seam. Sew leg seams.

CARDIGAN: Note: Always change colors on wrong side, picking up new strand from under dropped strand.

Yoke: Beg at neck edge, with G, cast on 16 sts. Work in ribbing of k 1, p 1 for 4 rows.

Row 5 (wrong side): P 3, place a marker on needle, p 2, marker, p 6, marker, p 2, marker, p 3. Sl markers each row.

Row 6: K, inc 1 st before and after each marker—8 sts inc.

Row 7: Purl. Repeat rows 6 and 7, 8 times—88 sts.

Divide for Sleeves: K 32 sts, removing 2 markers. Turn. P across 20 sts (sleeve). Work in stockinette st on 20 sts for 1¾″, end p row. Dec 4 sts on next k row, then work in ribbing of k 1, p 1 on 16 sts for 5 rows. Bind off in ribbing. Join G in st after sleeve, k across 44 sts, removing last 2 markers. Turn. P across 20 sts and complete 2nd sleeve as for first sleeve. Join G in st after sleeve, k across last 12 sts.

Body: Row 1: P across right front, back, left front—48 sts. Join R.

Row 2: * K 1 G, k 1 R, repeat from * across.

Row 3: * P 1 G, p 1 R, repeat from * across.

Row 4: * K 3 R, k 1 G, repeat from * across.

Row 5: P 2 G, * p 1 R, p 3 G, repeat from * across, end last repeat p 1 G.

Row 6: Repeat row 4.

Row 7: * P 1 G, p 3 R, repeat from * across.

Row 8: Repeat row 4.

Row 9: P 2 R, * p 1 G, p 3 R, repeat from * across, end last repeat p 1 R.

Row 10: * K 3 G, k 1 R, repeat from * across.

Row 11: * P 1 R, p 1 G, repeat from * across.

Row 12: Repeat row 2.

Row 13: Repeat row 11. Cut R. Work in ribbing of k 1, p 1 for 4 rows. Bind off.

FINISHING: Steam-press lightly. Sew sleeve seams. Beg at lower edge, work 1 row of sc up right front edge to neck. Ch 1, turn. Sc in each sc across. Ch 1, turn. With pins, mark position of 4 but-

tons, top button 1″ down from neck edge, bottom button ⅜″ up from lower edge, other two evenly spaced between. Work sc in each sc; at each marker, ch 1, sk 1 sc for buttonhole. Do not end off at neck edge; continue working sc around neck, then work 3 rows sc on left front edge. Sew on buttons.

HAT: With G, cast on 43 sts.
Row 1: Knit. Join R.
Row 2: P 1 R, * p 1 R, p 1 G, repeat from * across.
Row 3: K 1 R, * k 1 G, k 1 R, repeat from * across.
Row 4: P 1 G, * p 1 R, p 3 G, repeat from * across, end last repeat p 1 G.
Row 5: K 3 R, * k 1 G, k 3 R, repeat from * across.
Row 6: P 3 R, * p 1 G, p 3 R, repeat from * across.
Row 7: Repeat row 5.
Row 8: Repeat row 4.
Row 9: Repeat row 3.
Row 10: Repeat row 2. Cut R.
Row 11: Knit.
Row 12: K 1 row on wrong side for ridge.
Row 13: K 3, (k 2 tog, k 6) 5 times.
Row 14: (P 5, p 2 tog) 5 times, p 3.
Row 15: K 3, (k 2 tog, k 4) 5 times.
Row 16: (P 3, p 2 tog) 5 times, p 3.
Row 17: K 3, (k 2 tog, k 2) 5 times.
Row 18: (P 1, p 2 tog) 5 times, p 3.
Row 19: K 1, (k 2 tog) 6 times. Cut yarn, leaving an end for sewing. Draw yarn through remaining sts; pull up tight and fasten securely. Sew back seam.

BARBIE'S ROBE
Shown on page 207

SIZE: Fits 11½″ fashion doll.
MATERIALS: Fingering yarn, 3 ply, 1 oz. white (W), ¼ oz. gold (G). Knitting needles No. 2. Three hooks and eyes. Steel crochet hook No. 7. Three stitch holders. Large-eyed needle.
GAUGE: 8 st = 1″; 10 rows = 1″.
Pattern Notes: Note 1: Always change colors on wrong side, picking up new strand from under dropped strand.
Note 2: Sl all sl sts as if to p.
ROBE: Beg at lower edge with W, cast on 73 sts. P 1 row, k 1 row for 4 rows (hem), cast on 3 sts at end of last row.
Next Row: K across (for hemline), cast on 3 sts at end of row—79 sts.
Row 1: K 3, sl 1 (fold line), k to last 4 sts, sl 1 (fold line), k 3.
Row 2: Purl. Repeat last 2 rows once. Join G.
Rows 5 and 6: With G, repeat rows 1 and 2.
Rows 7 and 8: With W, repeat rows 1 and 2.
Row 9: K 1 G; with W, k 2, sl 1, k 2, * k 3 G, k 5 W, repeat from * 7 times, k 3 G; with W, k 2, sl 1, k 2; k 1 G. Continue to sl 4th st each side every k row.

Row 10: P 1 W, * p 1 G, p 3 W, repeat from * across, end last repeat p 1 W.

Row 11: K 2 W, * k 3 G, k 5 W, repeat from * across, end last repeat k 2 W.

Rows 12 and 13: With W, p 1 row, k 1 row.

Rows 14 and 15: With G, p 1 row, k 1 row. Cut off G. With W, work in stockinette st until piece measures 6″ above hemline, end p row.

Dec for Waist: K 3, sl 1, * k 2 tog, k 1, repeat from * to last 6 sts, k 2 tog, sl 1, k 3—55 sts. P 1 row.

Next Row: K 3, sl 1, k 1, * k 2 tog, repeat from * to last 4 sts, sl 1, k 3—32 sts. P 1 row.

Right Front Bodice and Sleeve: Next Row: K 3, sl 1, k 6, place remaining 22 sts on a holder, turn. P 1 row. Continue to sl 4th st at front edge every k row, inc 1 st at arm side every other row 6 times, then cast on 8 sts at arm side every other row twice—32 sts. Work even in stockinette st for 1″ above last cast-on sts, end p row (front edge).

Shape Neck: Bind off 9 sts at front edge once—23 sts. Work even for 4 rows. Sl sts on a holder. Break yarn leaving a 12″ strand for weaving shoulders tog.

Back Bodice and Sleeves: Sl next 12 sts from holder to needle. From right side, join W. K 1 row, p 1 row. Continue to work in stockinette st, inc 1 st each side every other row 6 times, then cast on 8 sts each side every other row twice—56 sts. Work even for 1″ above last cast-on sts. Cut yarn, sl sts on a holder.

Left Front Bodice and Sleeve: Sl remaining 10 sts from holder to needle. From right side, join W at arm side. K 6, sl 1, k 3. Work to correspond to right front, reversing shaping.

Place front bodice sts on one needle, back bodice sts on another needle. Weave tog back and front shoulder seams (23 sts) in Kitchener st, placing center 10 sts of back on a safety pin for neck.

Sleeve Facing: From right side, with W, pick up and k 16 sts around sleeve edge. K 1 row on wrong side for turning ridge. K 1 row, p 1 row, k 1 row. Bind off.

Collar: From right side, join W in 8th st from right front edge. Pick up and k 5 sts on right front neck, place the 10 sts from safety pin on left-hand needle and k, pick up and k 5 sts on left front neck, ending in 8th st from left front edge—20 sts. Work in stockinette st for 4 rows. K 1 row on wrong side for turning ridge. K 1 row, p 1 row for 4 rows. Bind off.

FINISHING: Steam-press lightly. Sew side and sleeve seams. Turn hem and facings to inside; sew in place. Sew 3 hooks and eyes on wrong side of front bodice so that when closed fronts will meet. With G, make 3 French knots on each front over hooks and eyes.

TIE SASH: With G and crochet hook, make chain 15″ long. With crochet hook, pull two 1½″ strands of W and G through first and last ch. Knot and trim for tassel. With a strand of W, make a small belt loop at each side of waist at underarms.

BARBIE'S SKI OUTFIT
Shown on page 207

SIZE: Fits 11½″ fashion doll.
MATERIALS: Lightweight sport yarn, ½ oz. each of blue (B), and white (W). Sets of dp needles Nos. 1, 2 and 3.
GAUGE: 13 sts = 2″ (No. 3 needles). 7 sts = 1″ (No. 2 needles).
PANTS: Beg at waist, with B, cast on and divide 26 sts on 3 No. 1 needles. Join; work in ribbing of k 1, p 1 for 3 rnds. Change to No. 3 needles.

Rnd 4: * K 1, inc 1 st in next st (k in front and back of same st), repeat from * around—39 sts. K around until piece measures 1½″ from start, inc 1 st on last rnd—40 sts.

Divide for Legs: Sl last 20 sts worked on a piece of yarn for one leg. Divide remaining 20 sts on 3 dp needles. K around for 1″.

Next Rnd: K 2 tog, k around—19 sts. K around until leg measures 3″.

Inc for Flare: Inc 1 st in next st (insert right needle in st below next st, k this st, then k st above it), k 9, inc 1 st in next st, k 8—21 sts. K around, repeat inc rnd every 5th rnd twice more working 1 more st between incs—25 sts. K around until leg measures 5″ or desired length. Bind off in purl. Work 2nd leg same as for first leg.

FINISHING: Steam-press lightly. Sew opening at crotch.

SWEATER: Collar: Working with two No. 2 dp needles and W, beg at neck edge, cast on 21 sts.

Row 1: Sl 1 as if to p, * p 1, k 1, repeat from * across.

Row 2: Sl 1 as if to p, * k 1, p 1, repeat from * across. Repeat these 2 rows twice more.

Shape Raglan Sleeves: Row 7 (right side): Sl 1, k 4, * inc 1 st in next st (k in front and back of same st), place a marker on needle, inc 1 st in each of next 2 sts, place a marker on needle, inc 1 st in next st *, k 3, work from * to * once, k 5—29 sts.

Row 8: Sl 1, p across slipping markers.

Row 9: Sl 1, k across, inc 1 st before and after each marker—8 incs.

Row 10: Sl 1, p across. Repeat last 2 rows until there are 13 sts before first marker, 16 sts between sleeve markers, end p row—77 sts.

Divide for Sleeves:Next Row: Sl 1, k 11, sl 1, sl next 16 sts on a piece of yarn, slip the sl st back to left needle, k sl st and next st tog for underarm, k 17, sl 1, sl next 16 sts on a piece of yarn, slip the sl st back to left needle, k sl st and next st tog for underarm, k 12—43 sts. Sl 1, p across.

Next Row: Sl 1, k across. Divide sts on 3 No. 2 needles. Join; k 31, k 2 tog (left underarm); mark for end of rnd—42 sts. K 2 rnds even.

Pattern: Rnd 1: Join B; * k 1 B, k 1 W, repeat from * around.

Rnd 2: * K 1 W, k 1 B, repeat from * around.

Rnd 3: Repeat rnd 1. Cut B. K 4 rnds. Change to No. 1 needles. Work around in ribbing of k 1, p 1 for 6 rnds. Bind off loosely in ribbing.

Sleeves: Divide 16 sts of one sleeve on 3 No. 2 dp needles. Attach W at underarm. Join; k around for 8 rnds. Work pat rnds 1-3. With W, k 3 rnds. Change to No. 1 needles. Work in ribbing of k 1, p 1 for 5 rnds. Bind off in ribbing. Make other sleeve the same.

FINISHING: Steam-press lightly. Sew underarm openings. Using 3 strands of B, make a tight braid about 10″ long. Lace through front as shown.

HAT: With W, cast on and divide 28 sts on 3 No. 3 dp needles. Join; k 2 rnds. Work pat rnds 1-3 same as for sweater. K 1 rnd W.

Next Rnd: * K 7, put a marker on needle, repeat from * 3 times.

Dec Rnd: Sl 1, k 1, psso, * k 3, k 2 tog, sl marker, sl 1, k 1, psso, repeat from * twice, end k 3, k 2 tog—20 sts. K 1 rnd even.

2nd Dec Rnd: Sl 1, k 1, psso, * k 1, k 2 tog, sl marker, sl 1, k 1, psso, repeat from * twice, end k 1, k 2 tog—12 sts. K 1 rnd, removing markers.

Next Rnd: K 2 tog around—6 sts. Cut yarn, draw through remaining sts, pull up and fasten securely.

Earlap: Mark center back (end of rnd). Count 3 sts to the left. From right side, with W and 2 No. 1 needles, pick up and k 1 st in each of next 8 sts. P 1 row, k 1 row, p 1 row.

Next Row: Sl 1, k 1, psso, k 4, k 2 tog. P 1 row.

Next Row: Sl 1, k 1, psso, k 2, k 2 tog.

Next Row: P 1, p 2 tog, p 1—3 sts.

Tie: Sl 1, k 2, turn; sl 1, p 2, turn. Work these 2 rows until tie measures 2″ long, end wrong side. K 3 tog. End off.

Sk next 7 sts. Work 2nd earlap same as for first earlap. Make a tiny B pompon. Attach to top.

BARBIE'S PAJAMAS
Shown on page 207

SIZE: Fits 11½″ fashion doll.
MATERIALS: Mercerized knitting and crochet cotton, 1 ball. Steel crochet hook No. 5. Round or narrow elastic, 6″ piece.
GAUGE: 9 hdc = 1″; 6 rows = 1″.
PANTS: Beg at top, ch 42. Sl st in first ch to form ring.

Row 1: Ch 1, hdc in each ch across—

42 hdc. Join with sl st to first hdc, ch 1, turn each row.

Rows 2-12: Hdc in each hdc across.
Row 13: Hdc in each of 21 sts, ch 3 for crotch, join to first hdc. Ch 1, turn.
Row 14: Hdc in each ch and st across— 24 hdc. Join, ch 1, turn. Working on these leg sts only, work as before until leg is 5″ from crotch, or desired length. Join yarn at crotch, work 24 hdc around for 2nd leg. Cut elastic to waist measurement; join ends securely. Turn ¼″ at waist down over elastic; sew edge in place being careful not to catch elastic.
JACKET: Beg at lower edge, ch 50.
Row 1: Hdc in 3rd ch from hook and in each ch across—48 hdc. Ch 1, turn each row.
Rows 2-16: Hdc in each hdc across.
Row 17: Hdc in 10 sts, ch 1, turn. Working on these sts only for right front, dec 1 st at outside edge each row for 5 rows— 5 sts. Dec 1 st each end of next row— 3 sts. End off. Join yarn 10 sts in from other end of last long row, work across last 10 sts for left front. Finish as for right front.
Back: Sk 4 sts on last long row for underarm, join yarn in next st, ch 1, hdc in each of 20 sts. Ch 1, turn. Dec 1 st each side of next row, then every 2nd row 3 times more—12 hdc. End off.

From wrong side, join yarn at beg of neck edge on left front, ch 1, hdc in 3 sts of front, hdc in 12 sts of back, hdc in 3 sts of right front. Ch 1, turn. Sc in each st around entire edge of jacket. Sl st in first sc. Do not turn. Ch 1, sc in each sc around. Join; end off.
Sleeves: Join yarn at top of armhole, ch 1, make 1 hdc, sl st in side of armhole, ch 1, turn; make 2 hdc, sl st in other side, ch 1, turn. Continue in this manner, adding 1 hdc each row and joining to sides until there are 10 sts at underarm. Do not turn; work hdc in corner of armhole, 4 hdc across underarm, hdc in other corner of armhole—16 hdc. Join, ch 1, turn. Inc 2 hdc evenly spaced on next row, then work even on 18 hdc for 14 rows, joining and turning each row. Work 1 row sc around edge. End off.
Belt: Ch 86. Hdc in 3rd ch from hook and in each remaining ch, 4 hdc in last ch. Working on other side of ch, hdc in each ch across, 4 hdc in last ch. Join to first hdc; end off. Ch 8 for each belt carrier; sew one to each side.

BRIDE'S GOWN, CROWN
Shown on page 208

MATERIALS: Mercerized knitting and crochet cotton, 1 250-yd. ball white. Steel crochet hook No. 6. Two small snap fasteners. White net, piece 12″ x 3″.
GAUGE: 3 shells (dc, ch 1, dc, ch 1, dc, ch 1, dc) = 2″.

GOWN: Beg at top, ch 26.
Row 1: Sc in 2nd ch from hook and in each ch across—25 sc. Ch 1, turn.
Row 2: Sc in first st, * ch 1, sk 1 st, (dc, ch 1) 4 times in next st, sk 1 st, sc in next st, repeat from * across—6 shells. Ch 3, turn.
Row 3: Shell of 6 dc with ch 1 between dc's in center sp of each shell across, dc in last st. Ch 3, turn.
Row 4: * Sk first ch-1 sp of next shell, work shell of 4 dc with ch 1 between dc's in 2nd ch-1 sp, sk next ch-1 sp, shell of 4 dc with ch 1 between dc's in next ch-1 sp, repeat from * across, dc in top of turning ch—12 shells. Ch 3, turn.
Row 5: (Shell of 4 dc with ch 1 between dc's in center sp of next shell) twice, ch 3 for underarm, sk 2 shells, (shell of 4 dc with ch 1 between dc's in center sp of next shell) 4 times (front), ch 3 for underarm, sk 2 shells, (shell of 4 dc with ch 1 between dc's in center sp of next shell) twice, dc in top of turning ch. Ch 3, turn. Work all shells in this way for dress.
Row 6: Shell in each of first 2 shells (back), sk 1 ch of ch 3, dc in center ch, shell in each of next 4 shells, sk 1 ch of ch 3, dc in center ch, shell in each of last 2 shells, dc in turning ch. Ch 3, turn.
Rows 7 and 8: Shell in each shell across, dc in turning ch. Ch 3, turn at end of row 7. Ch 1, turn at end of row 8.
Waistline: Row 9: Sc in first dc, ch 3, sc in center of first shell, (ch 3, sc in center of next shell) 7 times, ch 3, sc in turning ch. Ch 1, turn.
Row 10: Sc in first sc, 3 sc in next sp, (sc in next sc, 2 sc in next sp) 8 times, sc in last sc. Ch 3, turn.
Row 11: Dc in first sc, * ch 2, 2 dc in next sc, repeat from * across. Ch 3, turn.
Row 12: Shell in each ch-2 sp across, dc in turning ch—28 shells. Ch 3, turn.
Row 13: Shell in center sp of each shell across. Sl st in top of ch 3 at beg of row to join skirt at center back. Ch 3, turn.
Rows 14-29: Repeat row 13. At end of row 29, do not ch 3.
Row 30: Sl st to center of first shell, ch 1, sc in center sp, ch 3, sc in same sp, * ch 1; in center of next shell work 6 tr with ch 1 between tr's, ch 1, sc in center sp of next shell, ch 3, sc in same sp, repeat from * around, end sl st in first sc. End off. Sew snap fasteners to neckline and waistline.
HEAD DRESS: Ch 32 to fit closely around doll's head.
Row 1: Sc in 2nd ch from hook and in each ch across. Ch 1, turn.
Row 2: Sc in first sc, * ch 1, sk 2 sc, shell of 4 dc with ch 1 between dc's in next sc, ch 1, sk 2 sc, sc in next sc,

repeat from * across, end sc in last sc. End off. Sew ends tog. Gather 12″ edge of net to measure 3″. Sew to inside of headband, leaving center front of headband free.

BRIDESMAID'S SET
Shown on page 208

MATERIALS: Mercerized knitting and crochet cotton with metallic thread, 1 175-yd. ball turquoise. Steel crochet hook No. 6. Two small snap fasteners.
GAUGE: 3 shells (2 dc, ch 2, 2 dc) = 2″.

DRESS: Beg at top, ch 42.
Row 1: Sc in 2nd ch from hook and in each ch across—41 sc. Ch 1, turn.
Row 2: Sc in first sc, * ch 1, sk 1 sc, 2 dc, ch 2, 2 dc in next sc (shell), ch 1, sk 1 sc, sc in next sc, repeat from * across—10 shells. Ch 3, turn.
Row 3: Shell of 2 dc, ch 2, 2 dc in ch-2 sp of first shell, shell in ch-2 sp of next shell (back), ch 3 for underarm, sk 1 shell, shell in ch-2 sp of next shell, shell in each of next 3 shells (front), ch 3 for underarm, sk 1 shell, shell in each of last 2 shells (back), dc in last st. Ch 3, turn.
Row 4: Shell in each of first 2 shells, dc in 2nd ch of ch 3 at underarm, shell in each of next 4 shells, dc in 2nd ch of ch 3 at underarm, shell in each of last 2 shells, dc in top of turning ch. Ch 3, turn.
Rows 5 and 6: Shell in each shell across, dc in top of turning ch. Ch 3, turn. At end of row 6, ch 1, turn.
Row 7 (waistline): Sc in first st, ch 1, sc in first shell, * ch 3, sc in next shell, repeat from * across to last shell, ch 1, sc in top of turning ch. Ch 3, turn.
Row 8: Shell in ch-1 sp, * shell of 2 dc, ch 2, 2 dc, ch 2, 2 dc in next ch-3 sp, repeat from * across, shell in ch-1 sp, dc in sc. Ch 3, turn.
Rows 9 and 10: Shell of 2 dc, ch 2, 2 dc in each ch-2 sp across, dc in top of turning ch. Ch 3, turn each row. At end of row 10, sl st in top of ch 3 at beg of row to join skirt at center back. Ch 3, turn.
Rows 11-16: Shell in each shell across. Sl st in top of ch 3. Ch 3, turn.
Row 17: 6 dc in each shell across. Sl st in top of ch 3. End off. Sew snap fasteners at neckline and waistline.
HAT: Ch 5, sl st in first ch to form ring.
Rnd 1: Ch 3, 11 dc in ring. Sl st in top of ch 3.
Rnd 2: Ch 3, dc in same ch as sl st, 2 dc in each dc around. Sl st in top of ch 3.
Rnd 3: Ch 3, sk next dc, shell of 2 dc, ch 2, 2 dc in next dc, * sk next 3 dc, shell in next dc, repeat from * around, sl st in top of ch 3—6 shells.
Rnds 4 and 5: Ch 3, shell in each shell around. Sl st in top of ch 3.

Rnd 6: Ch 3, shell of 2 dc, ch 2, 2 dc, ch 2, 2 dc in each shell around. Sl st in top of ch 3.

Rnd 7: Ch 3, shell of 2 dc, ch 2, 2 dc in each ch-2 sp around. Sl st in top of ch 3.

Rnd 8: Ch 3, shell of 7 dc in each shell around. Sl st in top of ch 3. End off.

SHELL STITCH SET
Shown on page 209

SIZE: Fits 11½" doll.
MATERIALS: Knitting and crochet cotton, 1 ball pink. Steel crochet hook No. 7. Three snap fasteners.
GAUGE: 3 shells = 2".
TUNIC: Beg at neck, ch 26. **Row 1:** Sc in 2nd ch from hook and in each ch across. Ch 1, turn.

Row 2: Sc in first sc, * ch 1, sk next sc, (2 dc, ch 2, 2 dc) shell in next sc, ch 1, sk next sc, sc in next sc, repeat from * across—6 shells. Ch 3, turn.

Row 3: (2 dc, ch 2, 2 dc, ch 2, 2 dc) in each ch-2 sp across, dc in last st. Ch 3, turn each row.

Row 4: (2 dc, ch 2, 2 dc) shell in each ch-2 sp across, dc in top of turning ch.

Row 5: Shell in each of first 2 shells, ch 3, sk 2 shells, shell in each of next 4 shells, ch 3, sk 2 shells, shell in each of last 2 shells, dc in top of turning ch.

Row 6: Shell in each of first 2 shells, dc in center of ch 3, shell in each of 4 shells, dc in center of ch 3, shell in each of last 2 shells, dc in top of turning ch.

Rows 7-9: Shell in each shell across, dc in turning ch.

Row 10: Shell in first shell, (2 dc, ch 2, 2 dc, ch 2, 2 dc) inc shell in each of next 2 shells, shell in each of next 2 shells, inc shell in each of next 2 shells, shell in last shell, dc in turning ch, sl st in ch 3 at beg of row to join back. Ch 3, turn.

Rows 11-14: Shell in each shell, sl st in top of ch 3. Ch 3, turn.

Row 15: 6 dc in each shell across. Join. End off. Close back opening with 2 snap fasteners.

SLACKS: Ch 28. **Row 1:** Sc in 2nd ch from hook and in each ch across. Ch 3, turn.

Row 2: Dc in first sc, * dc in each of next 2 sc, 2 dc in next sc, repeat from * across, dc in last 2 sc—36 dc, counting ch 3 as dc. Ch 3, turn.

Row 3: Dc in first st, dc in each of 16 dc, 2 dc in each of 2 dc, dc in each of 16 dc, 2 dc in turning ch. Ch 3, turn.

Rows 4 and 5: Repeat row 3 having 2 more dc between incs each half each row—48 dc. Ch 3, turn.

Row 6: Shell of (2 dc, ch 2, 2 dc) in 2nd st, * sk 3 sts, shell in next st, repeat from * 4 times, sk 1 st, dc in next st, sl st in top of ch 3 at beg of row. Ch 3, turn.

Rows 7-19: Work in shell pat, joining and turning each row.

Row 20: 6 dc in each shell. Join; end off. Work 2nd leg the same. Close back opening with snap fastener.

CAP: Ch 5; sl st in first ch to form ring.
Rnd 1: Ch 3, 11 dc in ring. Sl st in top of ch 3. Ch 3, turn.

Rnd 2: Dc in same place as sl st, 2 dc in each dc around. Join. Ch 3, turn.

Rnd 3: Sk next st, shell in next st, * sk 3 sts, shell in next st, repeat from * 4 times. Join. Ch 3, turn.

Rnds 4 and 5: Shell in each shell around. Join, ch 3, turn each rnd.

Rnd 6: 5 dc in each shell around. Join. End off.

BEACH OUTFIT
Shown on page 209

SIZE: Fits 11½" doll.
MATERIALS: Knitting and crochet cotton, 1 ball multicolored. Steel crochet hook No. 5. Three small buttons. Three snap fasteners.
GAUGE: 9 sts = 1".
TOP: Beg at waistline, ch 33. **Row 1:** Sc in 2nd ch from hook and in each remaining ch. Ch 2, turn.

Row 2: Dc in each sc. Ch 2, turn each row.

Row 3: Dc in each dc, inc 6 dc evenly across—38 dc.

Row 4: Dc in each dc.

Row 5: Repeat row 3—44 dc.

Row 6: Repeat row 4.

Row 7: Dc in first 10 dc, ch 8, sk 4 dc, dc in next 16 dc, ch 8, sk 4 dc, dc in last 10 dc. Ch 1, turn.

Row 8: Sc in each st across.

Skirt: Join thread at waistline. Ch 1; working on opposite side of starting ch, work sc in each ch across. Ch 2, turn.

Row 2: Dc in each sc, inc in every 4th st. Ch 2, turn each row.

Row 3: Dc in each dc.

Row 4: Dc in 14 dc, (inc 1 dc in next st) twice, dc in 6 dc, (inc 1 dc in next st) twice, dc in each dc to end.

Row 5: Dc in 15 dc, (inc 1 dc in next st) twice, dc in 9 dc, (inc 1 dc in next st) twice, dc in each dc to end.

Rows 6-9: Work even in dc. End off.
FINISHING: Work 2 rows of sc down front, across lower edge and up other front edge. Make a ch 12" long. Run through 1 st at each front edge at waistline. Sew 2 snap fasteners to top front edges. Sew 3 buttons to right top front edge.

PANTS: Beg at waist, ch 33. **Row 1:** Sc in 2nd ch from hook and in each remaining ch. Ch 2, turn each row.

Row 2: * Dc in 2 sts, 2 dc in next st, repeat from * across, dc in last 2 sts —42 dc.

Row 3: Dc in each dc across, inc 6 sts evenly across—48 dc.

Rows 4 and 5: Dc in each dc across. At end of Row 5, sl st in top of first dc to join into rnds. Ch 2, turn.

Rnds 6 and 7: Dc in each dc around, sl st in first dc. Ch 2, turn.

Rnd 8: Dc in 24 dc, join to first dc for first leg. Ch 1, sc in each dc around. End off. Work 2nd leg in same way.
FINISHING: Sew crotch. Join thread in first ch at waist, ch 4, sc in 2nd ch and in each of next 2 ch for tab, sc in each st around waist. End off. Sew snap fastener to tab and right back opening at waistline.

BARBIE'S SHAWL
Shown on page 210

SIZE: 8½" long, plus fringe.
MATERIALS: White J. & P. Coats Knit-Cro-Sheen. Steel crochet hook No. 6.
SHAWL: Ch 15.

Row 1: Sc in 5th ch from hook, (ch 2, sk 1 ch, sc in next ch) 5 times. Ch 3, turn.

Row 2: Holding back last lp of each dc, 2 dc in first lp, yo and through 3 lps on hook (dc cluster made), * ch 1, 3-dc cluster in next lp, repeat from * across. Ch 3, turn.

Row 3: * Sc in next ch 1, ch 3, repeat from * across, end ch 3, sc in last st. Ch 3, turn. Repeat rows 2 and 3 19 times. End off.

Cut 24 pieces of thread 4" long. Fringe 2 pieces tog in each lp at ends.

BARBIE'S GREEN DRESS
Shown on page 210

SIZE: Fits 11½" doll.
MATERIALS: Fingering yarn, 1 oz. Knitting needles Nos. 3 and 1. Steel crochet hook No. 7. One dp needle. Three snap fasteners.
GAUGE: 8 sts = 1" (No. 3 needles).
DRESS: Beg at lower edge, with No. 3 needles, cast on 46 sts.

Row 1: (P 1, k 6) 6 times, (p 1, k 1) twice.

Row 2 (wrong side): (p 1, k 1) twice, (p 6, k 1) 6 times.

Row 3: (P 1, k 2, yarn in back, sl next 2 sts as if to p, k 2) 6 times, (p 1, k 1) twice.

Row 4: (P 1, k 1) twice, (p 2, yarn in front, sl next 2 sts as if to p, p 2, k 1) 6 times.

Row 5: * P 1, sl next 2 sts as if to p to dp needle, hold in back, k next sl st, k sts from dp needle (right cross st made), sl next sl st to dp needle, hold in front, k next 2 sts, k st from dp needle (left cross st made), repeat from * across, end (p 1, k 1) twice.

Rows 6-9: Repeat rows 2-5.

Row 10: Repeat row 2.

Row 11: P 1, k to last 4 sts, (p 1, k 1) twice.

Row 12: (P 1, k 1) twice, p to last st, k 1. Repeat these 2 rows 4 times.

Rows 21-30: Repeat rows 1-10.

Row 31: Change to No. 1 needles. Cast on 3 sts at beg of row, (k 1, p 1) twice for 4-st rib underlap, k across to last 4 sts, work (p 1, k 1) twice.

Rows 32-40: Keeping 4-st rib at beg and end of rows, work in stockinette st.

Rows 41-50: Repeat rows 1-10, keeping 4-st rib at beg and end of rows.

Rows 51-58: Change to No. 3 needles, repeat row 32.

Divide for Armholes: Left Back: Row 59: Working on 12 sts, work 4-st rib, k 6, p 1, k 1. Keeping 2-st rib at armhole, work pat rows 2-10. Bind off.

Front: Row 59: Working on 25 sts, k 1, p 1 (armhole edge), k 3 (½ pat), p 1, k 6, p 1, k 6, p 1, k 3 (½ pat), p 1, k 1 (armhole edge).

Row 60: P 1, k 1, p 3, (k 1, p 6) twice, k 1, p 3, k 1, p 1.

Row 61: K 1, p 1, sl 1, (k 2, p 1, k 2, sl 2) twice, k 2, p 1, k 2, sl 1, p 1, k 1.

Row 62: P 1, k 1, sl 1, p 2, k 1 (p 2, sl 2, p 2, k 1) twice, p 2, sl 1, k 1, p 1.

Row 63: K 1, p 1, sl 1 st to dp needle, hold in front, k 2, k 1 from dp needle, work from * to * on row 5 twice on next 14 sts, p 1, sl next 2 sts to dp needle, hold in back, k sl st, k sts from dp needle, p 1, k 1.

Rows 64-67: Repeat rows 60-63.

Row 68: Repeat row 60. Bind off.

Right Back: Work to correspond to left back.

FINISHING: Steam-press. Sew center back seam to underlap, sew underlap in place. Sew shoulder seams (5 sts). Work 1 row sc around neck edge. Work 1 row sc around bottom edge. Close back opening with 3 snap fasteners.

BARBIE'S SHELL AND SLACKS
Shown on page 210

SIZE: Fits 11½″ fashion doll.
MATERIALS: Fingering yarn, small amounts of one or more colors. Knitting needles No. 2. Two small snap fasteners.
GAUGE: 8 sts = 1″.
SHELL: Beg at lower edge, cast on 42 sts. Work in ribbing of k 3, p 3 for 3″, changing colors as desired.

Shape Top: Keeping to pat, work 8 sts, bind off 6 sts for armhole, work 15 sts, bind off 6 sts, finish row.

Next Row: Cast on 6 sts over bound-off sts. Work in pat for 4 rows.

Next Row (right side): * K 1, k 2 tog, p 1, p 2 tog, repeat from * across. Work in k 2, p 2 ribbing for 3 rows.

Next Row: * K 2 tog, p 2 tog, repeat from * across. Work in ribbing of k 1, p 1 for 1 row. Bind off in ribbing.

Weave center back seam, leaving 2″ opening at top. Work 1 row sc around back opening. Close opening with snap fasteners.

For slacks, see page 224.

BARBIE'S RED EVENING GOWN
Shown on page 210

SIZE: Fits 11½″ fashion doll.
MATERIALS: J. & P. Coats Knit-Cro-Sheen, 1 ball red. Steel crochet hook No. 6. Two snap fasteners.
GAUGE: 1 small shell = ½″.
DRESS: Beg at top, ch 44.

Row 1: Sc in 2nd ch from hook, * sk 2 ch, 5 dc in next ch, sk 2 ch, sc in next ch, repeat from * across, end 5 dc in next ch, sk 2 ch, sc in last ch—7 shells. Ch 3, turn.

Row 2: 2 dc in first sc, * sc in center dc of next shell, 5 dc in next sc, repeat from * across, end 3 dc of half shell in last sc. Ch 1, turn.

Row 3: Sc in first dc, * 5 dc in next sc, sc in center dc of next shell, repeat from * across, end sc in top of ch 3 turning ch. Ch 3, turn.

Row 4: Repeat row 2.

Row 5: Sc in first dc, * 3 dc in next sc, sc in center dc of next shell, repeat from * across, end sc in top of turning ch. Ch 3, turn.

Row 6: Dc in first sc, * sc in center dc of next shell. 3 dc in next sc, repeat from * across, end 2 dc in last sc. Ch 1, turn.

Row 7: Repeat row 5.

Row 8: Repeat row 6.

Row 9: Sc in first dc, * ch 3, sc in center of next shell, repeat from * across, end ch 3, sc in last st—7 waistline loops. Ch 1, turn.

Row 10: Sc in sc, * 5 dc in next lp, sc in next sc, repeat from * across. Ch 5, turn.

Row 11: Sc in center of first shell, * ch 4, sc in center of next shell, repeat from * across, end ch 4, dc in last sc. Ch 3, turn.

Row 12: 6 dc in first lp, sc in sc, * 6 dc in next lp, sc in next sc, repeat from * across, end 6 dc in last lp. Ch 5, turn.

Row 13: Sc in center of first shell, * ch 5, sc in center of next shell, repeat from * across, end ch 5, dc in last st. Ch 3, turn.

Row 14: 7 dc in first lp, sc in sc, * 7 dc in next lp, sc in next sc, repeat from * across, end 7 dc in last lp. Ch 5, turn.

Row 15: Sc in center of first shell, * ch 5, sc in center of next shell, repeat from * across, end ch 2, dc in last st, sl st in 3rd ch of ch 5 at beg of row to join back of skirt. Ch 3, turn to right side.

Row 16: 3 dc in first sp, sc in sc, * 7 dc in next lp, sc in next sc, repeat from * across, 3 dc in last sp. Sl st in top of ch 3. Do not turn each row; work all rows from right side.

Row 17: Ch 1, sc in first st, * ch 5, sc in center of next shell, repeat from * across, end ch 5, sl st in first sc.

Row 18: Ch 1, sc in sc, * 7 dc in next lp, sc in next sc, repeat from * across, 7 dc in last lp, sl st in first sc.

Row 19: * Ch 7, sc in center of next shell, repeat from * across, end ch 3, sl st in 3rd ch of first ch 7.

Row 20: Ch 3, 3 dc in first sp, * sc in next sc, 9 dc in next lp, repeat from * across, end 4 dc in last sp, sl st in top of ch 3.

Row 21: Repeat row 17 with ch-7 lps.

Row 22: Repeat row 18 with 9 dc.

Row 23: Repeat row 19.

Row 24: Repeat row 20, working 4 dc in first sp, 9 dc shells.

Row 25: Repeat row 17 with ch-7 lps.

Row 26: Repeat row 18 with 9 tr shells.

Row 27: Repeat row 19.

Row 28: Repeat row 20 with 9 tr shells.

Row 29: Repeat row 17 with ch-7 lps.

Row 30: Repeat row 18 with 9 tr shells.

Row 31: Ch 7, sc in center of next shell, * ch 9, sc in center of next shell, repeat from * around, end ch 4, sl st in 3rd ch of ch 7.

Row 32: Ch 4, 5 tr in first sp, sc in sc, * 11 tr in next lp, sc in next sc, repeat from * around, 5 tr in last sp. Join.

Row 33: Repeat row 17 with ch-9 lps.

Row 34: Ch 1, sc in first st, * 11 tr in next lp, sc in next sc, repeat from * around, sl st in first sc.

Row 35: Ch 7, * sc in center tr of next shell, ch 9, repeat from * around, end ch 4, sl st in 3rd ch of ch 7.

Row 36: Ch 4, 2 tr in next sp, ch 3, sl st in top of last tr for picot, 3 tr in same sp, * sc in sc, (4 tr, ch 3 picot) twice in next lp, 3 tr in same lp, repeat from * around, end 4 tr, picot, 1 tr in last sp. Join. End off.

FINISHING: From right side, join yarn in first ch at top of dress, sc in first 9 ch, ch 11 for shoulder strap, sk 4 ch, sc in next 17 ch, ch 11 for shoulder strap, sk 4 ch, sc in last 9 ch. End off. Sew snap fasteners at waist and top of back.

BARBIE'S CAPE
Shown on page 210

SIZE: 2″ deep.
MATERIALS: White J. & P. Coats Knit-Cro-Sheen. Steel crochet hook No. 6.
CAPE: Ch 25.

Row 1: Sc in 2nd ch from hook and in each ch across. Ch 3, turn each row.

Row 2: Dc in first st (inc), dc in 4 sc, 2 dc in next sc, (ch 1, 2 dc in next sc, dc in 4 sc, 2 dc in next sc) 3 times.

Row 3: Dc in first st (inc), dc in 6 dc, (2 dc in next dc, ch 1, 2 dc in next dc, dc in 6 dc) 3 times, 2 dc in last dc.

Row 4: Sc in first st, (ch 3, sk 1 st, sc in next st) 21 times. Ch 5, turn.

Row 5: Sc in first lp, (ch 4, sc in next lp) 20 times, ch 4, sc in last sc. Ch 5, turn.

Row 6: Sc in first lp, (ch 5, sc in next lp) 20 times, ch 2, dc in last lp. Ch 4, turn.

Row 7: Sc in first lp, (ch 4, sc in next lp) 20 times, ch 3, turn.

Row 8: 3 dc in first lp, (2 dc in next lp, 3 dc in next lp) 10 times. Ch 1, turn.
Row 9: Sc in first st, (ch 4, sl st in 3rd ch from hook for picot, ch 1, sk 1 st, sc in next st) 26 times. End off.

Beg at lower edge, sc along right side edge to top, ch 30 for tie. Ch 30, sc down left side edge to bottom. End off.

BARBIE'S TOTE
Shown on page 211

MATERIALS: Knitting worsted, ¼ oz.; few inches contrasting color for trim. No. 5 knitting needles. Crochet hook, size E.
TOTE: Cast on 10 sts.
Rows 1-10: Knit across.
Row 11: K 2 tog, k 6, k 2 tog.
Row 12: K 2 tog, k 4, k 2 tog.
Rows 13 and 14: Knit across—6 sts. Inc 1 st each end of next 2 rows. K 10 rows. Bind off.
FINISHING: Sew side seams; turn right side out. For handles, attach yarn to left side of opening with crochet hook, ch 16, attach to right side of opening. Weave contrasting color yarn around center of tote and tie in bow on front.

BARBIE'S TAM
Shown on page 211

MATERIALS: White baby yarn, small amount. Crochet hook size C.
GAUGE: 6 sc = 1″.
TAM: Ch 2.
Rnd 1: 6 sc in 2nd ch from hook.
Rnd 2: 2 sc in each sc around.
Rnd 3: (Sc in next sc, 2 sc in next sc) 6 times.
Rnd 4: (Sc in 2 sc, 2 sc in next sc) 6 times.
Rnds 5-7: Continue to inc 6 sc each rnd—42 sc.
Rnds 8-10: Work even on 42 sc.
Rnd 11: (Sc in next sc, work next 2 sc tog) 14 times.
Rnd 12: (Sc in 2 sc, work next 2 sc tog) 7 times—21 sc. Sl st in each sc around. End off. Trim top with small pompon.

BARBIE'S BATEAU-NECK DRESS
Shown on page 211

SIZE: Fits 11½″ fashion doll.
MATERIALS: Mercerized crochet cotton, size 20, 1 ball. Steel crochet hook No. 9. Small snap fastener.
GAUGE: 12 sts = 1″.
DRESS: FRONT: Beg at lower edge, ch 33.
Row 1: Sc in 2nd ch from hook and in each ch across. Ch 3, turn.
Row 2 (right side): Sk first st, dc in next sc and in each sc across—32 dc, counting ch 3 as 1 dc. Ch 3, turn.
Row 3: Dc in next dc, * ch 1, sk 1 st, dc in next 2 dc, repeat from * across. Ch 3, turn.
Row 4: Dc in next dc, * dc in ch-1 sp,

dc in next 2 dc, repeat from * across. Ch 3, turn.
Rows 5-23: Repeat rows 3 and 4 alternately, end row 3. At end of row 23, ch 14.
Row 24: Dc in 4th ch from hook (counts as 2 dc), dc in each ch, dc in each dc and ch-1 sp across; drop yarn. Join a separate strand of yarn to last st of row 23, ch 12. End off. Pick up dropped yarn, dc in each ch across. Ch 3, turn.
Rows 25-30: Repeat rows 3 and 4. End off.
BACK: Work as for front through row 23.
Row 24: Dc in 4th ch from hook, dc in each of next 10 ch, dc in next 15 sts, 2 dc in next st. Ch 3, turn. Working on right back only, work in pat for 6 more rows.
Left Back: Join yarn in next dc of row 23. Ch 3, dc in same st, work in dc across, adding 12 sts as for front, for sleeve. Finish as for right back.
FINISHING: Sew side and underarm seams. Sew top of sleeves and shoulder seams for 18 sts from each side. Close back of neck with snap fastener. Make a braid of colorful cottons or use ribbon for belt. Run through row 19.

BARBIE'S JUMPSUIT
Shown on page 211

SIZE: Fits 11½″ fashion doll.
MATERIALS: J. & P. Coats Knit-Cro-Sheen, 1 ball yellow. Steel crochet hook No. 6. Two snap fasteners.
GAUGE: 9 sts = 1″.
JUMPSUIT: Beg at top, ch 47.
Row 1: Dc in 4th ch from hook (counts as 2 dc) and in each ch across—45 dc. Ch 3, turn.
Row 2: Sk first dc, dc in each dc across. Ch 3, turn.
Row 3: Repeat row 2.
Row 4: Dc in next dc, * ch 1, sk 1 dc, dc in next dc, repeat from * across, skipping 2 dc twice in row, end dc in last 2 dc—20 sps. Ch 3, turn.
Row 5: Dc in next dc, dc in each dc and ch-1 sp across, working 2 dc tog 4 times in row—39 dc. Ch 3 turn.
Row 6: Repeat row 4—17 sps. Ch 3, turn.
Row 7: Dc in next dc, * ch 1, dc in next dc, repeat from * across, working 2 dc tog during row to dec 1 sp—16 sps. Ch 3, turn.
Row 8 (waistline): Work in dc, dec 3 dc in row—32 dc. Ch 3, turn.
Row 9: Dc in first st (inc), dc in 14 dc, 2 dc in each of next 2 dc, dc in 14 dc, 2 dc in last dc—36 dc. Sl st in top of first dc to join. Do not turn.
Row 10 (right side): Ch 3, dc in first st, dc in 16 dc, 2 dc in each of center 2 dc, dc in 16 dc, 2 dc in last st. Join each rnd.
Row 11: Work as for row 10 with 18 dc between incs.

Row 12: Work as for row 10 with 20 dc between incs.
Row 13: Work even in dc—48 dc.
Row 14 (legs) Ch 4, dc in next dc, (ch 1, sk 1 dc, dc in next dc) 11 times, ch 1, sl st in 3rd ch of ch 4—13 sps.
Row 15: Ch 3, dc in each sp, dc in each dc around leg. Join.
Row 16: Work 13 sps around. Join each rnd.
Row 17: Repeat row 15.
Row 18: Work in sps, inc 1 sp in rnd.
Row 19: Repeat row 15, inc 2 dc in rnd.
Row 20: Repeat row 18—15 sps.
Row 21: Repeat row 15.
Rows 22-32: Work even, alternating rows of 15 sps and 30 dc.
Row 33: Ch 1, sc in each dc and sp around. Join, end off.

Join yarn at crotch, ch 4, work 2nd leg the same.
FINISHING: Join yarn at top back; working across original ch, sc in each of 10 ch, ch 11, sk 4 ch, sc in each of next 17 ch, ch 11, sk 4 ch, sc in each of last 10 ch. End off. Sew snaps to waistline and top edge of back.

BARBIE'S RED SLACKS SUIT
Shown on page 211

SIZE: Fits 11½″ fashion doll.
MATERIALS: J. & P. Coats Knit-Cro-Sheen, 1 ball red. Steel crochet hook No. 5.
GAUGE: 9 sc = 1″.
VEST (can be tied in back as shown, or tied in front): Beg at lower edge, ch 47.
Row 1: Sc in 2nd ch from hook and in each ch across—46 sc. Ch 1, turn each row.
Rows 2-27: Work even in sc.
Row 28: Sc in 10 sc, ch 1, turn.
Rows 29-33: Work in sc, dec 1 sc at center edge every row—5 sc. Work even on 5 sc for 1 row. End off.

Sk 4 sc on row 27, sc in 18 sc. Ch 1, turn. Work even on 18 sc for 7 rows. End off.

Sk 4 sc on row 27, sc in last 10 sc. Ch 1, turn. Work as for first side.

Working across top, dec 2 sc across 5 sc of first side, ch 2, sc in 18 sc, ch 2, dec 2 sc across 5 sc of 2nd side. Ch 1, turn. Working across top, dec 1 sc at beg of row, sc in each ch and sc across, dec 1 sc at end of row. End off. Make 2 rows of sc around outer edge. Make one or more ch-80's for ties. Pull tie through edge of vest, tie in front or back.
HIPHUGGERS: Beg at top, ch 42. Sl st in first ch to form ring. Ch 1, turn.
Rnd 1: Sc in each sc around. Ch 1, turn each rnd.
Rnd 2: Sc in each sc around.
Rnds 3-12: Repeat rnd 2, inc 1 sc every other rnd 4 times—46 sc.
Rnd 13: Sc in 23 sc, ch 2 for crotch, sl st in first sc. Ch 1, turn.
Rnd 14: Sc in each ch and sc around. Work in sc until leg is 4½″ from crotch,

inc 1 sc at 1″ and 3″. Work 2nd leg the same.

NOEL AFGHAN
Shown on page 230

SIZE: 53″ × 76″.
MATERIALS: Unger's Fluffy, 1¾-oz. balls, 10 balls white, 7 balls red, 2 balls green. Crochet hook size I (5½ mm).
GAUGE: Large motif = 10″ from point to opposite point. Medium motif = 6″ from point to opposite point.
AFGHAN: LARGE MOTIF: First Motif: Rnd 1: With white, ch 4, join with sl st in first ch to form ring. Ch 3, 15 dc in ring, sl st in top of ch 3—16 dc (ch 3 counts as 1 dc).
Rnd 2: Ch 3 (counts as hdc and ch 1), * hdc in next dc, ch 1, repeat from * around, sl st in 2nd ch of ch 3.
Rnd 3: Ch 3, 3 dc in same place as sl st, drop lp from hook; insert hook in top of ch 3, draw dropped lp through (popcorn made), 2 dc in ch-1 sp, dc around post of hdc (insert hook down to the right of st, up to the left of st), 2 dc in ch-1 sp, * 4 dc in next hdc, drop lp from hook; insert hook in first dc of 4-dc group, draw lp through, 2 dc in ch-1 sp, dc around post of hdc, 2 dc in ch-1 sp, repeat from * around. Sl st in first dc after popcorn.
Rnd 4: Ch 3, dc in next dc, dc around post of next dc, dc in each of next 2 dc, * ch 2, dc in each of next 2 dc, dc around post of next dc (post dc made), dc in each of next 2 dc, repeat from * around, end hdc in 3rd ch of ch 3 (counts as ch-2 sp).
Rnd 5: Ch 3, 2 dc in sp, sk 2 dc, post dc around post dc, * 3 dc, ch 3, 3 dc in next ch-2 sp, post dc around post dc, repeat from *, end 3 dc in first sp, ch 1, dc in 3rd ch of ch 3 (counts as ch-3 sp).
Rnd 6: Ch 3, 2 dc in sp, ch 1, post dc around post dc, ch 1, * 3 dc, ch 3, 3 dc in next ch-3 sp, ch 1, post dc around post dc, ch 1, repeat from *, end 3 dc in first sp, ch 1, dc in top of ch 3.
Rnd 7: Ch 3, 3 dc in sp just formed, ch 1, post dc around post dc, ch 1, * 4 dc, ch 3, 4 dc in next ch-3 sp, ch 1, post dc around post dc, ch 1, repeat from *, end 4 dc in first sp, ch 3, sl st in top of ch 3. End off.
2nd Motif: Work as for first motif through rnd 6.
Rnd 7: Ch 3, 3 dc in sp just formed, ch 1, post dc around post dc, ch 1, 4 dc in next ch-3 sp, ch 1, sc in any ch-3 sp of first motif, ch 1, 4 dc in same sp of 2nd motif, ch 1, post dc around next post dc, ch 1, 4 dc in next ch-3 sp, ch 1, sc in next ch-3 sp of first motif, ch 1, 4 dc in same sp of 2nd motif (2 points of 2nd motif joined to 2 points of first motif), ch 1, finish rnd as for first motif.
3rd, 4th and 5th Motifs: Work as for 2nd motif, joining to 2 points opposite pre-

vious joinings. (**Note:** There are 2 free points on each side of each joined motif.)
6th Motif (2nd row of motifs): Work as for 2nd motif, joining points to 2 free points on side of first motif.
7th, 8th, 9th and 10th Motifs: Work as for 2nd motif, joining 2 points to 2 points of previous motif and next 2 points to free points on side of motifs of first row.

Work 5 more rows of 5 motifs joining motifs in rnd 7 as before, until there are 7 rows of 5 motifs.
MEDIUM MOTIF: Rnd 1: With red, ch 4, join with sl st in first ch to form ring. Ch 3, 3 dc in ring; drop lp from hook, insert hook in top of ch 3, draw dropped lp through (popcorn), ch 2, dc in ring, ch 2, * 4-dc popcorn in ring, ch 2, dc in ring, ch 2, repeat from * twice, sl st in top of ch 3.
Rnd 2: Ch 3, 3 dc in same place as sl st, form popcorn, ch 1, 2 dc in ch-2 sp, ch 1, post dc around next dc, ch 1, 2 dc in next sp, ch 1, * 4-dc popcorn in next popcorn, ch 1, 2 dc in next sp, ch 1, post dc around next dc, ch 1, 2 dc in next sp, ch 1, repeat from * twice, ch 1, sl st in top of ch 3.
Rnd 3: Ch 3, 3 dc in same place as sl st, form popcorn, ch 1, dc in ch-1 sp, dc in each of 2 dc, ch 1, post dc around post dc, ch 1, dc in each of 2 dc, dc in ch-1 sp, ch 1, * popcorn in popcorn, ch 1, dc in ch-1 sp and in each of 2 dc, ch 1, post dc around post dc, ch 1, dc in each of 2 dc, dc in ch-1 sp, ch 1, repeat from * twice, sl st in top of ch 3.
Rnd 4 (joining rnd): These medium motifs are joined to the large motifs in the 24 spaces between 4 large motifs. Ch 3, 3 dc in same place as sl st, form popcorn, sc over joining of 2 large motifs, ch 1, dc in ch-1 sp and in each of 3 dc, ch 1, post dc around post dc, sc around post dc of large motif, ch 1, dc in each of 3 dc and in ch-1 sp, ch 1, * work popcorn, sc over joining of large motifs, ch 1, dc in ch-1 sp and in each of 3 dc, ch 1, post dc around post dc, sc around post dc of large motif, ch 1, dc in each of 3 dc and in ch-1 sp, ch 1, repeat from * twice, sl st in top of ch 3. End off.
HALF MEDIUM MOTIF: Row 1: With red, ch 4, join with sl st in first ch to form ring. Ch 3; repeat from * of rnd 1 of medium motif until there are 3 popcorns, dc in ring. End off.
Row 2: Join yarn to top of ch 3 at beg of row 1. Ch 3; repeat from * of rnd 2 of medium motif, end popcorn in popcorn, dc in dc. End off.
Row 3: Join yarn to top of ch 3 at beg of row 2. Ch 3; repeat from * of rnd 3 of medium motif, end popcorn in popcorn, dc in dc. End off.
Row 4 (joining row): These half motifs are joined to 2 joined large motifs in the 20 spaces around edge of afghan. Join yarn to top of ch 3 at beg of row 3. Ch 3, sc in ch-3 sp of large motif, popcorn in popcorn, ch 1, dc in ch-1 sp and in

each of 3 dc, ch 1, post dc around post dc, sc around post dc of large motif, ch 1, dc in each of 3 dc and in ch-1 sp, repeat from * of rnd 4 of medium motif once, end popcorn in popcorn, sc in ch-3 sp of large motif, dc in dc. End off.
SMALL MOTIF: These small motifs are joined to large motifs in the 58 spaces between each 2 large joined motifs. With green, ch 6, join with sl st in first ch to form ring. Ch 3, 3 dc in ring, ch 1, sc around post dc of large motif, ch 1, 4 dc in ring, ch 1, sc around joining of medium motif, ch 1, 4 dc in ring, ch 1, sc around post dc of large motif, ch 1, 4 dc in ring, ch 1, sc around joining of medium motif, ch 1, sl st in top of ch 3. End.
BORDER: Join white at beg of any half motif. * Work 2 dc over each dc to center of half motif, dc in center ring, 2 dc over each ch 3 along edge, dc in joining, 2 dc in ch-3 sp of large motif, dc in each of next 4 dc; holding back on hook last lp of each dc, dc in each of next 2 ch-1 sps, yo and through 3 lps on hook; dc in each of next 4 dc, 2 dc in ch-3 sp, dc in joining, repeat from * around, working 3 dc in each ch-3 sp of large motifs at corners.

POINSETTIA
Shown on page 231

SIZE: 42″ x 52″.
MATERIALS: Knitting worsted, 5 4-oz. skeins white, 4 skeins green, 3 skeins red, 1 skein yellow. Crochet hook size J.
GAUGE: 10 sts = 3″. Motif is 8″ from side to opposite side.

AFGHAN: MOTIF (make 32): With yellow, ch 4, join with sl st to form ring. **Rnd 1:** Ch 3 (counts as 1 dc), 11 dc in ring. Sl st in top of ch 3. Cut yarn.
Rnd 2: Join red in any dc, ch 8, * sc in 2nd ch from hook, hdc in next ch, dc in next 2 ch, hdc in next ch, sc in next ch, sc in next dc, ch 7, repeat from * 10 times, sc in 2nd ch from hook, hdc in next ch, dc in next 2 ch, hdc in next ch, sc in last ch, sl st in first ch of first petal. Cut yarn.
Rnd 3: Join green in any sc between petals; ch 5; * working in back of petals, dc in next sc between petals, ch 2, repeat from * around, sl st in 3rd ch of ch 5.
Rnd 4: Ch 9, * sc in 2nd ch from hook, hdc in next ch, dc in next ch, tr in next ch, dc in next ch, hdc in next ch, sc in next ch, 2 sc in ch-2 sp, sc in dc, ch 8, repeat from * 10 times, work last ch 8 as before, 2 sc in ch-2 sp, sl st in first ch of first leaf. Cut yarn.
Rnd 5: With white, sc in each of 3 sc between leaves, * ch 1; working behind leaves, sc in each of next 3 sc,

repeat from * around, end ch 1, sl st in first sc.

Rnd 6: Ch 1, sc in first sc, sc in next sc, * insert hook in sc at tip of red petal and into next sc of rnd 5 at same time, draw yarn through, complete sc, 2 sc in next ch-1 sp, sc in each of next 2 sc, repeat from * around, end 2 sc in last ch-1 sp, sl st in first sc.

Rnd 7: Ch 3 (counts as 1 dc), dc in each of next 3 sc, * ch 2, sk 1 sc, dc in each of next 4 sc, repeat from * around, end ch 2, sl st in top of ch 3.

Rnd 8: Ch 3, dc in each of next 3 dc, * dc in ch-2 sp, sc in sc at tip of leaf, dc in each of next 4 dc, repeat from * around, end dc in ch-2 sp, sc in tip of last leaf, sl st in top of ch 3.

Rnd 9: Ch 1, sc in each of first 5 dc, * sc in sc at tip of leaf, sc in each of next 2 dc, 3 dc in next dc (corner), sc in each of next 2 dc, sc in sc at tip of leaf, sc in each of next 5 dc, repeat from * around (6 corners), end sc in each of last 2 dc, sc in sc at tip of leaf, sl st in first sc. End off.

FINISHING: Sew motifs tog through back lp of each st. Sew 5 motifs tog in a strip (width of afghan), joining opposite sides of motifs. Make 3 more strips of 5 motifs. Make 3 strips of 4 motifs. Alternating 5-motif and 4-motif strips, sew strips tog (length of afghan). With white, work 2 rows of sc around afghan, working in back lps only, making 2 sc in each point and skipping sc's at inner corners to keep edging flat. Cut 5″ strands of white for fringe. Knot a fringe in each st around outer edge of afghan.

ANIMAL MITTENS
Shown on page 232

SIZES: Directions for small size (1-2) and medium size (3-4). **Note:** Needles and gauge determine size.

MATERIALS: Knitting worsted, 2 ozs. of main color (MC), small amounts of other colors given in individual directions.

For Small Size: Set of dp needles Nos. 2 and 4. **For Medium Size:** Set of dp needles Nos. 4 and 6. Tapestry needle.

GAUGE: 6 sts = 1″ (No. 4 needles). 5 sts = 1″ (No. 6 needles).

GENERAL DIRECTIONS: LEFT MITTEN: Cuff: With smaller needles and MC, cast on loosely 28 sts; divide on 3 dp needles—10-9-9. Mark end of rnd. Join; work in ribbing of k 1, p 1 for 2½″. Change to larger needles.

Hand: Rnds 1-9: Knit.

Rnd 10: K 7, drop yarn; with a strand of a 2nd color, k 5 (thumb), sl these 5 sts back on left-hand needle; pick up MC, finish rnd.

Rnds 11-24: Knit.

Shape Top: Rnd 25: (K 1, k 2 tog, k 8,

k 2 tog in back of sts, k 1) twice—24 sts. K 1 rnd.

Rnd 27: (K 1, k 2 tog, k 6, k 2 tog in back of sts, k 1) twice—20 sts. K 1 rnd.

Rnd 29: (K 1, k 2 tog, k 4, k 2 tog in back of sts, k 1) twice—16 sts. K 1 rnd.

Rnds 31 and 32: K 2 tog around—4 sts. Break yarn, draw through remaining sts. Fasten on wrong side.

Thumb: Being very careful, draw out 2nd color yarn strand from 5 sts at base of thumb. Pick up and divide the 9 lps (5 from bottom, 4 from top of thumb base) on 3 larger dp needles. Join MC; k around, pick up and k 1 st at each side of thumb—11 sts. K around for 9 rnds.

Shape Tip: Next Rnd: K 2 tog, k 1, (k 2 tog) twice, k 2 tog—7 sts.

Next Rnd: K 1, (k 2 tog) 3 times—4 sts. End same as top of mitten. Steam-press.

RIGHT MITTEN: Work as for left mitten through rnd 9.

Rnd 10: K 2, drop yarn; with a 2nd color, k 5 (thumb), sl these 5 sts back on left-hand needle; pick up MC, finish rnd. Complete as for left mitten.

EMBROIDERY: Following chart, embroider features on left mitten in duplicate st.

LION: Small amount of green, black and red. Following general directions, make mittens in orange (MC).

Tail: With 2 larger dp needles and MC, cast on 4 sts.

Row 1: K across. Do not turn; push sts to other end of needle. With yarn at back of work, repeat row 1 for 2″. K 2 tog twice. End off. Sew cast-on sts to center back of right mitten on rnds 11 and 12.

Make 11 1″ MC pompons. Sew a pompon to end of tail. Embroider features. Sew 9 pompons around back of left mitten, one to center above ribbing.

RABBIT: Small amount of black and white. Following general directions, make mittens in light gray (MC).

Ears (make 2): With larger needles and MC, cast on 6 sts—2-2-2. Join; k 4 rnds.

Rnd 5: (Inc 1 st in next st, k 2) twice—8 sts. K 1 rnd.

Rnd 7: (K 3, inc 1 st in next st) twice—10 sts. K 2 rnds.

Rnd 10: (Inc 1 st in next st, k 4) twice—12 sts.

Rnds 11-19: Knit.

Rnd 20: (K 2 tog, k 4) twice—10 sts. K 2 rnds.

Rnd 23: (K 3, k 2 tog) twice—8 sts. K 1 rnd.

Rnd 25: (K 2 tog, k 2) twice—6 sts. K 1 rnd.

Rnd 27: (K 1, k 2 tog) twice—4 sts. K 1 rnd.

Rnd 29: K 2 tog twice. End off leaving long end for sewing.

With MC, make 1″ MC pompon; attach to center back of right mitten at

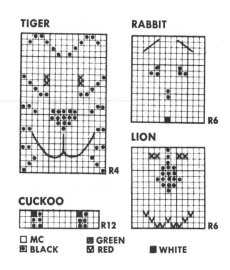

TIGER — R4
RABBIT — R6
LION — R6
CUCKOO — R12

☐ MC   ▨ GREEN
▥ BLACK   ▧ RED   ■ WHITE

rnd 12. Sew cast-on edge of ears to back of left mitten as indicated on chart. Embroider features.

CUCKOO: Small amount of black, white and orange. Following general directions, make mittens in turquoise (MC).

Tail: With larger needles and MC, cast on 15 sts—5-5-5. Join; k 6 rnds.

Rnd 7: K 7, k 2 tog, k 4, k 2 tog—13 sts. K 2 rnds. Drop MC. Divide sts on first and 3rd needles. With free needle, sl first st of first needle, last st of 3rd needle, * next st on first needle, next st on 3rd needle, repeat from * until all sts are on free needle—13 sts. Working back and forth with 2 needles, work as follows:

Next Row: With MC, k 1, * p 1, k 1, repeat from * across.

Next Row: P 1, * k 1, p 1, repeat from * across. Work 1 row in ribbing as established. Cut MC, join white yarn. Work 1 row in ribbing as established. With white, bind off as follows: K 1, * sl this st back on left-hand needle, k same st, p next st, pass k st over p st, sl p st back on left-hand needle, p same st, k next st, pass p st over k st, repeat from * until all sts are bound off. Sew cast-on edge across rnds 12 and 13 on center back of right mitten.

Beak: With larger needles and orange, cast on 16 sts—5-5-6. Join; k 1 rnd.

Rnd 2: K 3, k 2 tog, k 11—15 sts.

Rnd 3: Knit

Rnd 4: (K 1, k 2 tog) twice, (k 2, k 2 tog) twice, k 1—11 sts.

Rnd 5: (K 2 tog, k 1) twice, (k 2 tog) twice, k 1—7 sts.

Rnd 6: K 3 tog, (k 2 tog) twice—3 sts. End off; fasten securely; stuff lightly.

Embroider features. With k 3 tog on rnd 6 as lower beak, sew beak to back of left mitten below eyes as shown.

TIGER: Small amount of black, red and bright green. Following general directions, make mittens in yellow (MC).

Tail: Work tail as for lion. If desired, embroider on black stripes.

Ears (make 2): With larger needles and MC, cast on 18 sts—6-6-6. Join; k around for 5 rnds.

Rnd 6: (K 1, k 2 tog, k 3, k 2 tog, k 1) twice—14 sts.

Rnd 7: (K 1, k 2 tog, k 1, k 2 tog, k 1) twice—10 sts.

Rnd 8: (K 1, k 3 tog, k 1) twice—6 sts.

Rnd 9: K 3 tog twice—2 sts. End off; fasten securely. Gather cast-on edge of ears slightly; sew to sides of left mitten. Embroider features in running st.

PUPPY MITTENS
Shown on page 233

SIZES: Directions for 3 years. Changes for 4-5 and 6-7 years are in parentheses.

MATERIALS: Knitting worsted, 2 ozs. light green (LG), small amounts white (W) and brown (B). Knitting needles Nos. 6 and 8. Two stitch holders. Four black shank buttons. Scrap of pink felt.

GAUGE: 4 sts = 1″; 6 rows = 1″ (stockinette st, No. 8 needles).

Note: Work with double strand of yarn unless otherwise indicated.

RIGHT MITTEN: With double strand LG (see Note) and No. 6 needles, cast on 22 (22-24) sts. Work in ribbing of k 1, p 1 for 11 (13-15) rows. Change to No. 8 needles. Beg with a p row, work in stockinette st (k 1 row, p 1 row) for 5 (7-7) rows.

Inc for Thumb: K 12 (12-13), cast on 1 st, k 1, cast on 1 st, k 9 (9-10). P 1 row.

Next Row: K 12 (12-13), cast on 1 st, k 3, cast on 1 st, k 9 (9-10). P 1 row.

Next Row: K 12 (12-13), cast on 1 st, k 5, cast on 1 st, k 9 (9-10). P 1 row.

Divide for Thumb: K 12 (12-13), sl these sts on a holder (back of hand), inc 1 st in next st, k 6, sl remaining 9 (9-10) sts on a holder (palm).

Thumb: Work in stockinette st on 8 sts for 5 (7-8) rows.

Next Row: Work 2 tog across—4 sts. Cut yarn leaving an end for sewing; draw through remaining sts. Pull up, sew seam.

Hand: From right side, sl sts from first holder (back of hand) to needle; join double strand LG, pick up 1 st at base of thumb, k sts from 2nd holder (palm)—22 (22-24) sts. Work in stockinette st for 11 (13-15) rows, end p row.

Shape Top: Row 1: K 1 (1-0), * k 2 tog, k 1, repeat from * across—15 (15-16) sts. P 1 row.

Row 3: K 0 (0-1), * k 2 tog, k 1, repeat from * across—10 (10-11) sts. Finish as for thumb.

LEFT MITTEN: Work as for right mitten, having 9 (9-10) sts (palm) before thumb, 12 (12-13) sts (back) after thumb on k rows.

Face: With one strand W and No. 8 needles, cast on 12 sts. Work in stockinette st for 2″ (2½″-3″). Bind off.

Features: Sew button eyes to face. With B, embroider small straight sts for nose, embroider mouth in outline st. Cut pink felt tongue; sew in place.

Sew face to back of mitten on 3 sides, leaving bottom open for tissue.

Ears (make 2): With one strand B and No. 8 needles, cast on 5 sts. Work in stockinette st for 10 rows. Cut yarn, leaving an end for sewing; draw through sts, pull up and fasten. Sew ears to sides of face.

Twisted Cord: With two strands of LG, make twisted cord 40″ long. Sew an end to inside of each cuff.

SNOWMAN MITTENS
Shown on page 233

SIZES: Directions for 2-3 years. Changes for 4-5 years and 6-7 years are in parentheses.

MATERIALS: Knitting worsted, 2 (2-3) ozs. green; small amounts of red, black, white. Crochet hook size F.

GAUGE: 4 sc = 1″; 5 rows = 1″.

MITTEN: PALM: With green, ch 22 (25-28). **Row 1:** Sc in 2nd ch from hook and in each ch—21 (24-27) sc. Ch 1, turn each row.

Row 2: 2 sc in first sc (top), sc in each sc across.

Row 3: Sc in each sc—22 (25-28) sc.

Rows 4 and 5: Repeat rows 2 and 3—23 (26-29) sc.

Row 6: Sc in each sc across.

Row 7: Sc in each of 10 (11-12) sc, ch 16 (18-20) for thumb, sc in same st as last sc, sc in each sc to top.

Row 8: Sk first sc, sc in each sc and ch across—39 (44-49) sc.

Row 9: Sc in each sc.

Row 10: Sk first sc, sc in each sc across—38 (43-48) sc.

Row 11: Sc in each sc. End off. Make another palm. Sew up thumb, being sure to reverse for 2nd mitten. Work 1 (1-2) rows of sc around sides and top of palm.

BACK: Work as for palm, omitting thumb: inc at top edge on rows 2 and 4, dec at top edge on rows 8 and 10.

Sew palm to back. If desired, make 34″-36″ chain with double yarn to go through sleeves. Sew to backs of mittens at edge.

SNOWMAN: Head: With white, ch 2. Make 6 sc in 2nd ch from hook. On next rnd, 2 sc in each sc—12 sc. On next rnd, inc in every other sc—18 sc. Work 1 rnd even. End off. Sew to mitten wrong side out; stuff lightly with yarn. Embroider black eyes, red mouth.

Scarf: With red, ch 22. Sc in 2nd ch

from hook and in each ch. Ch 1, turn. Sc in each sc across. End off. Fold and sew on. Add fringe.

Hat: With black, ch 8. Sc in 2nd ch from hook and in each ch—7 sc. Work 6 more rows of sc. Gather last row slightly; sew to mitten above head. For brim, make a ch using yarn double; sew in place.

COLOR CAPS
Shown on page 234

SIZE: Fits all sizes.

MATERIALS: Knitting worsted: Striped Cap: 2 ozs. green and 4 ozs. assorted colors. Black and white cap: 4 ozs. black and 2 ozs. white. Zigzag cap: 2 ozs. raspberry and 1 oz. each of maroon, gold, yellow, scarlet, beige, hot pink, rust or any desired colors. Set of dp needles No. 9. Large-eyed needle.

GAUGE: 9 sts = 2″; 5 rows = 1″.

Pattern Notes For Black and White and Zigzag Caps: Always change colors on wrong side, picking up new strand from under dropped strand. Carry color not being used loosely across back of work. Cut and join colors when necessary.

STRIPED CAP: Beg at top edge, with any desired color, cast on 22 sts; divide on 3 dp needles. Join, being careful not to twist sts. Put and keep a marker on needle between last and first sts of rnd. Work around in stockinette st (k each rnd), inc 1 st in each st for 2 rnds—88 sts. Work around in stockinette st, changing colors as desired until piece measures 16½″ from start. With green only, work even until piece measures 22½″ from start. Turn work inside out (p side is right side of work).

Next Rnd: P 2 tog around—44 sts. Repeat last row—22 sts. Bind off tightly.

FINISHING: Steam-press tube lightly. With matching yarn, draw sts tog tightly on both ends; fasten securely. Fold solid color end to wrong side forming cap.

BLACK AND WHITE CAP: Beg at top edge, with black, cast on 22 sts; divide sts on 3 dp needles. Join, being careful not to twist sts. Put and keep a marker between last and first sts of rnd. Work around in stockinette st (k each rnd), inc 1 st in each st for 2 rnds—88 sts. K 1 rnd.

Pattern: Following chart 1 (see Pattern Notes), work pat in stockinette st, starting at arrow on rnd 1 and repeating pat to end of rnd. Work to top of chart (82 rnds). With black only, work around in stockinette st until piece measures 22½″ from start.

Next Rnd: K 2 tog around—44 sts. Repeat last rnd—22 sts. Bind off tightly.

FINISHING: Work as for striped cap.

ZIGZAG CAP: Beg at top edge, with maroon or any desired color, cast on

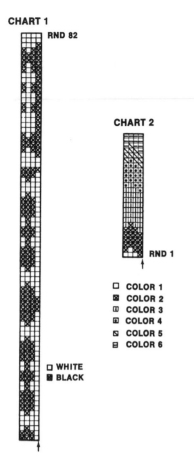

CHART 1
RND 82

CHART 2
RND 1

☐ COLOR 1
⊠ COLOR 2
⊞ COLOR 3
⊡ COLOR 4
◩ COLOR 5
⊟ COLOR 6

☐ WHITE
■ BLACK

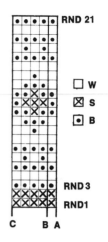

RND 21

☐ W
⊠ S
⊡ B

RND 3
RND 1

C   B A

22 sts; divide sts on 3 dp needles. Join, being careful not to twist sts. Put and keep a marker between last and first sts of rnd. Work around in stockinette st (k each rnd), inc 1 st in each st for 2 rnds—88 sts. K 5 rnds.

Pattern: Following chart 2 (see Pattern Notes), work pat in stockinette st, starting at arrow and repeating pat to end of rnd. Work to top of chart (25 rnds) then continue to work in pat as established, changing colors as desired and working desired number of rnds between color changes until piece measures 16½" from start. Keeping to pat as established, work next color change with raspberry. Working with raspberry only, work even until piece measures 22½" from start.

Next Rnd: K 2 tog around—44 sts. Repeat last rnd—22 sts. Bind off tightly.

FINISHING: Work as for striped cap.

MISSES' SNOW SET
Shown on page 235

SIZE: Medium.

MATERIALS: Knitting worsted, 6 ozs. scarlet (S), 2 ozs. each black (B) and white (W). Sets of dp needles Nos. 5 and 8. Stitch holder. Yarn needle. For ascot: ¼ yard 44" lining material.

GAUGE: 5 sts = 1"; 6 rows = 1" (No. 8 needles).

Pattern Notes: Always change colors on wrong side, picking up new strand from under dropped strand. Carry unused color loosely across back of work. When working ascot, cut and join colors as needed.

HAT: Hem and Hemline: With S and No. 8 needles, cast on loosely and divide 100 sts on 3 dp needles. Mark end of rnd. Join; work around in stockinette st (k each rnd) for 4 rnds. P next rnd for hemline.

Pattern: Rnds 1-21: Following chart 1, k and repeat pat from B to C around. Cut off B and W. With S, work in stockinette st until piece measures 8½" above hemline.

Next 2 Rnds: K 2 tog around—25 sts.
Next Rnd: K 2 tog around, end k 1—13 sts. Cut yarn leaving a 10" end; draw remaining sts tog. Fasten on wrong side.

FINISHING: Turn hem on hemline to wrong side; sew in place loosely.

POMPON: Wind B 75 times around a 2½" piece of cardboard, then wind W 75 times around same cardboard. Tie one end securely; cut lps on other end. Trim; fasten to top of hat.

FRINGE: Cut 50 lengths each of B and W, 3½" long. Fold strand in half. With crochet hook, draw folded lp through p st at hemline, inserting hook from back to front. Pull strands through lp. Alternating colors, knot a strand in every p st at hemline. Trim.

RIGHT MITTEN: With S and No. 8 dp needles, cast on loosely and divide 38 sts on 3 dp needles. Work in stockinette st for 4 rnds. P next rnd for hemline.

Pattern: Rnds 1 and 2: With S, k.
Rnds 3, 5, 7, 9 and 11: With B, k.
Rnds 4, 8 and 10: With W, k.
Rnds 6 and 12: (K 1 B, k 1 W) around.
Rnd 13: With B, k. Change to No. 5 dp needles. With S, k 1 rnd.
Rnds 15-20: With S, work in k 1, p 1 ribbing around. Change to No. 8 needles.
Rnds 21-27: Repeat rnds 5-11. Cut off B and W. With S, k 2 rnds.
Thumb Gore: Rnd 1: K 2, sl marker on needle, inc 1 st in next st (k in front and back of same st), k 1, inc 1 st in next st, sl marker on needle, work to end of rnd.
Rnd 2: Knit, slipping markers.
Rnd 3: Work to marker, sl marker, inc 1 st in next st, k to 1 st before 2nd marker, inc 1 st in next st, sl marker, k to end of rnd. Repeat rnds 2 and 3 until there are 15 sts between markers. K 1 rnd.
Next Rnd: K to 1 st beyond first marker, sl next 14 sts to holder to be worked later, cast on 2 sts, work to end of rnd. Work even on 38 sts until piece measures 4½" above cast-on sts at

thumb, or 1" less than desired length, end 2 sts before end of rnd. Put marker on needle.

Shape Top: Rnd 1: (Sl 1, k 1, psso, k 15, k 2 tog) twice—34 sts.
Rnd 2: (Sl 1, k 1, psso, k 13, k 2 tog) twice—30 sts. Continue to dec 4 sts in this manner every rnd, having 2 sts less between decs until 6 sts remain.
Next Rnd: (Sl 1, k 2 tog, psso) twice—2 sts. Break yarn leaving an end. Pull yarn through sts; fasten securely on wrong side.

Thumb: Sl 14 sts from holder to No. 8 dp needle; join S, pick up 2 sts over cast-on sts and 1 st in each corner. Divide 18 sts on 3 dp needles. Mark end of rnd. K 1 rnd, dec 1 st at each corner—16 sts. K around until thumb is 2" or ½" from tip of thumb.

Shape Tip: Rnd 1: (Sl 1, k 1, psso, k 4, k 2 tog) twice—12 sts.
Rnd 2: (Sl 1, k 1, psso, k 2, k 2 tog) twice—8 sts.
Rnd 3: (Sl 1, k 1, psso, k 2 tog) twice—4 sts.
Rnd 4: (K 2 tog) twice—2 sts. Break yarn leaving an end. Pull yarn through sts; fasten securely on wrong side.

LEFT MITTEN: Work as for right mitten to thumb gore.

Thumb Gore: Rnd 1: K to last 5 sts of rnd, sl marker on needle, inc 1 st in next st, k 1, inc 1 st in next st, sl marker on needle, k 2. Finish to correspond to right mitten.

FINISHING: Turn hem on hemline to wrong side; sew in place loosely.

ASCOT: With S, using 2 No. 8 needles, cast on 35 sts. Work back and forth in stockinette st (k 1 row, p 1 row) for 2", end k row.

Pattern: Rnds 3-21: P 5 S; following chart 1, p from A to B once, from B to C 6 times; p 5 S. Working in stockinette st, continue in this manner to top of chart. Cut off B and W. With S, work in stockinette st for 7", end p row. Piece should measure about 12" from start.

Shape Neck: Dec Row: K 2 tog across,

end k 1—18 sts. Work in stockinette st until piece from dec row measures 17″, end p row.

Inc Row: K 1, * inc 1 st, k 1, repeat from * across—35 sts. **To Inc:** Place right needle behind left needle and, from top down, insert right needle in st below next st, knit this st. St above when knitted counts as 1 k st.

Work in stockinette st for 7″, end k row. Work in pattern as before. With S, work in stockinette st for 2″, end p row. Bind off.

FINISHING: Run in yarn ends on wrong side. Steam-press lightly. Using ascot as pattern, cut lining. Line ascot.

FRINGE: Cut 36 W and 34 B yarn lengths, 6″ long. Starting with W, knot a strand in each cast-on and bound-off st, as for hat. Trim to 2½″ length.

HAND-HOLDER SET
Shown on page 235

SIZES: Mittens: Directions for medium size. Any changes for large size are in parentheses. **Double Mitten:** Directions fit medium and large size.

MATERIALS: Knitting worsted, 1 4-oz. skein green, main color (MC) and 1 1-oz. skein white, contrasting color (CC). Set of dp needles No. 6. Two stitch holders for double mitten.

GAUGE: 11 sts = 2″; 7 rnds = 1″.

MITTENS: Cast on 36 (40) sts loosely. Divide on 3 dp needles. Mark end of rnd. Join, being careful not to twist sts.

Cuff: With MC, work around in ribbing of k 2, p 2 for 3 rnds. With CC, work around in ribbing of k 2, p 2 for 2 rnds. Repeat last 5 rnds 3 times. Cut CC; with MC, k 3 rnds.

Inc for Thumb: Rnd 1: With MC, k 2, put a marker on needle, inc 1 st in next st, put another marker on needle, k to end of rnd—37 (41) sts.

Rnd 2: K around.

Rnd 3: K around, inc 1 st in st after first and before 2nd marker—2 incs. Continue in this manner, inc 2 sts for thumb every other rnd until there are 12 (14) sts between markers. K 2 rnds even.

Palm: Rnd 1: K 2, sl next 12 (14) sts on a piece of yarn; cast on 7 sts under thumb, k to end of rnd—42 (46) sts. K around until piece measures 3½″ (4½″) from thumb opening. Dec 0 (4) sts evenly spaced on last rnd—42 sts.

Shape Tip: First Dec Rnd: (K 5, k 2 tog) 6 times—36 sts. K 1 rnd.

2nd Dec Rnd: (K 4, k 2 tog) 6 times—30 sts. K 1 rnd.

3rd Dec Rnd: (K 3, k 2 tog) 6 times—24 sts. K 1 rnd.

4th Dec Rnd: (K 2, k 2 tog) 6 times—18 sts. K 1 rnd.

5th Dec Rnd: (K 1, k 2 tog) 6 times—12 sts. K 1 rnd.

6th Dec Rnd: K 2 tog around—6 sts. Break yarn leaving a long end for sewing. Thread end in needle, draw through remaining sts and fasten securely on wrong side. Weave in end.

Thumb: Place 12 (14) sts for thumb on 3 dp needles. Join MC, pick up and k 7 sts at base of thumb—19 (21) sts.

Next Rnd: K around, dec 2 sts at base of thumb—17 (19) sts. K around until thumb measures 2″ (2½″), dec 2 (1) sts on last rnd—15 (18) sts.

First Dec Rnd: * K 3 (4), k 2 tog, repeat from * twice—12 (15) sts. K 1 rnd.

2nd Dec Rnd: * K 2 (3), k 2 tog, repeat from * twice—9 (12) sts. K 1 rnd.

3rd Dec Rnd: * K 1 (2), k 2 tog, repeat from * twice—6 (9) sts.

On Large Size Only: K 1 rnd.

4th Dec Rnd: (K 1, k 2 tog) 3 times—6 sts.

On Both Sizes: Break yarn, finish as for tip of hand.

DOUBLE MITTEN: With MC, cast on 36 sts. Divide evenly on 3 dp needles. Mark end of rnd. Join; work cuff same as for mittens. Cut CC; with MC, k 3 rnds.

Shape Palm: Inc 1 st in first st, k around. K 2 rnds. Repeat these 3 rnds 4 times—41 sts. Sl sts on 2 holders. Break yarn. Work 2nd mitten in same manner; do not sl sts on holders; do not break yarn. Sl last 30 sts worked on one dp needle, first 11 sts on 2nd dp needle.

Join Mittens: With free dp needle, k across 26 sts on first mitten; with free dp needle, k last 15 sts on first mitten and continue to k 11 sts from 2nd mitten; with free needle, k last 30 sts on 2nd mitten—82 sts.

Palms: K around until palms measure 4″ above joining, dec 2 sts on last rnd—80 sts.

Shape Tip: Rnd 1: (K 2 tog, k 8) 8 times—72 sts. K 1 rnd.

Rnd 3: (K 2 tog, k 7) 8 times—64 sts. K 1 rnd.

Rnd 5: (K 2 tog, k 6) 8 times—56 sts. K 1 rnd.

Rnd 7: (K 2 tog, k 5) 8 times—48 sts. K 1 rnd.

Rnd 9: (K 2 tog, k 4) 8 times—40 sts. K 1 rnd.

Rnd 11: (K 2 tog, k 3) 8 times—32 sts. K 1 rnd.

Rnd 13: (K 2 tog, k 2) 8 times—24 sts. K 1 rnd.

Rnd 15: (K 2 tog, k 1) 8 times—16 sts. K 1 rnd.

Rnd 17: K 2 tog around—8 sts. Break yarn, finish as for tip of hand.

FINISHING: Run in yarn ends on wrong side. Weave joining at palm on double mittens. Steam-press.

STRIPED MITTENS
Shown on page 235

SIZES: Directions are for children's size 5-7 years. Changes for size 8-10 years are in parentheses.

MATERIALS: Knitting worsted, 2 ozs. deep turquoise (DT), 1 oz. each royal blue (RB) and white (W). Knitting needles No. 6. Two stitch holders.

GAUGE: 11 sts = 2″; 15 rows = 2″.

Notes: Carry unused colors loosely up side edge, twisting colors every other row. When working thumb, join separate strands of yarn.

PATTERN STRIPE: Work * 2 rows RB, 4 rows W, 2 rows RB, 4 rows DT for pattern stripe; repeat from * having 3 pattern stripes on hand, 2 pattern stripes on thumb; complete mitten with DT.

RIGHT MITTEN: With RB, cast on 29 (33) sts.

Row 1 (right side): (K 1, p 1) across, end k 1.

Row 2: (P 1, k 1) across, end p 1. Cut RB, join DT. K 1 row. Beg with row 2, work in ribbing until piece measures 3″ from beg, end row 2, inc 3 sts evenly spaced on last row—32 (36) sts. Following pattern stripe, work in stockinette st (k 1 row, p 1 row) for 6 rows, end p row.

Inc for Thumb: K 16 (18), put a marker on needle, inc 1 st in next st (to inc, place point of right needle behind left needle and, from top down, insert it in st below first st on left needle; k this st, then k st above it in usual way—1 inc made), k 1, inc 1 st in next st, put a marker on needle, k 13 (15). P 1 row.

Next Row: K, inc 1 st in st after first and before 2nd marker. P 1 row. Continue in this manner, inc 2 sts for thumb every other row until there are 11 (13) sts between markers. P 1 row.

Divide for Thumb: K 16 (18), put these sts on a holder (back of hand), k 11 (13) for thumb, casting on 1 st each side of thumb; put remaining 13 (15) sts on a holder (palm).

Thumb: Work in pattern in stockinette st on 13 (15) sts for 1½″ (1¾″), end p row, dec 1 (0) st on last row—12 (15) sts.

Shape Tip: (K 2 tog, k 1) 4 (5) times—8 (10) sts. P 1 row.

Next Row: (K 2 tog) across—4 (5) sts. Break yarn leaving end for sewing. Thread end in needle, draw through remaining sts; draw up tightly and fasten. Sew seam with matching colors.

Hand: From right side, sl sts from first holder (back of hand) to needle; join yarn, pick up and k 2 sts on base of thumb, k sts from 2nd holder (palm)—31 (35) sts. Work even in pattern stripe until piece measures 4½″ (5″) above

Continued on page 259

NOEL AFGHAN

Crochet our lovely afghan in motifs of shell stitch and popcorns (53″ × 76″). Use soft mohair-like yarn in Christmas colors. Noel Afghan, page 225.

HOLIDAY AFGHAN

Say "Merry Christmas" with a cheery afghan, crocheted in festive red, white and green. Petals and leaves of poinsettias are raised for a three-dimensional pattern. Directions, page 225.

CAPTIVATING ANIMAL MITTENS

A special Christmas gift, mittens are sized for youngsters 1–4 years old. Left mitten is "front" of lion, rabbit, tiger and cuckoo; right mitten has the tail. Directions, page 226.

FUN
MITTENS
FOR
KIDDIES

Puppy mittens can play a hand puppet's game.
Face is a tiny pocket for hankies; knitted
ears, button eyes, pink felt tongue are sewed
on. Worked with a double strand of
knitting worsted on two needles, for 3–7 year-olds;
page 227. Bright green mittens, worked
in single crochet, have well-dressed snowmen
appliqued on their backs. Mittens, for
sizes 2–7 years, are joined with a crocheted
chain. Snowman Mittens, page 227.

THREE HATS SIX WAYS

Three changeable caps, tubes made of knitting worsted in patterned stockinette stitch, ends closed and one end stuffed inside the other. See Color Caps, page 227.

SEVEN WINTER WARMUPS

Red, white and black set makes one or more great gifts; Misses' Set, page 228. Hand-holder set is for good friends; page 229. Children's striped mittens, page 229. Color-bright scarf and cap set, page 259.

HAND WARMERS

Easy-knit mittens in children's sizes and easy-crochet mitts for big girls are here for the gift-making. Clockwise from top: Rudolph Mittens, with knit-in reindeer, page 260; Easy Striped Mittens, extra warm in doubled yarn, page 261; Appliqued Mittens with Humpty-Dumpty in felt, page 260; Crocheted Mittens, page 261; Duck, Dog and Bunny designs in duplicate stitch, page 260.

FOOT WARMERS

Six pairs of ladies' slippers, all variations on a single theme of crochet, are six happy answers to a gift list. All in single crochet, with sturdy soles of rug yarn and colorful uppers of four-ply Orlon, slippers are quick-to-make, fun to crochet, and inexpensive, too! Pair at bottom center has woven insteps, made by old-fashioned darning. See Gift Slippers, page 262.

LITTLE AFGHANS

Two children's coverlets are crocheted in afghan stitch and colorfully embroidered. Crib Blanket, page 263. Henry Hedgehog crocheted toy, page 264. Norse Afghan, page 264.

Hedgehog designed by Sue Penrod.
Child's rocker by Beka Inc.

HOODED BUNTING

Adorable baby bunting is for the experienced knitter only. Hooded Bunting, page 265.

PIXIE PONCHO

Cute-as-can-be cover-up is impishly easy, keeps children cozy in comfort! Stitch a poncho for all your favorite pixies aged 1–3 years—here's how:

Start with warm, four-ply knitting worsted yarn in the color of your choice. Simply knit the poncho in two stockinette pieces, then seam at the sides.

Add the pixie hood with braided yarn drawstring. Crochet beading around poncho hem and loop with thick fringe. Complete Pixie Poncho directions can be found on page 265.

PAMPER BABY IN QUILTED SOFTNESS!

Knit a downy-soft set for baby. Coverlet and suit are knitted in two colors, "quilted" with diagonal running stitches of contrasting yarn. Set and animals on page 266.

Baby's coverlet is knitted in two layers—white and yellow —then quilted and trimmed with a knitted ruffle. Lace the coverlet edges together with yarn—it becomes a bunting!

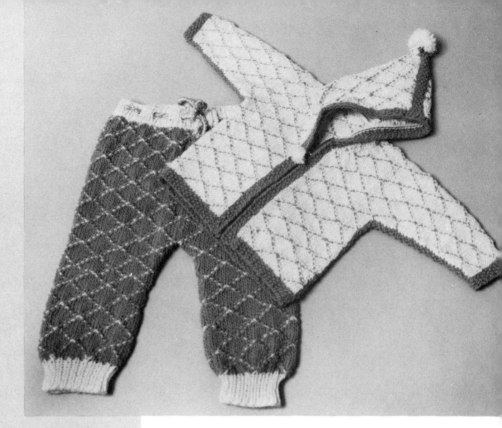

Baby suit, sized for 6 months to 1 year, has drawstring pants and zip-up jacket. Use leftover yarn to knit Freddie Frog and Katy Kat!

Photography by Arthur Klonsky.

Red vest and scarf set
is on page 268. Red and white
vest and tam, page 268.

GIFTS
TO
CROCHET

Snowflake Sets have cross-stitch embroidery; page 268.

Snowflake sets designed by Ruth Fulwiler

TOTS' TOGS

Zip-up jacket, in double crochet, has crocheted ribbings for a snug fit, flower appliques on fronts and matching hat for a happy note; page 269.

Easy-knit jumper is charmingly trimmed with embroidered flowers, crocheted scalloped edgings; page 270.

PATTERNED FOR WINTER

Reindeer muff's wintry design is in duplicate stitch; page 271. Clusters and popcorns texture a crocheted Aran muff; page 271. Reindeer Pants Set is knit in the round; page 272.

LADYBUGS

**Bright red ladybugs add cheer
to T sweaters, knit in the round.
Directions for girls' sizes 4
to 12, page 273.**

ACCESSORY SETS FOR TOTS

Your favorite girl says "hello" in a hat, muffler and muff trio, worked in half double crochet and "furry" loop stitch. For Scarf, Muff, Hat Set, see page 274.

Your favorite boy waves "good-bye" in his winter warmers knit in Quaker and stockinette stitch patterns. Directions for sizes 2–8. Scarf, Mittens, Hat Set, page 275.

SLIPPERS AND LOUNGE

BOOTS FOR GIFTS

Great slippers for apres ski, or any occasion that calls for cozy feet, are crocheted in an assortment of colors in a variety of stitches. Soles can be cut from leather, suede or vinyl; crochet uppers right to soles, shape as you go. Greenland Boots, page 275.

Seed-stitch bootees for adults and children can be made any size. Knit a square, fold and sew to form cuffed slippers, trim with pompons. Other trimmings can be added: fringe or a rippled edge on the cuffs. Bed Slippers, page 276.

SETS
FOR
CHILDREN

Sets in four-ply worsted yarn are children's favorites. Knit "fisherman" cables (left) in candy apple green. Directions, page 276. Trim our blue stockinette-stitched set (above) with embroidered white snowflakes. Directions on page 277.

Knit a set for baby; sizes for 6 months or
small (1–2). Use a warm knitting worsted to create
the raised tree-of-life variation on cardigan
front, back, and on crown of the cap; page 277.

Directions for
golf club covers,
page 278.

Fisherman knits keep you cozy from "heads" to toe!

Hat and mittens, page 279;
mittens and socks, page
279–280; hat, scarf
and mittens
(inset),
page 280.

Photography by Sal Corbo.

Marvelous gifts!

KNIT A GIFT

If you know how to knit and purl,
make a gift hat or scarf from a skein of yarn.
Directions, page 281.

STRIPED MITTENS
Continued from page 229.

ribbing or 1″ less than desired length, end p row, dec 1 (0) st on last row—30 (35) sts.

Shape Top: Row 1: (K 2 tog, k 3) 6 (7) times—24 (28) sts. P 1 row.

Row 3: (K 2 tog, k 2) 6 (7) times—18 (21) sts. P 1 row. Continue to dec 6 (7) sts in this manner every other row having 1 st less between decs until 6 (7) sts remain. Break yarn leaving end; thread end in needle, draw through remaining sts, pull up tightly and fasten. Sew side seam with matching colors.

LEFT MITTEN: Work as for right mitten having 13 (15) sts (palm) before thumb and 16 (18) sts (back) after thumb on k rows.

COLOR-BRIGHT SET
Shown on page 235

SIZES: Hat: Small fits 16″-17″ head-size. Changes for medium (18″-20″) are in parentheses. **Scarf:** Small size, 7″ x 34″. Changes for medium size, 8″ x 41″, are in parentheses.

MATERIALS: Knitting worsted, 1 4-oz. skein each of scarlet (A), dark red (B), green (C), gold (D), royal blue (E) and turquoise (F). Set of dp needles No. 9. For scarf: felt for lining, ¼ yard 42″ wide. Matching sewing thread. Cellophane tape, ½″ wide. Large-eyed needle.

GAUGE: 9 sts = 2″; 5 rows = 1″.

Pattern Notes: Always change colors on wrong side; pick up background color from under dropped pattern color; pick up pattern color over dropped background color. Carry color not being used loosely across back of work. Cut and join colors when necessary.

Following chart specified, work pat in stockinette st (k each rnd) starting at arrow on rnd 1. Repeat pat to end of rnd.

HAT: CUFF: Beg at top edge, with A and dp needles, cast on loosely and divide 66 (78) sts on 3 dp needles. Mark end of rnd. Join; work around in ribbing of k 1, p 1 for 1 rnd. With A, k 1 rnd. Following chart 2, work pat (see Pattern Notes) in stockinette st (k each rnd) from rnd 1 through rnd 7.

Next Rnd (eyelet rnd)**:** With D, * yo, k 2 tog, repeat from * around. With D, k 1 rnd; with A, k 4 rnds; with C, k 1 rnd; with A, k 1 rnd; with C, k 1 rnd; with A, k 2 rnds. Turn work. Following chart 3, work pat in stockinette st from rnd 1 through rnd 9.

Next Rnd: With B, k around, dec 2 sts around—64 (76) sts. Work rnds 11-20.

Next Rnd: With E, k around, inc 2 sts around—66 (78) sts. Work rnds 22-33.

Next Rnd: With E, k 2 tog around—33 (39) sts. Repeat last rnd, end k 1. Cut E, leaving a 10″ end of yarn; draw remaining sts tog. Fasten securely on wrong side.

POMPON: Wind A 100 times around a 2½″ piece of cardboard. Tie one end; cut other end. Trim; fasten to top.

FINISHING: Run in yarn ends on wrong side. Turn cuff on eyelet rnd to right side; hem in place. Steam-press.

SCARF: NOTE: Scarf is tubular and is cut after knitting is completed.

Beg at lower edge, with A and dp needles, cast on loosely and divide 36 (40) sts on 3 dp needles. Mark end of rnd. Join, work around in ribbing of k 1, p 1 for 1 rnd. Following chart 4 throughout, work pat in stockinette st (k in each rnd), from rnd 1 through rnd 11.

Next Rnd: With B, k around, inc 0 (2) sts around—36 (42) sts. Work rnds 13-46.

Next Rnd: With A, k around, dec 0 (2) sts around—36 (40) sts. Work rnds 45-58.

Next Rnd: With A, k around, inc 0 (2) sts around—36 (42) sts. Work rnds 60-84.

Next Rnd: With E, k around, dec 0 (2) sts around—36 (40) sts. Work rnds 86-90 (86-95).

On Medium Size Only: Next Rnd: With E, k around, inc 2 sts around—42 sts. Work rnds 97-117.

Next Rnd: With E, k around, dec 2 sts around—40 sts. Work rnds 119-124.

On Both Sides: Work rnds 125-128.

Next Rnd: With E, k around, inc 0 (2) sts—36 (42) sts. Work rnds 130-154.

Next Rnd: With A, k around, dec 0 (2) sts—36 (40) sts. Work rnds 156-166.

Next Rnd: With A, k around, inc 0 (2) sts—36 (42) sts. Work rnds 168-201.

Next Rnd: With B, k around, dec 0 (2) sts around—36 (40) sts. Work rnds 203-213. With A, work in ribbing of k 1, p 1 for 1 rnd. Bind off in ribbing same tension as sts.

FINISHING: Baste a straight line between marker and last bound-off st down length of scarf. Cover basting firmly with a strip of cellophane tape. Cut along basting line. Machine stitch twice, ¼″ apart, at each side edge, inside of tape, using a loose tension and small sts. Remove tape. Using scarf for pat, cut lining. With right sides facing, making ½″ seams, machine stitch side edges of scarf and lining tog. Turn scarf to right side. Steam-press lightly.

Fringe: Cut about 64 (72) 9″ strands of A. Thread needle with 4 strands. Pull strands through scarf and lining at bottom edge; remove needle. Knot

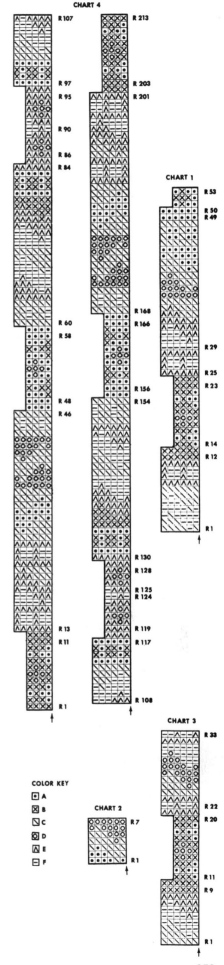

CHART 4

R 107
R 97
R 95
R 90
R 86
R 84
R 60
R 58
R 48
R 46
R 13
R 11
R 1

R 213
R 203
R 201
R 168
R 166
R 156
R 154
R 130
R 128
R 125
R 124
R 119
R 117
R 108

CHART 1

R 53
R 50
R 49
R 29
R 25
R 23
R 14
R 12
R 1

CHART 3

R 33
R 22
R 20
R 11
R 9
R 1

COLOR KEY

A
B
C
D
E
F

CHART 2

R 7
R 1

ends of yarn close to scarf. Repeat fringe about 1″ apart on each end.

RUDOLPH MITTENS
Shown on page 236

SIZE: 6-7 years.
MATERIALS: Knitting worsted, 2 ozs. green; few yards white. Knitting needles No. 5. Yarn needle. Four ¼″ black buttons. Two small red balls from ball fringe. Two stitch holders. Two bobbins.
GAUGE: 5 sts = 1″; 7 rows = 1″.
RIGHT MITTEN: With green, cast on 30 sts. Work in k 1, p 1 ribbing for 14 rows.
Row 15: K, inc 4 sts across row— 34 sts.
Rows 16-20: Work even in stockinette st, end p row. Wind 1 green, 1 white bobbin.
Row 21: K 7 green; working from chart, k 3 white from bobbin; with green, k 6, inc 1 st in each of next 2 sts, k 16.
Row 22: P to last 10 sts; drop green; with white, p 3; with bobbin of green, p 7. Always twist colors at color change to prevent holes. Following chart for white sts, inc for thumb as follows:
Row 23: K 16, inc 1 st in next st, k 2, inc 1 st in next st, k 16. P 1 row.
Row 25: K 16, inc 1 st in next st, k 4, inc 1 st in next st, k 16. P 1 row. Continue to inc 1 st each side of thumb every k row until there are 10 sts between incs. P 1 row.
Divide for Thumb: K 17; sl sts to a

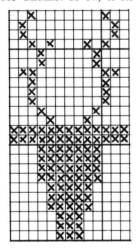

holder; k 12 sts on thumb; put remaining 17 sts on another holder. Work even on thumb sts for 11 rows, end p row.
Next Row: (K 1, k 2 tog) 4 times.
Next Row: (P 2 tog) 4 times. Run yarn through sts, pull up and fasten securely. Sew up side of thumb.
Hand: Sl first sts on right needle, last sts on left needle. Picking up 1 st at base of thumb, work across last sts.

Work to end of chart, using separate white strands for antlers and decreasing 1 st on last row.
Next Row: * K 1, k 2 tog, k 12, sl 1, k 1, psso, repeat from * once. P 1 row.
Next Row: * K 1, k 2 tog, k 10, sl 1, k 1, psso, repeat from * once. P 1 row. Continue decreasing 4 sts each k row in this manner for 2 more dec rows. Weave top edges tog in Kitchener St. Sew side seam. Sew on eyes and nose. If desired, crochet a row of white sc around cuff.
LEFT MITTEN: Work as for right mitten starting reindeer on back of mitten as follows:
Row 21: K 16, inc 1 st in each of next 2 sts, k 6; k 3 white from bobbin; k 7 green from bobbin.

DUCK, DOG, BUNNY MITTENS
Shown on page 236

SIZES: Directions for 7-8 years. Any changes for sizes 9-10 years and 11-12 years are in parentheses.
MATERIALS: Knitting worsted, 2 ozs. main color (MC): royal blue for duck mittens, green for dog mittens, dark red for bunny mittens; small amounts of design colors: yellow (Y), coral (C) and aqua (A) for duck; tan (T), black (B), white (W) and red (R) for dog; light blue (LB), natural (N) and pink (P) for bunny. Knitting needles No. 7. Two stitch holders. Tapestry needle.
GAUGE: 5 sts = 1″; 6 rows = 1″.
RIGHT MITTEN: With MC, cast on 28 sts. Work in ribbing of k 1, p 1 or k 2, p 2 (for larger sizes) for 4 rows. Change to striped pat: work 2 rows Y, 2 rows C, 6 rows MC for duck pat; 4 rows T, 6 rows MC, for dog pat; 2 rows LB, 2 rows MC, 6 rows N for bunny pat. Work in MC hereafter.
Hand: Row 1: Inc 1 st in each of first 2 sts, k across, inc 1 st in each of last 2 sts—32 sts.
Row 2 and All Even Rows: P.
Row 3: K 15, place a marker on needle, inc in each of next 2 sts, place a marker on needle, k 15.
Row 5: K 15, sl marker, inc in next st, k 2, inc in next st, sl marker, k 15. Continue to inc 1 st after first marker and before 2nd marker every k row until there are 12 sts between markers.
Row 12: P 16; sl sts to a holder, removing marker; p 10 (thumb); sl remaining 16 sts to another holder.
Thumb: Work even for 6 (8-8) rows. K 2 tog across next row. Break yarn; leave end for sewing. Run yarn through remaining sts, draw up tightly and fasten. Sew thumb seam.
Top: Join MC at beg of 2nd holder, p to end of row. Work even on 32 sts for 14 (16-20) rows.

Shape Top: Row 1: (K 2 tog, k 2) 8 times.
Row 2: P.
Row 3: (K 2 tog, k 1) 8 times.
Row 4: P.
Row 5: K 2 tog across. Break yarn; run through remaining sts and fasten.
FINISHING: Steam-press mitten. Embroider back of each mitten in duplicate st, following desired chart. Dog has black whiskers and red mouth made with long sts, a few short black sts in red collar. Bunny has blue whiskers, 3 long sts each side of nose. Sew side seam when embroidery is completed.

APPLIQUED MITTENS
Shown on page 236

SIZES: Directions for small size (2-4 years old). Changes for medium size (5-7 years old) are in parentheses.
MATERIALS: Knitting worsted, 2 ozs. Knitting needles No. 4. Two stitch holders. Tapestry needle. Scraps of yellow and blue felt. Embroidery floss: red, yellow, blue, black. Two small buttons.
GAUGE: 6 sts = 1″; 8 rows = 1″.
GENERAL DIRECTIONS: RIGHT MITTEN: Cast on 28 (32) sts. Work in ribbing of k 2, p 2 for 2″ (2½″), inc 3 (2) sts on last row—31 (34) sts. Work in stockinette st (k 1 row, p 1 row) for 4 rows, end p row.
Inc for Thumb: K 15 (17), put a marker on needle, inc 1 st in next st (k in front and back of same st), k 1, inc 1 st in next st (2 incs for thumb), put another marker on needle, k 13 (14). P 1 row.
Next Row: K, inc 1 st in st after first and before 2nd marker. P 1 row. Continue in this manner, inc 2 sts for thumb every other row until there are 11 sts between markers—39 (42) sts. Work even for 3 rows, end p row.
Divide for Thumb: K 15 (17) sts, put these sts on a holder (back of hand); k 11 (thumb), casting on 1 st each side of thumb; put remaining 13 (14) sts on a holder (palm).
Thumb: Work in stockinette st on 13 sts for 1″ (1¼″), end p row and dec 1 st in center of last row—12 sts.
Shape Top: Next Row: (K 2 tog, k 1) 4 times—8 sts. P 1 row.
Next Row: (K 2 tog) 4 times—4 sts. Break yarn, leaving an end for sewing. Thread end in needle, draw end through remaining sts. Draw up tightly; sew seam.
Hand: From right side, sl sts from first holder (back of hand) to needle; join yarn. Pick up and k 2 sts on base of

thumb, k sts from 2nd holder (palm) —30 (33) sts. Work even until piece measures 4″ (5″) above ribbing or ½″ less than desired length, end p row, dec 2 (1) sts on last row—28 (32) sts.
Shape Top: Row 1: (K 2, k 2 tog) 7 (8) times—21 (24) sts.
Rows 2 and 4: Purl.
Row 3: (K 1, k 2 tog) 7 (8) times.
Row 5: (K 2 tog) 7 (8) times—7 (8) sts. Break yarn, leave end for sewing. Thread end in needle, draw through remaining sts; fasten on wrong side. Do not sew side seam. Steam-press; do not press ribbing.
LEFT MITTEN: Work as for right mitten having 13 (14) sts (palm) before thumb and 15 (17) sts (back) after thumb on k rows.
APPLIQUES: Trace Humpty-Dumpty pattern. Cut 2 tops from yellow felt, 2 bottoms from blue felt. Appliqué to backs of mittens with outline st worked close to edge, using matching floss. Embroider blue eyes, black eyebrows and nose, red mouth. Sew on buttons. Sew side seams.

CROCHETED MITTENS
Shown on page 236

SIZES: Directions for size 6-6½. Changes for size 7-7½ are in parentheses.
MATERIALS: Knitting worsted, 2 ozs. each of blue and green, 1 oz. each of rose and fuchsia. Crochet hooks J and G.
GAUGE: 3 sc = 1″; 3 rnds = 1″ (double strand of yarn, size J hook).
Note: Mittens are worked with double strand throughout.
RIGHT MITTEN: Beg at tip, with 1 strand each of blue and green (see Note) and size J hook, ch 5.
Rnd 1: Sc in 2nd ch from hook, sc in each of next 2 ch, 2 sc in last ch; working on opposite side of starting ch, sc

in each of next 2 ch, sc in same ch with first sc. Sl st in first sc—8 sc.
Rnd 2: Ch 1, 2 sc in first sc, sc in each of next 2 sc, 2 sc in each of next 2 sc, sc in each of next 2 sc, 2 sc in last sc—12 sc. Join each rnd in first sc.
Rnd 3: Ch 1, 2 sc in first sc, sc in each of 4 sc, 2 sc in each of 2 sc, sc in each of 4 sc, 2 sc in last sc—16 sc. Drop blue and green.
Rnd 4: With 2 strands of rose, ch 1, 2 sc in first sc, sc in 6 sc, 2 sc in each of next 2 sc, sc in 6 sc, 2 sc in last sc—20 sc. Drop rose.
Rnd 5: With 2 strands of fuchsia, work even. Drop fuchsia.
Rnds 6-8: With blue and green, work even.
Rnd 9: With rose, work even.
Rnd 10: With fuchsia, work even.
Rnd 11: With blue and green, ch 1, 2 sc in first sc, sc in 8 sc, 2 sc in each of next 2 sc, sc in 8 sc, 2 sc in last sc—24 sc.
Rnds 12 and 13: Work even.
Rnd 14: With rose, work even.
Rnd 15: With fuchsia, work even.
Rnd 16: With blue and green, work even. For size 7-7½ only, work 1 more rnd, inc 1 st each side—24 (26) sc. Put work aside.
Thumb: With blue and green and size J hook, ch 2.
Rnd 1: 4 sc in 2nd ch from hook. Join in first sc each rnd. Drop blue and green.
Rnd 2: With rose, ch 1, 2 sc in each sc around—8 sc. Drop rose.
Rnd 3: With fuchsia, ch 1, work even. Drop fuchsia.
Rnd 4: With blue and green, inc 1 (2) sc in rnd—9 (10) sc.
Rnds 5 and 6: Work even. Drop blue and green.
Rnd 7: With rose, work even.
Rnd 8: With fuchsia, work even.
Rnd 9 (10): Work 1 (2) rnds even with blue and green. End off, leaving 6″ end.

Join Thumb: With blue and green, ch 1, sc around mitten to 6th (7th) sc before end of rnd, leaving 5 (6) sc unworked. Having joinings of thumb rnds on same side as joinings of mitten rnds, sc in 5(6) sc of thumb, sc in last sc before joining on mitten; join. With 6″ end, sew inner edge of thumb to skipped sts on mitten.

Working even and keeping to striped pattern, work 3 more rnds. Change to size G hook, work even to end of 6th blue and green section. Cut blue and green. Change back to size J hook, work 1 rose rnd. Cut rose.
Scalloped Edge: With fuchsia, sl st in first st, * 3 sc in next st, sl st in each of next 2 sts, repeat from * around. Join; end off.
LEFT MITTEN: Work as for right mitten up to Join Thumb.
Join Thumb: Ch 1, sc in first sc, having joinings of thumb rnds on same side as joinings of mitten rnds, sc in 5(6) sc of thumb, sk 5(6) sc on mitten, sc in each sc around; join. Sew inner edge of thumb to skipped sts on mitten. Finish as for right mitten.

EASY STRIPED MITTENS
Shown on page 236

SIZES: Directions for 3 years. Changes for 4-5 and 6-7 years are in parentheses.
MATERIALS: Knitting worsted 2 ozs. brown; few yards each of red, green, yellow, blue. Knitting needles Nos. 6 and 8. Two stitch holders. Yarn needle.
GAUGE: 4 sts = 1″; 6 rows = 1″ (double strand of yarn, No. 8 needles).
Note: Mittens are worked with a double strand of yarn throughout.
RIGHT MITTEN: With No. 6 needles and double strand of brown (see Note), cast on 22 (22-24) sts. Work in ribbing of k 1, p 1 for 11 (13-15) rows.

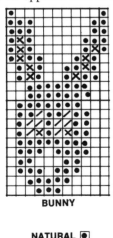

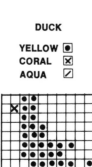

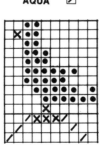

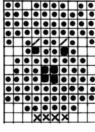

DUCK

YELLOW ⊡
CORAL ☒
AQUA ⧄

DOG

TAN ⊡
BLACK ▣
WHITE ⊘
RED ☒

BUNNY

NATURAL ⊡
PINK ☒
LT. BLUE ⧄

Charts for Duck, Dog and Bunny Mittens

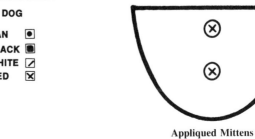

Appliqued Mittens
pattern

Change to No. 8 needles, p 1 row. Drop brown. With red, work in stockinette st (k 1 row, p 1 row) for 2 (4-4) rows. Cut red. With brown, k 1 row, p 1 row.

Inc for Thumb: K 12 (12-13), cast on 1 st (by looping yarn over right-hand needle), k 1, cast on 1 st, k 9 (9-10). P 1 row.

Next Row: K 12 (12-13), cast on 1 st, k 3, cast on 1 st, k 9 (9-10). P 1 row. Drop brown.

Next Row: With green, k 12 (12-13), cast on 1 st, k 5, cast on 1 st, k 9 (9-10). P 1 row. Cut green.

Divide for Thumb: With brown, k 12 (12-13), sl these sts on a holder (back of hand), inc 1 st in next st, k 6, sl remaining 9 (9-10) sts on a holder (palm).

Thumb: Work in stockinette st on 8 sts for 5 (7-8) rows.

Next Row: (Work 2 tog) 4 times. Cut yarn leaving an end for sewing; draw through remaining sts. Pull up tightly; sew seam.

Hand: From right side, slip sts from first holder (back of hand) to needle; join yarn, pick up 1 st at base of thumb, k sts from 2nd holder—22 (22-24) sts. Work in stockinette st for 11 (13-15) rows. Changing to yellow for 2 (4-4) rows after 6 brown rows, end p row, dec 0 (0-2) sts on last row—22 sts. Shape top, changing to 2 rows of blue after 6 brown rows.

Shape Top: Row 1: (K 2 tog, k 9) twice.
Rows 2 and 4: P.
Row 3: (K 2 tog, k 3) 4 times—16 sts.
Row 5: (K 2 tog) 8 times. Finish as for thumb.

LEFT MITTEN: Work as for right mitten, having 9 (9-10) sts (palm) before thumb, 12 (12-13) sts (back) after thumb on k rows.

GIFT SLIPPERS
Shown on page 237

SIZES: Directions for size 5-5½. Changes for sizes 6-6½, 7-7½ and 8-8½ are in parentheses.

MATERIALS: Rug yarn, 1 70-yard skein for soles. Knitting worsted weight yarn, 2 ozs. main color, 1 oz. each of contrasting colors. Crochet hook size G. Tapestry needle.

GAUGE: 3 sc = 1″; 7 rows = 2″ (rug yarn). 7 sc = 2″; 9 rows = 2″ (knitting worsted).

GENERAL DIRECTIONS: SOLE: With rug yarn, beg at back, ch 5. **Row 1:** Sc in 2nd ch from hook and each remaining ch. Ch 1, turn each row.
Row 2: 2 sc in first sc, sc in next 2 sc, 2 sc in last sc—6 sc.
Row 3: 2 sc in first sc, sc in next 4 sc, 2 sc in last sc—8 sc. Work even on 8

sc until sole is 4″ (4½″-5″-5½″) long. (For small narrow feet, make sole 6 sc wide; for large wider feet, inc to 10 sc.) Inc 1 st at beg of next 2 rows. Work even until sole is 6½″ (7″-7½″-8″) long. Sk 1 sc at beg of next 5 rows. At end of last row, ch 1; do not turn. Sc around sole, working 1 sc in end of each row and in each st at front and back. Sl st in first sc. End off.

UPPERS: All uppers are worked in sc. Patterns and colors are given with individual directions. When 2 or more colors are used in a row, lay unused colors along top of work and work over them until they are needed.

BLUE SLIPPERS WITH PINK INSTEP: Soles are beige. Main Color (MC) is dark blue, other colors are teal blue (T) and pink (P).
Uppers: Rnd 1: With T, beg at back of sole, sc in back lp of each sc around sole. With MC, sl st in first sc. Drop T.
Rnd 2: With MC, sc in each sc around. Sl st in first sc.
Rnd 3: Join P, pick up T. With MC, work 1 sc; working 1 sc in each sc, work in the following pat: * 1 P, 1 MC, 1 T, 1 P, 1 T, 1 MC, repeat from * around. Cut P and T.
Rnd 4: Repeat rnd 2.
Rnd 5: With T, repeat rnd 2. End off.
Instep: Beg at toe, with P, ch 4.
Row 1: Sc in 2nd ch from hook and in each ch. Ch 1, turn each row.
Rows 2-11: 2 sc in first sc, sc in each sc across—13 sc.
Rows 12-18: Work even. (For larger sizes, add 1 or 2 more rows.) End off. With T, from right side, work 1 sc in each st across top of instep, sc in end of each row down side of instep, sc in each st across toe, sc in end of each row up side of instep. Drop T off hook.

FINISHING: Pin center front T st of instep to center front T st on last rnd of uppers. Pin sides of instep into uppers so that sts of both pieces match. Insert hook in corresponding st of uppers, pick up dropped T lp and pull through. Working through corresponding sts of uppers and instep, sl st pieces tog. Continue around ankle, working 2 rnds of T, then 2 rnds of MC sc. End with 1 rnd of MC in hdc. End off.

BROWN SLIPPERS WITH RUST EDGING: Soles are beige. Main color (MC) is brown, other colors are rust (R), green (G) and yellow (Y).
Uppers: Rnd 1: With R, beg at back of sole, sc in back lp of each sc around sole. Cut R. With MC, sl st in first sc.
Rnd 2: With MC, sc in each sc around. Sl st in first sc.
Rnd 3: Join G, work * 1 MC, 1 G, repeat from * around. Cut G.

Rnd 4: Repeat rnd 2.
Rnd 5: Join Y; work * 1 MC, 1 Y, repeat from * around, cut MC.
Rnd 6: With Y, sc in each sc around. Join; end off.
Instep: Beg at toe, with MC, ch 4. **Row 1:** Sc in 2nd ch from hook and in each ch. Ch 1, turn each row.
Rows 2-7: 2 sc in first sc, sc in each sc across—9 sc. Work even on 9 sc until piece is 3½″ (4″-4½″-5″) long. Join Y. With MC, sc in first sc, * with Y, sc in next sc; with MC, sc in next sc, repeat from * across. Drop MC. With Y, sc in end of each row down side of instep, sc in each st across toe, sc in end of each row up side of instep, sc in each st across top. Drop Y.

FINISHING: Pin center front Y st of instep to center front Y st on last rnd of uppers. Pin sides of instep into uppers so that sts of both pieces match. Insert hook in corresponding st of uppers, pick up dropped MC lp and pull through. Working through corresponding sts of uppers and instep, sl st pieces tog. End off.

Working around ankle in sc, work 1 rnd of 1 Y, 1 MC, repeated around, 3 rnds MC. Finish with 1 rnd R in hdc.

NAVY SLIPPERS WITH TEAL EDGING: Soles are brown. Main color (MC) is navy, other colors are teal (T), bright blue (B) and apple green (G).

Uppers: Rnd 1: With MC, beg at back of sole, sc in back lp of each sc around sole.
Rnd 2: Join G and B. Working in sc, work * 1 MC, 1 G, 1 MC, 1 B, repeat from * around. Join each rnd. Cut G and B.
Rnd 3: With MC, sc around.
Rnd 4: Join T. Work * 1 MC, 1 T, repeat from * around. Cut MC.
Rnd 5: With T, sc around. End off.
Instep: Beg at toe, with MC, ch 4.
Row 1: Sc in 2nd ch from hook and in each ch. Ch 1, turn each row.
Rows 2-9: 2 sc in first sc, sc in each sc across—11 sc.
Rows 10-15: Work even.
Row 16: Work (1 MC, 1 G, 1 MC, 1 B) twice, 1 MC, 1 G, 1 MC. Cut G and B.
Row 17: Work even in MC.
Row 18: Work * 1 MC, 1 B, repeat from * across, end 1 MC. End off. With G, work 1 sc in end of each row to toe, sc in each st across toe, sc in end of each row up other side of instep. End off G. With T, work 1 sc in each st across top of instep. End off T.

FINISHING: Pin center front st of instep to center front st on last rnd of uppers. Pin sides of instep into uppers so that sts of both pieces match. From right side, join MC in first G st on edge of instep. Working through corresponding sts of instep and uppers, sl st pieces tog. Do not end off. Working from wrong side, with MC, sc around ankle of uppers to other side of instep. Ch 1, turn. Working around ankle, work 2 rnds MC. Join each rnd. From wrong side, work 1 rnd T. Ch 1, turn. Work 1 rnd hdc with T. End off.

PINK AND NATURAL SLIPPERS: Soles are brown. Main color (MC) is natural, other colors are pink (P) and olive green (G).

Uppers: Rnd 1: With G, beg at back of sole, sc in back lp of each sc around sole. Join each rnd. Join MC.

Rnd 2: Working in sc, work * 1 G, 1 MC, repeat from * around. Cut G. Join P.

Rnd 3: Working in sc, work * 1 MC, 1 P, repeat from * around. Drop MC.

Rnd 4: With P, sc around. Cut P.

Rnd 5: With MC, sc around. End off.

Instep: Beg at toe, with MC, ch 3.

Row 1: Sc in 2nd ch from hook and in next ch. Ch 1, turn each row.

Rows 2-7: 2 sc in first sc, sc in each sc across—8 sc.

Row 8: Join P; work 2 MC sc, 4 P sc; drop P; 2 MC sc.

Row 9: Work 2 MC sc, 4 P sc; drop P; 2 MC sc. Repeat rows 8 and 9, 5 times. Cut P. Work 4 rows MC. End off. With P, sc in each sc across top of instep, ch 2, dc in end st of each row down side of instep to about halfway to toe, hdc in each row to start of P section of instep, sc in each row to toe, sc in each st of toe and each row on other edge of instep to start of P section; finish rnd with hdc and dc to correspond to first side, ch 2, sl st in first sc. End off.

FINISHING: Pin center front of instep to center front of uppers. Pin sides of instep into uppers so that sts of both pieces match. Beg with dc on instep about 1¼″ below top edge, with MC, sl st instep to uppers, working through corresponding sts. End 1¼″ below top edge of instep. End off. With MC, work 4 rows of sc on remaining sts of uppers. With P, from right side, sc in end of each of 4 MC rows just made, 2 hdc in corner st, hdc in each st around to next corner, 2 hdc in corner st, sc in end of each of next 4 rows. End off. With P, sew side edges of uppers to free side edges of instep, sewing through back lps.

BROWN, GOLD AND WHITE SLIPPERS: Soles are brown. For main color (MC), use the brown rug yarn or worsted. Other colors are gold (G) and white (W).

Uppers: Rnd 1: With MC, beg at back of sole, sc in back lp of each sc around sole.

Rnd 2: Join G. Working in back lp of each sc, work * 1 MC, 1 G, repeat from * around. Join each rnd. Drop MC; join W.

Rnd 3: Work * 1 G, 1 W, repeat from * around. Cut W.

Rnd 4: Work * 1 MC, 1 G, repeat from * around. Cut G.

Rnd 5: With MC, sc around. Join; end off.

Instep: Beg at toe, with G, ch 4. **Row 1:** Sc in 2nd ch from hook and in each ch. Ch 1, turn each row.

Row 2: 2 sc in first sc, sc in next sc, 2 sc in last sc.

Row 3: Working over W, with G, 2 sc in first sc, sc in next sc, W sc in next sc, G sc in next sc, 2 sc in next sc—7 sc.

Row 4: 2 G sc in first sc, sc in next sc, W sc in each of next 3 sc; G sc in next sc, 2 sc in last sc—9 sc.

Row 5: 2 G sc in first sc, sc in next sc, W sc in each of next 5 sc; G sc in next sc, 2 sc in last sc—11 sc.

Row 6: G sc in 2 sc, W sc in 3 sc, G sc in next sc, W sc in 3 sc, G sc in 2 sc.

Row 7: G sc in 2 sc, W sc in 2 sc, G sc in next sc, MC sc in next sc, G sc in next sc, W sc in 2 sc, G sc in 2 sc. Repeat row 7, 12 times. Cut MC and W. With G, sc in each st across. Ch 1, turn. Work 1 rnd sc around instep, working sc in each st across top of instep, 1 sc in end of each row to toe, sc in each st across toe, 1 sc in end of each row to top. End off.

FINISHING: Pin center front st of instep to center front st on last rnd of uppers. Pin sides of instep into uppers so that sts of both pieces match. From right side, beg 1″ down from top of instep, with G, sl st instep to uppers, working through corresponding sts. End 1″ down from top of instep on other side. From wrong side, join G in first free st on uppers. Working in front lps only, sc in each st around back to last free st. Ch 1, turn. Working back and forth on these sts, working in both lps, work 1 row G sc, 2 rows of 1 G sc, 1 W sc, repeated across. End off. With G, from wrong side, sc along front edge of back section just made, sc around top of back section, sc along other front edge of back section. End off. With MC, from right side, work sc in each sc of last row. End off.

GREEN SLIPPERS: Soles are green. Main color (MC) is dark green, other colors are bright green (G) and dark red (R).

Uppers: Rnd 1: With MC, beg at back of sole, sc in back lp of each sc around sole. Join each rnd. Join G.

Rnd 2: Working in sc, work * 1 MC, 1 G, repeat from * around.

Rnd 3: Repeat rnd 2, working G in

MC st, MC in G st. Drop G. Join R.

Rnd 4: Working in sc, work * 1 MC, 1 R, repeat from * around, working MC in G st, R in MC st. Drop MC.

Rnd 5: With R, sc around. Cut R.

Rnd 6: Repeat rnd 2.

Rnd 7: With MC, sc around.

Rnd 8: Repeat rnd 2. End off.

Woven Instep: Join MC on last rnd of uppers about halfway between center back and front, ch 9 and join in other side of uppers directly across from first joining. End off.

Thread a tapestry needle with several yards of MC. Beg in center ch, draw yarn halfway through ch. Weave down through center st at toe, up through next toe st to one side and through next ch to same side; * down through next st at toe, up through next st and through next ch; repeat from * until all chs on one-half of ch have been used. Repeat with 2nd half of yarn on other side of instep. There should be 2 strands from each ch, but only 1 strand in each st at toe. Now weave from side to side through vertical strands: bring needle under sc at side, weave across instep, bring needle under sc at opposite side and back under next sc; * weave across instep, bring needle under same sc on first side and back under next sc; weave across instep to 2nd side, bring needle under same sc on 2nd side and back under next sc; repeat from * to toe. Run in yarn ends.

FINISHING: From right side, with MC, work sc in each ch across instep, sc in each sc around ankle, ch 1, sc in each sc across instep, ch 1, sl st in first sc on ankle. End off.

CRIB BLANKET
Shown on page 238

SIZE: 32″ x 36″.

MATERIALS: Coats & Clark's Red Heart 4 Ply Wintuk, 5 3½-oz. skeins Yale Blue. Coats & Clark's Red Heart Persian Type Needlepoint & Crewel Yarn, 3 ply: 4 12-yard skeins dark blue; 3 skeins each of dark green, light yellow, dark yellow, and dark red; 2 skeins each of white and light green; 1 skein each of gold, light blue, and light red. Afghan hook J or 10 (6 mm). Crochet hook size I or 9 (5½ mm). Tapestry needle.

GAUGE: 10 sts = 3″; 8 rows = 3″.

BLANKET: Ch 94. Work in plain afghan st on 94 sts for 90 rows.

Edging: Change to crochet hook. **Rnd 1:** Sc in each st across, 3 sc in corner st, * sc in each of next 5 sts on edge, 2 sc in next edge st, repeat from * down side, 3 sc in corner st, sc in each st across lower edge, 3 sc in corner st,

work from first * to second * up other side, 2 sc in corner, sl st in first sc.
Rnd 2: * Ch 3, sk 1 sc, sc in next sc, repeat from * around, working sc, ch 3, sc in each corner sc.
Rnd 3: * Ch 3, sc in 3rd ch from hook for picot, sc in next ch-3 sp, repeat from * around, working sc, picot, sc in each corner sp. Sl st in first st. End off.
EMBROIDERY: Following chart, embroider designs in cross-stitch. Open band at top is for child's name. Arrange letters in space, leaving 3 squares free between letters (or 2 for long name). Embroider letters in different colors.

HENRY HEDGEHOG
Shown on page 238

SIZE: 6″ long.
MATERIALS: Rug yarn, 1 70-yd. skein each of dark green (DG) and light green (LG). Crochet hook size J or 10 (6mm). Stuffing. Scrap of black felt. Glue.
GAUGE: 3 sts = 1″.

HEAD AND BODY: Beg at tip of nose, with DG, ch 4. Sl st in first ch to form ring. **Rnd 1:** 2 sc in each ch around.
Rnds 2-6: Working in back lp only of each sc, * sc in 2 sc, 2 sc in next sc, repeat from * around—32 sc.
Rnds 7 and 8: Work even. Stuff.
Rnds 9-12: * Sc in 2 sc, sk next sc, repeat from * around. Stuff. Sl st in every other st around until body opening is closed. End off.
EARS: Join DG in front lp of any sc on rnd 4. In same lp work sc, hdc 3 dc, hdc, sc. End off. Sk 3 sts on rnd 4, work 2nd ear the same.
FEET: Join DG in st between rnds 5 and 6 at side bottom edge of body. Work as for ear around upright bar of st. Work another foot on same rnd at other side bottom edge of body about 3″ from first foot. Work 2 back feet 2″ apart between rnds 9 and 10.
BACK TRIM: Join LG in front lp of sc just above left front foot. * Ch 4, sc in next st, repeat from * in each front lp across row to right front foot; ch 4, sc in lp of next row. Working back and

forth from side to side in every st, cover back and sides of toy with ch-4 lps.
FINISHING: Cut 2 black felt ½″ circles for eyes, ½″ semicircle for nose. Glue on.

CHILD'S NORSE AFGHAN
Shown on page 239

SIZE: 39″ x 60″, plus fringe.
MATERIALS: Bucilla Softex, 5 4-oz. balls light gold #25; 3 balls royal blue #89; 1 ball each of white, light taupe #69, dark gold #27, spring green #50, red #85. Afghan hook size J or 10 (6 mm). Tapestry needle.
GAUGE: 7 sts = 2″; 3 rows = 1″.

AFGHAN: With light gold, ch 132. Work in plain afghan st on 132 sts for 27 rows. Cut light gold, finish last st of row 27 with light taupe. With light taupe, work 1 row. Cut light taupe; finish last st with royal blue. With royal blue, work 24 rows. Cut royal blue; finish last st with light taupe. With light taupe, work 1 row. Changing colors as before, work 65 rows light gold, 1 row

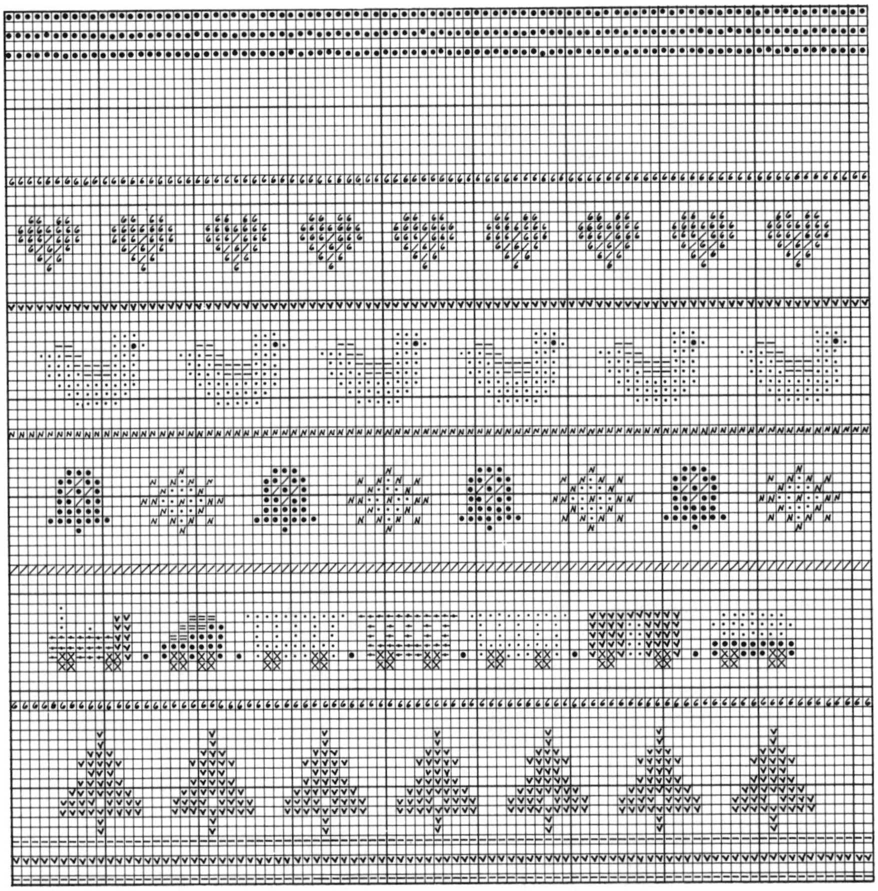

- ◉ DK. BLUE
- ☒ LT. BLUE
- ◪ DK. RED
- ⊡ LT. RED
- ☑ DK. GREEN
- ⊟ LT. GREEN
- Ν DK. YELLOW
- ⊡ LT. YELLOW
- ⊘ WHITE
- ⊟ DK. GOLD

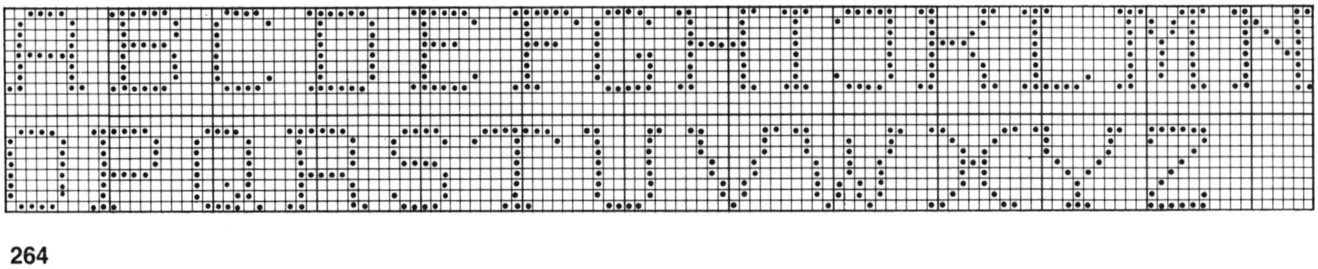

light taupe, 24 rows royal blue, 1 row light taupe, 27 rows light gold. Sl st in each st across. End off.

EMBROIDERY: Following chart, embroider design in cross-stitch on first end of afghan. Chart gives right half of border. For left half, read chart back from center to edge. When first end is finished, turn afghan around and work border on second end in same way.

FRINGE: Cut royal blue in 15″ lengths. Holding 6 strands tog, knot fringe in every 3rd or 4th st across both ends.

PIXIE PONCHO
Shown on page 241

SIZE: Fits 1-3 year olds.
MATERIALS: Yarn of knitting worsted weight (wool, orlon, etc.), 3 4-oz. skeins. Circular needles Nos. 6 and 10 (24″ or 29″). Steel crochet hook No. 0. Two stitch holders.
GAUGE: 4 sts = 1″; 5 rows = 1″.
BACK: With needle No. 10, cast on 177 sts. Do not join; work rows back and forth.
Row 1: K 88, put a marker on needle, k 89.
Row 2: Purl, slipping marker.
Row 3: K 1, k 2 tog, k to within 2 sts of marker, sl 1, k 1, psso, sl marker, k 1, k 2 tog, k to last 3 sts, sl 1, k 1, psso, k 1—4 sts dec. Repeat last 2 rows until 25 sts remain, end p row. Sl sts on a holder.
FRONT: Work same as for back. Weave side seams.
HOOD: Beg at right shoulder, with needle No. 6, working from sts on back

holder, inc 1 st in each of first 12 sts, p 1 (mark this st for center st), inc 1 st in each of last 12 sts on back holder. Working on sts from front holder, (k 2, p 2) 3 times, k 1, k 2 tog, (p 2, k 2) twice, p 2. Turn.
Next Row: Work first 24 sts in ribbing as established, p 24, k center st, p 24. Turn.
Next Row: K 24, p 1, k 24, finish row in ribbing as established.
Next Row: Bind off very loosely in ribbing first 24 sts (front), p to center st, k 1, p across. Change to No. 10 needle. Working back and forth, work in stockinette st (k 1 row, p 1 row) keeping center st in p rib on right side, in k rib on wrong side as established until piece measures 7½″ from start of hood, end wrong side. Bind off loosely.
FINISHING: Steam-press lightly. Fold hood on center st; weave top seam. Close small opening at side of hood.
Beading: From right side, work 1 row sc around hood, beg at right side seam and ending at left side seam, keep work flat. Turn.
Row 2: Ch 4, * sk 1 sc, dc in next sc, ch 1, repeat from * across, end dc in last sc.
Drawstring: Cut 9 strands of yarn 32″ long. Knot all strands together, 2″ from end (for tassel). Divide strands evenly in 3 parts; braid lightly. Pull knot through first beading space, weave braid through beading in every 3rd ch-1 space. Pull braid up for desired hood size; knot 2nd end; trim tassel to 2″.

Work 1 row sc around lower edge. Do not turn. Work row 2 as for hood,

end sl st in 3rd ch of ch 4.
Fringe: Cut yarn in 5″ lengths. Holding 2 strands together, knot a fringe in every ch-1 space around lower edge. Trim fringe evenly all around.

HOODED BUNTING
Shown on page 240

SIZE: Infants.
MATERIALS: Coats & Clark Red Heart Worsted Sport Yarn, 4 ozs. yellow (Y); 2 ozs. each of Red (R), Amethyst (A), Vibrant Orange (O), Paddy Green (G). Knitting needles No. 4. Crochet hook size F. One stitch holder.
GAUGE: 6 sts = 1″; 8 rows = 1″.
BACK: Beg at lower edge, with Y, cast on 60 sts loosely.
Foundation Triangle Row: * K 1, turn; p 1, turn; k 1, k next cast-on st, turn; p 2, turn; k 2, k next cast-on st, turn; p 3, turn; k 3, k next cast-on st, turn; p 4, turn; k 4, k next cast-on st, turn; p 5, turn; k 5, k next cast-on st, turn; p 6, turn; k 6, do not turn. Repeat from * 9 times—10 foundation triangles. Cut Y.
First Block Row: Starting Triangle A: With O, cast on 1 st at end of right-hand needle, turn; with O, p the O and next Y st tog (p 2-color tog made), turn; k 1, turn; k in back lp of O st, do not drop O st off left-hand needle; through front lps, p same O st and next Y st tog, turn; k 2, turn; k in back and p in front of first O st (inc made), p next O and next Y st tog (p 2-color tog made), turn; k 3, turn; inc in first st, p 1, p 2-color tog, turn; k 4, turn; inc in first st, p 2, p 2-color tog, turn; k 5, turn; inc in first st, p 3, p 2-color tog, do not turn.
Block A: Pick up as if to p 6 sts evenly spaced on side edge of same Y triangle, turn; * k 6, turn; p 5, p 2-color tog, turn; repeat from * 5 times, do not turn at end of last repeat. Work 8 more blocks in same manner—all previous color sts have been worked across. Do not turn.
End Triangle A: Pick up as if to p 6 sts on end triangle of previous color, turn; k 6, turn; p 4, p 2 tog, turn; k 5, turn; p 3, p 2 tog, turn; k 4, turn; p 2, p 2 tog, turn; k 3, turn; p 1, p 2 tog, turn; k 2, turn; p 2 tog. Cut O and pull through st on needle.
2nd Block Row: Starting Block: From right side, with R and free right-hand needle, pick up and k 6 sts evenly spaced on straight side of end triangle, turn. * (P 6, turn; k 5, sl 1, k next st of previous color, psso, turn) 6 times; do not turn at end of last repeat.
Block B: With R, pick up 6 sts on side of next block. Turn; repeat from * on starting block 9 times. Cut R; do not turn.
Third Block: Starting Triangle B: With A, cast on 1 st at end of right-hand

WHITE ⊙   **DK. GOLD** ☒   **RED** Ⓝ   **GREEN** Ⓥ

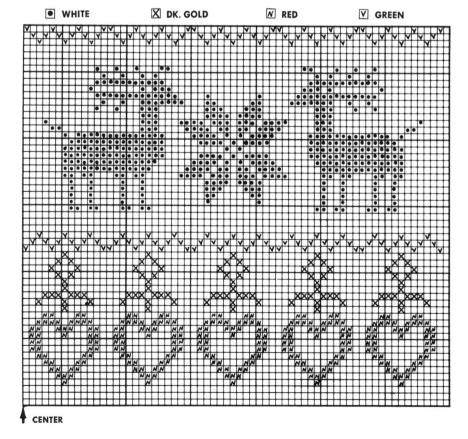

↑ **CENTER**

265

needle; work same as for starting triangle A.

Block C: Pick up as if to p 6 sts evenly spaced on side edge of R block, turn. (K 6, turn; p 5, p 2-color tog, turn) 6 times (C block worked over B block). Do not turn at end of last repeat. Work 8 more C blocks in same manner. Do not turn.

End Triangle B: Pick up as if to p 6 sts evenly spaced on last block of previous row, turn; complete same as end triangle A, turn. Repeating 2nd and 3rd block rows alternately for pat and working in color sequence as follows, work 1 block row G, 1 block row Y, 1 block row O, 1 block row R, 1 block row A. Work in color sequence as established to end of 4th G block row.

First Small Block Row: Small Block A: From right side, with Y and free right-hand needle, pick up and k 4 sts evenly spaced on side of end triangle, turn. P 4, turn; k 3, sl 1, k next 2 sts of previous color tog, psso, turn; p 4, turn. (K 3, sl 1, k next st of previous color, psso, turn; p 4, turn) twice, k 3, sl 1, k next 2 sts of previous color tog, psso; do not turn. Picking up 4 sts along side of previous color blocks, make 9 more small blocks in same manner. Cut Y; do not turn.

2nd Small Block Row: Small Starting Triangle: With O, cast on 1 st at end of right-hand needle, turn; with O, p the O and next Y st tog, turn; k 1, turn; k in back lp of O st, do not drop O st off left-hand needle; through front lps, p same O st and next Y st tog, turn; k 2, turn; inc in first st, p 2-color tog, turn; k 3, turn; inc in first st, p 1, p 2-color tog, do not turn.

Small Block B: Pick up as if to p 4 sts evenly spaced on side edge of Y block, turn. (K 4, turn; p 3, p 2-color tog, turn) 4 times; do not turn at end of last p 2-color tog. Work 8 more small B Blocks in same manner. Do not turn.

Small End Triangle: Pick up as if to p 4 sts evenly spaced on last block of previous color, turn; k 4, turn; p 2, p 2 tog; k 3, turn; p 1, p 2 tog, turn; k 2, turn; p 2 tog. Cut O and pull end through st on needle. Keeping in same color sequence as established, work to end of 2nd small Y block row.

Right Sleeve, Back Yoke and Left Sleeve: Sl all sts on a holder. With O, cast on 20 sts for right sleeve.

Small Foundation Triangles: * K 1, turn; p 1, turn; k 1, k next cast-on st, turn; p 2, turn; k 2, k next cast-on st, turn; p 3, turn; k 3, k next cast-on st, turn; p 4, turn; k 4, do not turn. Repeat from * 4 times; with k side facing you, sl back sts from holder to left-hand needle; with O work in pat across back. Cut O. With O cast on 20 sts on free needle for left sleeve; working

across left sleeve sts, work small foundation triangles over cast-on sts; do not turn. Keeping to pat and color sequence, work to end of 2nd small A block row. Turn.

Finishing Triangle Row for Shoulder and Sleeve: With G, pick up as if to k 4 sts on side of first triangle, turn; p 4, turn; k 3, sl 1, k 1, psso, turn; p 2, p 2 tog, turn; k 2, sl 1, k 1, psso, turn; p 1, p 2 tog, turn; k 1, sl 1, k 1, psso, turn; p 2 tog, turn; k 2 tog, do not turn. * Pick up 4 sts on side of next block, turn; p 3, p 2 tog, turn; k 3, sl 1, k 1, psso, turn; p 2, p 2 tog, turn; k 2, sl 1, k 1, psso, turn; p 1, p 2 tog, turn; k 1, sl 1, k 1, psso, turn; p 2 tog, turn; k 2 tog, do not turn. Repeat from * across. End off.

FRONT: Work as for back to end of 2nd small Y block row.

Left Sleeve and Left Front: Work as for right sleeve, working small foundation triangles. Having triangles on right-hand needle and front on left-hand needle, divide for front opening as follows: Work in pat across front until 5 small blocks are completed. Sl remaining sts on a st holder. Do not turn. With R, cast on 1 st, work a small starting triangle and work in pat across. Work even to end of 2nd small A block row. With G, work finishing triangle row across shoulder and sleeve edge as for back.

Right Front and Right Sleeve: Sl sts from holder to left-hand needle; work 5 small O blocks; cast on 20 sts for left sleeve. Complete same as for left front and sleeve.

FINISHING: Run in yarn ends on wrong side. Block pieces. Leaving 3″ opening at each lower edge for side slits, sew side and underarm seams. Beg at wrist, sew sleeve and shoulder seams, leaving 6″ free at center back for neck opening. From right side, with crochet hook and Y, work 1 rnd sc around neck and front opening, being careful to keep work flat. Join with a sl st in first sc. End off. Work 1 rnd sc around lower edge of bunting; work 1 rnd sc around lower edge of each sleeve.

HOOD: Beg at front edge, with Y, cast on 48 sts. Work small foundation triangles same as for sleeves—12 small triangles. Work small block rows and color sequence as on bunting to end of 3rd small block Y row. With O, work small finishing triangles. End off. Fold hood in half; weave bound-off edge tog.

NECKBAND AND TIES: With Y, cast on 6 sts.

Row 1: * K 1, p 1, repeat from * across.

Row 2: * P 1, k 1, repeat from * across. Repeat last 2 rows until piece measures 37″. Bind off in pat. Leaving 12″ at each end free for ties, sew band to

neck edge of bunting, easing in to fit. Sew neck edge of hood to band, placing front edges of hood in line with center front opening.

BABY SET AND ANIMALS
Shown on pages 242 and 243

SIZE: Directions are for 6 mos. to 1 yr. size.
Body Chest Measurement: 20″-22″.
Blocked Chest Measurement: 25″.
MATERIALS: Dawn Sayelle, 5 4-oz. skeins each of White (MC), and Baby Green (CC). Knitting needles, 1 pair size 6. 24″ circular needle, size 9. 36″ circular needle, size 13. Crochet hook size G. 10″ separating zipper.
GAUGE: Pat st, size 9 needles: 4 sts = 1″; 16 rows = 3″. Size 13 needles: 5 sts = 2″; 16 rows = 6″.
PATTERN STITCH (multiple of 10 sts plus 3):
Row 1 (right side): * K 5, p 3, k 2; repeat from * across, end k 3.
Row 2: P 4, * k 2, p 1, k 2, p 5; repeat from * across, end p 4.
Row 3: * K 3, p 2; repeat from * across, end k 3.
Row 4: P 2, * k 2, p 5, k 2, p 1; repeat from * across, end p 2.
Row 5: * P 3, k 7; repeat from * across, end p 3.
Row 6: P 2, * k 2, p 5, k 2, p 1; repeat from * across, end p 2.
Row 7: Repeat row 3.
Row 8: Repeat row 2. Repeat rows 1-8 for pat.
NOTE: Work back and forth on circular needle.
JACKET: BACK: With size 6 needles and CC, cast on 43 sts.
Seed St: Row 1 (right side): K 1, * p 1, k 1; repeat from * across. Repeat row 1, 4 times more. Cut CC, join MC. Change to size 9 needle. P 1 row. Work even in pat st for 44 rows (5½ pats).
Shape Sleeves: Keeping to pat and working added sts into pat, cast on 4 sts at beg of next 12 rows, then 6 sts at beg of next 2 rows—103 sts. Work even until 9 pats from beg are completed.
FRONT: Divide and Shape Neck: Work in pat across first 42 sts, join 2nd ball of MC and bind off next 19 sts for neck, work in pat to end—42 sts each side. Working each side separately, work 4 rows even. At each neck edge, inc 1 st in next row, then every other row 6 times more, then cast on 4 sts—53 sts each side. Work even until 4½ pats at sleeve edge are completed. At each sleeve edge bind off 6 sts once, then 4 sts 6 times—23 sts each side. Work 44 rows even—5½ pats. Cut MC, join CC. Change to size 6 needles. K 1 row. Work in seed st for 5 rows. Bind off in pat.
HOOD: With size 9 needle and MC, cast on 33 sts. Work 2 rows even in pat.
Shape Neck Edge and Crown: Next Row:

K 2 tog (neck edge dec), work in pat to within last 2 sts, inc 1 st in next st (crown inc), work last st. At neck edge, dec 1 st every row 14 times more; **at same time,** at crown edge inc 1 st every 6th row 3 times more, then every row 6 times—28 sts. Work even until 32 rows from beg are completed—4 pats. At crown edge, dec 1 st in next row, then every row 6 times more, then every 6th row 3 times; **at same time,** at neck edge work even for 11 rows, then inc 1 st every row 15 times—33 sts. Work 1 row even. Bind off.

FINISHING: From right side, with size 6 needles and CC, pick up and k 23 sts evenly along sleeve edge. Work 5 rows in seed st. Bind off in pat. From right side, with size 6 needles and CC, pick up and k 45 sts evenly along each front edge. Work 5 rows in seed st. Bind off.

With right side of back facing, with size 6 needle and CC, pick up and k 67 sts evenly between lower edge of back band and lower edge of sleeve band. Work same as front bands. Work 2nd side and underarm band to correspond. Sew side and sleeve seams.

Hood: From right side, with size 6 needle and CC, pick up and k 32 sts evenly along one half of crown edge, beg at front edge and ending at first dec row of shaping. Work 5 rows in seed st. Bind off in pat. Fold hood in half, sew bound-off edge of band to opposite edge of crown. Along front edge, pick up and k 68 sts; work same as band on crown edge. Sew shaped neck edge of hood to neck edge of jacket, matching front edges. Sew in zipper from lower edge of jacket to neck edge.

QUILTING: Thread MC in tapestry needle and work a running st between the 2 p sts that form diagonal rows.
Pompons: Wind MC around a 1¼" piece of cardboard about 200 times. Tie very tightly at one end, cut opposite end. Roll in palm of hand to form ball, trim evenly to a 2"-diameter ball. Sew to top of hood. Wind MC around a ¾" piece of cardboard about 100 times. Finish as for large pompon. Trim to 1" diameter. Attach to zipper tab.

PANTS:Right Half: With size 6 needles and MC, cast on 53 sts for waistband. Work in k 1, p 1 ribbing for 3 rows.
Eyelet Row: * Rib 3 sts, k 2 tog, yo; repeat from * across, end rib last 3 sts. Work k 1, p 1 ribbing for 3 rows more. Cut MC, join CC. Change to size 9 needle. P 1 row.
Back Shaping: Work short rows to shape back as follows:
Short Row 1 (right side): Work in pat across first 10 sts. Turn.
Short Row 2: Sl 1, work in pat to end. Turn.
Short Row 3: Work in pat across first 20 sts. Turn.

Short Row 4: Sl 1, work in pat to end. Turn.
Short Row 5: Work in pat across first 30 sts. Turn.
Short Row 6: Sl 1, work in pat to end. Turn.
Next Row: Work in pat across 53 sts. At back edge, inc 1 st every row 5 times—58 sts. Work even until 40 full rows of pat are completed—5 pats at front edge. Mark for crotch. Work 2 rows even.
Leg: Dec 1 st each side edge in next row, then every other row twice more, then every 4th row twice—48 sts. Work even until 88 pat rows from waistband are completed, about 8" from crotch, end with wrong side row. Cut CC, join MC. Change to size 6 needles.
Cuff: Dec Row: * K 4, k 2 tog; repeat from * across—40 sts. Work in k 1, p 1 ribbing for 9 rows. Bind off in ribbing.
Left Half: Work as for right half, reversing back shaping.
FINISHING: Sew center front and back seams, sew leg seams. With size G hook and 1 strand each of MC and CC, make ch 24" long. Fasten off. Weave drawstring through eyelet row at waist. Knot each end.
QUILTING: Thread MC in yarn needle. Work running st between the 2 p sts that form diagonal rows. Work all diagonal rows in this manner.
BLANKET: With size 13 needle and MC, cast on 87 sts.
Row 1 (right side): K 7, * p 3, k 11; repeat from * across, end k 7.
Row 2: P 6, * k 2, p 1, k 2, p 9; repeat from * across, end p 6.
Row 3: K 5, * p 2, k 3, p 2, k 7; repeat from * across, end k 5.
Row 4: P 4, * k 2, p 5; repeat from * across, end p 4.
Row 5: K 3, * p 2, k 7, p 2, k 3; repeat from * across, end k 3.
Row 6: P 2, * k 2, p 9, k 2, p 1; repeat from * across, end p 2.
Row 7: P 3, * k 11, p 3; repeat from * across, end p 3.
Row 8: Repeat row 6.
Row 9: Repeat row 5.
Row 10: Repeat row 4.
Row 11: Repeat row 3.
Row 12: Repeat row 2.
Repeat rows 1-12, 11 times more. Bind off.
Edging: From right side, with size 13 needle and CC, pick up and k 87 sts evenly spaced across bound-off edge, 1 st in corner, 95 sts along one side edge—183 sts.
Row 1: * P 3, k 1; repeat from * across, end p 3.
Row 2: Inc 1 st in first st, k 2, yo, p 1, yo, * k 3, yo, p 1, yo; repeat from * across, end k 2, inc 1 st in last st.
Row 3: P 4, * k 3, p 3; repeat from * across, end p 4.
Row 4: K 4, p 3, k 3; repeat from *

across, end k 4. Bind off in ribbing pat. Work edging on remaining 2 edges in same manner. Sew corners of edging tog. Work quilting same as on jacket with CC.

Work 2nd blanket in CC. Work edging in MC. Quilt with MC.

FINISHING: Wrong sides tog, sew blankets tog along all 4 edges at base of edging. To form bunting, fold in top and bottom of blanket to meet at center. With 2 strands of CC, make 2 chs 40" long. Weave blanket ends tog, beg about 12" below top edge and working to bottom edge, weaving ch in and out of yo sts of edging; weave ch back up to top edge. Tie ends tog at top. Trim ends with tassels. Weave lower edge in same manner.

FREDDY FROG: FRONT: With size 9 needle and CC, cast on 18 sts. Work in stockinette st (k 1 row, p 1 row) for 36 rows. Mark last row for top edge.
BACK: Row 1: * K 1, p 1; repeat from * across.
Rows 2 and 4: Purl.
Row 3: * P 1, k 1; repeat from * across. Repeat rows 1-4, 8 times more. Bind off.
FINISHING: Fold in half on marked row; sew side edges tog. Stuff firmly, sew lower edges tog. To form eyes, pinch top corners tog and sew into rounded shapes. Embroider black eyes and red mouth in outline st. To form head, on 20th row from lower edge, weave a strand of CC across front from side seam to side seam; pull strand tight enough to gather slightly, fasten securely.
Back Legs (make 2): Wind yarn around a 12" piece of cardboard 21 times. Tie tightly at one end, cut opposite end. Divide 42 strands into 3 groups and braid tightly, knot end. Sew tied ends to lower corners of body; loop legs to the outside and tack knotted end in place.
Front Legs (make 2): Wind yarn around a 6" piece of cardboard 12 times; finish as for back legs. Sew tied ends to side seams just below gathered row. Tack knotted ends in place on front.
KATY KAT: With size 9 needles and MC, cast on 18 sts. Work in garter st (k each row) for 30 rows. Work in stockinette st (k 1 row, p 1 row) for 18 rows for face. Mark last row for top of head. Work in garter st for 52 rows for back. Bind off.
FINISHING: Fold in half at marked row, sew side seams. Stuff firmly and sew lower edges tog. To form ears, pinch top corners tog and sew into triangular shapes. Embroider green eyes, black pupils, pink nose and mouth and black whiskers. With CC, make a ch 14" long. Tie around neck, pulling body in slightly to form head shape. Tack collar in place. Make 4 1" pompons and sew to front for feet. Wind yarn around an 8" piece of cardboard 9 times. Tie tightly at one

end, cut opposite end. Divide 18 strands into 3 groups and braid tightly. Tie end of braid with strand of CC. Sew to lower edge at center back for tail.

VEST AND SCARF SET
Shown on page 244

SIZES: Directions for small size (2-3). Changes for medium size (4-6) and large size (8) are in parentheses.
Body Chest Size: 21″-22″ (23″-24″; 26″).
Blocked Chest Size (closed): 22″ (25″-27½″).
MATERIALS: Knitting worsted, 2 (2-3) 4-oz. skeins. Crochet hook size I. 4 (4-5) buttons.
GAUGE: 3 sts = 1″; 5 rows = 2″.
To Dec 1 St: At beg of a row, ch 1, pull up a lp in each of first 2 sts, yo and through 3 lps on hook; **at end of a row,** pull up a lp in each of last 2 sts, yo and through 3 lps on hook. **Next Row:** Work in pat as established (sc over dc and dc over sc).
To Bind Off: At beg of a row, sl st loosely across specified number of sts; **at end of a row,** leave specified number of sts unworked.
VEST: Body: Beg at lower edge of back and fronts, ch 69 (77-85).
Row 1: Sc in 2nd ch from hook, * dc in next ch, sc in next ch, repeat from * across, end dc in last ch—68 (76-84) sts. Ch 1, turn.
Row 2: * Sc in dc, dc in sc, repeat from * across. Ch 1, turn. Repeat last row for pat until piece measures 7″ (8″-9″) from start. Check gauge; piece should measure 22⅔″ (25⅓″-28″) wide.
Shape Neck: Next Row: Keeping to pat as established, dec 1 st each side (see To Dec 1 St)—66 (74-82) sts. Work 2 rows even.
Divide Work: Right Front: Ch 1, dec 1 st at beg of row, work in pat across next 14 (16-18) sts—15 (17-19) sts. Ch 1, turn. Working in pat, dec 1 st at arm side every other row 1 (2-2) times; **at the same time,** dec 1 st at front edge every other row 6 (6-7) times—8 (9-10) sts. Work even, if necessary, until armhole measures 4½″ (5″-5½″) above start of armhole.
Shape Shoulder: Bind off 3 sts (see To Bind Off) at arm side of next row—5 (6-7) sts. End off.
Back: Sk 3 sts on last long row for right underarm, work in pat across next 28 (32-36) sts. Ch 1, turn. Keeping to pat as established, dec 1 st each side every other row 1 (2-2) times—26 (28-32) sts. Work even until armholes measure same as front armhole.
Shape Shoulders: Bind off 3 sts each side of next row. End off.
Left front: Sk 3 sts on last long row for left underarm, work in pat across, dec 1 st at center edge—15 (17-19) sts. Ch 1,

turn. Work same as right front, reversing shaping.
FINISHING: Block pieces. Sew shoulder seams. From right side, work 1 row sc around each armhole edge. Beg at lower right front edge, work 1 row sc around center front and neck edges. Steam-press edges lightly. Sew buttons, evenly spaced, on right front edge, first button 1″ above lower edge, last button at start of neck shaping. Spaces between sts form buttonholes.
SCARF: Ch 11 (13-15). Work in pat on 10 (12-14) sts for 28″ (30″-32″) or desired length. End off. Steam-press lightly.
Fringe: Cut yarn into 6″ lengths. Holding 4 strands together, knot 4 (5-6) fringes evenly spaced on each end of scarf. Trim fringe evenly.

VEST AND TAM
Shown on page 244

SIZES: Directions for size 4. Changes for sizes 6 and 8 are in parentheses.
Body Chest Size: 23″ (24″-26″).
Blocked Chest Size: 24½″ (26-27¾″).
MATERIALS: Knitting worsted, 1 (2-2) 4-oz. skeins each of red (R) and winter white (W). Crochet hook size I.
GAUGE: 11 sts = 4″; 2 rows = 1″.
To Dec 1 St: At beg of row, pull up a lp in each of 2 sts, yo hook and through 3 lps on hook; **at end of row,** work to last 2 sts, pull up a lp in each of last 2 sts, yo hook and through 3 lps on hook.
To Bind Off: At beg of row, sl st loosely across specified number of sts; **at end of row,** leave specified number of sts unworked.
VEST: BODY: Beg at lower edge of back and front, with R, ch 69 (73-77).
Pattern: Row 1 (right side): Sc in 2nd ch from hook, sc in next ch, * dc in each of next 2 ch, sc in each of next 2 ch, repeat from * across, end dc in each of last 2 ch. Drop R; join W. Turn.
Row 2 (wrong side): With W, ch 1, * sc in each of 2 dc, dc in each of 2 sc, repeat from * across. Drop W; do not turn.
Row 3 (wrong side): Pick up R, ch 2, * dc in each of 2 sc, sc in each of 2 dc, repeat from * across. Drop R; turn.
Row 4 (right side): Pick up W; with W, repeat row 3. Drop W; do not turn.
Row 5 (right side): Pick up R; with R, repeat row 2. Drop R; turn.
Row 6 (wrong side): Pick up W; with W, repeat row 2. Drop W; do not turn. Continue in pat as established, working 1 row R, 1 row W alternately until piece measures 8″ (9″-10″) from start or desired length to underarm. Check gauge; piece should measure 24½″ (26″-27¾″) wide.
Divide Work: Back Yoke: Keeping to pat, bind off 2 sts (see To Bind Off), work across next 30 (32-34) sts. Work-

ing on these 30 (32-34) sts, keeping to pat as established, dec 1 st (see To Dec 1 St) each side every row twice—26 (28-30) sts. Work even until armholes measure 4¾″ (5″-5½″) above armhole shaping.
Shape Shoulders: Bind off 4 sts each side of next row, 4 (4-5) sts next row—10 (12-12) sts remain. End off.
Side Front Yoke: Sk 4 sts on last long row for underarm; working with color to be used, work across next 15 (16-17) sts. Working in pat as established on these 15 (16-17) sts, dec 1 st at arm side every row twice; **at the same time,** dec 1 st at center edge every row 5 (6-6) times—8 (8-9) sts. Work even until armhole measures same as back.
Shape Shoulder: Bind off 4 sts at arm side of next row—4 (4-5) sts remain. End off.
Side Front Yoke: With color to be used, work in pat across next 15 (16-17) sts on last long row. Work same as for first front yoke.
FINISHING: Run in yarn ends on wrong side. Block. Sew shoulder and side seams. From right side, with R, work 2 rnds sc around each armhole and neck edge, working off 3 sc at center front neck as 1 sc on 2nd rnd to form V.
TAM: Beg at center top, with R, ch 2.
Row 1: 7 sc in 2nd ch from hook. Do not join; ch 1, turn.
Row 2: 2 sc in first sc, 3 sc in each of next 6 sc—20 sc. Ch 2, turn.
Row 3: 3 dc in each sc across—60 dc. Ch 2, turn. Work in pat same as for vest for 10 rows. Cut W.
Next Row: With R, * sc in each of 2 sts, dec 1 st over next 2 sts, repeat from * around—45 sc. Drop R. Sew back seam. Pick up R; work 1 rnd sc, decreasing, if necessary, to fit headsize. End off. Make R and W pompon; attach to top of tam.

SNOWFLAKE SETS
Shown on page 245

SIZES: Directions are for child's medium size. Changes for adult's medium size are in parentheses.
MATERIALS: Knitting worsted, 4-ply yarn, 1 4-oz. skein each of white (W) and red (R) for each set. Afghan hook size G. Crochet hook size G. Large-eyed tapestry needle.
GAUGE: 5 sts = 1″; 4 rows = 1″.
AFGHAN STITCH: Row 1: Keeping all lps on hook, pull up a lp in 2nd ch from hook and in each ch across.
To Work Lps Off: Yo hook, pull through first lp, * yo hook, pull through 2 lps, repeat from * across. Lp that remains on hook always counts as first st of next row.

Row 2: Keeping all lps on hook, sk first vertical bar (lp on hook is first st), pull up a lp under next vertical bar and under each vertical bar across. Work lps off as before. Repeat row 2 for afghan stitch.

To Dec 1 Afghan St: At beg of row, insert hook under 2nd and 3rd vertical bars and pull up a lp. **At end of row,** insert hook under 3rd and 2nd vertical bars from end and pull up a lp.

To Bind Off: Sl st loosely across sts.

CAP: SECTION (make 4): Beg at lower edge, with W and afghan hook, ch 17 (20). Work in afghan st on 17 (20) sts for 15 (19) rows. Check gauge; piece should measure 3½″ (4″) wide.

Shape Top: Dec 1 st each side (see To Dec 1 St) every row 7 (8) times—3 (4) sts.

Next Row: Keeping all lps on hook, sk first vertical bar, pull up a lp under next 2 (3) bars. Yo hook, pull through all 3 (4) lps on hook. End off.

Embroidery: Following chart, embroider each section in cross-stitch.

Edging: From right side, with crochet hook and R, sc in top point, * ch 1, sk next row or st, sc in next row or st, repeat from * around, working 3 sc in each corner. Join with a sl st in first sc. End off.

FINISHING: Working through back lps, with R, weave sections tog.

Lower Edging: From right side, with R and crochet hook, sc in any sc, * ch 1,

sc in next sc, repeat from * around, end ch 1, sl st in first st.

Next Rnd: Work same as last rnd. Join; end off.

For Child's Cap Only: EARLAPS (make 2): Beg at upper edge, with W and afghan hook, ch 11. Work in afghan st on 11 sts for 2 rows. Dec 1 st each side every row 3 times—5 sts remain. Bind off (see To Bind Off).

Edging: With crochet hook and R, work edging around earlaps same as for sections. Leaving 3″ free across center of one section for back of neck, weave earlaps to lower edge of cap.

Ties: From right side, join R at upper edge of earlap, sc in first sc, * ch 1, sc in next sc, repeat from * to lower point, ch 55; work 5 sc in 2nd ch from hook and in each of next 8 ch, sc in each remaining ch; working on other side of earlap, work from first * to 2nd * to upper edge of earlap. End off.

For Both Caps: Make 1 R pompon; attach to top of cap.

MITTENS (make 2): **Cuff:** Beg at side edge, with W and crochet hook, ch 15 (20).

Row 1: Sc in 2nd ch from hook and in each ch across—14 (19) sc. Ch 1, turn.

Row 2: Sc in back lp of each sc across. Ch 1, turn. Repeat last row until 18 (23) rows from start. At end of last row, sc back lp of each sc tog with starting ch, forming cuff. Do not end off.

Hand Back: With afghan hook, pick up

13 (16) lps along side edge of 9 (12) rows. Work off lps. Work in afghan st until 16 (22) rows from start.

Shape Top: Dec 1 st each side every row 3 times—7 (10) sts. Bind off.

Hand Front: With W, pick up 13 (16) lps on other half of cuff; work same as for back.

Embroidery: Following chart, embroider back of mitten.

Thumb: With afghan hook and W, ch 4. Work in afghan st for 1 row.

Next Row: Pull up a lp in horizontal strand before vertical bar (1 st inc), pull up a lp in each vertical bar to within last bar, pull up a lp in horizontal strand before last vertical bar (1 st inc), pull up a lp in last vertical bar. Repeat last row 2 (4) times—10 (14) sts. Work 3 (5) rows even. Dec 5 sts evenly spaced across next row. Bind off, leaving a long end for sewing. Draw bound-off sts tog tightly; fasten securely on wrong side. Weave side seam of thumb tog, leaving lower 3 (5) rows open.

FINISHING: Pin lower 3 (5) rows of thumb to back and front of mitten.

Edging: From right side, with crochet hook and R, work sc, ch 1 around outer edge of each mitten half, working through thumb and mitten as pinned (do not work sides of mitten tog). Working through back lps, weave back and front of mittens tog.

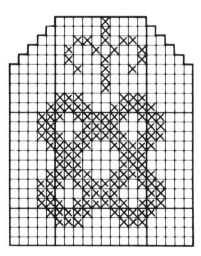

CHILD'S MITTEN

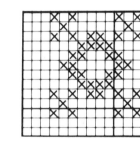

CHILD'S CAP

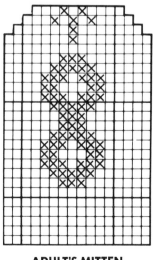

ADULT'S CAP

ADULT'S MITTEN

ZIP-UP JACKET
Shown on page 246

SIZES: Directions for size 4. Changes for sizes 6, 8 and 10 are in parentheses.

Body Chest Size: 23″ (24″-27″-28½″).

Blocked Chest Size (closed): 24″ (25″-27½″-30″).

MATERIALS: Knitting worsted, 3 (3-4-4) 4-oz. skeins denim color; small amounts of scarlet (A), yellow (B) and green (C). Crochet hooks sizes E and G. Separating zipper.

GAUGE: 7 dc = 2″; 2 rows = 1″ (size G hook).

To Bind Off: At beg of row, ch 1, sl st loosely across specified number of sts; **at end of row,** leave specified number of sts unworked.

To Dec 1 St: At beg of row, ch 3 (counts as 1 dc), sk first dc, yo hook, draw up a lp in each of next 2 sts, yo hook and through 2 lps, yo and through 3 lps, work in pat across; **at end of row,** work to last 2 sts, yo hook, draw up a lp in each of next 2 sts, yo and through 2 lps, yo and through 3 lps.

To Inc 1 St: At beg of row, ch 3, dc in first st; **at end of row,** work 2 dc in top of turning ch.

JACKET: BACK: Ribbing (worked from side seam to side seam): With size E hook, ch 13 (13-15-15).

Row 1: Sc in 2nd ch from hook and in each ch across—12 (12-14-14) sc. Ch 1, turn.

Row 2: Sc in back lp of each sc across. Ch 1, turn. Repeat row 2 until 42 (44-48-52) rows from start. Change to size G hook. Ch 3, do not turn.

Pattern: Row 1: Working across side edge of ribbing, sk first row, dc in next row and in each row across—42 (44-48-52) dc, counting ch 3 as 1 dc. Turn.

Row 2: Ch 3 (always counts as 1 dc), sk first dc, dc in next dc and in each dc across—42 (44-48-52) dc. Turn. Repeat last row until piece measures 6½″ (7″-7½″-8″) from start or desired length to underarm. Check gauge; piece above ribbing should be 12″ (12½″-13¾″-14¾″) wide.

Shape Armholes: Bind off 2 sts each side of next row. Dec 1 st (see To Bind Off and To Dec 1 St) each side every row 2 (2-3-4) times—34 (36-38-40) dc. Work even until armholes measure 4½″ (5″-5½″-6″) above first bound-off sts.

Shape Shoulders: Bind off 5 sts each side of next row, 5 (5-6-6) sts next row—14 (16-16-18) sts. End off.

RIGHT FRONT: Ribbing: Work same as for back ribbing for 21 (22-24-26) rows. Change to size G hook. Ch 3, do not turn.

Pattern: Row 1: Working across side edge of ribbing, sk first row, dc in next row and in each row across—21 (22-24-26) dc, counting ch 3 as 1 dc. Work same as for back until piece measures same as back to underarm. Mark end of last row for side edge. (On left front, mark beg of last row for side edge.)

Shape Armhole: Bind off 2 dc at side edge of next row. Dec 1 dc at same edge every row 2 (2-3-4) times—17 (18-19-20) dc. Work even until armhole measures 3″ (3½″-4″-4½″) above first bound-off sts.

Shape Neck: Bind off 5 (6-6-7) sts at center edge of next row. Dec 1 st at same edge every row twice.

Next Row: Bind off 5 sts at arm side—5 (5-6-6) sts. End off.

LEFT FRONT: Work same as for right front, reversing shaping.

SLEEVES: Ribbing: Work same as for back for 22 (24-26-26) rows. Change to size G hook. Ch 3, do not turn.

Pattern: Work same as for back on 22 (24-26-26) sts for 2 rows. Inc 1 st (see To Inc 1 St) each side of next row, then every 3rd row 4 (4-4-5) times more—32 (34-36-38) dc. Work even until piece measures 10½″ (11½″-13″-14½″) from start or desired length to underarm. Check gauge; piece above last inc row should measure 9¼″ (9¾″-10¼″-10¾″) wide.

Shape Cap: Bind off 2 sts each side of next row. Dec 1 st each side every

row 2 (2-3-4) times—24 (26-26-26) sts. Work 1 row even.

Next Row: Sl st across first st, ch 3, sk next st, dec 1 st over next 2 sts, work to within last 3 sts, dec 1 st over next 2 sts, do not work in turning ch—2 sts dec each side. Repeat last row 3 (4-4-4) times—8 (6-6-6) sts. End off.

COLLAR: Beg at neck edge, with size G hook, ch 44 (46-46-48).

Row 1: Dc in 4th ch from hook and in each ch across. Turn. Working in dc, inc 1 st each side of next row, then every other row 2 (2-3-3) times—48 (50-52-54) dc. End off.

FINISHING: Smooth pieces out, wrong side up, on a padded surface. Place rust-proof pins at top, bottom and sides of each piece. Do not pin ribbings. Steam pieces carefully, making sure steam penetrates knitting. Let dry. With backstitch, sew shoulder seams; sew in sleeves. Sew side and sleeve seams. Sew foundation ch of collar to neck edge of jacket. Beg at lower left front edge, work 1 row sc up left front edge, around collar, down right front edge, working 3 sc in each collar corner. Sew in zipper.

APPLIQUES: Flower: With size G hook and B, ch 2.

Rnd 1: 6 sc in 2nd ch from hook; join with a sl st in first sc. End off.

Rnd 2: Join A in any sc; work 2 sc in each sc around—12 sc. Join with a sl st in first sc.

Rnd 3 (petals): * Ch 4, sc in 2nd ch from hook and in each of next 2 ch, sl st in each of next 2 sc, repeat from * 5 times.

Stem: With C and size G hook, ch 14, sc in 2nd ch from hook and in each ch across. End off.

Leaves (make 2): With C and size G hook, ch 5, sc in 2nd ch from hook and in each ch across. End off. Make two appliqués and sew, wrong side up, with matching color yarn to fronts as pictured.

HAT: With size G hook, ch 4, sl st in first ch to form ring.

Rnd 1: Ch 3 (counts as 1 dc), 11 dc in ring—12 dc. Sl st in top of ch 3.

Rnd 2: Ch 3, dc in same ch with sl st, 2 dc in each of next 11 dc—24 dc. Sl st in top of ch 3.

Rnd 3: Ch 3, dc in same ch with sl st, dc in each of next 2 dc, * 2 dc in next dc, dc in each of next 2 dc, repeat from * around—32 dc. Sl st in top of ch 3.

Rnd 4: Ch 3, dc in same ch with sl st, dc in next dc, * 2 dc in next dc, dc in next dc, repeat from * around—48 dc. Sl st in top of ch 3.

Rnd 5: Ch 3, dc in same ch with sl st, dc in each of next 5 dc, * 2 dc in next dc, dc in each of next 5 dc, repeat from * around—56 dc. Sl st in top of ch 3.

Rnds 6-12: Ch 3, dc in next dc and in each dc around—56 dc. Sl st in top of ch 3. End off. (Ends of rnds are back of hat.)

BRIM: Turn work so that wrong side faces you. **Rnd 13:** Join double strand of yarn in front lp of dc at back of hat. Sc in front lp of each dc around. Sl st in first sc.

Rnd 14: Ch 1, sc in same sc with sl st and in each of next 11 sc, 2 sc in next sc, * sc in each of next 12 sc, 2 sc in next sc, repeat from * twice—60 sc. Join.

Rnd 15: Ch 1, sc in joining and in each of next 4 sc, 2 sc in next sc, * sc in each of next 5 sc, 2 sc in next sc, repeat from * around—70 sc. Join.

Rnd 16: Ch 1, sc in joining and in each of next 5 sc, 2 sc in next sc, * sc in each of next 6 sc, 2 sc in next sc, repeat from * around—80 sc. Join.

Rnds 17 and 18: Working in sc, continue to inc 10 sc evenly spaced around—100 sc.

Rnds 19-22: Sc in each sc around. End off. Join one strand of yarn in free lp of any dc on rnd 12. With inside of crown facing you (right side of dc rnds is inside of crown), ch 1, sc in free lp of each dc on rnd 12 around. Join.

Next Rnd: Sc in each sc around. Join; end off.

FINISHING: Steam-press brim lightly. Make two appliqués same as for jacket. Sew to brim as pictured.

EMBROIDERED JUMPER
Shown on page 247

SIZES: Directions for size 4. Changes for sizes 6, 8 and 10 are in parentheses.
Body Chest Size: 23″ (24″-27″-28½″).
Blocked Chest Size: 24″ (26″-28″-30″).
MATERIALS: Knitting worsted, 2 (3-3-4) 4-oz. skeins pink. Small amount white for edgings. Small amount red and olive green crewel embroidery yarn. Knitting needles Nos. 5 and 7. Crochet hook size E. Three stitch holders. Large-eyed embroidery needle.
GAUGE: 5 sts = 1″; 7 rows = 1″ (No. 7 needles).
JUMPER: BACK: Skirt Panels (make 3): Beg at lower edge, with No. 7 needles, cast on 34 (36-38-40) sts. Work in stockinette st (k 1 row, p 1 row) for 1″ (1½″-2″-2½″), end p row. Check gauge; piece should measure 6¾″ (7¼″-7½″-8″) wide. Dec 1 st each side of next row, then every 1″ 7 times—18 (20-22-24) sts. Work even until piece

measures 8½″ (9″-9½″-10″) from start, end p row. Sl sts on a st holder. Weave edges of panels tog for back skirt.

Waistband: From right side, sl sts on No. 5 needles—54 (60-66-72) sts. Work in ribbing of k 1 for 6 rows, end wrong side.

Next Row (eyelet row): * K 1, p 1, yo, k 2 tog, repeat from * across.

Next Row: * K 1, p 1, repeat from * across. Work in ribbing as established for 4 rows. Change to No. 7 needles. Work in stockinette st until piece measures 14″ (15″-16″-17″) from start, end p row.

Shape Armholes: Bind off 3 (4-5-5) sts at beg of next 2 rows. Dec 1 st each side every other row 3 (4-5-7) times—42 (44-46-48) sts. Work even until armholes measure 4″ (4¼″-4¾″-5¼″) above first bound-off sts, end wrong side.

Shape Neck and Shoulders: K 13 (14-15-16), drop yarn, join another strand of yarn, bind off center 16 sts, finish row—13 (14-15-16) sts each side. Working on both sides at once, with separate strands of yarn, bind off 3 sts at beg of each neck edge once, 2 sts once. Dec 1 st at beg of each neck edge 1 (1-1-2) times—7 (8-9-9) sts each side. Work even if necessary until armholes measure 5″ (5¼″-5¾″-6¼″) above bound-off sts. Bind off.

FRONT: Work same as for back until armholes measures 1½″ (1¾″-2¼″-2¾″) above first bound-off sts, end p row.

Shape Neck and Shoulders: K 13 (14-15-16), drop yarn, join another strand of yarn, bind off center 16 sts, finish row—13 (14-15-16) sts each side. Working on both sides at once, bind off 2 sts at beg of each neck edge twice. Dec 1 st at beg of each neck edge 2 (2-2-3) times—7 (8-9-9) sts each side. Work even until armholes measure same as back. Bind off.

FINISHING: Block pieces. Sew side and shoulder seams.

Edging: From right side, with Blossom, work 1 rnd sc around neck, armhole and lower edge.

Next Rnd: Join white in any sc, * ch 3, sl st in next 2 sc, repeat from * around. Join with a sl st in joining. End off. Work same edging around all edges.

Embroidery: With red, work five lazy daisy st petals for each flower, green straight st between each petal. Embroider flowers on front bodice and around lower edge of skirt as pictured. Steam-press lightly on wrong side.

CORD: With White, make chain 44″ (48″) long. Sl st in each ch across. End off. Weave chain through eyelets; tie ends into bow.

ARAN MUFF
Shown on page 248

SIZE: About 11″ x 8½″.

MATERIALS: Columbia-Minerva Performer, 2 4-oz. balls. Crochet hook size G. ⅓ yard lining fabric. Polyester stuffing. Matching sewing thread.

GAUGE: 4 sts = 1″; 9 rows = 2″.

STITCH PATTERN: Note: Do not work in stitch directly behind raised dc or double raised dc, or in eye of a cluster.

CLUSTER: (Yo hook, draw up a lp in st) 4 times, yo and through all 9 lps on hook. Ch 1 tightly to form eye. (Cluster is worked from wrong side but appears on right side.)

RAISED DC: Dc around upright bar of dc 1 row below, inserting hook behind dc from front to back to front, for ridge on right side.

DOUBLE RAISED DC: Holding back last lp of each dc on hook, make 2 dc around upright bar of st 1 row below, yo and through all 3 lps on hook.

POPCORN: 4 dc in st, drop lp off hook, insert hook in top of first dc, pick up dropped lp and pull through.

MUFF: Ch 44 to measure about 11″.

Row 1: Sc in 2nd ch from hook and in each ch across—43 sc. Ch 1, turn each row.

Row 2 (wrong side): Sc in each of first 5 sts, (cluster in next sc, sc in each of next 15 sts) twice, end cluster in next st, sc in each of last 5 sts.

Row 3 (right side): Sc in each of first 3 sts, * work dc around post of next sc 1 row below (row 1), sk sc on row 2 behind raised dc (see Stitch Pattern: Note), sc in next sc, sk eye of cluster, sc in cluster, sc in next sc, dc around post of next sc 1 row below, sk sc on row 2 behind raised dc, sc in each of next 4 sc; holding back last lp of each dc on hook, make 2 dc around next sc 1 row below, yo and through 3 lps on hook, sk sc on row 2 behind double raised dc, sc in next sc, sk 1 sc on row 1, make double raised dc around next sc as before, sk sc on row 2 behind double raised dc, sc in each of next 4 sc, repeat from * once, end (dc around post of next sc 1 row below, sk sc behind raised dc, sc in each of next 3 sts) twice.

Row 4: Sc in each of first 4 sts, (cluster in next st, sc in next st, cluster in next st, sc in each of next 13 sts) twice, end cluster in next st, sc in next st, cluster in next st, sc in each of last 4 sts.

Row 5: Sc in each of first 3 sts, * (raised dc in raised dc, sc in each of next 3 sts) twice, (double raised dc in double raised dc, sc in each of next 3 sts) twice, repeat from * once, end (raised dc in raised dc, sc in each of next 3 sts) twice.

Row 6: Repeat row 2.

Row 7: Sc in each of first 3 sts, * raised dc in raised dc, sc in each of next 3 sts, raised dc in raised dc, sc in each of next 2 sts, double raised dc in double raised dc, sc in each of next 5 sts, double raised dc in double raised dc, dc in each of next 2 sts, repeat from * once, end (raised dc in raised dc, sc in each of next 3 sts) twice.

Row 8: Repeat row 4.

Row 9: Sc in each of first 3 sts, * raised dc in raised dc, sc in each of next 3 sts, raised dc in raised dc, sc in next st, double raised dc in double raised dc, sc in each of next 3 sts, popcorn in next sc, sc in each of next 3 sts, double raised dc in double raised dc, sc in next st, repeat from * once, end (raised dc in raised dc, sc in each of next 3 sts) twice.

Row 10: Repeat row 2.

Row 11: Repeat row 7.

Row 12: Repeat row 4.

Row 13: Repeat row 5.

Row 14: Repeat row 2.

Row 15: Sc in each of first 3 sc, * raised dc in raised dc, sc in each of next 3 sts, raised dc in raised dc, sc in each of next 4 sts, double raised dc in double raised dc, sc in next st, double raised dc in double raised dc, sc in each of next 4 sts, repeat from * once, end (raised dc in raised dc, sc in each of next 3 sts) twice. Repeat rows 4-15 for pat 4 times (63 rows), then repeat rows 4-14. Work 1 row sc. End off.

STRAPS (make 2): Ch 5. Sc in 2nd ch from hook and in each remaining 3 ch —4 sc. Ch 1, turn. Work in sc until strap measures 42″. End off.

FINISHING: Cut lining same size as knitted piece. Stitch ends of piece tog, forming ring. Stitch ends of lining tog, forming ring. Fold 3 sts at each side of muff to wrong side. Insert 1½″ layer of stuffing into muff. Turn under ½″ seam allowance on raw edges of lining, hem to inside of muff. Attach a strap to each side of muff. Tie ends at back of neck.

REINDEER MUFF
Shown on page 248

SIZE: About 10½″ square.

MATERIALS: Columbia-Minerva Nantuk Sports Yarn, 2 2-oz. balls each of red (A), white (B) and green (C). Knitting needles No. 6. Large-eyed embroidery needle. ⅓ yard felt or lining material. Polyester stuffing. Matching sewing thread.

GAUGE: 5 sts = 1″; 7 rows = 1″.

Pattern is embroidered in duplicate st when muff is completed.

MUFF: With A, cast on 53 sts.

Row 1 (right side): Knit.

Row 2: K 1, p 51, k 1. Repeat last 2 rows until piece measures 11″ from start, end wrong side. Repeating last 2 rows, work 2 rows B, 2 rows C, 6 rows B, 2 rows C, 28 rows B, 2 rows C, 6 rows B, 2 rows C, 2 rows B. With A, work even until piece measures 21″ from start, end wrong side. Bind off in k same tension as sts.

EMBROIDERY: Following chart, working in duplicate st, embroider front of muff on the 6 and 26 B rows.

FINISHING: Run in yarn ends on wrong side. Steam-press lightly. Cut lining ½″ larger on all edges than knitted piece. Weave bound-off edge to cast-on edge, forming ring. Sew ends of lining tog, forming ring; insert lining in muff. Fold ½″ of lining at one end of opening to wrong side; hem to muff. Insert a ½″ layer of stuffing between muff and lining; hem other edge of lining to muff.

REINDEER PANTS SET
Shown on page 249

NOTE: Body of pullover to shoulder is tubular. Armholes are cut later.

SIZES: Directions for small size (8-10). Changes for medium size (12-14) are in parentheses.

Body Bust Size: 31½″-32½″ (34″-36″).

Blocked Bust Size: 41″ (44″).

MATERIALS: Knitting worsted, 7 (8) 4-oz. skeins scarlet (A); 2 skeins green (B) and 1 skein white (C). 29″ circular needle No. 10; set of dp needles No. 10. Aluminum crochet hook size G. Two stitch holders. Seam binding. One yard ½″ elastic.

GAUGE: 4 sts = 1″; 11 rows = 2″.

Pattern Notes: Always change colors on wrong side; pick up background color from under dropped pattern color; pick up pattern color over dropped background color. Carry color not being used loosely across back of work. When more than 5 sts between colors, twist colors every 3rd or 4th st. Cut and join colors when necessary.

PULLOVER: BODY: Beg at lower edge of back and front, with A and circular needle, cast on 164 (176) sts. Put and keep a marker on needle between last and first sts of rnd. Join, being careful not to twist sts.

Hem: Work in ribbing of k 1, p 1 for 3 rnds.

Next Rnd (eyelet rnd): * Yo, k 2 tog, repeat from * around. K 4 rnds.

Pattern: Rnds 1-9: Following chart 1, work pat in stockinette st (k each rnd) starting at arrow on rnd 1. Repeat pat to end of rnd. Check gauge; piece should measure 41″ (44″) around. With A, k 4 rnds.

Next Rnd: Following chart 2, * k from A to B 7 (8) times, k from B to C once,

repeat from * once. Work in this manner to top of chart. With A, k 4 rnds, dec 2 sts on last rnd—162 (174) sts. Following chart 3, repeat the 8 rnds until piece measures 23″ (24″) above eyelet rnd or desired length from lower edge to top of shoulder.

Next Rnd: With A, work 21 (23) sts, bind off loosely next 21 (23) sts for left front shoulder, k until 39 (41) sts from bound-off sts, sl these sts on a holder for front neck; bind off next 21 (23) sts for right front shoulder, put a marker on work in last st; bind off next 21 (23) sts for right back shoulder, k until 39 (41) sts from bound-off sts, sl these sts on a holder for back neck, bind off next 21 (23) sts for left back shoulder; leave marker on work.

SLEEVES (make 2): Beg at lower edge, with A and dp needles, cast on 48 (52) sts; divide on 3 dp needles. Mark end of rnd. Join, being careful not to twist sts. Work same as for body to end of rnd 9 on chart 1. With A, k 4 rnds, inc 0 (2) sts on last rnd—48 (54) sts.

Next Rnd: Following chart 2, k from A to B 8 (9) times. Work in this manner to top of chart. With A, k 3 rnds. Following chart 3, repeat the 8 rnds until piece measures 11″ above eyelet rnd. Check gauge; piece should measure 12″ (13½″) around. Inc 1 st each side of marker every 1″ 6 times, working added sts into pat—60 (66) sts. Work even until piece measures 18″ above eyelet rnd or desired sleeve length. With A, bind off loosely.

FINISHING: Run in yarn ends on wrong side. Block pieces.

Slash Armholes: Baste a straight line from shoulder edge down for 7½″ (8¼″) at each arm side between sts of front and back (at marker and at last bound-off st). Machine stitch twice, using a loose tension and small sts, ¼″ each side of basting. Slash along basting line.

With A, sew shoulder seams. Fold armhole edge of sleeve in half between underarm incs; placing inc edge of sleeve at underarm of body and center top of sleeve at shoulder seam, sew in sleeves from right side, lapping sleeve over armhole (to conceal raw edge). Steam-press raw edges toward sleeves. Cover wrong side of armhole seams with seam binding. Turn hems to wrong side on eyelet rnd; sew in place.

Collar: Beg at front neck, from right side, sl 39 (41) sts each of front and back neck on 3 dp needles. Join; with A, k 2 rnds, inc 2 sts on first rnd—80 (84) sts. Following chart 1, work rnds 1-9. With A, k 2 rnds.

Next Rnd (eyelet rnd): With A, * yo, k 2 tog, repeat from * around. K 13 rnds. Bind off loosely.

Fold collar on eyelet rnd to wrong

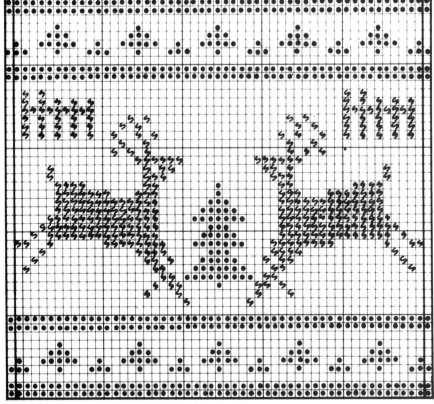

Embroidery Chart for Reindeer Muff

side; sew in place loosely. Steam-press collar.

PANTS: LEG: Beg at lower edge, with A and dp needles, cast on 84 (92) sts; divide on 3 dp needles. Mark end of rnd. Join, being careful not to twist sts. Work same as for pullover body to end of rnd 9 on chart 1. With A, work in stockinette st for 4 rnds, dec 0 (2) sts on last rnd—84 (90) sts.

Next Rnd: Following chart 2, work from A to B 14 (15) times. Work in this manner to top of chart. With A, k around until piece measures 28" above eyelet rnd or desired leg length to crotch. Check gauge; piece should measure 21" (22½") around.

Shape Crotch: Next Rnd: Bind off 12 sts, finish rnd—72 (78) sts. Sl sts on a holder. Make other leg in same manner. Leave sts on dp needles.

Join Legs: From right side, sl sts from dp needles to circular needle. K around sts on holder—144 (156) sts. Work in stockinette st until piece measures 9" (10") above crotch.

Next Rnd (eyelet rnd): * Yo, k 2 tog, repeat from * around. Bind off loosely in k.

FINISHING: Run in yarn ends on wrong side. Block. Weave bound-off sts at crotch tog. Turn hem to wrong side on eyelet rnd; sew in place. Cut elastic to waist measurement; weave through eyelets at waistline. Sew ends securely.

LADYBUGS ON GREEN
Shown on page 250

Note: Body of pullover to shoulder is tubular. Armholes are cut later.

SIZES: Directions for small size (4). Changes for medium size (6-8) and large size (10-12) are in parentheses.

Body Chest Size: 23" (24"-26"; 28"-30").

Blocked Chest Size: 25½" (29"-32").

MATERIALS: Knitting worsted, 2 (3-4) 4-oz. skeins green (G), 1 skein white (W); 1 2-oz. skein of black (B) and red (R). 24" circular needle No. 8; set of dp needles No. 8. Two stitch holders.

Seam binding. Matching sewing thread.
GAUGE: 5 sts = 1"; 11 rows = 2".
Pattern Notes: Always change colors on wrong side; pick up background color from under dropped pattern color; pick up pattern color over dropped background color. Carry color not being used loosely across back of

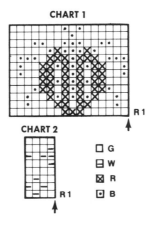

CHART 1

CHART 2

☐ G
🄴 W
☒ R
🄱 B

work. Cut and join colors when necessary.

PULLOVER: BODY: Beg at lower edge of back and front, with G and circular needles, cast on 128 (144-160) sts. Put and keep a marker on needle between last and first sts of rnd. Join, being careful not to twist sts. Work in ribbing of k 1, p 1 for 1¼" (1½"-1¾"). K 3 rnds.

Pattern: Rnds 1-10: Following chart 1, work pat in stockinette st (k each rnd) starting at arrow on rnd 1. Repeat pat to end of rnd. Work to top of chart (12 rnds). Check gauge; piece should measure 25½" (29"-32") around. With G, k 5 rnds. Following chart 2, starting at arrow on rnd 1 and repeating pat to end of rnd, work to top of chart, then repeat the 8 rnds of chart until piece measures 16" (18½"-21½") from start or desired length from lower edge to top of shoulder, end pat rnd 4 or 8.

Next Rnd: With G, bind off loosely 14 (16-19) sts for left front shoulder, k until 36 (40-42) sts from bound-off sts,

sl these sts on a holder for front neck; bind off next 14 (16-19) sts for right front shoulder, put a marker on work in last st; bind off next 14 (16-19) sts for right back shoulder; k until 36 (40-42) sts from bound-off sts, sl these sts on a holder for back neck, bind off next 14 (16-19) sts for left back shoulder; leave marker on work.

SLEEVES (make 2): Beg at lower edge with G and dp needles, cast on 48 (52-56) sts; divide on 3 dp needles. Mark end of rnds. Join, being carful not to twist sts. Work ribbing same as for body. K 1 rnd.

Pattern: Following chart 2, repeat the 8 rnds of chart until piece measures 5" (5½"-6") from start or desired sleeve length, end pat rnd 4 or 8. With G, bind off loosely.

FINISHING: Run in yarn ends on wrong side. Block pieces.

Slash Armholes: Baste a straight line from shoulder edge down for 5" (5½"-6") at each arm side between sts of front and back (at marker and at last bound-off st). Machine stitch twice, using a loose tension and small sts, ¼" each side of basting. Slash along basting line.

With W, sew shoulder seams. Fold armhole edge of sleeve in half at end of rnd marker; place this edge at underarm. Stretching sleeve to fit armhole, sew in sleeves from right side, lapping sleeve over armhole (to conceal raw edges). Steam-press raw edges toward sleeves. Cover wrong side of armhole seams with seam binding.

Collar: Beg at front neck, from right side, sl 36 (40-42) sts each of front and back neck on 3 dp needles—72 (80-84) sts. Join; with G, k 1 rnd. Folloiiing chart 2, work pat rnds 1-8. With G, k 1 rnd.

Next Rnd (eyelet rnd): * Yo, k 2 tog, repeat from * around. With G, k 10 rnds. With G, bind off loosely.

Fold collar on eyelet rnd to wrong side; sew in place. Steam-press collar.

☐A ⊡B ☒C

CHART 2

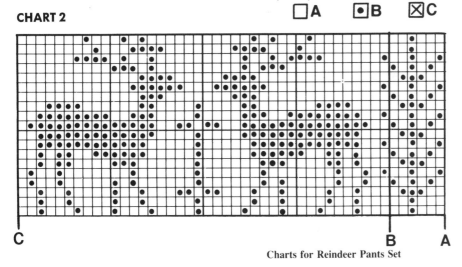

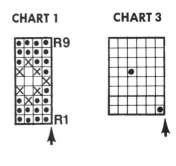

CHART 1 **CHART 3**

C   B   A

Charts for Reindeer Pants Set

LADYBUGS ON WHITE
Shown on page 250

Note: Body of pullover to shoulder is tubular. Armholes are cut later.

SIZES: Directions are for small size (4). Changes for medium size (6-8) and large size (10-12) are in parentheses.

Body Chest Size: 23" (24"-26"; 28"-30").

Blocked Chest Size: 25½" (29"-32").

MATERIALS: Knitting worsted, 2 (3-3) 4-oz. skeins white (W); 1 skein each of red (R), black (B) and green (G). 24" circular needle No. 8; set of dp needles No. 8. Two stitch holders. Seam binding. Matching sewing thread.

GAUGE: 5 sts = 1"; 11 rows = 2".

Pattern Notes: Always change colors on wrong side; pick up background color from under dropped pattern color; pick up pattern color over dropped background color. Carry colors not being used loosely across back of work. Cut and join colors when necessary.

PULLOVER: BODY: Beg at lower edge of back and front, with W and circular needle, cast on 128 (144-160) sts. Put and keep a marker on needle between last and first sts of rnd. Join, being careful not to twist sts. Working in ribbing of k 1, p 1, work 4 W rnds, 2 R rnds, 1 W rnd, 2 G rnds, 2 W rnds. K 2 W rnds.

Pattern: Following chart, work pat in stockinette st (k each rnd) starting at arrow on rnd 1. Repeat pat to end of rnd. Repeat this rnd to top of chart, then repeat rnds 1-30 1 (2-2) times. For sizes 4, 10 and 12 only, repeat rnds 1-16 once. Check gauge; piece should measure 25½" (29"-32") around; about 14" (16½"-19½") above ribbing.

Next Rnd: With W, bind off loosely 14 (16-19) sts for left front shoulder, k until 36 (40-42) sts from bound-off sts, sl these sts on a holder for front neck; bind off next 14 (16-19) sts for right front shoulder, put a marker on work in last st; bind off next 14 (16-19) sts for right back shoulder; k until 36 (40-42) sts from bound-off sts, sl these sts on a holder for back neck, bind off next 14 (16-19) sts for left back shoul-

der; leave marker on work.

SLEEVES (make 2): Beg at lower edge with W and dp needles, cast on 48 (52-56) sts; divide on 3 dp needles. Mark end of rnds. Join, being careful not to twist sts. Work ribbing same as for body, then k 2 W rnds, inc 1 st at end of last rnd—49 (53-57) sts.

Pattern: Rnd 1: K 1 (3-5) W; following chart, work from arrow across 3 times, k 0 (2-4) W. Work in pat as established to end of rnd 13 (16-16). Check gauge; piece above ribbing should measure 9¾" (10½"-11½") around. For size 10-12 only, k 3 W rnds. For all sizes, bind off loosely.

FINISHING: Run in yarn ends on wrong side. Block pieces.

Slash Armholes: Baste straight line from shoulder edge down for 5" (5½"-6") at each arm side between sts of front and back (at marker and at last bound-off st). Machine stitch twice, using a loose tension and small sts, ¼" each side of basting. Slash along basting line.

With W, sew shoulder seams. Fold armhole edge of sleeve in half at end of rnd marker; place this edge at underarm. Stretching sleeve to fit armhole, sew in sleeves from right side, lapping sleeve over armhole (to conceal raw edges). Steam-press raw edges toward sleeves. Cover wrong side of armhole seams with seam binding.

Collar: Beg at front neck, from right side, sl 36 (40-42) sts each of front and back neck on 3 dp needles—72 (80-84) sts. Join; following chart, work rnds 17-28.

Next Rnd (eyelet rnd): * Yo, k 2 tog, repeat from * around. With W, k 12 rnds. With W, bind off loosely.

Fold collar on eyelet rnd to wrong side; sew in place. Steam-press collar.

SCARF, MUFF, HAT
Shown on page 251

SIZES: Muff: One size. Scarf And Hat: Directions for size 2-4. Changes for size 6-8 are in parentheses.

MATERIALS: Bear Brand Win-Knit, 2 4-oz. Twin-paks. Crochet hook size G. ¼ yard lining fabric. Polyester stuffing. Matching sewing thread. ¾" cardboard or plastic strip.

GAUGE: 7 sts = 2".

LOOP STITCH PATTERN (worked on wrong side): Hold cardboard in back of work, insert hook in first st, wind yarn around cardboard from back to front, yo hook and draw lp through st, yo and through 2 lps on hook, * insert hook in st last worked in, wind yarn around cardboard, yo hook and draw through st, insert hook in next st, wind yarn around cardboard, yo hook and draw through st,

yo and through 3 lps on hook, repeat from * across. Ch 2, turn.

SCARF: First Half: Beg at lower edge, ch 22 (26).

Row 1 (right side): Hdc in 3rd ch from hook and in each ch across—20 (24) hdc. Ch 2, turn each row.

Row 2: Work in lp st pat across (see Loop Stitch Pattern).

Row 3: Hdc in each st across. Repeat rows 2 and 3, 2 (3) times. Repeat row 3 until piece measures 21" (22") from start or half desired scarf length. End off. Work 2nd half in same manner.

FINISHING: Steam-press lightly; do not press loops. With wrong sides facing, weave last row of each half tog.

MUFF: Ch 26. Work rows 1-3 same as for scarf, then repeat rows 2 and 3 until piece measures 12" from start, end row 2. End off, leaving a long end for sewing.

FINISHING: Cut lining ½" larger on all edges than crocheted piece. Weave last row to foundation ch, forming ring. Sew ends of lining tog, forming ring. Insert lining in muff. Fold ½" of lining at one end of opening to wrong side; hem to muff. Insert a ½" layer of stuffing between muff and lining; hem other edge of lining to muff.

TIES (make 2): Ch 20" or desired length; sl st in each ch. End off. Attach a ch to each side of muff. Tie ends at back of neck.

HAT: Ch 3.

Rnd 1: 7 hdc in 3rd ch from hook. Sl st in first hdc; turn.

Rnd 2: Ch 2, 2 hdc in first hdc and in each hdc around, hdc in sl st—16 sts, counting ch 2 as 1 hdc. Sl st in top of ch 2; turn each rnd.

Rnd 3: Ch 2, 2 hdc in next st, * hdc in next st, 2 hdc in next st, repeat from * around, sl st in top of ch 2—24 hdc.

Rnd 4: Hdc in next st, 2 hdc in next st, * hdc in each of next 2 sts, 2 hdc in next st, repeat from * around, sl st in top of ch 2—32 sts.

Rnd 5: Ch 2, hdc in each of next 2 sts, 2 hdc in next st, * hdc in each of next 3 sts, 2 hdc in next st, repeat from * around, sl st in top of ch 2—40 sts.

Rnds 6-8: Continue to inc 8 sts evenly spaced around—64 sts.

For Size 6-8 Only: Next Rnd: Inc 5 sts evenly spaced around—69 sts.

For All Sizes: Rnd 9 (10): Ch 2, hdc in next st and in each st around—64 (69) sts. Repeat last rnd 6 (7) times.

Next Rnd: Work in lp st around. Join; turn.

Next Rnd: Hdc in each st around. Turn.

Next Rnd: Work in lp st around. Join; turn.

Earlap: Sl st in each of next 3 sts, ch 2, hdc in each of next 19 (21) sts. Ch 2, turn.

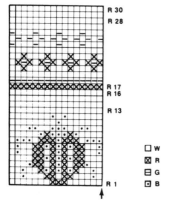

R 30
R 28

R 17
R 16

R 13

R 1

☐ W
☒ R
⊟ G
⊡ B

Next Row: Yo hook, pull up a lp in each of next 2 sts, yo and through 3 lps on hook, yo and through remaining 2 lps (1 st dec), hdc in each st to within last 2 sts, dec 1 st over next 2 sts. Ch 2, turn. Repeat last row until 3 sts remain. Ch 2, turn.

Next Row: Pull up a lp in each of next 3 sts, yo and through 3 lps on hook, yo and through remaining 2 lps.

Tie: Ch 10" long, sl st in each ch, sl st in last st on earlap. End off.

2nd Earlap: From right side, sk next 21 (22) sts for front of hat, hdc in next st and in each of next 18 (20) sts—19 (21) hdc. Complete same as for first earlap.

SCARF, MITTENS, HAT
Shown on page 251

SIZES: Directions for small size (2-4). Changes for medium size (6-8) are in parentheses. SCARF: 4" x 35" (40"), plus fringe.
MATERIALS: Bear Brand Win-Knit, 2 4-oz. Twin-paks. Knitting needles Nos. 5 and 9. Crochet hook size G. Two stitch holders for mittens.
GAUGE: 7 sts = 2" (No. 9 needles).
SCARF: With No. 9 needles, cast on 120 (140) sts. (K 1 row, p 1 row) twice, k 2 rows, (p 1 row, k 1 row) twice. Repeat these 10 rows 1 (2) times; then (k 1 row, p 1 row) twice. Bind off in k same tension as sts.
FINISHING: Steam-press lightly.
Fringe: Cut strands 13" long. Fold 3 strands in half and knot a fringe in every 3rd row on each end. Trim ends.
MITTENS: Cuff: With No. 9 needles, cast on 22 (26) sts. (K 1 row, p 1 row) twice, k 2 rows (p 1 row, k 1 row) twice, (k 1 row, p 1 row) twice, k 1 row. Change to No. 5 needles.
Hand: Beg with a k row, work in stockinette st (k 1 row, p 1 row) for 2 (4) rows.
Inc For Thumb: K 10 (12), put a marker on needle, inc 1 st in each of next 2 sts, put a marker on needle, k 10 (12). P 1 row, k 1 row, p 1 row.
Next Row: K to marker, sl marker, inc 1 st in next st, k to within 1 st of next marker, inc 1 st in next st, sl marker, k to end of row. P 1 row, k 1 row, p 1 row. Continue in this manner, inc 1 st after first marker and 1 st before 2nd marker every 4th row until there are 8 (10) sts between markers. Work 3 rows even, end wrong side.
Divide for Thumb: Work 10 (12) sts, sl these sts on a holder, k 8 (10), sl remaining 10 (12) sts on a holder.
Thumb: Next Row: P across, cast on 1 st at beg and end of row—10 (12) sts. Work even for 1" (1¼"), end p row.

Shape Tip: K 2 tog across—5 (6) sts. P 1 row. Break yarn leaving a 10" end. Thread needle, draw up tightly through remaining sts; sew thumb seam.
Hand: From right side, sl sts from first holder to No. 5 needle, pick up and k 2 sts on base of thumb, work sts from 2nd holder—22 (26) sts. Work even until piece measures 1¾" (2¼") above base of thumb, end p row.
Shape Top: Row 1: (K 1, sl 1, k 1, psso, k 5 (6), k 2 tog, k 1) twice—18 (20) sts. P 1 row.
Next Row: (K 1, sl 1, k 1, psso, k 3 (4), k 2 tog, k 1) twice—14 (16) sts. P 1 row.
Next Row: (K 1, sl 1, k 1, psso, k 1 (2), k 2 tog, k 1) twice—10 (12) sts. P 1 row.
Next Row: K 2 tog across—5 (6) sts. Break yarn leaving a 12" end. Thread needle, draw up tightly through remaining sts; sew side seam. Work 2nd mitten in same manner.

HAT: With No. 9 needles, cast on 64 (68) sts.
Cuff: Work same as for mitten cuff for 14 rows, end p row. Mark last row for right side of cuff. Change to No. 5 needles. Work in ribbing of k 1, p 1 for 6 rows. Change to No. 9 needles. Beg with a p row, work in stockinette st until piece measures 2¼" (3") above ribbing, dec 0 (4) sts evenly spaced across, end p row—64 sts.
Shape Top: Next Row: (K 6, k 2 tog) 8 times—8 sts dec. P 1 row.
Next Row: (K 5, k 2 tog) 8 times. P 1 row. Continue to dec 8 sts every other row, having 1 st less between decs until 8 sts remain. Cut yarn leaving a 14" end. Thread end into needle, draw remaining sts tog; fasten securely on wrong side. Weave back seam.

FINISHING: Steam-press hat lightly; do not press ribbing. Fold cuff to right side.
Earlaps: From right side, sk 3 sts from center back (back seam) at lower edge of ribbing; from right side, with No. 9 needle, pick up and k 20 (22) sts across first row of ribbing. Working back and forth, beg with a p row, work in stockinette st, dec 1 st each side every other row until 2 sts remain. Bind off.
2nd Earlap: Sk next 18 sts on lower edge of ribbing for front; with No. 9 needle, pick up and k 20 (22) sts across first row of ribbing, leaving remaining 3 sts to center back for back of neck. Work same as for first earlap.
Earlap Edging and Ties: From right side, with crochet hook, work sc down one side of earlap, end at point, ch 15", sl st in each ch, sc on other side of earlap. End off. Work same on 2nd earlap. Steam-press earlaps and ties lightly.

GREENLAND BOOTS
Shown on page 253

SIZE: Any woman's size.
MATERIALS: Knitting worsted weight yarn, up to 8 ozs. (depending on size) of assorted colors. Colors in boots shown are purple (P), olive green (O), white (W), light blue (LB), fuchsia (F), aqua (A), royal blue (RB), nile green (N). Steel crochet hooks Nos. 7 (or finer) and 0. Suede, smooth leather, or vinyl, piece large enough for 2 soles. Foam-type insoles, 1 pair men's large size. Glue. Large tapestry needle. Hammer and nail or awl (for punching leather (1).

GAUGE: 9 sts = 2".

BOOTS: Soles: Make pattern for sole by drawing around outline of foot on paper. Cut leather for soles ⅛" larger all around, reversing pattern for 2nd sole. Cut foam insoles ¼" smaller all around. Mark a line on leather soles ¼" in from edge. Punch holes ¼" apart along this line all around.
Rnd 1: With P, make lp on No. 7 hook. Working from right side of sole, insert hook in hole at center back of sole, bring yarn through, yo and through 2 lps on hook, * ch 1, sc in next hole, repeat from * around, end ch 1, sl st in first st. Change to No. 0 hook.
Rnd 2: Ch 1, sc in back lp of each st around. Sl st in first sc.
Rnd 3: Ch 3, sk first sc, dc in back lp of each sc around. Sl st in top of ch 3. End off.
Rnd 4: With 0, sc in back lp of each dc around. Join; end off.
Instep: Row 1: With W, sl st in back lp of st at point opposite widest part of sole, sc in back lp of next st; working across toe in back lp of each st, hdc in next st, dc in each st to 3 center front sts, hdc in next st, sc in next st, hdc in next st, dc in each st to opposite side of instep, hdc in next st, sc in next st. End off.
Row 2: With LB, sl st in back lp of sc 3 sts before beg of last row, sc in back lp of next st, hdc in back lp of next st; working across row 1 in back lp of each st, dc in each st to 3 center front sts, hdc in next st, sc in next st, hdc in next st, finish row to correspond to beg of row. End off.
Row 3: With F, work as for row 2 to 5 center front sts, dec 1 dc in next 2 sts (to dec, (yo hook, draw up a lp in next st, yo and through 2 lps) twice, yo and through 3 lps), dc in center st, dec 1 dc in next 2 sts, finish row to correspond to beg of row. End off.
Top: Rnd 1: Join W at center back of sole, ch 3. Working in back lps of sole

and instep sts, dc in each st around. Join; end off. Try on boot. On following 6 rnds, dec across front section as necessary for desired fit.

Rnd 2: Join A at center back, ch 3; working in back lps only, dc around. Join; end off.

Rnd 3: Join RB at center back, ch 3; repeat rnd 2.

Rnd 4: Join O at center back, ch 3; dc in back lp of each of 2 sts, * long dc in back lp of A st of rnd 2, dc in back lp of each of 3 sts, repeat from * around. Join; end off.

Rnd 5: Join F, sc in back lp of each st around decreasing as necessary. End.

Rnd 6: Join LB; * sc in back lp of 3 sc, ch 3, repeat from * around. Join; end off.

Rnd 7: Join W, ch 3; dc in back lp of each of 2 sc, * sc in 2nd ch of ch 3, dc in back lp of next 3 sc, repeat from * around. Join; end off.

Rnd 8: Join A in top of ch 3; * sk next st, dc in back lp of next st, dc in back lp of skipped st, repeat from * around. Join; end off.

Rnd 9: Join W, sc in back lp of each sc around. Join, ch 1.

Rnds 10 and 11: Sc in each sc around. Join each rnd. End off W.

Rnd 12: Join O, ch 3. Sk first st, dc in each of next 2 sts, * sk next st, dc in next st, dc in skipped st, dc in each of next 3 sts, repeat from * around. Join; end off.

Rnd 13: Join LB, ch 3. Sk first st, dc in back lp of each of next 2 sts changing to P in last st (always change colors by working last dc of one color until 2 lps remain on hook, draw near color through last 2 lps); * with P, dc in back lp of 3 dc, with LB, dc in back lp of 3 dc, repeat from * around. Join.

Rnd 14: Work as for rnd 13, reversing colors. Join; end off LB and P.

Rnd 15: Join RB; work sc in back lp of each dc around. Join, ch 1.

Rnds 16-18: Work even in sc. Join; end off.

Rnd 19: Join A, ch 3. * Cluster st in next st (to make cluster st, (yo hook, draw up a lp in st) 4 times, yo and through 8 lps on hook, yo and through 2 lps), ch 1, sk 1 st, repeat from * around. Join; end off.

Rnd 20: Join F; sc in back lp of each st around. Join; end off.

FINISHING: Turn boot inside out, weave in yarn ends on wrong side. Glue foam insoles to inside of sole. Let dry. Turn boot right side out.

Embroidery: Run double strand of LB through rnd 1. Run double strand of N through bottom and top of rnd 4. With single strand of N, work crosses over rnds 9-11. With single strand of F, work crosses close tog over rnd 17.

BED SLIPPERS
Shown on page 252

SIZE: Directions for infants' size. Changes for childs' and adults' sizes are in parentheses.

MATERIALS: Infants': Baby pompadour yarn, 1 2-oz. ball. Childs' and adults': Knitting worsted, 1 4-oz. skein. Knitting needles No. 8. For infants' only: Knitting needles No. 4 for ruffle. Large-eyed needle.

GAUGE: 9 sts = 2" (No. 8 needles). **Note:** Infants' slippers are worked with 2 strands of yarn; ruffle with 1 strand of yarn.

SLIPPERS: With 2 (1-1) strand of yarn, (see Note) and No. 8 needles, cast on 29 (39-49) sts.

Row 1: K 1, * p 1, k 1, repeat from * across. Repeat row, having k 1 over a p st and p 1 over a k st until piece is square (about 6½" (8½"-10½")). Bind off in pat, leaving an 18" end for sewing.

FINISHING: Steam-press lightly. Thread yarn end into needle. Fold square into triangle. Weave tog one edge for sole and 2" (3"-4") up other edge for back seam. Fold open point to right side for cuff.

Infants' Ruffle: With one strand of yarn and No. 4 needles, cast on 50 sts. K 1 row, p 1 row.

Next Row (inc row): * K 1, inc 1 st in next st, repeat from * across—75 sts. P 1 row. Repeat last 2 rows once—112 sts. Bind off. With side edge of ruffle at back seam, sew cast-on edge of ruffle to cuff edge.

Childs' Fringe: Cut yarn in 2½" lengths. Knot 1 strand in each st around cuff edge.

Gather center front on infants and childs' slippers for 1" (1½") from point. Fold point to right side on adults' slippers; tack securely. Sew pompon to each toe on all slippers; sew a pompon to tip of front cuff on adults' slippers.

CABLED SET
Shown on page 254

SIZES: Directions are for 2-3 year old. Changes for 4-5 are in parentheses.

MATERIALS: Knitting worsted, 1 4-oz. skein apple green. Knitting needles Nos. 5 and 7. Cable or dp needle. Two stitch holders. Yarn needle.

GAUGE: 5 sts = 1"; 7 rows = 1" (stockinette st, No. 7 needles).

PATTERN STITCH (worked on 8 sts):

Row 1 (right side): P 1, k 6, p 1.

Row 2: K 1, p 6, k 1.

Row 3: P 1, k 2, yarn in back, sl next 2 sts as if to p, k 2, p 1.

Row 4: K 1, p 2, yarn in front, sl next 2 sts as if to p, p 2, k 1.

Row 5: P 1; with dp needle, sl next 2

sts as if to p, hold in back, k next sl st, then k sts from dp needle (right cross st made), sl next sl st to dp needle, hold in front, k next 2 sts, then k st from dp needle (left cross st made), p 1. Repeat rows 2-5 for pattern stitch.

CAP: With No. 5 needles, cast on 79 (83) sts.

Ribbing: Row 1 (wrong side): P 1, * k 1, p 1, repeat from * across.

Row 2: K 1, * p 1, k 1, repeat from * across. Repeat these 2 rows for 3", end wrong side, inc 1 st on last row—80 (84) sts. Change to No. 7 needles. Work as follows:

Row 1: K 6, * work row 1 of pat st on next 8 sts, k 12 (13), repeat from * across, end last repeat k 6 (7).

Row 2: P 6 (7), * work row 2 of pat st on next 8 sts, p 12 (13), repeat from * across, end last repeat p 6. Continue in this manner until piece measures about 4" above ribbing, end row 5 of pat st. Change to No. 5 needles.

Next Row: P 1, * k 2 tog, p 2 tog, repeat from * across, end last repeat p 1—41 (43) sts.

Next Row: K 1, * p 1, k 1, repeat from * across. Work in ribbing as established for ¾" (1"). Break yarn leaving a 12" end. Thread yarn needle; draw sts tog; fasten securely. Sew back seam.

FINISHING: Steam-press very lightly. Fold ribbing in half at lower edge to wrong side. Sew in place loosely.

Top Trim: With No. 7 needles, cast on 11 sts. Work in stockinette st for 8 rows.

Next Row: K 2 tog across, end k 1—6 sts. Draw remaining sts tog; fasten; sew seam. Attach to top of hat.

RIGHT MITTEN: With No. 5 needles, cast on 25 (29) sts. Work in ribbing as for cap for 2", inc 3 sts on last row—28 (32) sts. Change to No. 7 needles. Work as follows:

Row 1: K 4 (5), work pat row 1 on next 8 sts, k 16 (19).

Row 2: P 16 (19), work pat row 2 on next 8 sts, p 4 (5). Work in pat as established for 2 more rows.

Inc for Thumb: Work 15 (17) sts, put a marker on needle, inc 1 st in next st (k in front and back of same st), k 1, inc 1 st in next st, put another marker on needle, k 10 (12). Work 1 row even.

Next Row: Inc 1 st after first and before 2nd marker. Work 1 row even. Continue in this manner, inc 2 sts for thumb every other row until there are 9 sts between markers. Work 3 rows even, end wrong side.

Divide for Thumb: Work 15 (17) sts, sl these sts on holder (back of hand), k 9 (thumb), cast on 1 st each side of thumb, sl remaining 10 (12) sts on holder (palm).

Thumb: Work in stockinette st (p 1 row, k 1 row) on 11 sts for 1" (1¼"), end p row, dec 1 st in center of last row.

Shape Top: K 2 tog across—5 sts. P 1 row. Break yarn leaving an end. Thread

end in yarn needle, draw up tightly through remaining sts; sew thumb seam.
Hand: From right side, sl sts from first holder (back of hand) to No. 7 needle; join yarn, pick up and k 2 sts on base of thumb, work sts from 2nd holder (palm)—27 (31) sts. Work until piece measures 4″ (5″) above ribbing, end pat row 2.
Shape Top:Row 1: K 1, k 2 tog across—14 (16) sts. Purl 1 row.
Row 3: K 2 tog across—7 (8) sts. Break yarn leaving end for sewing. Thread end in needle, draw through remaining sts; fasten securely; sew side seam.
LEFT MITTEN: Work as for right mitten having 10 (12) sts (palm) before thumb and 15 (17) sts (back) after thumb on right side rows.
FINISHING: Steam-press lightly.

SNOWFLAKE SET
Shown on page 254

SIZES: Directions are for children 5-7 years. Changes for 8-10 years are in parentheses.
MATERIALS: Knitting worsted, 3 (4) ozs. royal blue. For embroidery and pompon, small amount white light-weight knitting worsted or 4-ply sport yarn. Knitting needles No. 6. Two stitch holders. Yarn needle.
GAUGE: 11 sts = 2″; 15 rows = 2″.
HAT: Cast on 100 (104) sts loosely. Work in k 2, p 2 ribbing for 1½″. Work in stockinette st (k 1 row, p 1 row) until piece measures 6″ from start, end p row.
First Dec Row: (K 2 tog) across—50 (52) sts. P 1 row. Repeat last 2 rows once—25 (26) sts.
Next Dec Row: (K 2 tog) across, end k 1 (0)—13 sts. P 1 row.
Next Dec Row: (K 2 tog) across, end k 1—7 sts. Break yarn leaving a long end. Pull yarn through sts, draw up tightly, fasten securely.
RIGHT MITTEN: Cast on 32 (36) sts loosely. Work in k 2, p 2 ribbing for 3″. Work in stockinette st for 4 (6) rows.
Inc for Thumb: K 16 (18), put a marker on needle, inc 1 st in next st (k in front and back of same st), k 1, inc 1 st in next st, put a marker on needle, k 13 (15). P 1 row.
Next Row: K, inc 1 st in st after first and before 2nd marker. P 1 row. Continue in this manner, inc 2 sts for thumb every other row until there are 11 (13) sts between markers. P 1 row.
Divide for Thumb: K 16 (18), put these sts on a holder (back of hand), k 11 (13) for thumb, casting on 1 st each side of thumb; put remaining 13 (15) sts on a holder (palm).
Thumb: Work in stockinette st on 13 (15) sts for 1½″ (1¾″), end p row, dec 1 (0) st on last row—12 (15) sts.
Shape Tip: (K 2 tog, k 1) 4 (5) times—8 (10) sts. P 1 row.

Next Row: (K 2 tog) across—4 (5) sts. Break yarn leaving end for sewing. Thread end in needle, draw through remaining sts; draw up tightly and fasten. Sew seam.
Hand: From right side, sl sts from first holder (back of hand) to needle; join yarn, pick up and k 2 sts on base of thumb, k sts from 2nd holder (palm)—31 (35) sts. Work even until piece measures 4½″ (5″) above ribbing or 1″ less than desired length, end p row, dec 1 (0) st on last row—30 (35) sts.
Shape Top: Row 1: (K 2 tog, k 3) 6 (7) times—24 (28) sts. P 1 row.
Row 3: (K 2 tog, k 2) 6 (7) times—18 (21) sts. P 1 row. Continue to dec 6 (7) sts in this manner every other row having 1 st less between decs until 6 (7) sts remain. Break yarn leaving end; thread end in needle, draw through remaining sts, pull up tightly and fasten securely.
LEFT MITTEN: Work as for right mitten having 13 (15) sts (palm) before thumb and 16 (18) sts (back) after thumb on k rows.
FINISHING: Steam-press hat; do not press ribbing. Fold mittens in half; pin out carefully; steam-press lightly.
Embroidery: See Contents for Stitch Details. Work embroidery with single strand of white yarn. If desired, trace designs on tissue paper; embroider over tissue. Embroider straight lines in straight stitch, curved line in fly stitch, dots in French knot. Alternate these two patterns around hat, filling in with star stitches in various sizes. To make a star stitch, embroider, in straight stitch, eight equal lines radiating from center; embroider French knot in center. Embroider mittens as shown.

Sew hat and mitten seams. Steam-press seams open flat.

Pompon: Wind white yarn 100 times around a 2″ piece of cardboard. Carefully remove cardboard. Tie a double strand of yarn tightly around center. Cut

loops; trim into a ball. Fasten to top of hat.

TREE-STITCH BABY SET
Shown on page 255

SIZES: Directions for infants' size (6 mos.). Changes for small size (1-2) are in parentheses.
Body Chest Size: 19″ (20″-21″).
Blocked Chest Size: 20″ (22″).
MATERIALS: Yarn of knitting worsted weight, 2 4-oz. skeins. Knitting needles Nos. 7 and 9. Dp needle for cable. Stitch holder. Crocket hook size E. Four buttons.
GAUGE: 4 sts = 1″ (stockinette st); 9 sts = 1½″ (pat); 13 rows = 2″ (No. 9 needles).
Pattern Notes: Note 1: Sl all sl sts as if to p.
Note 2: Right Cross St (rc st): With dp needle, sl next st and hold in back of work, k 1 through back lp, then p st from dp needle.
Note 3: Left Cross St (lc st): With dp needle, sl next st and hold in front of work, p 1, then k st from dp needle through back lp.
PATTERN STITCH (worked on 9 sts):
Row 1 (right side): P 3, k 3 through back lps, p 3.
Row 2: K 3, p 3 through back lps, k 3.
Row 3: P 2, rc st (see Note 2) on next 2 sts, k 1 through back lp, lc st (see Note 3) on next 2 sts, p 2.
Row 4: K 2, (p 1 through back lp, k 1) twice, p 1 through back lp, k 2.
Row 5: P 1, rc st on next 2 sts, p 1, k 1 through back lp, p 1, lc st on next 2 sts, p 1.
Row 6: K 1, (p 1 through back lp, k 2) twice, p 1 through back lp, k 1.
Row 7: Rc st on next 2 sts, p 1, k 3 through back lps, p 1, lc st on next 2 sts.
Row 8: P 1 through back lp, k 2, p 3 through back lps, k 2, p 1 through back lp. Repeat rows 3-8 for pat.
CARDIGAN: BACK: Beg at lower edge, with No. 9 needles, cast on 46 (50) sts. Work in ribbing of k 1, p 1 for 1½″.
Pattern: Row 1 (right side): K 13 (15), work next 9 sts in pat, k 2, work next 9 sts in pat, k 13 (15).
Row 2: P 13 (15), work next 9 sts in pat, p 2, work next 9 sts in pat, p 13 (15). Repeat these 2 rows until piece measures 7″ (7½″) from start or desired length to underarm. Check gauge; piece should measure 10″ (11″) wide.
Shape Armholes: Bind off 4 sts at beg of next 2 rows—38 (42) sts. Work even until armholes measure 4″ (4½″) above first bound-off sts.
Shape Shoulders: Bind off 5 (6) sts at beg of next 4 rows. Place remaining 18 sts on a holder.
Buttonhole Note: For boy's cardigan, work right front first, for girl's cardigan,

work left front first. When first front is completed, with pins mark position of 4 buttons evenly spaced on center band, first one 1″ above lower edge, last one ½″ below start of neck shaping. When making 2nd front, form buttonholes as follows:

Buttonholes: Beg at center edge, work first 2 sts, bind off next 2 sts, finish row.
Next Row: Cast on 2 sts over bound-off sts.
RIGHT FRONT: Beg at lower edge, with No. 9 needles, cast on 26 (28) sts. Work in ribbing of k 1, p 1 for 1½″, forming buttonhole opposite marker on girl's cardigan (see Buttonhole Notes), end wrong side.
Pattern: Row 1 (right side): Work first 5 sts in ribbing (center band), next 9 sts in pat, k 12 (14).
Row 2: P 12 (14), work next 9 sts in pat, last 5 sts in ribbing. Repeat these 2 rows, forming buttonholes opposite markers on girl's cardigan until piece measures same as back to underarm, end arm side.
Shape Armhole: Bind off 4 sts at beg of next row—22 (24) sts. Work even until armhole is 3¼″ (3¾″), end center edge.
Shape Neck and Shoulder: Bind off 4 sts at beg of center edge 3 times; **at the same time,** when armhole measures same as back, bind off 5 (6) sts at beg of arm side twice.
LEFT FRONT: Cast on, work as for right front for 1½″, forming buttonhole on boy's cardigan, end wrong side.
Pattern: Row 1 (right side): K 12 (14), work next 9 sts in pat, last 5 sts in ribbing as established (center band).
Row 2: Work first 5 sts in ribbing, next 9 sts in pat, p 12 (14). Keeping to pat as established, complete left front as for right front.

With backstitch, sew shoulder seams.
SLEEVES: With No. 9 needles, from right side, pick up and k 34 (36) sts evenly around armhole edge. Work in stockinette st (k 1 row, p 1 row) for 2″. Check gauge; piece should measure 8½″ (9″) wide. Dec 1 st each side of next row, then every 1″ 4 times more—24 (26) sts. Work even until sleeve measures 7″ (8″) from picked-up sts, or 1½″ less than desired sleeve length. Change to No. 7 needles. Work in ribbing of k 1, p 1 for 1½″. Bind off loosely in ribbing.
COLLAR: From wrong side, beg and ending ¾″ in from each front edge, with No. 7 needles, pick up and k 15 (17) sts on right neck edge, k across 18 sts on holder, pick up and k 15 (17) sts on left neck edge—48 (52) sts. Work in ribbing of k 1, p 1 for 2 rows. Inc 1 st each side of next row, then every other row 6 times more, working added sts into ribbing—62 (66) sts. Work 1 row even. Bind off loosely in ribbing.
FINISHING: Steam-press cardigan lightly. Sew sleeve and side seams. Work

buttonhole st around buttonholes. Sew on buttons.
HAT: Beg at lower edge, with No. 9 needles, cast on 70 (74) sts. Work in ribbing of k 1, p 1 for 2½″ (3″), inc 1 st at end of last row—71 (75) sts.
Pattern: Row 1 (right side): P 3, * work next 9 sts in pat, p 5 (6), repeat from * across, end last repeat p 3.
Row 2: K 3, * work next 9 sts in pat, k 5 (6), repeat from * across, end last repeat k 3. Repeat these 2 rows until piece measures 4″ (4½″) from start, end wrong side.
First Dec Row: P 2 tog, p 1, * work next 9 sts in pat, p 1 (2), p 2 tog, p 2, repeat from * across, end last repeat p 1, p 2 tog—65 (69) sts.
Next Row: K 2, * work next 9 sts in pat, k 4 (5), repeat from * across, end last repeat k 2. Work even for 2 more rows.
2nd Dec Row: P 2, * work next 9 sts in pat, p 1, p 2 tog, p 1 (2), repeat from * across, end last repeat p 2—61 (65) sts.
Next Row: K 2, * work next 9 sts in pat, k 3 (4), repeat from * across, end last repeat k 2. Work even for 2 more rows.
3rd Dec Row: P 2 tog, * work next 9 sts in pat, p 2 tog, p 1 (2), repeat from * across, end last repeat p 2 tog—55 (59) sts.
Next Row: K 1, * work next 9 sts in pat, k 2 (3), repeat from * across, end last repeat k 1.
4th Dec Row: P 1, * work next 9 sts in pat, p 2 tog, p 0 (1), repeat from * across, end last repeat p 1—51 (55) sts.
Next Row: K 1, * work next 9 sts in pat, k 1(2), repeat from * across, end last repeat k 1.
For Size 1-2 Only: 5th Dec Row: P 1, * work next 9 sts in pat, p 2 tog, repeat from * across, end last repeat p 1—51 sts.
Next Row: K 1, * work next 9 sts in pat, k 1, repeat from * across.
For Both Sizes: * K 1, p 1, k 2 tog, p 1, repeat from * across, end last repeat k 2 tog, p 2 tog—40 sts. Work in ribbing of k 1, p 1 for 3 rows.
Next 2 Rows: K 2 tog across. P 2 tog across—10 sts. Cut yarn leaving a long end. Draw through remaining sts, pull up and fasten. Sew back seam.
Earlaps (make 2): With No. 9 needles, cast on 14 sts. Work in ribbing of k 1, p 1 for ¾″.
Next Row: K 2 tog, work in ribbing across to last 2 sts, k 2 tog. Work 1 row in ribbing as established. Repeat last 2 rows until 2 sts remain. K 2 tog; do not end off. Place remaining lp on crochet hook. Make a 5″ chain. Turn. Sl st in 2nd ch from hook and in each ch across, then sl st all around earlap, having a ch 1 at corners. End off.
Fold ribbing on hat in half to right side. Sew earlaps in place at sides of hat.

STRIPED CLUB COVERS
Shown on page 256

MATERIALS: Knitting worsted weight yarn, 4 ozs. natural (MC), 2 ozs. rust (CC). Knitting needles, No. 8 (5½ mm). Crochet hook size H (5 mm).
GAUGE: 9 sts = 2″; 11 rows = 2″.
SOCK 1: Cast on 34 sts. Work in k 2, p 2 ribbing for 5″.
Next Row (right side): K 2 tog, * p 2 tog, k 2 tog; repeat from * across—17 sts. Work in k 1, p 1 ribbing for 3 rows.
Inc Row: Inc 1 st in each st across—34 sts. P 1 row. Work in stockinette st (k 1 row, p 1 row), working 8 rows more of MC, 3 rows CC, 9 rows MC.
Dec Row 1: With MC, * k 2 tog; repeat from * across—17 sts.
Dec Row 2: * K 2 tog; repeat from * across, end k 1—9 sts. Break yarn, leaving a 12″ end. Thread end in yarn needle and draw through sts, slipping sts from needle. Draw up sts tightly and fasten securely. Sew side seam.
SOCK 2: Work same as sock 1 through Inc Row—34 sts. P 1 row. In stockinette st, work 6 rows more MC, 3 rows CC, 4 rows MC, 3 rows CC, 4 rows MC. With MC, work dec rows and finish same as sock 1.
SOCK 3: Work same as sock 1 through Inc Row—34 sts. P 1 row. In stockinette st, work 3 rows more MC, 3 rows CC, 3 rows MC, 3 rows CC, 3 rows MC, 3 rows CC, 2 rows MC. With MC, work dec rows and finish same as sock 1.
SOCK 4: Work same as sock 1 through Inc Row— 34 sts. P 1 row. In stockinette st, * work 3 rows CC, 2 rows MC; repeat from * 3 times more. With MC, work dec rows and finish same as sock 1.
POMPONS (make 4): Holding 1 strand each of MC and CC tog as 1, wind yarn around a 1½″ piece of cardboard about 150 times. Tie very tightly at one end, cut opposite end. Roll in palm of hand to form ball; trim evenly. Attach 1 pompon to top of each sock.
LINKING CORD: With size H hook and 1 strand each of MC and CC, join with sl st to 1 st in first dec row at top of sock 1, ch 24, join with sl st to 1 st in first dec row at top of sock 2, ch 24, join to sock 3 as for sock 2, ch 24, join to sock 4 as for sock 2. Fasten off.

CABLED CLUB COVERS
Shown on page 256

MATERIALS: Knitting worsted weight yarn, 5 ozs. of MC, 3 yds. of CC for numbers. Knitting needles Nos. 4 (3½ mm) and 6 (4½ mm). Crochet hook, size H (5 mm). Cable needle. Four ½″ plastic rings. Macrame cord, 15″ length.

GAUGE: Stockinette st, No. 6 needles, 5 sts = 1"; 13 rows = 2".

COVER (make 4): With No. 4 needles, cast on 36 sts. Work in k 2, p 2 ribbing for 5".

Inc Row: Working in ribbing, inc 1 st in every 3rd st 11 times—47 sts.

PATTERN: Row 1 (right side): * (K 1, p 1) twice, sk next st, k in front 1p of next st leaving st on needle, k in front 1p of skipped st (twist st), sl both sts from needle (twist st), twist st over next 2 sts, p 1, k 1, p 2, k 6, p 2, k 1, p 1, (twist st) twice, p 1, k 1, p 1 *, place marker on needle, (k 1, p 7) twice, k 1, p 1. Carry markers.

Row 2 and All Even Rows: K all k sts, p all p sts.

Row 3: * K 1, p 1, k in front, back, front, back and front of next st then pass first 4 sts over last st (bobble), p 1, (twist st) twice, p 1, bobble, p 2, sl next 3 sts to cable needle and hold in back of work, k next 3 sts, k 3 sts from cable needle (cable twist), p 2, bobble, p 1, (twist st) twice, p 1, bobble, p 1 *, k 1, p 6, k 3, p 6, k 1, p 1.

Row 5: Repeat between *'s of row 1 once, k 1, p 5, k 5, p 5, k 1, p 1.

Row 7: * K 1, p 1, bobble, p 1, (twist st) twice, p 1, bobble, p 2, k 6, p 2, bobble, p 1, (twist st) twice, p 1, bobble, p 1 *, k 1, p 4, k 7, p 4, k 1, p 1.

Row 9: * (K 1, p 1) twice, (twist st) twice, p 1, k 1, p 2, cable twist, p 2, k 1, p 1, (twist st) twice, p 1, k 1, p 1 *, k 1, p 3, k 9, p 3, k 1, p 1.

Row 11: Repeat between *'s of row 7 once, k 1, p 2, k 11, p 2, k 1, p 1.

Row 13: Repeat between *'s of row 1 once, k 1, p 1, k 13, p 1, k 1, p 1.

Row 15: Repeat between *'s of row 3 once, k 1, p 2, k 11, p 2, k 1, p 1.

Row 17: Repeat between *'s of row 1 once, k 1, p 3, k 9, p 3, k 1, p 1.

Row 19: Repeat between *'s of row 7 once, k 1, p 4, k 7, p 4, k 1, p 1.

Row 21: Repeat between *'s of row 9 once, k 1, p 5, k 5, p 5, k 1, p 1.

Row 23: Repeat between *'s of row 7 once, k 1, p 6, k 3, p 6, k 1, p 1.

Row 25: Repeat row 1.

Row 27: (K 2 tog) 4 times, p 1, k 1, p 2, (k 2 tog) 3 times, p 2, k 1, p 1, (k 2 tog) 3 times, p 1, k 1, (p 2 tog) 3 times, p 1, k 1, p 1, (p 2 tog) 3 times, k 1, p 1—31 sts.

Row 28: K 1, (p 1, k 4) twice, p 1, k 1, p 3, k 1, p 3, k 2, p 1, k 1, p 4.

Row 29: (K 2 tog) 3 times, p 2 tog, sl 1, k 2 tog, psso, (p 2 tog) twice, k 2 tog, p 2 tog, k 1, (p 2 tog) twice, k 1, (p 2 tog) 3 times—16 sts.

Row 30: * P 2 tog; repeat from * across—8 sts.

FINISHING: Break yarn, leaving a 12" end. Thread end in yarn needle and draw through sts, slipping sts from needle.

Draw up sts tightly and fasten securely. Sew side seam.

POMPONS (make 4): Wind yarn around a 1½" piece of cardboard about 300 times, tie very tightly at one end, cut opposite end. Roll in palm of hand to form ball, trim ends evenly. Attach 1 pompon to top of each cover.

NUMBERS: With size H hook and CC, leaving a 10" end at beg for sewing, make a ch about 4" long for each of the 4 numbers. Fasten off, leaving end for adjusting. On the stockinette st diamond of each cover, form a number 1, 3, 4 and a 2 or 5 (golfer's preference). Pin in place and sew, adding or removing chs as needed. Sew 1 ring under each pompon. Thread cord through rings and knot securely.

CHILD'S HAT AND MITTENS
Shown on page 257

SIZE: One cap size fits all. Mittens, 6-10 years.

MATERIALS: Knitting worsted weight yarn, 5 ozs. Knitting needles, Nos. 6 and 8 (4½ mm and 5½ mm). 1 cable needle.

GAUGE: Stockinette st: 4 sts = 1"; 6 rows = 1".

CAP: With No. 6 needles, cast on 85 sts. Work in k 1, p 1 ribbing for 14 rows, inc 7 sts evenly spaced in last row—92 sts. Change to No. 8 needles.

PATTERN: Row 1 (right side): * K 2, p 3, k 6, p 1, k 2, p 2, sk next st, k in back 1p of next st leaving st on needle, then k skipped st in front 1p, sl both sts from needle (twist st), p 1, k in front, back, front, back, and front of next st and sl first 4 sts over last st (popcorn), p 1, twist st, repeat from * across.

Row 2 and All Even Rows: K all k sts and p all p sts.

Row 3: * P 2, k 2, p 1, sl next 3 sts to cable needle, hold in front of work, k next 3 sts, k 3 sts from cable needle (cable twist), p 3, k 2, twist st, p 3, twist st, repeat from * across.

Row 5: Repeat row 1.

Row 7: * P 2, k 1, k 6, p 3, k 2, twist st, p 3, twist st; repeat from * across.

Row 9: * K 2, p 3, cable twist, p 1, k 2, p 2, twist st, p 1, popcorn, p 1, twist st; repeat from * across.

Row 11: Repeat row 7.

Row 12: Repeat row 2. Repeat rows 1-12 once more, then repeat rows 1-6 once.

Next Row: * K 2 tog; repeat from * across—46 sts. P 1 row. Repeat last 2 rows 3 times more—6 sts. Break yarn, leaving a 15" end.

FINISHING: Thread end in yarn needle and draw through sts, sl sts from needle. Draw sts up tightly and fasten securely. Sew back seam.

POMPON: Wind yarn around a 2" piece

of cardboard about 300 times. Tie very tightly at one end, cut opposite end. Roll in palm of hand to form ball. Trim ends evenly. Attach pompon to top of cap.

MITTENS: RIGHT HAND: With No. 6 needles, cast on 28 sts. Work in k 1, p 1 ribbing for 20 rows, inc 7 sts evenly spaced in last row—35 sts. Change to No. 8 needles.

Row 1: K 3, place marker on needle, k 2, p 1, sl next 3 sts to cable needle and hold in front, k next 3 sts, k 3 sts from cable needle (cable twist), p 1, k 2, place marker on needle, k 20. Carry markers.

Row 2 and All Even Rows: P all p sts, k all k sts.

Row 3: K 3, p 3, k 6, p 3, k 20.

THUMB GUSSET: Row 5: K 5, p 1, k 6, p 1, k 2, k 1, place marker on needle for gusset, inc 1 st in next st, k 1, inc 1 st in next st, place marker for gusset, k 16—37 sts. Carry all markers.

Row 7: K 3, p 3, cable twist, p 3, * k to next marker, inc 1 st in next st, k to within 1 st of next marker, inc 1 st in next st, k to end *—39 sts.

Row 9: K 3, k 2, p 1, k 6, p 1, k 2; repeat between *'s of row 7 once—41 sts.

Row 11: K 3, p 3, k 6, p 3; repeat between *'s of row 7 once—43 sts.

Row 13: K 3, p 3, cable twist, p 3, k 1; dropping gusset markers, sl next 11 sts to holder for thumb, cast on 2 sts, k to end—34 sts.

HAND: Working pat between markers as established in rows 1-12 and remaining sts in stockinette st, work even until 4½" above ribbing or 1½" less than desired length to fingertips, end with wrong side row.

Next Row: Keeping pat, * k 1, k 2 tog, repeat from * across. P 1 row. Repeat last 2 rows twice—11 sts. Break yarn, leaving a 12" end. Thread end in yarn needle and draw through sts, sl sts from needle. Draw sts up tightly and fasten securely. Do not cut yarn.

THUMB: With right side facing, sl 11 sts to size 8 needle, cast on 1 st at beg, k across, cast on 1 st at end—13 sts. P 1 row. Work in stockinette st for 1½".

Next Row: * K 2 tog, repeat from * across—6 sts. P 1 row. Repeat last 2 rows once—3 sts. Break yarn, leaving a 6" end. Finish as for top of mitten, sew seam. Sew side seam of mitten.

LEFT HAND: Work ribbing same as right mitten. Change to No. 8 needles.

Row 1: K 20, place marker on needle, k 2, p 1, cable twist, p 1, k 2, place marker, k 3. Finish as for right mitten, reversing shaping.

ADULT MITTENS
Shown on page 257

SIZE: Women's size.
MATERIALS: Knitting worsted, 2 ozs.

Knitting needles No. 8. Dp needle.
GAUGE: 4 sts = 1".

RIGHT MITTEN: Cast on 36 sts, work in k 1, p 1 ribbing for 4".

PATTERN: Row 1: K 4, p 2, * sl next 2 sts as if to p on a dp needle, hold in back, k next 2 sts, then k sts from dp needle, sl next 2 sts on a dp needle, hold in front, k next 2 sts, then k sts from dp needle, * p 2, k to end of row.
Row 2: P 20, k 2, p 8, k 2, p 4.
Row 3: K 4, p 2, k 8, p 2, k 2, inc 1 st in next st (thumb inc), k 1, inc 1 st in next st (thumb inc), k to end.
Row 4: P 22, k 2, p 8, k 2, p 4.
Row 5: K 4, p 2, k 8, p 2, k 2, inc 1 st in next st, k 3, inc 1 st in next st, k to end.
Row 6: P the p sts, k the k sts.
Row 7: K 4, p 2, work from * to * of row 1 for cable, p 2, k 2, inc 1 st in next st, k 5, inc 1 st in next st, k to end.
Row 8: Repeat row 6.
Row 9: K 4, p 2, k 8, p 2, k 2, inc 1 st in next st, k 7, inc 1 st in next st, k to end.
Row 10: Repeat row 6.
Row 11: K 4, p 2, k 8, p 2, k 2, inc 1 st in next st, k 9, inc 1 st in next st, k to end.
Row 12: Repeat row 6.
Row 13: K 4, p 2, work from * to * of row 1 for cable, p 2, k 2; sl next 13 sts to a holder; cast on 3 sts; k to end.
Row 14: Repeat row 6.
Row 15: K 4, p 2, k 8, p 2, k to end. Repeat last 2 rows, working cable twist every 6th row, until 7 cable twists have been made or until mitten is 1" less than desired length, end wrong side.
Shape Top: Row 1: K 1, sl 1, k 1, psso, k 1, p 2, k 8, p 2, k 1, k 2 tog, k 1, sl 1, k 1, psso, k to last 3 sts, k 2 tog, k 1.
Row 2: P the p sts, k the k sts.
Row 3: K 1, sl 1, k 1, psso, p 2 tog, sl 1, k 1, psso, k 4, k 2 tog, p 2 tog, k 2 tog, sl 1, k 1, psso, k 1, sl 1, k 1, psso, k 4, (k 2 tog, k 1) twice.
Row 4: Repeat row 2.
Row 5: *K 1, k 2 tog, repeat from * across, end k 1. Cut yarn, leaving long end. Run through remaining sts, gather in sts slightly, sew top seam. Sew side seam after thumb is completed.
Thumb: Pick up and k 3 sts on cast-on sts at thumb, k across thumb sts. Work even on thumb sts for 1½", end p row.
Next Row: * K 1, k 2 tog, repeat from * across, end k 1. P 1 row.
Next Row: * K 2 tog, k 1, repeat from * across. Cut yarn, leaving end for sewing. Run through remaining sts, draw sts tog tightly; sew thumb seam.

LEFT MITTEN: Work as for right mitten through ribbing.

PATTERN: Row 1: K 20, p 2, work cable pat on next 8 sts, p 2, k 4. Finish as for right mitten, reversing shaping.

SLIPPER SOCKS
Shown on page 257

SIZE: Socks will fit 8"-10" foot.
MATERIALS: Knitting worsted weight yarn, 1 3½-oz. skein for calf length, 2 skeins for knee length. Knitting needles, No. 8 (5 mm). 1 cable needle.
GAUGE: 9 sts = 2"; 6 rows = 1".
FOOT: Cast on 76 sts. K 1 row.
Row 2: K 38, place marker on needle, k to end. Carry marker.
Row 3: * K 1, inc 1 st in next st, k to within 2 sts of marker, inc 1 st in next st, k 1; repeat from * once making last inc 1 st from end—80 sts. K 1 row. Repeat last 2 rows twice more—88 sts. Work even in garter st (k each row) for 14 rows more—11 ridges each side.
SHAPE INSTEP: Row 1: K to within 5 sts of marker, p 2, k 6, p 2 (last 10 sts form cable panel), k 2 tog. Turn. Drop marker.
Rows 2, 4, 6 and 8: Sl 1, k 2, p 6, k 2, k 2 tog. Turn.
Row 3: Sl 1, p 2, sl next 3 sts to cable needle and hold in back, k next 3 sts, k 3 sts from cable needle (cable twist), p 2, k 2 tog. Turn.
Rows 5 and 7: Sl 1, p 2, k 6, p 2, k 2 tog. Turn. Repeat rows 3-8, 3 times more, then rows 3 and 4 once more—60 sts.
Next Row: Sl 1, p 2, k 6, p 2, k to end.
Next Row: (P 1, k 1) 5 times, * p 1, k 1, (p 2, k 1) twice, p 1 *, k 8, p 6, k 8; repeat between *'s once, (k 1, p 1) 5 times.
LEG: Row 1: (K 1, p 1) 6 times, sk next st, k in front lp of next st leaving st on needle, then k in front lp of skipped st, sl both sts from needle (twist st), p 1, twist st, p 1, k 1, p 2, p 2 tog, p 4, cable twist, p 4, p 2 tog, p 2, k 1, (p 1, twist st) twice, (p 1, k 1) 6 times—58 sts.
Row 2: (P 1, k 1) 5 times, * p 1, (k 1, p 2) twice, k 1, p 1 *, k 7, p 6, k 7; repeat between *'s once, (k 1, p 1) 5 times.
Row 3: (K 1, p 1) 5 times, * k in front, back, front and back of next st and sl first 3 sts over last st (popcorn), (p 1, twist st) twice, p 1, popcorn *, p 2, p 2 tog, p 3, k 6, p 3, p 2 tog, p 1; repeat between *'s once, (p 1, k 1) 5 times—56 sts.
Row 4: (P 1, k 1) 5 times, * p 1, (k 1, p 2) twice, k 1, p 1 *, k 6, p 6, k 6; repeat between *'s once, (k 1, p 1) 5 times.
Row 5: (K 1, p 1) 5 times, * k 1, (p 1, twist st) twice, p 1, k 1 *, p 1, p 2 tog, p 3, k 6, p 3, p 2 tog, p 1; repeat between *'s once, (p 1, k 1) 5 times—54 sts.
Row 6: (P 1, k 1) 5 times, * p 1, (k 1, p 2) twice, k 1, p 1 *, place marker on needle, k 5, p 6, k 5, place marker on needle; repeat between *'s once, (k 1, p 1) 5 times. Continue in pat, repeat rows 3-6 for sts outside markers, and work established cable twist and reverse stockinette st over sts between markers, until 1" less than desired length, end with right side row. Drop markers.

Next Row: (P 1, k 1) 13 times, p 2 tog, (k 1, p 1) 13 times. Work in k 1, p 1 ribbing for 1". Bind off loosely in ribbing.
FINISHING: Break yarn, leaving a 24" end. Sew back and foot seam.

ADULT SET
Shown on page 257

SIZE: One size fits all.
MATERIALS: Knitting worsted weight yarn, 4 4-oz. skeins. Susan Bates or Marcia Lynn 16" circular knitting needle No. 9. Set of double-pointed needles No. 9. Susan Bates "Trim-Tool"™ for fringe.
GAUGE: 9 sts = 2"; 7 rows = 1".
PATTERN: Row 1 (wrong side): Purl.
Row 2: Knit.
Row 3: P 1, * p 1 wrapping yarn twice around needle, p 2, p 1 wrapping yarn twice, p 1; repeat from * across.
Row 4: K 1, * sl 1 dropping 2nd wrap, k 2, sl 1 dropping 2nd wrap, k 1, yo, k 1, yo, k 1 all in next st; repeat from * across, end last repeat k 1.
Row 5: P 1, * sl 1, p 2, sl 1, k 5; repeat from * across, end last repeat p 1.
Row 6: K 1, * sl 1, k 2, p 5; repeat from * across, end last repeat k 1.
Row 7: P 1, * sl 1, p 2, sl 1, k 2 tog, k 3 tog, pass k 2 tog st over k 3 tog st; repeat from * across, end last repeat p 1.
Row 8: K 1, * drop first long st off needle to front, sl next 2 sts, drop next long st off needle to front, pick up first long lp and sl back to left needle, sl 2 sl sts back to left needle, pick up 2nd long lp and sl back to left needle, k 5; repeat from * across. Repeat rows 1-8 for pat.
Note: When working pat in rnds, k all p sts on odd rows, and, in row 5, work k 5 as p 5; in row 7, work k 2 tog, k 3 tog as p 2 tog, p 3 tog. As decs and pat beg, sl sts to preceding or following needle as necessary.
SCARF: With circular needle, cast on 40 sts. Do not join, work back and forth in rows. K 1 row.
Next Row (right side): K 12, place marker on needle, work pat row 2 across next 16 sts, place marker on needle, k 12.
Next Row: K 4 for garter st edge, p 8, sl marker, work pat row 3 to next marker, sl marker, p 8, k 4 for garter st edge. (Note: Carry markers throughout.)

Working pat between markers, repeat last 2 rows for side sts. Work even until 60" from beg, end with right side row. K 1 row. Bind off.
Fringe: With Trim-Tool™, cut 7" fringe lengths. Using 2 strands for each fringe, knot a fringe in every other st across each short end.
HAT: With dp needles, cast on 80 sts. Divide sts on 3 needles as follows: 22 sts on first needle, 20 sts on 2nd needle, 38 sts on 3rd needle.

Rnd 1: With care not to twist sts, join, * k 4, place marker on needle, work in pat across next 16 sts (see pat note for working in rnds), repeat from * around—4 k panels, 4 pat panels. Carry markers. Repeat rnd 1 until 1½″ from beg.

Next Rnd: * K 1, k 2 tog, k 1, work in pat across next 16 sts; repeat from * around—76 sts. Work even in pat as established until 4″ from beg, end with pat row 8. Work 2 rnds more, replacing old markers with a marker on center st of k panels.

Next Rnd: Work around, dec 1 st each side of each marked st and working only the center 6 sts of each pat panel in pat, k remaining sts—68 sts.

Next Rnd: Work even. Repeat last 2 rnds 3 times more, discontinuing pat after 2nd dec rnd—44 sts.

Next Rnd: Dec 1 st each side of each marked st and 2 sts across 6-st panel—28 sts. K 1 rnd.

Next Rnd: * K 2 tog; repeat from * around—14 sts. Cut yarn, leaving a 6″ end. Thread end in tapestry needle, draw through sts and sl from needle. Draw up tightly and fasten securely.

BRIM: From right side, with circular needle, pick up and k 80 sts along cast-on edge. Join and k 2 rnds. Inc 10 sts evenly spaced in next rnd, then every 3rd rnd 6 times more—150 sts. K 2 rnds. P 1 rnd for turning ridge. K 2 rnds. Dec 10 sts evenly spaced in next rnd, then every 3rd rnd 6 times more—80 sts. K 2 rnds. Bind off. Fold brim to wrong side along ridge. Sew in place with care not to pull sts too tight.

MITTENS: Right Hand: With dp needles, cast on 36 sts. Divide evenly on 3 needles. With care not to twist sts, join and work around in k 1, p 1 ribbing for 5 rnds, dec 6 sts evenly spaced in last rnd—30 sts. Work in pat for 16 rnds, omitting first st (work only the sts following the *). See pat note for working in rnds. K 4 rnds.

SHAPE THUMB: K 4, place marker on needle, inc 1 st in each of next 2 sts, place marker on needle, k to end. K 3 rnds even. Carry markers.

Next Rnd: K to marker, inc 1 st in next st, k to within 1 st of next marker, inc 1 st in next st, k to end. Repeat last 4 rnds 3 times more—12 sts between markers; 40 sts. K 1 rnd.

Next Rnd: K to marker, sl next 12 sts to holder, cast on 2 sts, k to end—30 sts. Work even until 1½″ less than desired length to fingertips.

Shape Top: Next Rnd: * K 2 tog, k 4; repeat from * around. K 1 rnd. Repeat last 2 rnds, having 1 less st between decs in each successive rnd, until 10 sts remain. Break yarn, leaving a 6″ end. Thread end in tapestry needle, draw through sts and sl from needle. Draw up tightly and fasten securely.

Thumb: Sl 12 sts to 3 needles. Join yarn at inside edge and pick up 1 st in each of the 2 cast-on sts of hand—14 sts. K 1 rnd, dec 1 st at each inside corner—12 sts. Work even until thumb measures desired finished length. K 2 tog all around. Finish same as top.

Left Hand: Work same as right mitten.

EASY-KNIT HAT
Shown on page 258

MATERIALS: Knitting worsted, 1 4-oz. skein. Knitting needles No. 8, 9 or 10. Yarn needle.

GAUGE: 5 sts = 1″.

HAT: Starting at lower edge, cast on 100 sts.

Rows 1-4: K all sts.

Rows 5-8: * K 1, p 1, repeat from * across. Repeat these 8 rows until piece is 8″ long, end row 8 of pattern.

Next Row: K 1, * k next 2 sts together, repeat from * across to last st, k last st —51 sts.

Next Row: K 1, * k next 2 sts together, repeat from * across—26 sts. Bind off. Cut yarn, leaving 24″ end. Thread end in yarn needle, run through top of hat, gathering sts. Sew back seam with backstitch.

Pompon: Wind yarn 200 times around a 3″ cardboard. Tie windings together tightly at one edge. Cut through yarn to opposite edge. Trim pompon into a round ball. Tie to top of hat with matching yarn.

EASY-KNIT SCARVES
Shown on page 258

SIZE: About 6″ wide x 50″ long.

MATERIALS: Knitting worsted, 1 4-oz. skein. Knitting needles No. 8, 9 or 10.

GAUGE: 5 sts = 1″.

YELLOW SCARF: Cast on 30 sts.

Row 1: * K 1, p 1, repeat from * across.

Row 2: Repeat row 1.

Row 3: Repeat row 1.

Row 4: * P 1, k 1, repeat from * across.

Repeat rows 1-4 until one yard of yarn is left. Bind off.

PURPLE SCARF: Cast on 30 sts.

Row 1: * K 1, p 1, repeat from * across.

Row 2: Repeat row 1.

Row 3: Repeat row 1.

Row 4: Repeat row 1.

Row 5: * P 1, k 1, repeat from * across.

Row 6: Repeat row 5.

Row 7: Repeat row 5.

Row 8: Repeat row 5. Repeat rows 1-8 until one yard of yarn is left. Bind off.

RUST SCARF: Cast on 30 sts.

Rows 1-4: K all sts.

Rows 5-8: * K 1, p 1, repeat from * across. Repeat these 8 rows until a few yards of yarn are left, ending with row 8 of pattern. K 4 rows. Bind off.

Steam-press scarves very lightly on wrong side; do not flatten pattern.

PACKAGE TRIMS
Continued from page 48

turn. Work 3 more rows of 9 sc. Change to red, dec 1 sc at each end. Work 8 rows even on 7 sc. At end of 8th row, ch 5; sc in 2nd ch and next 3 ch, sc in each sc across—11 sc. Ch 1, work across 11 sc, ch 2. Sc in 2nd ch and in 11 sc. Work 2 rows even on 12 sc. Dec 1 sc each end of next row. End off. Glue on 2 green felt holly leaves and 2 red sequins.

SANTA: With pink, ch 9; sc in 2nd ch and in each ch across. Ch 1, turn. Work 8 more rows of 8 sc. Change to white; work 2 rows even. Change to red; work 2 rows even. **Next Row:** Dec 1 sc each side. Work 2 rows even. Dec 1 sc at center of next 3 rows. Work 3 rows even. Dec 1 sc on next row. Work 3 rows even. Work 2 sc tog. End off.

Pompon: With white, ch 4; sc in 2nd ch and next 2 ch. Work 2 rows even on 3 sc. Sew through 4 corners of piece, pull up into a ball and sew to tip of cap.

Sew on loops of white yarn for hair and beard. Glue on mustache. Cut blue felt eyes, black pupils, red crescent mouth. Glue on. Glue tip of cap to side of head.

TO ATTACH TRIMS: Put glue on back of trim, leaving snowman's scarf, angel's wings, chenille sticks, or whatever you want free. Place trims on Contact plastic on plastic side, weight down and allow to dry. When dry, cut out around trim. To use trim, remove paper from back and press onto package.

DECORATIVE TOUCHES FOR HANDKNITS

BUTTONHOLES FORMED WITH KNITTED BIAS BINDING

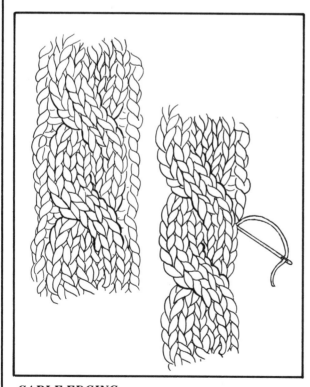

CABLE EDGING

DECORATIVE TOUCHES
FOR HANDKNITS

There are many ways to decorate handknits. They can be embroidered with sequins or beads; more casual knits in stockinette stitch can be embroidered with wool.

Wool Embroidery: Work embroidery after pieces have been blocked, and if possible, before they have been sewn together. Place tissue paper over the design you want to embroider and trace the outlines. Leaving a margin of paper around design, cut out motif. Baste in place.

Many yarns are suitable for embroidering sweaters: crewel wool, fingering yarn, knitting worsted, mohair, etc. Any yarn except a nubbly or bulky yarn may be used. Thread yarn in a chenille needle (sharp-pointed yarn needle). Embroider design over tissue paper, then carefully tear tissue away.

Embroidered Appliques: If design is a large solid motif such as a flower worked entirely in satin stitch, the design can be traced or stamped on organdy and embroidered. The embroidered motif is then appliqued to the sweater.

Duplicate Stitch: Cross-stitch or needlepoint designs which are given in chart form may be used for duplicate stitch embroidery on stockinette stitch. For the embroidery, use same weight yarn as sweater was knitted in. For Duplicate Stitch directions, see Index. In choosing the design, consider that each little square of the design will cover one stitch of the knitting. Since there are more rows to the inch than stitches to the inch in stockinette stitch, the design will appear somewhat shorter from bottom to top after it is worked on the sweater.

Bias Tubing: Satin or velvet makes attractive trimming for knitwear. It can be curved to follow the lines of the garment or formed into scrolls and other applied designs. For a flat effect, remove all or part of the stuffing in the tubing and press flat. To use tubing as binding for necklines, collars, cuffs and pocket edges, open up seam of tubing and remove filler. With right sides together, stitch one edge of binding to edge of knitwear. Fold binding to wrong side; hem.

Knitted Bias Binding: A binding knitted in stockinette stitch of the same yarn as the garment, in matching or contrasting color, gives a couturier look to a suit or jacket. Cast on stitches required for width of binding desired taking into consideration that binding will be folded in half. Work for required length, increasing in first stitch and knitting two stitches together at end of every knit row. Sew along edge of piece to be bound with right sides together, turn and press. Sew other edge to wrong side of garment. Vertical buttonholes can be made automatically by leaving spaces when sewing on binding.

Knitted Cable Edging: A knitted cable can be

made to edge coats, suits and dresses. Sport yarn weight is excellent for most purposes but knitting worsted can be used for bulkier cable trims. To make cable trim, cast on 10 stitches. Work a 6-stitch cable at center with 2 stitches each side in reverse stockinette stitch to be turned under. One edge of trimming, when turned under, forms a deeper scalloped edge than the other. Using this deeper edge for outer edge. Stitch outer edge of trimming to wrong side of garment taking in two stitches of trimming. Turn trimming to right side; turn under two stitches on opposite edge and hem in place.

Rolled edges: A corded finishing on knitwear can be made by rolling crocheted edges over cable cord. Cable cords can be bought in several thicknesses. Work a row of single crochet from wrong side along edge to be trimmed. Work back and forth in single crochet until edging is deep enough to roll forward to right side over cable cord. A ready-made braided piping can be inserted along the edge of the roll and stitched in at the same time as the rolled edge is sewed down to the right side.

Folded Grosgrain Ribbon Trim: This makes a pointed decorative border for jackets and cardigans. Use 1″ wide grosgrain ribbon in matching or contrasting color. Fold ribbon on the bias for all folds and press each fold flat as you work. In making the folds, never bring two edges of the ribbon together.

Fold right end of ribbon to back diagonally; Fig. 1.

Working from right to left, fold ribbon to front diagonally forming a point; Fig. 2.

Continue to fold diagonally to front forming points at top and bottom for desired length of trimming; Fig. 3. Trimming can be used in this form if a saw-tooth edge is desired. Or, fold trimming through center and press; Fig. 4.

Knitted Fringe Trimming: A fringe can be knitted and sewed to the lower edges of casual sweaters, stoles and ponchos. Use knitting worsted and a pair of knitting needles No. 5. Cut a piece of cardboard as wide as you want the fringe and about 3″ long.

Cast on 8 to 10 stitches. The number of stitches you cast on will determine the depth of the knitted border above the fringe.

Row 1: Insert needle in first stitch in the usual way, place the cardboard behind your needles and in front of the yarn close up to first stitch. Hold cardboard between thumb and forefinger of left hand. Pass yarn along back of cardboard, up front and around point of right needle. Knit off the stitch. Knit to end of row.

Row 2: Slip first stitch, knit to end of row. Repeat these two rows alternately for desired length of fringe trimming. Bind off. When cardboard is full of loops, slip some loops off end and slide remainder of loops towards end of cardboard to make room for more loops. Fringe may be kept in loops or cut.

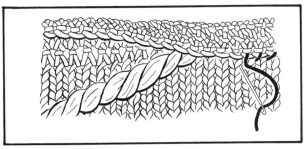

CROCHETED EDGE ROLLED OVER CABLE CORD

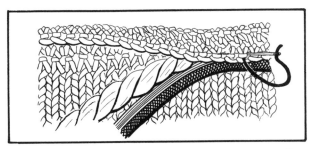

PIPING INSERTED FOR EXTRA TRIMMING TOUCH

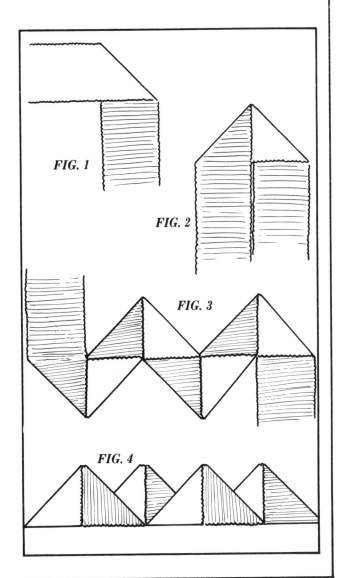

FIG. 1

FIG. 2

FIG. 3

FIG. 4

LAUNDERING HINTS

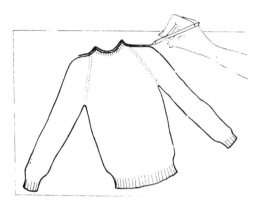

HOW TO LAUNDER SWEATERS

To maintain the proper shape, before washing a sweater, trace the outline on clean brown wrapping paper. Spread the paper out on a clean, flat surface. Put several layers of newspaper or bath towels under it to prevent damage to the surface caused by moisture. (For Orlon Sayelle, see special instructions below.)

Wools, including Angora, should be washed in lukewarm water (comfortable wrist temperature) and soap or light-duty detergent suds. Squeeze garment gently through suds and constantly support it with your hands both in sudsing and rinsing to prevent stretching. Do not twist or wring. Rinse thoroughly in water of the same temperature until all soap or detergent is removed. Do not lift out of the water as the weight of the wet garment will stretch it. In last rinsing use a softening and fluffing agent. Squeeze water out gently, as much as possible without wringing or

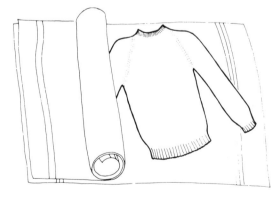

twisting. Place turkish towels under and over garment, roll and squeeze to remove water. Carefully place garment on brown paper, shaping to outline; pin with rust-proof pins if necessary.

If sweater is made of Angora, shake it gently to fluff up surface hairs before garment is completely dry; return to drying process. Refluff when dry.

If sweater is very fragile, with open pattern, baste it to a piece of white sheet before laundering it to help it retain its shape.

Another good way to reshape a knitted sweater is to use a cardboard form, cut to the size and shape of body and sleeves before washing. Cut away cardboard sleeve shapes from rest of form so that they can be inserted separately. Place washed garment on a paper-covered surface, insert cardboard forms, pat knitted fabric to fit form. Let dry flat. During drying, garment will adjust itself to the form, which can be saved and used again.

Usually a knitted sweater needs no pressing after laundering, but a light steaming may be desirable. Use a steam iron or a regular iron with a damp cloth. Hold iron just above knitwear, so steam penetrates without applying any actual pressure.

Nylon, orlon and other synthetics should be laundered in same way as wool, but warmer water may be used. Use fluffing and softening agent in last rinse water. Dry in same manner as wool.

HOW TO LAUNDER CROCHETED LACE

Make a lather of soap or detergent and hot water, taking care to have all particles well dissolved. Dip lace in suds and squeeze gently until clean. Rinse in several changes of lukewarm water, once in cold water. Wrap in towel to press out excess moisture and dry immediately, starching and blocking if desired.

Starching: Use elastic starch and cold water, 2 level tablespoons of starch to each cup of water. Dissolve starch completely, dip lace in solution until saturated, roll in turkish towel, then block immediately.

Blocking: For a square or any rectangular piece, draw desired outline on padded board with pencil, taking care to make corners square. Pin lace, right side down, to outline, using only rust-proof pins. For round doily, pin center securely; for an oval doily, pin the center section in a straight line. Smooth out edges from center and pin, checking distance from center with a ruler and keeping patterns evenly spaced around. Press thoroughly through a dry cloth until all moisture has been absorbed.

1. To make a professional blocking table, tack rug padding to edges of a table or board at least 40" x 60". Cover tightly with muslin.

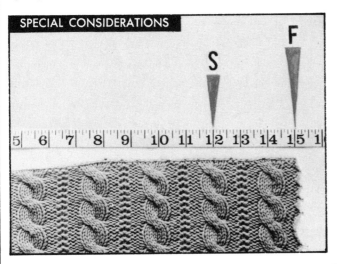

SPECIAL CONSIDERATIONS

2. Examples of knitted pieces are shown with markers S and F. S = Start = knitted measurement. F = Finish = blocked measurement.

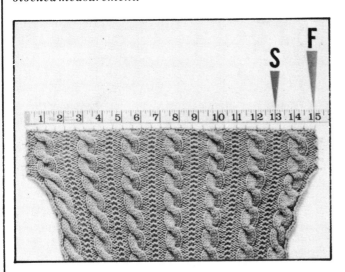

3. Pieces knitted in cable or ribbing patterns should be blocked wider, as they tend to pull in. Stretch such pieces 1" to 2" wider.

PROFESSIONAL BLOCKING

Blocking is the method used to set the separate knitted pieces of a garment to desired shape, size, and texture. Blocking in a professional manner can often make the difference between a beautiful garment and a mediocre one. A perfectly knitted sweater can be ruined by slipshod blocking and finishing, while even a poorly knitted one can be made smart by careful blocking and finishing.

Before blocking your knitted pieces, write down the blocking measurements for each piece. The knitting directions give you the width each piece should be after the words "Check gauge". The length of each piece is also given in the directions. If you have changed the width or length of any section from the directions, make a note of these changes. If you are not sure how wide a piece should be at any given point, you can figure this easily by referring to the directions and dividing the number of stitches across at that point by the stitch gauge.

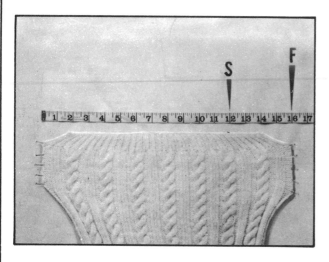

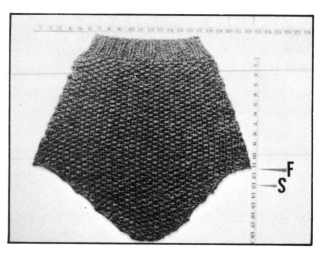

4. *Pieces containing 50% or more nylon should be blocked 2" or 3" wider. If a piece is knit in a cable pattern, block even wider.*

7. *Extra-heavy or loosely knitted garments tend to lengthen when they are worn. Block heavy or loosely knitted pieces shorter and wider.*

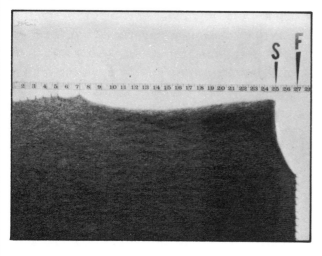

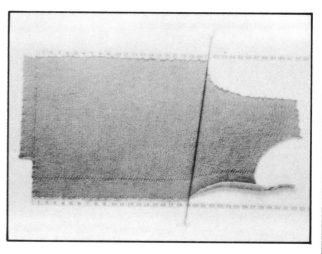

5. *Mohair pieces tend to shrink back in length rather than width. In blocking pieces knit of mohair, stretch a little extra in length.*

8. *A full-busted figure needs a bustline dart. To leave room for the dart, stretch the side edge of the front longer than the center edge.*

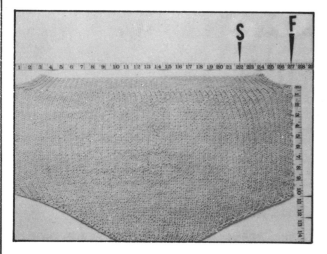

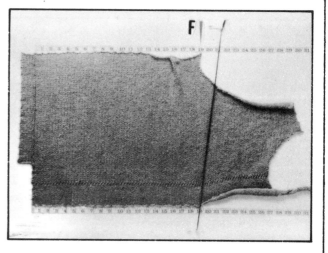

6. *Some knit pieces measure longer when they are held up than when they are lying flat. Block these pieces both shorter and wider.*

9. *Illustration shows extra fullness for dart pinned in, bringing side edge back to original length. The dart will be sewn in later.*

10. If a bustline dart is needed and the front should not be pressed flat because of yarn or stitch, insert a pad under side edge.

11. Pin side edge over pad to stretch the edge for dart. A shoulder pad of type shown is perfect for stretching edges in blocking.

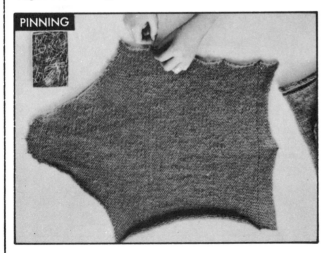

12. All pieces should be blocked before they are sewn together. Pin one section at a time, wrong side up, using rustproof pins.

13. Following measurements, place pins around edges not more than ½" apart. Insert pins through edge and into the padding as shown.

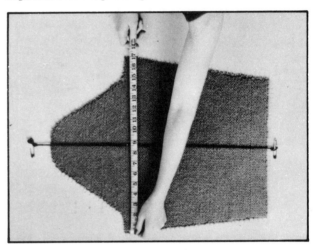

14. String attached to a safety pin at each end and pinned to the blocking surface is helpful in marking the exact center of each piece.

15. Steam knits with raised patterns and yarns which should not be flattened. Hold iron close to piece; move slowly over surface.

16. *Pieces knitted with smooth yarns in stockinette stitch should be pressed flat. First cover piece with an organdy pressing cloth.*

17. *Using maximum amount of steam, lower iron so that weight rests on cloth. Raise and lower iron over entire piece. Do not iron.*

18. *If yarn is bulky, you will need extra steam for flat pressing. To provide more steam, use a damp pressing cloth or a spray iron.*

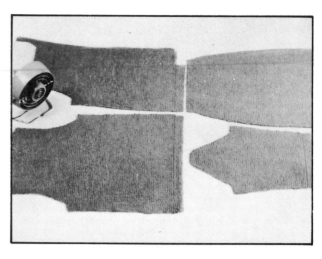

19. *After pieces have been steamed or pressed, leave them pinned until dry. A small electric fan or hand dryer will hasten drying.*

20. *If a piece has a duplicate, block the first piece. When removing from table, leave an outline of pins all around shape of piece.*

21. *Set duplicate piece into outline of pins; pin to shape and block. Block the sleeves, fronts of sweaters, skirt pieces this way.*

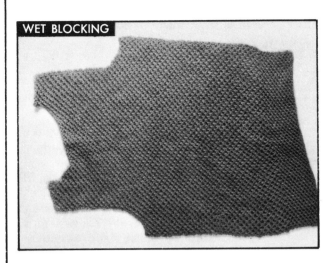

22. Wet blocking is the method used for pieces that go bias because of the pattern stitch and for soiled pieces that need washing.

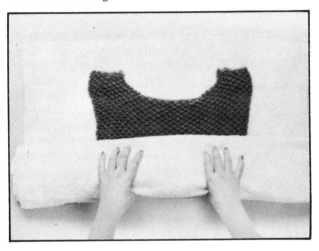

23. Wet bias piece thoroughly, or, if piece is soiled, wash and rinse it. Squeeze out and roll in a towel to remove excess moisture.

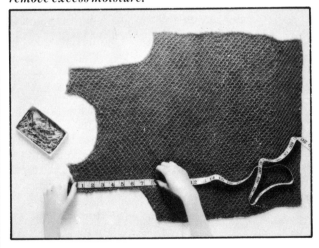

24. While piece is still damp, pin it to measurements on the table, using rustproof pins. Leave pinned until piece is thoroughly dry.

25. Bias pieces can also be straightened by steam blocking. First mark the center stitch with a basting thread down the length of the piece.

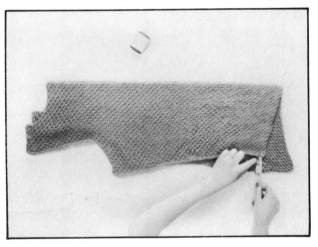

26. To measure exactly how much bias amounts to, fold piece in half along basting line. Measure the difference between side edges.

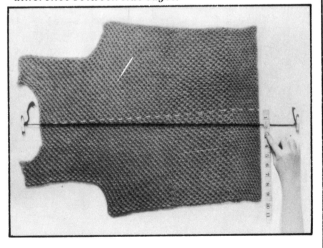

27. Block piece same amount in opposite direction. For example, if piece has a 2″ bias to left, it should be blocked 2″ to right.

KNITTING AND CROCHET HOW TO'S

TO CAST ON

Methods Of Casting On Stitches: There are several ways to cast on.

The simplest one-needle method is shown in Figures 1-5. Make a slip loop on needle; Fig. 1. Loop yarn around left thumb; Fig. 2. Insert needle in loop; Fig. 3. Remove thumb; Fig. 4. Pull yarn, to tighten stitch; Fig. 5. This method is suitable if the cast-on edge will not show or receive wear.

Another one-needle method is shown in Figures 6 and 7. Start with a slip loop the same number of inches from end of yarn as number of stitches to be cast on; e.g. 30 stitches, 30″ from end of yarn. Hold needle with slip loop in right hand. * With short end of yarn make a loop on left thumb by bringing yarn up around thumb from left to right; Fig. 7. Bring yarn from ball under and over needle, draw through loop on thumb, tighten short end with left hand. Repeat from * for required number of stitches.

The two-needle method for casting on makes a firm knitted edge. First make a slip loop over left needle. * Pass right needle through loop from left to right, yarn under and over right needle. Draw yarn through loop and transfer loop on right needle to left needle by inserting left needle in loop from right to left; Fig. 8. Repeat from * for desired number of stitches. This method is used when stitches must be added to the side of your knitting as, for example, when sleeves are knitted with the body of the garment. In this case, the first added stitch is made in the end stitch of your knitting.

To Cast On Stitches Loosely: For most garments, it is best to cast on stitches loosely. If you tend to cast on tightly, use a larger needle for casting on than for knitting the garment.

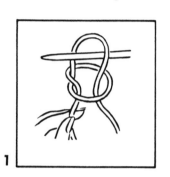

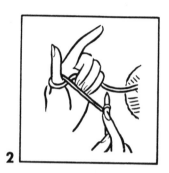

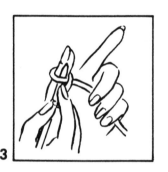

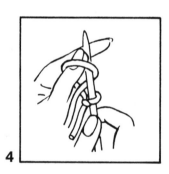

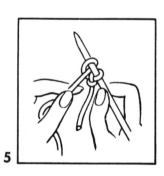

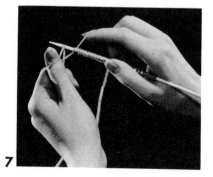

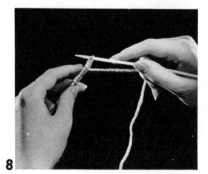

TO BIND OFF

To Bind Off Stitches: Binding off is usually done in the pattern stitch of the garment; that is, each stitch to be bound off is worked in the way it would be if you were not binding off. Unless the directions read "bind off tightly," or "bind off loosely," the bound-off edge should be the same tension as the knitting. If you tend to bind off too tightly, use a larger needle for binding off than for knitting the garment. On a high ribbed neckline, it is absolutely essential to bind off loosely.

MEASURING YOUR GAUGE

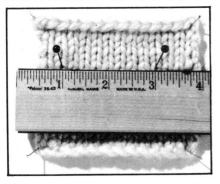

Gauge: All knitting directions for garments include a stitch gauge. The stitch gauge gives the number of stitches to the inch with the yarn and needles recommended in the pattern stitch of the garment. The directions for each size are based on the given gauge. The gauge (or tension) at which you work controls the size of each finished piece. It is therefore essential to work to the gauge given for each garment if you want the garment to fit. To test your gauge, cast on 20 or 30 stitches, using the needles specified. Work in the pattern stitch for 3″. Smooth out your swatch and pin it down. Measure across 2″ and place pins 2″ apart as shown. Count number of stitches between pins. If you have more stitches to the inch than directions specify, you are knitting too tightly; use larger needles. If you have fewer stitches to the inch, you are knitting too loosely; use smaller needles.

Most patterns give a row gauge too. Although the proper length of a finished garment does not usually depend upon the row gauge (directions usually give lengths in inches rather than rows), in some patterns it is important to have the proper row gauge too.

Multiple: In pattern stitches, multiple means the number of stitches required for one pattern. The number of stitches on needle should be evenly divisible by the multiple. If pattern is a multiple of 6 stitches, number of stitches to be worked might be 180, 186, 192, etc. If directions say "multiple of 6 sts plus 2," 2 extra stitches are required: 182, 188, 194, etc.

Yarn Over: This is an increase stitch. It is used primarily in lace patterns or for the openwork increases on raglan sleeve shapings.

To Make a Yarn Over When Knit- ting: Bring yarn under right needle to front, then over needle to back, ready to knit next stitch.

To Make a Yarn Over When Purling: Bring yarn up over right needle to back, then under needle to front, ready to purl next stitch.

To Increase One Stitch: Method 1: Knit 1 stitch in the usual way but do not slip it off left needle. Bring right needle behind left needle, insert it from right to left in same stitch (called "the back of the stitch") and make another knit stitch. Slip stitch off left needle. To increase 1 stitch on the purl side, purl 1 stitch in the usual way but do not slip it off left needle. Bring yarn between needles to back, knit 1 stitch in back of same stitch.

Method 2: Pick up horizontal strand between stitch just knitted and next stitch, place it on left needle. Knit 1 stitch in back of this strand, thus twisting it.

Method 3: Place right needle behind left needle. Insert right needle in stitch **below** next stitch, knit this stitch; then knit stitch above it in the usual way.

To Decrease One Stitch: On the right side of work, knit 2 stitches together either through the front of the stitches (the decrease slants to the right) or through the back of the stitches (the decrease slants to the left). On the purl side, purl 2 stitches together.

To Slip a Stitch: Insert needle in stitch as if to knit stitch (unless directions read "as if to purl") and slip stitch from left needle to right needle without knitting or purling it.

PSSO (pass slip stitch over) is a decrease stitch. When directions say "sl 1, k 1, psso," slip first stitch, knit next stitch, bring slip stitch over knit stitch as in binding off.

To Count Stitches When Binding Off: At the beginning of a row, when directions read "bind off 7 sts," knit 2 stitches; * insert left needle under first stitch on right needle and lift it over the second stitch. This is 1 stitch bound off. Knit 1 more stitch and repeat from * 6 times—7 stitches bound off (8 stitches have been knitted to bind off 7 stitches but 1 stitch, already knitted, is on right needle).

When binding off within a row (as for buttonholes), knit the required number of stitches to point of binding off, then knit next 2 stitches to bind off first stitch. Bind off required number of stitches (1 stitch is already knitted after bound-off stitches). When directions read "knit until 7 sts after bound-off stitches," this means to knit 6 more stitches or until there are 7 stitches after bound-off stitches.

To Pick Up Dropped Stitch: Use a crochet hook. In stockinette stitch, from knit side of work, insert hook through loop of dropped stitch from front to back of work, hook facing upward. * Pull horizontal thread of row above stitch through loop on hook; repeat from * to top.

To Pick Up and Knit Stitches Along Edge: From right side of work, insert needle into edge of work, put yarn around needle, finish as a knit stitch. When picking up on bound-off or cast-on edge, pick up and knit 1 stitch in each stitch (going through 2 loops at top of each bound-off stitch). On front or side edges, pick up and knit 1 stitch in each knot formed on edge of each row.

To Tie in a New Strand of Yarn: Join a new ball of yarn at beginning of a row by making a slipknot with new strand around working strand. See illustration. Move slipknot up to edge of work and continue with new ball. If yarn cannot be joined at beginning of row, splice yarn by threading new yarn into a tapestry needle and weaving it into the end of the old yarn for about 3″, leaving short end on wrong side to be cut off after a few rows have been knitted. If the yarn cannot be spliced (e.g. nubby yarn), leave a 4″ end of yarn, work next stitch with new yarn leaving a 4″ end. Work a few rows, tie ends together and weave them into work.

CHANGING COLORS

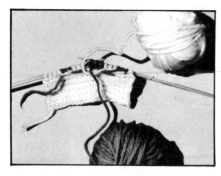

To Change From One Color To Another: When changing from one color to another, whether working on right or wrong side, pick up the new strand from underneath dropped strand. This prevents a hole in your work. Carry the unused color loosely across back of work. Illustration shows wrong side of work with light strand being picked up under dropped strand in position to be purled.

To Ravel Out Knitting: When it is necessary to ravel work and then pick up stitches again, remove needles from work. Rip down to row of error. Rip this row stitch by stitch, placing each stitch (as if to purl) on a fine needle. Then knit these stitches onto correct size needle.

To Mark Work: When directions read "sl a marker on needle," put a commercial ring marker, small safety pin, or paper clip on needle. In working, always slip marker from one needle to another. To mark a row or stitch, tie contrasting thread or put a pin around end of row or stitch to be marked.

Work Even: This term means to work in same stitch without increasing or decreasing.

To Measure Armhole: Mark row on which first stitches have been bound off for armhole by putting a pin through the row 1″ or 2″ in from the bound-off stitches. Place work on a flat surface; smooth out. Measure straight up from marked row.

To Measure Work: Spread article on flat surface to required width before measuring the length at center of the piece.

To Block Knitwear: Smooth pieces out, wrong side up, on a padded surface. Using rustproof pins, place pins at top and bottom of each piece, measuring to insure correct length. Pin sides of pieces to correct width. Place pins all around outer edges, keeping patterns straight. Do not pin ribbings. **For flat pressing technique** (stockinette stitch, flat rows of crochet, other smooth surfaces): Cover with damp cloth. Lower iron gently, allowing steam to penetrate knitted fabric. Do not press down hard or hold iron in one place long enough to dry out pressing cloth. Do not slide iron over surface.

For steaming technique (mohair and other fluffy yarns, raised pattern stitches): Support weight of iron in your hand; hold as close as possible to piece without touching it and move slowly over entire piece, making sure steam penetrates knitting. If yarn is extra heavy, use a spray iron or wet pressing cloth to provide extra steam. When blocked pieces are dry, remove pins and sew garment together. Steam-press seams from wrong side, using a steam iron or damp cloth and dry iron and same blocking method.

To Launder Knitwear. First trace around outline of garment on brown paper. Cut out paper pattern. Use cold-water soap following manufacturer's directions; or, make suds with detergent or mild soap and lukewarm water. Work suds through garment. Do not rub or twist. Support article in the hands when squeezing out water so it will not pull out of shape. Rinse in lukewarm water, squeezing article between hands to remove suds. Do not twist or wring. Squeeze out as much water as possible and roll in Turkish towel to absorb excess moisture. Spread on a flat surface over a dry Turkish towel. Shape garment according to desired measurements, using paper pattern as a guide. Allow to dry thoroughly, away from artificial heat and direct sunlight. Do not hang knitwear to dry.

KNITTING WITH TWO COLORS
An easy way to knit in a design by using both hands to hold colors

Knit all main color stitches in usual way by throwing yarn around needle with right index finger. Knit design stitches as shown in illustration, pulling yarn from left index finger through stitch.

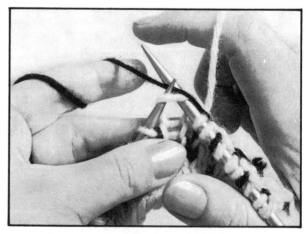

Catch in design color every 4th stitch to avoid loose strands between stitches of design, insert needle in stitch, bring design color over needle as shown, then knit stitch with main color only.

FINISHING STITCHES

To Sew Seams With Backstitch: Most seams should be sewn with backstitch. Pin right sides of pieces together, keeping edges even and matching rows or patterns. Thread matching yarn in tapestry needle. Run end of yarn through several stitches along edge to secure: backstitch pieces together close to edge. Do not draw yarn too tight. See illustration.

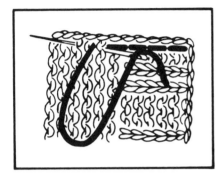

To Weave Seams Together: Straight vertical edges, such as those at the back seam of a sock, can be woven together invisibly from the right side. Thread matching yarn in tapestry needle. Hold edges together, right side up. Bring needle up through first stitch on left edge. Insert needle down through center of first stitch on right edge, pass under 2 rows, draw yarn through to right side. Insert needle in center of stitch on cor-

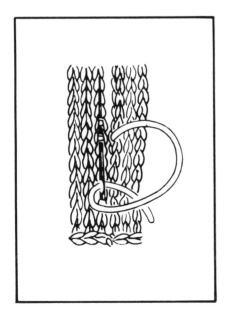

responding row of left edge, pass under 2 rows as before, draw yarn through to right side. Continue working from side to side, matching rows. Keep seam flat and elastic.

To Weave Top Edges of Stockinette Stitch: Two equal top edges of stockinette stitch can be joined by an invisible seam. In this case, the stitches are not bound off, but are kept on the needles or stitch holders until they are ready to be woven. Thread yarn in tapestry needle. Lay the two pieces together so that the edge stitches match. Draw up yarn in first stitch of upper piece, inserting needle from wrong side; insert needle from right side in first stitch on lower piece, bring up through next stitch on lower piece, from wrong side. Draw up yarn, * insert needle from right side in same stitch as before on upper piece, bring up through next stitch on upper piece from wrong side. Draw up yarn, insert needle in same stitch as before on lower piece. Repeat from * until all stitches are joined.

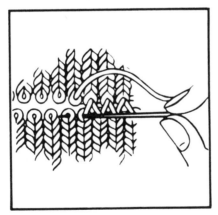

To Sew in Sleeves: Place sleeve seam at center underarm and center of sleeve cap at shoulder seam. Ease in any extra fullness evenly. Backstitch seam.

To Crochet Edge on Knitting: From right side, unless otherwise specified, work 1 sc (1 single crochet) in each stitch on bound-off or cast-on edges; work 1 sc in each knot formed on edge of each row on front or side edges; work 2 or 3 sc at cor-

ners to keep work flat. To make a single crochet, start with a loop on hook, insert hook under 2 loops of stitch on edge, draw yarn through, yarn over hook and through both loops on hook. To end off, make a sl st (slip stitch): Insert hook under both loops of stitch. Catch yarn with hook and draw through stitch and loop on hook.

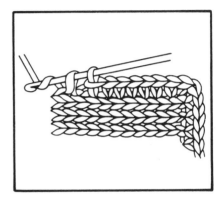

To Weave with Kitchener Stitch: Stitches are evenly divided on two needles and held parallel, with yarn coming from first stitch on back needle. Break off yarn, leaving about 12″ end on work. Thread this end into a tapestry needle. Working from right to left * pass needle through first stitch on front needle as if to knit and slip stitch off needle, pass yarn through 2nd stitch on front needle as if to purl but leave stitch on needle, pass yarn through first stitch on back needle as if to purl and slip stitch off needle; pass yarn through 2nd stitch on back needle as if to knit, but leave on needle. Repeat from * until all stitches are woven.

KNITTING NEEDLES

U. S.	0	1	2	3	4	5	6	7	8	9	10	10½	11	13	15
English	13	12	11	10	9	8	7	6	5	4	3	2	1	00	000
Continental — mm.	2¼	2½	3	3¼	3½	4	4½	5	5½	6	6½	7	7½	8½	9

CROCHET HOOKS (ALUMINUM OR PLASTIC)

U. S.	1/B	2/C	3/D	4/E	5/F	6/G	8/H	9/I	10/J	10½/K
English	12	11	10	9	8	7	6	5	4	2
Continental — mm.	2½	3		3½	4	4½	5	5½	6	7

KNITTING ABBREVIATIONS

k—knit
p—purl
st—stitch
sts—stitches
yo—yarn over
sl—slip

sk—skip
tog—together
rnd—round
psso—pass slip stitch over
inc—increase
dec—decrease

beg—beginning
pat—pattern
lp—loop
MC—main color
CC—contrasting color
dp—double-pointed

CROCHET ABBREVIATIONS

ch—chain stitch
st—stitch
sts—stitches
lp—loop
inc—increase
dec—decrease
rnd—round
beg—beginning

sk—skip
p—picot
tog—together
lp—loop
sc—single crochet
sl st—slip stitch
dc—double crochet
hdc—half double crochet

tr—treble or triple crochet
dtr—double treble crochet
tr tr—treble treble crochet
bl—block
sp—space
cl—cluster
pat—pattern
yo—yarn over hook

HOW TO FOLLOW DIRECTIONS

The asterisk (*) is used in directions to mark the beginning and end of any part of the directions that is to be repeated one or more times. For example, "* k 9, p 3, repeat from * 4 times" means to work directions after first * until second * is reached, then go back to first * 4 times more. Work 5 times in all.

When parentheses ( ) are used to show repetition, work directions in parentheses as many times as specified. For example "(k 9, p 3) 4 times" means to do what is in ( ) 4 times altogether.

CROCHET HOOKS:

Crochet hooks come in a large range of sizes, from a very fine steel hook No. 14, used with the finest crochet cotton, to larger hooks of aluminum, plastic or wood, used with one or more strands of thicker yarns. In general, the hook size to use for any crochet work is the hook that can carry the yarn easily, without catching in the work.

STEEL CROCHET HOOKS
These are 5″ long and come in sizes 00 (large) to 14 (very fine). Steel hooks in the finer sizes are used for cotton threads, but the larger sizes are often used with other yarns.

PLASTIC AND ALUMINUM HOOKS
Plastic crochet hooks are 5½″ long and come in sizes D to J. These hooks often carry a number as well as a letter, but the numbers are not standardized.

Aluminum crochet hooks are 6″ long and come in sizes B to K. In sizes D to J, plastic and aluminum hooks are usually interchangeable. Plastic hooks are flexible; aluminum hooks are rigid and are advisable for stiff yarns and tight work.

Afghan hooks of aluminum and plastic are 9″ to 14″ long and have a straight, even shaft. They range from sizes 1 to 10 and F to J. When afghan hooks are sized by number, the shaft of each hook is roughly equal to the same size in knitting needles. When they are sized by letter, they are equivalent to crochet hooks of the same letter.

WOODEN CROCHET HOOKS
These are 9″ or 10″ long and are used for jiffy work, usually with 3 or more strands of yarn.

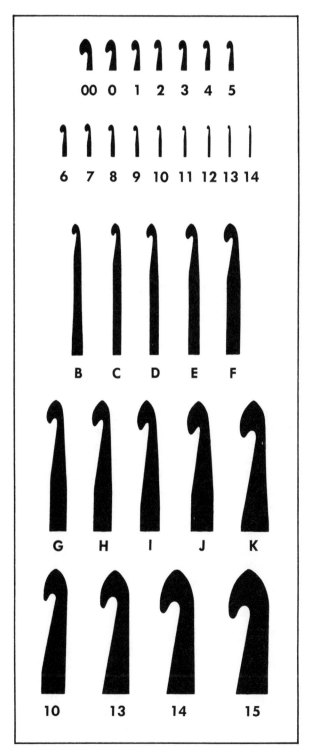

SLIP STITCH (SL ST)

Insert hook in chain or stitch, yarn over hook and pull through stitch and loop.

SLIP STITCH FOR JOINING

When directions say **join** always use a slip stitch. Insert hook from front under 2 top threads of stitch. Yarn over hook and with one motion draw through stitch and loop on hook.

JOINING WITH SLIP STITCH

TO INCREASE

When directions call for an increase, make 2 stitches in 1 stitch. This forms an extra stitch in row.

TO DECREASE SINGLE CROCHET

Work 1 single crochet until there are 2 loops on hook, then begin another single crochet in next stitch until there are 3 loops on hook (Figure 1). Yarn over hook and through 3 loops at once (Figure 2).

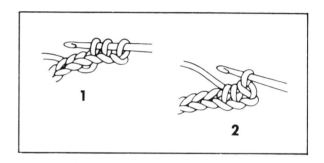

DECREASING SINGLE CROCHET

TO DECREASE DOUBLE CROCHET

Work 1 double crochet until there are 2 loops on hook, then begin another double crochet until there are 4 loops on hook (Figure 1). Yarn over hook and through 2 loops (Figure 2), yarn over hook and through last 3 loops (Figure 3).

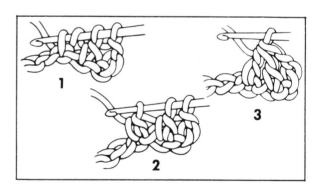

DECREASING DOUBLE CROCHET

HOW TO TURN YOUR WORK

At the end of a row, a certain number of chain stitches (ch) are needed to bring work into position for next row. Then work is turned so reverse side is facing the crocheter. Follow the table below for the number of chain stitches required to make a turn.

Single crochet(sc)	Ch 1 to turn
Half double crochet (hdc)	Ch 2 to turn
Double crochet (dc)	Ch 3 to turn
Treble crochet (tr)	Ch 4 to turn
Double treble crochet (dtr)	Ch 5 to turn
Treble treble crochet (tr tr)	Ch 6 to turn

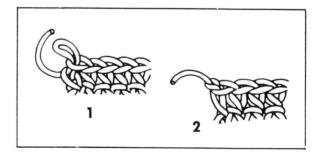

ENDING OFF WORK

HOW TO END WORK

Do not make a turning chain at end of last row. Cut working strand about 3 inches from work (Figure 1). Bring loose end through final loop remaining on hook and pull through. This fastens the end of the work (Figure 2). Thread end in yarn needle and weave back into body of work so it is hidden.

FINISHING TOUCHES

HOW TO MAKE POMPONS

One method is to cut two cardboard disks the desired size of pompon; cut out ¼″ hole in center of both disks. Thread needle with two strands of yarn. Place disks together; cover with yarn, working through holes. Slip scissors between disks; cut all strands at outside edge. Draw a strand of yarn down between disks and wind several times very tightly around yarn; knot, leaving ends for attaching pompon. Remove disks by cutting through to center. Fluff out pompon and trim uneven ends.

HOW TO MAKE A TASSEL

Wind yarn around cardboard cut to size of tassel desired, winding it 20 or more times around, depending on plumpness of tassel required. Tie strands tightly together around top as shown, leaving at least 3″ ends on ties; clip other end of strands. Wrap piece of yarn tightly around strands a few times, about ½″ or 1″ below tie and knot. Trim ends of tassel.

TWISTED CORD

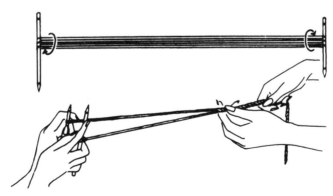

Method requires two people. Tie one end of yarn around pencil. Loop yarn over center of second pencil, back to and around first, and back to second, making as many strands between pencils as needed for thickness of cord; knot end to pencil. Length of yarn between pencils should be three times length of cord desired. Each person holds yarn just below pencil with one hand and twists pencil with other hand, keeping yarn taut. When yarn begins to kink, catch center over doorknob or hook. Bring pencils together for one person to hold, while other grasps center of yarn, sliding hand down at short intervals and letting yarn twist.

HOW TO MAKE FRINGE

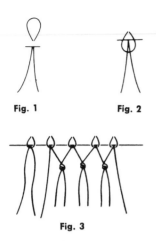

Fig. 1   **Fig. 2**

Fig. 3

Cut strands of yarn double the length of fringe desired. Fold strands in half. Insert a crochet hook from front to back of edge where fringe is being made, pull through the folded end of yarn strand as shown in Fig. 1. Insert the two ends through loop as shown in Fig. 2 and pull ends to tighten fringe. Repeat across edge with each doubled strand, placing strands close together, or distance apart desired. For a fuller fringe, group a few strands together, and work as for one strand fringe.

The fringe may be knotted after all strands are in place along edge. To knot, separate the ends of two adjacent fringes (or divide grouped fringes in half); hold together the adjacent ends and knot 1″ or more below edge as shown in Fig. 3. Hold second end with one end of next fringe and knot together the same distance below edge as first knot. Continue across in this manner. A second row of knots may be made by separating the knotted ends again and knotting together ends from two adjacent fringes in same manner as for first row of knots.

DUPLICATE STITCH

To Make Duplicate Stitch: This embroidery stitch looks the same as knitted-in designs and it's worked after garment is finished. Thread tapestry needle with yarn of contrasting color. Draw yarn from wrong side of work to right side through center of lower point of stitch. Insert needle at top right-hand side of same stitch. Then holding needle in horizontal position, draw through top left-hand side of stitch and insert again into base of stitch to left of where needle came out at start of stitch. Keep yarn loose enough to lie on top of work and cover knitted stitch. See illustration.

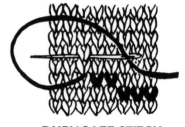

DUPLICATE STITCH

AFGHAN STITCH

Plain Afghan Stitch: Work with afghan hook. Make a ch desired length.

Row 1: Keeping all lps on hook, sk first ch from hook (lp on hook is first st), pull up a lp in each ch across; Figure 1.

To Work Lps Off: Yo hook, pull through first lp, * yo hook, pull through next 2 lps, repeat from * across until 1 lp remains; Figure 2. Lp that remains on hook always counts as first st of next row.

Row 2: Keeping all lps an hook, sk first vertical bar (lp on hook is first st), pull up a lp under next vertical bar and under each vertical bar across; Figure 3. Work lps off as before. Repeat row 2 for plain afghan stitch.

Edge Stitch: Made at end of rows only to make a firm edge. Work as follows: Insert hook under last vertical bar and in lp at back of bar, pull up 1 lp; Figure 4.

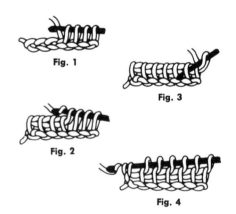

Fig. 1

Fig. 2

Fig. 3

Fig. 4

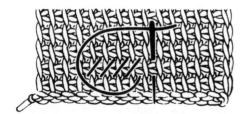

HALF CROSS-STITCH ON AFGHAN STITCH

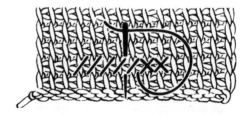

CROSS-STITCH ON AFGHAN STITCH

STITCH DETAILS

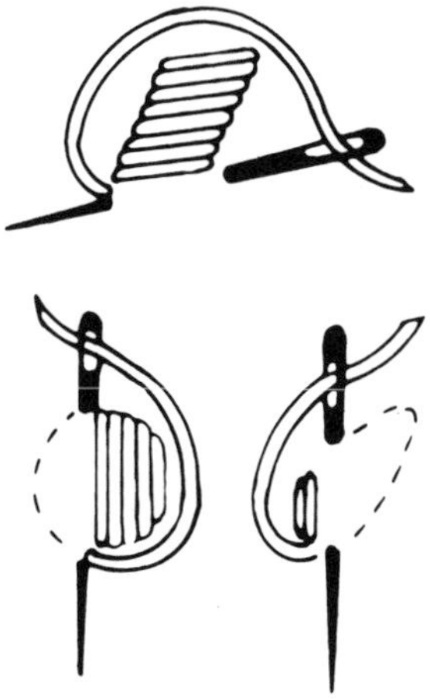

Outline Stitch

Satin Stitch

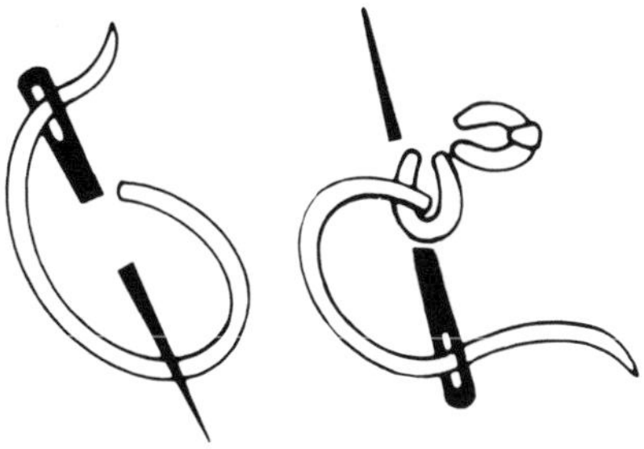

Lazy Daisy Stitch

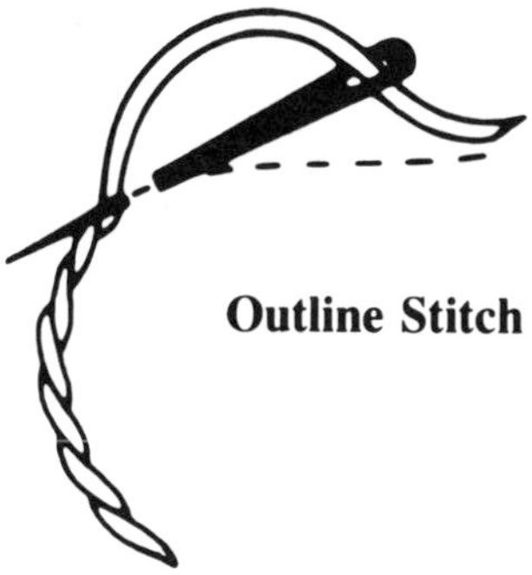

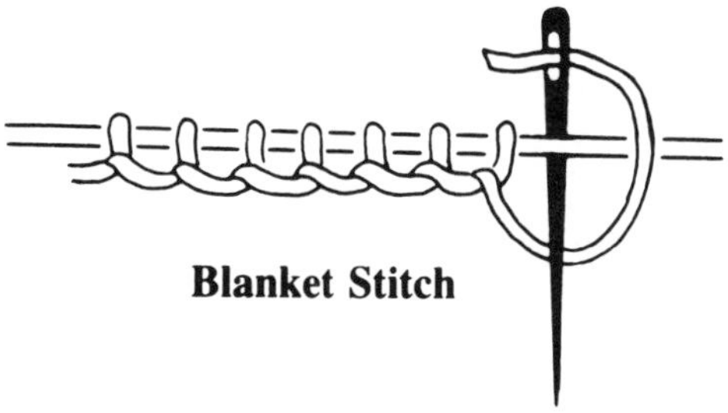

Blanket Stitch

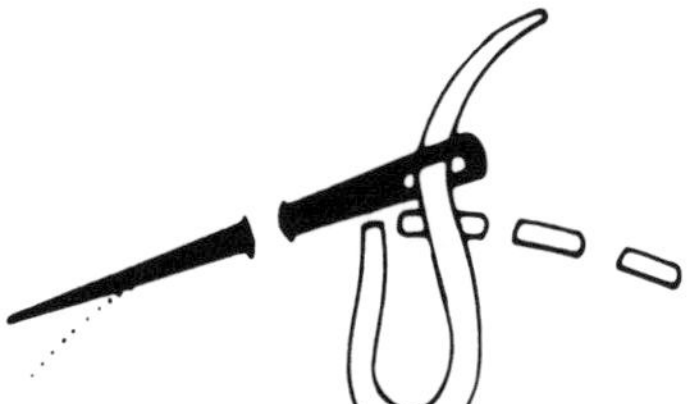

Running Stitch

Cross-Stitch

Chain Stitch

French Knot

Straight Stitch

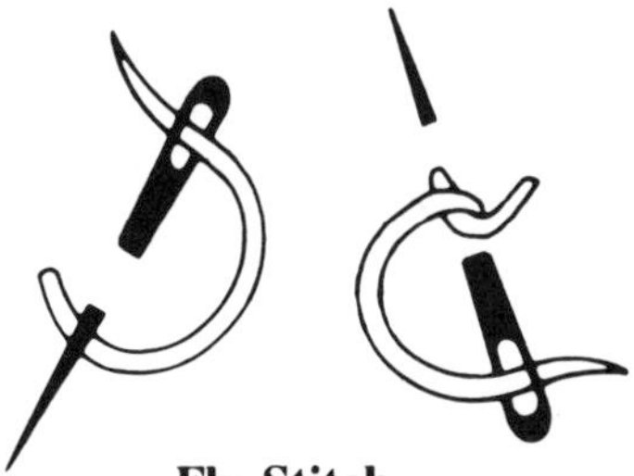

Fly Stitch

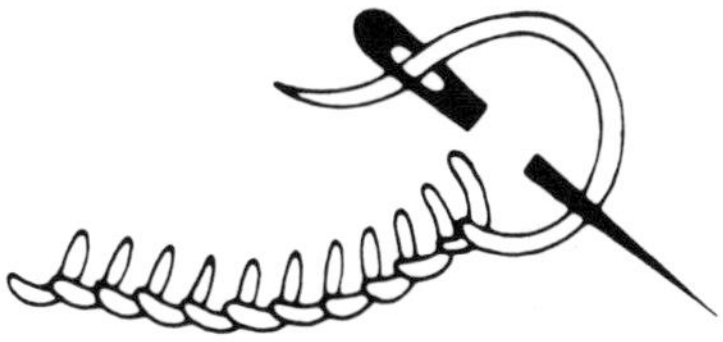

Buttonhole Stitch

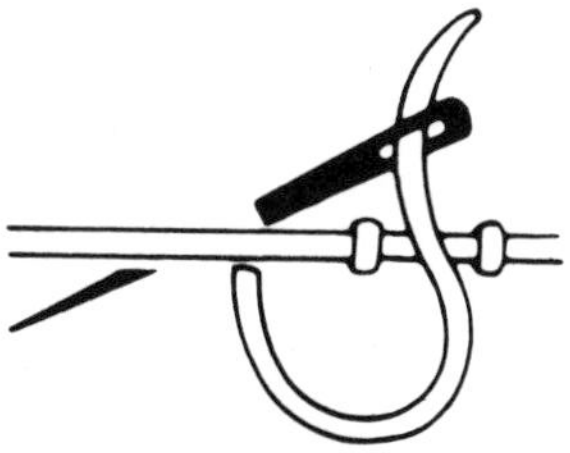

Couching

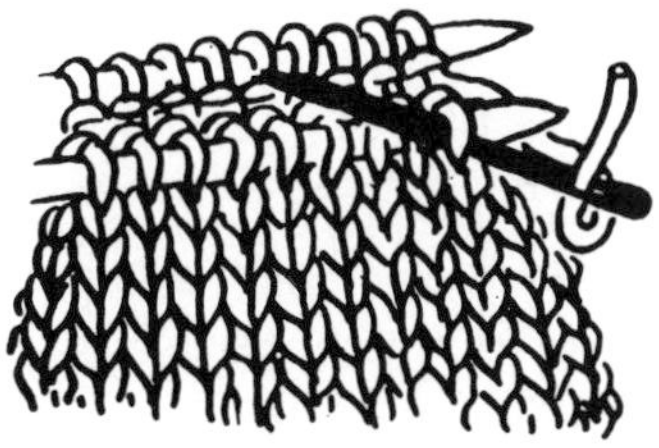

Kitchener Stitch

INDEX

Page numbers in **bold** indicate illustrations.